D1599936

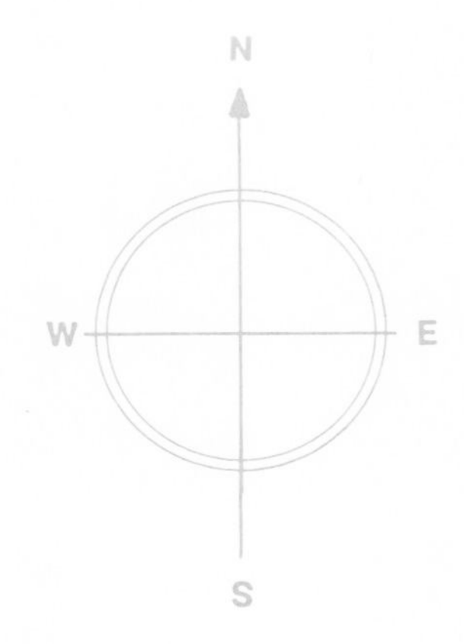
N
W
E
S

Santa Ana
(St. Ann's Bay)
Las Chorreras
(Ocho Rios)
villa la Nueva
Puerto De Melilla
(Port Maria)
Los Bermejoles
Rio Nuevo
Puerto Guayguata
(Annotto Bay)
Puerto Anton
(Port Antonio)
Sierra de Bastidas
(The Blue Mountains)
Liguanea
(Kingston - St. Andrew)
Guanaboa
Los Angeles
bacoa
Pen)
Santiago de la Vega
(Spanish Town)
Anaya
Rio Minho
Morante
Ayala
(Yallahs)
Morant Bay
Yama
(Vere)
Bahia de la Vaca
(Old Harbor Bay)
Puerto de Caguaya
(Port of Kingston)
Cayo de Careno
(Port Royal)
Caguaya
(Passage Fort)

History of the Catholic Church in Jamaica

History of the Catholic Church in Jamaica

Francis J. Osborne, S.J.

Loyola University Press
Chicago

Loyola University Press
3441 North Ashland Avenue
Chicago, Illinois 60657

Library of Congress Cataloging in Publication Data

Osborne, Francis J.
History of the Catholic Church in Jamaica / Francis J. Osborne.
p. cm.
Originally published: Aylesbury, Bucks, U.K.: Caribbean Universities Press, c1977.
Includes index.
Bibliography: p.
ISBN 0-8294-0544-5
1. Catholic Church—Jamaica—History. 2. Jamaica—Church history.
I. Title.
BX1455.2.084 1988 87-38072
282'.7292—dc19 CIP

Designer: C. L. Tornatore

The map appearing on the endsheets is from The Hermon Dunlap Smith Center for the History of Cartography and is the work of Tom Willcockson.

CONTENTS

Foreword

It is a pleasure to contribute this foreword to a new edition of Father Osborne's book. For the first edition came out in a rather unsatisfactory format, and that has perhaps deterred some readers from taking up what is in fact a wide-ranging work of Jamaican history. Father Osborne was able to draw upon a variety of Jesuit archives, in addition to the ones freely consulted by lay historians, and this gives parts of his book a new authority and originality.

In fact, in the continuing absence of any recent substantial history of Jamaica as a whole, his book offers the best available account of several general historical themes. These include the culture and religious beliefs of the Arawaks, the general condition of the island under the Spaniards, and some aspects of the British conquest.

Historians of religion will find much to ponder in the experiences of the Catholic church on the island. The Christian denominations have long been curiously tolerant of each other, from the time of Father Churchill in the 1680s—where but at Port Royal would you have found an Anglican church, a Catholic chapel, a low church meeting-house, and a synagogue in the same town?—down to the revival of Catholicism in the nineteenth century, and even to the present day. Since the established church was Anglican, Catholic groups tended to appear as a result of sporadic waves of immigration, whether of Spanish merchants in the seventeenth century, or of French refugees in the eighteenth, or of Gibraltarian evacuees in the twentieth.

It was, indeed, out of the nucleus established in the time of the French refugees of the 1790s that the modern Jamaican Catholic church would spring, first establishing itself in Kingston and then, in the 1830s, moving outside the capital. The 1850s were a crucial decade in which high schools were founded for both boys and girls, and in which the Franciscans arrived to join the Jesuits; from that time onwards there was a steady expansion.

The story impinges upon other aspects of Jamaica's history, such as the advent of the Chinese, whose general conversion to Catholicism is interestingly explained here. It also deals with the church's role in many different aspects of social development, such as education, health care, housing and the foundation of credit unions. Father Osborne's tale comes to an end with the appointment of Archbishop Carter, the first Jamaican leader of the Jamaican Catholics. With him the missionary phase may be said to come to an end, as a native church increasingly takes over its own destiny.

DAVID BUISSERET
The Newberry Library
Chicago

Preface

This work represents the story of the Catholic Church in the tropical island of Jamaica, West Indies, during the 1494 to 1986 period, with an apology for the lacunae when the Church ceased to exist or existed so tenuously that it had no visible effects on the populace. Based on documents available to scholars, it is the fruit of seventeen years of research and writing.

A long list of characters parades through its pages emphasizing the human element, subjecting dates and places to the people, both men and women, who created this story.

Such a work could not have been written unless interested scholars and institutions had offered their knowledge by opening their repositories to the author. To these the author is most grateful and acknowledges his debt to: Mr. C. Bernard Lewis, Director of the Institute of Jamaica; to Mr. Clinton V. Black, Government Archivist; to Miss Elith Magnus who researched the Government Archives, Spanish Town; to the archivist of Propaganda Fide, Rome; to the archivists of the Society of Jesus both in Rome and London; to the Keeper of the Public Record Office, London; to William L. Lucey, S.J., who read the manuscript and offered constructive criticism; to Hugh Rodman, S.J., who advised on style, and Robert B. Clark, S.J., who edited the manuscript and saw the work through the press.

Since the author acquired an extensive knowledge of the Catholic Church in Jamaica, he felt that this knowledge should be shared with you the reader; hence he offers this work with the hope that you will find its reading a pleasure and its contents informative.

FRANCIS J. OSBORNE, S.J.

15 June 1987
Campion College
Kingston,
Jamaica

One

Arawak Country

Columbus's Discovery of Jamaica

A cry went up from the watch aboard the *Niña* that land loomed on the southern horizon. In the far distance appeared separate peaks rising from out the sea, the outline of an island as these peaks coalesced into Jamaica on the afternoon of discovery, 5 May 1494.[1] Columbus was searching for this island when he set his course southeast from Cabo de Cruz, Cuba, on 3 May to sail in the direction pointed out by friendly Arawak Indians.[2] Head winds lengthened the short ninety-mile run into two full days. Before him lay one of the most attractive tropical islands in the world. Gleaming white sand contrasted sharply with the lush green vegetation of tropical trees in the hinterland. High above the white beaches rose steep hill country culminating in the peak of Blue Mountain, 7402 feet high. Columbus had seen more of the Western world than any mortal of his age, but here was terrain of such astonishing beauty that only one expression in the navigator's vocabulary described the island: Santa Gloria.[3]

Approach was easy. The *Niña, San Juan,* and *Cadera* swung gracefully through the narrow opening in the arc-shaped reef which extended its protecting arm out into the Caribbean to separate rough ocean seas from the calm waters of St. Ann's Bay.[4] Columbus had discovered a new land; Spain had added another colony to her string of West Indian islands. To have reached thus far in his search for China could only have been accomplished by a man of Columbus's stature, a giant in perseverance and courage, a genius in maritime navigation.

The Quest of Columbus

Much in contrast to the serenity of this May afternoon in Jamaica was the turbulent uncertainty of Columbus's life. Three years earlier, footsore, weary, and in extreme penury, Columbus had knocked at the monastery gate of La Ribida, Spain, to claim his young son Diego. He had entrusted Diego to the care of the friars while he himself endeavoured to interest various courts of Europe in his fantastic scheme of sailing west over the Ocean Sea to discover a new route to China and Japan. But now he would give up all hope of finding a patron. It was a crucial moment in history when fortunes of millions hung in delicate balance. At this moment, when all seemed lost and his lifelong ambition an unrealizable dream, Friar Juan Perez, whom Columbus first met in 1484, again came into the life of the admiral, stimulating enthusiasm and turning the great navigator's despair into the resolute will of making one last attempt to interest Isabella in his oriental project. Perez had been confessor to Isabella, and he obtained another audience for Columbus at court. Even this failed to interest a patron, for the royal council to whom the crown referred this phase of the enterprise considered the honours, titles, and revenues demanded by Columbus too extravagant. Columbus packed his few personal effects, saddled his mule, and, accompanied by the faithful Perez, rode out from the unsuccessful audience on the January morning of 1492.[5]

But Columbus's visit to the court paid off from an unexpected angle. Unknowingly, he had made a friend in the influential person of Luis de Santangel, keeper of the privy purse. The shadow of Columbus had scarcely passed through the city gates of Santa Fe when Santangel was on his way to the queen requesting her to reconsider the council's objections and use her own keen sense of judgment, weighing how little risk there was in an enterprise which offered glory to God and his Church, to say nothing of lasting renown to her realm. Was it money the queen needed? If so, Santangel himself would finance the fleet. Should there be urgent need of funds, the queen's jewels stood ready to be pledged. Money was not really, though, the important matter at the present. Lack of time demanded that a messenger be sent to Columbus as quickly as possible. The queen agreed and her courier overtook the discouraged man at Pinos-Puente, four miles from Santa Fe. Assured of the queen's interest, Columbus's clouded countenance brightened with the good news. Hope turned to fulfillment when Isabella, Santangel, and several others invested 2,000,000 maravedis to outfit three ships.[6]

These ships—*Niña, Pinta* and *Santa Maria*—crossed the Atlantic, opening up the New World on 12 October 1492; not this world of two vast continents but the ancient world of China had been the goal of Columbus, admiral of the Ocean Sea. Columbus tried four times to reach the Far East and four times he failed, simply because his nautical calculations were off by some 14,000 miles, and an impenetrable barrier of land reaching from pole to pole lay in his path. One factor for Columbus's persistent certainty he could reach the Far East was his correspondence with Paolo dal Pozzo Toscanelli, a Florentine mathematician and astronomer who agreed that a sea voyage to China was feasible, and he actually calculated the distance as 5,000 nautical miles.[7] Columbus's own calculations reduced this distance to 2,250 nautical miles.[8] This would have placed Japan a mere 2,000 miles from Europe; hence on all four voyages Columbus sought one of the Japanese islands. Whenever land appeared on the horizon, his hopes ran high—this was it, the key to ancient China and the fulfillment of all he had read in the *Il milione* of Marco Polo about fabulous Cathay.

The Conquest of Jamaica

This thought was uppermost in his mind the afternoon he sailed into St. Ann's Bay. Was this an outpost of Japan? Had he at last found the object of his intense search? Before the question could be answered, angry Arawak warriors swarmed over the bay in pirogues, gesticulating furiously as they brandished wooden spears, defying the foreign power which molested their native hearths. One blank salvo from the fleet reduced their bravery to frightened flight, leaving the foreigners in possession of the bay.[9] Early next morning Columbus sailed eighteen miles westward where another Arawak village, perched on a vantage point four hundred sixty feet above the sea and under a different cacique, watched the strange ships enter the harbour.[10] Alarm was sounded and warriors hurried into canoes to battle the invader. If they were not prudent, they were courageous in the defense of their homes. Not wishing to do battle, Columbus gave the order for his ships to leave the harbour.[11] Then, lest the Indians think they had frightened away the mighty power of Spain, he returned and let fly a shower of arrows from crossbows, which found their marks among the canoes, wounding many of the Arawaks. Continuing the pursuit on land, he set a fierce dog upon them "who bit them and did them great hurt, as a dog is worth ten men against Indians."[12] When they had been terrified into submission, Columbus heaped acts of kindness on these simple creatures, proffering coloured beads, mirrors, knives, hawks' bells, and such like trading truck he had brought along to pacify the Indians. From their village the Indians sent six of their number with propitiatory gifts of cassava, fruit, and fish which the admiral accepted as a pledge of peace during the remainder of his stay at Puerto Bueno.[13]

No landing party had been ashore on 5 May when the explorers sailed into St. Ann's Bay. Not until the next day, 6 May, when he anchored at Puerto Bueno, did Columbus raise the standard of Castile and León on its sandy shore, claiming the island for his patron, and renaming it Santiago in honour of Spain's St. James of Compostela.[14] It was known as Santiago for some years until it reverted to its original Arawak name Jamaica.

Clear evidence from Peter Martyr's *Fifth Book* of his *Decades* indicates that when Columbus discovered Jamaica he had a chaplain with him, a friar of the Order of Our Lady of Mercy.[15] Shortly after Columbus discovered Jamaica, he sailed to Cuba where the friar celebrated the Holy Sacrifice of the Mass on 7 July 1494, at Rio de las Misas.[16] Silence by Peter Martyr concerning the first Mass in Jamaica does not imply that Mass was not celebrated here from the sixth to the ninth of May 1494, for Columbus's chaplain had more reason to celebrate Mass on this solemn occasion of taking possession of and naming Jamaica than he had for saying Mass in Cuba two months later, since Cuba had been discovered on the 1492 voyage, although this was the occasion of the first Mass also in Cuba. Only a few months previously, on 6 January 1494, Mass had been celebrated for the first time in the New World at Hispaniola.[17] So it is possible that the honour of the second Mass may be claimed by Jamaica.

Weighing anchor again, Columbus left Rio Bueno and sailed forty-two miles west to Montego Bay which he entered on 14 May and named El Golfo de Bien Tempo.[18] It was well designated for it afforded the expedition relief from the foul weather that had plagued Columbus during the first days of May. After a short stay, a good-bye was waved to Montego Bay and the following day the *Niña, San Juan* and *Cadera* sailed for the south coast of Cuba. It was on this leg of the journey that chronicler Peter Martyr recorded the Mass celebrated by the Mercederian chaplain.[19]

Columbus's Survey of Jamaica

Fascination drew Columbus back to Jamaica on 21 July to explore the western and southern coasts over a period of two months.[20] He found enough of interest in the Indians and their way of life to detain him for this relatively long time. One such interest was the number of Indian villages, for his survey indicated that Arawak settlements every fifteen miles apart ringed the coast, and he also stated that there were a number located in the hinterland. But this could have been only a rough approximation, for to estimate accurately the number and location of Indian villages would have consumed more than two months. Columbus's second interest was in the natural resources of the island. Judgment of these could be made from the profusion of ornaments worn by the Arawaks on festive occasions and if gold, it would be a lodestone for future colonization. An abundant use of gold by the Indians would have indicated some rich immediate source but, as it turned out, bright coloured feathers were more in evidence as Arawak finery than the yellow metal, indicating a lack of gold in Jamaica. Spanish colonists who combed the island for mines and found none later confirmed this judgment.[21]

Columbus Marooned in Jamaica

On 19 August Columbus left Jamaica for Hispaniola.[22] Thence he returned to Spain to prepare for this third try, in 1498, for a route to China. It is, however, his fourth and last voyage in 1502 which concerns Jamaica, for on her shores were dashed forever the great navigator's hope of ever discovering a western sea route to the lands of spice and silk. Neither love of tropical beauty nor interest in gold but pressure of necessity compelled Columbus to hurry his sinking ships riddled by teredos into St. Ann's Bay on 24 June 1503.[23] He beached them and hoped to send word to the Spanish colony in Hispaniola that he was stranded in Jamaica. News did reach Hispaniola but was of little help to Columbus; a ship dropped wine and food but hurried back to the mother colony without taking any of Columbus's sailors aboard.

This voyage all but ended Columbus's earthly career as he experienced the terrifying sensation of his ship gradually sinking under his feet and all efforts to keep it afloat a hopeless task. The *Capitana* and *Santiago* were veritable sieves with teredos boring through every inch of their rotting hulls.[24] Only two remained of the four caravels which began the fourth voyage, for he had to abandon the *Gallega* and *Vizcaina* on the sands of Central America,[25] leaving the *Capitana* and the *Santiago* to make the run for Hispaniola before the teredos ate every last plank of the ships. Lashing rains along the south coast of Cuba so contested every inch of the way that the only hope was to turn south to Jamaica. The navigator approaching Jamaica from the sea would sight two neighbouring harbours in midnorth shore which could easily be mistaken for one another. Misjudging that Puerto Seco was Puerto Bueno, Columbus was puzzled to find that no river emptied into its harbour. With no time to spare, he left Puerto Seco and hurried east to St. Ann's Bay at the eleventh hour, just in time to beach his two caravels on a sandbar in twelve feet of water, minutes before the ships would have settled of their own accord to the bottom of the Caribbean.[26]

The position of the ships, fifteen hundred feet from the shore, provided protection from an Arawak surprise attack and deterred the crew from venturing ashore without the admiral's permission. Hull to hull, shored up on both sides, with cabins constructed fore and aft on the decks, and strong enough to resist Arawak attack, the *Capitana* and *Santiago* remained until teredos, tropical storms, and salt sea reduced them to mere keels on the bottom of the bay.

The discoverer of the New World was now back in the very spot he had so ecstatically proclaimed Santa Gloria in 1494. In that year he had seaworthy ships and could sail away from Jamaica; this time he and one hundred sixteen men were without means to break the four-hundred-mile barrier of the Caribbean to the nearest Spanish settlement in Hispaniola. They had expected one or two months of exile in Jamaica, at most, before communications would be set up with Hispaniola, but they reckoned not with Don Nicholas de Ovando, knight of Alcántara, founder of Spain's Indies' empire and governor of Hispaniola. Though Ovando could have rescued these men, he let them experience the pangs of anxiety for one full year.

In a crisis such as Columbus was now facing, there is always one man upon whom the leader may rely; for him it was Captain Diego Méndez. Departing with a good supply of bright-coloured cloth, hawks' bells, mirrors, and scissors, Méndez traded these in Indian villages and returned to St. Ann's Bay with a large canoe filled with food and the promise from friendly Arawaks to send a regular supply for the stranded Spaniards.[27] Méndez again was Columbus's choice when he needed someone to paddle over to Hispaniola for help.

Méndez's first try was a failure, but he made it on the second attempt.[28] He had to endure terrible sufferings under a burning tropical sun and the loss of several oarsmen. When he arrived in Hispaniola, Méndez met with cold, delaying indifference from Nicholas de Ovando, a petty tyrant who allowed personal ambition to stand in the way of dispatching a rescue ship to Jamaica, for he feared that Columbus's glory might overshadow his own and bring his retirement from his highly lucrative position as ruler of Spain's outpost.[29]

In Jamaica, days of delay lengthened into weeks of impatient waiting as every exile daily scanned the horizon for the expected relief. Would it ever come? Had Méndez reached Hispaniola? Questions grew into murmurings and murmurings into mutiny. On 2 January 1504 the Porras brothers, Francisco of the *Santiago* and Diego, crown comptroller, together with fifty followers, seized ten canoes and paddled to Holland Bay in the far eastern end of the island.[30] There they launched three unsuccessful attempts to reach Hispaniola, attempts buffeted by furious northers—high winds of December through January on the north coast—which forced them to abandon their venture. Returning to St. Ann's Bay, the mutineers spewed their vehement disappointment on every poor Arawak village in their path, finally battling the sailors loyal to Columbus near Maima, with the Arawaks spectators of this unique event of white man fighting white man in Indian country. The disaffected were defeated and Francisco de Porras spent the rest of the year in chains.

The Rescue of Columbus

While the Porras brothers had been making a futile attempt to leave Jamaica, Ovando sent a ship to St. Ann's Bay which dropped meat and wine then quickly sailed away without so much as taking a single exile on board. Marooned, Columbus had faced mutiny, and now came this tantalizing relief. How bad could the exiles' situation get? It was now one year since they had run their leaking ships on to a sandbar in St. Ann's Bay, and all this time there was no sign of rescue. But faithful Méndez had not forgotten his promise, and just as the months were rounding into a full year, he chartered a small caravel under command of Diego de Salcedo. There it was on the horizon one fine June morning.[31]

Columbus had drawn aside the veil of the unknown from tropical Jamaica, but it remained for conquistadors to subdue and colonize the island, forging it as another link in the vast network of possessions Spain was binding to herself in the New World, on which no intruder might so much as set foot. Jamaica was to remain within the Spanish orbit for one hundred and sixty years until England pried it loose in 1655.

Throughout the Bahamas and Greater Antilles, Columbus had been in contact with Indian settlements whose culture, customs, and religious beliefs revealed a homogeneous family of common origin under the generic name of sub-Taino, all speaking the Arawak language. These Indians left no literature, no architectural monuments, nor even any present-day descendants, and so it was incumbent upon the science of archaeology to dig into the past and reveal the origin, culture, and religion of these Arawaks. Where did they come from? What was their manner of life? What were their religious beliefs?

Jamaica in the Time of Columbus

Jamaica is the third largest of the Greater Antilles, 144 miles long, nineteen to forty-nine miles wide. Only ninety miles from the Oriente Province of Cuba, it lies between 76° 11′ and 78° 32′ west longitude; between 17° 43′ and 18° 32′ north latitude, which locates the island within the tropics. This mountainous land of 4,411 square miles is covered with tropical vegetation; its precipitous hills often begin at water's edge and stretch back onto a high ridge forming a solid backbone of the Blue Mountains, culminating in a peak 7,402 feet high.

The Arawak People

All civilizations fit into the general pattern of the human family. From a common point of origin, they had spread over the earth in divers directions impelled by search for food, the desire to improve living conditions, and in pursuit of that elusive goal called happiness. One such civilization worked itself into Venezuela from Asia and thence into Jamaica. Unglazed pottery, simple diet, and a limited mode of agriculture characterize this primitive culture. Their religion was based on elementary natural reason corrupted by idolatry until the sixteenth century contact with the Church offered them the opportunity of becoming Christians. The Arawak Indian of Jamaica lived in a primitive neolithic world which had survived in the Caribbean long after the Stone Age had yielded to the Age of Metals in Europe.

One important function performed by these primitives of the Antilles was to draw the Church from its limited fifteenth-century geographical position in Europe into the wide world of the western hemisphere, there to encounter the more advanced civilizations of the Maya, Aztec, and Inca, and even beyond into the Pacific, where her missionaries transformed the non-Christian Philippines into the only Catholic nation of the Orient. All this missionary success began with the Antillean Arawaks.

The Indian settlement of Jamaica came after a slow migration by means of a very limited mode of transport from one island in the Antilles to the next until Jamaica was reached. The story of these Indians has recently been revealed by scientific research.[32] An arc of islands extending from northeastern Venezuela to southern Florida separates the Atlantic Ocean from the Caribbean Sea. Geographically, these islands fall into two natural groups: the Lesser Antilles, consisting of the Leeward and Windward Islands, and the Greater Antilles, Cuba, Hispaniola—Haiti and the Dominican Republic—Puerto Rico, and Jamaica. The Lesser Antilles are inconspicuous islands but the Greater Antilles terminate in the large island of Cuba, six hundred ninety miles long. Like stepping stones they formed the path along which migrant Indians found their way from South America into the Antilles.

Mongoloid features place the remote origin of these Arawak Indians in Asia, but their immediate origin was on the northeast coast of South America. There are three major groupings of these peoples: the paleo-, the meso- and the neo-Indians. The paleo-Indian lived from 15,000 B.C. to 5000 B.C.; the meso-Indian from 5000 B.C. to 1000 B.C.; the neo-Indian from 1000 B.C. to 1500 A.D.[33]

Recent evidence indicates that the paleo-Indian was present in the Greater Antilles in the year 5000 B.C. The meso-Indian appears to have left Venezuela, migrated to Cubagua and Margarita since beginning his trek about 2500 B.C. Latest archaeological evidence indicates that the meso-Indian came via Central America.[34] Evidently the meso-Indian had developed considerable seafaring skill to reach even these offshore islands of Cubagua and Margarita since their only means of transport was a dugout canoe gouged out of a log by primitive stone tools after the interior section had been burned. By some means or other, these meso-Indians bypassed the Lesser Antilles and colonized the Greater Antilles. This could have been done by accident, as canoe parties were caught in the prevailing current and carried against their will onto these northern shores.

Transition from the meso-Indian to the neo-Indian took place along the Orinoco River where the Indian had developed agriculture as a principal means of subsistence. Pushing his way through the Orinoco delta onto the coast, the neo-Indian came into contact with the remnant of the meso-Indian who taught him the art of fishing and seafaring.[35] He migrated into the Lesser Antilles and by a series of island hopping reached Puerto Rico by 200 A.D. Jamaica became the home of the neo-Indian by 650 A.D.[36]

Arawak Manner of Life

These neo-Indians, known as Arawaks from their Arawakan language, made violent contact with Columbus that May afternoon when he sailed into St. Ann's Bay. Recorded Spanish observation of Arawak culture in Cuba is equally true of the same Indian in Jamaica for the same language, the same tribal structure, the same religious beliefs, and the same mode of life reveal a close kinship between the inhabitants of Cuba and those of Jamaica, ninety miles to the south. The Indian who was Columbus's interpreter could be understood by his fellow Arawaks throughout the Greater Antilles and even among the Caribs of the Lesser Antilles where captive Arawak women, incorporated into those fierce tribes, had carried their own language. In Cuba each village was under a chieftain called a cacique, and in turn the villages were subject to an overlord who ruled a series of settlements called a province. In Jamaica the same system prevailed. Each village was ruled by a cacique and the whole island of one hundred fifty settlements was divided into ten provinces ruled by ten great caciques.[37] Stability in these settlements required a regular supply of food obtained by hunting, fishing, and cultivating. Cultivation of the land yielded maize, cassava, sweet potatoes, tomatoes, pulse, and a highly prized pepper called ajes. The nearby Caribbean furnished a tasteful variety of seafood: parrot fish, jack, sea turtle, grunt, grouper, terrapen, snapper, bass, hogfish, and even a species called squirrel fish.[38] In the primitive forest the Arawak hunter sought out the coney and hutia to balance his heavy fish diet. Women did the cooking over open fires close to the hut in unglazed clay vessels which showed a high degree of simple ceramic art of limited style that might be either circular or boat shaped.[39] This style was named Meillacoid from its close affinity with Haiti.[40] But Jamaica did develop a style distinctly its own, which has been given the name of White Marl from its principal source located at the Arawak village of the same name on the south coast near to the present Spanish Town.[41]

Proximity to the sea made fishing a major industry for the Arawaks. Fish might be caught in the conventional way of using a net weighted with a stone sinker, lowering the net enough to entrap whatever swam into it, or fish might be caught with a lamprey allowed to swim freely on a long cotton line until it attached its sucker onto a victim fish.[42] The canoe from which the Indian fished was his own construction. In order to make it, he burned the centre of a large cottonwood tree, and then hacked away at the interior with a stone hafted by thongs to a stout stick. These implements which the Arawak used were made from the blue river stone,[43] some six inches long, petaloid in shape with one end elliptical; the other end brought to a point with edges bevelled to razor sharpness, whose shape and exact bevelling might rival modern workmanship. This petaloid celt might be used as a tool or a lethal weapon.

The women were assigned the task of preparing the corn meal and cassava which formed the basic Indian diet. Corn was reduced[44] to meal and cassava to flour on elaborately shaped stone grinders[45] consisting of the metate and the pestle: the metate carved from one piece of sandstone, standing eighteen inches high with three supporting legs, one in front and two in the rear joined together by a curved back ten inches wide, terminating in front with a zoomorphic representation, gave the impression of a stone animal. The pestle was a heavy elliptical river stone worn smooth by years of grinding. The corn meal and cassava flour were baked on a clay griddle, elliptical in shape, about twelve inches in diameter and one inch in thickness, having a slight indentation so that the viscous dough would not run over the sides.[46] Cassava bread had the advantage over bread made from wheat in that it did not readily spoil but could be kept for weeks and still remain fresh.

The Arawak village huts were of simple but effective construction consisting of stout poles set three feet apart, driven into the ground to form a circle ranging from ten to thirty feet in diameter.[47] The spaces between the poles were artfully interwoven with a pliable reed, leaving an opening for the doorway. The cone shaped roof was so closely woven of thatch that even torrential rains could not penetrate it. This mode of construction offered a surprisingly cool interior and a most welcome escape from the burning rays of the tropical sun. Instead of a bed, the Arawak had invented the hammock made from strands of woven cotton, an invention later taken over by the European.[48]

Religious Beliefs of Arawaks

As with all people who have fallen into idolatry, plurality of gods makes it difficult to place their religious beliefs in rigid categories; when to this first obstacle there is the added disadvantage of no written language through which to trace their beliefs, reliance must be placed on observers who may not have interpreted their ceremonies with the accuracy they deserved, for such a person could easily have read his own belief into their religious practices. With no influence from Christianity or contact with Judaism, the Arawaks held a primitive belief in a Supreme Being, according to authorities close to the time of Columbus. Called by the Arawaks "Yocahu Vagua Moacrocotii," this Supreme Being was invisible, dwelt in the heavens, was not addressed in supplication by the Indians, and had no practical influence in their lives. This Supreme Being was further acknowledged as "Aiomun Kondi" (Dweller in the Height) and "Ifilece W'acinaci" (Great Our Father), as well as "W'amurrecti Kwonci" (Our Maker).[49]

Despite all such acknowledgments, no acts of adoration were paid the Supreme Being. The Arawak reasoned that, since he might expect no harm from him, there was no need to propitiate him—only the lesser gods who might harm him. No inconsistency was seen in assigning to the Supreme Being a father and mother, as these Indians did. The father could be addressed under five titles: Allabbeira, Mamona, Guacarpita, Liella, and Guimazea; the mother under six titles: Alubei, Jemao, Guacar, Apito, Zumaco and Atabex.[50]

The religion of the Arawak may be called *zemiism.* Although he did not pay honor to the Supreme Being, he was very careful to worship the zemis that had the power to harm him. Zemis were not only accorded worship but were consulted as advisers or possessors of knowledge of the future and curers of ills. Antedating the making of zemis of wood, baked clay or stone, ancestor worship had manifested itself in a more primitive form. This ancient stage had been characterized by skeletal remains of departed relatives preserved by the beneficiary in the hut and the greatest respect was shown to these remains from which magical power was expected, for the soul was thought to dwell in these bones.[51]

The next chronological step was to encase some of these skeletal remains in wood, carved in the form of an image.[52] The final stage was reached when images were carved from wood which by predetermined signs showed that the soul of the departed had taken up his abode.

For public worship by the whole village, it was the soul of the cacique which was deified and not the person of the common Arawak. Indian belief in the survival of the soul after death was the basis of this ancestor worship.[53] Life and death were two important phases of Arawak thought, for these Indians differentiated between the soul in this life, which was called *Goenz,* and the soul of the departed, which was called *Opea.*[54] Feasting and dancing were important functions of the whole Indian village, not only for the living but also for the dead who enjoyed their feasts and dances in the forests where they were thought to have had their abode. It was here in the forest that the soul of the dead cacique took up his abode in a tree, and hence it was the duty of the village to determine the tree in which he dwelt and then carve an image from the tree and place it in a special hut for the whole community to worship. Both the cacique zemi and the hut became the property of the incumbent cacique of the village.

That a particular tree was the abode of a dead cacique could be noted in two ways: the first was by observing the movement of the roots of the tree;[55] the second was by finding a wooden beam in a pit where a hunted animal had taken refuge.[56] In either case an image was carved from the tree of omen and the zemi worshiped by the whole village. Although there was communal worship offered to some zemis, there was no objection to the common people having their own private zemis either in their huts or on their person, but they were not given the same honours by the whole village as accorded the cacique who had become a god. Most of the zemis worshiped privately by the common people were of baked clay and only a few inches high.

The cult of zemiism had its functioning priesthood, intermediaries who had their own particular function in the cult: Bohutio, Buhibitos, Peaeman, and Beheques were mediums of the zemis, each having its own cultic role—one to cure the sick, another to predict the future, another to see that the idol was not neglected by the people. They might also be used by the village cacique to impose his will on the people by oracular utterances in favour of the chieftain.[57]

The zemis' attendant, Bohutio, a medicine man, was one of the village's most important functionaries; for if the cacique fell ill, he was called to perform a rite.[58] Powdering tobacco finely, the Bohutio inserted a reed tube into the patient's mouth and bade him inhale the snuff. Simultaneously using another tube, the Bohutio followed the same procedure for himself. As many as possible of the cacique's subjects gathered around the medicine man, their faces blackened by charcoal. In order that they might enter into the ritual with purified souls, herbs were made into a nauseating paste which each bystander swallowed, and evil spirits lodged in their stomachs were expelled by vomiting. The entire assembly then intoned a magic chant while hand held lighted torches made shadows dance necromantically over blackened faces. The chant ended, the Bohutio closed the patient's mouth with quivering hands. Applying his own mouth to the cacique and at the same time breathing heavily, he feigned to extract something from the ill man's body. Coughing and gesticulating as if he had eaten something bitter, the medicine man extracted a piece of bone from the patient's body which he had previously concealed in his own mouth, claiming that it had been placed there by some zemi whom he had neglected to worship. Should the cacique die despite the Bohutio's ministration, relatives of the dead man decided in council if the fault lay with the Bohutio who neglected to perform the ceremony properly—then the medicine man was subjected to painful punishment from which he himself might die.

One occasion when the whole village gathered to propitiate the zemis was at the harvest festival.[59] Presided over by the peaeman, the ceremony opened with an arieto, an ancient religious song accompanied by a ritualistic dance. Within the rustic temple, a handsomely polished table in the form of a dish was placed in the centre of the room and on it powdered tobacco. A portion of the snuff was sprinkled on the head of each idol while the remainder was drawn into the nostrils of the worshipers by reed tube. As they snuffed, they uttered incantations. Cassava offerings were then proffered to the zemis by the women. The priest took these sacred cakes, presented one cake to each participant, who was to carry it back to his hut and preserve it until the next festival as a safeguard against earthquakes, thunderstorms, hurricanes, and like manifestations of zemi anger. On the occasion of these community gatherings, the cacique would often take advantage of expressing his will on tribal matters through a talking idol. A reed inserted into the mouth of the idol led to a shaman hidden under leaves in a dark corner of the idol's hut and, from this position, he would utter the cacique's will, appearing as though it were the will of the zemi.[60] Spanish conquistadors coming upon such a performance exposed the fraud to the village over the protestations of the cacique who wished his revelation kept secret that he might more effectually control his tribe.

While most of these idols were carved from wood, others, much smaller, were made of clay. Early conquistadors observed that they were also of goffan pine cotton, folded or wreathed and stuffed within the image.[61] These latter were made to sit upright much as contemporary Spanish art had depicted evil spirits upon their walls. This cotton zemi was bound by a cotton cord to the forehead of the Arawak warrior as a protection against the enemy during battle.

Until 1955 no stone idols had been found in Jamaica, but in that year one was discovered at Portland Point, in a district known as Mahoe Gardens, a tiny fishing village in Vere, Clarendon.[62] The cave is in a most inaccessible spot, three hundred feet up the side of a very steep hill. Here within the dark recess of a cave is a three foot high stone idol, a crude artifact whose mouth, nose, and eyes distinctly mark it as an Arawak zemi. Curiously enough, the head of this zemi has a very definite cleavage through the centre of the cranium, dividing it into two sections and forming a cup at the rear of the skull where worshipers placed sacrifices to this god. It is perilous to conjecture why this idol was placed in such an out-of-the-way cave where the number of worshipers on any given occasion was necessarily limited by reason of the terrain and the narrowness of the location. Perhaps some esoteric ritual limited the worshipers to an initiated few.

The Spanish and the Arawak, two opposing cultures, met face to face in Jamaica. The European had much to offer the Arawak, widening his horizon beyond his insular home to give him a glimpse of the culture of Europe. The primitive Indian came to know the white man's great cities with their dense population, his highly organized government with its hierarchy of officials culminating in the king. He became acquainted with the white man's institutions of learning, which offered instruction from the elements of reading and writing to the highest level of university education. Through the Spaniard, knowledge of the Unknown God, the Supreme Being, the "Our Maker," the "Our Father," whom hitherto he had acknowledged in a vague, far-off manner, but to whom he had never paid divine worship. The European taught him the wonderful works of God manifest through his divine Son, whom he had sent to reveal more fully the Supreme Being. Lastly, he incorporated the Arawak into the Mystical Body by baptism.

The Indian in turn had something to contribute to the European, for the Arawak had learned to live on a small island, isolated from the rest of humanity and had here enured himself to the tropics. He could subsist on a practically meatless, monotonous diet, under circumstances no European settlement would have endured, for either the lack of comforts or discouragement would have made the European abandon Jamaica. The Indian acted as a buffer between the European and the hardships of this primitive island.

The European found in the Indian a ready source of manual labour without which the infant colony would not have survived, for a labour force was necessary in the search for gold. Had gold been discovered, it would have been needed to mine it. Indian labour was essential for plantation and ranch, for without it the Spaniards would have had to import many slaves. The Arawak products of cassava and maize were adopted by the Spaniards early in colonization and more intensely cultivated until they formed the staple commodities of the colony's economy.

The struggle between the two cultures began the day the European set foot on Arawak country; when large sailing ships completely overshadowed the Indian canoe; when steel swords, cannon and crossbows overwhelmed wooden spears and petaloid celts. Village life, cacique government, language, and even their very persons were assimilated by the more powerful European culture. Disease, death, and intermarriage helped reduce the once-ruling Arawak to impotency before the onrush of conquest and colonization.

The naive have fancied savage life as an idyllic, simple, pastoral country life far removed from belching black smoke of factories, the rush of modern transport, and the impersonal humanity of modern cities; but this is the fruit of imagination of men who have never had contact with the primitive. After long study of Antillean savages, Admiral Samuel Eliot Morison comes nearer to the truth when he says:

> If the natives of these islands had really lived in a sort of golden age, as Peter Martyr described them, with plenty to eat, all possessions held in common, innocent of covetousness, untouched by the vices of civilization, our feeling might be otherwise, but the reality was different. The Indian, as the philosopher Hobbes said of men "in a state of nature," lived in continual fear of danger of violent death, and his life was poor, nasty, brutish and short.

Even on an island the size of Jamaica, there were eight or ten different caciques who indulged in war for the most trivial reasons. Jamaica was also within raiding radius of the Carib warriors from Broiguen and the Lesser Antilles, who carried off slaves both for labour and for eating, whose dietary habits gave rise to the word *cannibal*. This was far from a *pax americana* when Columbus broke down the isolation of the New World. In Central America one bloody empire succeeded another: Toltec conquered Maya, and Aztec conquered Toltec. In North America, the five nations, the Iroquois Confederacy, had every bordering nation terrified by their energy in war and the exquisite cruelty with which they tortured their captives. The Arawaks who inhabited this island were its first inhabitants; but their cousins in Cuba had driven the Sihoney to the western part of the island. Not least of Spanish achievements was to bring the Americas from Florida to Patagonia under one law, one administration; if we could do half so well in our closely integrated world through the United Nations, we could afford to sneer at the Spaniards.

* * * *

If then, we weigh what the Indians had against what Columbus and his successors brought to the New World, there can be only one conclusion. All that we value in modern life—liberty under law, representative government and democracy, freedom of religion, freedom to choose our own career or occupation, enjoyment of technological advances of civilization—are direct consequences of Columbus's discovery."[63]

The Western World took on a new look from the days of discovery, for its untapped natural resources made it one of the most desirable spots on earth, so that from isolated Indian settlements it grew into great cities with populations in the millions.

Jamaica could not offer the Western World any great mineral resources, but it did offer deep fertility of soil and agricultural produce which made it the bread basket of expanding colonization. Upon Jamaica depended many of the infant colonies which pushed Spanish conquest farther and farther into the direction of the setting sun. Its cassava, cattle, pigs, and horses made it a valuable base from which to launch marching conquistadors into the unknown of Mexico, Peru, even north into California. Jamaica played a Cinderella but important role in Spanish conquest.

Two

Conquistadors

The conquistador was born into a world that for centuries had been geographically static, but now in the dying fifteenth century this same world was expanding with such dynamic energy that every red-blooded Spanish youth turned his eyes westward where the unknown suddenly became the known. Gold and pearls and aromatic spices lured the Spaniards with dreams of wealth and ease as the reward for a few short years spent in the high adventure of conquest and colonization. The eighty conquistadors who stepped ashore on Jamaica's sand in November 1509 carried with them the Old World dreams of adventure, wealth, and renown.[1] Theirs was the task of forging Jamaica as a link in the chain of empire, of mining gold, and of establishing a great city on the north coast. Only the first of these was ever completed; the other two were failures. Although these projects may be written off the credit sheet, the extensive overall missionary effort to christianize the New World achieved astounding success. Whether on a small island like Jamaica, or on a vast continent like South America, every city, every town, every tribal settlement which Spain found pagan, she made supreme efforts to christianize—this because crown and Church cooperated to carry out the terms struck in the Patronato Real de las Indias which formed the very foundation of imperial and ecclesiastical structures from the Straits of Magellan to the California missions.

The patronato did not appear spontaneously; it was a climax to a series of papal concessions having root in the famous Grant of Granada.[2] Patronato documents reveal a gradual unfolding of papal favours to the Spanish crown beginning with Eugene IV.[3] In 1436 he established the precedent for Innocent VIII to issue in 1486 his grant for the whole of Granada, wherein advancing Spanish armies wrested city after city from the Moors.[4] At the same time the Catholic monarchs made extensive land grants for the support of ecclesiastical foundations in the conquered territory. Julius II, anxious to improve the quality of episcopal candidates, allowed Ferdinand and Isabella the right of patronage.[5] This gave the monarchs the privilege of proposing suitable clerics of their own choice to the sees in newly conquered Moorish territory.[6] Soon Alexander VI added his own concessions in five papal documents which ranged from dividing the New World between Portuguese and Spaniard to the donating of ecclesiastical tithes to Spain.[7] These latter were given as a help to defray the enormous expense incurred in the early days of discovery and the establishing of colonies when little revenue came to her, in contrast to later days when so much gold and silver flowed into her treasury that she became the wealthiest nation of Europe.

A crucial date in history was 28 July 1508, for Ferdinand then won from Rome the celebrated *Universalis Ecclesiae Regimini*.[8] This decree placed every church, every monastery, and every future ecclesiastical establishment under the patronage of king and queen. It formed the very basis of her American empire for Spain, and for the Church the greatest missionary success she has ever known. The impact of the Patronato Real de las Indias can never be overemphasized, for not only churches but hospitals, refuges, loan funds, schools, universities, and seminaries must be added to the credit column of this epochal grant. The good it accomplished far outweighed the human failings which must inevitably be encountered in such an enterprise. The prime object of the Patronato Real was the christianizing of the New World; it granted to the crown the choice of missionaries, their despatch into specific fields overseas, the establishment of policies, the expansion and retrenchment of operations, a subordination of all secular clergy to civil administration.[9]

Jamaica was drawn into this orbit of the Patronato Real by early colonization ensuing from a territorial dispute between Ferdinand and Diego Colon.[10] On 20 October 1508, Ferdinand appointed Diego, son of Christopher Columbus, governor of the Indies. Christopher had died two years previously on 20 May 1506. When Ferdinand appointed Diego governor of the Indies, he did not include the mainland in his jurisdiction. This choice piece of continental territory fell to Alonso de Ojeda and Diego de Nicuesa.[11] Ferdinand assigned them the colonization of Tierra Firme, as the geographically vague land west of the Caribbean islands and across the Yucatán Strait from Cuba was known.

Ojeda and Nicuesa needed a base of operations, and they chose Jamaica.[12] They established themselves on the south coast of Jamaica at Parotee Point, at a settlement called Oristán. Later this base was moved westward to Bluefields. Diego offered no objection to Ojeda and Nicuesa as conquistadors of the continent, but he did object vehemently to Jamaica coming under their jurisdiction, for this was his patrimony, and he intended to keep it so.[13] A reply from Ferdinand approved Diego's claim that Jamaica belonged to the Colón family; should Ojeda and Nicuesa show up in Jamaica, Diego was to appoint a fiscal to regulate their actions. To forestall Ojeda's and Nicuesa's claim, Diego, with the approval of Ferdinand, appointed Juan de Esquivel as his lieutenant governor for the island.[14] Ferdinand had every reason to look with favour upon Esquivel, for as a captain he had served the crown with distinction at the battle of Higuey when he overcame the cacique Cotubano, a decisive factor in the pacification of Hispaniola.[15] Now Esquivel was on a new adventure as the pioneer governor of Jamaica.

In November 1509 Esquivel with his eighty conquistadors stepped ashore at St. Ann's Bay to begin the foundation of New Seville.[16] Esquivel had reason to select this spot for he had sailed this same harbour with Columbus on his voyage of discovery, May 1494.[17] He also had reason to name the capital Seville, for he had been born in the old city of Seville in Spain.[18] St. Ann's Bay was selected for practical reasons too, for it had a good harbour, well protected by an offshore reef, and afforded an easy approach to Cuba on the north and Hispaniola on the east.

One of the first tasks confronting Esquivel was to provide shelter for his men. Timber was the only readily available material, and houses and churches were constructed with it; roofs were thatched in the manner of Arawak huts. As time progressed more substantial material—brick and cut stone—were used for the walls, and clay tiles for the roofs. The bricks were baked by the Indians and the stone cut in nearby quarries under the direction of Spanish artisans. Seville's centre, flanked by the governor's castle fort and the church, was the very heart of the settlement.[19]

The Repartimiento System

Every person—governor, settler, and Indian—had a part to play in this drama of colonization. For the native it meant manual labour on the ranches, on the farms, in making brick or burning lime for public buildings and settlers' homes; for the hidalgo, though he may have been a bootblack in Spain, he was a gentleman in the New World—to him was assigned the task of ruling, of governing farms and ranches, of acting as entrepreneur. Never an assignment of a servile nature, for he was superior to the Indian and must hold a position in the community to show this superiority. In early Spanish Jamaica, eighty days of service was required of the Indian, after which he might return to his native village.

This was the beginning of the *repartimiento* system: an apportionment or allotment of natives to the colonists.[20] Closely related was the term *encomiendas* which signified that the

> conquered territory was divided into areas of jurisdiction and each area, comprising several villages, was 'comende' by the Crown to a conquistador or colonist, who became its 'encomendero.' It was the encomendero's duty to maintain law and order within his jurisdiction, protect people from their enemies, come to their aid in their necessities, and provide them with the opportunity to learn the Christian faith. In exchange for these services, he had the right to levy tribute and statute labour, subject to government regulations.[21]

In this important duty of pacifying Indians, Esquivel was not entirely successful, for instead of running with open arms to embrace the civilization proffered by the Spaniards, the Arawaks ran into the hinterland. Judging their ancient freedom of more value than a regime that would force them into organized labour, for neither by nature nor desire were they suited for the work that Europeans wished to impose upon these children of the forest. No Arawak wished to exchange generations of freedom for slavery, nor could he see the logic of suddenly becoming the workhorse of Spanish invaders who had seized Arawak territory and would now subjugate every man, woman, and child in order to search for gold or raise cattle and cultivate land which the aborigines claimed as their own by the mere fact of possession.

The object of every colonist was gold: find it and he would be rich. But he could not find it, despite thorough search by the Indians, for the simple reason that there was no gold in Jamaica. The Spaniard was quick to realize that the country was admirably suited for agriculture and the raising of cattle. But no conquistador would be found performing the manual labour of the ranches and the haciendas: that was for the Arawak. This reasoning seemed illogical to the Indian. The Spaniard had seized his country, now he had seized his person and would have him work for the aggrandizement of a foreign power he had never known until fifteen years ago.

Ferdinand's letter of 25 July 1511 told Diego to have Esquivel and his colonists make a special effort to discover gold.[22] This meant that the burden of search was placed on the Indians. The primitive terrain of Jamaica would suggest that only a small number of caciques and their subjects were actually involved in this search; those living in the vicinity of St. Ann's Bay. Shortly afterwards the king himself had to admit that the search for gold was futile; he asked Esquivel to make the Arawaks grow as much food as possible. This would take from the mother country much of the burden of transporting food which could easily have been grown in Jamaica. So favourable were the conditions for cultivation that Ferdinand fancied a profit might be made. He was correct, for Jamaica became the supplier of food for the infant colonies on the mainland. By the king's command the Indians ceased searching for gold and employed their energies exclusively in cultivation.[23] The first Spanish cultivation was a continuation of what the Arawaks had grown: maize, cassava, and cotton, but on a more extensive scale. Cotton cloth manufacture grew from a pioneer to a mature industry in these very early days of colonization, being made into clothes and hammocks exported to Cuba, Cartagena, Nombre de Dios, and Santa Marta. Since the Indian was one of the chief users of the hammock, Esquivel was ordered to supply every Arawak with one.[24]

The Spaniard was not only interested in the economy of the country, but he also cherished the desire to spread Christianity. The first hint of early missionary endeavour comes from a letter Esquivel wrote to Ferdinand in which he enthusiastically related the conversion of many Arawaks. Although the king was elated and praised Esquivel for his zeal, he had learned from past experience that conversions coming so quickly were liable to be based on a meagre knowledge of the faith, since brevity of time and the language barrier militated against a solid catechetical foundation of their Christianity. In reply, Ferdinand cautioned Esquivel that, since the faith was being planted in Jamaica for the first time, it should be well planted with all converts properly instructed before baptism.[25] This precaution would avoid the mistake made in neighbouring Hispaniola where the Indians were merely Christian in name because of hasty baptism without proper instruction. The Arawak language presented a formidable obstacle to the conveying of sublime truths, for it was a medium which expressed inadequately spiritual concepts, and to this difficulty must be added the imperfect knowledge of this language by the first missionaries. Las Casas complained that the Indians in Jamaica were not being taught properly nor was any more care taken of them than if they had been wild beasts.[26] Yet, according to this same critic, who never set foot in Jamaica, they were the best disposed in the whole world to become Christians.

Ferdinand took steps on 27 June 1512 to make missionary work in the Caribbean more effective.[27] Under the terms of the Patronato Real, Ferdinand had power to choose missionaries and dispatch them to specific fields overseas. The Franciscans, growing in numerical strength and in zeal for the propagation of the faith in the New World, were Ferdinand's choice. The king formally requested the Franciscan provincial in Hispaniola to send forty friars to Cuba, San Juan in Puerto Rico, the mainland, and Jamaica.[28] Since Jamaica was a promising settlement at this time of its history, she received a fair share of these missionaries. At least ten Franciscans arrived in 1512. In a letter to Gil González Dávila, dated 10 December 1512, Ferdinand approved of supplies that had been sent by the government to the monks in Jamaica and Cuba.[29] In this letter the king clearly implied that the Franciscans had already undertaken their missionary work. This would place them among the first to evangelize the New World. From the geographical area of the West Indies, the Franciscans moved into Mexico, Central and South America, and even as far north as California, where they established the string of missions along the Camino Real to bring Christianity and civilization to the Indians of the Pacific coast of the United States; but the beginning was in the Caribbean.

All was not going well in Jamaica. Suspicious reports from Diego Colón to Ferdinand prompted his majesty to send an agent, Miguel de Pasamonte, to investigate Esquivel's administration.[30] No complaint could be lodged against Esquivel's successful farms or cattle ranches; it remained for his critics to complain of his failure to search diligently for gold and of the infrequency of his official reports to the home government.[31] Search for gold was a hopeless task, yet some colonists persisted in the belief that gold could be found in Jamaica. A more serious complaint against Esquivel was that he was remiss in the conversion of the Arawaks, a report that could have come from the missionaries.[32] On 12 December 1512, Ferdinand condensed these complaints in a strong note to Diego Colón, alleging that Esquivel had served him negligently in the conversion and pacification of the Indians as well as in failing to increase the royal revenue;[33] finally both settler and native had suffered from his hands. Diego was ordered by Ferdinand to replace Esquivel by a governor who would act in the best interests of the colonists and the conversion of the Arawaks.

Hardly were these words penned than Esquivel was dead.[34] Possibly Esquivel, who had initiated his administration with so much zeal for the conversion of the Indian, was too physically ill in 1512 to be interested in anything, secular or ecclesiastical, for in this year a serious pestilence struck the island, taking a large toll of lives, particularly among the Indians.[35] It appears that Esquivel succumbed to this same sickness.

Two years after the death of Esquivel, Francisco de Garay assumed office in 1515. The interim government was filled by Captains Perea and Camargo and the royal treasurer Pedro de Mazuelo.[36] The two captains treated the Indians cruelly—both were unsuited by nature to rule the infant colony; but Mazuelo was the chief offender.

Governor Francisco Garay's Administration

Garay arrived on 15 May 1515 with full authority.[37] He intended to curb the excesses of Royal Treasurer Mazuelo who had appropriated choice farms to himself and had forced five hundred Indians into his personal service during the interim. In a report to Ferdinand, Garay blamed Mazuelo for the exodus of many Indians from Jamaica, principally by the harsh treatment meted out to them by the acting governor.[38] No number is given, but Garay implies that all who could do so left the island probably going to Cuba or even to distant Yucatán.

Garay himself experienced Mazuelo's arrogance when he sought to take up residence in the governor's apartments attached to the castle fort, built under Esquivel.[39] The royal treasurer refused to surrender his comfortable quarters to the new governor. Instead of resorting to force, Garay let the situation continue for a time while he sought temporary shelter with one of the colonists until he overcame Mazuelo's delaying tactics.[40] When Garay arrived with his wife, he knew little of what had happened on the island before his arrival. Mazuelo explained that Captains Pera and Camargo fled Jamaica under a cloud when charges were preferred against their administration and left the castle fort in custody of the Seville mayors.[41] Since Garay took a year to arrive in Jamaica after his appointment in 1514, it seemed proper to Mazuelo that he himself should occupy the governor's quarters.[42] A more serious allegation by Garay claimed that Mazuelo falsified reports to the king, for the quantity of cassava bread and beef was much less than stated by the treasurer, and that he could not have made the large profit at the recent cattle market if he stated correctly what it actually cost him.[43] Then three hundred farm implements sent out by the king were lying idle because there was no one to teach the Indians how to use them.[44]

Garay's administration was not only productive for Jamaica but it was important to Spain's expanding empire which was experiencing a serious supply problem as lifelines stretched farther and thinner to the west. A six-year partnership begun in 1514 between king and governor establishing farms and ranches so that provisions might be supplied to Castilla del Oro brought relief to the mainland whose colonists were on the verge of abandoning the settlement.[45] Garay's agricultural venture also attracted an increase of settlers to Jamaica, bringing the total up to five hundred colonists.[46] On 6 September 1519 this contract was about to expire, but so effective had been these farms and ranches in supplying provisions to governor, troops, and settlers of Castilla del Oro that Garay reminded Ferdinand's successor that, should the partnership be dissolved, hardship would ensue for the mainland settlements depending upon Jamaica for their food supply. Upon this advice, the king extended the agreement for three more years.[47] Cassava bread, corn, salted beef, bacon, and other pork products were shipped to new colonial centres as they were settled by colonists eager to take advantage of the opportunities which the West offered them.

On 6 September 1521 Charles I ordered Garay to ship forty cows, fifty calves, one thousand pigs, two hundred sheep, and two hundred hampers of cassava bread to the newly founded city of Panama on the Pacific side of the isthmus.[48] This meant that the animals had to be herded from the Atlantic to the Pacific over almost trackless country.

Jamaica had proved such a rich agricultural country that Garay took advantage of its fertile soil to introduce sugarcane to the island.[49] This product, in later years to become king among Jamaican produce, was brought to the Indies by Aquilón from the Canary Islands.[50] Garay's sugar mill at Seville produced one hundred twenty-five tons of sugar annually, a remarkable performance for so early colonization. That first one hundred twenty-five tons has grown into thousands of tons annually and has become one of the basic products of the Jamaican economy.

Colonists were migrating to Jamaica in those early days, to the ranches and farms for that elusive thing called fortune. So many colonists, in order to make their fortunes quickly, overextended their credit and fell into bankruptcy which so seriously affected Jamaica's economy that the crown had to issue an order, 20 July 1515, forbidding credit for all but essential goods. The order reads as though it were issued in the twentieth century.

> As many of the colonists of Jamaica are in debt through purchasing on credit goods that are not necessary and consequently many of them pass so much time in prison and are absent from their plantations, and there have been many quarrels and law suits, it is ordered that henceforth no one shall buy or sell anything on credit except cattle, slaves and tools for working farms and mines.[51]

The first reference to slavery comes from a document dated 5 June 1513 in which the king gave permission to the Esquivel family to import three slaves who must be Christians.[52] Another early reference is a letter of Charles I dated 20 February 1524 to officials of the Chamber of Commerce, Seville, Spain, wherein he stated that they were aware that he gave permission to his chief steward, Lorenzo de Garrebad to transport to the Indies and the mainland four thousand black slaves over a period of eight years. The colonists asked that, when Garrebad's license expired, all be allowed to import their own slaves in a general permission to all settlers. These colonists, having protested this monopoly, were allowed to bring four thousand slaves: Hispaniola 1400; Fernandina (Cuba) 700; San Juan, Puerto Rico 500; Jamaica 300; the mainland under the government of Pedro Aria Dávila 500; New Spain under the government of Hernando Cortés and Francisco Garay 600. These slaves were to include women as well as men, duty being paid on each one. A further covenant limited the type of slave. They were to be untrained negroes; and it was urged that, upon arrival, they were to become Christians. These slaves were assigned to domestic work in the homes of colonists, leaving the farm and ranch labour to the Arawaks.

The life of every Arawak in Jamaica was affected by the royal decree dated 26 July 1515.[53] In the first year of Garay's administration, Ferdinand convoked his theologians together with canon and civil lawyers on the methods to be adopted to convert the New World Indians; to give proper direction to their decision, conquistadors who had been in the Indies and who had an intimate knowledge of Arawak life and customs, were called to advise this body. Uppermost in Ferdinand's mind was the obligation, under the Patronado Real, to propagate the faith in the newly conquered Indies. The conferees unanimously agreed that solid conversion could come only by continued, unbroken contact with Christian colonists. Sad experience had proved that, when converted Indians returned to their own villages after the eighty-day working period for the colonists, they fell back into idolatry and the vices common to the semi-savage. Christians they were while with the Spanish colonists; zemi worshipers when they returned to their native settlements. Conquistadors attending the conference observed that what Indians learned or pretended to learn of the Christian faith while in the company of colonists they soon forgot once they returned to their own estancias. The king's council saw only one solution: the Arawaks must be assigned to the permanent care and custody of the colonists.

This drastic decree of 26 July broke up the Arawak village settlements and assigned Indians to live permanently with Spanish settlers. The king added his own note of caution: the Indians were still to own their properties and no one was to deprive them of the right of private ownership. This order forestalled any Spaniard from claiming both the person of the Indian and his estates as his own. Three hundred of these Arawaks were allotted to Diego Colón to keep them under his charge, teach and maintain them on his own plantation and the plantation owned by the king. Ferdinand was also careful to add that these Indians were to be allotted as employees and not as slaves. Under this covenant, the Arawaks were to be paid a wage for their labour which characterized all future relations between the colonists and Arawaks.

The ensuing years, 1515–19, may be classified as the most fruitful in the conversion of the Indians. On 29 August 1519 Charles I, who had succeeded Ferdinand, had high praise for Garay's efficient implementing of the decree of 1515. "I approve and thank you for the care you have taken that the caciques and Indians of the island are instructed in our holy faith and removed from the rites and bad habits in which they used to live."[54]

Charles's chief anxiety was that the caciques and Indians be well treated, that they live and increase, and that they be carefully instructed in the faith. The king reiterated his command that Garay pay special attention to the royal ordinances concerning the aborigines, assuring Garay that in nothing could he serve him better than by carrying out these decrees conscientiously; but should Garay fail in this matter, he would do a great disservice to his king. Charles placed the conversion and good treatment of the Arawak squarely upon Garay's conscience.

Garay served Jamaica in several other ways which proved of advantage to the island: he insisted that all colonists marry as soon as convenient, and to these married men he offered special help in building brick homes.[55] Hans Sloane, an observant scientist, noted in 1688 that these houses stretched for two miles along the road at Seville.[56] A second service rendered to the populace was to remove the town of Seville in 1519 from its swampy lowland to a more healthy elevated site directly south and less than one quarter mile distant.[57] At the same time he also removed the town on the south side of the island, Oristán, to the vicinity of Bluefields which was the choice of the inhabitants. Charles I, in a letter to the Jamaican officials, related that the inhabitants of both Seville and Oristán were contented with Garay's arrangements. Garay made his own search for gold, not satisfied with the negative results of his predecessors, and reported to the king that there seemed to be evidence that there was gold in Jamaica. Charles I in replying to Garay showed more interest in the welfare of the Indian than in the suspected presence of gold, for he warned Garay that Indians used for the search were not to be ill treated; and if they were employed in the mines, the labour should be as moderate as the work done on the farms in accordance with the ordinances issued by the king. There was no need of this warning because again it had to be admitted that there was no gold in Jamaica.

When Cortés's proposed expedition to Mexico rumoured through the Caribbean, both lowly colonist and high official had his imagination fired with dreams of adventure and gold. In November 1519, when Pedro Xuarex Gallinato de Porra sailed his caravel into St. Ann's Bay to stock food for Cortés's expedition to Mexico, Governor Garay was badly bitten by the fever of adventure.[58] Then and there he determined to embark on his own conquest of Mexico, for Jamaica's most capable governor had too much of the conquistador in his blood to allow him to settle for long on a small island.[59] The whole world was his, particularly the world of Mexico. On his way to Mexico, Garay stopped at Xagua, Cuba only to find that Cortés had beaten him to Pánuco, Mexico and had established a colony there. On St. James's day, 25 July 1519, Garay anchored at the mouth of the river Pánuco and sent his kinsman, Gonzalo de Campo, up the river in a brigantine to reconnoiter the country. After four days Gonzalo reported to Garay that he found the country poor and uninhabited. Taking four hundred soldiers and some horses, Garay marched to the town of Pánuco only to find that Cortés had left for San Esteban del Puerto. With supplies running low and his men in a state of imminent mutiny, Garay was in a perilous state and had no alternative save to strike a military bargain with the conqueror of Mexico. A favourable reply came back from Cortés. But treachery immediately followed these fine words. Cortés attacked Garay's cavalry at Mochaplan, and forty of Garay's men under Captain Alvarado were arrested as usurpers of the land. Thoroughly annoyed by this deceitful act, Garay demanded that Pedro de Vallejo release his men, claiming that his own authority to explore and found a colony in Mexico came from the king. Vallejo's answer was that he would believe it when he saw Garay's credentials.

Cortés was informed of Garay's arrival and was on the point of setting out to meet him when Francisco de las Casas and Rodrigo de Paz arrived with letters from Charles I appointing Cortés governor of New Spain in all the land he had conquered. Garay raised the question whether this included Pánuco. Diego Ocampo, Cortés's lieutenant, claimed it did; he ordered Garay's ships in the harbour to surrender or sail away.

Garay then exhibited the royal decrees which allowed him to establish his colony at Rio de las Palmas, some distance north of Pánuco. Garay wrote to Cortés who accepted the authorization; but Garay's men deserted ship, alleging that they were not obliged to follow him beyond the Pánuco. In desperation, Garay went to Cortés; Cortés again agreed to Garay's colony north of the Pánuco at Rio de las Palmas, and furthermore promised to aid him with arms and men.

Garay never set foot in his proposed colony, for he fell ill with pneumonia shortly after Christmas day 1523, and died. Garay is one of the few early governors whose life we can trace from the day he landed in Jamaica until he died in Mexico.[60]

* * * *

The first vocation to religious life in Jamaica was that of Luis Sánchez de la Torre in 1519.[61] He had been a royal supervisor of smelting and marketing gold in the island and left his sinecure to enter the monastery of St. Francis in Hispaniola.

The Franciscans were the only missionaries in Jamaica at this period of history, and hence they had the obligation to take stock of their friars and ecclesiastical institutions by making periodic canonical visitations. Following a visitation, emphasis might be placed on a different aspect of their work and some clerics replaced by others. This first canonical visitation occurred in 1522, ten years after the first Franciscans arrived in Jamaica when two priests were sent out to evaluate the work of the missionaries in the island. As was customary, the civil officers were informed by Charles I in a letter of 31 August 1522, addressed to Diego Colón, "Our Vice Admiral and Governor of the Island of Hispaniola and those other islands discovered by the industry of your father the Admiral, and to the Governor, Justices and Officials of the island of Jamaica."

> Let it be known that Friar Juan de Tecto and Friar Juan de Arevalo, religious of the Order of St. Francis, are going by commission of their provincial and with our consent to visit the Friars of their Order who reside in the said islands, in order to judge who are useful and fit to remain there for the profit and instruction of the inhabitants and also for other business pertaining to their office. Those who do not measure up to the standard are to return to their monasteries as will be seen by their commission. It is my will that they be given all the assistance and favour they require to carry out the purpose of their visitation. For this is for the greater service of God, Our Lord. So I order you and make you responsible to aid them in everything they may need to carry our their commission.[62]

The Jamaican scene which greeted Tecto and Arevalo was much different from that experienced by their pioneer confreres in 1512. The first Franciscans found only the beginnings of European civilization, pioneer colonists waging war against tropical nature and little by little conquering the virgin forest. The Spanish colonists in 1522 had established farms and ranches throughout the island, and the Arawak labourers on these settlements had been brought into contact with the missionaries and had been converted to Christianity. The Franciscan visitors, Tecto and Arevalo, could witness sure signs of ecclesiastical progress in the conversion of the Indians and the sight of two churches, one in Seville on the north coast, the other in Oristán on the south coast. Although these were wooden structures with tile roofs, they did indicate that the Church was here to stay for the duration of Spanish occupation. Ranches and farms widely scattered over long distances on the island placed the Franciscans in the category of itinerant missionaries travelling from ranch to ranch celebrating Mass and conferring the sacraments at the homes of colonists for both Spaniard and Arawak; at best it was a lonely life for these holy adventurers.

Life on the north coast of Jamaica in 1533 could be monotonous, and after the first fervour of adventure wore off, daily routine on ranch and farm was no place to fire the imagination with dreams of wealth, of fame, or of conquest. Stories trickling in from the west told of vast lands yet unconquered by the Spaniard. If colonists were to depart from Jamaica, the more pious their motive, the better the chance that the crown would grant their petition. In 1532, Sánchez de Valliere of Seville wrote to the crown on behalf of the Council of Justice, the aldermen, knights, esquires, and officials that some Jamaican colonists wished to sail in caravels and brigantines to the mainland to christianize the Indians and turn them from their idolatry and heinous crimes by making war on them.[63] Charles was absent from Spain, but on 16 February 1533 the queen granted the Jamaican petition and hoped that the Council of Justice, the aldermen, knights, esquires, and officials would protect the rights of the crown and observe faithfully and diligently the orders of the Council of the Indies. Should the royal officials be unable to accompany the colonists, they must send two religious persons or priests, and a notary must observe that the correct form be observed. When the Indians had been summoned and examined, and it should appear that with justice war can be made on them, the royal officials may then declare war. Any Indian taken prisoner was to be held in slavery.[64] The queen knew that this was contrary to previous royal decrees and stated that, notwithstanding any previous decree forbidding Indians being made slaves, the present decree was to stand and any person who should make it void or act contrary to it, would incur the displeasure of the crown and be subject to a fine of 10,000 maravedis. History would pronounce the whole venture as naive, if not unjust. It was never put into effect.

Private letters to the crown give us a glimpse into the colonial life of the Seville era. Some concern inheritances, others domestic problems like the one written by Francisca Flórez, an inhabitant of Ciudad Rodrigo, Spain, in which she complained to the king that about twenty-eight years before she had married Marcos Martínez.[65] They had lived as man and wife for two years or more. About twenty-five years before, Marcos left for the Indies; during these years he had neither written nor provided for her support. She suffered very much from this neglect. She learned that he had married a daughter of Retamales in Jamaica, and she had presented this information to the Council of the Indies. Francisca asked that the officials in Jamaica apprehend the person of Martínez, that they seize and sell the goods he accumulated in Jamaica, and that the money from the sale be sent to the king's officials in the city of Seville, Spain, and further that Marcos return to conjugal life with her. Francisca received a sympathetic hearing from the queen, who wrote to the royal officials in Jamaica on 20 April 1533, saying that as soon as they received her letter, they were to summon Marcos, hear the parties concerned, and administer summary justice so that no further complaint might reach the queen.

Inheritance was another worry for both king and queen. Juan Ruiz died in Jamaica in 1522.[66] In his will he left his wife and three sons, Martin López Melendo, Juan Ruiz Melendo, and Hernad Ruiz, citizens of Vaena, Spain, much property and personal effects. He had entrusted to fellow colonists his possessions including two hundred gold pesos to one Diego de Villanueva. Fourteen years had elapsed since Ruiz's death, but his widow and sons had not collected their inheritance. They were poor people and had not the means to pursue the case at law. In writing to the crown, they asked that the effects of the deceased be brought to the Chamber of Commerce, Seville, Spain, that the heirs might claim them. Again it was the queen who replied from Valladolid on 14 July 1536, saying that the alcaldes in Jamaica were to make inquiries and ascertain what jewels, gold, silver, and other effects belonging to Ruiz might have remained in possession of colonists. These, together with all papers concerning the effects of the deceased, were to be sent by the first ship leaving for Spain.[67]

The daughter of a former governor of Jamaica, Licentiate Gil González de Avila, asked for her father's salary which was still due him from the crown. Doña María de Alva, wife of Doctor Galaza, said that her father, who had been governor of Jamaica from 1533 to 1534, had never received his salary. The crown replied from Valladolid 18 May 1533, telling the alcaldes to verify Doña María's claim; if it were found correct, they should send the salary to the Chamber of Commerce, Seville, Spain. This too was to be sent by the first ship leaving for Spain but at the risk of the heiress. Doña María received her father's salary.[68]

Another heiress, Elena de Ledesma, claimed that her son, Juan de Bolanos, died, leaving certain effects which belonged to his mother as rightful heiress. On 6 September 1538, the king wrote to the alcaldes of Seville that they send the effects of the deceased together with his will, after they have ascertained if anyone in Jamaica had legal claim on the property. The royal officials were to do justice to all concerned, and should they act unjustly they would incur the king's displeasure and a fine of 20,000 maravedis.[69]

The heirs of another governor, Juan de Mendegurren, complained that he had died in Jamaica, leaving gold, silver, and other effects in the possession of Pedro Cano, an inhabitant of the island, and they asked that inquiries be made whether Cano had them in his possession or whether they be in the possession of any other person. The heirs asked that they be returned to them in Spain. As in the other cases, the crown commanded that justice be accorded the heirs of former Governor Juan de Mendegurren.[70]

Even the king of Portugal lodged a complaint, stating that he had sent certain ships of Suhnias under licence from the king of Spain to Hispaniola. Through bad weather one ship sprang a leak but made port in Jamaica. Juan Pedro Montero, who had charge of the *Suhnias* sold the goods, the greater part on credit and at a low price. On 22 January 1536, the king of Spain ordered his Jamaican governor to have them collected at once and if paid in gold, silver, or precious stones, to arrange that sufficient value in bonds be given in Jamaica and a duplicate be sent to officials in Seville, Spain, and all possible assistance be given to the agents of the king of Portugal in settling the matter.[71]

Three

Absentee Abbots

The First Abbot: Dr. Sancho de Matienzo, 1516–1522

As early as 1514 the Church in Jamaica began to assume some degree of pioneer importance; colonists had increased to five hundred, Seville could boast of a church, and the Arawaks were being converted. Christian influence was spreading along the coast wherever Spaniards settled to carve out plantations and ranches from virgin forest. Such progress demanded a coordinating of ecclesiastical efforts under the aegis of an Ordinary. In order to implement this plan, Ferdinand wrote to his ambassador at Rome, Don Geronymo Vichy, on 29 January 1515, to request Leo X to appoint a prelate for Jamaica.

Ferdinand said that in 1515 the islands of the Indies were being settled more and more every day, and so to royal officials in these islands he had recommended diligent care that the aborigines should be well trained and fully instructed in Christian tenets.[1] The Patronato Real had placed a serious obligation on the king's conscience to promote both the temporal and spiritual welfare of his newly acquired subjects. In some of the Indies, ecclesiastical life was placed on a solid foundation by the appointment of bishops. Santo Domingo, Santiago de Cuba, and San Juan could boast of their own prelates because their revenues suffice to support a bishop as his episcopal state demanded.[2] But for Jamaica, neither the king's revenues nor the island's yearly income was sufficient to maintain a bishop.[3] Ferdinand's solution was to establish an abbacy for Jamaica. This was the office of a prelate inferior only to that of a bishop's see. The holder of this office, called an abbot, would have power of jurisdiction, faculty of correction, visitation, and provision. This latter signified that he had the right to issue a decree or writ in the same manner as a Spanish tribunal. Such was the office Ferdinand wished the Holy See to establish in lieu of the see of a bishop, a customary procedure where there was no bishopric. It would correspond in modern days to the office of a vicar apostolic who was not a bishop. Ferdinand nominated his own chaplain, Don Sancho de Matienzo, a canon of the church of Seville, Spain, for the office of abbot. Ferdinand ordered Ambassador Don Vichy to present his petition together with an enclosed letter to His Holiness, asking that he erect an abbacy in Jamaica under the administration of an abbot with jurisdiction in spiritual and temporal matters. In his letter Ferdinand noted that the pope would be granted one tenth part of the revenue as was the custom where there was no bishopric.[4]

No reply came to Ferdinand's petition. Annoyed by the seven month delay, he asked for an explanation.[5] Ferdinand discovered that the fault lay not with the pope: he had signed the document. But a countersigning official wanted a fee of fifty ducats for affixing his signature to the document. Even a king found reason to question the payment of fifty ducats for a mere signature.[6] Ferdinand let Rome know that he considered the request excessive.[7]

Ferdinand did not live to see his chaplain appointed abbot of Jamaica; this was reserved for his successor, Charles I. Charles announced the event to Don Diego Colón in a letter dated 17 July 1516, saying that Leo X had created and erected an abbacy for the whole of Jamaica, appointing Sancho de Matienzo the first abbot.[8] In missionary zeal Matienzo could hardly be classed with Paul, Augustine of Canterbury, or Xavier, for he had no qualms about collecting profits, rents, and emoluments attached to the abbacy, but when it came to the inconvenience of leaving Spain to take up residence in colonial Jamaica, he preferred to act through a vicar.[9] It is fairly clear why Charles I did not compel the first abbot to reside in the island. Charles in 1519 was a mere youth of nineteen years, a novice in matters ecclesiastical, and would have respected the wishes of an older man who had spent his entire clerical life in the comparative comfort of his native Spain. Advanced in years and sickly, Matienzo died in 1522, only six years after his appointment.

The Second and Third Abbots:
Don Andrés López Frias, 1522–1523
Don Luis de Figueroa, 1522–1524

The appointment of the second abbot was made amid some unnecessary confusion, for while Charles I was absent from Spain—this was the period of the paralyzing French wars—Diego Colón presented Prothonotary Apostolic Andrés López Frias as the appointee to fill the position of abbot of Jamaica left vacant by Matienzo.[10] Charles admitted the legality of Colon's action: "a report has been made to me that the governor of these realms in my absence, by our commission, presented to Andrés López the abbacy of Jamaica."[11]

Diego's presentation of Frias, confirmed by Adrian VI, 25 December 1522, was evidently not in accord with the mind of Charles I, who on 27 March 1523, offered his own candidate, the Jeronimite Don Luis de Figueroa. Behind the choice of Jeronimite Figueroa lay a plan to rectify harsh conquistador treatment of the Indians.[12] This was a change of policy by the crown, not in its fundamental humane attitude toward the Indian, but a change in policy towards the conquistadors, compelling them to observe strictly the royal decrees issued for the amelioration of the aborigines. This change was brought about chiefly by Las Casas's constant, but not always fair, criticism of colonial officials.[13] Definitely, something had to be done if Arawak civilization was to survive.

Strict, zealous Figueroa was the man for the task. In his person he was to combine both spiritual and civil authority, for he was both abbot of Jamaica and bishop of La Vega de la Concepción, Hispaniola, and president of the powerful Council of the Indies of the Audiencia in Hispaniola, which controlled colonial policy in the Americas.[14]

A Jeronimite was the perfect choice for this work of reform. A religious congregation of hermits founded in the fourteenth century under the Rule of St. Augustine, they became noted for generous almsgiving throughout Spain and Italy. By reason of the sanctity of their lives, the Holy See employed them to reform other religious orders which had lost their pristine spirit.

Reformation was no new experience for these holy men. On one occasion, being sent to investigate the evils which had crept into the *repartimiento* system in Jamaica, they discovered that, contrary to law, absentee landlords were using Indians on their estates.[15] The Jeronimites rectified this irregularity by reassigning these Indians to actual inhabitants of the island.

With the appointment of Figueroa, everything was in readiness to set rolling the wheels of reform. But Figueroa never reached Jamaica. He died in 1523, and with him died all hope of immediate reform of the vast network of colonial officialdom.[16]

Figueroa was dead, but Frias was much alive, crying for his tithes. Although deprived of office, Don Frias was quick to point out that he had been legally proposed by Diego Colón and canonically appointed by Adrian VI to the abbacy of Jamaica. He was therefore entitled to all the profits and income that had accrued.[17] Charles I amicably settled the matter by ordering the governor to pay Frias all the profits, income, and tithes that were due to the abbot from 25 December 1522 to 27 March 1523 when the king had proposed Figueroa for the office.[18] Two years later, in 1525, Frias donated these tithes toward the erection of a new stone church at Seville, Jamaica.[19]

Of great pith and moment were profits, income, and tithes, but the personal administration of the infant Church was of little importance in the everyday life of these abbots.[20] For the colonists, however, the question of tithes was a thorny one, and they questioned the right which these abbots called for tithes and yet neglected to perform the religious duties incumbent on their office. The income from the Jamaican Abbacy was now on a par with the sees of Cuba and San Juan of Puerto Rico, and yet no bishopric was granted to Jamaica. No light burden was placed on struggling cattlemen and farmers by paying heavy tithes, so that they reluctantly parted with hard-earned income to ecclesiastics ensconced in Old World comfort, unwilling to leave Spain for the tropical, exotic, but nevertheless primitive, north side Jamaica. Had the effort to take up residence in Jamaica been equal to their zeal in collecting tithes, the Church would have enjoyed resident abbots and greater progress would have been made in the spiritual life of the colony. Absenteeism has never helped the Church; Jamaica was no exception.

Fourth Abbot: Don Pedro Martyr d'Anghiera, 1524–1526

If the importance of an office may be judged from the eminence of the person chosen to fill the position, the abbacy of Jamaica ranked high in Spain and in Rome, in the minds of king and pope, for both agreed upon Peter Martyr d'Anghiera as the fourth abbot.[21]

In all Spain there could not be found another to equal Peter Martyr in humanistic studies and in knowledge of the Indies; in both fields he was a master. Born 2 February 1457, at Arona, near Anghiera, Italy, Peter sought his fortune at the age of twenty in Rome, where his superior talents attracted some of the greatest humanists of the age, Pomponius Laetus, Cardinal Arcimbolo and Cardinal Ascanio Sforza. In August 1487 Peter fortuitously accompanied Ambassador Don Iñigo de Mendoza to Spain, where he remained for the rest of his life. In 1488, by special invitation, he lectured at the University of Salamanca where the presence of Castile's intelligentia at his lectures so enhanced his reputation that he was introduced to the court in 1492 and there taught the nobles and many of Spain's most prominent citizens. If Peter Martyr's reputation as a humanist was preeminent, as a historian of the Indies he had no peer in his day. Appointed official chronicler in 1511, Peter had access to all documents which passed through the powerful Council of the Indies. Not only had he access to all official documents, but he was personally acquainted with Columbus and other famous names of discovery and colonization. At great labour, Peter acquired firsthand knowledge of what was currently happening in the New World, and from his studies came his well-known *Decades* upon which historian and geographer have leaned heavily for a picture of people, places, and events in early sixteenth century America. These were the qualifications of Don Peter Martyr d'Anghiera who was presented to Pope Clement VII by Charles I for abbot of Jamaica on 19 December 1523;[22] he was confirmed shortly afterwards by the pope in 1524.

First Stone Church

On his spouse, as Peter Martyr affectionately called his Church in Jamaica, he lavished all emoluments of office, and he even begged additional funds from Charles to carry out necessary improvements at Seville. His first consideration was to appraise the condition of the edifice used for divine worship. He found that on two occasions the wooden church had suffered disaster—timber and wattle had burnt to the ground. Peter launched a campaign to erect a structure not only fire resistant but one architecturally worthy of colonial Seville and the dignity of his abbacy. Constructed of limestone quarried locally by Arawaks a mile or so back in the hills, squared and decorated by Spanish craftsmen talented in sculpturing the most intricate designs, this edifice was planned by Peter Martyr to rival any church of its size in Europe.

Construction began sometime in 1524, for in a letter dated 21 March 1524 Charles I noted that it had been reported to him that Peter Martyr had made a gift of the income of the first year from his abbacy to defray expenses in building the chapel of the principal church and this had received royal approval.[23] In the same letter Charles revealed some pertinent facts concerning early building construction at Seville, declaring that within a period of fourteen years, Spanish artisans had taught semisavage Arawaks the arts of masonry and brick-making. They were now employed in helping construct houses, the fort, and the governor's castle. Peter Martyr requested that these Indians skilled in building construction be employed to build his church.[24] Pioneer work had its human side. Indians had to be fed, and this was a problem until one Seville official discovered that a large quantity of yucca and ajes—a species of pepper—valued at one hundred fifty gold pesos had been placed in the custody of certain citizens by the Jeronimites when they made their visitation. Since their ownership had now become mooted, the Seville official applied to Charles that these delicacies be used to support the cacique and his Indians working on the new church. The king approved the request. More money was added to the growing funds for the Church when Peter Martyr persuaded former Abbot Frias to allocate all rents and profits that belonged to the abbacy during his incumbency.[25] This also met with the approval of the king who was anxious to build the main chapel of stone and brick to avoid the dangers that had destroyed the former church built of timber and wattle. Not to be surpassed in almsgiving, Charles I instructed his treasurer to allocate an amount of money equal to the combined donations of Peter Martyr and Andrés Frias. This was to be paid into the hands of a trustworthy person, who was to administer it conjointly with the vicar general, Peter Martyr's representative in Jamaica.[26]

Charles I was a man of meticulous exactness to detail, though it should concern a remote area of his empire, it was considered worthy of his undivided attention. Thus, on the eve of defeating Francis at Pavia, 24 February 1525, he was as much concerned with his Church overseas in Seville as he was in waging a full-scale war against France. He knew down to a fine detail that the cacique who had become an expert in making lime and brick for the government fortress in St. Ann's Bay was to be engaged in constructing the Seville church. Fearing lest coercion be used, the king cautioned the governor that the cacique and his people were to work of their own free will and were to be paid a wage. A second caution from Charles demanded that the cost of construction be kept as low as possible, and all expenses were to be met by Peter Martyr from funds made available to him.[27] To show how minutely the king was informed of colonial affairs, he knew that some lime, bricks, and other material had been left over from the building of the fort; these he consigned into the hands of the governor and vicar general as a further contribution to the church.[28]

In 1526 the Church received an additional grant of 100,000 maravedis.[29] This generous sum had originally been assigned to construct a new hospital, but on second consideration the hospital was not considered urgent, since few colonists were ill in Seville and such sick who came from other parts of the island were well-cared for in private homes.[30]

A letter of 9 September 1526 reveals that construction of the stone church was well under way.[31] One month later, on 15 October, Charles announced the sad news to the colonists that Abbot Peter Martyr, who showed such keen personal interest in their new church, was dead.[32] Shortly before his death, Peter Martyr had experienced annoyance from colonial officials. Pedro Mazuelo, who had caused Governor Garay no end of trouble in 1515, removed the Indians constructing the church to repair the fort. For this act Mazuelo and his fellow officials received a severe reprimand from Charles I, who commanded that they observe strictly the royal order concerning these Arawaks and permit no other work to interfere with the work of the church.[33] Five years passed and in 1533 came complaints by the aldermen, knights, esquires, and other citizens of Seville that the stone church to which Peter Martyr had donated eight hundred pesos, and to which the crown had allocated another eight hundred, was badly in need of money if it were to be completed.[34]

One hundred fifty years later, it was a sad spectre standing amid the cane fields. Hans Sloane, founder of the British Museum, penned a picture of its unfinished ruins:

> The Town [Seville] is now Captain Hemming's plantation. The church was not finished. It was 20 paces broad and 30 paces long. There were two rows of pillars within. Over the place where the altar was to be were some carvings under the ends of the arches. It was built of a sort of stone, between freestone and marble, taken out of a quarry about a mile up in the hills. At the church lie several arched stones to complete it, which had never been put up, but lay among the canes. The rows of pillars were for the most part plain. . . . The west gate of the church was very fine work and stands entire. It is seven feet wide, and as high before the arch began. Over the door in the middle was Our Saviour's Head and a Crown of Thorns between two angels, on the right side a small figure of some saint with a knife struck into his head; on the left a Virgin Mary of Madonna, her arm tied in three places, Spanish style. Over the gate, under a coat of arms, this inscription:
>
> Petrus Martir ab Angleria Italus civis Medionalen. Prothon. Apos. Hujus. insulae Abbas Senatus Indici consiliarius ligneam prius aedem hanc bis igne consumptam latericio et quadrato lapide primus a fundamentis extruxit.
>
> [Peter Martyr of Angleria, an Italian citizen of Milan, Prothonotary Apostolic, Abbot of this island, Consultor of the Council of the Indies, was the first to construct of brick and squared stone from its foundation this building, formerly made of wood and twice destroyed by the fire.][35]

Had Peter Martyr lived, the church would have been completed and the stone inscription of its builder would never have found its way into the old slaughter house in St. Ann's Bay, where one section of it was discovered by a workman in 1953, some three feet long and eighteen inches wide, containing one sixth of the original inscription.[36] This find confirmed the tradition that stones from the church were used in the British conquerors' buildings in St. Ann's Bay.

Friar Miguel Ramirez, 1527–1535

There appear periodically on every human scene troublesome characters. Of such a nature was Friar Miguel Ramirez, O.P., who held combined the offices of bishop of Santiago de Cuba and of abbot of Jamaica. A man of strong temperament and energy, once set on a course he continued undeviating to the goal. Proposed for the office of abbot on 17 May 1527, he received its revenues retroactively to the death of Peter Martyr, 15 October 1526.[37] With documents from Charles I authorizing him to collect these tithes, he sailed for Jamaica. Santiago de Cuba was his destination; Jamaica merely a stopover on his way to his diocese.[38]

As Ramirez's carrack rounded the reef at St. Ann's Bay, the whole populace stood on the shore to welcome with that respectful enthusiasm a people of deep faith show for their prelate. His departure several months later was much in contrast to his arrival. Cheers changed into sullen resentment at the high-handed dealings. He used his civil authority by assigning Indians to some favoured colonists for his own aggrandizement and to the detriment of other settlers. Besides holding the offices of bishop of Cuba and abbot of Jamaica, he held in common with Governor Juan de Mendegurren the civil authority to assign Arawaks to colonists, if he found some of the Indians unemployed. Half of these he imprudently allotted to clerics of the island, the other half he kept for his own service.[39] He made another mistake by including in his distribution Indians who actually belonged to the king, and a further error by seizing two of the king's farms. Official Spain became aware of the abbot's depredations, and such a furor was aroused by his rash acts that a strongly worded letter was addressed to Ramirez on 22 December 1530. He was reminded that his office imposed a special concern for the Arawaks, and he was not permitted to have Indians for his personal service in order to be able to demand their humane treatment by others. This ruling applied not only to the abbot of Jamaica but to all prelates and protectors of Indians wherever they might live in the colonies. The queen's note personally to Ramirez was sharp:

> I, therefore command you, if you have any Indians allotted to you, or have acquired them in any manner, at once discharge them, you and our Governor, allot them to persons, inhabitants of the island who may be without them and henceforth you will not take any for yourself. Such is our will, and such also meet for the service of God, Our Lord, and the discharge of our conscience.[40]

In order to prevent future depredatory acts, the crown ordered the next governor, Gil Gonzales Dávila, to make an official enquiry into the manner in which Jamaican Arawaks were treated. He was ordered to investigate to what persons and for what reason these Indians had been allotted contrary to royal decrees, to note if preference had been given conquistadors and settlers without just reason, and to search out frauds and misdeeds, and to learn if Indians had been ill-treated. Those found guilty of ill-treating the Indians should be punished in their person as well as in their purse.[41] This particular document and many like it reveal a continual paternal benevolence by the Spanish rulers towards the Indian. Any cruelty or injustice must be placed squarely on subordinate Church and State officials as well as on settlers themselves.

Removal of Chief Town from North to South Side of the Island

In 1534, while Ramirez was abbot, the capital was removed from the north to the south side and renamed Santiago de la Vega. With its removal the curtain falls on the first epoch of Spanish Jamaica. The generally accepted reason for its removal was that the site on the north was unhealthy. This and more details were written in a letter by Charles I to Governor Gil Gonzales Dávila on 19 July 1534.[42] Mazuelo suggested moving the capital for, whereas, when the Indians were distributed under Garay in 1524, Seville had eighty conquistadors, only twenty were alive in 1534. The rest had succumbed to pestilence and disease caused by the unhealthy location of the town. Since swamps and creeks lie between port and town, the sea breeze passing over the miasma carried infected air to Seville. Again this same polluted air returned to the town after striking the high mountains rising in the south. The treasurer Mazuelo, who took five hundred Indians for his own personal service, and made life so miserable for the Indians that they fled Jamaica, drew a rosy picture of the south side of the island: no mountains, good water, soil easy to cultivate, extensive grazing lands, and two good harbours. He also claimed that the inhabitants were already cultivating crops on the south side and were contemplating removing their homes there to enjoy some comfort and a certain supply of good food.

But Mazuelo's complaint about continual sickness on the north side does not agree with a report to the king in 1526, which claimed that the people were healthy and were in no need of a hospital for which Charles I had allotted 100,000 maravedis:

> You know well that I [the king] made a grant of 100,000 maravedis drawn on our treasurer to assist building a hospital in which might be collected the sick men of the island as is more fully set forth in the decree on the subject that I ordered, and on the part of the said island a report has been made to me that there is no need for the said hospital because there are very few sick and when some come from other parts of the island, the inhabitants receive them, keep them in their houses and give them what they require.[43]

It would appear that the royal treasurer Mazuelo had a personal reason for relocating the capital. On the south side he had a sugar mill, and it was close to this mill that he requested the king to issue a license for the establishment of the new capital Santiago de la Vega.[44] It would also make it easier for Mazuelo to supervise the work.

Despite Mazuelo's suspected personal interest, the south side proved an ideal location for the capital, commanding the use of two excellent harbours, and near the great plain of Vere which could boast of some of the most fertile cane land in the world. Along this same coast developed the great Spanish *hatos:* Morant; Ayala (Yallahs), Liguanea (St. Andrew); Guanaboa; Guatibacoa (Old Harbour); Yama (Vere); Le Eado (Blue Fields); Cabanico (Savanna-la-Mar).[45]

Rarely can the career of a Spanish crown official in Jamaica be followed in such detail as that of Mazuelo from January 1515 until he left the island twenty years later. His ill treatment of the Indians, his refusal to relinquish the castle to Governor Garay, and his pressing into his personal service five hundred Arawaks, have been previously noted, but there were other complaints against the royal treasurer.

One colonist protested to Charles I in 1519 that Mazuelo took Indians from him when the distribution of the Arawaks was made. In reply the king commanded Governor Garay to summon and hear the parties concerned and to act justly so that no one be aggrieved. Again, in 1526, Charles had to send another directive, this time to Governor Juan de Mendegurren, telling him that all equipment taken by Mazuelo from the two sugar mills of the late Governor Francisco Garay, were to be returned to his heirs:

> Charles I: To our Governor and Officials of the island of Santiago, called Jamaica, on behalf of the heirs of Governor Francisco Garay, deceased:
> A report was made to me that the above-mentioned governor left in that island two sugar mills. One was completed and could grind 12,000 arrobas of sugar each year. Little had to be done to the second one to complete it. This would be the best and surest business for the uplift of the island and the support of the inhabitants.
>
> They say that Pedro de Mazuelo, treasurer of the island, because of the great enmity towards the aforementioned Francisco Garay, has endeavoured and is still trying to destroy those sugar mills. And he has stopped granting what money he has for their upkeep and management.
>
> Furthermore, certain properties and things were given to the above-mentioned Governor Garay as *encomiendo.* And I have been begged and requested to order whatever the said Governor Garay might have had in *encomiendo* be left intact so that the above mentioned sugar mills should be preserved. And I was requested to order that if anything has been taken away, that it be restored.
>
> So, seeing that the above-mentioned mills were beneficial to the inhabitants of that island, reflecting too on the many outstanding services rendered to us by the said Francisco Garay and it being right that his sons,

as far as possible, receive benefits and not hardships, I command you to see to all the above and take steps to carry out everything that the above-mentioned Governor Garay ordered to be done with his estate and for the service and maintenance of the above-mentioned mills.

If others have them, let them return them so that the true heirs may have them in their entirety.

Let there be no deceit under penalty of 10,000 maravedis for each one who might act contrariwise.

9 September 1526[46]

The most serious complaint came in the year 1533, from Ballabos, fiscal of the Council of the Indies, who reiterated Antonio Garay's claim that Mazuelo and another official, Juan Lopez de Torralba, were mismanaging the king's estates, properties formerly held in partnership with Governor Garay but dissolved since his death. They administered these properties as though they were their own personal estates. They sold Indians, slaves, horses, bread, birds, and other products to Spanish settlers in the new colonies of the west; when these products brought a high market price, they claimed them as their own; but when they brought a low price, they generously allowed the king to have the returns. But they had no power to sell the king's cattle or produce except at public auction and to the highest bidder. Eight thousand pesos were involved in this fraud.[47]

Such an accumulation of complaints could only arouse suspicion back in Spain that Mazuelo was not managing his office in the best interests of the crown. To confirm his suspicions, Charles I sent one of his most trusted servants, Manuel de Rojas, to act as governor and investigate the suspected irregularities.

Rojas arrived in Jamaica on 25 July 1534.[48] Since Mazuelo's accounts had been impounded when Governor González de Dávila died the previous June, they were released to Rojas, whose royal commission authorized him to examine the accounts and sue for any balance he found owing the king. Mazuelo alleged that Rojas would not allow him to complete his accounts or show what was due the king and Garay's heirs from the partnership between his Majesty and Governor Garay made in Madrid on 9 January 1514. Rojas refused to be fooled by subterfuge, seized Mazuelo's property, and sold it to obtain what he considered was owed to the royal treasury.

Mazuelo left Jamaica a ruined man. Just before the curtain falls, we see him begging the king to allow him to go to that colony on the mainland known as Nombre de Dios. No answer to this request is extant.[49]

Four

Resident Abbots

First Resident Abbot:
Don Amador de Samano, 1535–1539

Newly founded Santiago de la Vega needed both an abbot and a church, for Abbot Ramirez, O.P., had died in January 1535, and the incomplete church at Seville on the north side had been abandoned when the capital was removed to the south side in 1534.[1] Stones, bricks, stark pillars, and carefully worded inscriptions of the church that had been ruined by rains, winds, and tropical storms were all that was left on the north side. But on the south side things were different. There a growing population was anxious to have a place worthy of divine worship, for despite all their faults these early Spanish colonists were a religious people. The abbacy also needed a resident prelate who would perceive and solve her thorny ecclesiastical colonial problems. Considering the abbacy vacancy of more immediate importance, Charles I nominated Don Amador de Samano to the office of abbot on 1 March 1535.[2] He presented his nomination to Paul III through his ambassador, Count de Cifuentes, a relative of the king and chief standard bearer of Castile. Once Samano's name had been dispatched to Rome, events moved rapidly in the life of the abbot elect. Only two weeks had elapsed when Charles I, writing to him from Madrid on 15 March 1535, ordered Samano to proceed at once to Jamaica.[3] Charles had become impatient with appointees that sat at home by the comfortable fireside collecting with regularity tithes which colonists paid reluctantly to abbots they never saw. A labourer in the vineyard, not an absentee landlord, was the real need for Jamaica. Pending the transmission of papal bulls, Charles I granted him power to act in the capacity of abbot as far as lay in the power of the crown to do so. To make certain no obstacle would stand in Samano's path, Charles wrote to the governor and his royal officials in Jamaica on 23 May 1539 requesting them to allow Samano to take possession of his abbacy should he arrive in the island prior to the papal confirmation.[4] In the same letter, the king decreed that the officials in Jamaica pay the abbot all the emoluments of his office from the day he embarked from San Lucar Barrameda, Spain.[5] To these were to be added all the revenues that accrued since the death of his predecessor, Abbot Miguel Ramirez, which funds were now designated to construct and furnish a new church at Santiago de la Vega.[6] The annual abbacy revenues fluctuated with the island's economy; the average over the years of Spanish occupation was four hundred pesos. Revenue was collected from such items upon which government levied customs duty. Tax on profits made by ranches and farms was another source of income. A tithe on all revenues was assigned to the Holy See. In this case it went to the incumbent abbot. The method used to reap these tithes by the abbots, though contrary to the laws of the Indies, was countenanced by Jamaican government officials. This was to farm out the tithes to the highest bidder at an annual auction, a method which smacked of the publicans under the ancient Romans. And it led to abuses, for the person who bought the right to collect would not only make back what he had paid but would look for a profit; otherwise he would not be in business. Early Spanish residents objected to these taxes, saying they could see no reason why they should pay a tax on local lime, tiles, bricks, and fish to an abbot they never saw. Municipal authorities listened sympathetically to their protests and persuaded the crown to exempt them temporarily from the tax; this was in 1526.[7]

Again the queen came to Samano's rescue. She wrote on his behalf to that same body on April 22, 1535, and ordered the officials to loan Samano the 50,000 maravedis, provided he gave sufficient guarantee of repayment within two years.[8] Following this incident another minor problem arose: Samano did not have the servants customary for a person of his rank. Out in the colony it would look bad, and it might even lower his social status, should the creoles see him without servants. Samano asked for Jamaican Arawaks to serve him. Although it was contrary to royal policy for clerics to have Indians, an exception was made in his particular case; Samano was granted this faculty by the queen.[9] Should there be any Arawaks unemployed in Jamaica as domestic servants, he was free to use them provided they entered his service of their own will and without pay. The royal ordinance of providing these Indians with food and clothing was pointed out to the abbot.[10] That the queen had to remind the prelate that he must provide the Indians with the necessities of life seems superfluous, but instances in the past made this warning imperative. Despite royal anxiety to see Samano off, these annoying obstacles delayed his early departure.

Amador de Samano may have had his troubles before embarking, but they were minor compared with those when he stepped ashore at low-lying muddy Caguay (Passage Fort). Here he encountered a critical civil situation. The descendants of Christopher Columbus had filed suit to recover from the crown the island of Jamaica.[11] They claimed it was their patrimony. Diego Colón, son of Christopher, had married Doña María de Toledo and two sons were born of this union. Luis, the elder and heir to his father's titles, entered suit to regain what he claimed had been the rightful possession of his grandfather, the discoverer. Charles I finally allowed his claim.

Since Charles I was absent from Spain, the queen wrote Governor Manuel de Rojas on 8 September 1536 that the king had awarded Don Luis Colón the island of Jamaica with civil and criminal jurisdiction.[12] To Luis was now due all taxes and profits of the island. A superfluous addition granted to the heir "mines and mining, silver and gold." No precious metal had ever been discovered in Jamaica, but the king's lands and pastures and whatever he had in Jamaica were of value and went to Luis Colón. Charles conceded everything except supreme jurisdiction.[13] From the day Rojas received this letter, he was no longer to exercise the office of governor but was to yield to the person that Doña María de Toledo, acting in the name of her minor son Luis, should sent or appoint. The office of governor fell to Pedro Cano, a native of Jamaica.[14]

This choice was unfortunate for Abbot Samano. The day Samano assumed office, Cano, accompanied by inhabitants of Santiago de la Vega, appeared at the abbot's residence and demanded that the prelate produce the papal documents authorizing him to take over the abbacy. Since they had not arrived, Samano could not show them. Whereupon he was told by Cano in language ill-befitting a governor that he was not to exercise ecclesiastical jurisdiction.[15] Cano's opposition was a direct defiance of both abbot and king. He insulted the abbot by refusing to recognize the faculties granted by the cardinal archbishop of Seville. He defied the king's right under the Patronato Real to propose a candidate whose confirmation by the Holy See was always an assured fact. More sensitive nerves Cano could not have touched.

The feud between governor and abbot had split the town in two. Although the whole ecclesiastical body should have allied itself solidly on the side of the abbot, at least one priest, Fr. Juan Cano, possibly a relative of the governor, leagued himself on the side of the governor, defying ecclesiastical authority, and causing a disturbance in Santiago de la Vega. Since there was no abbot to personally guide the Church in the crucial years between Ramirez's death and Samano's arrival, the peril of an overly ambitious cleric assuming a role to which he had not been canonically appointed became a real danger in the person of Fr. Juan Cano. Licitly or illicitly, some power of jurisdiction had been granted Juan by the old municipality of Seville, and from this point of departure he assumed the role of ecclesiastical judge without canonical appointment in the new capital of Santiago de la Vega. Upon Samano's arrival he presumed to sit in judgment on the new abbot.

On 5 September 1539, Charles sent a sharp note to Cano. Disrespect had been shown the king's royal decree when Cano, accompanied by others, had gone to the house of the abbot and demanded he produce the papal documents appointing him abbot and on his own authority forbade Samano to exercise ecclesiastical jurisdiction. Cano must also have berated and threatened the abbot, for Charles accused Cano of using disrespectful words and of other things worthy of censure and punishment. It had been a wild day in the capital, one which had to be reported immediately to the king either by Samano or some official through a deed legally notarized and signed by competent witnesses. Charles's decision was swift and to the point. Since receiving these serious complaints, the king referred the case to the Council of the Indies, which suggested that Charles direct a royal order to Cano. It said that Cano was to appear before the president and judges of the audiencia in Hispaniola within fourteen days after the receipt of the decree to undergo trial for his offense. Should he fail to appear in person, he would incur the royal displeasure and suffer the loss of one half of his property.[16] Cano ceased to be governor shortly after his trial in 1539.

Under the same date of 5 September 1539, as the king's letter to Governor Cano, another letter showered royal wrath upon the cleric Juan for "presuming to act as an ecclesiastical judge, for publicly insulting the abbot, for causing a rebellious disturbance in Santiago de la Vega and many other incivilities."[17] All, so the royal epistle claimed, were harmful to the service of God. In this letter Charles I reversed the roles; Cano the judge was to be judged. Samano was to apprehend the person of Juan, send him under arrest to the bishop of Cuba who would render judgment in the case. The final barb from the king's pen decreed that Juan Cano was to pay his own fare to the judgement seat in Cuba.

The Abbey Church in Santiago de la Vega

If one had lived in Santiago de la Vega during the twenty year period from 1534 to 1554, one would have witnessed the few houses clustered around Mazuelo's sugar mill develop into as neat a sixteenth-century Spanish Colonial town as one might find in all the Indies. The very heart of the municipality was its plaza, an open quadrangle around which were framed its public buildings: the governor's palace, the abbey church, the Council Chambers, and the public offices. On the south side of Santiago de la Vega's plaza, Samano built his church. Edward Long, Jamaica's pioneer historian, saw the ruins of this ancient abbey church and pinpointed the site as the south side of the plaza where the guard room and British chapel stood in 1770.[18] Here he noted the huge eight foot square bases of brick, cemented with fine mortar, which supported two tall columns of the archway leading into the church. Long praised the Spanish clergy for having cultivated such elegant architecture in this remote part of the world and condemned the English invaders for their fanatic rage and heedless indifference in permitting the ruin of so splendid a work of art. The abbey church, served by the abbot and his secular priest, would correspond to a cathedral if Jamaica had a bishop for its ordinary in this Spanish period.

The Dominicans in Jamaica

Two other churches formed the nucleus of religious life in the capital. The Dominicans had constructed a substantial monastery of stone, and attached to this monastery was their church dedicated to Our Lady of Perpetual Help.[19] Its site was just north of the town limits, on the banks of the Río Cobre. It is possible that Abbot Ramirez, himself a Dominican, introduced members of his order into Jamaica from the very early days of the old capital at Seville. However, it would appear that the Franciscans antedated the Dominicans, and that from Seville they had removed to Santiago de la Vega where they constructed a monastery dedicated to the patron of Spain, St. James of Compostela, and a church dedicated to the Expectation of the Blessed Virgin Mary, situated about one-half mile south of the Dominican compound, on the grounds of the present Anglican cathedral.[20]

In colonial times, when the Church leaned heavily on the crown for financial aid in constructing ecclesiastical edifices, both the monastery and the Dominican church were built from funds collected from contributions among colonists of Jamaica. This offers a clue to the solid financial status of its inhabitants during this twenty-year period, when Spanish Jamaica was experiencing her most prosperous era, enriched by returns from fertile soil on the south coast extending down through the district of Vere, where even today is found some of the best cane producing land in the world, and this after being cultivated for four centuries. Only six miles to the west, another harbour offered its facilities. Unfortunately, Jamaica was off the ordinary Spanish shipping routes; so that when the fleet from Spain called into Santo Domingo, it split into two sections, one sailing to Cartagena, the other to Havana, bypassing Jamaica on its north coast. Had Santiago de la Vega been on one of the main shipping routes, there would have been more facilities to market its products.

Two other religious chapels, called hermitages, completed the number of edifices dedicated to divine service in the island. One was dedicated to St. Lucy,[21] the other to St. Barbara, where Mass was celebrated only on certain feast days. Both were outside the capital; one is thought to have been on the present site of the Jamaica School of Agriculture at Twickenham Park, a few miles east of Santiago de la Vega; the site of the other hermitage is not known. Since the number of churches was limited, the missionaries travelled to the great haciendas where they celebrated Mass and offered the inhabitants the opportunity to fulfill their religious duties.

Samano closed his career as abbot in 1539, and from that date until 1554 there is no indication of an incumbent in the office.[22] It is hardly possible that the Holy See would have allowed a fifteen year period to elapse without appointing a successor. The lacuna must be accredited to the fact that Jamaica was now in the hands of the Columbus family; hence royal documents are rare. The next four abbots, of whom we have very little history are Johanes Dávila (1554–?); Don Francisco Orsorio Mercado (1561–73); Don Mateo de Santiago (1573–78); Licentiate Luis Muñoz (1578–?). Of Abbot Johanes Dávila we have only the brief statement that he came to Jamaica in 1554 and in that same year made a sea voyage to consult Don Luis Colón, duke of Veragua; after he reached Honduras in Central America, the mantle of mystery falls on him.[23]

A period of twenty months had elapsed since Abbot Dávila left Jamaica and during this time the crown had designated Fr. Francisco Izquierdo as curate of the abbey church, but Governor Juan González de Hinojosa had, by virtue of the power vested in him by the king, appointed Juan Descobar to the same office. Descobar had been well-received by all the inhabitants for to his zeal the Church owed much of her prosperity. Fortunately, Izquierdo was also a zealous priest, so they came to an amicable agreement whereby each took a week's turn acting as curate for the abbey church.

Little documentary evidence is extant on the administration of Abbot Don Francisco Osorio Mercado, the next incumbent; but what there is helps to settle one important question: Jamaica's position in the hierarchy of the West Indies, then undefined. Was the abbot of Jamaica under the bishop of Cuba or under the archbishop of Santo Domingo? Whenever this question arose, no one could give a satisfactory answer. Since Jamaica was geographically closer to Cuba than to Hispaniola, it was assumed by the bishop of Cuba that the island fell within the sphere of his jurisdiction.

On 15 November 1570, Andrés de Carvajal, O.F.M., bishop of Puerto Rico, became archbishop of Santo Domingo.[24] The new archbishop laid claim to Jamaica, but had not reckoned with the fighting spirit of Bishop Don Juan del Castillo of Santiago de Cuba, who sailed posthaste to Hispaniola, presented his case before the archbishop and the audiencia, then appealed to the Council of the Indies. The council could not be accused of undue haste in coming to a decision, for not until four years later, on 26 October 1574, did it decree that the abbacy of Jamaica was subject to the see of Santiago de Cuba.[25]

Jamaica had now been settled for some sixty years, yet the sacrament of confirmation had never been administered in the island. Such was the claim of the next abbot, Mateo de Santiago, who held office from 1573–78. Incredible as it may seem, there is no reason to doubt his statement, for the abbots lacked the faculty to administer it. Philip II used his influence to persuade Bishop Don Juan del Castillo of Cuba to administer the sacrament, for the only other bishop to visit Jamaica in that sixty year period was Ramirez, and there is no record that he conferred it.[26] Some time in 1574 drab Port Caguay assumed holiday mood as Governor Juan de Gaudiel and civic officials dressed in full regalia of office, the abbot and his priests in black, brown, and white soutanes, extended the hand of cordial welcome to Bishop Don Juan del Castillo when he arrived in Jamaica from his Cuban see. Six miles over low, flat, dusty road brought the bishop and his entourage to Santiago de la Vega, where he conferred the sacrament of confirmation on Spaniard and Arawak alike.

Had Bishop Castillo confined his activities to confirmation, there would have been no account of his extended visit, but he did not. Jamaica had been assigned to his jurisdiction as part of the diocese of Santiago de Cuba, and under this title he instituted a formal visitation of the Church in the island to right wrongs and to put order into the ecclesiastical structure. Tithes were a fundamental problem, for Castillo considered the 500–800 ducats, the income of the abbacy, not as the personal property of the abbot, but funds to be used for the general support of the Church. He reapportioned these tithes: one part he allotted to the abbot, a second to the abbey church, and a third to two canons, a sacristan, and choir boys. The abbot was no longer free to seize the lion's share and dole out what he personally thought necessary for the support of the Church. Despite his financial solicitude for the Church in Jamaica, Castillo was not at all bashful about dipping his hand into the abbacy treasury and withdrawing 1500 ducats for his own use. Not content with the first 1500 ducats, as soon as he returned to Cuba, Castillo sent his vicar general to make another visitation and another dip into abbacy funds, this time to the extent of 1000 ducats.[27] A future abbot of Jamaica commenting on these acts accused these ecclesiastics of being blinded by greed.[28] There is no written protest from Abbot Santiago, who must have been long-suffering in allowing these ecclesiastical pirates to snatch funds from under his nose without a strong letter to higher authorities.

Jamaica presented a shocking contrast in her moral life to the sound family life Abbot Santiago had known in Spain. In the Indies the morals of the slaves were of no concern to their masters; they could live as they wished, provided they put a good day's work in field or household, for ability to work was the criterion of a good slave, not his moral life. Out in the fields, at a comfortable distance from the master's house, in a poorly constructed wattle hut, the slave entered into concubinage with the woman of his choice.[29] The owner raised no objection to the children born of this illicit union, for an increase in slave population meant more hands on the hacienda.

Slavery had antedated Santiago's regime by some sixty-four years, beginning when Esquivel introduced a few slaves into Jamaica from Cape Verde. On 5 June 1513 King Ferdinand granted the Esquivel family permission to import three slaves who had to be Christians and who could not be sold to another colonist.[30] On December 13, 1527 a royal licence granted Francisco García Bermejo the right to import twenty-two black slaves into Jamaica; twelve had to be men and ten women and could be from the Cape Verde Islands or Spain itself.[31] In 1523 there is mention of slaves being employed on the king's properties and even Abbot Medina Moreno, the last of the abbots, was allowed four black slaves.[32] Once these slaves were landed in Jamaica, little attention was paid to their moral life, but Abbot Santiago thought that his office placed upon him the obligation of safeguarding the morals of his people. Before his eyes were clear violations of the moral order; to remedy this situation, he summoned those whom he suspected of living in concubinage. Questioning the parties and finding his judgment to be correct, he warned them to separate—but for some it was a serious hardship. Such cases preferred to marry rather than break up their home life.[33] One obstacle stood in the way of the abbot's social reform program: Santiago's zeal for the slaves found no enthusiastic favour with the upper class Spaniards. Some thought his action oppressive and imagined serious difficulties; others openly protested they would not consent to the marriage of their slaves. All saw marriage as depriving them of long-standing rights over their slaves, particularly the freedom of the master to dispose of his slaves where it had not been specifically forbidden. Although the crown insisted that an equal number of women accompany the male slaves to Jamaica to establish family life among slaves, this had become a dead letter in Santiago's day. It was easier for a master to dispose of an individual than to sell an entire family. Here was a practical difficulty for social-minded Santiago. His solution was to promise to protect the rights of the masters, but they were not satisfied with a mere promise and sent complaints to Luis Colón. They failed to stop the abbot who replied to Colón that he was merely doing what a Christian must do and what the law required. Anticipating such a complaint the abbot carried the case to Philip II in a letter dated 5 October 1574, wherein he explained the moral condition of the slaves and the reform he had introduced.[34] Philip assured the abbot that the crown was in full accord with the amelioration of the slaves' moral lives. Since Santiago had the approval of the king, the slave owners had no choice but to submit. Santiago had every opportunity to enforce his reforms, since he continued in office for four more years until 1578.

Little is known of the abbot who followed Santiago beyond his name, licentiate Luis Muñoz, and the fact that he was appointed in 1578 and held office for three years until his successor, Abbot Villalobos, assumed office in 1581.

Five

The Great Abbot: Marqués Villalobos

Seven miles of harbour, becalmed after the morning breeze had died down, slowed a carrack to a leisurely approach as it neared Caguay's quay. It was 24 August 1582, and the eye of every Spaniard within and without the fort was strained to catch a glimpse of their new prelate.[1] From his vantage point on deck, Villalobos had a panoramic view of the coast as his ship rounded Careening Point, the terminus of a long, extended arm of land from the main, known later in history as the Palisadoes. The beauty of the island forced itself upon his eyes. Beauty was on the broad Liguanea plain stretching several miles along the shore, rising gently to the interior until suddenly it confronted mile high mountains. Beauty was in the lush vegetation of graceful trees and savanna grass, in the retreating mist on the mountain casting a blue tint around its summit. This Caribbean island, his home for the next twenty-four years, was one of the beauty spots of the world, so admitted the abbot as the carrack sailed into Caguay.

Six miles inland the primitive natural beauty of the coast yielded to man-made Santiago de la Vega. As the abbot approached the capital, he was received by the vicar general and then escorted by the people to the abbey church where, amid a colourful ceremony, Villalobos took possession of his abbacy. No papal documents were presented; he had none, for they had not arrived. Yet no voice of protest was raised like that of Cano's against Abbot Samano, for this abbot was a marquis—Don Francisco Marqués de Villalobos, and no one dared question the integrity of one whose social position was just below that of a duke.

Immediately before the hurricane season began in May, Villalobos had sailed with the fleet from Cadiz.[2] Protection against the mounting menace of Dutch and British pirates was sought in numbers, for as many as forty-one ships have been recorded to have left

Spain for the Indies on one of these annual sailings.[3] On the outward voyage passengers were transported together with such cargo as wine, figs, raisins, olives, kerseys, oil, linen, iron, and quicksilver for the mines. The return voyage from South America carried gold and silver plate together with tropical products. Sailing south from Spain to the Canaries, the fleet struck out across the Atlantic and sighted the Lesser Antilles a month later. Fresh water was taken on at Guadeloupe, and a chance to stretch one's sea legs in treacherous Carib country if one did not wander too far from the fleet's protection.[4] Some did wander astray on a later voyage and were captured and slain by Indians. Once within the Caribbean, the fleet dispersed: some to Santo Domingo, some to Jamaica, Margarita, Havana, Puerto Rico, or Campeche; but the majority sailed to Cartagena, South America, or Veracruz, Mexico.[5]

No ship sailed directly to Jamaica in 1582, so Villalobos had to travel to Cartagena, whence he later transshipped to this island.

Villalobos was Philip II's choice; he now asserted his right to nominate the abbot because he was not satisfied with the Colón appointees. There had also risen the legal question whether his father, Charles I, had the right to subdelegate this privilege—the Holy See had granted the Patronato Real to the king of Spain, with no provision of delegation to another party.

Governed by a vicar general for eight years, the Church in Jamaica had fallen into such a chaotic situation that Villalobos recognized his first duty was to initiate a canonical visitation wherein he followed the prescribed form and opened this ecclesiastical process in Santiago de la Vega where the clergy and most of the faithful were concentrated.[6] On the appointed day, dressed in pontifical robes, the abbot arrived at the entrance of the abbey church where he was received by the vicar general and all the clergy. When the entourage had entered the church, the abbot in a sermon told the assembled congregation the purpose of the visitation. Then vesting in black cope and simple mitre, he recited prayers for the deceased abbots. Afterwards a procession was formed to the cemetery where prayers were recited. Before returning to the Abbey Church, final prayers were recited before the high altar. Then substituting white vestments for the black, the abbot examined the tabernacle, altars, baptismal font, sacred oils, confessionals, relics, records, cemetery, and all edifices attached to the abbey church, ending with private prayers at the foot of the high altar. He recorded one complaint: he had found only one baptismal register, and it was stripped of its covers because, Villalobos claimed, former abbots had been more concerned with acquiring an income than attending to their duties.[7] The abbot noted that, in the country, the greatest concentration of people was on the *hatos:* Morant Bay, Yallahs, St. Andrew, Guanaboa, Old Harbour, Vere, Pedro Plains, Oristán, and Savanna-la-Mar. These were all on the south side of Jamaica; no settlement had existed on the north coast since Seville was abandoned in 1534.

His intimate knowledge and accurate judgment of the island indicated that Villalobos had made a searching visitation of his abbacy. In the course of his visitation, there came to light some irregularities both by abbots and governors. The Colón family had chosen abbots without approbation of the Holy See.[8] Greed marked their regimes; they collected rents for their own personal use, spent the tithes and bequeathed abbacy property, which they had no right to alienate, to whomsoever they wished without approval from Rome.[9] Nor was civic life any better. Villalobos attested to similar venality in the governors of his own day.[10] Lucas del Valle Alvarado had been sent as governor by the Colón family, his first tenure of office lasting from 1578–81, and again in the year 1583, a period of about fifteen months, during which time Villalobos claimed that he dipped his hand deeply into the treasury, taking all the money he could.[11] Also, he purloined funds from the estates of deceased persons and the six hundred hides, tithes belonging to Abbot Don Mateo de Santiago, claiming he was taking them for the abbot's heirs.[12]

When he departed from Jamaica in 1581, he left a creole, Pedro Lopez, a citizen of the town and a man of many relatives, as acting governor for the year 1582.[13] Lopez was appointed governor because he had befriended Lucas del Valle Alvarado whenever the governor found himself in straightened financial conditions.[14] Lopez was irascible and quarrelsome to both secular priests and friars. He even claimed that the abbot could not impose excommunication because he brought no papal documents.[15]

From the day the Colón family acquired Jamaica, Villalobos claimed that the island was plagued by a series of law suits, but he offered no indication of their nature.[16] He also accused the Colón family of manifesting no interest in improving the country, since their governors resided in more comfortable Hispaniola and governed Jamaica through a lieutenant.[17] When one governor[18] became rich, the Colóns sent another sycophant who did likewise and made light of the irregularities of his predecessor, knowing that he himself would leave glaring lacunae in the ledger when he retired from office. Villalobos further rebuked these Colón appointees for both ill-treating the people and forcing them into a state of near slavery in a governor's private service.[19] From these wrongs the populace could expect no redress either from the incumbent governor or from his successor.

The successor would not press charges against the outgoing governor thereby winning his favour, always a valuable asset. Should the afflicted people wish to present their grievances in person to the Audiencia of Santo Domingo, they would not be granted the due process of law nor the certified papers necessary to appear before that high tribunal, and should they attempt to mail letters to that supreme body, their letters got as far as the governor's waste basket in Jamaica. Jamaican officials intercepted any letters arriving from the Audiencia of Santo Domingo; no matter how the people tried to have wrongs rectified, their case was hopeless.[20]

Strategic Importance of Jamaica

In the late sixteenth century, not only the British but also the French and Dutch were casting ominous shadows over the Indies, portending a serious threat to Spanish sovereignty. Villalobos recognized the strategic importance of Jamaica in the forthcoming struggle for supremacy of the Indies and expressed his fears for all Spain's possessions in the New World should a powerful enemy occupy so important a military position.[21] The abbot noted that the island was such a convenient latitude that, should an enemy molest his Majesty, take possession and make a permanent settlement here, as some boasted they would, it would mean total loss of the neighboring islands such as Cuba, only ninety miles to the north, or Hispaniola, one hundred miles to the east, or even Puerto Rico, the easternmost island in the Greater Antilles; finally, it would be very dangerous to Spanish naval and mercantile fleets.

He also observed that Jamaica had deep and commodious harbours such as Caguay, the chief port; Maymon and Anaya on the south coast; Morante on the south east; Oristán and Negrillo on the west; St. Ann and Puerto Antonio on the north. Each was spacious enough to hold two hundred enemy sail. In addition to these advantages, there was a well-built fortress perched on a hill overlooking St. Ann's Bay, built in the days of Garay. Though the woodwork had decayed with age, the tower and the masonry were firm and strong. Should the enemy settle here, strengthen the fort and make it his base, he could sally forth from the north coast to attack Spanish merchant vessels sailing from the mainland which passed to the leeward side of Biboras; or he might place himself in a position to plunder ships that went to New Spain while keeping in sight of both Jamaica and Cuba.[22]

Villalobos's prescience was partially fulfilled when the British captured Jamaica and used it as a springboard to attack not only the

Plate fleet but every Spanish settlement in the Caribbean and, on the mainland, the colonies of Cartagena and the rich city of Panama.[23] Although Britain never occupied Cuba, Hispaniola, or Puerto Rico, she did divide the whole of the Lesser Antilles with the other enemies of Spain, France and Holland.[24]

Villalobos estimated that Jamaica was fifty leagues long and twenty-five wide. His estimate of the length is about correct, but the estimate of the width is nine leagues too large. Within these limits very few habitations broke the continuous terrain of mountain and savannas. Along the south coast of Jamaica stretched the great *hatos*, only nine in number, where the owners divided among themselves the one hundred fifty miles of rich land on which to graze their herds of cattle and horses.[25] On the north side, totally uninhabited by humans, wild cattle shared the ranges and forest with wild pigs. Periodically Indian and negro hunters were sent here to bring back hides from the cattle and lard from the pigs, leaving the carcasses for the vultures. In addition to ranching, the Spaniards cultivated great quantities of cassava, maize, and vegetables for both the domestic and export markets.

Villalobos's Description of Santiago de la Vega

The abbot noted that the capital, Santiago de la Vega, was located on an open level country and faced a north-south direction. On the eastern side flowed the river Caguay, an excellent source of water for the inhabitants. The river discharged into the chief port of Caguay two leagues from the capital. From the capital to the port ran a level cart road over which all exports were conveyed to the ships.[26] Close to the quay was a fort in the form of a stockade surrounding a tiled roof house.[27] The whole compound was protected by lignum vitae and earthwork which, though not militarily strong, afforded occasional protection against enemy fire. Above this fortification at the port's entrance was a high morro of stone where a guard was stationed to watch incoming ships, part of the constant, day-and-night watch along the coast for British, French, or Dutch ships.[28] In Villalobos's day there was a plan to construct a strong fort at the morro which was never carried out by the Spaniards to the detriment of the people.[29]

Domestic dwellers in the capital of only a hundred citizens could boast of no imposing architecture since they were low, one storey buildings,[30] constructed of timber with tiled roofs which were supposed to be hurricane proof and earthquake resistant. Even the abbey church which Villalobos inherited contributed little to the architecture of Santiago de la Vega, for it followed the general pattern of timber and tile.[31] The poorly constructed abbey church was a reflection of its poverty, for it had no great hacienda from which to draw income, since it was totally dependent upon its one-third share of the annual tithes. The Dominicans could likewise boast of extreme poverty both in financial income and in personnel, for with only two resident monks and no fixed income, they were entirely dependent upon the alms given them which were not overly generous in an island where poverty was so widespread.[32] The poverty of the two hermitages, St. Lucy and St. Barbara, is indicated by the fact that they could not even afford the services of a caretaker.[33]

Ownership of Jamaica

General dissatisfaction with the Colón family ownership of Jamaica was bluntly expressed by Villalobos in his letter to Philip II saying that he and others like him longed for the day when Jamaica would revert to the crown.[34] The abbot also had plans to increase the prosperity of the island. One scheme was for Philip II[35] to send Jamaica fifty slaves to cultivate cassava and maize and also to prepare meat from cattle and lard from pigs. He estimated that as many as six thousand loads of cassava and an equal number of maize together with much beef and lard could be exported twice a year.[36] He claimed that his plan would advance the economy of the island and considerably reduce the prices that his Majesty was paying for food supplied to the navy and the mercantile fleets. He suggested that the maize might also be used as food for the pack animals plying between Nombre de Dios and Panama City.[37]

When Villalobos further suggested that negro slaves be imported to reopen the gold mines which "are very good," he was either listening to old wives' tales or taking some other metal for gold, for in all her history, gold has never been found in sufficient quantity to mine in Jamaica.

The Woes of a Sixteenth-Century Jamaican Abbot

Pirates

Sleepy, tropical Santiago de la Vega woke up on the morning of 29 January 1596 to the excited cry ringing through its lazy streets, "Pirates!" Whatever personal cares and worries the individual citizen had that January morning were forgotten in the overall fright of the British adventurers. Eleven ships rode at anchor in the harbour.[38] One word of confirmation from the guard at Caguay that they were pirates was enough to rouse the whole town to action; possessions were hastily packed into every form of conveyance and the inhabitants beat a quick retreat into the mountains. Even Abbot Villalobos had no desire to make a personal acquaintance of the pirate captain, Sir Anthony Shirley.[39] Together the Dominican friars and the abbot hastened to the island in Old Harbour Bay called La Legua.[40] For forty days Sir Anthony and his men were in possession of Santiago de la Vega, plundering and looting and all the while demanding a fat ransom as a condition of their peaceful departure, as was the custom of these jolly gentlemen.[41] Forty days in hiding at La Legua wore down the resistance of Villalobos; he sent word by messenger to the governor that he should pay the ransom and rid themselves of this pest.[42] This was an error, for Shirley intercepted the communication which revealed the hiding place of the abbot. Whereupon Sir Anthony paid a personal courtesy call on Villalobos, but the abbot was unwilling to receive him, and so in the middle of the night he fled La Legua, leaving his baggage, his silver and gold plate, and his robes to become the property of this knighted bandit.

Not every attack on Jamaica succeeded as well as Shirley's. At dawn Friday, 24 January 1603, a negro slave belonging to Rodrigo Alonso de Flores knocked excitedly at the door of Governor, Don Fernando Melgarejo de Córdoba, breathlessly exclaiming that while on his way to his master's ranch, Morante, at sundown the previous evening, he espied eight ships sailing in the direction of Caguay.[43] The governor ordered the church bells rung, the call to arms; this awakened the sergeant major, Juan de Palencia Carrillo, who leaped out of bed, ran to the council chambers where the governor lived, only to find the chief executive already in the plaza narrating the slave's story.[44] The sergeant major unfurled his flags and had the drums beat to muster all the fighting men into their companies; meanwhile the governor ordered two mounted men to ride to the sea and observe the sails coming into the port.[45] Returning at dawn, the pair related that two ships were already riding at anchor and others were entering the harbour. Command was given for all soldiers to proceed towards the sea to encounter the enemy should they be on their way towards the capital. Half a league from the capital, Melgarejo ordered a halt while the sergeant major shared out a barrel of powder and a great quantity of bullets and fuse to soldiers who had none.[46] The march was resumed in formal military fashion until another halt was called within sight of the sea. Arms were inspected by the governor, and all whom he thought insufficiently supplied with powder and bullets were given their full quota.[47]

The British now landed in eight barges and set fire to the Indian defense hut on the promontory.[48] Melgarejo dispatched an intermediary, Francisco Cartagena de Fuentes, to find out who they were and what they wanted.[49] Returning shortly, he informed the governor that they were English on their way to settle in a place they would not reveal and were stopping here for a supply of meat and cassava; if refused these supplies, they would land fifteen hundred men, take the city, and raze it to the ground. Eight ships were already in the harbour and eight more would arrive at midday with their commanders.[50] Sir Christopher Newport was in charge of the land forces and William Parker, of the sailors and marines.[51]

Bullets not supplies was Melgarejo's answer as he prepared to give battle by stationing thirty-two harquebusiers in ambush.[52] Fifteen men and a corporal hid on one side of a hill, and a like force on the other side. They were ordered to skirmish with the enemy and then retire to another ambush and there carry out a similar action. Their next move was to retire to a fortified trench in a narrow defile, a quarter of a league from the capital where the governor had been working all morning to make it his final stand. On one side of a barricade he had built a corral into which he herded one hundred cattle which he would use tactically at the proper moment.

Not all the town's people favoured the governor's plan of resistance; the women particularly thought it foolhardy to resist such overwhelming odds as fifteen hundred British. These terrified women sought the mediation of both religious and secular priests to dissuade the governor from precipitate action against the enemy. The vicar general, Manuel Botello, O.P., and Diego de Orive, O.P., together with two Franciscans, Friar Alonso de Ortego and Friar García de Barrera, approached the governor on behalf of the women; his answer was that, should an angel come down from heaven with the same request, he would still fight.

On Saturday morning at 10.00, six drums beating, two fifes and bugles playing, five flags flying, five hundred British began marching along the road where the Spaniards were in ambush. When the advance guard of the British approached the defenders' hiding place, the Spaniards opened fire, then retired to their second place of ambush and again fired on the British marching in formal military ranks.

British dead and wounded fell at both ambushes. The harquebusiers then retired to the barricaded trench near the capital where Melgarejo had stationed thirty men together with soldiers on the hills of the defile to await the approaching enemy. Shouting and making a great noise, the British approached. The Spaniards opened fire; the British replied with a volley. Then Melgarejo broke open the corral, goaded the cattle to fury directly into the ranks of the oncoming soldiers.

Confusion reigned. Some British fired at the cattle; the cattle, frightened by the din, tried to force their way through the soldiers. Then Melgarejo ordered the artillery pieces and all muskets to fire on the confused ranks of the British.

In the face of this deadly barrage, British soldiers fell dying and wounded. Captain Olives, the British officer leading the attack, was one of the first to die. Melgarejo shouted "Victory" as the British retreated and threw their dead into River Caguay, and carrying their wounded on their backs or on stretchers made of blankets supported by pikes.[53]

The battle before the barricade lasted a short half hour—one of the most successful defenses of Jamaica against the British ever made by the Spaniards.

Thirty musketeers followed the retreating soldiers harassing the rear guard until the British embarked on their ships in disorder. Sir Christopher Newport remained in the harbour all day Saturday. On Sunday morning he sailed out of Caguay and along the coast to the west, stopping at Oristán, a cattle ranch, where he tried to persuade Francisco Fanfan, a cow hand, to butcher some cattle for him. While in the hands of the British, Fanfan had been told by Newport that Melgarejo had fought like a gentleman and should pay his soldiers well. Newport promised to return to Caguay and take the governor prisoner or carry his head to Elizabeth, queen of England; his threat was never fulfilled.

Melgarejo, who so successfully defended the island, was the only person to suffer a loss. While he was busy protecting his fellow citizens, negroes entered his house and stole many valuables.[54]

Hurricane

Pirates were only one of Villalobos's troubles; nature added her share in one of the most terrifying manifestations of power—a hurricane. Sixteenth century Jamaica had no meteorological warnings that a storm born in the Leewards was headed for the island. The first sign of impending disaster came during the previous day when an ominous stillness filled the atmosphere and not a leaf stirred on the trees. The morning sun was reported to have changed to an awesome orange hue in the late afternoon, while several hours previously storm winds began to stir, mounting in intensity as time progressed until black clouds darkened the heavens with heavy rains driven by the fury of the storm. Gusting up to one hundred miles an hour, the hurricane swept through the streets of Santiago de la Vega, driving the rain with such force that it entered every crevice, lifted roofs from their supports, and hurled them miles away, while walls collapsed like paper. The storm's clockwise action struck the town first from the south; then, after the eye's lull of fifteen minutes, struck it with the same fury from a northerly direction—four hours of merciless battering. The capital was in worse condition than Shirley had left it the previous year, and Villalobos was a much humbled prophet as he stood before his church on the morning of 2 August 1597 and viewed its ruined walls and gaping roof, then walked over to the Dominican monastery leveled to the ground. He recalled the words he wrote to Philip II, "Hurricanes there used to be, but by the grace of God, they have ceased."[55]

Financial Difficulties

Pirates and hurricanes increased his financial worries. The abbot lived in reduced circumstances, so poor that he could not afford to import wine and candles for the altar, but had to depend on his farm to supply them.[56] Yet he was better off than the Dominicans who had no farm. These friars lived in a state of near destitution despite their reputation as excellent preachers.[57] With incomes over the whole island so reduced and tithes down to a pittance, the abbot became daily more entangled in his financial labyrinth. There was no other recourse save to ask a gift of 500,000 maravedis from the Spanish crown for his own use and an additional 50,000 maravedis for his chaplain, canons and sacristan.[58]

Philip II was now king and, although British and French privateers were boldly attacking the Plate fleets after the defeat of his father's armada in 1588, much gold and silver continued to find their way into the royal treasury. Upon receiving Villalobos's detailed account of the disastrous state to which all ecclesiastical establishments had been reduced, and the further assurance that no assistance might be expected from impoverished Jamaica, Philip responded with a generosity worthy of his father. On 28 June 1599, he wrote to the officials of the city of Panama relating that the churches and chapels in Jamaica badly needed assistance both to repair their structure and to restore their furnishings. Philip informed Panama that he considered it only right that funds be allocated for this purpose, and so revenue from the state of Veragua was to be taken from the royal treasury and placed in the hands of whoever might have authority from the abbot and governor to receive the money in their names which would be two thousand ducats, the equivalent of 750,000 maravedis, to be spent by the abbot and governor solely on the repair of churches and chapels, and also to provide them with vestments and furnishings. These funds were not to be used *en bloc*, but were to be distributed from time to time by warrants issued conjointly by abbot and governor.[59]

No description of the reconstructed abbey church survives, but with such generous funds it is safe to conjecture that Villalobos constructed it along architectural lines common to such churches seen in every Spanish-American plaza. That it was a massive building is known from historian Long's own observation of its ruins that the bases of two columns which supported the large archway into the abbey church were eight feet square.[60] These columns, indicative of its size, would make the structure compare favourably with churches constructed during this same period throughout Central America and Mexico.

A Remnant of the Arawaks

In the closing years of the sixteenth century, Arawaks still lived in Jamaica and were employed on Spanish-owned ranches and farms for an annual wage, but their wage was a mere pittance. Governor Melgarejo, having always in mind the betterment of Jamaica, turned his attention to the Arawak problem in his community. He was aware that ranchers were taking unfair advantage of the Indians by not paying them a just wage for their labour. So, after giving the problem much thought, he decided to take steps to improve the condition of this race, once the sole occupants of the island. His plan was to establish an exclusively Indian town and rescue the Arawaks from the near slavery to which the ranchers had reduced the remnant of the race. Living apart in a separate community, the Arawaks would be less under the influence of the wealthy Spaniards and more able to manage their own affairs on the basis of a united body. In this way they could hire themselves to the whole Spanish community and not limit their labour to ranching and farming, and being thus united they might also demand higher wages than they received at the time.

These were the thoughts of Governor Melgarejo when, on 26 December 1597, invoking his supreme powers, he commanded all Arawaks, men and women, to appear before him and express their opinion on the idea of establishing a separate Indian town. He made it clear that the government would be willing to assign them a site, and in order to test the practicality of his idea he sought their opinion, making it a matter of free choice on their part. He would also seek the opinion of Don Francisco Marqués de Villalobos, abbot of Jamaica, and other respectable and conscientious gentry.[61]

The Indians assembled on the day the decree was issued and a notary, Jerónimo de Flores, was appointed to record the proceedings.

In the presence of the governor, there were the Arawaks, Villalobos, Licentiate Francisco de Novada Alvarado, Diego de Valdés and Diego Siesa, ordinary alcaldes, Pedro de Castillo, accountant and official judge, Captain Pedro López Bejarano, and other leading citizens of Jamaica. The Arawaks were asked if it would be better for them to have their own town together with small farms on which to cultivate produce for home consumption, or if they wished to serve the Spaniards for a wage as they did at present. All, with the exception of Miguel Bejarano, Antonio López, and Bartolomé Luys, Arawaks with Spanish names, said they preferred the town. These three did not agree with the majority decision and said they wished their status to remain unchanged. Next the leading Spanish citizens were asked their opinion, and the abbot, the cattlemen, and most of the Spaniards voiced their objection to the governor's scheme. If an Indian town were established, so they argued, and the Indians not compelled to serve the inhabitants as hitherto, then the cattle ranches would be deserted, the stock run wild, trade and commerce cease. Further, it was predicted that the greater part of the Indians, left to themselves, would practice predial larceny. The only Spaniard to favour the governor's scheme was Captain Francisco de Bejarano, who argued that it was not only proper but even necessary that the Arawaks should be taken from the exclusive control of the ranchers and put on their own. In this way the Indians could offer their services to a wider clientele and even poorer Spaniards might profit by their work, a thing not possible under the existing system. Bejarano added that the argument alleged by the cattlemen, that the cattle would become wild, was a specious one for opposing the governor; the real motive was the selfish desire to enjoy the exclusive use of the Arawaks' labour.

Seven months passed and by July 1598 no agreement had been reached. Melgarejo had no alternative but to write to Philip III, for the king himself had recommended that the remnant of the Arawaks in Jamaica be preserved from extinction. The king had offered no detailed plan; it was left to Melgarejo to implement Philip's decision. The governor explained to the royal council that he had proposed the separate town for the Indians because of the trifling wage which the ranchers paid the Arawaks. In the same letter he asked the king to confer with his council and advise the government of Jamaica what action should be taken. He promised to carry out faithfully whatever policy they chose.

There is no evidence that an Arawak town was established. It was one of those excellent projects of social justice obstructed by vested interest.

There was no question of the Arawaks falling back into idolatry as was the excuse given in the early days of colonization for breaking up the Indian village system, for these Arawaks in 1598 had a background of eighty-five years of Catholic tradition and environment which completely obliterated their former superstitions.

Villalobos was ageing and twenty-four years of continuous service in the trouble-riddled Spanish outpost had reduced his youthful enthusiasm to a burdensome weight from which he found no escape. Although the king's munificent gifts of two thousand ducats restored the church's buildings, it did not liquidate the abbot's personal debt of four thousand ducats. In March 1606, Villalobos wrote to Philip II that he could no longer remain in Jamaica and asked to be released from his exile.[62] Before the king could reply, the good old abbot has laid aside his earthly worries of pirates, hurricanes, and debts, for death mercifully relieved him of these burdens on 3 August 1606.[63] At the high Mass Don Francisco Marqués de Villalobos was buried before the main altar of his abbey church.

Interim between Death of Villalobos and Appointment of Successor

Within a year of Villalobos's death, the Church suffered a gradual but frightening decline in her spiritual life which awoke both common citizen and government to its seriousness.[64] This was the second occasion when the Church fell into chaos under a vicar general. Vicar General Juan de Cueto's exaggerated opinion of his personal importance offended both clergy and laity, and lack of cooperation with the acting head of the Church brought upon a state of deterioration. The clergy were not numerous, as there was no need for a large number among Jamaica's small population: a few diocesan priests and a handful of Franciscans and Dominicans made up the full complement. What was needed was someone from outside Jamaica to investigate fully ecclesiastical conditions in the island. Don Juan de las Cabesas Altamirando, bishop of Cuba, met this requirement, and to him was dispatched a request from ecclesiastical and civil authorities in Jamaica that he to pay a visit and establish order amid the present state of chaos.

Altamirando left Santiago de Cuba on 26 February 1608. The weather was so bad that he spent thirteen days at sea for a voyage which should have taken three days or less. On 11 March he arrived in Jamaica. It was a gala occasion for Santiago de la Vega when Governor Alonso de Miranda and all the people, clergy and laity, marched in procession to greet the bishop as he approached the capital. Arriving at the abbey church, the bishop gave his blessing to the assembled populace and explained the object of his mission. He had come to make a canonical visitation of the Church. Then he retired to the house prepared for him, but the governor insisted that the bishop be his house guest; there they might discuss the problems affecting Jamaica.

On the following Sunday Altamirando expressed his intention of opening the visitation in the abbey church, but he failed to reckon with Juan de Cueto, who claimed the office of vicar general. Through his secretary, Alonso de Vargas, Cueto notified his Most Reverend Lordship that he should not presume to exercise jurisdiction in Jamaica until he first presented his credentials to the ecclesiastical authorities and the civil cabildo. Altamirando abided by protocol, and that day remained away from the church. Next day, when governor Alonso de Miranda, the alcaldes, and the aldermen met in council, the notary, Diego de Ayala, exhibited an order and judgment from the Royal Audiencia of Santo Domingo as well as documents from His Holiness attesting the authority of the bishop of Cuba. These so satisfied the civil authorities that Altamirando possessed proper jurisdiction that he was received unanimously by the cabildo who proceeded to the bishop's residence where he was presented an address of welcome by the governor, the civil authorities, and the clergy.[65]

On the following Sunday, the first in Lent, Friar Juan Fuesteros, superior of the newly established monastery of St. James, was appointed by Altamirando to preach the visitation sermon, which he did as he himself admitted "with clarity and eloquence." Next in the pulpit, notary Diego de Ayala, read the general edict of the visitation "in a loud and intelligible voice that all might hear him."[66]

On Monday the actual visitation began with Altamirando presiding over a solemn Mass for the dead. He then inspected the altar, chrismatories, baptismal font, and church records. An inquiry was held into the conduct and acts of the clergy. Public offenses were punished and a remedy offered for abuses. One serious abuse was that certain priests had performed the marriage ceremony for a dozen parties without proper faculties. The general public was scandalized, and the couples themselves had had doubts about the validity of their marriages. Difficulties about proper faculties had arisen after the death of Villalobos. To whom were the clergy to turn to obtain the faculty to perform the marriage ceremony? The abbacy was considered without a head, so some of the clergy concluded they might take upon themselves the office of pastor. They seemed to have precedents in the cases of Venice and Lucca, where the clergy had been allowed to assume the office of pastor under like circumstances. Altamirando prudently remedied the difficulty by following the decrees of the Council of Trent in regard to the sacrament of matrimony and restored both public order and peace of mind to those who had been disturbed.[67]

On Holy Thursday Spaniards, Arawaks, and negro slaves crowded the abbey church to witness for the first time in Jamaica a bishop perform the Holy Week services. Holy Oils were consecrated, twelve men of the working class participated in the ceremony of the washing of the feet, and a sermon on the Mandatum was preached. In the afternoon occurred the most unique ceremony of the week. Altamirando conferred minor and major orders on theological students who had come to Jamaica with dimissorial letters from various parts of the Caribbean. These are the first recorded ordinations in Jamaica, but unfortunately no names are given. In seventeenth-century Spanish America, aspirants to the priesthood, where there was no resident bishop, found their path strewn with difficulties. They might prepare in a local Dominican or Franciscan monastery by a course in philosophy and theology, but they had to seek out a bishop to ordain them. As the number of bishops in the Indies increased, this difficulty resolved itself.

On Easter Sunday a solemn pontifical Mass was celebrated by the bishop, and during the first few days of Easter week he conferred the sacrament of confirmation on six hundred persons.[68] He then blessed a hermitage and the new Franciscan monastery of St. James. All these duties kept Altamirando busy until the end of Easter week and when the ecclesiastical functions ended, he still had to attend the festivities arranged by the governor, cabildo, and clergy in which the Spaniards held tournaments and the brown folk played games of ball.[69]

Altamirando's task was not completed until he put some order into the ecclesiastical life of the island by making an inventory of all church property, thoroughly examining all accounts, drawing up a list of alms, incomes, and taxes belonging to the Church. On the touchy point of ecclesiastical seniority, Altamirando had to tread cautiously, for here was the root of much trouble, since seniority meant honour for the clergy, indicating who was to be first, second, or last. Altamirando appointed Juan de Cuerto, the cleric who had questioned his authority, as ecclesiastical superior of Jamaica. As next in virtue of a royal order under the Patronato Real, he assigned Fr. Andrés Gallegos the curacy of Santiago de la Vega, and an order to this effect was published for all to read.

Honour was one source of dissension, money another cause—particularly the soliciting of alms for the clergy and Church. This too he remedied. Next, a just division of tithes was decreed by the bishop and stipends for Masses were limited according to the custom of the Indies. Fees for ecclesiastical services such as baptisms, marriages, and burials were given some uniformity. Chaplaincies were in a state of disorder; they had no rule, no calendar, nor were they properly established. These were given canonical status and their names entered in a separate register.

Unfortunately, there is no documentary record of the places of these chaplaincies; presumably they were at the estates of the more important families of the island living at a distance from Santiago de la Vega, and on the south coast there were nine such *hatos*. The bishop considered proper records very important, for he opened a register for deaths and burials and another for attendance at Mass. His final proposal was that Jamaica be given a bishop who could confer the sacraments of confirmation and holy orders.

From clergy, government officials, and common folk came loud praise for the bishop who had settled internal dissension and put order into what had been chaos before his arrival. Four months was all he needed for the task which left the people much happier and portended a reign of peace if the clergy faithfully carried out the provisions of the memorial.

From the port of Caguay Altamirando left early in July on a ship he hired at his own expense. Four months earlier he had come as a stranger; now he was parting as a friend to all the inhabitants.

> In the same manner in which they had received him, the governor, clergy, and all the people bade him farewell at the seacoast with many tears and much sadness, not departing until his Lordship had embarked and given them his blessing. He thereupon left the port of the island of Jamaica and came to this city of Havana.[70]

During the closing years of the sixteenth century, the Flemish made more frequent raids on Jamaica, attracted by the rich forests of brazilwood and in order to barter goods which had been stolen from ships in the Caribbean. Spanish law forbade trade by barter.

On 10 March 1599, a Flemish ship arrived at Port Caguay, and the captain announced that his intention was peaceful; he wished to barter, but was refused by Governor Fernando Melgarejo de Córdoba, who drove the Fleming from the harbour and forbade citizens to trade with the captain.[71] Sailing from Caguay, the ship anchored off Brazil Cay, where the sailors cut a large quantity of dyewood and were about to load it on the ship when Melgarejo surprised them and captured three of their number. Then Melgarejo burned both the wood they had cut and the trees they left standing.[72] From these three prisoners the governor gained the important information that the French and

Flemish ships had been plundering along the coast of Hispaniola. The competition between French and Flemish had become so great that this Flemish ship had left Hispaniola to seek richer rewards in Jamaica.

A Spanish vessel returning to Jamaica from Cuba encountered several of these corsairs at Negril Point on the extreme west of Jamaica. The Spanish ship would have become a victim of the raiders had not Melgarejo appeared on the scene, drove them off and released twelve Spanish prisoners. From his countrymen Melgarejo learned that these ships were French and Flemish, and while plundering Hispaniola they had encountered the Spanish fleet of Don Francisco Colona who gave chase as far as Cape St. Nicholas.

Four months later, on 7 August 1599, news was brought to Melgarejo that four English vessels had anchored at Morant Bay in the eastern end of the island, fifteen leagues from Caguay and had put men ashore to cut brazilwood. It was also reported that they had come to barter. Far removed from the eyes of the governor, the corsairs found Morant a safe place to carry on illegal trade for here they would rendezvous with trusted Jamaican accomplices. The English brought as their interpreter Alvero de Cuendo, a creole of Hispaniola, who had sold his service to them for seven hundred ducats a year. In him they had an agent who could deal confidently with the Spaniards of Jamaica who did not scruple to barter. News of the English ships brought Melgarejo to Morant Bay where he ambushed twenty-two English as they came ashore. Cuendo, one of them, refusing to surrender, was run through with a lance, and on his person was found an incriminating letter from no less a person than Friar Manuel Botello, O.P., of the Dominican monastery in Santiago de la Vega and vicar general of Jamaica.[73] Melgarejo had previously made the statement that no friar was involved in bartering.[74] This evidence that the vicar general was involved in this illegal traffic came as a complete surprise to the governor.

The first part of the incriminating letter contained domestic matters concerning Cuendo who expressed his opinion that his wife was dead, but Botello had seen her very much alive in Santo Domingo when on a visit to that city six months previously. She and other relatives were much grieved at Cuendo's long absence, but for him to return to Santo Domingo, now that he was in the employ of the English, would have been much too dangerous. The other part of the letter was more explicit about current activities of barter. In it Botello told Cuendo and his English employers to remain at Morant Bay where he might expect many people from Santiago de la Vega to contact them. Although the governor had forbidden such transactions with the corsairs, they were to pay no attention to him for it was Melgarejo's custom to issue such ineffective orders. Botello reminded Cuendo that the last barterer to come to Morant Bay was not an honest fellow in dealing with his customers. Since cloth was an article most desired and very difficult to buy in Jamaica, this barterer took advantage by using a measuring stick that was short by four and one-half units and his weights were one-eighth more than the same weights used in this island. Moreover, his bartering demands were excessive and did much harm to the trade. If Cuendo's employers would give good measure and make reasonable demands, they would be well patronized by all the inhabitants. Botello himself wanted many things and would pay cash, but at present he could send no money because the alms for sermons he had been ordered to preach had not been given to him, but he did expect the money within three days. The vicar general then sent a list of his needs to Cuendo and asked that the goods be delivered to him in Santiago de la Vega, and also that Cuendo go surety for him. He promised upon his word as a religious that he would keep his part of the bargain. Cuendo might also let Botello know if he needed any sheep, goats, or cattle, or in fact anything Jamaica produced, for the vicar general would be glad to serve him. Cuendo would find in the messenger's knapsack some sweet oranges, sour guavas, plums, paw-paws, good melon which resembled those of Asia, a pickled shoulder of pork, and a fat capon, all personal gifts to Cuendo. In Botello's letter to Cuendo there was mention of a large quantity of pearls which these same English had procured by barter from the people of the island of Margarita, but unfortunately this part of the manuscript is torn, but it does seem to indicate that Jamaican colonists were willing to barter for these pearls.

Melgarejo complained constantly to his superiors that he could not defend Jamaica's uninhabited coast line from these interlopers. Only twenty-two days after the English vessels had been at Morant Bay, a French ship, piloted by Gasper Hernández, a Portuguese, came into the same harbour to contact his relatives and friends in Jamaica to exchange cloth for hides.[75] Although Melgarejo captured the pilot at the Morante *hato,* the ship escaped because an Arawak in the governor's service deserted to the French and informed them that Melgarejo was advancing towards them both by land and sea. The governor learned from the captured pilot that the corsairs had come from Puerto Escondido, Cuba, where their large ship was anchored and that one Diego Ximinez, an inhabitant of Baracoa, brought them to Jamaica in his smaller vessel with the design to barter with Hernández's relatives and friends who lived here. The captured Portuguese, Gasper Hernández, now offered his services to Melgarejo, if the governor would construct a small vessel like the one he had piloted from Cuba and equip it with thirty soldiers. Hernández would then ferret out the corsairs who were plundering along the Cuban coast and thus relieve the pressure of these interlopers on Jamaica.

Two years previously Melgarejo had sent out such a vessel but as the sailors were inexperienced and the officials in Panama had not paid their wages, the experiment proved a failure. Melgarejo now informed Philip III that he was inclined to accept Hernández's offer since he was an experienced pilot. In the following March he wrote to Philip that he had inflicted much harm on the Cuba-based corsairs with his vessel equipped with one piece of artillery, twenty-five muskets, twelve pikes, and a good supply of ammunition. Some of the crew were criminals Melgarejo had sentenced to this work.

Two questions arose in the mind of the governor which he desired Philip to settle. First, what was he to do with the captured prisoners? He could not afford to maintain them in Jamaica but could ship them to Cartagena if the king would allow this. Secondly, the sailors were not being paid a wage, so Melgarejo offered them a share in the spoils of the captured vessels; would the king approve? There is no evidence that the king disapproved of Melgarejo's action, since it kept the corsairs away from the coast of Jamaica.

Candidates for Abbot

Villalobos had died on 3 August 1606. After two years no abbot had yet been appointed to replace him. Suddenly an array of influential candidates appeared. Did it mean that the Church in Jamaica had risen to a high degree of importance or had Altamirando's proposal that the next prelate be a bishop proved to be attractive bait for clerical ambitions? It was a formidable array of titled clerics: Dr. Antonio Gutierez Ossorio, who had the approval of the viceroy and audiencia of Mexico; Pedro Zarfate de Hinojosa, also approved by both viceroy and audiencia with the added note of the archbishop of Mexico; Dr. Antonio Mendez; Dr. Pedro Muñoz de Espinosa; Dr. Prudentia de Armendia; Dr. Lucas de Villareal; Dr. Jorge Fernández de Bealco, dean of Honduras; Don Francisco Sanchez Ortiz, chaplain of the discalced nuns.[76] Distinguished as were the qualifications of these clerics, they were all passed over in favour of the most illustrious man of letters to occupy the office of abbot of Jamaica: Don Bernardo de Balbuena.

Six

The Poet Abbot: Bernardo de Balbuena

Bernardo de Balbuena, an unexpected candidate, was chosen abbot of Jamaica on 29 April 1608 in preference to an array of doctors of divinity.[1] Previously, Jamaica had a well-known chronicler of the Indies, Peter Martyr; a marquis, Francisco de Villalobos; but never in her history so illustrious a poet as Bernardo de Balbuena.

Balbuena's Early Years

Mexico in the sixteenth century was a Spanish dreamland for acquiring fame and fortune. The Wild West of that day, it beckoned many an imaginative Spaniard to pull up roots in the Old and plant them in the New World. Such an adventurer was the elder Balbuena, born in 1522, who had sailed to this land of promise to seek fame and improve his fortune.[2] Some measure of success attended his efforts for he accumulated a modest fortune and held a minor political office for years. In 1560 he returned to Spain and there met Francisca Sanchez de Velasco. There is no record of their marriage,[3] but a son, baptized Bernardo, was born to them in 1562.[4]

In 1564 Balbuena returned to Mexico with his infant son. As a colonial, Balbuena was wealthy enough to give his son the best education that Mexico offered at the famed University of Mexico, whose reputation in scripture, canon and civil law, rhetoric, and grammar rivaled that of Salamanca, whose faculties and privileges this New World seat of learning shared.

Bernardo was ordained in 1586.[5] Shortly afterwards he was assigned to act as chaplain to the Audiencia of Guadalajara; six years later he was appointed pastor of two small parishes in a remote district north of Guadalajara where he wrote his famous narrative poem "Bernardo" and possibly his pastoral novel "Siglo de Oro" at this time.[6] A third work, "Grandeza Mexicana," a description of

Mexico City, must also be added to his major literary works.[7] These three will live as long as Spanish literature flourishes.

Believing that his superior talents should be recognized by ecclesiastical preferment, he left his country parish in 1602 for the more promising City of Mexico.[8] Four years in that city proved just as sterile as the country. In 1606 he returned to his native Spain, studied at the University of Siguenza, and won his doctorate in theology.[9] Bernardo's application for advancement, filed at Seville, Spain, in 1592[10] seemed destined to lie inert for the remainder of his mortal life, when without warning he was offered the office of abbot of Jamaica. True it was not a bishopric, but it might lead to one, so Balbuena accepted.

Philip III wrote to the chapter and clergy of Jamaica on 17 May 1609 and informed them that he had presented Don Bernardo de Balbuena, priest, to His Holiness Paul V as abbot of Jamaica.[11] The king requested the Jamaican clergy to allow Bernardo de Balbuena to act as abbot pending the arrival of the papal commission. An authority on Balbuena, Van Horn, offers a probable reason why Bernardo was chosen abbot.

> In seeking to determine why Balbuena was preferred to the eight candidates on the first list and to Juan de Cueto, one is tempted to assume the intervention of Conde de Lemos, President of the Council of the Indies. In 1604, Balbuena dedicated to him an edition of the "Grandeza Mexicana" and in October 1607, the "Siglo de Oro." In 1609 he secured the permit to print the "Bernardo" with the intention of dedicating it to the same patron. Further, Balbuena's description of Jamaica (1612) begins with the statement that Lemos had asked him to write it. It would appear probable that he owed his appointment to the famous patron of letters, and thus his literary productions contributed directly to his ecclesiastical advancement.[12]

Waiting for Passage

Sailing to the Indies in the seventeenth century was a major task; it was a matter of securing permission to go, of being cleared by the authorities, of providing one's own food and booking passage on one of the ships which sailed with the fleet only once or twice a year. This process might take a full year or even two years before the traveler actually set sail from Spain. An added reason delayed Balbuena; though the king had written to the authorities to allow Balbuena to function as abbot pending the arrival of papal documents, past experience had demonstrated that it was unwise to appear in the colony without written authorization from Rome.

The awaited documents from Rome did not come with the speed

Balbuena had hoped for. Correspondence between Pedro Cosidas, Spanish ambassador at Rome, and Contreras, secretary to Philip III, revealed that two questions had been raised: the question of Balbuena's legitimacy, and the question in what category to place the abbacy of Jamaica.[13]

On 3 May 1608, when Cosidas had received application for the bulls of abbacy from Dr. Bernardo Balbuena, it was clear from the documents that Bernardo was the natural son of his parents, not legitimate.[14] Nor had he been legitimated by a subsequent marriage. Here was a personal bar to the office of prelate. In the questionnaire answered by Balbuena, he claimed there was no obstacle and passed rather lightly over his illegitimacy; possibly he had obtained a dispensation in view to holding such an office. But this was questioned by the ambassador; a subsequent dispensation must have been granted because he did become abbot.

The second difficulty concerned the abbacy itself. In what category was it canonically?[15]

It could not be consistorial, the ambassador noted, because it did not have a stated income, so he judged it must be datarila, that is, it derived its income from tithes given by the people by either direct or indirect taxation. This meant that there was no fixed amount and the sum would vary with the state of Jamaica's economy. But the income of the previous abbots had to be known by Rome. In order to discover this information, the ambassador asked when Balbuena's predecessor had been appointed so that he might seek the papers in the archives and discover this financial statement among them. Predecessor Villalobos's papers, sought by the ambassador, had been pigeonholed in some forgotten place and not until one year later were they found.

Balbuena's funds were now running low, and he had no alternative save to request that the income from Jamaica be granted him until the papal documents arrived. On 8 April 1609, a letter written on Balbuena's behalf complained because of the missing documents. He had been detained in Spain for one full year and was so impoverished that he could not support himself in the capital.[16] Another month passed and still no answer. Balbuena's impatience grew into desperation and he could wait no longer. So on May 5 1609 he petitioned the Council of the Indies that documents or no documents, he be allowed to take one cleric, four servants, three negro slaves who would be exempt from taxation, personal effects free of taxes to the amount of one thousand ducats, jewels worth five hundred ducats, books connected with his studies to the value of five hundred ducats and sail for Jamaica.[17]

A royal decree dated 26 May 1609, addressed to the king's governors, judges, and officers of the Casa de la Contratación, Seville, Spain, directed that office to allow Fr. Balbuena, who had been nominated abbot, to sail to the island of Jamaica, and that a priest and four servants were to form part of his retinue, and that abbot and priest were exempt from obtaining credentials, but the rest of his entourage were not exempt, but were required to have descriptive papers drawn up in their place of residence before the local authorities with the assurance that they were not married men departing without their wives, nor of the category of those forbidden by the crown to live in the Indies.[18] A description of each person was to be added to the document, a counterpart of the modern passport with its photograph of the person. Two of these descriptions are worth quoting. The first is servant Simon Ruiz's credential, dated 2 January 1610, from Valdepenas,

> a man of medium stature, twenty-five years of age, one more or less, with dark complexion and black beard, a small mole on his right cheek, a little stooped shouldered, a citizen and native of the city of Valdepenas, married according to the regulations of Holy Mother Church. His family are and have been pure, good Christians who do not come nor are descended from Moors or Jews, nor have they been sentenced by the Holy Office for the crime of heresy, and with this reputation as Old Christians they have remained in this town, and there have been and in their lineage members of the Order of Calatrava and attendants of the Holy Office and Justices of the first instance and other honourable offices. . . . They do not come or descend from the Pizarros nor from any other person forbidden to go to the Indies.[19]

Simon Ruiz's wife, Andrea Carillo, had her person subject to close scrutiny in the testimony she gave at Amargo on 4 January 1610,

> indentations on her face that appear to be smallpox marks, with two moles, one near the right ear on the temple and the other on the same side of the neck under the ear, apparently of the age of about twenty-two years. Her parents are Old Christians, not Moors, nor those converted long ago, nor are they descendants of the Pizarros, nor any people forbidden to go to the Indies.[20]

While servants were obtaining credentials and the abbot planning his departure, some one found Villalobos's much-sought-after documents in Rome; by 13 February 1610, the bulls confirming Balbuena as abbot of Jamaica had been issued.[21] Although Balbuena was prepared to sail without the Roman documents, possession of them made his appointment official and forced the Jamaica authorities to recognize him as the lawful abbot. On the passenger list Balbuena was number thirty.

Balbuena's Description of Jamaica

It could be expected of Balbuena's literary talent that he would leave his impressions of Jamaica in writing. This he did in a letter to Philip III, dated 14 July 1611, in which he painted a gloomy picture of the island.[22] Every abbot had voiced a complaint about the abbacy church he had inherited from his predecessor, particularly when a long period lapsed between the death of one abbot and the arrival of another, during which interim no one seemed to have had much interest in the upkeep of the sacred edifice. Balbuena added his own complaints to the long list of his predecessors.

The church was poor. It was in ruins, leaking so badly that Mass could not be celebrated there when it rained. A search in the treasury failed to reveal any funds allocated for the emergency repair of the sacred edifice so that Governor and abbot planned a personal visit to every inhabitant in Santiago de la Vega to solicit funds.[23] It was a sight unique in the Indies to see the head of state and the head of the church knocking on every door begging alms to repair a leaky abbacy church roof. Balbuena's commenting on the results remarked that for all their labour, they collected very little money. Failing this expedient, the abbot had to reach into his own private reserves and repair the church as best he could from his own meagre funds. These repairs were in progress when Balbuena wrote to Philip III telling what little money he possessed personally and reminding the king that the income of the abbacy was so meagre for five months following the death of Villalobos that the tithes were leased for a mere one hundred pesos or eight reals;[24] and that for the whole of the following year, 1607, they amounted to a mere six hundred and ten pesos. This was a trifling sum to meet current expenses and at the same time restore the church so despoiled by three incursions of plundering enemies that there were hardly enough vestments left to officiate decently. Since his arrival in Jamaica, Balbuena had endeavoured with his feeble powers to make improvements which included, among others, the constructing of a neat frontal for the use on principal feasts, and had he more means at his disposal he would have made extensive improvements, but he could hardly pay for the repairs he had made: such was the content of his letter to the king. Balbuena was not unaware of the possibility of making money by way of exchange in the Indies whereby the church might be repaired and the island's economy improved without cost to the royal treasury. This was his idea: copper coin used for currency in Santo Domingo was also used in Jamaica.[25] The specie was sent to Jamaica with an added letter -S-, possibly standing for *Santiago,* the early Spanish name for Jamaica. In the transfer of the specie from Hispaniola to Jamaica, the value increased eight times, so that a real of silver which was worth seven quartos in Santo Domingo was worth fifty-six quartos in Jamaica. The abbot's scheme was to have the Church take advantage of this rate of exchange by allowing the abbot to draw on account from Hispaniola one thousand ducats in quartos and import them to Jamaica. What accrued in value to the specie by transfer to Jamaica would be used to repair the abbey church, since by the transaction the abbot would be richer by 528,000 quartos. It looked quite simple on paper, but Balbuena forgot that if there was to be such a transaction the government wished to benefit and not the abbot. The abbot's scheme was quickly forgotten.

Balbuena's Suggestion to Improve the Church in Jamaica

Balbuena made another proposal, one affecting the spiritual life of Jamacia. He claimed that the limited powers of the abbot were an obstacle to spiritual progress. So on 12 December 1612, he wrote to Philip III saying that these limitations had produced a spiritual impasse, but if the powers of the Jamaican prelate were widened by raising the abbacy to a bishopric, new life would be injected into the whole community.[26] If this first plan were not acceptable, an alternative would be to abolish the office of abbot in Jamaica and place the Church immediately under the diocese of Cuba. The Cuban bishop could then place a vicar in Jamaica as he was doing in Florida. This plan would insure Jamaica of the personal interest and the occasional presence of a bishop. At the same time the bishop would enjoy the income from the tithes and thus have means to defray the expenses of ocean travel, for the expense of travel was a major obstacle to the present titular head of the Church visiting Jamaica. Only when the king agreed could the bishop of Cuba legally visit Jamaica, and then he had to follow the prescriptions laid down by the Council of Trent. The present arrangement of the ruling prelate not being a bishop but only an abbot offered difficulties which fell under three headings—he could not, first, confer the sacrament of confirmation; secondly, confer holy orders; lastly, consecrate holy oils on Holy Thursday.[27]

Since only two or three bishops had ever visited Jamaica in its one hundred eighteen years as a Spanish possession, the sacrament of confirmation was neglected and the people died without receiving it. Seldom did a bishop chance the voyage from Cuba to Jamaica, since the seas were increasingly fraught with danger from British, Dutch, and French pirates who were redoubling their efforts in the Caribbean, always on the lookout for an episcopal prize whom they might ransom for precious gold ducats. Just at this time, too, the bishop of Cuba was transferring his see from Santiago de Cuba to Havana, thus lengthening the journey to Jamaica by several hundred miles and increasing the danger of capture by pirates.

A more serious difficulty was the abbot's powerlessness to confer Holy Orders on young men who had vocations to the priesthood. The Church flourishes through the medium of native vocations, for when she can call upon the youth of a country to fill the ranks of her priesthood, she is in a healthy, vigorous state. There was no lack of vocations among the youth of Jamaica, for young men inspired by the desire to serve God at the altar had entered the Franciscan and Dominican monasteries, but on completion of their studies found there was no bishop to ordain them; so discouragement overcame enthusiasm, they departed the monastery and returned to secular life.[28] Thus many vocations to the priesthood were lost to Jamaica. Three native vocations had been saved by the candidates working their way through a labyrinth of difficulties and finally attaining their goal. They were Don Alonso de Espinosa Centeno, Juan de Cueto, and Andrés de Segura.

Andrés de Segura lived in the days of Abbot Villalobos, and possibly this prelate had encouraged his vocation and his preliminary studies in one of the local monasteries of Santiago de la Vega where he might study philosophy and theology. But the impasse came when the abbot could not confer holy orders.[29] There was no alternative save to seek ordination outside Jamaica. Segura left Jamaica to find a bishop to ordain him. Six years later he became a priest. During those years he had been in Cuba, Santo Domingo, Santa Marta, Cartagena and Panama incurring heavy expenses, inconveniences, and illness as part of the price he had to pay to attain his goal. Segura offered no explanation why he wandered from place to place, for in each of the places mentioned there was a bishop. Could the answer have been that creoles were not encouraged as candidates for the priesthood? This is a possibility because they were looked upon as second-rate clergy. A creole in this case would be one born in the colonies, even though he was of Spanish parentage. After ordination Segura returned to Santiago de la Vega to become a parish priest. At Villalobos's death he was the recipient of a yearly grant of 100,000 maravedis from Philip III because he had not shared in the tithes of the abbot during his long service to Jamaica but had subsisted on stole fees gained from officiating at baptisms, funerals, and marriages.

His fellow ecclesiastic, Juan de Cueto, who acted as pastor during the interim between Villalobos's death and the arrival of Balbuena, suffered the same fate as Segura when he sought ordination.[30] Only after eight years of wandering, toil, and poverty in Cuba, Florida, and other Spanish territories did he reach the goal of ordination to the priesthood. Worn out and broken in health, he returned to his native Jamaica.

Some years later another Jamaican, Don Alonso de Espinosa Centeno, related his experiences, saying that when he had completed his preliminary studies in Jamaica, he matriculated at the University of Mexico, where he was graduated, receiving the degrees of bachelor of arts and canon law.[31] During the course of his studies he defended many theses with such mastery that his intellectual prowess won the acclaim of the university professors. Upon ordination he acted as confessor general in both the archdiocese of Mexico and the diocese of Puebla Los Angeles. Then he sailed for Spain to follow a course of studies at the Royal University of Avila, where he won his licentiate and doctorate in canon law. He remained in Spain for seventeen years while he lived at court and became a candidate for ecclesiastical office. He then returned to Jamaica where he served for many years in the principal church of the island. He modestly admitted that he gave satisfaction to both estates, the civil and the ecclesiastical, and with equal modesty he recounted his illustrious ancestry: his parents, grandparents, and great grandparents had served His Majesty on divers occasions. Gonzalo Perez and his father Alonso de Espinosa were ordinary alcaldes several times; his ancestors were among the conquistadors and colonizers of Jamaica; they had an allotment of Indians, showing they were important persons, while Diego Sanches de Espinosa, his paternal great-grandfather, was the permanent alcalde of the fortress on the north side of the island in the town of Seville and had even risked his life on several occasions to defend the fortress from the king's enemies. Centeno's boasting may be overlooked for at the time he wrote, this doctor of canon law was a mere curate in his home town seeking from superiors a merited ecclesiastical promotion, seemingly denied because he was a creole.

Although Balbuena's third argument for a resident bishop for Jamaica seems puerile today, it did have some weight in the seventeenth century. Balbuena advanced the argument that only with serious inconvenience could he obtain the holy oils used in the administration of the sacraments of baptism, confirmation, extreme unction, not to mention holy orders. Balbuena lived in a period of deep religious feeling. Tension was in the air, for the Reformation had split the Christian world into two opposing camps which encountered one another under almost every conceivable circumstance both on land and on sea. An encounter spelt trouble, and for this reason it was risky to transport such a sacred thing as the holy oils through pirate-infested seas. Nor was this danger a mere figment of the imagination. Examples could be cited like the following: a frigate bearing the holy oils from Cuba to Jamaica was attacked and boarded by corsairs; so sudden was the action that there was neither time nor place to hide them.[32] The cleric carrying them had only one choice, if he would prevent them from falling into sacrilegious hands—cast them into the sea. This he did. Balbuena could cite another example. Again the holy oils were transported from Cuba to Jamaica; again corsairs attacked and boarded the ship.[33] This time the cleric fastened the containers with a rope tied to the helm and cast the holy oils into the sea, hoping to recover them when the danger had passed. But this was an old trick, used to save gold and precious jewels from pirate hands. The pirate who discovered the leaden containers looked with disappointment on his find, but for the rest of the pirate crew they provided sacrilegious sport who made mockery and scorn of religious ceremonies with the holy vials. Despite the cogent arguments proposed by Balbuena, Jamaica remained under an abbot. There was no change of status during Spanish days.

Balbuena, like Villalobos, wrote his personal observation of Jamaica. In the year 1611 he noted that apart from the capital, Santiago de la Vega, the country had vast tracts of uninhabited, uncultivated land overgrown with lush vegetation where cattle roamed wild and in early seventeenth century Jamaica became a hunting ground for wild stock. Colonists who formerly had shares in domestic cattle on the great haciendas, now hunted these wild cattle within allotted areas and spent the entire year killing cows and bulls for their hides, leaving the meat for scavenger birds locally known as John Crows. In the mountains large herds of swine multiplied, the common property of all who wished to hunt them and from which great quantities of lard and barbecued pork were shipped to Spain and nearby colonies.[34]

Builders of seventeenth century sailing vessels also had their eyes open for timber that would resist the deadly encroachment of marine parasites, and to this Balbuena thought he had an answer in the hard woods of Jamaica, for on the hillside slopes grew untapped resources of cedar, mahogany, and brazilwood, all suitable for constructing sailing vessels. Galleons, so claimed Balbuena, might be built in Jamaica close to the source of this timber supply, and the low cost of labour would allow a considerable saving over building these same ships in other parts of the Indies. But Spain was interested in logwood from which a purple dye is obtained, and in 1611 the first experimental cargo was sent to Spain to see if the dye would be suitable for the wool and silk used so extensively in Europe. It proved most satisfactory and became one of the important exports of Jamaica.

Population of Jamaica, 1611

Balbuena ended his description of Jamaica with the lament that, despite these natural resources, the inhabitants, because of laziness, were so poor they could hardly manage to feed themselves with beef and cassava, the most plentiful and cheapest of all foods.[35]

With much poor human material the Church was not and could never be in a vigorous, flourishing condition; for not only were they ambitionless but they were also few in numbers so that after one hundred two years of colonization there were only 1,518 persons of all classes.[36] Broken down into categories, they were five hundred thirty-two Spaniards, men and women; one hundred seventy-three Spanish children; one hundred six free negroes; seventy-four Arawak Indians;[37] five hundred fifty-eight slaves; and seventy-five foreigners. Among the latter were some Englishmen who had deserted after Jackson's raid on Jamaica and had cast their lot in with the Spaniards.[38]

This meagre population in the early seventeenth century indicates that the fortune seekers had placed a low evaluation on Jamaica, since agriculture and ranching were the only two resources it could offer in contrast to the silver and gold of Mexico and South America. Colonists who did remain found themselves in a constantly dwindling population, so that in 1611 these families had so intermarried that all were related by some degree of consanguinity.

Tithes

Jamaican abbots depended, according to ecclesiastical law, on tithes both for their own personal support and for the maintenance of the church. Tithes, technically the tenth part of the income arising in Jamaica from land, stock, and customs duty allotted to the clergy for their support or devoted to religious and charitable use, were a source of contention from the days of the conquistadors. The very type of ecclesiastical office granted Jamaica was made to depend upon the value of the tithes, so that Jamaica was never granted a bishopric because its tithes could not support one.

Each abbot complained about the management of these tithes by his predecessor. Balbuena accused Villalobos of collecting tithes illegally, especially the funds which had accumulated between the death of Samano and the appointment of Villalobos, and it would appear that Villalobos did on his own authority and without leave from the king appropriate these tithes for his own use, whereas he should have consulted the crown, for in every instance where tithes amassed during the interregnum of abbots, it was the king who decided how these tithes were to be used.[39]

Conscience-stricken Villalobos, on his deathbed, willed eleven hundred pesos to the Church or to whom the money belonged.[40]

In 1611, five years after Villalobos's death, these tithes were still on deposit with the executor of the estate.[41] No one could discover the real owner, nor had the executor informed the king of Villalobos's desire to make restitution, so Balbuena took up the matter with the king, informing him that it was not clear to whom the eleven hundred pesos belonged.[42] Since there was uncertainty, Balbuena considered His Majesty the arbiter. Balbuena was careful to add that the Church could use this money to relieve the many necessities under which it was burdened; furthermore, Balbuena himself would find the money a decided help in defraying his passage to Jamaica and the debt he still owed for his Roman documents.

In Balbuena's day tithes were paid in Jamaica's most valuable asset, hides. These were delivered to the abbot, who consigned them to Manuel del Rio, his agent in Seville, Spain. Extant accounts show that on 2 August 1612, Captain Martin S. Romero of the *Magdalen*, registered and loaded aboard his vessel one hundred hides of cattle, both cows and bulls.[43] In 1614, seventy more hides bearing the abbot's brand were placed on Captain Sebastian Lopez's ship, and they were recorded to have been "salted, dried and in good condition, except one which was rotted at the loin."[44]

Tithes, as a barometer, indicated periods of prosperity or recession in Spanish Jamaica's economy. In the twenty years from 1534 to 1554, its most prosperous period, tithes were on a par with those of Cuba, Puerto Rico, and Santo Domingo, reaching the all-time high of one thousand pesos a year.[45] This was the period sugar manufacture formed an important economic item. Later the value of tithes declined to the rock bottom low of one hundred pesos in 1606; rose to four hundred ten pesos in 1608; then increased to five hundred and twenty-five pesos in 1609.[46] During the low period, British, French, and Dutch interlopers attacked Spanish ships. Jamaica itself had been subject to enemy raids which aimed at disrupting the economy of the country. Fewer and fewer Spanish ships found their way into Jamaican ports, and she became isolated from the rest of the Spanish empire.

Last Days of Balbuena

In 1619 Balbuena rounded out his tenth year as abbot, years not too happy for the poet-abbot; he felt frustrated that Jamaica proved a cul-de-sac for ecclesiastical advancement. He asked Philip III to have him appointed to a deanery in Mexico or Tlaxcala or even in far away Peru.[47] No one in Jamaica had ever questioned his zeal and piety as abbot, for he was well liked by the people; but Balbuena did not reciprocate their admiration. One source of his dislike for them was the question of money. These same Jamaican admirers owed him one-half of his tithes.

Balbuena determined to depart Jamaica as soon as the opportunity arose. This came when the see of Puerto Rico became vacant upon the elevation of Bishop Pedro Solier, who was chosen archbishop of Santo Domingo. Balbuena was named to fill the Puerto Rican see in 1619, but, for some reason, he remained in Jamaica until 1620, though he had ceased to be abbot from the previous year. On 27 January 1620, Archbishop Solier consecrated him bishop of Puerto Rico in the city of Santo Domingo. He remained in Santo Domingo to attend the synod of 1622, and did not take possession of his own see until 1623.[48] He lived for four years to enjoy episcopal honours and died in Puerto Rico in the year 1627.[49]

Seven

The Last of the Abbots

The final and crucial period of Spanish-Jamaican history opened with Don Mateo de Medina Moreno, the last of the abbots. Moreno was the choice of the Colón family. Don Juan Colón, marquis of Jamaica, in a letter to Philip IV dated 1620, recommended Licentiate Mateo de Medina Moreno.[1] The Holy See, acting with more than customary caution, delayed the confirmation for a full two years. Although Don Mateo had received his appointment from Gregory XV, it was not confirmed until shortly before 9 April 1622, for in a letter written then Moreno was informed by the crown that he might now proceed to Jamaica.[2] In his entourage he was allowed one priest, four servants, and four black slaves, while for his household use he could carry five hundred ducats in value of gold and wrought silverware. All were exempt from customs duty except the slaves.[3]

Little did the abbot reckon with maurauding pirates who at divers times paid unfriendly visits to Santiago de la Vega, where a display of Old World gold and silverware would be deemed fair prize. His slaves, should they live long enough, would one day flee into the mountains before the invading force of Penn and Venables. To history they would be known as the Maroons, a perennial thorn in the side of the English.

Abbot Moreno Arrives at Jamaica

In striking contrast to the comparative comfort of Old World Spain was primitive Santiago de la Vega of the Caribbean, which sorely tried the soul of the good abbot as he walked its narrow streets for the first time in 1622. Unpretentious dwellings of low, squat, one storey houses with no distinctive architecture, arranged along narrow crowded streets, indicated that the city was poor. Only the plaza gave evidence of a more glorious past in the governor's residence, government buildings, and the abbey church. As he gazed upon the church to which he had fallen heir, a structure badly in need of repair from the ravages of hurricanes, plaster-shattering earthquakes, and the avaricious pirates, Moreno was strongly tempted to return to the land and life he had left in Spain with his heavy wrought gold and silver plate, his servants and slaves, and his one clerical attendant. But there was something of the champion in the nature of the fifty-seven year old abbot, for despite depressing surroundings and quarrels with civil officials, he held tenaciously to his post for twenty-eight long and trying years. Only once did he leave Jamaica, and that was to attend the provincial synod at Santo Domingo in 1622. (See Appendix C) At this synod it was decreed that the abbot of Jamaica should come under the jurisdiction of the archbishop of Santo Domingo, a decree which took effect on 15 February 1624.[4]

Two worries were on Moreno's mind when he voyaged from Jamaica to attend the synod at Santo Domingo; one was financial. He had learned that no free passage was allowed him; so that he personally, without royal aid, would be responsible for chartering a vessel, a heavy expense cutting deeply into his meagre first year tithes. The other was fear of pirates, for there was danger that these jolly rovers might seize him for a fat ransom. Somehow the abbot was able to finance his passage, and no black flag with prominent skull and crossbones appeared on the horizon to give chase to his carrack while on the way to or from Hispaniola.

Dutch Attack Jamaica

Pirates did not seriously enter the abbot's life until two years later. On 1 August 1626 Philip IV wrote Governor Don Francisco Terril, warning him that he had received news by way of Flanders that the Dutch and English were planning to secure a foothold on the coast of Jamaica by taking possession of the fort at Anaya Point, and he advised the governor to take military precautions.[5] As early as 1580 the Dutch were making inroads into Spanish-claimed territory, for in that year they settled in the Guianas on the north coast of South America.[6] Further settlements in the same Guianas—at Essequibo in 1615 and Berbice in 1624—strengthened the Dutch foothold in the Caribbean. The Hollanders were interested not only in territorial gains but in trade as well, and this led to the incorporation on 3 June 1621 of the Dutch West India Company. Trade for this commercial company had a wider meaning than the ordinary significance of the word, for it also included piratical attacks on Spanish merchant vessels. This became evident a few years later in 1627, when it declared a dividend of 50 percent after Dutch Admiral Pieter Heyn attacked the

Plate Fleet off Mantanzas Bay and relieved the Spaniards of gold, logwood, and sugar which sold in the Netherlands for some 15,000,000 guilders. St. Croix of the Virgin Islands, captured in 1626, merely whetted their appetite for more territorial gains in the Antilles, for it could be used as a springboard for an attack on weakly held Jamaica, which looked like fair pirate prize.[7]

The decision to attack Jamaica at Point Anaya was a new military strategy. Hitherto attacks had come by way of Puerto Caguay with a six-mile march to the capital which could be impeded, and at times completely stopped, by ambushes from natural and man-made defenses. This unusual plan of attack by the Dutch would come from the west of Santiago de la Vega, and once the fort at Anaya was silenced, the whole plain of Vere was wide open to the invaders. The Spaniards would then have to oppose the Dutch on level open country with little opportunity for ambush, since there were neither natural nor military barriers to stop the enemy march on the capital, while women, children, and old men fleeing into the mountains would run directly into the arms of the advancing Dutch.

Taking the abbot into his confidence, Terril informed the prelate of the impending attack and promised it would be more than a mere raid; it would be a full-scale attempt to secure a foothold on the island. If it succeeded, it would spell disaster for both civil and ecclesiastical life in Jamaica.

Four hundred fighting men were mustered into service by Terril, and lookouts were placed along the coast at strategic points from Fort Morant to the Baziletto Mountains overlooking Anaya. This gave an advantage to the Spaniards, who could sight the enemy miles before he landed on Jamaican shores. Drill and military tactics were rehearsed every day and plans were laid how most effectively to meet the Dutch on the plain of Vere. One week passed, and another, until a full month was rounded out with no sign of the Dutch. Both governor and abbot, however, kept the fighting men keyed for the possibility of an unexpected attack.

One day ships did appear on the horizon; a closer approach definitely identified them as Dutch. Excitement ran high in Santiago de la Vega and on every *hato* in Jamaica, for true to report the enemy launched its attack on Anaya. But long weeks of military preparation told in favour of the Spaniards as they routed the Dutch so roundly that they never made another attempt to gain a foothold on the island.[8]

The last Dutch ship had scarcely turned its defeated prow towards more friendly shores than Abbot Moreno directed his zealous energy to matters ecclesiastical which demanded his attention. For three years before his arrival, the Church had had no competent leader. The synod and the Dutch had occupied his attention up to the present, but now he could put his ecclesiastical house in order. This made him a favourite with government and people, but not with the clergy. The documents state that his popularity was not found among the Dominican friars; their antipathy may have come from a lack of prudence in his declining years. He was one of those holy men who showed little wisdom in his dealings with others.

If the abbot was all but universally popular in the island, the same could not be said of his friend, Governor Francisco Terril. A man of domineering and obdurate character, he had ejected two governors sent to replace him.[9] In the second of these, Juan Martínez Arana, he met a resilient character who returned to Jamaica and forced Terril to leave.

During the 1637–50 period,[10] governors were replaced at a furious rate, some remaining only a year. To add to these internal troubles, was an external one: the British made two incursions, one in 1640, and the other in 1643.[11]

English Attack Jamaica

In the year 1640, on one of those delightful tropical mornings with the sun just peeping over the horizon, appearing afraid to awaken peaceful Jamaica from slumber, there became visible in the distance sails of seven ships flying the British flag, about to disturb the peace and calm of Santiago de la Vega. A few hours later these ships were riding boldly at anchor in Caguay harbour. Receiving the alarm from the watch, Governor Jacinto Sedeno promptly rode down to the port where personal observation confirmed that they were British and that four hundred soldiers with artillery had already landed on the shore. Sedeno hastened back to the capital, ordered the women and children to flee into the mountains and the men to remove the sacred vessels and vestments of the churches to a place of safety. Abbot, Franciscans, and Dominicans found ready hands to load these and their own personal belongings into carts and drive them through Guatibacoa into the mountains.

Fighting men drawn from four hundred Spanish citizens and two hundred negroes were mustered into three companies of infantry and one of cavalry. Sedeno stationed troops on the shore near the invading British, but the majority he placed in the capital awaiting the inevitable attack on the centre of the island's life.

The Spaniards down at the port, however, were in a fighting mood. When the British officers gave the order to attack, the Spaniards retaliated to give the invaders such a battering that the survivors were only too happy to seek refuge on their ships, weigh anchor, and sail away.[12]

Chased out ignominiously by a handful of Spaniards in 1640, the British were back again in 1643 with more ships and more men for another try. This time they succeeded. From eleven ships under the command of Captain William Jackson, they poured fifteen hundred men onto the beach and struck out for the capital, Santiago de la Vega, six miles away. Catching the Spaniards unawares, the British captured the town with little loss of personnel. It was Easter Sunday, 5 March 1643, when alleluias should have echoed within the sacred walls of the abbey church; instead these sacred walls resounded with imprecations of billeted soldiery.[13]

Six days the enemy occupied Santiago de la Vega, threatening to burn the capital unless supplied with beef and bread to provision their fleet. Since beef could be had from mere slaughter of cattle and bread from cassava, the ransom placed no heavy burden on the people. Governor Don Francisco Ladrón de Zegama agreed to the terms, supplied beef and bread to rid the island of Jackson and his unwelcome guests. On point of departure the British commander noted the fertility of the island and its excellent harbours, remarking that the English settlers were becoming too numerous for the tiny island of St. Kitts and would like to settle in Jamaica. He also made the understatement that Jamaica might support as large a population as eight thousand. Some of the crew must have thought in the same vein, for a good number deserted Jackson and threw their lot in with the Spaniards.[14]

This was the turbulent atmosphere in which the Church carried on her spiritual labours in the mid-seventeenth century, a precarious, uncertain existence of wondering from day to day if the lookout above Caguay would bring news of another raiding party. With each such alarm everyone hastily packed possessions and fled into the mountains, disrupting civil and ecclesiastical society. The abbot did not neglect his heavy wrought gold and silver plate valued at five hundred ducats but always carried them to safety.

If the Church was in a state of uneasiness from external causes, she had equal concern within the colony, since disturbances in civil government were clearly manifest. A real crisis was reached in October 1643, when Governor Don Francisco Ladrón de Zegama died a prisoner in his own house.[15] The alcaldes, municipal magistrates, then became the governing body. This state of affairs continued for two years until 1645, when the duke of Veragua nominated Captain Sebastian Fernández Gamboa governor. Alarmed at the situation, the

Audiencia of Santo Domingo sent a commission piloted by Licentiate Juan de Retuerta to investigate the seriousness of affairs in Jamaica.[16]

Thoroughly investigating all causes, Juan de Retuerta placed responsibility for the crisis squarely on the shoulders of the duke.[17] He declared in his report that the duke could neither defend the island from pirates, nor maintain justice, nor impose the obedience so necessary for good government. The absentee duke did what he could to remedy the situation by letter; he admonished and demanded observance of law and order. But his words were treated with no weight or authority since he was too far removed from Jamaica, and with an income reduced to a meagre six hundred ducats a year he found himself in the impossible situation of trying to maintain an efficient government without funds enough to pay a competent and honest governor for the colony. Five hundred ducats of quartos or its equivalent two hundred and fifty ducats of silver was the annual salary of the mid-seventeenth century Jamaican governors. By all standards of living, a governor needed more than this to support himself properly in the highest office of the land. Consequently, only down-at-heels officials were willing to accept employment. Jamaica got just what she paid for—men worth two hundred and fifty silver ducats a year.

More interested in making a quick ducat than in possessing a clear conscience, these local potentates had recourse to divers illegal acts. One took this form: every year slave ships on their way to Vera Cruz or another Caribbean port stopped at Jamaica. Although it was illegal for them to do so, they found one excuse or another to put into a Jamaican harbour by feigning either necessity of repairs or lack of food supplies. As many as twelve such vessels, carrying from three to four hundred slaves each, called every year and remained from seven to eight months. During their sojourn, crews and slaves in excess of four thousand, eight hundred persons, had to be fed. Here is where the governor augmented his salary, for only those approved by him were allowed to act as ship's chandlers, others daring to sell to the slavers being subject to severe penalties. From the sale of supplies, the governor received a sizeable commission.[18]

Another illegal but lucrative act was this: when slave ships, which had called at Jamaica, departed for their port of destination, they left a large number of slaves they were carrying in the island. Some had been registered on the ship's manifest, others had not. Those on the manifest had to be accounted for by the captain of the ship so he would tell the authorities in Vera Cruz that the slaves had died or he had been forced to sell them for the crew's maintenance. Later, after the ship had left Jamaica, these slaves would be sold in Havana, not in the name of the captain but in the name of a Jamaican citizen. The captain would collect his share of transaction at a future date. This thievery could not have taken place without the knowledge and bribery of the Jamaican governor.

Unhappy State of the Church

Unhappy as was investigator Juan de Retuerta's picture of civil society, unhappier still was his censure of the Church. He painted it in fading colours.[19] Moreno was ageing, close to eighty years old; the fiery enthusiasm of twenty-five years before was slowly deteriorating into lassitude. The abbey church, having weathered a full century of earthquakes and hurricanes, of pirate depredations and omnivorous termites, of torrential downpours and long hot days of piercing tropical sun, badly needed repairs. But Moreno was unable physically or financially to afford these repairs, so divine service was conducted only on rare occasions within the massive Spanish walls. Again, the religious orders, both Dominicans and Franciscans, were in serious need of rejuvenation—the Dominicans had four friars, the Franciscans three. Both Dominicans and Franciscans lived so poorly on scanty alms that they found it difficult to carry out properly the religious duties of regular community life.

Canonical procedures of the abbot were also criticized by Retuerta who claimed that two petitions presented to the abbot were sufficient to have a marriage declared invalid. Again, the ageing prelate thundered out so many excommunications that no one paid the slightest attention to them, for so frequently did the church bell ring to announce a new censure that its sound had hardly ceased before the abbot with equal ease lifted the ban.

These complaints may have been the hyperbolic language of one who wished to impress higher authorities with the serious state of ecclesiastical affairs, for Retuerta claimed that everything ecclesiastical was in such a state of utter confusion that a clever lawyer would find it an intricate task to unravel the disorder, which does seem somewhat exaggerated.

Sebastian Fernández Gamboa was appointed governor immediately after Retuerta's report to Philip IV in 1644.[20] He remained until 1646, when Pedro Caballero took his place.[21] This haughty and impetuous governor of twenty-eight years of age, whose black beard lent maturity to his slightly freckled face, raised a storm in the old capital and unwittingly occasioned the end of Moreno's regime as abbot.

It all began with a drought. Rain is very important to a tropical island; without it over a considerable period of the year, the lush vegetation will turn a sickly brown, grass will wither, the ground will become dry and hard, cattle will die, and the whole populace will suffer. This was the unhappy climatic state of Jamaica in 1648. During the months of June, July, and August, the drought had reached such severity that fear of starvation filled the whole island.[22]

On Friday evening, 26 August 1631, a great throng marched in penitential procession through the streets of Santiago de la Vega.[23] Peasant and governor, curate and prelate recited prayers for relief as they processed to the abbey church on the south side of the plaza where Friar Pedro Balbuena preached from the pulpit to the assembled government officials, clergy, and people.

There were vices in the capital—the chief public scandal was excessive gambling. No one could deny this; by reproving these gamblers Balbuena hoped to bring about a reform of life and with it more divine beneficence in the form of rain. So eloquent was Balbuena's condemnation of this vice that tears and groans could be seen and heard as the preacher pictured the distress of wives and children when the scanty income of the breadwinner was squandered at the gambling tables.

But one listener was neither moved to tears nor impressed by the friar's condemnation of his favourite sport: Governor Caballero. Gambling took place in the governor's house. Men were playing for such high stakes that many a worried wife poured her tale of woe into the friar's ear. Husbands would gamble from dusk to dawn, not only their own money but their property and cattle upon which their families depended for sustenance. This type of gambling would find its counterpart in later history, in the days of the plantocracy, when the estate Great House would witness fortunes lost at the turn of the cards.

Balbuena's sermon startled the whole town from the men involved down to the last peasant. Caballero felt that the censure included himself. He repressed his anger while in the church, but on the following day, Saturday, he vented his spleen when he met his accuser at the abbot's house. While Balbuena was paying his respects to the abbot, Caballero arrived and seeing the friar in company with Moreno remarked "A fine lance your Lordship has in his company." With mounting temper, the governor called the friar a liar and a dissolute monk. Threats followed. If they were not in the presence of the abbot, the governor would give the friar something to really talk about! There was no stopping the torrent of abuse by Caballero.

Balbuena did get one word in when he asked the governor that he at least have regard for the dignity which he professed. But abusive words kept spewing out of Caballero's mouth. Thoroughly frightened, Balbuena beat a hasty retreat into the street, followed by

Caballero still hurling insults at the fleeing Franciscan. Balbuena sought the refuge of his monastery, but Caballero caught him at the gate of the abbot's country house.

The pursuit cooled the governor's temper somewhat, for he made it clear to the friar that the king had given him authority to have games in his house. Balbuena had his own reply; in the opinion of many who had attended these games, especially men from the abbot's household, neither God nor king desired that Jamaicans should be ruined or deprived of their sustenance. This reply so excited the governor that besides the use of filthy and depraved words, he advanced towards Balbuena with upraised cane threatening to strike the friar. Balbuena was able to restrain Caballero by asking him to hasten and strike him that he might have the merit in the sight of God. With this the governor went into his own house, and Balbuena to his monastery. But before reaching his own gate, Caballero stopped near the town butchery, and there before a large crowd of townsmen he berated all priests, religious as well as secular, as if they were the scum of the earth.

This was not the first time Caballero had shown disregard for common decency. Three months previously two men pursued by law officers for some irregularity sought refuge in the Franciscan monastery.[24] Locked gates and high walls stopped the pursuers until Caballero arrived with twenty followers. Then the monastery was no obstacle. Door and gates barring their way, the governor and his henchmen unceremoniously scaled the wooden fence to remove the frightened fugitives from a refuge which by common consent was held inviolable.

Balbuena could recall other incidents in which Caballero had crossed swords with the clergy. Recently he had treated the vicar general as if he were the greatest rogue in the world simply because he wished to banish some men of evil lives.[25] The governor also wished to take precedence over the clergy in the abbey church at the offering of holy water and the kiss of peace. When he appeared at the Franciscan monastery, he expected the whole community to come out to meet him.

The abbot allowed neither these nor the previous incident to pass without a formal protest to higher authorities. The crown received a full report of the immature acts of Governor Caballero. If the abbot thought that a mere written complaint would curb Caballero's indiscretions, he was in error. Shortly after the sermon incident another imbroglio arose. This time the baptism of Caballero's infant son occasioned the altercation.[26]

Trouble over Baptism of Governor's Son

The baptism of a governor's son is an important event in any colony, and under ordinary circumstances calls for much rejoicing. This one caused a mild cataclysm, rocking the island and causing it to split into two parties due solely to the perverse and fiery-tempered governor. The contention arose over a bed. Caballero reasoned, but not canonically, that a bed with costly draperies, erected within the sanctuary, next to the altar, on which the infant would lie during the ceremony, would add both solemnity to the baptism and gubernatorial dignity to the Church's rite. One obstacle stood in the way of Caballero's pomposity: Moreno did not share the governor's enthusiasm. The abbot would not consent, and even the governor's liaison officer could not change the abbot's mind. There would be no bed in the sanctuary during the baptism.

Caballero was a person unwilling to take no for an answer. Brushing aside his envoy, he flew down the narrow street to the abbot's residence, burst in on the prelate, and tried to press home his point. With deadly temper mounting at each refusal, Caballero broke into abusive language, hurling choice epithets at the resolute abbot. The governor called him first a servant boy then a garlic-eating clown. The tirade ended with his threat to erect not one bed but a dozen beds in the church, his own included.

Omitting his own bed, Caballero did erect a bed for the infant, trappings and all. The abbot might endure insults, but an act of defiance of ecclesiastical authority he could not countenance. Into the hills he betook himself, lest his presence at the baptism seem to give even tacit consent to the irregular action of the defiant Caballero. Failing the abbot's consent, the governor now tried to persuade the vicar general to grant permission for the bed-in-sanctuary arrangement. He too refused. At this refusal, the governor went beyond himself as a gentleman and physically attacked the vicar general. Excommunication immediately followed on 28 May 1649.

This censure Caballero unsuccessfully tried to have removed. Some eight months later, on 1 January 1650, the censure continued to rest uncomfortably on Caballero's soul.[27] Such a continued state of excommunication which the abbot refused to lift, contradicts Retuerta's previous statement that, no sooner had the abbot announced an excommunication, than with equal ease he lifted the ban even before the church bells had ceased to ring. Here is one documentary proof that an excommunication of Jamaica's highest civil official was not treated lightly, but continued to press on Caballero for almost eight months.

Governor Caballero Removed from Office

The crown could not allow a series of complaints against this immature, violent-tempered disturber of the peace to pass unheeded. It referred these complaints to the fiscal of Santo Domingo, Francisco de Alarcon Coronado. In April 1649 a new governor was appointed, Jacinto Sedeno de Albornoz, who had previously served as governor, from 1639 to 1640. Coronado advised that the newly appointed governor hold an enquiry as soon as he arrived in Jamaica; if charges against Caballero were proved, to arrest him and confiscate his property.

Sedeno de Albornoz arrived in Jamaica on 2 May 1649, but did not reveal his position as governor-elect. For a time he acted as commissioner of accounts and audited the books of the royal treasurer. Both the treasurer and Caballero objected strenuously to this. There was only one course open to Sedeno. He produced his letters patent as governor of Jamaica and Caballero's rule came to an end.

On 26 May 1649, Captain Jacinto Sedeno de Albornoz was formally installed and acknowledged as governor of Jamaica by the cabildo of Santiago de la Vega.[28] Rejoicing was intense among all the citizens. Even those who had been ruining the island received the new governor with a show of friendliness. Sedeno recorded the names of these contentious persons: Adrian Cazetas Bayante, a perverse man; Duarte de Acosta Norguera, Lucas Borrero Bardezi, Pedro Perez de León, Cristóbal Bejarano and his sons—one of them, Juan de Chabes Bejarano, was commissary of the Holy Office—Don Francisco de Naveda Alvarado, Antonio Ponz Milanes, Juan de Aranziba, Juan Francisco Reduto, Francisco Rodriguez de la Cueba, Juan Martin Borundel, Ignacio Ramos, Roque Martinez de Munera, and Diego Nunez Roza. All were members of the cabildo, the governing body.

Crisis in the Colony

One of Sedeno Albornoz's first acts was to place a fine of fifty pesos silver on the former governor, charging him with having disturbed the peace.[29] At the same time he ordered Caballero to deliver some documents to him. Caballero refused repeatedly; with each refusal Sedeno increased the fine until it finally reached one thousand fifty silver pesos.

The imposition of the penalty did not win the benevolence of Caballero and his followers. Enmity again split the town and the abbot again wrote a complaint to the audiencia of Santo Domingo, alleging that Caballero was stirring up trouble for the new governor.

Those in favour of the present governor called themselves Sedenists; the followers of the former governor, the Caballeros.

This turmoil could not continue indefinitely. It came to a climax on New Year's Day, 1650.[30] Caballero had smarted under the ban of excommunication for almost eight months and did not want to begin the New Year under ecclesiastical ban. Summoning his courage, he decided to make a final effort to persuade the abbot to remove the ban. Perhaps on the first day of the new year the ageing abbot's heart would soften. Mulling over such thoughts, Caballero strolled over to the abbot's residence near the abbey church and arrived while Moreno was celebrating Mass. The former governor sat in the parlour to wait for the abbot.

At this time, a negro page of the abbot looked in. He wrongly concluded that Caballero was waiting there to murder his master.

The panic-stricken page ran to a nearby building where Governor Sedeno and the cabildo had assembled to choose officers for public posts, according to the custom at the beginning of each year. The excited boy burst in upon the assembly and screamed at the top of his voice that Caballero was waiting in the abbot's house to murder him.

The whole assembly rose in alarm. Sedeno hastily gathered a group of soldiers under Captain Blas de Figueroa. The all ran quickly across the plaza to defend Moreno.

Caballero's End

Seated quietly in the abbot's patio, Caballero was the most surprised man in Jamaica when the troop of highly excited men burst in. Sedeno opened with a barrage of questions, but then changed his tactics and accused Caballero of lying in wait to lay violent hands on the abbot. More words followed, and the unjustly accused Caballero leaped to his feet in a threatening manner. Suddenly Captain Figueroa stepped behind him and plunged his sword into the heart of the former governor. Caballero slumped to the floor. So vicious was the attack that Ornate, one of the Sedenists, held a tuft of the victim's hair in his hand as the dying man called for absolution. Clad in the sacred vestments, the abbot rushed into the patio and raised his hand in absolution over the prostrate body.

Here was murder before their very eyes. This horrible deed would call for a full explanation, since Caballero was more than an ordinary citizen. He was maestro titular of the Supreme Council of the Holy Office of the Inquisition, alcalde of its prison in Cartagena, and had held the office of governor of Jamaica. This act would call for redress by the highest authorities. As the news spread throughout

Santiago de la Vega, and the swelling crowd made excited enquiries, some acceptable explanation approximating the truth had to be made to the shocked public.

This was the explanation given: upon entering the abbot's house, Governor Sedeno in company with six other persons saw Don Pedro Caballero seated in a chair; he did not rise or uncover his head when the governor entered. The governor spoke to him, asking why he was making a disturbance. Thereupon Caballero rose from his chair, asked the governor why he spoke to him in this manner, then struck a blow at the governor with his crutch. The governor warded off the blow with his cane, breaking Caballero's crutch, and at the same time sought to seize him. Caballero put his hand to his sword. At this point the details become vague. Allegedly, Caballero's sword fell to the ground, ornamented trappings first. Although Caballero had definitely not drawn his sword from its scabbard, all the Sedenists agreed that the fatal wound was inflicted by Caballero's own broad sword.

Some may have believed the story, but not Doña Teresa de Guzman Caballero. She was not so credulous. Through her father, Pedro de Guzman of Cartagena, she immediately petitioned for an inquiry into the death of her husband. It was granted. On 8 June 1650, a deputation consisting of Bartolomé de la Toras, priest and commissary of the Holy Office in Cartagena, together with commissioners of the Holy Office in Jamaica, Francisco de Leybia Ysasi and Juan de Chaves Bejarano, undertook the inquiry after asking the cabildo of Santiago de la Vega assistance for the hearing.

Governor Sedeno Arrested

On 11 June 1650, just as Sedeno was preparing for bed, a boisterous mob burst in on him.[31] They had broken down the doors and were climbing through the windows to gain an entry. They called out that he was now a prisoner of the Holy Office of the Inquisition. Sedeno tried to quiet them by protesting that he had done nothing against the Catholic faith to warrant arrest, but they would not be silenced. One of them, Francisco de Leyba Ysasi, informed the governor that he and Commissioner Bejarano had already prepared his cell. Sedeno later blamed Ysasi and Bejarano for inflaming the people and intimidating them with the threat of excommunication if they did not assist them in arresting the governor.

Sedeno ceremoniously faced the mob with his staff of office in hand to show he was still the governor. But ceremony lasted only a moment, for the mob seized him before he could buckle his sword.

They hustled him off to the commissary inspector's house, where someone seized the staff of office from his hands and bound him in chains.

Two days later, Sedeno was placed in a cart and carried to Port Caguay, in sharp contrast to his ceremonious arrival of the previous year. Now he was a prisoner accused of murder to be locked in a narrow cell on board Ysasi's ship in the harbour. From 13 June to 14 August he was held incommunicado—not even a servant could visit his cell. He was alone in his leaky cabin where the wide spaces between the planks allowed the burning sun to beat down on him and the rain to soak his body.

The Abbot's Last Days

On 16 August as Sedeno was being transferred from his cabin to the quarter deck, he saw the old abbot being brought on board; he too was under arrest. His soutane was dirty, his person unkempt—no respect had been shown for his high office as abbot of Jamaica. Two fellow prisoners were with him—the vicar general, Don Duarte Figueroa, and his father, Captain Blas de Figueroa. Sailors placed mattresses in boxes for the abbot and the other prisoners, who all slept on the open deck. But the widow Caballero with her servants, travelling on the same ship, occupied cabins or more comfortable places on the deck.

They sailed across the Caribbean. The prisoners were under heavy guard, to prevent communication with one another. They arrived in Cartagena on 27 August 1650.[32] On the following night the officials of the Holy Office of the Inquisition took them into custody and lodged them in the common jail. The abbot was placed in the monastery of St. Dominic, while his vicar general had to be content with the bleak walls in the tower of the parish church.

At this point the documents draw a veil over the proceedings. Back in Jamaica, the abbot's possessions, including his pectoral cross, were seized and sold at auction. No reason is given for this unwarranted thievery, a tragic note on which to end his twenty-eight years of service.

No other abbot was ever appointed for Jamaica. Moreno brought to a close an ecclesiastical institution which had served the island for one hundred thirty-four years with these parting words: "Blessed be God, that at the end of twenty-eight years of pastorate, Jamaica has given me this reward."[33] On this poignant note the Age of the Abbots ends in Jamaica.

Eight

Conquest

Although Jamaica remained officially under Spanish rule until the Treaty of Madrid, 8 July 1670, ceded the island to Great Britain, the British invasion on 10 May 1655 fulfilled the worst fears of Abbot Villalobos.

Oliver Cromwell had long coveted Spain's American possessions, but he could not effect his "Western Design" until peace at home and encouragement from Thomas Gage brought the firm resolution to seize every Spanish colony not only in the West Indies but throughout the mainland of South, Central, and North America. Peace in 1654 was an important factor, but more decisive was Gage's *A New Survey of the West Indies,* which revealed the weaknesses of Spain's sprawling island and continental empire.[1] This seventeenth-century best-seller, excellent propaganda for a British incursion into exclusively Spanish preserves, caught the eye of Thomas Challoner, who recommended that Gage submit a memorandum to Oliver Cromwell on the prospects for an attack against Spanish possessions in the New World.[2]

Thomas Gage

In his memorandum Gage employed the same arguments he had advanced in his text. The whole area claimed by the Spaniards was sparsely occupied by them and throughout Central America they had no artillery or forts to defend their cities. The Indians were unarmed and would not rally to the support of their Spanish masters. The Spaniards themselves were too lazy and lustful a lot to defend their territory. If supplied with arms, negroes and mulattoes would rise against the Spaniards since both could be expected to support any nation that would proclaim liberty for them. Since jealousy had made a rift in relations between Spaniard and creole, there was not the united front which appeared from the outside. Finally, God would surely appear on the side of the upright English and oppose the Spanish sinners.

Thomas Gage was one of those very rare persons who had lived in Spanish colonies when it was absolutely forbidden for an Englishman so much as to set foot in Spanish America. Nor was this his only claim to distinction. Scion of an illustrious English family, he was second cousin to the martyr St. Robert Southwell, was Jesuit educated, and a Dominican missionary in Central America. Despite his long religious training and solid Catholic family background, he became an apostate from the faith.[3]

Early Years

Thomas Gage had been born in 1603, the second son of John and Margaret Gage.[4] Their two years imprisonment in the Tower for having harbored St. Henry Garnet, S.J., in 1592 furnished them with a decisive motive for sending their sons to the Jesuit-conducted college of St. Omers in French Flanders. One son, Henry, became an officer in the British army, another, George, became a secular priest, and Thomas a Dominican. Francis, a Jesuit, and John, a secular priest, were stepbrothers of Thomas, his father having married a second time.[5] From 1620–25, when Thomas suddenly appears in history as a Dominican, his life is shrouded in obscurity. It is thought that he entered the Society of Jesus but departed under a cloud, then made sensational charges which were emphasized by the enemies of the Jesuits. Gage carried this animosity towards the Jesuits to the grave.

Gage Goes to Mexico

One day in early 1625, Antonio Calvo, O.P., came to the friary in Jerez, Andalusia, seeking prospective missionaries for the Philippines.[6] Gage volunteered and was accepted. He sailed from Cadiz on 2 July 1625[7] and arrived in San Juan de Ulna, Mexico, on 12 September.[8] In Mexico City, Gage met a disgruntled missionary who painted such a black picture of the Philippines that he and three companions deserted the main party and fled south to Guatemala.[9]

Flight into Guatemala

Arriving in Guatemala, the fugitives knew not what to expect, but much to their surprise, they happened upon the Dominican provincial Pedro Alvarez, one of the kindliest of men, who sympathized with the runaways, imposed a normal penance, and received them into his province.[10] An order from the Dominican master general in

Rome regularized the change of Gage and his companions from the Philippines to Central America.[11]

Gage Leaves Guatemala

Gage remained twelve years in Guatemala.[12] In his early years he taught Latin to the youth of Chiapa, was then reader of the arts at St. Thomas Aquinas College, Guatemala City, and finally a bush missionary in the country. Dissatisfaction with missionary work developed while he was labouring among the primitive Indians. In 1636 he made up his mind definitely to return to England.[13] Since the provincial opposed his departure, Gage converted books, paintings, and household goods of the mission into ready cash to the value of nine thousand pieces of eight.[14]

Gage arrived in London a few days before Christmas 1637.[15] For the next twelve months he acted as chaplain to his uncle, John Copley, at Cheam Manor, Gratton.[16]

Two events shattered his life during the years 1638–39; he secretly attended Protestant services in London, and, with others of his order, he caused serious trouble for his provincial, Thomas Middleton.[17] In the summer of 1639, Gage left England to confer with the master general in Rome.[18] He requested that he be allowed to transfer to the Dominican monastery in Orleans, France.

Gage Apostatizes

Gage's request was granted, but he never arrived at Orleans. He returned to England, where eighteen months later he joined the established church and preached his recantation sermon on 28 August 1642 at St. Paul's.[19] Marriage ensued. On 22 December 1643 came his appointment as rector of St. Martin's Church, Acrise.[20] Then he shed his Anglicanism for Puritanism and followed the popular tide into the Cromwellian camp.[21]

Gage Outlines the Conquest of Spanish America

The final phase of Gage's life began with his influence on Oliver Cromwell and ended with his death in Jamaica. Cromwell had a serious financial problem to solve at this time. His government needed funds, needed them badly, and needed them immediately. The scheme had been growing in Cromwell's mind to wrest the Indies, with all its treasures, from Spain. It looked like a hopeless task until Gage gave Cromwell an account of the feebleness of Spain's vast American empire. Then he made up his mind to follow out the scheme and take every inch of territory Spain possessed across the Atlantic.

Dreams of empire and wealth determined Cromwell's decision to send an expedition to loosely-held Spanish-America. Dreams of high preferment coloured Gage's imagination of easy triumph: what an empire England would be with all Spain's possessions under Cromwell's government! It all looked so simple as the protector and Gage poured over maps and formed plans of conquest. Military strategists frowned upon Gage's enthusiasm for launching an immediate attack on Central America, but his alternative plan to take Hispaniola, move on to Cuba, and then attack Central America was agreed upon as good naval strategy.[22] It even took precedence over the suggestion of Thomas Modyford, who later became governor of Jamaica, that the fleet launch the initial attack on Trinidad and then take Cartagena, since from that geographical position the whole west would be open to British conquest.[23]

The Expedition Sails

Thirty ships of war under William Penn as admiral and Robert Venables as commander of the troops, sailed from Portsmouth, England, on 26 December 1654.[24] The *Fagon,* a newly launched frigate of two hundred twenty-two tons, carrying twenty-two guns, was despatched to pick up Gage at Deal, Kent.[25] Chaplain and chief architect of the expedition, he was a key man of the invasion force. The first stop was Barbados, an island occupied by Britain since 1625, a little to the east and outside the orbit of the Lesser Antillean arc. Here four thousand men were enlisted by the promise of freedom to bond servants. A muster at Barbados showed a complement of 6,973 men now in the expedition.[26] Another one thousand joined at St. Kitts.[27] Besides the infantry, there were one thousand sea soldiers; the whole fighting manpower was some nine thousand men.[28] The fleet took on eight ships at St. Kitts, bringing the total to thirty-eight warships, a formidable force to meet any Spanish opposition.[29]

Penn and Venables disagreed on how best to attack Santo Domingo. Venables wanted to land the troops close to Fort Jerome.[30] Penn claimed this was impossible, for his ships could not approach the shore close enough to disembark troops and insisted that they land them where Drake had put his men ashore, forty miles to the west of Santo Domingo. Penn's plan prevailed.[31]

Attack on Santo Domingo

But from the moment the troops disembarked, ill fate dogged their footsteps. An account of the attack written by an English captain to a friend provides us with some understanding of the prebattle and battle conditions.[32] One letter was written from Barbados, the second after the attack on Santo Domingo. The plan had appeared so simple: Hispaniola first, then Cuba, Jamaica, Mexico, and Central America. Lastly, Spain's treasure chest, Peru, would fall into British hands. Totally different was the outcome as narrated by an English officer. On the eve of Easter, General Venables landed eight thousand troops forty miles west of Santo Domingo, while another force disembarked close to the Spanish fort captured by Drake a few years before. The second force moved on the fortress commanded by the Spanish Maestro de Campo, who offered token resistance and then retreated towards Santo Domingo.

But within nine miles of the city the pursuing British called a halt. The writer then narrated in detail what had happened. The main body of troops under Venables made a tactical error by landing forty miles from its objective, and a second mistake by choosing the wrong road. It narrowed down to a mere path as the army marched through heavy underbrush and dense forest only to be met in this tropical maze by small bands of Spanish guerillas who disputed every inch of the way by allowing the British to discharge their cumbersome blunderbusses and then attacking with long lances before the British had time to reload.

Nor was the Spanish lance the only lethal weapon; thirst proved just as effective a killer as soldiers dropped by the wayside from lack of drinking water in this humid tropical heat for which they had received no previous conditioning or adequate preparation.

The other regiment, taking a different road than did Venables, encountered Fort Enrique, one mile from Santo Domingo, which the writer claimed could not be taken except by heavy bombardment, so high were its stone fortifications. In a battle near Fort Enrique, General Gaynes received a lance through the heart; Major Ferguson and several captains bravely laid down their lives. In contrast, twenty volunteers saved their own lives by fleeing ignominiously from the field of battle.[33]

All the British troops found themselves in a serious situation as days lengthened into weeks with no sign of relief from their supply ship. So desperate did the lack of food become that the soldiers were forced to eat their horses. When they exhausted this supply of meat, they slaughtered donkeys and the dogs that they caught roaming through the decimated regiments. If Spanish resistance and climatic conditions were serious obstacles to an assault on Santo Domingo, no less cruel were their own British naval officers who reduced the ration of bread and other necessities and then sold the soldiers a biscuit for two shillings and six pence and a quart of brandy for six shillings.[34]

The half-starved troops fell exhausted while these venal captains and stewards enriched their own pockets from troops crying out desperately for bread and water. The last straw which broke the soldiers' morale came with the destruction by fire of the supply ship, the *Discoverer.*[35] Fortunately for the British, no other ship caught fire, although they were anchored close to one another in the harbour.

Another writer added his version of the British attack on Santo Domingo. He noted that Hispaniola was covered with forests, that the majority of men were negroes or mulattos whose work was to slaughter cattle much as these same negroes did in Jamaica. When the invaders appeared, these men sought safety in Santo Domingo, driving their cattle into the city and leaving the British with no cattle to slaughter for the army. The writer claimed that there was an abundance of oranges which the soldiers plucked to slake their burning thirst, but unripe fruit caused dysentery from which many of the soldiers died. The writer was prone to forgive these acts of intemperance but not the act of cowardice which, he claimed, could never be forgiven in an army. As an example of cowardice, the writer gave his cousin, Adjutant General Jackson, in command of the free lancers. Jackson fled in fright during the second attack on Santo Domingo, leaving his troops in disorder when they encountered General Venable's army coming through a narrow defile. When this base action was investigated, many officers were in favour of the death sentence for Adjutant General Jackson. Saved from the firing squad, he was disgraced by having his sword broken over his head at Drake's fort.

The British now drew their troops in battle formation before the city of Santo Domingo. This was the moment for which Cromwell had so carefully planned and upon the outcome of which he had staked his dream of empire. Twice the British assaulted the city and twice they were repulsed by the Spaniards. When the smoke of battle cleared, a thousand British lay dead on Spanish soil.

All were disheartened and dejected, but no one as depressed as Thomas Gage, for the defenders of Santo Domingo had completely shattered his grandiose plan of conquest. It required no vivid imagination to picture the Lord Protector ending a violent peroration to Gage with a swift irrevocable sentence to the Tower.

The British Capture Jamaica

Penn and Venables could not return to Cromwell with no Spanish prize. The leaders called for a consultation with the commissioners—Edward Winslow, Daniel Searle, and Gregory Butler. All admitted that the soldiers under their command were so cowardly that they could not be trusted unless some minor success raised their spirits.

They then resolved to attack Jamaica. If Gage may be blamed in part for the abortive attempt on Santo Domingo, he may also be credited in some measure for the capture of Jamaica, for fundamentally the "Western Design" was his scheme.

Cautiously and a little fearful that Santiago de la Vega might be a repetition of Santo Domingo, a much chastened fleet, minus one ship and a thousand men, sailed into Caguay, Jamaica's largest harbour. It was Thursday, 10 May 1655, at 11.00 o'clock in the morning.[36] The tropical sun, high in the heaven, shone down on the low-lying shore line revealing the clear outline of weak battery defences, the sole shield of the capital, Santiago de la Vega, six miles inland. Not until 3.00 p.m. were troops landed on the shore.[37]

Just before disembarking the soldiers, Penn and Venables went aboard the *Martin Gaaley,* which fired on the Spanish shore defenses. The Spaniards returned the fire but had to abandon the fort under the heavy British barrage. With the cowardice of the troops at Santo Domingo fresh in mind, the order was issued that should a soldier attempt to run away, the man next to him should kill the deserter or be tried for his own life.

Since it was now three o'clock in the afternoon, the officers thought it better not to march that evening because they had no guides; should they again experience a lack of water, they would be in the same position as they had been at Santo Domingo. Next morning at dawn the troops began to march. So cautiously did they proceed that they took five hours to cover the six miles to the capital. At noon they approached the savanna of the town, and three Spaniards came out to meet them. Venables commanded a mounted trooper to ride out to meet the envoys. When asked what they wanted, the envoys replied they wished to make a peace treaty with the English. Venables answered that he would negotiate with them when he met an envoy authorized by the Spanish governor, whereupon they departed. Next morning a priest and a negro major came to the port to arrange the treaty and promised to supply whatever the English might ask within reason. Venables then made it clear that his was no mere hit-and-run attack. The British had come not to pillage but to plant.[38] In the interim, while negotiations were in progress, Venables demanded that the Spaniards supply him with one hundred cows and fresh bread daily. Without those supplies Venables would not begin negotiations. Thereupon the Spaniards sent the cattle but not the bread, alleging they had no surplus.

Capitulation

Spanish governor Don Juan Ramirez de Arellano too hastily concluded that the situation was hopeless. Old, sickly, and incapacitated, he had neither strength nor will to resist Penn and Venables. Ramirez was the wrong governor at this crucial moment. He had not been without knowledge of the proposed invasion, for information had been despatched immediately by the governor of Hispaniola when he learned from prisoners that Jamaica was the next island marked for invasion.

Morant Bay had first glimpsed the invaders' sails; two fishermen hurriedly paddled their canoes to Caguay in time to give the alarm.[39] Although crippled in hands and feet, Ramirez had himself carried to the port to see if anything might be done for the defence of the island. But thirty-seven ships riding at anchor convinced him that the situation was hopeless. To such strength he could offer no resistance, so the colonists abandoned port and capital, fled into the mountains with their families and whatever they could salvage quickly from their homes while the British marched triumphantly into Santiago de la Vega.

Terms of capitulation drawn up by the British were presented to Governor Juan Ramirez de Arellano for his official signature.[40] Their wording clearly indicated that the British laid full claim to Jamaica, for every vestige of defense—ships, forts, arms, and ammunition—came under the terms demanded by the British.[41] All inhabitants of the island who wished to depart would be transported to some part of New Spain in the Americas. An addendum cautioned these people to provide their own food and clothing for the voyage. All tradesmen who wished to remain in Jamaica were to enjoy freedom, provided they conformed to English laws. Everything belonging to the haciendas was to be left there. One article made it clear that the British who had deserted to the Spanish from Captain William Jackson's expedition were to enjoy no exemption and were to be handed over to the British invaders. In order to ensure that every inhabitant was accounted for, a list of inhabitants with their names, titles, occupations, and social position in the community, was demanded. Even the names of their wives, children, servants, and slaves were to be given to General Venables.

Hours after the British had entered Santiago de la Vega, Maestro de Campo Don Francisco de Proenza, commissary of the Holy Office, Juan de Chaves Bejarano, sargento mayor, Duarte de Acosta Noguera, Alcade Bernardino de Fuentes, Captains Don Francisco de Leiba Ysasi and Julian de Castilla, in company with many lesser lights, gathered around Governor Ramirez to discuss immediate plans. Ramirez had already decided to appear before Venables and negotiate a peace. Proenza violently disagreed and entreated Ramirez not to appear before Venables to negotiate a peace treaty.[42] The British were treacherous. The men sent by the Spaniards to negotiate were now prisoners, and the governor might expect no better treatment, for their only purpose was to trap the governor into signing terms favourable to themselves. Proenza made it clear where he stood. He, the maestro de campo, would neither accompany Ramirez to the town, nor would he respect orders of the governor issued from the enemy camp. Bejarano was asked his opinion. He could only caution the governor to avoid the occasion of danger. The assembled members of the cabildo agreed that, if the occasion demanded a parley, it should be held in an open field, not at the British headquarters in the town.

Sargento Mayor Don Francisco de Cavajal, impatient with negative replies, reminded the civic fathers that he had come from the enemy camp and had pledged his word that the governor would return with him to General Venables. Silence fell on the disputants. The one exception was Maestro de Campo Don Francisco de Proenza, who continued to oppose the governor's meeting with the British.

Carried by two negroes in a hammock, for he could neither walk nor ride, Ramirez proceeded towards Santiago de la Vega.[43] Maestro de Campo, the sargento Mayor, the accountant, the commissary of the Holy Office, and both Captains together with several others formed the entourage which stopped half a league short of the town. Proceeding alone into the town, Don Francisco de Cavajal sent back an adjutant with a pass allowing the governor to enter the British camp. They exchanged farewells and Ramirez was carried down the road. Then the dissenters turned back to their own camp in the west. At Santiago de la Vega, nine regiments of British infantry were drawn at attention on the parade grounds, each flying its distinctive regimental colours to welcome their distinguished visitor. After the preliminary courtesy of governor meeting general, Ramirez was carried to his lodging in the former residence of the high sheriff of the Holy Office, Ysasi's father.

The interval between the governor entering the British camp and the hour he signed the articles of capitulation was marked with noteworthy events. After he had provided for the safety of his family, Proenza marched with one hundred thirty infantry, fifteen negro bowmen, and chaplain Alonso Telles to the bridge two leagues from Santiago de la Vega.[44] Here scouts from Proenza's troops ambushed British soldiers as they ventured out into the country to replenish their dwindling stock of guinea hens, ducks, and chickens. Most of the enemy were slain, but one youth, George Nicholas Paine, begged for his life in Spanish. So unusual was it to hear the Spanish tongue coming from an Englishman that he was brought before the commander. He said he had been a merchant in Barbados and had been forced to join the Cromwellian forces because of his knowledge of Spanish to act as Venables's interpreter. From Paine the Spaniards learned the details of the successful resistance their compatriots offered to the British at Santo Domingo. He proffered the further information that the British fleet was determined to conquer not only the West Indian islands but all Spain's continental possessions.

Don Hieronimo Tello, nephew of Governor Ramirez, was not the most popular person when he arrived from the enemy camp to read the articles of capitulation signed by Ramirez and Cavajal on behalf of the Spaniards and by General Venables, Major-General Richard Fortescue, Vice Admiral William Goodson, Colonel Holdip, and Colonel Edward D'Oyley on behalf of the British.[45]

Guerilla Warfare

Out on the Bunducuc in the district of Guatibacoa in the presence of Maestro de Campo Proenza and the people, the articles of capitulation were read:

> That within 12 days from their date every faithful Christian was to present himself to the General [Venables], or to his deputies with all the money in gold, silver, and copper he might have, jewels, silverware, slaves, household effects, ranches, farms, sugar estates, mills, arms, munitions and merchandise. . . .
>
> Artificers, poor and rich, who might desire to remain in the island, might do so provided they agreed to live under the government and laws of England. No priest nor book might remain in the island. Each person was to bring his own victuals for a month and present himself at the end of 12 days. His Excellency would furnish ships to convey them to lower ports, that is, to Honduras and Campeche, allowing each person two shirts and one suit of clothes. The military officers to retain the arms and insignia.[46]

A unanimous shout of disapproval rent the air; all would rather die in the bush than see their wives and daughters in the power of the English. Proenza's worst fears were realized; weak-kneed Ramirez had capitulated without even a token show of resistance. At this moment in her history, Spanish Jamaica needed a Melgarejo, who would have fought it out with the British despite their superiority in numbers. Such resistance might have eventually saved Jamaica for Spain, since one thousand British soldiers died of disease or by the Spanish sword by May 1656. Dissension had spread throughout the ranks; all were for returning to England. A united front presented by a strong Spanish governor at this crucial point would have tipped the scales in favor of Spain.

Venables awaited the return of Tello, but Tello did not return. Had he tried to do so, a lance in the back would have pierced his body as soon as he turned his face towards the British camp in Santiago de la Vega. The Spaniards were not going to sit meekly and let a foreign power take their homes. If numbers did not allow a European style of war with flags flying and drums beating and soldiers marching in closed ranks, it did not prevent them from carrying on guerilla warfare.

Half a league from the bridge over Rio Negro, Spanish resistance showed itself. Eighty mounted British on their way to Guatibacoa sighted two Spanish scouts, Ensign Juan Gomez and Diego de Medina.[47] The Englishmen shouted: "Dogs, come to the army." Ignoring the order, Gomez and Medina spurred their horses as if to flee. The British colonel spurred his horse; when the Spaniards saw they had separated the British officer from his soldiers, they suddenly turned their horses and pierced him with both lances. Neither his side arms nor his pike availed to defend him from their deadly blows. Eighty mounted British galloped at full speed but were too late to defend their colonel.

The same British soldiers then spent the night at the Anaya ranch and in the morning moved on to reach Santiago, where they rounded up forty-seven head of cattle, rode on to Guatibacoa where they killed the cattle, butchered the meat, and carried it back to the capital with them.[48] On their way to Santiago de la Vega they met 1,200 troops despatched by Venables to crush all Spanish resistance on the south coast. The steady rhythmic beat of Red Coats marching toward Spanish-held Guatibacoa served notice to the guerillas that Cromwell was in dead earnest about planting the British standard permanently in Jamaica.

To impress upon the Spaniards the permanency of British occupation, the officers occupied all the farms and ranches in the environs of Santiago de la Vega, branded all Spanish horses and cattle as their own. Meanwhile the infantry planted beans, chick-peas and other vegetables, cultivated tobacco, cleaned up the yucca fields, killed cattle, cured the meat, and rendered tallow from wild hogs.

Outside the capital, colonels, captains and noncommissioned officers occupied many Spanish farms and ranches and worked them together with the common soldiers. The British pursued the same psychology the Spanish had followed in their colonization of Jamaica. The underdog was made to perform the menial tasks—plant, rear cattle, and hunt. The Spanish used Arawaks, the British used the infantry soldiers. Both reacted against this forced labour. The Indians ran into the hinterland or left the island. The British infantryman cried out that he wished to return to England—give him his pay and send him home, for he did not come out to Jamaica to be a labourer; he was a soldier, not a farm hand.

The British agrarian policy of occupying the Guatibacoa farms and ranches, and later the attack and occupation of the Anaguani ranch deprived the Spanish civilians of hideouts and places of safety. Unless they wished to entrust their persons to the precarious security of the bush, dwelling in a semisavage state, the Spaniards had to look for another land. They crossed the Caribbean to Santiago de Cuba in whatever was available—ships, skiffs, and frail canoes. With women and children safely in Cuba, the guerillas began a long siege of hit and run warfare against the British invaders.

Proenza had succeeded Ramirez, but he too was incapacitated. Almost blind, he also suffered from chills and fever and had a fistula in one leg which gave him great pain. With Proenza disabled, the mantle of command fell on physically sound Christóbal Arnaldo Ysasi. Early in 1656 Ysasi took command at the camp established in the Porras country. He immediately selected three officers, thirty soldiers, and fifteen negroes to reconnoiter the British at Guatibacoa.[49]

From two Spanish prisoners taken at Hato de Pereda, the British commander learned that Ysasi was near his own camp. Taking no chances, the British withdrew from Guatibacoa to Santiago de la Vega. Ysasi followed them, passing close to another British camp in the vicinity of Anaya. Reconnoitering, Ysasi learned that this camp was accustomed to send twenty-five men and a sergeant to collect water in barrels from the river. On 25 March Ysasi attacked this contingent and killed all but two, whom he took prisoners.[50] The prisoners informed the Spaniards that the British were quartered at a ranch called Los Angeles, some two and a half miles north of Santiago de la Vega, an estate formerly owned by Thome Estacio. The prisoners further revealed that on the following day, 26 March, two companies of British soldiers were to march from their quarters at Guanaboa, eight miles from Santiago de la Vega. Ysasi was now prepared to act. Concealing some men under Captains Diego Sanchez de Santella and Antonio de León, he issued orders to attack as soon as the British were on the march. As soon as the British appeared, Ysasi's men attacked them from ambush, killed eleven and carried away a large supply of tools, peas, rye and garlic.[51]

Meanwhile, Ysasi with Captain Diego de Medina, Adjutant Gomez de Posada, Sargeanto Mayor Christóbal de Leyba Ysasi, and fifteen soldiers stole down to Port Caguay to observe the British ships in the harbour and to ascertain if munitions were stored nearby.[52]

From a vantage point above Passage Fort they saw that munitions were stored under two large tents at Cayo de Carena. Seven pieces of artillery were positioned at Passage Fort pointing towards Santiago de la Vega. Just at that time in the morning, Ysasi caught sight of five horse-drawn carts loaded with provisions on the point of departing for the capital. Well behind them rode fifty British soldiers, little suspecting that the whole operation was under close surveillance.[53]

Ysasi concealed his men in a thicket and awaited the approach of the supply train, made a sudden sally, attacked and killed all five drivers before the soldiers could come to their resuce.[54] He then withdrew to another ambush and this time made so sudden an attack on the British soldiers that he killed eleven including the captain while the rest fled in terror. Ysasi was able to carry away only one cart, fearing that, should he delay at the place of attack, a stronger force of British might come to the rescue of the ambushees and wipe out his own men.[55]

Ysasi disappeared into the woods after the attack on the supply train and waited for darkness to make an attack on Santiago de la Vega. Under cover of darkness he crept into the plaza where the British troops were quartered. He saw that the abbey church had been converted into a fort and that the British general had made his headquarters in the former residence of Captain Don Felix de Fuentes which faced the open country towards the sea. To frighten the general, Ysasi set fire to nearby huts belonging to Mulatto Bartolo. When the general appeared in the doorway, Ysasi fired his gun into the air to frighten the occupation force.[56] Ysasi then withdrew from Santiago de la Vega after seven days of harassment. The British did not know where he would strike next.

Next Ysasi collected cattle from estates near the capital and drove them into his camp at Guatibacoa where he had two thousand head with their herdsmen.[57] After he saw the cattle safely in the corral, Ysasi marched down to Fort Anaya to see if he might stalk more British soldiers. His adjutant, Juan de Gomez, and two soldiers were sent to reconnoiter the vicinity of the river and came upon eight British soldiers. Judging them to be so few, Gomez engaged them in a fight, not knowing that other British soldiers were in ambush on an eminence above the river awaiting for such a move on the part of the Spaniards. Before Ysasi could rescue his men, the British had killed Gomez and one other soldier.[58]

When Ysasi arrived, he killed all the British except for one man who escaped. This man sounded the alarm at Anaya barracks. A hundred men sallied forth to capture Ysasi. But he fled, then doubled back to Anaya and set the barracks on fire. The British now marched twenty-five miles west to Ysasi's camp at Guatibacoa, hoping to raze it. But Ysasi marched throughout the night, herded as many cattle as he could, and fled into the mountains.[59]

During the year 1656, the British experienced growing discontent among soldiers who wanted no part with colonization. They were military men, had done their part in the conquest, and under no circumstances wished to settle down as planters. They threw every obstacle in the way of the officers' plans, destroyed as many as twenty thousand head of cattle, and created a food shortage with a slowdown in planting. So serious did the situation become that a near famine resulted.[60]

Ysasi claimed that many British soldiers offered to come over to his camp. But he did not trust them; he suspected that as long as they had a large body of troops, they would continue to fight with confidence. He did accept five who surrendered to him, a captain, an ensign of German origin, a sergeant, and two soldiers.[61] These he sent to Cuba with a letter stating that the British had held a military conference in which they decided to send Ysasi a Franciscan priest whom they captured at Riohacha, on La Guajira peninsula, South America.[62] The envoy had offered the Spanish ships to transport their men and slaves, if they would leave the island. Ysasi had rejected the offer.

Last Days of Thomas Gage

The presence of a captured priest is of interest in relation to the last days of Thomas Gage. Did the Spanish Friar receive the Puritan preacher back into the Church? On 1 May 1656 Vice Admiral Goodson had left Jamaica with a well-armed fleet bound for raids on Spanish territory.[63] On 4 May Goodson stopped at Hispaniola, made a quick incursion on the coast, then turned south across the Caribbean. The settlement at Riohacha on the north coast of South America was his next prey. It was easy. Defenses crumbled, and in no time he had much booty and one hundred twenty-five prisoners, including the Franciscan priest. Goodson then planned to attack Cartagena, but its defences looked so formidable that he turned north to Jamaica without firing a shot at the coastal city. On 23 May 1656 the raiding party returned to Caguay.[64] Was Gage dead before 23 May? We know that in 1656 British soldiers were dying by the hundreds from fever and malnutrition. In the month of April, the mortality reached its highest level. The only real evidence of Gage's death comes from his widow's application for a pension granted to families of soldiers who had died in Jamaica. This application is dated 18 July 1656.[65] Clearly Gage had died in Jamaica previous to this date. Since a sailing ship took some eight weeks to reach England, very little margin is left between his death and the arrival of the Spanish friar.

One wonders if Gage called for a priest in his last moments, for there was no lack of intercession on his behalf since the entire Gage family of England was praying for his return to the Church. His brother Francis, the Jesuit, was alive and would not have failed to remember Thomas daily at Mass. His cousin, the martyr St. Robert Southwell, was interceding for him. Lastly, there was the powerful efficacy of Thomas Holland, whom Gage had sent to the gallows at Tyburn. It cannot be stated that Gage came back to the Church, for there is no documentary evidence to substantiate this claim. Some future historian searching among the tomes of Spanish or English archives may give a definite answer to the enigma.

Nine

The British Defeat the Spaniards and Colonize Jamaica

The guerilla warfare of Ysasi irritated the British. Rid themselves of him they must, for no Englishman could settle peacefully on his farm while the threat of sudden, lethal raids hung ominously over his head. Every proposal of surrender, no matter how sugar-coated, brought the same reply from Ysasi, an emphatic no.

Ysasi Refuses to Surrender

But it was one thing to answer the enemy defiantly, another to reconcile differences of opinion on the proper military strategy in mountainous Jamaica within one's own ranks. The unfortunate conjunction of enemy pressure and internal disagreement resulted in defeat for the guerilla leader.

Dissension within Spanish ranks began on 7 July 1657, when five hundred eighty-five men fully armed with muskets, arquebuses, lances, and guns (bocas de fuego), under the supreme command of Captain Juan de los Reyes of Puerto Rico, and the subordinate commands of Christóbal de Aunez of Havana, Domingo de Silva of Santo Domingo, Lucas Borrero of Santiago de Cuba, and Francisco Cartagena de Leyba of Jamaica, disembarked at Las Chorreras.[1] Their supply ship is recorded to have brought eight hundred and thirty-two arrobas of cassava, sixty tierces of salt, six tierces of biscuits, sixty-six tierces of salted but putrid beef, twelve sacks of beans, thirty-four barrels containing fifty-two quintals of powder, sixty tierces of cord, five cases of rifle balls and nine thousand, two hundred balls for arquebuses, and one small medicine chest.[2] A delay of eight months passed from the day this contingent was mustered into service in Cuba until it set foot on Jamaican soil. The governor of Santiago de Cuba, Don Pedro de Bayona, was responsible for this procrastination—an avaricious, self-seeking official who placed personal ambition before the common good. In the early days of the evacuation of refugees from Jamaica, he had charged each person, including infants, the rate of ten to twelve pesos for passage to Cuba and he even sold cassava and vegetables for high prices to poor refuges in the Jamaican mountains.[3] In 1657, when the king ordered relief forces from Santo Domingo, Puerto Rico, Havana, and New Spain to assemble, before ordering the troops to Jamaica, Bayona asked Ysasi on which side of the island the men should land. "Land them on the south side" replied Ysasi.[4] Without personal knowledge of the island's topography, Bayona countered with his opinion that the disembarkation should be on the north side. Wearily Ysasi gave in to Bayona, telling the governor to send the men to the north coast, if he so wished, in any event, send the men—that was the important thing.

Since these soldiers had spent eight months in Cuba, their food supplies were almost depleted and their uniforms reduced to tatters. If it were not for the foresight of the viceroy in sending fifteen hundred yards of cloth, the troops would have been a sorrowful spectacle entering the little port of Le Maguana close to Las Chorreras, Jamaica.[5] For eight days before Reyes landed, Ysasi had trod the sands scanning the horizon for the expected ships. When they did not appear, sadly disappointed, he betook himself back into the mountains to his camp at Los Vermejales so that when Reyes finally landed, there was no one to meet him.[6]

From Las Chorreras on the coast, Reyes glanced up at the rugged, forbidding mountains where Ysasi had established his camp, twenty-four miles from St. Ann's Bay, equidistant from both north and south coasts.[7] One narrow road from the north coast led into the camp, another led from the camp into the south coast at Guatibacoa which Ysasi proposed to attack since it was now held by the British. Ysasi's position was militarily sound, for he could attack the British and then retire into his mountain camp at Los Vermejales, which the enemy would find difficult to besiege. But Reyes did not see it in this light. He warned Ysasi that there was a shortage of supplies.[8] To make matters worse, the Spaniards of Oristán on the southwest coast had lost all their horses to the British, which seriously hindered Ysasi from transporting the provisions and munitions of the Reyes's contingent to Los Vermejales. Reyes, speaking with respect for the governor, voiced the opinion of his fellow officers that it would not be advisable for Ysasi to remain at Los Vermejales nor to attack the enemy at Guatibacoa.[9] According to Reyes, should Ysasi run short of provisions and munitions during the attack, he would incur great risk with only raw recruits under his command. He should also take into consideration the tropical climate which could cause additional hardships to Reyes's untried troops. Then there was always the danger that, should Ysasi meet a superior enemy force and lose some of his men, under duress they might reveal the condition of his army, the hardships they were undergoing, where the soldiers were deployed, and where the munitions were cached. The enemy might even discover where the relief forces had landed and whence the despatches were sent to Cuba.

Since Ysasi planned to attack Guatibacoa, his former camp on the south of the island, Reyes warned him that he could rely on no more than fifty men should he call for immediate assistance. Further, there were few soldiers available as lookouts or special guards. Reyes added that two men had already died without confession and a third had gone unconscious before the chaplain reached him. If Ysasi had thought of capturing horses from the enemy with his own infantry, Reyes and Captain Don Domingo de Silva, who had military experience, warned him that he was taking a calculated risk. Even if Ysasi had sufficient supplies, a good plan of battle, and was vigilant, Reyes and his advisers were not in accord with Ysasi's plan to attack Guatibacoa.

Reyes, being a good soldier, left the final decision to the governor, with the statement that, as subordinates, theirs was to obey until they shed the last drop of their blood. Reyes did not really mean the last drop of his blood;[10] he was content to shed a few drops of sweat on his trek up the mountains to Ysasi's camp. After three days march over narrow tropical trails, he called a council of war in which a decision was reached to return to Las Chorreras.[11] In order to forestall mutiny, Ysasi ordered the disaffected to march back to the coast and named Reyes commander with instructions in writing that he was to remove the provisions and stores at Las Chorreras to a safe place in the port of Baycani where they were to be concealed and whence it would be more convenient to transport them to the south coast where Ysasi intended to carry on his campaign.[12] Disobeying orders, Reyes built a stockade around the provisions at Las Chorreras, and removed thither the powder Ysasi had safely hidden in another place.[13]

The inevitable happened. British vessels appeared in the harbour, and three hundred thirty soldiers swooped down on the Spaniards.[14] At the first charge Captain de Silva took refuge within the stockade; on the second charge, both Reyes and de Silva fled for their lives, leaving the provisions and munitions in the hands of the British. After the engagement, one hundred twenty Spaniards lay dead or wounded on the shores of Los Chorreras.[15] The hapless survivors, without food or munitions, sought refuge in the forest, in constant fear of discovery. Shortly after this fiasco, the "brilliant" strategist Reyes, together with two hundred forty-four men deserted Ysasi for the more friendly shores of Cuba where they could soldier with no risk to their lives.[16]

Battle of Rio Nuevo— Last Spanish Stand in Jamaica

Stubborn Bayona failed to profit by the Las Chorreras defeat. On 16 May 1658, when he despatched the Mexican contingent, five hundred fifty-seven strong, under command of Sargeanto Mayor Don Alvaro de la Raspuru, they were again disembarked on the north side by Bayona's order. The expedition left Cuba on the evening of the 18 May and had a safe voyage, since they neither saw any other vessel nor were they observed by the enemy.[17] On Saturday morning at eleven o'clock, the contingent arrived at the port of Rio Nuevo. As soon as the ships anchored, a launch with three captains, Don Juan Diaz del Castillo, Don Juan Francisco de Ynca, and Don Francisco Murillo, accompanied by some infantry were sent to reconnoiter the land and to discover if the governor, Don Christóbal Ysasi, was at Rio Nuevo; for Ysasi had written that he would await the expedition there. The captains made their search, but finding neither Ysasi nor his men, they returned to their ships and reported there was no sign of life on the shore. They had discovered only a half-covered empty hut. Juan de Herrera, the best pilot in Jamaica, was sent to seek the governor with diligence and haste along the coast in the places where he might be expected to have hidden. In the meantime, Raspuru completed constructing a hut on the shore and then added several new ones, for it was at Rio Nuevo that Raspuru presumed that Ysasi wished to establish camp. He disembarked some of the infantry on Saturday and on Sunday, at four o'clock in the afternoon, a large British ship appeared on the horizon.[18]

The port of Rio Nuevo, open to the sea, afforded the enemy the opportunity of observing the military operations of the Spaniards. Taking every precaution, Raspuru allowed a garrison to remain on the ships while he landed the greater portion of his men on the shore at Rio Nuevo together with provisions and munitions. Torrential rains continued day and night, necessitating the construction of four large huts to shelter provisions, and from the beach these supplies were labourously carried by the soldiers up the steep hill to Camp Concepción.

On Monday the British ship disappeared at sunset, but on Wednesday it was back again, and this time it was accompanied by another vessel.[19] Raspuru kept his men working incessantly transporting provisions and keeping a continuous watch on the spy ship and stationing guards at all points where it was feared this corsair might land a raiding party. Amid all this anxiety arose the problem of the owners of the vessels which had transported the Spanish contingent from Cuba, who wished to leave as soon as possible for fear of encountering the enemy at sea by too long a delay in Jamaica. Once these ships left, the Spanish soldiers were doomed to remain in Jamaica as the victors or the vanquished.

As late as Thursday 24 May, no news had been received from Ysasi, nor had they any idea of his whereabouts.[20] Eight days after Raspuru's arrival, Ysasi appeared.[21] His appearance was fortunate, because Raspuru fell so dangerously ill that the chief chaplain administered the last sacraments to the commander, who died on 20 June.[22]

After inspecting the troops and supplies, Ysasi wrote a long complaint to Bayona, whom he suspected of trying to sabotage the campaign and discredit him as governor of Jamaica. His opening complaint was that no supply ship was forthcoming from Santiago de Cuba since the arrival of the contingent, and Ysasi was much worried.[23] One month had passed since the troops had arrived from Cuba, and in that time Bayona had not even despatched a launch, though Ysasi knew that the king had one in Cuba for the very purpose of maintaining contact with Jamaica and of receiving news about the troops at Rio Nuevo. Ysasi asked that all able-bodied Jamaicans be sent back to the island, for Ysasi deemed their aid important for his guerilla warfare since they knew the island well; but Bayona ignored his request. He asked Bayona for two hundred lances, but he sent only fifty; he asked for provisions for eight months, but Bayona sent two months supply. Of the infantry which the duke of Albuquerque had assigned to Jamaica, Bayona kept the best troops for himself; and out of the one hundred ten soldiers sent under command of Don Francisco Salinas, only forty-one arrived. Ysasi had asked that the king's launch be sent if the contingent was not to sail within eight days of the appointed date. Bayona's reply was that it would be giving information to the enemy, but Bayona nevertheless despatched the contingent without knowing whether enemy ships were lurking along the coast of Jamaica. Because Bayona had not sent supplies prior to the arrival of the troops, many of Ysasi's men died and others had deserted to the British. For these calamities he blamed Bayona. If Bayona would not do these things for Ysasi, he might do them for the service of the king, so complained the governor of Jamaica. Ysasi warned Bayona that his designs were becoming clear and one day would be as bright as day to the whole world.

Ysasi continued his complaints. Jamaica needed beef not cassava; when he needed cassava he would inform Cuba. The twenty-five yards of coarse cloth sent by Bayona was of no use for the sail Ysasi wished to make; so useless was it that Ysasi had to purchase sailcloth out of his own money. On three occasions he had met the enemy in battle, and the linen sent by Bayona was now used up for drumheads and cartridges. A despairing request asked Bayona not to send any more linen shorts; this was a war, not a banquet. Powder and ball were in short supply, for the last three engagements were with musketry and artillery. He needed ten barrels of powder. In return Ysasi was sending Bayona forty cannon balls and one bar shot picked up from the enemy. Neither cannon balls nor the bar shot fitted Ysasi's own artillery but might be useful in Cuba. He also was returning eighty-six firearms perfectly useless and in the same damaged condition in which they had come from Cuba. At least they could have been sent in a better condition, for there was no armourer to repair the infantry arms which were now in a very poor state. He reminded Bayona that he knew that Governor Don José de Aguirre had earmarked fifty lances for Jamaica, but they never got beyond the hands of Bayona's alcaldes. Ysasi asked Bayona to do him the favour of requesting these gentlemen to release them and add three hundred more lances to the memorandum in which he had set forth the necessities of the war.

On 28 May a British warship arrived to reconnoiter the port of Rio Nuevo.[24] Sighting the Spanish vessels, it began to fire on them. The Spaniards returned the fire. When the British ship had spent her ammunition she put out to sea, but in the evening returned with two others from the fleet under her convoy and entered the port with her sprit sails prepared to board the Spanish ships. Troops on the Spanish ships attacked the British trying to board, killing many, while at the same time the Spaniards pressed the attack with land based artillery, forcing the British ships to retire. The following day, though within sight of the shore, the British ships dared not return to attack the Spaniards. Ysasi then ordered the Spanish ships which had conveyed the troops to Jamaica to run the blockade. This they did successfully under cover of darkness. The British captain then despatched a vessel to Santiago de la Vega to inform Edward D'Oyley of the latest Spanish attempt to land troops. Five British ships now returned to Rio Nuevo and under cover of their artillery attempted to land troops. Again land-based guns gave the foremost ship two dangerous hits and she was obliged to cut her cable, leave her anchor in the water, and sail away. The second British attack ended in failure.[25] When news of the latest Spanish landing reached the British capital, Colonel Edward

D'Oyley, alarmed at the report, called a council of war and proposed the question: would it be more advantageous to allow the Spaniards to remain and hope that the ravages of tropical sickness would decimate them, or to fall on them at once without warning?[26] Enthusiasm ran high among the officers for immediate action, so D'Oyley ordered seven hundred fifty men to sail for an attack on Fort Concepción. The fort was not quite complete, a large portion of the stockade facing the back country to the south being still in the process of construction, when on 25 June D'Oyley appeared on the horizon with seven warships manned for action.[27] D'Oyley gave orders to disembark on the east side of the Bay.[28] Here two companies of Spanish soldiers and negro hunters were drawn up to dispute their landing. Land the British did, leaving a captain and twenty-three Spanish soldiers dead on the shore. Although within six hundred yards of Spanish artillery fire, D'Oyley brought the remainder of his men ashore, suffering few casualties. Supplies followed and camp was pitched on the hill opposite the Spanish fort. D'Oyley spent most of the day reconnoitering for a weak spot in the Spanish defences. A frontal attack by sea or river looked impossible since formidable cliffs topped by a strong stockade made the fort impregnable from that angle. Before the assault D'Oyley sent his drummer, in proper seventeenth century prebattle protocol to demand Ysasi's surrender. It would be an honourable one, the Spaniards marching out "with bag and baggage, arms in their hands, matches lighted and bullets in their teeth."[29] With equal courtesy Ysasi replied:

> Lord General:
>
> Don Christopher Arnadlo Ysasi, Governor for his Majesty, the King of Spain, lord of the island of Jamaica, answering your letter, wherein you require me to deliver the fort of Rio Nuevo, and what else is therein, I say that his Majesty, whom God preserve, has appointed me governor of this island, being his own property, and has remitted me unto it a regiment of Spanish infantry and twenty-four companies to defend it. The forts and castles of his Majesty are not yielded with so much facility. I have received no attack from your batteries, nor have you made any advance. I am in no want of powder, nor musket ball, nor gallant men that know how to die before they are overcome. God keep your honour many years in these commands that you desire.[30]

Formalities completed, Ysasi presented the drummer with twenty-five pieces of eight and sent D'Oyley a jar of sweetmeats. The stage was now set for the attack.

At muster before dawn, D'Oyley went from company to company encouraging the men and officers to carry the day, for England's honour was at stake. Two British ships were sent sailing west as a ruse to make the Spaniards think that a landing was to be made further down the coast. The remainder of the fleet drew close to the shore and cannonaded the fort furiously. British infantry marched through tangled underbrush until they came opposite the ravine. There they observed a party of Spaniards on the hill constructing a breastwork from which the ford of Rio Nuevo could be protected. The working party tried to stop the British with a well-directed volley but they came on, forcing the defenders to retreat within the fort. Climbing the hill, the English rested a while before the final assault. The British had taken the correct route, as before them lay the unfinished palisades, wide open to a frontal attack. Since this was such a low section, it was simple for the infantry to scale the walls with ladders, hurl grenades, and make an open breach for the main body of troops to enter the fort. When the smoke cleared, Sergeant Major Christóbal de Leyba and three hundred men lay dead. One hundred Spaniards were taken prisoners.[31] It was England's greatest Jamaican victory, Spain's most disastrous defeat. The curtain was about to come down on Spanish Jamaica. With all supplies burnt and men scattered in hiding, Ysasi called a council of war. Since the British had five thousand five hundred armed men and six hundred horses as well as negro guides who had surrendered to them and ships to cruise around the island, the council decreed that the sick and wounded together with those officers whom the governor should appoint, should embark for Cuba and be sent to Governor Don Pedro de Bayona as refugees in the city of Santiago de Cuba.

The straw that broke the Spanish resistance was the defection of Juan de Bolas and his camp of negro followers.[32] He and two hundred slaves fled into the mountains at the time of the British invasion in 1655, forming themselves into three camps and remaining faithful to their Spanish masters. They fought for the Spaniards and supplied them with meat from hunted cattle. Although flattering offers were made by the British, these negroes remained faithful until 1660, when Juan de Bolas and his camp defected. All Spanish officers were of the opinion that to remain in Jamaica would mean certain death for every one of their men, since these negroes knew the mountains and could lead the British to every Spanish camp site.[33] From that date Jamaica became an undisputed British possession and it only remained for the Treaty of Madrid, 8 July 1670, to make it legally so.[34]

The British Set up a Government

Fundamental differences between Spanish and British colonization manifested themselves early in British occupation. Spain approached the New World seeking quick returns from investments in her voyages of discovery; gold was the prime objective. She searched each and every mainland settlement to fill her depleted treasury. An island like Jamaica with no gold was readily abandoned for the more promising mineral-producing mainland. A few Spanish colonists had been left in Jamaica to extend Arawak cultivation, introduce sugar, cattle, and hogs for the support of Tierra Firme settlements.

England came with a dream of total conquest of all Spanish settlements in the New World. Everywhere the Spanish standard was to be replaced by the Union Jack. When she found herself bogged down on the third largest island of the Greater Antilles, Britain accepted the *status quo* and threw her manpower into the development of Jamaica's chief natural resource, agriculture. England could afford to concentrate her efforts in Jamaica, for it was the most promising of her West Indian possessions.

Spain on the contrary had to spread her colonizing manpower thin though the Caribbean, into Mexico and Central America, South and North America, and as far out into the Pacific as the Philippines. The conquistador was primarily a seeker of fortune and glory; where these could be found, there he could be found. The British colonist, on the other hand, was bred on the land, valued it high among his possessions, and sought his fortune in its careful cultivation.

Jamaica was for Spain just another link in that chain that bound her New World to an absolute monarchy. Crown paternalism invaded every phase of public life. British contrast appeared immediately upon the establishment of civil government in 1663/4.[35] Settlers are wont to judge the laws which govern them in the homeland the ideal also for them in some faraway colony. This was particularly true of the British colonist in Jamaica whose rights under English common law he would not wish to lose simply because he had transported himself five thousand miles from Britain. Lord Windsor, sent to Jamaica as governor, published Charles II's proclamation on 14 December 1661, in which the king promised "that all children of any of our naturalborn subjects of England to be born in Jamaica shall from their respective births be reputed to be, and shall be free denizens of England and shall have the same privileges to all intents and purposes as our free-born subjects of England."[36] Although no specific mention was made of the laws of England, yet Windsor interpreted it to include these laws. Arriving in Barbados on his journey to Jamaica, he issued a proclamation declaring that "justice shall be administered agreeably to the laws of England or such laws not repugnant thereto as shall be enacted by the consent of freemen of this island."[37]

Windsor's sojourn in Jamaica was brief, a mere two months. His successor, Deputy Governor Sir Charles Lyttleton, convoked the first assembly on 20 January 1663/4 with the consent of the council.[38] This assembly passed an act declaring the laws of England to be in force in Jamaica. Windsor's proclamation was now placed on a statutory basis. Charles II had granted Jamaica the same form of government enjoyed by Barbados: a governor appointed by the crown, a nominated council, and a representative assembly chosen by the freemen of the island. The legislature was a convocation of all three: governor, council, and assembly. After the colony enjoyed this system of government for fifteen years, the crown saw reason to repent its generosity, because the Assembly of Jamaica had begun to show signs of intolerable independence and even infringed upon a prerogative of the governor by attempting to circumscribe the power of the militia.

Back in England, a body known as the Lords of Trade was the watchdog that jealously guarded prerogatives of the crown. This board decreed that the independence of the Jamaican Assembly must be restrained and that official rights of the crown be not only maintained but extended. Legal opinion in England considered the crown had every right to alter the system of making laws in Jamaica, since its constitution rested on Charles II's instructions to Windsor in 1661.[39] Again, Jamaica was a conquered island and its form of government depended solely upon the will of the king.[40] In order to bridle the recalcitrant assembly, the same method of lawmaking as prescribed for Ireland under the Poyning Law was to be enacted for Jamaica.[41] This meant that all laws were made in England, then sent to the Jamaican Assembly for their approval, taking away the deliberative voice and reducing it to a mere ratifying body.

Resentment in Jamaica was universal. The assembly presented Governor Carlisle with their objections to the new constitution:

a) Being English subjects they claimed the right to be governed as such.
b) That by Lord Windsor's proclamation they were granted freedom and denization.
c) For sixteen or eighteen years they have been governed by the laws of England.
d) That the new frame of government would be unworkable by reason of the distance.
e) That the Irish method was designed to support the English against the Irish.
f) That the proposed change would cause many to depart from the island.
g) That they alone of all the colonies ought not be deprived of their privileges.[42]

The difficulty resolved itself into this question: had the crown deprived itself of the power to establish whatever form of government it chose for Jamaica? Since Jamaica was a conquered territory, it was recognized that the king had the right to establish whatever form of government he chose. Had he done so by the acts of 1661? It was the contention of the assembly that this was not a mere experiment to be altered at the whim of the crown. Rather it had been the royal intention in that year to place Jamaican subjects on an equal footing with the king's other plantations in regard to rights and privileges.

The Lords of Trade interviewed two former governors together with several Jamaican merchants. After much wrangling, they agreed that the method of making laws in Barbados be applied also to Jamaica. This was a triumph for the assembly, which could continue to make its own laws and govern itself as it had done since the days of Governor Windsor. Due in large measure to this form of government, Jamaica made rapid economic strides, and thus many of the great fortunes of England had roots in the cane fields of this tropical island. Within fifteen years after the capture of Jamaica, the English colonists numbered 15,198 persons, a striking contrast to the few who occupied the island under Spanish rule.[43] These people, appreciating the rich soil which the colony offered, had patented 209,020 and one half acres by the year 1670.[44] Their plantations had 57 sugar works producing 1,700 thousandweight of sugar, 47 cocoa walks yielding 188,000 pounds of nuts, and 49 indigo works producing 49,000 pounds of dye per year. There were 3 salt ponds containing 4,000 acres, yielding 10,000 bushels of salt per year. The mountains were full of pimento, producing 50,000 pounds annually. On the savannas the English had increased the cattle from 60 to 6,000 head within six years. Sheep, goats, and hogs were plentiful. England saw Jamaica's promise of rich harvest, and early in colonization took advantage of it.

The statistics for 1670 noted that there were privateers, hunters, sloop and boat men to the number of two thousand able, virile men.[45] These were the infamous buccaneers who roamed the Caribbean in search of Spanish prey.

The Days of the Buccaneers

It all began with Thomas Modyford. On 4 June 1664 Sir Thomas Modyford arrived in Jamaica to take up his duties as governor.[46] Born in Devonshire, England in 1627, he migrated in 1647 to the West Indian island of Barbados for political reasons. The name Modyford is linked historically to that of Morgan, buccaneer "par excellence," for Modyford opened Port Royal as a rendezvous to this most brutal, feared, hated, legalized band of pirates ever to plunder the Spanish Main. Letters of marque, issued by the governor of Jamaica to the buccaneers, placed them legally outside the category of pirates and allowed them to carry on their depredations in the name of the Jamaican government.

In the footsteps of pioneers who open up a country come the inevitable adventurers who live by their wits and have recourse to violence when necessary to maintain their control of affairs. Physically powerful, with little or no conscience, they prey on victims where there is no strong arm to curb their licence. Such were the buccaneers of the seventeenth century. Spain had claimed, through the discoveries of Columbus, exclusive rights to the entire West Indies. This all-embracing title was questioned by France, Britain, and Holland. From time to time colonizers from these nations settled in the peripheral islands and disputed Spain's right to remove them. If physically able, Spain rejected the intruders; if not, she suffered these foreigners within her territorial claims.

The initial British, French, and Dutch intruders were mariners. In order to secure food supplies they would anchor off the northwestern end of Haiti and hunt the wild cattle which the Spaniards had abandoned when they removed to the more fertile south eastern end of Hispaniola. In the course of time, some of these seamen settled in Haiti hunting cattle for hides, curing the meat in Carib Indian fashion, and selling both products to passing ships. Tortuga, a small turtle shaped island, just off the north coast of Haiti, became the rendezvous for buyers and vendors. At this early period in their history they became known as buccaneers, a name acquired from the method of curing meat they adopted from the Indians.[47] Bones removed, the meat was cut into convenient strips, salted and placed over a gridiron framework of green wood close to a slow-burning fire. The meat thus cured was given the name *boucan,* and from this word these men became known in French as boucaniers, and later the English equivalent, buccaneers.

The local Spanish government did not look with favour upon the buccaneer settlement in Tortuga. In 1638 it despatched a strong force from Santo Domingo to wipe out the intruders.[48] The soldiers carried out their orders faithfully, slaying every buccaneer they met. Fortunately for the buccaneers, most of their number were in Haiti hunting cattle at this time. Three hundred buccaneers came back to their smouldering buildings and ruined plantations on Tortuga after the Spanish soldiers had departed. This time they put some order into their lives by electing one of their number leader. By 1641 there was a split in their ranks; a French governor managed by stratagem to gain control of Tortuga and forced the British to seek another habitat. Ejected from Tortuga, they took to a seafaring life, preying on Spanish treasure-laden ships as legitimate prize. Both French and British governors abetted these depredators, for it was clear profit every time a treasure ship or "prize"—as D'Oyley called it—was escorted into their harbours.[49] Besides favouring the buccaneers, these governments were developing a ready instrument which, on a moment's notice, could be used for military purposes. A whole series of armed ships, manned by experienced fighting men, for whose maintenance neither the French nor the British assumed responsibility, was a boon to island governments so precariously dependent on the home government thousands of miles across the Atlantic. A free hand in raiding Spanish shipping kept the buccaneers supplied with funds and up-to-date fighting experience.

Henry Morgan, Buccaneer

The greatest name in buccaneering was that of Henry Morgan. Morgan and Port Royal will always be joined in disreputable association. This city at the tip of the palisadoes became the pivot for raids throughout the whole Spanish Main. Back to Port Royal came triumphant Morgan to squander Spanish plate on dubious characters who profited by his daring raids.

Born in Wales about 1635, Morgan migrated at an early age to Bristol. Kidnapped and placed aboard a West Indian vessel, he found himself an unwilling bond servant on a Barbados plantation. After seven years of servitude, he joined the buccaneers, first at Tortuga, later in the more hospitable Port Royal. The barbarous exploits of this scoundrel were broadcast throughout the Caribbean: Camagüey, Gibraltar, Maracaibo, Porto Bello, Panama City, were places that heard the dread name of Morgan ring in their streets.

The Attack on Panama City

One of the never-to-be-forgotten Morgan raids was on the treasure-rich city of Panama in 1670.[50] Two thousand buccaneers made this raid, striking first at Fort Lorenzo at the entrance of the River Chargres. Against this fortification Morgan sent four hundred men under command of Bredely, a seasoned campaigner. Their initial attack beaten off by the Spaniards, the attackers effected an entrance when the fort's magazine exploded. The Spaniards still resisted until two hundred of them fell under buccaneer swords. These desperadoes then paddled down the River Chargres, carrying canoes, weapons, and baggage over spots where the river had run dry. Twelve hundred buccaneers pushed their way through heavy tropical jungle until the ninth day rewarded them with a sight of the Pacific Ocean and the unfortified city of Panama. Taken completely by surprise, the

Spaniards in astonishment watched the buccaneers march on their city. So confident had the Spaniards been that no army could possibly attack from the Atlantic side on account of the natural barrier of dense tropical forests and rough terrain that they had raised no adequate defense embattlements around Panama City. On 27 January 1671, Morgan faced every available Spanish male hastily inducted for the defence of the city, two thousand foot, four hundred mounted, young men and old, slaves and freemen determined to defend their homes. By nightfall the superior fighting experience of the buccaneers began to tell, and next morning six hundred Spaniards lay dead. The city completely in their hands, these barbarians stole, looted, seized everything of value, torturing inhabitants to give up money and valuables, treating religious and priests with even more vicious cruelty than the laity. When Morgan left, one hundred seventy-five mules carried the spoils, six hundred inhabitants marched as prisoners, many pressed into service to carry loot.[51] Others of high social position, among them the bishop, were held for ransom. These frightened people looked back upon the charred ruins of Panama as they began their long trek to the Caribbean.

The wanton burning of the city was placed on the shoulders of Henry Morgan by Esquemelin, one of the buccaneers: "The same day, about noon, he [Morgan] caused certain men privately to set fire to several great edifices of the city, nobody knowing whence the fire proceeded nor who were the authors thereof, much less what motives persuaded Captain Morgan thereto, which are unknown as yet to this day."[52]

The sack of Panama left a bad taste in Europe, for this wanton attack took place hardly after the Treaty of Madrid had been signed on 8 July 1670. Modyford, abetting Morgan, had acted contrary to instructions issued him by the king in his commission as governor, and was removed from office. On 22 August 1671, both governor and buccaneer were sent back to England in chains. For the next two years these rogues exchanged a free and easy life of the Caribbean for the confining life of the Tower. But by 1675, Modyford was back in Jamaica as chief justice, while Morgan's imprisonment had the alchemic effect of transforming him into an official gentleman: he returned to Jamaica knighted with the title of Sir Henry. Later, on two occasions, the reformed buccaneer became lieutenant governor, first from 1677–78, again from 1680–83.[53]

Early English Immigration

In this buccaneer-dominated society, the Catholic Church was not allowed to function publicly.[54] There is some evidence that Catholics lived in Jamaica during this period. This shows up in her immigrant population. To augment the white population of Jamaica, five hundred Irish, men and women, were transported to the island between the years 1671 and 1675. They came as bond servants, carried in Bristol ships which had called at southern Ireland ports for provisions before sailing for the British West Indies.[55] Here these ships took aboard the Irish, willingly or unwillingly. On the West Indian sugar plantations the life of the bond servant was little better than that of the slave, and for as long as seven years these whites were obliged to labour for the plantation owner before being freed of their bonded obligation. In addition to the Irish, twelve hundred to fourteen hundred English arrived each year.[56] They were either free men or bond servants for a one year period. It may be affirmed with much probability that most of the Irish were Catholics and that among so many English a number were of the same faith. Thirteen years later, James II sent Fr. Thomas Churchill to be pastor of his majesty's Catholic subjects, clearly indicating there were many in Jamaica.

Ten

Churchill-Castillo 1688

Brief Revival of the Church in 1688

An historic date in England was 6 February 1674/5.[1] Hope ran high among the minority group of English Catholics that the accession of James II would begin a new era for the Church. James had been reconciled to the Church before the death of his second wife, Mary of Modena, in 1671. In the following year, 1672, he made public avowal of his faith. As king, he allowed Mass to be celebrated publicly, forbade sermons against the faith, and suspended the Test Act which had prohibited Catholics from holding high army posts and important offices of state.

The effect of this revival was felt in Jamaica. Despite the large number of Protestant settlers, there were also many Catholics, not only among the Irish immigrants, but in the ranks of prominent English, such as Sir Richard Dereham. The Catholics petitioned James II that a priest be sent to minister to the faithful in the island.[2] Their mediator was a Fr. Thomas Churchill, known both to the petitioners and to James II.[3] James II asked for volunteers among the clergy; when no one came forward, Churchill, though in his sixtieth year, offered his services.[4]

Churchill, Pastor of Jamaica

James II was pleased at this show of generosity and chose Churchill chief pastor of all his Catholic subjects in Jamaica.[5]

Thomas Churchill was born in London in 1628, the son of Edward Churchill and his wife, Catherine Hazelwood.[6] On the death of his mother in 1638, Thomas was sent by his uncle James Hazelwood, a priest, to Wales and there brought up a Catholic. Matriculating at Douay in 1646, he studied for the priesthood and was ordained at Cambrai in 1663.

The Jamaican petition for a priest was sent to England in 1685, the year Sir Philip Howard, a prominent Catholic, was appointed governor of Jamaica. The death of Sir Philip delayed matters until his successor, the duke of Albemarle, a Protestant, received the appointment in 1687.[7] James II issued special instructions to the duke of Albemarle, dated 15 August 1687. "You are to give all protection, countenance and encouragement to our Roman Catholic subjects in our island of Jamaica, and particularly unto Doctor Churchill, whom we have appointed chief pastor over them in that our island, unto whom you are to give credit and assistance as there shall be occasion."[8]

This was dated four months before Albemarle landed in Jamaica. Practical minded James II, knowing Churchill would need money for his support, saw that a grant of £200 per year was made to him from the exchequer. Albemarle generously added another £100 to this to help Churchill defray household expenses.[9] Three hundred pounds sterling a year gave the chief pastor a certain financial independence.

Accompanied by his physician, Sir Hans Sloane, Governor Albemarle arrived in Jamaica on 20 December 1687 and Churchill followed a month later.[10] When Albemarle stepped ashore at Port Royal, he found a strong body of Catholics, despite laws that had forbidden the open practice of their religion for thirty-two years.

In appreciation for what Albemarle had done to ease the laws restricting Catholic worship, a committee addressed the following to the new governor:

> To his Grace, Christopher, Duke of Albemarle, Lieutenant General and Governor of his Majesty's island of Jamaica and territories therein depending:
>
> May it please your Grace:
>
> The extraordinary benefits we have already received by your accession to the government, and that we have of future happiness under so auspicious an influence, oblige us with the deepest sense of gratitude, to express favourably and publish our acknowledgement and beg your Grace will be pleased to receive these our hearty tenders of duty and affection, which as well on behalf of ourselves as the rest of the Catholics of this island, we humbly offer and do therefore illustrious prince, return you our unfeigned thanks for your repeated assurances of safety and protection to us, equal with the rest of his Majesty's subjects under your government, [and] the Divine Will, that directed his Majesty to convey to us the blessings, and the satisfaction which the rest of his subjects enjoy at home by virtue of his late declaration, through the person of so good and gracious a prince: as we are confident there never was more mercy, more goodness and clemency or more justness and compassion contained in fewer expressions than in his Majesty's said late declaration for liberty of conscience: so we dare affirm there never was choice made of a more apt

and proper member for the advancement and distribution of those royal attributes than your Grace, to whom moderation and temperance, loyalty and constancy, virtues inherent to that memorable and princely flock from which you are descended, are so natural, that in compliance with his Majesty's pleasure and commands, you do but second your own inclination; whereof, we being the proper objects here, have sufficiently tested, and which gives us encouragement humbly to recommend ourselves to your Grace's favourable representative of us to his Majesty, with this assurance to our obedience and conformity to your Grace's command and government, shall evidence both our loyalty to the King and duty to his Governor, which, with out daily prayers for the prosperous and long continuance of your Majesty's government over us in this island, concludes the signed testimony of our thoughts and intentions, and which is subscribed by:

Your Grace's
Most obedient and humble servants,

Thomas Churchill, chief pastor of his Majesty's Catholic subjects of this island.

John Jones
Francis Thomas
Redmond M'Raugh
William Linwood
Bryan M'Grah
James Wate

John Stapleton
George Pigott
Edward Anthill
Richard Morton
William Worley
James Lispenass
(or Lettpenasse)[11]

The Church Acquires its First Property

Churchill discovered two generous benefactors among his Catholic flock. Dr. and Mrs. Joseph Smallwood had purchased the old Dominican monastery in Santiago de la Vega from a Catherine Smith, who in turn received title to it from Charles II on 23 March 1678. On 21 March 1687/8 the Smallwoods deeded this property to Churchill. Here he established his first chapel under the new order of religious freedom for English Catholics in Jamaica.[12]

Fr. Churchill Establishes Four Parishes

Celebration of Mass had ceased when the Spaniards abandoned Jamaica in 1660. Churchill, commissioned by James II as chief pastor, had the authoritative support of Governor Albemarle and therefore was in a unique position to revive Catholic worship. In a letter he revealed what he accomplished. "I opened chapels. I preached and said Divine service. I visited the sick and buried the dead publicly. I got leave for my priests to go out in a distinct habit and orders that if anyone did molest them, they should be severely punished. In fine I got the foundations for four parishes. All in less than a year."[13] Two of these parishes are known, one at Santiago de la Vega, and the other at Port Royal. Evidently, the others were in districts where Catholics were concentrated, probably centred around the great house of a prominent Catholic like Sir Richard Dereham.

Port Royal where Castillo had his Chapel

Port Royal demands attention, for history does not associate the rendezvous of buccaneers, the great slave mart of the Indies, and the wickedest city in the Caribbean, with a Catholic priest offering the Holy Sacrifice of the Mass in Old King's House or preaching the word of God, or consigning the bodies of the dead to the cemetery in the Palisadoes.[14] Before Churchill's advent, Mass was celebrated at the house of James Castillo, Assiento agent.

James Castillo, Slave-Agent

When James Castillo, a native of Barcelona, Spain, arrived at Port Royal in November 1684, he came as a representative of the Assiento, engaged in the lucrative but dishonourable trade in slaves.[15] English slave trade had its official origin in the Company of Royal Adventurers when in 1671, two hundred investors underwrote the company's capital to the amount of £111,100.[16] This company was to deal chiefly in negroes whose labour was growing in demand both in British and Spanish colonies. From 1640–71 the Spanish Government had made no attempt to supply negroes to its colonies, and in such default allowed the colonies to buy negroes supplied by the Dutch.[17] But the Spanish government could not allow this indiscriminate trade in slaves to continue without some official supervision, so in 1662 it revived the Assiento and negotiations were opened both with the Dutch India Company and the English Royal Adventurers to supply negroes to Spanish colonies. But the Second Dutch War so crippled the Company of Royal Adventurers that it became insolvent and by 1668 had practically abandoned the slave trade in favour of a new company known as the Royal African Company of England.[18] This new company was allotted lands in Africa from Cape Blanco in the north to Cape Bona Speranza in the south.[19]

From 1686 the Spaniards were trading in Jamaica and had an agent in the person of James Castillo, who acted for the Spanish factor, Don Nicholas Parcio.[20] But Castillo did not have a monopoly, for another agent, Alexander Olivero, who represented the Dutch factor Balthasar Coyman, with whom Castillo was frequently at loggerheads, was also a slave agent. On one occasion a bill of chancery was brought by Olivero against Castillo, who retaliated by suing Olivero for defamation, claiming £10,000. The suit came to the attention of the Duke of Albemarle, who declared that Castillo had this suit brought against his rival to discourage the Olivero faction from trading in Jamaica and had Castillo's suit thrown out of court. Albemarle had also learned that the king of Spain favoured Olivero because there were serious suspicions on the part of the governors of Panama and Cartagena that Castillo was making fraudulent use of assiento funds and both officials requested that Castillo be brought to trial. Albemarle, as governor of Jamaica, expressed his willingness to do so as soon as definite proofs arrived to charge Castillo with defalcation; until they did arrive, he was powerless to indict Castillo since accounts showed that the assiento was in debt to him.[21]

When Castillo arrived in Jamaica as assiento agent in 1684, Lieutenant Governor Hender Molesworth befriended him by allowing Castillo his choice of the best slaves brought into Port Royal from Africa. For such services rendered in a single year, Molesworth received 10,777 pieces of eight and six reales from the Spanish assiento.[22] Molesworth further befriended Castillo by granting him letters of naturalization in March 1685, thus making him a British subject. Milesworth's granting Castillo the choice of slaves brought strong protest from the Jamaican planters as seen in the report to James II of 18 September 1688:

> and now it may please your majesty, notwithstanding some thousands of negroes, which in these six years last past have been imported into your Majesty's island. . . . yet such is our misfortune that the quantities imported within your harbour, few fell to the planters' share, and these refuse to . . . work.
>
> The Assiento (once it had) settled, the negro ships were picked and culled to furnish them with such as they liked; the factors, and all their particular friends still reaping all the advantages as well to the detriment of the most substantial planters.[23]

Castillo was not only involved in civil difficulties but he also became enmeshed in things ecclesiastical. The roots of this involvement may be seen in his applying to Cuba that his chief chaplain be appointed vicar general. ". . . from the day I arrived in Jamaica, I had a chapel in my house, though there was no liberty of worship for Catholics. I had a chapel built capable of holding 300 persons in which divine services were held, I maintaining the priests at my own expense. For greater validation, I arranged for the Dean and Chapter of Cuba to give the title of Vicar General to my chief chaplain."[24]

When Churchill arrived in January 1688, he spent eighteen days at Castillo's Port Royal residence, where he had an opportunity of viewing the local ecclesiastical situation personally. Not being pleased with it, he tried to introduce some order into Church procedure. For this purpose he called together both clergy and parishioners.[25] But Castillo would have no part with the convocation, claiming that Churchill had no authority, since Jamaica was still ecclesiastically under the jurisdiction of Cuba and not under England. Castillo violently opposed Churchill and threatened to put a quietus to his activities.[26] Churchill responded by placing Castillo's chapel under interdict so that no religious services might be held there legally.[27] Smarting under this grievance, Castillo despatched a messenger to Cuba asking that a manifesto be issued to remove the interdict from the Port Royal Chapel and that Churchill be forbidden to function in Jamaica.

Castillo Publishes the Cuban Manifesto

The manifesto was issued on 26 April 1688, and the document was published on Sunday night 6 May 1688 in Castillo's chapel by Fr. John Baptist Dempsy.[28]

> By what we have been informed by reliable information of some excesses of Thomas Churchill alias Charchel, presbyter cleric who arrived on the island of Jamaica, and who at present enjoys the title of Vicar General sent by the titular Bishop of Adramiten, Greece, who without further jurisdiction than that which has been referred to, and as it is clear has attempted by other means to disturb or make trouble for the Catholic and Christian zeal of Captain Don Santiago del Castillo, authorized agent and general administrator for the introduction of negro slaves into the Indies and Captain Don Nicholas Parcio who is in charge of this with the consent given by your Majesty (May God keep you). Now by means of the chapel that he maintains at his own house at his own expense which is also the home of the missionaries which his Christian Majesty of Great Britain sent to the above-mentioned island and who presented themselves by means of letters, and one of them came personally to the Dean and begged for the vacant See, realizing that for the validity of his ministry respecting ecclesiastical jurisdiction they would need your permission and power because the above-mentioned island of Jamaica was connected from its early foundation on account of its proximity to this Bishopric by apostolic concession applied for, and within whose right it has always been maintained, and even though your Majesty (May God keep you) ceded the temporal right of the above mentioned island to the very Christian sovereign of Great Britain, you did not touch, nor should you do so, the spiritual right; but only the See of the Bishopric of Cuba could do so which in times past conceded to missionaries ample jurisdiction and faculties for administrating the holy sacraments in the other islands to the faithful Christians as also to those who being infidels and heretics should wish to become members of our Holy Catholic Faith, giving thanks to the

above-mentioned Captain Santiago del Castillo for the patronage of his chapel and for the protection of the above-mentioned missionaries and other priests and congregations in it, and he prayed in his house for a happy issue from his zeal which is the propagation of the Christian religion in the above-mentioned island, which at the moment is increasing due to the permission which the above-mentioned sovereign of Great Britain has given. . . . Therefore because of the urgency of the matter we are agreed that these missionaries ought to function in (Jamaica) and the above-mentioned Captain del Castillo retain possession of his chapel . . . in consequence of which we remit this notice to the above-mentioned Captain del Castillo that in virtue of this he should continue with his chapel . . . and that in it the above-mentioned missionaries, especially Don Juan Baptista Dempsy, priest, cleric, as his [Castillo's] chaplain should celebrate the Sacrifice of the Mass and administer the holy sacraments to those whom the above-mentioned concession granted it, without the above-mentioned Thomas Churchill, alias Charchel, interfering or impeding or disturbing him in any way under any pretext from the prosecution of his [Dempsy's] right . . .

Given at Santiago de Cuba
the 26th day of April 1688
by the order of the Vicar General, Chrysostom de Valdes

Churchill immediately informed Albemarle that a manifesto had been obtained surreptitiously from Cuba, much to the prejudice of James II's prerogatives, and that it endeavoured to obstruct Churchill in the discharge of his duties. Albemarle called for a copy of the manifesto which Castillo placed in his hands on 7 May.[29] On Wednesday, 9 May, Albemarle convened a meeting of the council: Sir Francis Watson, Thomas Freeman, Thomas Ballard, Thomas Fuller, John White, and James Walker.[30] Witnesses were called to substantiate Churchill's allegations.

Mr. John Stapleton being sworn made oaths that the said Dempsy owned to him that he had published the said paper, and that the said Castillo would justify every word of it.

Antonio de la Pas, Friar of the Order of Mary for the Redemption of Captives, and Leonard Godfrey of the Spanish nation being sworn . . . the said Antonio de la Pas affirmed on Sunday last he went to Church at Castillo's Chapel, but being sick of the belly was forced to go out again and was afterwards told that the paper sent by the Bishop of Cuba was published in the chapel by Fr. Dempsy. The said Antonio de la Pas further declared that Castillo persuaded him to sign as a witness for a statement against Fr. Churchill saying it would be a great service to his Grace, for the Duke had told him, that Fr. Churchill was too great and he must clip his wings but that he (de la Pas) did not read the said paper nor does he know the contents of it.

The said Leonard Godfry being shown a copy of the paper delivered to his Grace and signed by Castillo made oaths that the same was published by Dempsy in Castillo's chapel on Sunday last.[31]

Having heard the case, the Council decided that Castillo had introduced a foreign ecclesiastical power into Jamaica which in turn made derogatory remarks about his Majesty, the King of Britain. Castillo was ordered to give surety that he would answer to his Majesty and not depart from Jamaica for twelve months or until such time as the King's pleasure be known.[32] Castillo refused to give surety to answer the charges in Jamaica, whereupon the governor signed an order to Provost Marshall Smyth Kelly that he take Castillo into custody. "Whereupon it is ordered that the Provost Marshall do forthwith take into custody the body of the said Castillo and him safely keep until he shall give sufficient security or that his Majesty's pleasure be further known herein or that the same Castillo be otherwise discharged by due course of Law."[33]

Castillo's "body" was never taken into custody. His good friend the Provost Marshall informed Castillo privately of the warrant for his arrest and gave him plenty of time to escape. Castillo was seen walking freely about the streets of Port Royal from 6.00 o'clock in the morning until 10.00 o'clock in the evening of 8 May.[34] The marshall made no attempt to carry out the Council's orders; but he had to make some show of performance of duty, so at 3.00 o'clock the following morning, 9 May, Smyth Kelly appeared at the governor's residence in Spanish Town asking if he might break down the door of Castillo's house in Port Royal to arrest Castillo.[35] Kelly had consulted the attorney general, who cautioned the provost marshall to seek Albemarle's permission. A weary, suspicious governor gave his half-awake assent.[36] Castillo's door was broken and even the tabernacle in the chapel desecrated, but Castillo was on the high seas bound for Havana in a sloop manned by seven sailors.[37] He landed there on 17 May.[38]

What began as an ecclesiastical quarrel had wider repercussions. The provost marshall was replaced by Thomas Waite.[39] This had not been Kelly's only brush with executive authority. Several charges of misdemeanor had been leveled at him in the last legislative assembly, one on account of his undue and exorbitant execution of office to such a degree that he became a general nuisance to both colonial and royal interests.[40]

Waite confronted Kelly with documents showing the provost marshall's discharge from office. Kelly not only refused to submit, but seized the person of Waite and imprisoned him in the gaol.[41] Kelly was then ordered to appear before the council to answer for this action; like his friend Castillo, he fled the island leaving no indication of his whereabouts.[42] Attorney General Musgrave, also under suspicion of having connived at Castillo's escape, lost his office and was replaced by Sir Richard Dereham, a Catholic, while Roger Elleston became chief justice, replacing Hender Molesworth. A new House of Assembly was elected in 1688 and sworn in on 23 July 1688.[43] According to the historian Long, they were mostly Catholics. Careful research reveals the probable Catholic members of this Assembly—Port Royal: Ralph Knight and William Mathews; St. Catherine: John Ellis and William Worley; St. Ann: William Bragg; Clarendon: John Peake and Richard Dawkins; St. Elizabeth: Richard Scott and John Harrow; St. John: George Reed and Edward Winter; St. David: Thomas Rives and John Lobley; St. Thomas in the Vale: Robert Noell. To these must be added the names of Attorney General Sir Richard Dereham and the Provost Marshall Thomas Waite.[44]

When Castillo left Jamaica on 8 May with his Jesuit and St. John of God priests, he had the assurance of Molesworth, who was on his way to England, that he would call for Castillo at Havana and take him to James II. Castillo, having arrived at Havana on 27 May with his two companions, the Jesuit and the St. John of God priests, went immediately to call on the governor, Don Diego de Viana, who received them with hospitality and listened to the account of events in Jamaica:

> . . . having given him a clear account of our troubles, he (the Governor) promised every assistance and as soon as the ships should arrive in sight he would have us put on board one of them. . . .
>
> The next day the Governor of Havana told me that he had a cedula from his Majesty (King of Spain) by which he commanded him to arrest me and send me to the Kingdom of Castile for not having rendered the accounts of what had been under my charge in connection with the business of the Assiento, but that he would not carry it out considering my voyage was so important to the service of God and both Majesties (Spain and England).
>
> I answered him on the point that if the royal cedula referred to my not having rendered the account of what concerned the Assiento, his Majesty had been badly informed for they arrested me in Jamaica just when the deposition from Coyman arrived. I made up the accounts and they made me deliver up everything. I had, notwithstanding that after the accounts had been balanced, proved I was a creditor of the Assiento to the sum of 34,550 pesos and six reales . . . consequently, the royal will was complied with and there was no more discussion over this matter as he (Don Diego de Viana) was satisfied with the authentic and original papers.
>
> As the ships that were to come for me were hourly expected, I asked him on the third day to give me the permit to leave the port in a launch in order not to detain the ships. Calling the Secretary, he ordered him to sanction it, but from another source I was informed that the Governor expected a sizeable gratuity, if not, he would act on the royal cedula. Considering the great harm that could follow to the Vicar General who was under arrest (in Jamaica),—for I have no doubt that if redress is not sought at once they will sentence him to death—and also the evident danger to the other Religious and laity, to the service of his Majesty and

> the loss to the Assiento, if I were detained to go to Spain in the fleet when on this occasion the remedy had to be sought in London where it was very necessary I should go to make it known that there were enough negroes in Jamaica in case his Majesty restored the administration of his Assiento to my principal.
>
> Therefore taking into consideration what is above referred to, I thought it right to give first place to this service and make him an offer of 500 pesos to which he did not agree as he wanted 1000. As at this time I had little means, only what was necessary for the voyage which would have been impossible for me to make if I gave him what he demanded, I was obliged to suffer the despotism. He took me in his coach to the Castle of la Printa where he left me a prisoner.
>
> The next day the Governor came to visit me and proposed that I should make a report and give him a memorandum with my explanation proving that the royal cedula, by virtue of which I was a prisoner, had been carried out in Jamaica and how I had behaved in the matter and the services rendered to his Majesty and his vessels. It was done forthwith and presented to him. He handed it over to his Lieutenant General Don Francisco Manuel de Roa, his legal adviser who was of the opinion that the Governor neither could nor should detain me as it was clear that his Majesty's will had been complied with and that my voyage meant much good for God and the royal service. . . . Upon that opinion the Governor sent me his Secretary to learn what I would do. I replied that I could not give him more than 500 pesos. As he had already made up his mind to get the 1000 pesos, he called together some lawyers to say that he should not allow me to leave. . . . As I could not move him from his resolve without the 1000 pesos, he sent me a prisoner in the Admiral's ship of the fleet (Spanish). . . .
>
> From the Admiral's ship of the Fleet
> October 25, 1688
> To his Excellency the Marquis de los Valez [45]

When Castillo departed from Jamaica, Churchill transferred Catholic services from Castillo's chapel to Old King's House in Port Royal where he continued to make progress by putting some order into matters ecclesiastical, now that there was no interference from Castillo.[46]

Fr. Churchill Leaves Jamaica

A civic matter arose at this time which sent Churchill on a trip to England. Foreign agents were buying up the most able-bodied slaves and shipping them to Spanish possessions, only the sickly and physically unfit being left for the local planters. Within a period of six years, one third of the slaves purchased by the Jamaican planters had died. At a joint meeting of the Executive Council and the Assembly, resolutions were drawn up to curb the activity of these foreign agents.

On 18 September 1688, a memorial was addressed to King James II.[47] Churchill was chosen courier to present the planters' case to his Majesty. Landing at Falston, near Hide in Kent, England, on 15 October 1688, Churchill wrote to the Jamaican planters on 16 November, saying that he had been graciously received by the King who was pleased to have personal news about Jamaica, and in particular about Albemarle.[48] Unknown to James II and Churchill, the governor had died on 5 October 1688.[49] The death of Albemarle was a blow to the progress of the Church; but a more serious calamity, and one from which the Church did not recover for more than a century, followed immediately when James II lost his throne and had to flee to France for safety. Ever zealous in promoting the interests of the Church, James II made the serious error of pursuing too vigorous a policy against the Establishment. Although Anglicans might disagree among themselves, they presented a united front against their common enemy, James II. He experienced this hostility in April 1687, when he published a Declaration of Indulgence, freeing Catholics and dissenters from penal statutes and allowing Catholics to be elected fellows in the universities and hold office in all departments of the state and municipal corporations. The climax was reached when James II forced the Established clergy to read this Declaration of Indulgence from their pulpits. Upon his royal head fell the wrath of the whole Establishment.

Since 1678 Protestant gentry had been in contact with William of Orange, husband of James II's daughter, Mary. On 30 June 1688 they sent a definite invitation by Admiral Herbert offering William and Mary the throne of England. They accepted and landed an army at Tor Bay on 5 November 1688. James offered resistance, but the military engagements were in favour of the foreign prince. On 23 December 1688 James fled to France where Louis XIV offered him asylum at St. Germain.

Hope for the Church in Jamaica faded on 22 February 1689, when William of Orange sent instructions to the Executive Council appointing Hender Molesworth lieutenant governor.[50] Molesworth removed Elletson, Dereham, and Waite from office; henceforth, no Catholic was allowed to hold public office in the island.

Fr. Churchill's Last Days

Churchill, like his friend James II, spent his last days in exile. He retired to Dunkirk where he wrote a letter dated 18 September 1704, which revealed that he was in a state of destitution. Pope Clement XI generously granted the former chief pastor of the Jamaican mission a pension, but he did not live long to enjoy it; he died in the same year of 1704.[51]

James Castillo Returns to Jamaica

From Spain Castillo found his way to England where he ingratiated himself into the friendship of William and Mary and was appointed commissary general for supplying Spanish colonies with slaves. On the same occasion the British sovereigns conferred upon the slave agent the honour of knighthood.[52] He was henceforth Sir James Castillo.

Destruction of Port Royal

Three years after Castillo returned to Jamaica, Port Royal was struck with a most devastating earthquake from which the city never fully recovered.

In Spanish days ships were scraped of barnacles and made seaworthy at Careening Point on the Palisadoes, a settlement of no importance until the British, who took the island in 1655, dropped military supplies there, laying the foundation of Port Royal. Houses were built on this healthy spot, which enjoyed the advantage of a continual sea breeze, making the promontory cooler than the swampy shore of the mainland. Seven years after conquest the town was well established with four hundred men, two hundred women, three hundred soldiers, and fifty negroes. During Churchill's residence the population was reckoned at more than five thousand inhabitants and twelve hundred houses vying in architectural construction with those in London.[53] It was a period of prosperity with some of its profits coming from the middlemen who channeled stolen Spanish goods into ready markets. Other profits came from the handling of honest merchandise for planters and other residents of the island.

June is always hot in Jamaica, and this particular Wednesday, 7 June, dawned unusually sultry, with no breeze ruffling the becalmed Caribbean. Ships in the harbour, having just returned from a raid on a Haitian settlement, were riding at anchor, their loot safely in the already bulging warehouses. The Council, in session, had just adjourned for the morning when, seventeen minutes before the hour of noon, a thunder-like sound echoed in the St. Andrew hills, followed by three distinct shocks mounting in intensity until the third was so violent that it struck terror into every living being.[54] The Anglican minister, Mr. Heath, had been earlier in St. Peter's Church reading his prayers, as was his custom since his appointment as rector of the parish church, saying that he performed this daily act of devotion to keep up some evidence of religion amongst a most ungodly people.[55] After prayers he walked over to a nearby meeting place of merchants, where he met his friend John White, president of the Council. White invited Heath to a glass of wine to whet his appetite for dinner. While Heath was drinking his wine, White lighted his clay pipe. Heath grew uneasy waiting for White to finish his pipe, since he had been invited to dine at Captain Ruden's house. At this point the ground began to roll under Heath's feet. Frightened, he turned to White for an explanation, who assured him that the earthquake would soon pass. Instead of diminishing, it grew in intensity. The church and its tower crashed to the ground. Out in the street confusion reigned, and Heath ran towards the open ground in Morgan's fort. Fortunately he never reached the spot, for the earth opened up and completely swallowed all within the fort's compound. Captain Ruden, his wife, children, and all his dinner guests had been among those killed. But Heath lived to write one of the few eyewitness accounts of the destruction of Port Royal, in which some three thousand persons perished.

After the earthquake Castillo bought a property at the eastern approach to Kingston, on the Windward Road, from his friend Smyth Kelly, who had now been reinstated as provost marshall.[56] On 11 September 1693, by royal letter patent, issued by Sir William Beeston, Castillo was empowered to enclose his estate with embattled walls for the defence of his house, plantation, and slaves.[57] The journals of the Assembly note that Castillo's "fortified house was very serviceable against the French and a bulwark between them and Kingston."[58] Realizing the importance of the fortification on Windward Road, the Assembly aided Castillo by defraying part of the construction expenses in two grants of £600 and £400 respectively.

Not everyone looked with favour upon Castillo's fortified house guarding the approach to Kingston. Brigadier General Selwyn wrote to the Council of Trade and Plantations in 1701, asking for instructions concerning Castillo's fortified house. "Whereas Sir James Castillo is in possession of a fort situated upon an important pass in Jamaica, I desire that it be an instruction either to garrison it or demolish it."[59]

The answer came back from England that Castillo's house was to be garrisoned. It was no mere cottage, for the building could lodge two hundred soldiers who occupied it for five years. They gave it such rough treatment that Dame Mary Castillo, Sir James's widow, petitioned the House of the Assembly in 1711 for funds to repair the property which she had inherited from her late husband.

> A petition of Dame Mary Castillo setting forth that her late husband, having at great charge and expense in building a fortification by consent of the government and the same order of her Majesty was taken into possession by her Majesty's forces and held for a space of five years, during which time it had greatly run down into ruins, to repair the damage she humbly prays the consideration of the honourable House.[60]

John Colfy, one of the committee appointed to consider Mary Castillo's petition, reported that

> The Committee found the allegation of my Lady Castillo to be just and true and are of the opinion that more than £200 would not put the house in repair and good order, as they were when taken from her for the use and service of her country. That the sum of £200 be paid to my Lady de Castillo and to make her a further satisfaction for the damages she has sustained by the continuance of the same in the hands of her Majesty's forces.[61]

This fortified house on the Windward Road could have been used also as a chapel by Castillo. Although there was no liberty of worship for Catholics upon Castillo's return to Jamaica in 1689, the same officials who had countenanced his chapel at Port Royal were now returned to power and may have allowed Castillo to have a private chapel in his house for the benefit of Jamaican Catholics.

Church Officially Proscribed

That there were Catholics and that they were increasing may be inferred from an item in the Journals of the Assembly dated 5 October 1705. "Hugh Totterdale, chairman of the committee for bringing a bill for preventing the growth of popery, reported the opinion of the committee. It was therefore put to a vote whether the House concurred with the report. It was carried."[62]

On the following day, 6 October, it was ordered "that the bill preventing the growth of popery be read and passed the first time."[63]

As far as was humanly possible, the opposition left no loophole for the continuance of the Church in Jamaica. For a long period no priests were allowed to set foot on Jamaican soil. Sixty-five years after the great earthquake, Dr. Richard Challoner, vicar apostolic of the London district, writing to Rome on 14 September 1757, related that "In Jamaica there are many Catholics, and two priests in our time have made some attempt to settle there but could not succeed."[64]

Battle of the Saints—
French Catholic Prisoners in Jamaica

The only priests to pierce this barrier came unwillingly as prisoners of war. During the American Revolutionary War 1775–83, Admiral

Count de Grasse felt that the key to British power in the Caribbean lay in the island of Jamaica. Once this was captured, all British West Indian possessions would fall. His strategy was for the combined fleets of France and Spain, numbering more than fifty sail, manned by twenty thousand men, to meet at Santo Domingo and from there to launch an attack on Jamaica. It was never executed, for the brilliant victory by Admiral George Rodney crushed de Grasse's hopes and broke French naval power in the Indies.

News of the French fleet in Antillean waters had brought Rodney out of retirement and back to active duty. On 12 January 1782, he sailed with his fleet from England, arriving in Barbados on 19 February, where Hood joined him. Their combined fleets numbered thirty-four sail, and carried 2,460 guns. They sailed for St. Lucia and anchored at Gros Islet Bay, twenty-five miles from de Grasse at Martinique. From that vantage point Rodney kept a strict watch on the French. On 8 April de Grasse slipped out of Martinique with the hope of joining the Spanish fleet at Santo Domingo. Rodney followed. De Grasse had no intention of engaging Rodney until the combined French and Spanish fleets faced him. But one of de Grasse's ships, the *Zele,* gave no end of trouble. First it collided with another ship and then struck two others on the following day. Against his better judgment, de Grasse slowed down to aid the unfortunate member. This was all Rodney needed. With the British within firing range, de Grasse could only stop and fight.

On 12 April the two fleet challenged one another in what became known as the Battle of the Saints, fought off tiny islands just north of Dominica, Les Saintes. Both fleets spread out and from 11.00 in the morning until 6.00 in the evening the fighting raged furiously. The climax came when Rodney broke the French line and caught the French flagship *Ville de Paris* between murderous cross fire, battering it to a pulp. Disorganized and disabled, the rest of the French fleet limped off to Guadeloupe. Six prizes of war and seven hundred prisoners were taken to Jamaica. Three hundred of the wounded were quartered in Kingston. Never had Jamaica so many Catholics.

One of the prisoners, Fr. Charles Maurice Whelan, deserves attention. While residing in the Capuchin monastery of Bar-sur-Aube in Champagne, France, he answered the call of Louis XVI for chaplains to serve with the fleet.[65] He was accepted, and assigned to the warship *Jason.* His chaplaincy was no armchair sinecure, for fourteen sea engagements were recorded before the Battle of the Saints. This last was his most serious and most dangerous. The *Jason* limped into Kingston, a prize of war.

After defeat, the big problem was the spiritual care of the wounded and the dying. When he suggested to his brother chaplains that they visit their respective sick, through some queer twist of mind they refused. They said that they too were prisoners and hence exempt from any obligation to attend to them. Taking all the work upon himself, Whelan could report that not a man died within the sacraments.[66] Whelan remained in Jamaica for thirteen months, ministering to three hundred French, eighty Spaniards, and thirty-five Americans who eventually died from wounds or yellow fever. The site where the Kingston Station of the Jamaica Railway now stands on West Street was known as the Strangers' Burial Ground; it is probable that these dead were buried there.

War came to an end with the Treaty of Versailles on 3 September 1783. Whelan returned to Ireland, whence he proceeded to New York. There he ministered to Catholics until trustee troubles forced him to depart. After years of service to the Catholics of Kentucky, he retired to live with the Jesuits in Bohemia Manor, Maryland, where he died 21 March 1806.

Eleven

Rebirth 1792

For one hundred thirty-seven years the Church had played no role in Jamaican life. Practically it was dead, if we exempt the brief Churchill-Castillo interlude. The year 1782, however, witnessed the Church's resurrection. Spanish merchants from South America and the Antillean islands had already been settling in increasing numbers and had formed an important nucleus of mercantile life. Far from being welcomed by the British citizenry, they were at best merely tolerated, as may be inferred from the House of Assembly, 29 November 1791.

> We are ordered by the House to wait on your Honour [the attorney general] and request you will be pleased to issue his Majesty's royal proclamation prohibiting all Spaniards trading in this island from landing themselves or slaves without your Honour's special licence . . . that the constables or senior magistrates in the precincts forthwith make a return of all Spaniards resident in their several districts.[1]

Despite this restraining order, Spaniards residing in Jamaica presented a petition to the government requesting that a priest be allowed to settle here and minister to their spiritual needs.

Petition Sent at Propitious Moment in English History

This request was made at a most auspicious moment in English history, for in 1791 a parliamentary act, far-reaching in effect, had been passed. Penal laws in force since 1558 were so mitigated that a Catholic could no longer be prosecuted for the sole reason that he was a Catholic. He could now be educated in his faith and hear Mass, could no longer be summoned to London to take the Oath of Supremacy, did not have to register his wills and estates. The profession of law was open to him with its varied careers of councilor, barrister, attorney, solicitor, and notary. He could enter a religious order. A priest was allowed to celebrate Mass publicly, provided the place of assembly had been certified at Quarter Sessions and the name of the priest recorded by the Clerk of Peace. The enactment was a long stride towards eventual complete emancipation.

This parliamentary act had its effect in Jamaica. The government now had a precedent for allowing a priest to function in this island. The request for a priest was received with favour by Rt. Rev. John D. Douglass, vicar apostolic of the London district, under whose ecclesiastical jurisdiciton Jamaica had come since his consecration in 1790. Priests were few in England, and for Douglass to assign even one missionary to this outpost, where Catholics could be counted by the handful and prospects of conversions very slim, was a real sacrifice.

Fr. Anthony Quigly, Recollet

A Franciscan had inaugurated missionary life at the dawn of Spanish colonization; a Franciscan Recollect, Anthony Quigly, reopened the second phase of the Church's life in this West Indian island. The first was on the north coast at Seville, the second on the south coast at Kingston.

Gifted with one of the most spacious harbours in the world, Kingston nestled in the idyllic tropical setting of the Liguanea plain with the high Blue Mountains as a backdrop. Kingston was celebrating its centenary when Quigly opened his mission on West Street.

The City of Kingston

Founded on 24 June 1692, immediately after the great earthquake had destroyed Port Royal, Kingston was destined to supplant Spanish Town as the capital and eventually become the second most populous city in the West Indies, surpassed only by Havana.[2] On 9 August 1692, the plan for the new city of Kingston, proposed by John Goffe, was approved by the council. The Goffe draft was later extended by a military engineer, Colonel Christian Lilly, who projected the dimensions of the original plan to give the city the general appearance it has today. Three of its boundaries had the prosaic names of North Street, East Street and West Street. The fourth was not called South Street but Harbour Street. But William Beeston put a Port Royal Street between Harbour Street and the sea, thus perpetuating the buccaneer port on the Kingston side of the harbour. Through the centre of the city ran the main north-south thoroughfare, named King Street. Its sixty-foot width made an impressive seventeenth century highway. Parallel to

King Street ran other streets fifty feet with intervening lanes twenty feet wide.[3] The main street, running east-west, intersecting King Street, was named Queen Street. Streets and lanes parallel to Queen Street north and south followed the same pattern as streets parallel to King Street.

Kingston was not only a city, it was also a civil parish. As a city, its boundary was confined within an approximate one square mile; as a civil parish it extended some six square miles. Thirty thousand inhabitants lived within the parish limits in 1792: nine thousand whites, two thousand free negroes, and fifteen thousand slaves. Of this total only a handful were Catholics, some being Spaniards of the commercial class and a few being refugees from neighbouring Haiti.

Effect of the French Revolution on Jamaica

The French began to arrive in 1791, for in the Journals of the Assembly dated 28 February 1792, it was ordered that the custos of the Town and Parish of Kingston on or before Tuesday 6 March make a return of all free mulattoes and free negroes who had arrived in Kingston since 10 December 1791.[4] To these were added all the free mulattoes and negroes from Haiti who were resident in the Town or Parish of Kingston together with the names of the people who were acting as surety for such persons. Again on 19 November 1793 there is another mention made in the Journals of the Assembly stating that on 3 April 1793 a proclamation was issued requiring all magistrates to consider any French person found at large in the island and not properly registered with the authorities an enemy of the state. Eighty persons were apprehended. Fifty-one French subjects and their families, seventy-one persons in all, were granted licenses to reside with their domestics in Jamaica, provided they were on their good behaviour and offered security during residence.[5] These refugees from Haiti were to form the core of the Church in Jamaica, so imprinting their national character that for years it was known as the French Church. Nor was it without reason that the Jamaican government viewed these refugees from Haiti with suspicion.

Until 1791, Haiti was much like any other West Indian island: sugar and coffee produced by the sweat of slaves enriched many a French family both on the island and in France. Great fortunes were built upon the labour of hundreds of thousands of Africans transported against their will from their native home to work for white masters who considered them just as much their property as the cattle in the field. In 1789 the Haitian colonists heard rumblings of revolution in faraway France. Since an ocean intervened, they considered themselves perfectly safe, more than four thousand miles distant, in their island home. They were safe until two years later, when in 1791 what they thought could not happen, did happen, and with ferocious savagery.

It all began with the burning of a trash house on Chabaud's plantation at Cap François.[6] Behind the burning lurked the serious plot of revolution. The incendiary, a negro from Desgrieux's plantation, when caught and interrogated confessed that all the drivers, coachmen, domestics and trusted negroes of the neighbouring plantations and adjacent districts had formed a plan to set fire to the plantations and murder all the whites. Four of the ring leaders lived on Flavelle's plantation at Acuel. The attorney[7] for Flavelle refused to believe that any of his slaves were involved in the plot, but more violence erupted between 22–23 August, when twelve negroes seized the apprentice sugar refiner at Noe's plantation, Acuel, dragged him before the Great House—where he died under their savage blows—then proceeded to the home of the head refiner and assassinated him in his bed. At daybreak the uprising had spread over the whole plain, houses and canes set afire and inhabitants massacred.

Treachery characterized the uprising in Haiti, for the slaves at Flavelle's plantation had sworn fidelity to the attorney, yet armed themselves, entered the houses of the whites, and murdered five of them. The attorney's wife, on her knees, besought them to spare the life of her husband, but they disregarded her plea and murdered him in cold blood. Mr. Robert, a carpenter employed on the same plantation, was bound between two planks and sawed in two. Canes were set afire, buildings were added to the flames as the revolt spread rapidly throughout the whole country and atrocities increased. The body of a white infant was impaled on a stake and used as a standard by the revolting negroes. M. Oedluc, who had befriended his own slaves, as they themselves acknowledged, was found with a hundred weapons in his body.[8]

Nor did the French Assembly help matters. First they favoured one side, then they retracted their support in favour of the other. Neither whites nor mulattoes knew where they stood. On 15 May 1791 the Paris Assembly decreed that all free persons of whatever shade of colour, born of free parents, were to be treated as equals. Since many mulattoes had been born of slave mothers, the Paris decree placed them beyond the pale of equal rights with the whites. Resenting the decree, mulattoes rose in a rebellion supported by thousands of slaves, and a terrible massacre of whites took place.

On 24 September 1791 whites and mulattoes came to terms.[9] But almost immediately it was learned that the Paris Assembly had revoked its former decree by another dated 24 September 1791.[10] This inconsistency of the assembly infuriated the mulattoes who felt that the white man could not be trusted. Allying themselves with the slaves, they began a war of extermination of the French. On 4 April 1792, the National Assembly of France again changed its mind by a new decree which placed all free men on an equal footing without distinction.[11] Leger Felicitie Santhonax, a mulatto, made himself dictator. France sent two commissioners, Poverel and Ailaud, supported by six thousand soldiers who arrived on 13 September 1792.[12] Opposed by whites, they secured the support of slaves by promising freedom and license to plunder. Heavy fighting resulted. Faced with an impossible situation, the whites left Haiti, some fleeing to the United States, others to England, while a large number found their way to the neighbouring island of Jamaica. Haiti was now in chaos; revolution and counterrevolution followed in rapid succession with repercussions in Jamaica. On 23 December 1799 Sas Portas, a Haitian spy, was hanged in the Parade Kingston.[13]

The question arose whether Portas was an isolated individual or was there a real plot by Haiti to invade Jamaica? The Maroon country of St. James, Jamaica, would have been an ideal place to foment this revolt, for this community of runaway slaves had been a thorn in the side of British officials for years. Three mulattoes from Haiti, one of whom was a friend of the chief of the Maroons, were told to make contact with Maroon Town. Contact was made, and the Maroons were promised that there would soon be an insurrection in the civil Parish of St. James. To aid the insurrection, one hundred French from Haiti, mostly mulattoes, were landed in Jamaica.[14] Another part of the plan was to recruit ten thousand mulattoes in Haiti, land them east of Kingston on the coast between Port Antonio and Port Morant, each armed with an extra musket and broadsword which were to be given to Jamaican negroes joining the revolution.[15] "Liberty" was to be the rallying cry of the invaders who hoped to rouse the countryside to armed insurrection while the Maroons were to come down from the hills and join forces with them. This powerfully combined force of invaders and Maroons would then make its way to Kingston. Nor was this all theory, for a French officer who bore an inveterate hatred for the English was to lead the expedition. Several times he had been to Jamaica secretly and had established communications with Jamaicans who held themselves in readiness to furnish scouts and guides to the invaders. By October 1799 the Haitians expected Jamaica to be in their power.[16]

This was the critical situation Quigly encountered when he took up residence in a house rented from Peter McTavish, a stone mason.

The site of the house is identified today as 9 West Street, located immediately below the corner of Barry and West Streets on the southwest side, the lot being number 289, known from the Michael Hay plan of 1795 (established by water marks), but undoubtedly copied from an earlier drawing dating between 1738 and 1747. Within the walls of his West Street residence, Quigly opened his first chapel in 1792 to serve all Catholics of Jamaica: Spaniards, French, English, and Irish. In 1795 he purchased this West Street property from McTavish, and in the same year his name appeared for the first time on the Tax Roll under the heading of "landlord," with the additional qualifying word "own."[17] From this tiny chapel the Church would spread to every nook and corner of Jamaica. It would grow from a handful of foreigners to more than 139,508 native Jamaicans in 1967.[18]

The Spaniards had asked for the priest, but the French offered him a growing stable congregation. With the French refugees came several priests who, like the laity, had to flee Haiti. William Le Cun, O.P., prefect apostolic, was one of them.

Only after repeated pleas by his congregation did Fr. Le Cun flee Haiti. On the very day he was to be handed over to the executioner, yielding to the advice of his people, he left at 4.30 o'clock in the evening.[19] For a month he secreted himself in Port-au-Prince. On 15 February 1798, disguised as a sailor, he left the island by ship, without money and with only the clothes on his back, remaining hidden in the hold of the vessel bound for New York. Coming out of hiding, he was transferred by the captain to a passing French ship bound for Cuba. This was six days after he had left Haiti and there a British warship transported him to Jamaica, where he landed on 9 March.[20]

Le Cun's Description of the Revolution in Haiti

Le Cun had left behind scenes of horror that remained seared in his memory until he died in Kingston in 1808. Departure of the French army from Haiti had left the country completely in the hands of the revolutionaries. Le Cun had hoped to save his churches and continue divine worship, and by this means turn the people from acts of violence. This motive induced him to remain as long as possible, even at the peril of his life.

Upon the free men of colour Le Cun placed the blame for the infuriated violence which characterized the uprising. After the French withdrew, the Haitian government was composed of two classes of men, the mulattoes and the blacks. Le Cun claimed these two classes showed hatred not only for Frenchmen but for whites of every nation. Of these two classes, the mulattoes were more embittered than the blacks against the whites. Le Cun also asserted that without mulatto urging, the mass of the black population would never have perpetrated this terrible carnage, because they had respect for religion and its ministers. Precisely because these mulattoes saw that the missionaries were opposed to their wickedness, they proscribed Le Cun and put to the sword all priests who fell into their hands. All churches except those in Port-au-Prince, St. Marc, and Les Cayes were destroyed by arson. Le Cun was not sanguine about the survival of the other churches. All missionaries except five were either exiled or murdered, and in many parishes the blacks seized what was left of the sacred vessels and vestments, making them their own, some going so far as to sacrilegiously simulate the administration of the sacraments and the celebration of Mass.[21]

The Spanish Chapel on West Street

While these scenes of horror were being enacted in Haiti, Quigly was busy in Kingston organizing his handful of parishioners into regular parochial life. From 1792–99 he conducted religious services in his residence.[22] In 1799 he opened a public chapel in the adjoining property, now 11 West Street.[23] Since his first parishioners were Spanish, it acquired the popular name of Spanish Chapel.[24] In an old church register, a detailed inventory has preserved a picture of this chapel. Although this description labours the obvious, it is well to record, for it shows that Quigly's chapel was not a primitive wattle hut but an edifice that might compare favourably with its counterpart in eighteenth-century Europe.

A Description of the Spanish Chapel

The cradle of the Church in modern Jamaica was a wooden structure facing north-south at the corner of Barry and West Streets.[25] Peering through the front entrance, one could observe that damask covered the wall behind the altar which was of native wood, while over it was suspended a baldachin of expensive lace done in a varied flower pattern. On feast days the tabernacle was covered with the same damask. A bronze crucifix with its corpus and base of the same metal stood above the tabernacle. An antependium of damask screened the lower part of the altar, while the whole sanctuary was covered with a blue carpet having a white design running through it. On the top altar step was another carpet, while the lighting of the chapel was by four glass oil lamps. The seating arrangement was simple consisting of six prie-dieux and three long benches; evidently the prie-dieux were for the gentry. In the rear of the chapel was a confessional. A large mirror also occupied a prominent position in the rear of the chapel, but no explanation is offered of its function. This offers a description of the main body of the chapel. There was also a sacristy with the usual sacred vestments, all of reversible style so that two rubrical colours might be used on the one vestment. The chalice used on ordinary days was of silver whose paten was gold-plated, while on special feasts the chalice was gold-plated, with cruets and bell of the same metal. A chrismatorium for reserving the holy oils with a silver vessel having a spout for anointing the dying was kept in the wall cabinet. Corporals, purificators, a Spanish antependium, albs and yards of linen interwoven with small gold flowers were deposited in the sacristy for use on appropriate occasions. Despite their few numbers, the Jamaican congregation, mostly Spaniards, took pride in the appointments for divine worship used in their West Street chapel.

During the 1792–99 period Quigly faithfully recorded his baptisms and burials. Unfortunately, the very early records of 1792–94 are in poor condition, for the ravages of tropical insects have left little of the writing from which to glean statistics. A sample of the extant baptismal record reads as follows: "April 26, 1798, I do certify that I baptized according to the rite of the Roman Catholic Church, a slave boy by name of Joseph Antonio the property of Alberto, a Spaniard. A. Quigly."[26]

Another of the same year reads as follows: "April 24, 1798: I do certify that I baptized a quadroon male child by name of Luis, the property of Madam Bess: godfather and godmother, Madam Bess' two children. A. Quigly."

His burial records give intimate details as may be seen from the following. "September 1, 1795: I do hereby certify that I have conducted to the consecrated ground of the town of Kingston the dead body of Rose Lerret, otherwise Madame Sanchier, spouse to Francis Sanchier and there performed the ceremonies according to the rites of the Roman Catholic Church. She died in the large house belonging to Patterson's garden the 31st of August, age 26. A. Quigly."

The burial of one of the Haitian refugee priests is recorded in more detail.

> In the year 1798, on November 28, was buried in the cemetery of Kingston, Jamaica, the body of the late Dom Ambrose Marie Provost, a Benedictine of the Congregation of St. Maure, formerly Professor of Theology of the same Congregation, and lately Missionary Apostolic at the Mission of Affranches in the island of San Domingo (Haiti), born at Avranches Parish of St. Gervais in Normandie on December 5, 1762, lawful son of Maître Louis Ambrose Provost Attorney of the Crown for that district and

of Dame Catherine Allain. He died yesterday evening in the city of Kingston; the burial took place in the presence of the Catholic clergy and of several other prominent parishioners who together with us have signed the above statement.

Fr. W. Le Cun, Prefect Apostolic of St. Domingue De L'Espinasse
Rochanson, Missionary Apostolic
F. Isbey, Missionary Apostolic
The Abbot Monchet, Testamentary Executor
M. Rostare
Clr. de DeDillon
Collette, wife of DeDillon
Anthony Quigly, Roman Catholic Priest of Kingston, Jamaica

Refugees from Haiti

Although refugees from Haiti began to arrive in 1791, not until the years 1793–98 did they come in considerable numbers. A vivid picture of horror in Haiti had been seared in their memory. Now resettled in the neighbouring island of Jamaica, whose people, language, and customs were foreign to them, they persevered despite obstacles and formed there the groundwork of the Church in modern times.

The refugee priests—Provost, Rochanson, Monchet, and L'Espinasse—had begun their odyssey in 1791, when they were expelled from France.[27] Crossing the English Channel, they were sent by their bishops to Haiti where they were assigned temporarily to the mission of Jeremie. Here they worked under Le Cun, prefect apostolic of the mission.[28] Stole fees, shared with Le Cun, were their principal source of livelihood. Seven years later they were again on the move, this time to Jamaica where only Le Cun, L'Espinasse, and Rochanson remained after the death of Provost. Had L'Espinasse also departed, the Church would have been much happier, for he was one of those characters whose perverse will constantly upsets harmonious order.

L'Abbé L'Espinasse

In August 1798, when all other priests followed the proper procedure and used Quigly's West Street Chapel for divine service, L'Espinasse refused to do so.[29] He set up a chapel of his own in a rented house without Quigly's consent and directly opposed to the pastor's wishes. In the following April of 1799, L'Espinasse was again the source of serious annoyance to Quigly. This time l'abbé cast an avaricious eye on the coffee trade, and persuaded a wealthy refugee, Charles de Parouty, to advance him a considerable sum of money which he invested in coffee.[30] Two other refugees were hired to manage the coffee estate while l'abbé personally directed the commercial end of the enterprise. Suddenly on 13 August 1799, the coffee business was concluded.[31] No reason for its demise was given, but we are allowed to infer from l'abbé's words that its termination was an act of sublime virtue on his part. He also stated that the enterprise was originally launched in the interest of two noble but indigent laymen whose names he did not divulge.

The Death of Quigly

To lay the foundation of the Church single-handed in a strange land, to placate diverse ethnic groups, to care for an influx of refugees, and to bear with an eccentric fellow priest, were the burdens which Quigly laid aside at a comparatively early age. Less than a year after the death of Provost, Quigly too was dead. Few details are recorded, nothing beyond the mere statement that he died at 6.00 o'clock in the evening at his residence, near the Spanish Chapel, on 17 September 1799 and was interred next day by the officiating priest William Le Cun, O.P.[32] L'Espinasse and Rochanson were present at his burial, together with two laymen, Patrick Peacan and Thomas Hinds, merchants of Kingston, as official witnesses to the interment. The sole biographical note given was that he was a professed religious of the order of Recollects in Ireland and about fifty-five years of age.[33]

To Quigly must be afforded the honour of being the founder of the resurrected Church in Jamaica. It is a story of growth, slow and almost imperceptible, the history of difficulties from within and obstacles from without, but at no time seriously impeded by open persecution.

Le Cun Takes Charge

Quigly was dead. Vicar Apostolic John Douglass lived in London, some four thousand miles away. The question arose as to who should assume charge of the mission. Le Cun, former prefect apostolic in Haiti, stepped into the void and took charge under an unusual faculty granted him by Pius VI, on 12 February 1797.[34] This faculty allowed Le Cun to administer the sacraments to the faithful in any place where there was no bishop or his representative in the person of a vicar or parish priest. On 20 September 1799, Le Cun announced to all the Catholics in Jamaica that by reason of a decree from the Holy See, he now had faculties to administer the sacraments.[35] In the same letter he granted faculties to l'Abbé L'Espinasse and placed him in charge of the West Street chapel for the interim; but Le Cun made it clear that the chapel was subject to his own authority. The pronouncement was read at Mass on two successive Sundays and affixed to the chapel door in French, Spanish, and English. On 26 September 1799, Le Cun informed Bishop Douglass in London of Quigly's death. Mail by sailing vessel took ten weeks from Jamaica to England, so it is not surprising that Douglass did not reply until 6 January 1800 when he said:

> I received your letter dated September 26, 1799, on the fourth of last month in which you announce the death of Fr. Quigly, Missionary Apostolic at Kingston, Jamaica. I have read your letter and approve all your actions. I consider it a piece of good fortune that you and so many other confessors of the faith were there when our Missionary died in Kingston, and you had the goodness to take charge of the spiritual welfare of the people, offering to God the Holy Sacrifice of the Mass, administering the sacraments and preaching the word of God, and (I am thankful for the ministry of Mr. L'Espinasse who can speak our language . . .) I pray you, Reverend Father, to accept our humble thanks and we on our part grant you faculties to continue to exercise [the ministry] in Jamaica for three years from the date of this letter. In that letter, the faculties which were given you by our Holy Father Pius VI, were born of extraordinary circumstances and subject to changes which circumstances might make necessary later.[36]

L'Espinasse was more the greedy business man than the zealous pastor. Not only did he have an interest in a coffee plantation, but he became a partner with M. Boulangerie in a bakery business, opened a wine shop next to the soldiers' barracks, and made a business trip to Central America. His pastorate on West Street offered a further opportunity of improving his finances from stipends and stole fees. In October 1799 l'abbé asked twelve gourdes for celebrating seven Masses, whereas the accepted stipend was seven gourdes.[37] Also in October he refused to bury a man unless twelve gourdes were offered him by Rose Delbois, the person responsible for the burial, and he made another demand of twelve gourdes from Madame Brisson before he would conduct a funeral. Every duty he was asked to perform added up to the magic number of twelve gourdes.[38]

The Baron and L'Abbé L'Espinasse

October 1799 was an ill-starred month for l'abbé. Stole and stipend fees were only part of his troubles. His hasty temper led him into a serious situation. The episode took place on 13 October.[39] On that Sunday, Baron De Verteuil attended Mass and benediction in L'Espinasse's West Street chapel and met l'abbé after the services. The documents offer no reason for the sudden outburst of temper on the part of the priest, but there must have been smouldering resentment occasioned by real or imagined injury. L'abbé fixed his eyes so menacingly on the baron that this gentleman declared that the whole world seemed to fall on him while at the same time l'abbé extended his hand in welcome, not to the baron, but to the man standing beside him, saying as he did: I am pleased to greet a gentleman, but in the other person [the baron] I do not see anything resembling a gentleman." L'abbé's eyes were still fixed menacingly on the embarrassed baron leaving the chapel.

A few days later, on 18 October, the baron appeared at l'abbé's residence with a letter in hand intended for the priest. The contents merely asked that justice be shown the baron and some amends be made for the insult on the previous Sunday. Not only did l'abbé refuse to accept the epistle but called the astonished baron a few choice unprintable names and ended the encounter by seizing a stout stick and bringing the full force of it down upon the baron's person and challenging him to a duel. If the bewildered nobleman thought his troubles ended with this latest insult, he was in error. An hour later the baron was more astonished to see two policemen, led by I'Espinasse, enter his house and announce that he was under arrest. The representatives of the law led the dumbfounded baron off to a magistrate to confine the unfortunate and highly sensitive Frenchman in the gaol.

The following day the baron was marched through the streets of Kingston to stand trial before a judge. Never before had this officer of the French Royal Navy been so shockingly humiliated. Fortunately, the baron had staunch friends to prove his innocence and to release him from the clutches of the law and l'abbé.

Le Cun Takes Action

With such an incident disturbing parishioners of the West Street chapel, Le Cun had to take action. What action was he to take? The only other priest beside l'abbé was Rochanson, not a desirable character because of alleged immorality in Haiti. This would preclude him from taking l'abbé's place. The diplomatic manoeuvre seemed to be to transfer the West Street chapel to another location where it and L'Espinasse would be under Le Cun's watchful eye.

Accordingly, on 9 November 1799 Le Cun notified all Catholics of Jamaica that he was removing the West Street chapel to a larger, more spacious building on High Holborn Street.[40] This building was also to be headquarters for the recently organized Charitable Bureau, a group of prominent French citizens formed to care for the many poor who had lost all in the Haitian upheaval.

To make this change Le Cun needed the sanction of the earl of Balcarres, the governor of Jamaica, and also the permission of the Custos of Kingston, the Honourable John Jaques. These sanctions were obtained 8 November 1799, and it was on Sunday, 17 November, that he hoped to conduct the first divine service at the new location. In a personal note to L'Espinasse on 19 November, before he had received a reply from Douglass, he wrote

> As I expressed to you previously that for reasons of religion, prudence and humanity, and with the approval of His Excellency, the Governor, and the Custos of Kingston, I have determined that on Sunday the 17th of this month, the Catholic Chapel will be located in the Great House on High Holborn Street. Secondly, I alone am charged with the exercise of the ministry, but it will be with your assistance, if it is agreeable to you and Fr. Rochanson, until it shall please the Vicar Apostolic of the London district to decree otherwise. . . . I hope and am convinced that you will approve of this plan . . . for the glory of God, the salvation of souls, the relief of the poor and the edification of the public.[41]

The following day, 10 November, L'Espinasse sent a protest to Le Cun, saying that the West Street Chapel should not be removed to High Holborn Street, arguing that the location of West Street had the approval of Governor Balcarres, and that it was the site selected by the late pastor, Anthony Quigly, who had been sent to Jamaica by Bishop Douglass of London. L'Espinasse carried his protest to the governor, who on 15 November 1799, reversed his decision and ordered the Spanish Chapel to remain on West Street.[42] But then, for some unknown reason, L'Espinasse, on his own authority, removed the West Street Chapel into a private house owned and occupied by some women, "good people, but a place less decorous than an edifice devoted exclusively to Divine worship."[43]

Early in 1800 Bishop Douglass received mutual recriminations from Le Cun and L'Espinasse. Douglass replied on 3 March 1800.

> These letters grieve me. At this distance of London from Jamaica, it is not easy to discern who is right, and who is wrong. . . . I desire, therefore, peace and harmony. . . . This dissention is from the devil who sees the great good you are doing among the faithful of Kingston. . . . Do not cooperate with his envy and malice but be long-suffering and by your patience with one another as becomes brothers in Jesus Christ, foster the public welfare. It is my desire and will that you continue to exercise the spiritual faculties which I granted in my letter of January 5th, and that Mons. L'Espinasse serve the public, especially the British subjects.[44]

The bishop's letter urging harmony between the antagonists did little to pacify the two clerics. L'abbé continued to cause trouble until Balcarres, weary of the contention, appointed Sir Henry Shirley, a member of the Assembly, well versed in French, to act as investigator and arbitrator in the dispute.

Shirley met with Count de Savilleon, protector of French immigrants, at the beginning of Holy Week in 1800, to discover a means of ending the differences. Both Le Cun and L'Espinasse were examined under oath.[45] Witnesses were called, and most of them favoured Le Cun. During the investigation, Le Cun suspected that Shirley was biased in favour of L'Espinasse. Independently of the commission, Le Cun sent two men from door to door securing the signatures of two hundred persons favouring his cause.[46] This independent petition was sent to Balcarres. On Wednesday of Holy Week, the governor ordered l'Espinasse to suspend services until he might make a definitive judgment in the case. Balcarres's mandatum was delivered to l'abbé at 8.00 o'clock on Wednesday evening. L'Espinasse reacted immediately by claiming that of the total two hundred signatures, only twenty were those of reputable persons, seven being names of infants, nine of children under eleven years of age, and others of mulatto women of questionable reputation.[47] He further represented to the Governor that a suspension of the mandatum during Holy Week would be welcomed by the Catholic community. These reasons won the benevolence of Lord Balcarres, who revoked the first command and allowed l'abbé to celebrate Mass on Holy Thursday.

L'Espinasse had a natural faculty for fomenting trouble. Instead of limiting his Holy Thursday sermon to an appropriate topic, he launched into a tirade against Le Cun.[48] He falsely alleged that Le Cun had been excommunicated for taking the civil oath on Haiti and all subsequent acts of his ministry were invalid.

Consternation spread through the French community; some concluded that all marriages performed by Le Cun were invalid and their children illegitimate.

Not only were the French parishioners disturbed; the Spaniards were also angry at the development of events under l'abbé, for he had removed their chapel to a private house, and was now falsely accusing Le Cun. Soon after Holy Week the Spaniards petitioned Balcarres for a separate chapel. Permission was granted on 18 April 1800, under the condition that a Spanish priest officiate in their chapel.[49]

At the beginning of the nineteenth century, priests were not readily available in the British West Indies, much less a Spanish priest. The congregation had to wait until the latter part of the year before inducing one to come to Jamaica. The name of Fr. Euservio de Naxeras appears for the first time in the Spanish Chapel records on 15 November 1800.[50] He seems to have remained there until 1802—his last entry is dated 19 April of that year. Two other priests assisted him for a short time: a German, Fr. H. J. Stocher, helped on the mission from 20 September 1801 until 1 March 1802; the other, Fr. Patrick Mulligan, remained but a few weeks. His first entry in the baptism register is dated 17 January 1802, and his last on 28 January 1802. Although he originally signed his name as Patrick Mulligan, priest of Ireland, he later became Patrick Mulligan Robinson, following the Spanish custom of writing names of both parents to show he was of legitimate birth.

Another Spaniard, Fr. Francisco Algarian, began to officiate on 17 February 1802, and was appointed pastor when de Naxeras left the island. Algarian remained until 19 May 1804, the longest of the itinerant priests to serve the Spanish chapel.

After the Holy Thursday incident there was only one course open to Le Cun: an appeal to Rome. He had a trusted friend in Luke Concannon, O.P., assistant to the superior general of the Order of Preachers. Le Cun had sought his advice when L'Espinasse began to give trouble in October 1799. In a letter dated 28 February 1800, Concannon informed Le Cun he was not surprised to learn that he was harassed by the emigré priest, for the greater number of them had given more trouble than edification in every place they had been called to work.[51] The letter also throws light on Bishop Douglass, for Concannon added that Douglass seemed to have been ill informed about these emigre's and favoured them unduly. He advised Le Cun that if he was thwarted in the exercise of his ministry by these priests, he should conduct himself with prudence and send his complaints to the Sacred Congregation of Propaganda.

Le Cun followed this advice after the Holy Thursday incident. In a deposition he gave all his charges against L'Espinasse, which he sent to Concannon, who received it 18 May 1800. Concannon forwarded it immediately to the Sacred Congregation of Propaganda. This body, with the sanction of Pius VII, pronounced the sentence of excommunication on l'Abbé L'Espinasse 7 December 1800.[52] A letter bearing the penalties was sent to Bishop Douglass by Cardinal Gerdill, Prefect of Propaganda, for it devolved upon Douglass to execute the sentence.[53] Douglass wrote to L'Espinasse informing him of his excommunication but l'abbé had a powerful friend in Lord Balcarres, who forbade its promulgation in Jamaica.

Douglass was at a loss on how to act in this tense situation. He wrote to Pius VII, explaining the impasse.

> When I received the letter of the Sacred Congregation, I wrote without delay to Rev. L'Espinasse and informed him of the sentence pronounced by their Eminences, advising him to submit humbly. But Lord Balcarres, a non-Catholic, Governor of the whole island and representative of the

> King, would not allow it and resisted the execution of the sentence of their Eminences. What, therefore, am I to do? I am not able to carry out the decree of their Eminences.[54]

When it became evident that Balcarres would not allow its publication, Le Cun had it printed in the French island of Martinique and distributed in Jamaica. A copy fell into the hands of Balcarres and infuriated him.[55] He advised L'Espinasse to send a copy to Douglass. The governor considered Le Cun's act most unjust. This was on 18 July 1801. A short time later, on 29 July, a new governor, George Nugent, replaced the Earl of Balcarres, whose five year term had expired.[56]

For three more years L'Espinasse continued to exercise his priestly functions. In 1804 Le Cun appealed to Nugent to end this disagreeable ecclesiastical situation. After studying the documents, Nugent wrote to L'Espinasse on 17 March 1804.

> It is the positive order of the Lt. Governor General Nugent, Governor and Commander-in-Chief of Jamaica, that you deliver up the Spanish chapel in Kingston to Rev. Padre Basilio Suarez DeLema, who has been chosen by the Spanish residents of Kingston, and you are hereby enjoined in the future not to exercise the holy functions of the priesthood in this island, in consequence of the excommunication passed upon you at Rome by their Excellencies the Cardinals in Conclave, and approved by His Holiness the Pope, Pius VII, dated at Rome 7 December 1800.[57]

Despite this order, l'abbé did continue to function as a priest until the end of the month. His last entry recorded in the church register is on 31 March 1804.[58] Shortly afterwards he departed from Jamaica for the predominantly French city of New Orleans, U.S.A. A letter of Bishop John Carroll of Baltimore, dated 17 November 1806, mentions a Fr. Espinasse who wanted to function as a priest in that city.[59] Carroll added that he knew nothing of his antecedents. At this point l'abbé became an obscure figure in history.

Fr. Basilo Suarez de Lema

The Spaniards rejoiced that they had, at last, found a zealous pastor in Basilio DeLema, Knight of the Inquisition. His records for the first two years indicate faithfulness to his trust for during this time he conducted funeral services for 204 persons and his books were kept in orderly fashion.[60] There was no indication why, in 1807, he should be detained in the public gaol by the civil authorities. Le Cun offered no reason for DeLema's detention, merely calling him the "condemned priest." Not only did he run foul of the civil law but he carried off the sacred vessels, altar ornaments, registers, and all church property committed to his care. He further expressed a determination to sell the chapel.

On 23 May 1807, Le Cun wrote to Colonel Walshe, secretary to Sir Eyrie Coote, lieutenant governor, requesting that steps be taken to recover Church property from DeLema. Governor Coote took a personal interest in the affair and on 27 May, in the presence of Le Cun, ordered DeLema to deliver up the Spanish chapel on West Street with all its appointments to the rightful owner.[61]

Le Cun Removes to Hanover Street

Why Le Cun gave up his residence and chapel on High Holborn Street and removed it to a place called Harmony Hall on Hanover Street is not known, but his new chapel-residence had the advantage of being more centrally located in a rapidly expanding city whose Catholic population was growing proportionally. Both the residence on High Holborn Street, called Jasper Hall, and the one on Hanover Street, named Harmony Hall Gardens, were two of Kingston's most spacious residences. The Harmony Hall chapel served Catholics of all nationalities when the Spanish chapel was closed after DeLema departed from Jamaica at the request of his majesty's government.

While Le Cun still occupied Harmony Hall, it was sold, and he was given notice to vacate. This posed a problem, where a place, suitable and spacious, could be found to house both chapel and residence. After exhausting all possibilities, Le Cun had no alternative save to return to the old Spanish Chapel on West Street. He wrote to the government for permission to reopen this chapel on 19 June 1807, stating that Harmony Hall had been sold and there was need for a place of worship for the Catholics of Kingston.[62] On 27 June Colonel Walshe replied that Governor Sir Eyrie Coote was unwilling to grant permission unless Le Cun first secured the sanction of the Kingston magistrates.[63] Evidently he was unable to obtain this sanction. All sacred vessels and church ornaments were removed from West Street to the Hanover Street chapel and an inventory attested to by Constable David de Castro on 2 July 1807, thus bringing to a close the chapel where Quigly resurrected the Church in Jamaica.[64]

Last Days of Fr. Le Cun, O.P.

Ecclesiastical affairs were reduced to an extremity when, early in October 1807, Le Cun fell seriously ill. On 10 October he realized he would not survive. He made his will, sealed it, and gave instructions that it was to be opened immediately after his death. His long missionary career was drawing to a close. Born in the parish of Fridarezec, near the town of Freguier in the province of Lower Brittany, he had entered the Order of Preachers and had gone out to Haiti where he was appointed superior of the mission and later prefect apostolic. In 1798 he was forced to flee to Jamaica. During his last illness he manifested deep religious sentiments. His one regret was that in all Jamaica there could not be found another priest to administer to him the last sacraments. He died in his room, near the Catholic chapel on Hanover Street, at 8.00 o'clock in the evening, Friday 15 October 1807.[65] His will, when opened by his executors, stated expressly that at his funeral no minister whatsoever except a Catholic priest was to officiate. Since there was no priest in all Jamaica, his body was to be clothed in sacred vestments and laid out at the foot of the altar until 2.00 o'clock in the afternoon, when the congregation was to recite the prayers for the dead. His last wishes were faithfully carried out by the parishioners. On the following day, 16 October, they bore his body to the cemetery of the city of Kingston and laid it to rest.

Twelve

Early Nineteenth Century

Le Cun's death left the Catholics without a priest, even among the prisoners of war, but the heroic work of Quigly and Le Cun, on the verge of collapse, was saved by Carlos Esteiro, a native of Galacia and prominent merchant who had interested himself in every phase of the Church's struggle to maintain a foothold in Jamaica. In the present crisis he did not sit idly by and allow the work of fifteen years to perish. Since no instructions had been left by Le Cun to contact Douglass in London, neither Esteiro nor anyone else knew where to turn for a priest. Fortunately Esteiro had a good friend in Vera Cruz, Mexico, to whom he appealed that the Church might not again become a historic memory.

Fr. Juan Jacinto Rodriguez de Araujo

In the city of Vera Cruz, Juan Jacinto Rodriguez de Araujo, an Augustinian friar, performed his daily duties with a routine born of peace and contentment in the service of God.[1] Few extraordinary events disturbed the even tenor of his life until he received from Don Carlos Esteiro the letter telling of Le Cun's death and the dire distress of the Church in this British island. There was no priest to administer the sacraments. Would Araujo come to this priestless country? It would mean living in a foreign land; language, customs and people would be different from any he had known; he would cut himself off from the pleasant companionship of his fellow Augustinians; he would be alone without even an assistant. He made his decision. In the month of April 1808, Araujo sailed into the harbour of Kingston to begin his long missionary career.[2] He observed that on the shore rose no familiar steeple with its cross to mark the Church he would serve. He was now in a land which, if not openly inimical to his faith, at least regarded it with cool aloofness, as the religion of a small minority, incompatible with the current English way of life.

Kingston, 1808–16

The Kingston of Araujo's day was rapidly becoming the island's political, cultural, and commercial centre. By reason of its magnificent harbour, seven miles long, and its sweeping Liguanea plain, it was quickly surpassing the capital, Spanish Town, in importance. Kingston boasted a population of 30,000, half of whom were slaves.[3] When Araujo had time to assess his own congregation, he estimated it to be nine hundred, the largest ethnic group being the French, numbering about six hundred.[4] This was exclusive of the 1,452 Catholic slaves, mostly owned by the French, whom they had brought from Haiti. These French refugees were a source of concern to the Jamaican government;[5] many were without means of support and were thrown on the mercy of public welfare. Again, some of their slaves were infected with revolutionary ideas, a dangerous contagion to the Jamaican negro population.

The presence of refugees and the suspected subversive element among their slaves was the immediate cause of Kingston being raised to the status of a city, just six years before Araujo arrived. Under the governmental form of vestrymen and justices, the Town of Kingston did not possess sufficient legal and judiciary powers demanded by the circumstances.[6] In February 1801, the vestrymen and justices petitioned the House of Assembly to create a corporation so that there might be a body with power to preserve law and order, a body demanded by the new circumstances facing Kingston. The Act was passed and ratified in 1802, substituting for vestrymen a mayor, aldermen, and a commonalty of the City and Parish of Kingston. The newly created city was granted a seal, and the freeholders were "ordained, constituted and declared to be one body corporate and politic."[7]

Kingston boasted of three thousand houses built upon a gradually rising ground which began at the land reclaimed from the swamps near the sea, and reached its highest level in St. Andrew.[8] Residences were constructed of brick and mortar, one or two storeys high, having ample porches running around the buildings to relieve the burden of the unwelcome tropical sun. Among all these buildings, Araujo looked in vain for a Catholic Church. An Anglican, a Presbyterian, a Jewish synagogue he might see, but not a cross-topped spire of his own faith. This defect would be remedied immediately.

Don Carlos Esteiro, the zealous Spanish merchant, had anticipated Araujo's wish. Before the missionary arrived, through a generous donation from his own pocket, he had purchased a site on the northwest corner of Duke and Sutton Street in the very heart of the city, equidistant from the old West Street Chapel and the later French chapel on Hanover Street.[9] In selecting the site Don Carlos had in mind the union of all Catholics in one place of worship whether French, Spanish, English, Dutch, or Irish. This new location, he thought, would have the psychological effect of introducing harmony into the Catholic community. Construction began in 1810 and was completed one year later in 1811.[10] At first it was a modest brick structure. Partially destroyed by fire in 1843,[11] it was rebuilt and enlarged in 1844, renovated and lengthened in 1858 at the cost of £2,000.[12] It accommodated two thousand people and was one of the finest churches in Jamaica. And so it remained until the devastating earthquake of 1907 reduced it to rubble and stark walls.

The great work of the Holy Trinity completed, Araujo employed his talents in welding the Kingston congregation into a harmonious unity which hitherto it had not enjoyed. He did this chiefly by setting an example of devotion to duty. Araujo's unspectacular daily routine, pursued over a period of sixteen years, from 1808–24, was a powerful influence among the diverse ethnic groups which comprised his congregation. Twelve of these sixteen years were spent as the only priest in Jamaica. His carefully kept records, both in French and Spanish, show that he performed 1,157 baptisms, including 46 baptisms of slaves and conducted the funerals of 700 parishioners.[13]

Among Araujo's baptisms there is one of note. It is unusual to find in his records the name of an American among the predominantly French and Spanish names, but there is one, a medical doctor, Franklin Litchfield, twenty-six years old, a native of Carlisle, Massachusetts, U.S.A.[14] He was the son of Reverend Paul Litchfield and his wife Mary Bailie Litchfield, natives of Situate, Massachusetts, U.S.A.[15] Paul Litchfield was born in Situate on 12 March 1752, the eldest of a family of twelve children.[16] He was graduated from Harvard College in 1775.[17] Leaving Harvard, he taught in the Latin School of Situate and later studied theology under Dr. Stephen West of Stockbridge, Massachusetts. On 7 November 1781 he was ordained first pastor of the church in Carlisle which had been opened the previous February.[18] For forty-six years he held this pastorate, until he died on 7 November 1827.[19]

Franklin Litchfield was of solid Yankee ancestry.[20] He was born in Carlisle, on 18 August 1790, and was graduated from Harvard College in 1810. After his college course, he studied medicine under the renowned Dr. David Ramsay in Charleston, South Carolina. Migrating to the West Indies, he practiced medicine with marked success in Kingston, the most populous city of the British West Indies. While in

Kingston he met the daughter of a prominent Venezuelan family, Maria de Jesús Gracia de Lena. Maria was a resident of Kingston, the daughter of the late Ramón Gracia de Lena, a native of Mostoles in the Spanish Peninsula, and the late Manuela Loretto de Silva y Lena, a native of Caracas.

On 28 June 1816 Araujo received Franklin Litchfield into the Church.[21] On 4 July 1816 he married Maria de Lena in Kingston.[22] Araujo also baptized their first child, Maria Carolina Litchfield, 23 April 1817. Dr. and Mrs. Litchfield migrated to Porto Cabello, Venezuela, where President Monroe appointed Dr. Litchfield United States consul on 22 December 1823. There he died in 1844.[23]

If Araujo had experienced joy in receiving Dr. Litchfield into the Church, he had been saddened by the loss of Don Carlos Esteiro, who died on 22 February 1814, at 7.00 o'clock in the morning after receiving the last sacraments.[24] He was buried near the main altar of Holy Trinity Church in respect for having been its founder and principal benefactor.

The Days of Slavery

There was one sight which Araujo could not fail to observe in the Jamaica of his day, the vast number of negro slaves. Upon the shoulders, hands, and feet of some 323,827 human beings labouring in servitude on plantations in every corner of the island, rested the whole economy.[25]

Sugar and slavery were linked as interchangeable terms in the minds of West Indian planters. Without slavery, it was thought, there could be no sugar, and sugar was the most profitable product of the Indies.[26] In order to retain the rich cane lands stretching in an arc from Trinidad to Florida crowned heads of Europe fought fierce naval engagements. Indigo, tobacco, coffee, and cocoa were other products, but the greatest was sugar, which required the labour of many hands, labour as cheap as one could get, preferably the labour of slaves. This demand for slave labour was met by the none too tender consciences of merchants of Bristol, England.

An interesting question about any race is where did it come from? Where was its geographical centre of migration? How did it arrive at its present terminus? What means of transportation? African slaves had been introduced into Jamaica during Spanish days, but in limited numbers. With the advent of the British and because sugar needed cheap labour, thousands of slaves were transported to Jamaica from Africa every year. Some years the number ran as high as ten thousand; an all-time high of 18,448 occurred in 1774.[27] The social and geographical background of these people is important, for upon them would the Church in Jamaica be built eventually when they surpassed the French, Spanish, and English in the number of Catholics. They would bring to the Church their native characteristics which would lend a distinct flavour to their Christianity. Indeed, because Spanish, French, British, and American missionaries failed to recognize the African characteristics inherent in the modern Jamaican, the Church has made such painful progress. Instead, a European or American-oriented culture had been the goal consciously or unconsciously set by the missionaries.

Voyage to West Indies

These Africans were a people who were forced into this western geographical setting and into work for which they had no taste. Bought, bartered for, or stolen, they were shipped in wretched vessels to the West Indies. One of the most profitable ways of securing slaves was to make a raid and carry off as many as possible to a waiting ship. Such a raid is recorded in the Vice-Admiralty Court. In 1792 the slave ship *Hero* carried out a raid on a fort at the mouth of the Benin River on the Slave Coast of Africa. In the dead of night, the crew set the fort on fire and captured the surprised villagers running to escape the flames. By six o'clock the next morning, the raiders had returned to their waiting ship, driving their captives into a trans-Atlantic prison. One of these captives proved to be the daughter of the king of Benin River.

Thrown onto shelves built between decks, the unfortunate captives were shackled no more than three feet apart to preclude escape. Necessity rather than human compassion required that the slaves be brought on deck periodically and their foul quarters be washed with highly saline seawater. Often the captain of the ship was forced to suffer pecuniary loss by forcing slaves overboard, however unwilling they might be, to leave the ship, when it became obvious that rapacious pirates would overtake the heavily laden slaver.

Unpalatable salt beef, hardtack, and fetid water caused many to die on this middle passage. Six, eight, or even ten weeks of this misery and the unwilling passengers were glad to see the Blue Mountains of Jamaica. Where they would spend their lives in Jamaica they did not know, until they were sold on the block at the Borden or Harbour Street mart, and from there they could look forward to a lifetime of servitude on the plantations.

Work on Plantations

Once purchased by a planter at the current price of £45[28] and transported to his plantation, no time was lost assigning the new slave to his work. A conch shell blown at dawn was the signal that time for sleep had ended and that work was to begin. Marched into the field in a gang of sixty, he worked all day, with the exception of a two-hour rest at noon, under the watchful care of whip and overseer.

Crop time was most trying. In shifts he worked round the clock, seven days a week: in the field cutting cane, in the mill yard crushing cane, in the mill house filling the huge coppers. Slaves continuously fed the fire of the boiling house, watched the sugar crystalize in the curing house, filled the great wooden casks with sugar and the puncheons with rum for transportation to the plantation wharf where a barquardier waited impatiently to sail to England.

Runaway Slaves

This pointless life of the slaves tempted some to run away. Old estate journals record many such an incident.

> Mercury getting tired of the excessive labour of the crop, takes council with March and Mark, and they, followed by Mackrie, are away to the hills and rocks. The others soon tire of this illicit freedom and return home, but when Mercury, the incorrigible, is brought home in the second week of January 1821, he, after a few days in confinement is, on January 15th, sent to Montego Bay gaol. On the 29th of the same month his name appears for the last time on the Journal—Mercury died in Montego Bay gaol.[29]

Long and arduous labour in the cane fields called for substantial diet and plenty of it. Each slave was allowed a small plot of land on which to raise his own vegetables. For the most part this diet was vegetarian. Meat and fish were supplied by the planter, but as one author observes: "Any taste they might have for butcher's meat was diligently discouraged."[30] The favoured one was the house slave, dedicated to the domestic work of the master's Great House. Chosen because of their intelligence, these slaves performed the duties of cook, butler, maid, governess, and did general domestic work.

Never-ending toil was the sum total of the slave's life, yet there were bright spots when the sun shone through the dark clouds and made life a little more liveable. Christmas, New Year, and Easter holidays were a joy to conjure when the monotony of cane cutting seemed unbearable. Or one could look forward to Sunday market where slaves from the neighbouring estates met to sell their produce, or when daily work had ended and one might sit before the hut and tell stories of old Africa and sing in beautiful harmony under a smiling tropical moon.

These were the people Araujo met in Jamaica; everywhere he saw them, for they comprised the vast majority of the population. It would be a herculean task to give them even a veneer-thin knowledge of Christianity. Araujo did learn, however, that they had a vivid sense of the supernatural which they had transported from Africa. Unfortunately, it took the form of superstition.

The Kormantine Negro

The slaves most favoured for the Jamaican plantation were shipped from the Dutch fort Kormantine (Cormantyne) on the Gold Coast (Ghana). They possessed great physical courage and intolerance of subservience, traits which led to several serious rebellions. Because their superb physiques rendered them capable of hard work, they were preferred to the milder African tribesmen, despite their recalcitrant natures. The Kormantines maintained a commanding influence over the other negroes and imposed their own peculiar superstitions and religious practices upon them. These practices would offer Araujo a further obstacle to their conversion.

Religious Beliefs and Practices

One authority is convinced that the African negro held a firm belief in a Supreme Being that was not derived from Christianity nor from Islam.[31] But in addition to the Supreme Being, he also believed in a multiplicity of gods. "Every Ashanti temple is a pantheon in which repose the shrines of gods, but the power or spirit that on occasions enters into these shrines is directly or indirectly derived from the one God of the sky, whose intermediaries they are."[32]

Obeah

Worship of a multiplicity of lesser gods leads to superstition. Among the African superstitions the practice of Obeah is associated with the Ashanti negro. Its function is to injure or harm an enemy. Since it is a common frailty of man to make enemies, this superstition rested on the instinct of man to preserve his honour by revenge for wrongs, real or imaginary. Hence Obeah had an appeal to these primitive peoples and entered into every phase of their lives. Obeah was the superstition the Ashanti carried with him to the West Indies, and leaders of this cult became powerful agents of evil on the Jamaican plantation.

The most potent factor in Obeah is fear, striking terror into its victim. It could reduce the powerful physique of the plantation negro to a prostrate inert form, causing death in many instances. The Jamaican government recognized the evil potency of Obeah. "Considering the multitude of occasions which may provide the Negroes to exercise the power of Obi (Obeah) against one another, and the astonishing influence of this superstition upon their minds, we cannot but attribute a very considerable part of the annual mortality among the Negroes of Jamaica to this fascinating mischief."[33]

A government observer was convinced that the original professors of Obeah had brought this pseudoscience to Jamaica, for throughout the island Obeah was so universally practiced that few of the larger estates were without one or more of the practitioners. The oldest and most crafty were the Obeah men who attracted the greatest devotion and confidence of the natives, those of hoary head, and in aspect peculiarly harsh and diabolical, who possessed skill in medicinal and poisonous plants qualified for successful imposition upon the credulous. Negroes whether Africans or Creoles revered, consulted, and abhorred them. A government report spelled out in detail the method and activity of these Obeah men.

> To these oracles they [negroes] resort and with implicit faith upon all occasions, whether for cure of disorders, the obtaining of revenge for injuries or insults, the conciliating of favour, the discovery and punishment of the thief or the adulterer and the predicting of future events.
>
> The trade which these wretches carry on is extremely lucrative. They manufacture and sell Obies adapted to different cases and at different prices. A veil of mystery is studiously thrown over their incantations, to which the midnight hours are allotted, and every precaution is taken to conceal them from the knowledge and discovery of white people. The deluded negroes, who thoroughly believe in their supernatural power, become the willing accomplices in this concealment, and the stoutest among them then tremble at the very sight of the ragged bundle, the bottle, or the eggshells which are stuck to the thatch or hung over the door of the hut or upon the branch of the plantain tree to deter marauders.
>
> In the case of poison, the natural effects of it are by the ignorant negroes ascribed entirely to the potent working of Obi (Obeah).[34]

It was difficult for the white proprietor to discover these Obeah men, for no one would reveal them through dread of incurring revenge which the Obeah man fulminated against the person who would dare betray him. There was no way of distinguishing the Obeah man from any other negro slave on his plantation, but the effect was electrifying.

> They no sooner find Obi set for them near the door of their homes or in the path which leads to it, than they give themselves up for lost. When a

> negro is robbed of a fowl or a hog, he applies directly to the Obeah man. It is then made known among his fellow blacks that Obi is set for the thief. As soon as the latter hears the dreadful news, his terrified imagination begins to work. No recourse is left but the superior skill of some more eminent Obeah man of the neighbourhood who may counteract the magical operation of the other. But if none can be found of higher rank and ability, or if after gaining such an ally he should fancy himself affected, he presently falls into a decline, under the incessant horror of impending calamities. The slightest painful sensation in the head, or in any other part of the body confirms his apprehensions, and he believes himself the victim of an invisible and irresistible agency. Sleep, appetite, and cheerfulness forsake him, his strength decays, his disturbed imagination is haunted without respite, his features wear the settled gloom of despondency . . . he contracts a morbid habit of body and gradually sinks into the grave.[35]

Such mischievous superstition would have had a disruptive effect upon the whole community unless proscribed by law. Severe punishments were enacted against those found guilty of its practice. Though it continued surreptitiously, civil law was always on the alert to strike a blow whenever it raised its head.

Why the Vast Majority of Jamaicans are Protestants

Araujo found that superstition was one deterrent for the negro coming into the Church; another was the fact that the vast majority had already made their choice of Christianity in one of the Protestant bodies long before Araujo arrived in the island, so that he found them Anglican, Baptist, Methodist, Moravian, and Presbyterian, but not Catholic. Political and religious conditions explain why so many slaves became Protestants. At the dawn of British Jamaican history, the Catholic Church and its clergy was practically nonexistent, since only clergy of Protestant denominations were allowed to function. It is very early in British-Jamaican history we find the first reference to Protestant clergy in the Statistical papers of the Acts of the Assembly dated 1 October 1664. There had been seven civil parishes established by this time.

> In these parishes there are now five ministers: *videlicet,* Mr. Webb and Mr. John an old army preacher not yet in orders, and Mr. Maxwell left by Sir Charles, and Mr. Houser and Mr. Sellers two Germans brought hither by the lieutenant-general; one Mr. Nicholas a passenger on the Westgate was well settled at Port Morant but died of the disease that many of the ship perished in.[36]

The Anglican clergy, intimately associated with the planter class, considered the instruction of slaves not within the orbit of their parish duties and in order to discourage any planter who might wish his slaves baptized, the stole fee was set at £3.4.0.[37] This attitude persisted for generations until the many conversions made by the non-Conformists awakened them to the realization that if they did not work among this depressed class, the whole slave population would be Moravian, Baptist, Methodist, or Presbyterian, and the Established Church would be left with the small minority of planters and British officials.

Efforts of the Non-Conformists: The Moravians

Foremost among the non-Conformists to make systematic efforts to convert the slaves were the Moravians. On 9 December 1754 three ministers, Zacharias G. Caries, Gottlieb Haberecht, and Thomas Shallcross came from England to work on four plantations in the civil parish of St. Elizabeth.[38] These plantations were owned by William Foster and Joseph Foster Barham, who had become Moravians. But the Moravian ministers ran into a snag. The overseers of these estates were reluctant to allow the slaves time from their work to be catechized. The ministers were forced to give what little instruction they could going from hut to hut, endeavouring to give them some limited knowledge of Christ while the slaves were preparing their evening meal. Owners Foster and Barham righted this inconvenience by despatching a Moravian from England to act as attorney for their Jamaican estates. Under more favourable conditions these ministers soon had five preaching stations on the Foster and Barham estates, in addition to offering instruction on neighbouring plantations. In the first year they baptized twenty-six slaves.[39] In the second year they baptized more than seventy-seven and had some four hundred under instruction.

The Baptists

The Baptists came next in order of time. George Liele and Moses Baker had immigrated to Jamaica from Virginia during the American Revolutionary War, for like many loyalists they found it unwise to remain in the United States.[40] Both were negroes. Liele had been granted his freedom from his master who was a deacon in the Baptist Church of Virginia.[41] Immediately upon arrival in Jamaica, Liele began to preach at the Race Course, Kingston.[42] It was so novel that it attracted hundreds of listeners. Removing his open-air pulpit from the Race Course to a shed on Windward Road, he ran afoul of the law, was charged with inciting slaves to rebellion, tried on this charge and acquitted. But the opposition would find a way to stop him. They did it on the lesser charge of failure to pay the debt on his chapel; but they had not reckoned with generous friends who paid off the debt and released Liele from gaol.[43] Moses Baker was baptized by Liele in 1787.[44] In the following year he was appointed religious instructor to the slaves on an estate in St. James owned by Isaac Winn, a Quaker.[45] From this point Baker projected the work of Liele throughout the western end of Jamaica.

Although Liele inaugurated the Baptist mission, Thomas Burchell and William Knibb, English missionaries, put system into the work.[46] On 23 February 1814 the second founding of the Baptist mission began.[47] The churches were subdivided into classes with a negro leader appointed over them. These leaders were expected to become personally acquainted with each member of the class and to visit them as often as possible. They also reported from time to time to the minister on the conduct of both members and catechumens. This personal contact with a member of their own race placed the Baptist mission on a solid foundation. In the course of time, these same leaders were allowed to hold services among their own people; gradually the erection of what were called Class-Houses became common in every negro village. So effective was the Knibb-Burchell system that the number of Baptists increased from year to year. In 1827 there were eight Baptist churches with 5,246 members.[48] In 1831 the churches had increased to twenty-four, presided over by fourteen ministers with a total of 10,838 members.[49]

The Wesleyan-Methodists

Wesleyan Methodist missionary work was begun by Dr. Thomas Coke on 19 January 1789, when he began preaching in a private house in Hannah Town, Kingston, until the more spacious quarters of a concert hall in the centre of the city was offered him.[50] It was not without violent opposition that he held services at this new location. Despite this obstruction, Coke continued to preach with some two hundred slaves attending. When Coke left Jamaica, he appointed Mr. William Hammett in his place. As long as Hammett confined his services to a rented house in Hannah Town, he was not molested.[51] But once he purchased a large dwelling on the East Parade, Kingston, trouble began. A mob tore down the gate and would have destroyed the chapel but for the timely arrival of the town guard.[52]

Non-Conformists Under Suspicion

The principal opposition came from the Assembly, which forbade the gathering of slaves in any meeting place after dark, a precaution against an uprising. Continued opposition in Kingston forced Hammett to accept an invitation from estates in the country to preach to their slaves. Within a few years the Wesleyans had established missions as far east as the civil parish of St. Thomas. Here again they met with hostility in the person of the custos, Simon Taylor, through whose influence the Assembly passed an act to prevent preaching by any person not duly qualified by law. Baptists and Wesleyans were looked upon with suspicion by the Jamaican government, which lived in dread of slave uprisings. Any catalytic agent which might set off a chain reaction to cause a revolution was an enemy of the commonwealth. One authority writing on this point has this to say of both missionaries and the Jamaican Assembly:

> Neither side of the controversy even suspected the real root of the difficulty. The Methodist missionaries felt that they were victims of the rankest bigotry and cried aloud in protest. If they only realized that they were offering themselves as martyrs to revivify and extend absolute paganism with a veneer of Christianity in the resuscitated Myalism that was parading as Revivalism, they might have been less outspoken in their denunciation of the Assembly. If the Planters, on the other hand, who honestly recognized the unrest caused by the activities of the Methodists among the slaves, the significant forerunners of serious disturbances, if they had only been able to really analyse the situation and distinguished between strong Myalistic tendencies and the Methodist emotional susceptibilities, they might have been able to direct the latter influence into less dangerous channels and have opened the eyes of its proponents to what was actually afoot. But each side of the controversy was deaf to the arguments of the other, just as they were blind to the real nature of the terrible forces of harm that were accumulating among the mass of the blacks.[53]

Uprising of Slaves

The much anticipated uprising broke out on the night of 28 December 1831, when some fifty thousand negroes on the northwest end of the island, under the leadership of a highly intelligent slave, Samuel Sharpe, a prominent member of the Baptist Church, exploded in open revolt.[54] Ten white men and more than four hundred slaves were killed in the fighting. After regular army troops crushed the revolt, one hundred negroes, including their leader, Sharpe, were executed. The House of Assembly assessing the cause of the uprising, placed the blame partly on the shoulders of the non-Conformists. The Report of 1832 read in part: "And lastly . . . the preaching of the religious sects called Baptists, Wesleyan-Methodists and Moravians (but particularly the sect termed Baptists), which had the effect of producing in the minds of the slaves a belief that they could not serve both a spiritual and temporal master. . . .[55] Wherever the blame for this unpleasant situation is to be placed, the significant fact is that the vast majority of the descendants of the slaves are today members of the non-Conformist churches. How can we explain this except that their ministers, first to instruct these pagan animists, fought and suffered for these negroes. Naturally the slaves, seeing the interest these missionaries had in their amelioration, eagerly accepted their doctrine.

Feeble Efforts of Church to Convert Slaves

While the non-Conformists were converting thousands of plantation slaves, the lone Catholic priest, Araujo, looked on with a sense of helplessness. Evangelizing the plantation was not possible since Araujo could not leave Kingston for long periods at this crucial moment in history, when the faithful needed his constant, watchful attention. Neither England nor the United States could be expected to supply priests when priests were very limited in numbers in both countries. The best Araujo could do was to struggle single-handed and accomplish what he could under the circumstance, merely striving to keep the faith alive. Araujo did not entirely neglect the slaves, but conversions were restricted to those owned by Catholic masters. For the most part these owners were French or Spanish, but occasionally we find an Englishman like James Harley, who had Araujo baptize sixteen slaves.[56]

The first reported Catholic baptism of slaves was in 1795.[57] The last was in 1 August 1834. During this thirty-nine year period, 230 slaves were baptized in Kingston. This is a small number, but it does indicate that the Church was interested in the spiritual welfare of the slaves despite the trying circumstances under which she was functioning in the early nineteenth century. When on 1 August 1836 311,075 negroes emerged from the status of apprenticeship to that of free men, they were Anglicans, Moravians, Wesleyan-Methodists, Baptists, and Presbyterians, and a handful of Catholics. The stubborn fact remains, however, that the Church did not take advantage of this important social epoch, no matter what may be the reason or excuse.

Fr. Araujo Gains an Assistant

For sixteen years this was the socio-religious panorama constantly presenting itself to Araujo's mind. For twelve of these years he was helplessly alone, without the companionship of a fellow missionary until political disturbances in South America drove three priests to seek asylum in the more nationally stable Jamaica. Fr. Bathelemy

Jacinthe Souza, fleeing from South America, became Araujo's assistant.[58] His first entry in the Kingston records is on 10 June 1820, and his last on 13 July 1822. After two years in Jamaica he departed for a country which had a more Spanish atmosphere. Another was Dr. Don Miguel Marco de Yarza, canon of the Cathedral of Santa Marta, Colombia.[59] His only record is dated 28 October 1821. He too left Jamaica shortly after his arrival. The third priest, Benito Fernandez, became one of the greatest missionaries Jamaica has ever known. He saw the need for priests in the island and, gifted with perseverance, settled down to a long career of thirty-five years.

Fr. Benito Fernandez

A revolution in New Granada, Colombia, South America, was the fortuitous occasion of bringing to Jamaica the one who would prove himself a missionary giant.

Benito Fernandez was born on 10 January 1782, in the diocese of Calahorra, Castile, Spain. When he was thirteen years old, his parents emigrated to Bogotá, New Grenada. After he finished college, Benito entered the Friars Minor, and steeled himself to spend the rest of his days in the more or less uneventful work-a-day duties of a Franciscan friar. After ordination he exercised the ministerial duties with such zealous success that he was appointed superior of a house of his order.

While he was devoting his energies to this office, a revolution broke out which would change the whole course of his life. Insurgents in New Granada wished to separate from the mother country, Spain, and form an independent republic. Fernandez was of the party which stood loyally by Spain. A successful coup by the revolutionaries spelled disaster for the royalists. Benito was thrown into prison and calmly awaited execution before the firing squad on an early Colombian morning.

The sequence had the ring of a movie thriller. On the eve of his scheduled execution, the royal Spanish fleet sailed into the harbour of Cartagena, drove out the insurgents, and freed all political prisoners. Having escaped execution on one occasion, Benito saw that, should he remain in New Granada, he would again be in danger as soon as the fleet sailed and the insurgents regained control of the country. Cuba looked inviting, for there he might exercise his priestly office under more peaceful conditions, so to Cuba he sailed. En route he stopped off at Kingston for two months. Once in Cuba, Fernandez gave serious thought to the paucity of priests in Jamaica. In Cuba he would be of some help to the Church, while in Jamaica he would be a necessity. With these thoughts in mind, Benito sailed back to Jamaica, never to leave it. From 1821–24 he was the devoted co-worker of Araujo; they were the only two priests in the island.

Araujo had done a yeoman's job. He was afflicted with that failing common to the human race, old age. Sixteen years he had laboured, building up the Church in a country which was foreign to him. Thoughts of his native land beckoned him home.

On 14 April 1824[60] Araujo performed his last baptism, that of Augustine Tayla.[61] He then entrusted the Church into the competent hands of Benito Fernandez and sailed for his native Lisbon, where he died in 1839.[62]

Thirteen

Eve of Emancipation

If Benito Fernandez had ever experienced the loneliness of an exile, it was the day he bade good-bye to Araujo, watched the four-master sail labouriously out of Kingston harbour, then returned to his rectory at 74 King Street to muse over the current position of the Church in Jamaica. He was now in the same circumstances that his predecessor had been in for a dozen years. The whole spiritual welfare of the faithful rested squarely on his shoulders alone. His first task was to reconcile those ill disposed towards him, for Kingston's polyglot parish had strong likes and dislikes. By tactful prudence he succeeded in bringing a large percentage of the parishioners to the regular practice of their religious duties.

A further consideration had to be given to the stability of their pastor. The ecclesiastical situation demanded the habitual and continued service of a priest who could not be removed at a moment's notice. Since Fernandez, as a member of a religious order, was under obedience to his superiors who could determine where he should labour and for how long, there was danger he might remain in Jamaica for only a short time. This would disrupt the Church once more, and again leave Catholics without the services of a priest. For a religious this was no easy decision to make. Benito decided to petition the Holy See to release him from his vows as a Franciscan that he might become a secular priest to remain the rest of his days in this faltering mission. The document granting Benito his release was signed at Rome by Carlo Cardinal Odescalchi on August 28, 1828.[1]

A New Vicar Apostolic for the British West Indies

It is not uncommon to learn from the daily press, prior to official notice, that a change had taken place in ecclesiastical circles. This was Fernandez's experience when one day after breakfast he read the *Morning Journal* and learned that a new vicar apostolic had been appointed for the British West Indies, Bishop Daniel MacDonnell. With diplomatic courtesy, Fernandez addressed a letter of welcome to MacDonnell on 7 September 1829, congratulating him upon his safe arrival in Port of Spain, Trinidad, and offering obedience to his Lordship vested with the title of vicar apostolic for the Antilles.

In a few lines Fernandez acquainted MacDonnell with conditions prevailing in Kingston: Catholics had only one Church, erected at the expense of Don Carlos Esteiro and the zeal of Juan Rodriguez de Araujo, O.S.A. Araujo was its first pastor, who upon departing Jamaica had left Holy Trinity in charge of Fernandez by a faculty granted him in 1823 by Bishop James Buckley, MacDonnell's predecessor.[2] The congregation consisted of Spaniards, French, Dutch, some Italians, and about twelve Irish. The letter ended with these words:

> We are endeavouring to do all we can for the advancement of religion, conformable to the rites of the Church, and in keeping with the few means afforded by the conditions of the country and the fervour of the parishioners. We have just finished work on our Church which will render it more roomy than before, and it is now sufficiently large to celebrate the divine services with the solemnity and decorum that becomes them.

Mail between Jamaica and Trinidad was no faster than service from London to Jamaica. Not until 4 May 1830 did MacDonnell reply to confirm faculties granted by his predecessor and request Fernandez to prepare for a canonical visitation which he might expect some two or three months hence, adding that as many as possible were to be prepared for confirmation. A warning was issued to Fernandez that he was to receive no priest who did not present faculties signed by MacDonnell, together with an introductory letter dated not earlier than 4 May 1830.[3] This was a wise precaution to prevent emigré priests showing up unexpectedly and claiming faculties and privileges which might upset right order.

The bishop was unable to fulfill his promise of a visitation until one year later, in June 1831. When he did arrive, the hard persevering work of Fernando and his eminent gift of organization were so clearly manifest that MacDonnell declared that he had not found in any of the islands subject to his jurisdiction a congregation better governed than that of Kingston.[4]

Reverend Edmund Murphy Appears on the Scene

Character is difficult to judge accurately. Even when a good analysis has been made, the judgment may prove wrong. An error in judging the character of Rev. Edmund Murphy was made by a bishop and an attorney general. The Honourable Anthony Dowell O'Reilly, attorney general for Jamaica, was the instrumental cause of introducing Murphy into this mission. This unfortunate cleric gave as much trouble as did l'Abbé Espinasse in the days of Le Cun.

While vacationing in Great Britain, O'Reilly met Murphy, and because of the dire need of priests, either the attorney general suggested that Murphy come to Jamaica or he listened to a plea from the cleric that he be allowed to accompany O'Reilly on his return to the island. From whom the initiative came is not known, but the fact is that Murphy did sail with the attorney general.

A zealous layman from one of Ireland's most influential families, O'Reilly was prominent in the affairs of state and an ardent advocate of Catholic emancipation. Superior talent led to an appointment in one of the top positions of colonial service. Despite his high social status and official position, he did not hesitate to support the freedom of the slaves and to criticize the apprenticeship system as it was practiced. Yet he retained the respect of the planters, and visitors to Jamaica found him attractive, generous, and independent. The Rev. James A. Thome and J. Horace Kimble, members of the American Anti-Slavery Society appointed to investigate the apprenticeship system in the West Indies, wrote that O'Reilly was "one of the noblest men in the island, distinguished for that simplicity of manners, that warmheartedness, and flow of natural benevolence which are the characteristics of the Irishman."[5]

They were well aware that he was a Roman Catholic and so described him, refraining from the accustomed disparaging term of papist. These Abolitionists discovered O'Reilly's attachment to the cause of freedom was genuine while "his hostility to the apprenticeship" demonstrated "his sincerity and independence." He kindly furnished them with letters of introduction to planters in order to expedite their own investigation.

An ardent Catholic abolitionist of the nineteenth century, O'Reilly sought every opportunity to promote both civic and religious welfare. Murphy, he thought, would second the efforts of overworked Fernandez. On the voyage out, the happy travelers stopped at Trinidad to call on Bishop MacDonnell. MacDonnell welcomed the visitors and granted faculties to Murphy together with a letter of introduction to Fernandez dated 15 June 1832.[6] Everybody was in high spirits, O'Reilly because he had been instrumental in introducing Murphy, the bishop because he had another willing missionary in his Antillean vicariate, Murphy because Jamaica was virgin territory where he might act completely independent of Fernandez. This seemed to be Murphy's manner of interpreting MacDonnell's faculties, for he disembarked at Kingston with the preconceived and erroneous notion that he had no superior in Jamaica, but was under the immediate and direct jurisdiction of the vicar apostolic in Trinidad, since MacDonnell had issued no directive to make it clear that Murphy was to serve under Fernandez.

Fr. Murphy Throws Church into Disorder

Trouble started within a few months after Murphy had taken up residence with Fernandez at Holy Trinity in Kingston.[7] It was a feast day and Fernandez was celebrating a High Mass when Murphy mounted the pulpit to preach a homily of the day. Instead of a sermon, the congregation listened to a tirade against the astonished Fernandez, accusing the pastor of being ignorant and negligent of English religious culture. After Mass, the mild-mannered Fernandez contented himself with admonishing Murphy privately for his lack of charity and for giving public scandal. Fernandez added that if Murphy felt greater zeal than the pastor, he should use it for the glory of God and not in a public tirade. Bad blood had been roused the previous Saturday night when Fernandez admonished Murphy for abandoning himself to excessive drinking. Following the pulpit incident, Murphy left the rectory and hired a room where he set up his own chapel and continued to declaim against Fernandez, introducing division into the hitherto united congregation. This was in October 1832. Fernandez could not sit passively by and allow the hard work of years to be snatched from him; in the same October he wrote a detailed account of the evil afflicting the Kingston congregation to the vicar apostolic in Trinidad.

St. Patrick's Chapel

Murphy's chapel on High Holborn Street was situated in Jasper Hall, one of the historic showplaces of its day. Four prominent and wealthy merchants had placed a wager on who could construct the most palatial residence. One became Hibbert House on Duke Street, Kingston, later used by the government as Headquarters House, the seat of government. The second, Bull House, was situated on the northwest corner of North and East Street. The third, Harmony Hall, was on Hanover Street. The fourth, Jasper Hall, was completed 1 June 1756. Historian Cundall awards the prize to Jasper Hall, not only for its architectural excellence but also for its library and fine art collection which were the best private collections in the island.[8] On two occasions Jasper Hall served as a Catholic chapel: once in Le Cun's day and now in Murphy's, who named it St. Patrick's.

Addressing another letter to MacDonnell on 2 March 1833, Fernandez protested vigorously at the high-handed, overbearing manner and complete disregard for authority manifested by Murphy in opening St. Patrick's. MacDonnell's reply was dated 5 May 1833.

> I take occasion to renew my assurance of reliance on your enlightened and pious endeavours for the promotion of Religion, the honour and contentment of your fellow-labourer Mr. Murphy; the undisturbed and undiminished and secure transmission to the Church of all interests entrusted in Kingston to your Ecclesiastical administration. I address myself to you as senior and chief. I request you will communicate this to your Rev. Brother and that kindly, generously, discreetly working together you may agree in all things for the advantage of our holy religion in your colony and you will mutually and disinterestedly assist, solace and sustain each other.[9]

This was all but a duplicate of the advice Le Cun received from Douglass when L'Espinasse was giving him endless trouble. Had Murphy been a more pliable character, it would have been effective.

In this same letter MacDonnell gave Fernandez permission to open another mission chapel in any other part of the island. Since Fernandez had made no such request, this was a subtle way of allowing him a diplomatic escape from the present difficulty by granting Murphy permission to continue at St. Patrick's, if Fernandez so willed. Since Fernandez had been told to communicate the contents to Murphy, he did so. Murphy acknowledged receiving MacDonnell's letter, but interpreted it as a victory for himself. He went further and wrote to Fernandez on 24 May 1833, saying that he was ready to listen to any proposals Fernandez might offer relative to the establishment of another mission. He hoped Fernandez would choose a mission outside Kingston, and allow Murphy to fall heir to the entire Kingston congregation. With this in mind Murphy laid down the following conditions in his letter: first, Fernandez should secure to him the transmission of all the interests in Kingston now entrusted to Fernandez's ecclesiastical administration; secondly, Fernandez should, until these arrangements were carried out, fix a stipend which would enable Murphy to live according to the desires of the Bishop with honour to his exalted station and personal contentment, for he was never content under the same roof with Fernandez.[10] Fernandez did not accede to either demand and the passage of time only widened the rift.

The new congregation at St. Patrick's, composed principally of

Irish and English, grew and prospered under two advantages possessed by Murphy: he was a British subject, perfectly familiar with the English tongue; he was an eloquent, persuasive speaker.[11]

While the Murphy-Fernandez contention was raging in Kingston, a third party, Fr. Don Maria Antonio Oberto, innocently stepped into the fray on 3 July 1834.[12] Whence he came is not known, but his Spanish name would indicate a refugee from politically unsettled South America. Fleeing from a national revolution, Oberto found himself in a private one. Oberto wrote to MacDonnell for faculties to work in Jamaica. Immediately Murphy's suspicions were aroused since he reasoned that, should Oberto be allowed to function in Kingston, Fernandez might place him in charge of St. Patrick's. Anticipating such an act, Murphy wrote Oberto a sharp note, warning him against what he termed the consequences of the inconsiderate advice of others and his own rashness in exercising functions to which the bishop was far from calling him, since he had already nominated a priest who knew the language and wants of the British faithful. As soon as possible Oberto left for the quieter island of Trinidad.

Bishop McDonnell Visits Jamaica

Letters from Fernandez to MacDonnell brought no response from the vicar apostolic, while another letter, dated 11 June 1833, was treated with the same silence. Not until 26 November 1834 did MacDonnell announce his intention of visiting Jamaica to investigate complaints he was receiving from both Jamaica and elsewhere. When he arrived in January 1835 to appraise the situation, MacDonnell did nothing to relieve the tension. He left Murphy in charge of St. Patrick's, for either he judged that the situation was not as serious as represented by Fernandez, or he hoped that with the passage of time everything would eventually right itself. Whatever his reason, the status quo remained unchanged.

New Site for St. Patrick's

Now that the vicar apostolic had given him sanction, the congregation at St. Patrick's so prospered that in 1835 Murphy was busily engaged in collecting funds to purchase a new site. The subscription list, an indication of Murphy's interest, contained the names of prominent gentry throughout the island and abroad. His efforts were rewarded when he secured valuable property in the heart of the city on East Queen Street at the corner of Hanover Street and George's Lane, for here was to rise the new St. Patrick's.

On 19 March 1836 the cornerstone was laid. In the eyes of Murphy, the occasion called for all the flourish and fuss a colonial government might lend to the ceremony. No less a personage than the Earl of Altamont, governor general of Jamaica, would lay the cornerstone. The *Jamaica Despatch* for 21 March carried a detailed account of the occasion.

> On Saturday, the 19th instant, the Committee of Management met at the residence of Mr. Bartholomew Seymour in North Street where arrangements were made for conducting the ceremonies on the occasion. They proceeded thence to Miss Burke's lodgings on Duke Street to wait on the Earl of Altamont and conduct His Lordship to the grounds, where they arrived at five o'clock. The cortege proceeded in the following order:
>
> Captain Dillon and Bartholomew Seymour, Esq., next, half the Committee in carriages, then His Lordship accompanied by the Hon. Capt. Brown and Onsly Higgins, Esq., followed by Rev. Mr. Murphy with his clerical attendants; after them came the other half of the Committee in carriages, and they were followed by a large number of friends also in carriages, many of whom were decorated with green scarves ornamented with the crown, the harp, and national emblems, the thistle and the shamrock.
>
> An immense concourse of people attended, thousands having assembled previously in the grounds to witness this novel and imposing ceremony. When the cortege arrived at the spot destined for the laying of the first stone, the choir of St. Patrick's Church commenced chanting the 63rd psalm. Towards the close of it the Earl of Altamont, assisted by several gentlemen of the Committee proceeded with the ceremony, with silver trowel, square, mallet etc., during which the choir sang the 87th psalm, Fundamenta Ejus. After the usual dedication of the building to its patron Saints [St. Patrick and St. Martin], the Rev. Mr. Murphy read the following beautiful prayer from the ritual of the Church: "Omnipotent and merciful God, who out of the universal abode of the elect in heaven has framed an eternal dwelling for thine infinite Majesty, give to this edifice a heavenly increase that whatsoever has been commenced under Thy sanction may be completed through Thy most bountiful aid and through the merits of Christ our Lord, Amen."
>
> After the prayer, the Domine Salvum for his Majesty the King of England, closed the ceremony, the cortege retired in the same order as it arrived.[13]

Some time during the following month of April, Murphy departed from Jamaica leaving no forwarding address. It was discovered that he went to London, taking with him the funds he had collected to build the new St. Patrick's. Fernandez gave a sigh of relief to be rid of Murphy, but could hardly condone the money being taken from the Church. Fernandez then allowed the construction of St. Patrick's to be carried out under the direction of a committee representing the English-speaking Catholics of Kingston. The building was completed towards the end of 1839.

Although Murphy had departed, there remained uneasy tension in the mind of Fernandez and the congregation since both wondered how to prevent a future collapse of ecclesiastical discipline. The answer seemed to come from a Turin merchant, Louis C. Maury, whom Fernandez had met in 1834, while Maury was visiting Kingston. Fernandez made Maury his confidant in the unhappy Murphy affair. After Maury had left Jamaica, Benito wrote to him in Alexandria, Egypt, penning a long account of ecclesiastical conditions in Jamaica and asking the Turin merchant to place it in the hands of the Holy Father. On 30 June 1835 Maury wrote to a Jesuit friend of his, Antonio Bresciani, in Rome, enclosing Fernandez's letter and adding his own eyewitness account of the troubled mission.[14] He asked Bresciani to see that both accounts came to the attention of the pope. Six months passed without a reply. Again, on 25 January 1836, Maury wrote Bresciani from Turin, inquiring what had happened.[15] Was Bresciani enjoying the cloistered life of the novitiate while fire destroyed the Church in a West Indian island? In the same letter Maury begged for two Jesuit missionaries and threatened that if not successful with Father General, he would appeal to Gregory XVI. By 28 July 1836 Propaganda had received both letters, and on that date an acknowledgement was sent by the Sacred Congregation to Maury. Replying to Propaganda on 10 August 1836, Maury related the history of the events.[16] He had the pleasure of dealing confidentially with Fernandez for several days in 1834, and he had sent accounts of the Murphy affair to Bresciani, who relayed them to the Jesuit general for proper channeling to the pope. At this date Maury learned through a third party that negotiations for the requested Jesuit missionaries were making progress and that the British government had also made the same proposal. While Maury's negotiations were in progress, some Catholic men of Kingston had sent a memorial to Rome on 27 March 1838 imploring a remedy to cure the afflicted mission.[17] They proposed a twofold solution: 1) To separate Jamaica from the jurisdiction of the vicar apostolic of the West Indies due to the difficulty of communications; and 2) To place Jamaica under the archbishop of Cuba, only three sailing days distant, and allow Jamaica to have its own perfect apostolic or vicar apostolic. Accompanying the letter was a testimonial from Hector Mitchel, mayor of Kingston, in which his Honour vouched for the gentlemen who had signed the petition, saying that they were the most reliable of the Catholic congregation.

These letters and petitions had their effect upon Rome, for the Jesuits were told to send missionaries to Jamaica. On 6 August 1836 the Superior General, Fr. John Roothaan, wrote to Propaganda, "For Jamaica two English Fathers have been named (nor can the English province spare more). To whom are added one French Father and one Spanish. The Superior among them will be the English Father, William Cotham."[18]

Jamaica Becomes a Vicariate

The changes suggested by the memorial sent by the Kingston congregation were received with favour in Rome. On 10 January 1837, by a motu proprio, Gregory XVI formed Jamaica into a separate vicariate and placed British Honduras and the Bahamas under its jurisdiction.[19] The next step was to appoint a vicar apostolic. For this office the pope wished to choose a Jesuit, but Roothaan objected. He thought Benito Fernandez should be appointed, since he had served the Church unflinchingly through the many storms. Accordingly, on 10 January 1837 Benito Fernandez was appointed the first vicar apostolic of the newly formed Vicariate of Jamaica, British Honduras, and the Bahamas.[20] It was a happy choice, for few have given such a lifetime of service to the Church in this island as had Fernandez.

Jesuits Come to Jamaica

The original plan of sending four Jesuits to Jamaica was changed and only two arrived, one Englishman, William Cotham, and one Frenchman, James E. Dupeyron. Neither a second Englishman nor the Spaniard, Fr. Fonda, came. Cotham and Dupeyron arrived in Kingston on the historic date 2 December 1837.

William Cotham was born in St. Helens, Lancashire, England, 21 December 1791. He studied humanities at Stonyhurst and entered the Society of Jesus 7 September 1809. After his course in philosophy and theology, he was ordained at Ushaw College by Bishop Smith on 17 December 1818. On 30 March 1819 he made a public defense of theology. After a period of teaching at Hodder and Stonyhurst, he did mission work at Wigan and Hereford. He pronounced his final vows on 2 February 1831. Being superior at the adjoining seminary of Stonyhurst, instructor of tertians, and consultor of the province filled the intervening years until on 24 August 1837 he was appointed superior of the Jamaican mission.

Dupeyron arrived in England from France on 7 September 1837.[21] The two missionaries sailed on the *Thames,* a 450 ton ship under Captain Barclay.[22] They sighted the last of England at Gravesend on 6 October, stopped at Madeira on 30 October, and after a slow but tranquil voyage across the Atlantic arrived at Kingston 2 December 1837.

Dupeyron wrote Roothaan 6 December 1837, recording his first impressions of the mission.

> a little while after disembarking, we were taken to the residence of F. Fernandez who welcomed us royally. For two or three months he and L'Abbé Duquesnay were waiting patiently for us to arrive. We were embarrassed at their kindness towards us. The reception which the Catholic laity has shown us is no less indulgent. This is not astonishing because they are very much attached to the Vicar Apostolic. What pleases him also pleases them. The excellent Fr. Benito Fernandez commands their undivided confidence, and merits it by his edifying conduct which speaks for itself and does not lie dormant. A dazzling proof of his last 14 years in Kingston. One knows a pastor by his sheep. The Catholic population is about 4 or 5000 souls. Communions are very numerous, whereas before the arrival of Fr. Fernandez they were very few. Divine service is conducted with as much ceremony as is becoming. Last Sunday there was a High Mass. At vespers we had the pleasure of listening to the organ and a good number of musicians. I believe that many a city in France would call itself fortunate to possess what Kingston has. The faithful show by their exterior conduct, great respect for the sanctuary.
>
> Last Sunday the Vicar Apostolic preached in French and at Vespers I preached in the same language which is understood by nearly everybody in Kingston. In the country, that is to say in nearly all the rest of the island, they speak only English.
>
> . . . I have shown you the bright side, now I must show you the reverse. . . . It is of a priest whose name you know (Murphy), who has given more than one species of scandal. In order to show he was here, it is sufficient to read the letters he wrote against L'Abbé Duquesnay and which he published against the latter as well as against Benito Fernandez in a Kingston newspaper. Thank God he has left the island these many months. He was in London when I passed through there. They hope he will never return for the added reason that he carried away quite a considerable sum of money, the proceeds of a collection made for the construction of a chapel which will probably remain only on paper. His departure, however, has not done away with all the difficulties. For he left behind a successor, an Irishman like himself (John Curtin) who already has been in four dioceses of America. He is not overwhelmed with attention, and because of the very small number of persons of low birth (in his congregation) who are not capable of supporting him, it is very probable that want will soon oblige him to leave Kingston.[23]

Cotham and Dupeyron, like all who see the tropics in the winter, were quick to be fascinated by the flowers, the fruit, and the weather. On 12 December Attorney-General O'Reilly drove the two missionaries to Spanish Town, thirteen miles from Kingston. Along the road they saw trees, shrubs, flowers, and even grasses of such species unlike any they had ever seen in Europe. Fruit was in abundance. Large oranges sold for 5d a dozen; bananas, plantains, shaddocks, pineapples, grapes, and watermelons could be had for a few pennies.

But the wines were not good, and the meat very tough most of the time. Their European clerical clothes were too heavy, but everyone perspired whether they wore clerical black or white. The lowest temperature was noted at 69 degrees Fahrenheit, and the highest in the shade 86 degrees. Cotham made the following observations on 20 December concerning the temperature: at 6:30 a.m., 69 degrees; noon until 2.00 p.m., 86 degrees; 3.15 p.m., 73 degrees. One day when the sun was shining through the window, he recorded the temperature at 113 degrees. Blankets were superfluous, though most people used both a sheet and a light coverlet at night. Cotham was the only one in the rectory to use a mattress; the others merely placed a sheet on their bedstocks.

By New Year Cotham and Dupeyron had settled down to steady employment. Suited by training for teaching, they were assigned to the secondary school started by Duquesnay in September 1836.[24]

Fr. Duquesnay, Native Priest Returns to Jamaica

Arthur W. L. Duquesnay, a native of Jamaica, was born of Haitian parents in Kingston on 29 December 1808. His father was Phillipe le Mercier Duquesnay, a native of Gonaives, Haiti, and his mother, Marie Françoise Duverger Duquesnay, a native of St. Marc in the same island. Following his course of studies at St. Aloysius College, Montmouillon, Poitou, France, Arthur entered the Jesuit novitiate but did not remain. He transferred instead to a seminary in Rouen to study for the secular priesthood. Ordained in 1833, he returned to Jamaica in January 1834 to become Fernandez's assistant. With Benito he shared the vituperation spewed by the Reverend Edmund Murphy on those not of his ilk.

Two years later in 1836, Duquesnay opened a high school on Orange Street, Kingston. Forty-six pupils followed a liberal arts curriculum of English, Latin, French, Spanish, and religion. In writing to Rome on 16 May 1837, Kingston parishioners expressed their appreciation of the work Duquesnay was doing to educate the Catholic youth, thereby preventing them from falling under non-Catholic influence.[25] In 1838 the school was removed to 74 King Street, then the premises of Holy Trinity rectory.

Teaching can be a very trying profession, and it is not surprising that Duquesnay in a letter to a Jesuit friend in Rome, dated 8 December 1837, expressed his doubts that his school would ever amount to anything of value.[26] Despite Duquesnay's feeling of discouragement, this little school was the cradle of all future Catholic education in Jamaica. It would grow from one school of forty-six pupils in 1836 to 138 schools of 52,588 pupils in 1980.[27]

Two Jesuits Witness the End of Slavery

Cotham and Dupeyron happened upon a critical period in Jamaican history. Slave trade between Africa and Jamaica had been abolished by an act of the British Parliament since it was decreed that after 1 March 1808 no more slaves should be brought to the island. This did not end slavery, which continued until 1 August 1834, when the apprenticeship was introduced.[28]

Under the apprenticeship system the field slave was bound for six more years to his master, and the house slave for four years. During the apprenticeship the slave was required to give forty and one half hours of free labour each week to the master; for all practical purposes this kept the negro in subjection. It was estimated that he had only thirteen working hours a week which he could rightly call his own. Apprenticeship was a misnomer for freedom. In order to supervise the system, the British Government appointed stipendiary magistrates whose duty it was to see that the former masters took no unfair advantage of the ex-slave.[29] The magistrates were in a peculiar position. Officially they had to protect the ex-slave and initiate him into the ways of the free man, but want of hostels throughout the country forced them to accept the hospitality of the planters as they moved from plantation to plantation in making their rounds of duty. It was only natural that the apprentice, seeing the magistrates living at the great house, should identify them with the interests of the planter class. Despite this embarrassing situation, these magistrates performed their duties with impartial justice, since they protected the new freeman from the importunate demands of the planter.

The stipendiary magistrate had control over the apprentice up to the point when, for misbehavior or refusal to work, he was committed to the gaol. At this point the local magistrate took over control of the culprit and flogging or the treadmill could be the punishment.

The treadmill was dreaded.[30] Invented by an engineer named Cubitt in 1818, the first used in English prisons, the treadmill consisted of a large, hollow, wooden cylinder, round the circumference of which was a series of steps. Persons undergoing punishment trod on these steps, their weight causing the cylinder to revolve, compelling them to move quickly from step to step as the cylinder turned. If anyone slipped or fainted while on the mill, he hung by his wrists from the overhead hand-rail while the revolving steps battered him or her.[31]

It was precisely this cruel gaol treatment which had a reactionary effect against the apprenticeship system, bringing it to a premature end and thereby granting complete freedom to the negro. A committee appointed by the House of Commons to enquire into the working of the apprenticeship reported that, despite the difficulties inherent in the system, it was operating satisfactorily. This finding was not accepted by the more radical abolitionists. In 1836 Joseph Sturge with three fellow abolitionists paid a visit to the West Indies to make a personal evaluation of conditions. These investigators exposed conditions of the gaol, emphasizing the treadmill as a form of cruel punishment. In this report of the abolitionists and in a book published by Sturge, unfair, sweeping allegations were made that the stipendiary magistrates had become tools of the planters.

The result was that antislavery again became a burning issue in England. Public opinion was so aroused that in 1838 Parliament passed an act amending the Abolition of Slavery Acts, whereby flogging or the use of the treadmill to punish female slaves was forbidden. But the British government refused to abolish the apprenticeship, claiming that legally this was part of the compensation promise to the slave owners. Government was prepared to discontinue the system only if the colonial legislature voted its abolition.

Shortly afterwards another question arose. Numbered among the field slaves were the plantation artisans—carpenters, coopers, blacksmiths, and numerous other skilled workmen. Legal opinion on this point was that these could not be classified as predial labourers and therefore had to be released from the apprenticeship at the same time as the house slaves were freed. This legal opinion in regard to the status of artisans and the restrictions imposed by the amendment to the Abolition of Slavery Act persuaded the legislature of all the colonies to terminate the apprenticeship system and free all the slaves completely on 1 August 1838.[32]

State of Country Immediately Following Emancipation

When 1 August 1838 dawned, 311,000 negroes in Jamaica found themselves free. Emancipation was a reality. From the capital, Spanish Town, to every corner of the island joyous celebrations marked the event. Despite the blessing of freedom, however, it was a confused, deteriorating society, one that would require years of adjustment before it would return to normal. Insecurity now plagued both former master and former slave. Hitherto the slave had lived in his cottage on the plantation, raised his own vegetables both for his own use and for sale in Sunday market; now he was on his own. November was the month set when all who did not continue working on the plantations had to find other quarters. Plantation owners after this date charged rent for cottages and provision ground.[33] While in some cases it was as low as one shilling a week, in others the planter charged one shilling a week for each member of the family—father, mother, and children. One estate claimed to have drawn £1300 per year in rents. In other cases no rent was charged provided the family gave some free labour to the owner; should a member of the family absent himself, 6d was charged the culprit for each day. If the owner raised the rent and the family protested, cattle would be turned into their provision grounds, crops destroyed, cottages pulled down, leaving the family without means of support or shelter. Such overbearing acts of intimidation did not encourage the negro to remain on the plantation. Some took themselves into the deep woods to squat on Crown lands; others, with the help and encouragement of Baptist ministers, settled in what became known as Free Villages.

> The first of these, started in 1835 by Rev. Phillipo for freed slaves, was Sligoville—named in honour of the governor—situated in the hills behind Spanish Town. Three years later Knibb with Joseph Sturge's help, settled seventy families on a 500 acres estate in St. Ann and established the village—complete with church and school house—now known as Sturge Town. The other Baptist missionaries Clarke, Dendy and Burchall, encouraged and assisted the setting up of free villages and, in doing so, helped the process which was to change the emancipated slaves into peasant proprietors or freeholders. Within five years, nearly two hundred of these villages, including Bethany, Buxton, Clarksonville, Wilberforce, had been established; by 1840 there were about eight thousand peasant freeholders, within five years the number jumped to nineteen thousand. These farmers were almost self-supporting, earning cash for their needs from the sale of provisions grown on their small allotments.[34]

If the former slave was having difficulty adjusting himself to the new life, the planter, deprived of free labour, was experiencing a like headache. Free villages were enticing labourers away from work on the plantations just at a time when their help was critically needed. Wages were also a source of constant worry to the planter, for ready cash had to be found to meet regular labour bills. From wealth to ruin was the safari of many a planter. All efforts to avert bankruptcy seemed hopeless, and even the very banks formed to meet his needs for ready capital were on insecure foundations. Agricultural societies founded throughout Jamaica which encouraged the planter to grow indigo, cocoa, coffee, and sugar likewise failed. The crippling blow came in 1846 when England abolished the protective tariff on sugar, rum, and coffee, leaving no defense against similar products grown more cheaply in slave-economic countries. Further distress was in store for the planter when

> in 1847, a commercial crisis in Britain caused by over speculation, led to the bankruptcy of several prominent West Indian merchants who in the

> past had provided credit to planters, and banks in the West Indies also failed. A further fall in the price of sugar completed the ruin of many of the planters and a number of sugar estates in Jamaica and elsewhere were allowed to become derelict, while on those that survived the wages of the labourers were drastically reduced. Strikes and disorders followed in some colonies and distress in all was acute.[35]

Many large estates became too overburdened with debt to continue sugar on a profitable basis, the Great House falling into decay, the fields to ruin, and the ensemble becoming a mere pretext of its former luxury and wealth. Kingston, chief commercial mart of the island, reflected this general decay, business falling off in its shops, dwelling houses becoming badly in need of repair and even its streets becoming gullies, mere conveyors of excessive tropical rains into the sea.

All this had effect upon the Church in Jamaica. As early as 1833, on the eve of Emancipation, the Kingston congregation was unable to offer Fernandez sufficient support for the Church.[36] On 24 October 1833 they were placed in the embarrassing position of having to appeal to the government for aid. The congregation expressed its regret that it found it necessary to address the House of Assembly in a tone of supplication at a time of public distress. The Assembly was reminded that the petitioners were loyal to the throne of Great Britain and they contributed to the public revenues in the same proportion as members of any other religious body. The priest of the petitioners, Fr. Benito Fernandez, had lived in Jamaica some thirteen years and had performed his sacred duties in such a manner as to acquire the esteem of all the inhabitants of Kingston. The only emolument he enjoyed came from marriage, baptismal, and burial fees together with a small annual pew rent. Even the pew rent had been drastically reduced due to present economic distress. Thus ran the essence of their argument; the government considered it, but granted no aid to help the Church.

Expansion of the Church

Spiritually Kingston was making progress. The vicar apostolic, a short stout man of fifty-four years, enjoyed his missionary duties. Cotham appraised him in these words: "The good he has done in Kingston is very great, for I fancy that we have the best congregation in the West Indies. He is universally esteemed by persons of all religions and dearly beloved by all Catholics with very few exceptions."[37] Kingston was only one corner of the island, and there were Catholics elsewhere. On 30 May 1838 the vicar apostolic and Cotham set out to seek these rural Catholics who had no opportunity of receiving the sacraments except on a visit to Kingston.[38]

Spanish Town, thirteen miles distant, was their first stop. Here they spent a week and found 130 Catholic soldiers and some one hundred civilians, but not one person received the sacraments of penance or Holy Eucharist. The response was not encouraging. On 7 May they pushed on to Old Harbour, twelve miles west of Spanish Town, but caught in a tropical afternoon shower, they beat a hasty retreat to Spanish Town.[39]

Spiritual vacuity opened Fernandez's eyes to the need for regular services in the capital. Cotham was assigned to spend each weekend there, celebrate Mass at the attorney general's home, and reclaim lax Catholics. Concubinage, the chief impediment, was exceedingly common among all classes so that, even with weekly Mass, progress was slow among a people deprived of spiritual ministration for years. The last sacraments to a dying woman, one reception of Holy Communion, and two confessions of a couple about to marry, was the sum of Cotham's early efforts. All who received the sacraments were Irish. Fernandez concluded from this evidence that a resident priest was needed to establish more personal contact.

On 14 December 1838 Cotham and Dupeyron were established in an old house in Spanish Town rented at £24 per year which served as rectory, chapel, and school.[40] In fine weather it was comfortable, but in the rainy season umbrellas had to be used in the hallways and staircases. When the Catholic citizens of Spanish Town thought of purchasing the building, the owner increased his price from £450 to £800. A school was opened with five scholars who paid 1/5 per week. Discouragement is manifest in Cotham's letters; one dated 3 February 1839 reveals the slow progress of the mission.

> The Lord knows what good we shall do here, our prospects appear very gloomy to me at present: but things can scarcely be in a worse state: a great many have never once been to chapel, only about five have made their last Easter Communion, possibly there may be eight or ten next Easter; very few of the children come for instructions. A Protestant lady called for instructions of the Catholic doctrine but we have not seen her for several weeks and her Catholic husband has never been to Mass. . . . As a specimen of the drunkenness of the soldiers, Sunday before Mass no less than six of the sentinals at the gate of the barracks of Spanish Town were unarmed, stripped of their belts and coats, handcuffed and tumbled off into confinement for being drunk; this was at ten in the morning. When soldiers are going to church, the officers are obliged to examine them by parading them for some time to see which of them are too drunk to go to prayers.[41]

Fr. Dupeyron's First Journey into the Country

Dupeyron by his very nature could never be an armchair missionary. Never could he accept the status quo of the church, but he must plant it over the next mountain where it did not exist in his day. Even while stationed at Spanish Town, he rode fifty miles into the civil parish of Manchester on 22 June 1838 and returned on 4 July 1838 with one marriage validated. On 25 May 1839 he stated that he had visited St. Thomas in the Vale, thirty-two miles from Spanish Town, on two occasions.[42] Duquesnay had first discovered some three hundred descendants of Haitian refugees in the hills eighteen miles north of Kingston. On Dupeyron's second visit three made their first Holy Communion, and he held out the hope that on his third visit at least three more would do the same. The Spanish Town mission proved a failure, and on 15 October 1839 this ill-fated mission was closed. Cotham and Duquesnay returned to live with Fernandez in Kingston.

Not every missionary experience was gloomy. Now and then the humorous side appeared. Cotham related such an incident which occurred shortly after he and Dupeyron had returned from the defunct Spanish Town mission.

> On the 1st of this month the Attorney-General invited us to dine with him. Fr. Dupeyron and I accepted the invitation. According to our good Fr. Benito's ideas, but much against my will, we were obliged to go in a gig, Fr. D. undertook to drive, also much against my will, as he knows nothing of driving or of the streets (rough with great holes enough to upset or break down an ordinary carriage), and I am an old driver of gigs. He began by poking the whip almost into my face, and before we have gone 100 yards he nearly ran over a couple of young pigs lying in the street. What remains is melancholy enough. In returning we had gone a few yards, when I told him he was running against some steps and would upset us; he tried but did not know how to turn the horse and presently my prediction was lamentably verified. We ran against the steps leading into a house and were immediately overturned. I must have fallen on him, as I was neither dirtied nor seriously hurt, but only a little sprain in one finger; but as for him, his right shoulder was dislocated and his right leg was much hurt. He was carried back to the house of the Attorney-General and in a few minutes his shoulder was again in joint. In the course of an hour or two he was brought home. His sufferings have been very great ever since; though he is getting better, he cannot raise his arm to his head without great difficulty. Yesterday he said Mass for the first time since his misfortune. I felt very grateful that nothing worse happened either to him or to me.[43]

Whether Dupeyron ever mastered the intricate driving of a gig is not known, but he did become an expert in the saddle with some thirty odd years of experience.

Controversy at St. Patrick's

Events were stirring at St. Patrick's a month after the two missionaries had returned from Spanish Town. Fr. John J. Curtin, Murphy's successor as pastor at St. Patrick's, died on 17 November 1839 of malignant fever.[44] On 19 November William Shannon, editor of *The Jamaica Despatch,* and one of the trustees of St. Patrick's, having quarrelled with the other members of the church committee, called a meeting of the parishioners in the chapel. A Presbyterian who was leading a scandalous life presided. Shannon made a violent speech filled with misstatements and abusive language against the vicar apostolic, the archbishop of Cuba, and the Holy See. Shannon proposed a resolution to petition the vicar apostolic of the London district to send Murphy back to Jamaica.

On 26 November another meeting was convened in the chapel of the vicar apostolic at 74 King Street; the attorney general presided. The gathering was composed of the most respectable Catholics, both those who had always favoured Fernandez and members of St. Patrick's congregation who now opposed Shannon. A resolution condemning Shannon was passed. On the following day an address signed by fourteen hundred people was presented to the vicar apostolic expressing their sorrow at the insults and making evident their determination to stand by him in this crisis. Shannon's diatribe had one good effect: it reunited the good element of the Kingston congregation solidly on the side of the vicar apostolic.

Both the vicar apostolic and the reconciled parishioners of St. Patrick's asked the two Jesuits to take over the administration of the ill-fated chapel. Cotham had no doubt about their precarious position.

> We are here at Jasper Hall (St. Patrick's) like strangers, for we have been invited to take upon ourselves this mission only till some other priest can arrive to turn us out. We have brought only part of our goods. I have not the necessary furniture, no table for study, no clothes press or bureau, and I am to my great inconvenience standing while I write to you. The brother of Fr. Curtin lives in the house and eats and drinks when he thinks proper, gratis; if we were to remain, he would be of service to us at the beginning as he would introduce us to his brother's friends. Some of the congregation seem to be good Catholics ready to do anything for the Chapel and for us. . . . Would you fancy that almost all this Irish congregation of St. Patrick's are French and many of them understand English poorly?[45]

Murphy's expected return threw the parishioners into a state of uncertainty. Some even abstained from receiving the sacraments, awaiting their administration by their former pastor. Cotham called his mission in Kingston far from consoling.[46] He said that he thought no country in Europe had the proportion of bad Catholics as had St. Patrick's. Immorality and neglect of religion were astonishing. Not one man had received Holy Communion since he and Dupeyron had taken charge, and of the forty children they had baptized, only three were born in wedlock. Many of the parishioners never attended Mass on Sunday and not more than ten men had been present at any one time. One consoling thing was the number of good pious women who frequented the sacraments.

Perhaps Cotham was too much of the schoolman to envisage the future. He could not peer into the future of the Kingston against which he complained and see the many thousands of Catholics who would one day attend Mass and the same thousands who would receive Holy Communion on Sunday, nor could he foresee the eleven churches that would rise in the Kingston-St. Andrew area. This would be one hundred twenty years later; no one could be expected to envisage such growth from such unpromising initial material.

Fourteen

Lights and Shadows

For a period of forty-seven years, 1792–1839, the Church's apostolate in Jamaica was confined to Kingston and environs, if we except the attempt to establish a mission in Spanish Town in 1838. Limited personnel and the failure of the Catholics of Spanish Town to respond appreciatively to the Church's efforts restricted activity to the environs of Kingston, for here most of the Catholic population was concentrated. Then, with the immigration of thousands of Scots, Irish, Germans, and Portuguese during the apprenticeship years from 1834–38, Catholics among them settled in the Jamaican countryside.[1] Unaccustomed to work under the tropical sun, they perished in great numbers. The survivors constantly requested the ministration of a missionary, but no one could be spared until Dupeyron stepped into the breach, saving the faith of these isolated Europeans and at the same time widening the Church's influence among native Jamaicans living on the plantations and in the mountains.

Cotham had not yet closed the Spanish Town mission when one of these immigrants stopped at the rectory. Writing back to England, Cotham had this to say of the event:

> The most interesting news that we have is this, that on the 28th of September [1839], a German [John Bierbusse] called here on his road to Kingston in search of a priest. He told me that four years ago 300 Germans, 200 of them Catholics, settled about 24 miles from Kingston. When they came, a priest promised to follow them, if they sent him a good account of affairs. This they have written, but have received no answer. I fear that nearly all of them can speak no other language but German, so that no priest in the island will be able to instruct them. The messenger speaks English pretty well. He is of the 3rd Order of St. Francis. He acts as their missionary: they have built a school and a chapel where they assemble on Sundays for lectures of piety, prayer, psalms and hymns, etc. I expect to see him on his return.[2]

The question arose how Fernandez could have been ignorant of so many Catholics concentrated in a single community and for a period of four years. It is perfectly understandable when it is realized that these people, transported from Germany, merely made their port of entry call at Port Royal and were then shipped into the deep forest of the hinterland without being allowed any communication with Kingston. Five hundred acres of bush country at Seaford Town were allotted to the immigrants, making them prisoners in their isolation.

It was through Catholics of Montego Bay that, after four years in this wilderness, they discovered that a vicar apostolic resided in Kingston. Even today descendants of the first German settlers live an isolated life in a mountain-bound district with roads made passable for motor traffic only in recent years. There is no electricity, and water must be had from rain catchments or from a standpipe at the roadside. Many of the immigrants who could afford to pay their passage left Jamaica immediately when they saw they had been fooled by glittering promises.

Two weeks after the German catechist, John Bierbusse, called on Cotham and Dupeyron, the Spanish Town mission closed and Cotham resumed teaching at Duquesnay's high school. Dupeyron was now free to begin his long life of missionary excursions throughout the length and breadth of Jamaica. On 28 October 1838 Dupeyron, swinging into his saddle, rode through the presbytery gate of 74 King Street to make history for the Catholic Church in Jamaica.[3] His objective was Montego Bay. The morning sun shone through moisture-laden clouds forecasting fair weather as Dupeyron rode towards Spanish Town over low, flat ground, swampy in spots, but green and fresh from recent October rains. Spanish Town had its opportunity and failed, so into the open country the rider turned. Sugarcane again became a familiar sight as he passed through Innswood estate to the town of Old Harbour and rode into territory redolent with memories of Spanish defense against marauding seventeenth-century pirates. At Free Town he turned south along the road that skirts Old Harbour Bay, and when the rich sugar lands of Vere came in sight, Dupeyron ended the first leg of his journey. Wearily he alighted from a very tired horse at Moreland estate where he was received with warm Jamaican hospitality at the Great House by Thomas McMahon, one of the Catholic immigrants from England who had settled in the remote Jamaican countryside.

The Feast of All Saints, 1 November, was the historic day Dupeyron began his ministry.[4] He received Sarah Benket into the Church, performed the marriage ceremony between her and Thomas McMahon, baptized their child, and celebrated the Holy Sacrifice of the Mass. On 2 November the missionary saddled his horse for a long, fatiguing ride into the high mountain country. Search was made for the mule packed with vestments, breviary, and supplies needed for the journey, but nowhere could the animal be found. The previous night he had wandered off on his own, perhaps a bit weary of missionary life. Cotham, commenting on this event said: "Dupeyron was so imprudent as to set off before its [the mule's] return. You may fancy his vexation in being several days without office, Mass etc."[5] Seven days later the mule was found and sent from Kingston to Dupeyron, then seventy miles away.

From the Moreland estate, minus mule, Dupeyron turned north through Vere over impassable roads. He spent one and half hours travelling each of the next seventeen miles of the journey; the only compensation was the cool November morning air. But the tropical sun was high in the heavens when he passed through the settlement of May Pen, and shining mercilessly when Four Paths appeared in view. Somewhere along the road he had to stop for the night, perhaps at Clarendon Park where the planter would have welcomed the traveler to the hospitality of the Great House with a hearty dinner and a good night's rest in exchange for pleasant conversation and news of the outside world.

Next day all was flat, open country until he reached Porus where the real mountain climb began. There a slope of seven miles led into the Don Figuerero Mountains until, beyond Mandeville, Dupeyron viewed with wonder the sweeping panorama of the plain below stretching through the haze out into the blue Caribbean: a delightful compensation for the hitherto monotony of flat, unvaried countryside. The captivating scenery was only accidental, for he had a destination to reach. From the mountains he descended into savanna land where a welcome at the Holland estate refreshed horse and rider. From this point travel was all uphill through sparsely settled districts over the YS road, a mere bridle path which led into the very heart of the mountain country Dupeyron had set out to evangelize.

Dupeyron's next stop was a settlement whose sole claim to distinction was its biblical name of Pisgah, whence Moses viewed the Promised Land. From the Jamaican Pisgah, located in the civil Parish of St. Elizabeth bordering Westmoreland, stretches a lovely valley some twenty miles long owned by small farmers whose bananas, coconuts, and sugarcane guaranteed a moderate subsistence. But in the environs of Pisgah the peasantry eked out a hard living from mountainside cultivation.

A Scotsman named MacDonald was the object of Dupeyron's visit. He had found his way to Jamaica after leaving the seminary in

Scotland where he had been studying for the priesthood, had married and settled amid these scenic but remote hills. On 16 November 1839, sixteen days after he had ministered to the McMahons, Dupeyron performed three baptisms at Pisgah.[6] That he took so long to reach this settlement is no surprise to anyone acquainted with the rough terrain; the wonder is that Dupeyron had the courage to attempt such a journey with primitive transportation.

Continuing into the mountains, Dupeyron headed west to one of the most unusual villages in the island, Seaford Town. It was from here that Johannes Bierbusse, the twenty-eight-year-old German catechist, had set out to find a priest. An apostle of Catholic Action, he had kept alive the faith of his countrymen in this inaccessible hinterland. From 2 October 1836 to 15 September 1839 Bierbusse had baptized twenty children born of Catholic parents bearing such surnames as Meikenback, Gutenberg, and Eisenger—proof of their German origin.[7] Dupeyron recorded these baptisms and added two more of his own while staying at Seaford Town from 19–24 November.[8]

The immigration of these Germans is closely linked to the emancipation of the slaves in Jamaica. Anticipation of freedom had pervaded the air for some years prior to 1 August 1838. The negro slaves were aware that a strong abolitionist group in England was espousing their cause of freedom; the Jamaican planters were also aware that the old social order of slavery would soon yield to a new one of complete freedom for the slaves who now toiled in their plantations.

Freedom was certain to come: so argued John Myers, a Jamaican Pen keeper.[9] What the country needed was the concrete example of a European labouring class which would serve as an incentive to the negro that he might continue to work on the plantation making it his life's work in order that no disruption occur in the social order. A Jamaican resident of German origin, Myers determined to persuade German laborers to settle in this island. During the week of 20 May 1834, Myers arrived in Jamaica with sixty-five German immigrants composed of thirteen families.[10] He had spent one year in his native country recruiting and had now returned to Jamaica with his mission successfully accomplished. Before he left, Myers had been denounced as a dreamer and his enterprise chimerical; but when he returned with labourers, the *Jamaican Despatch* on 27 May 1834 lauded his persistence and predicted future successes when more Germans arrived.[11] His scheme was to establish a white labouring community of farmers and artisans isolated from the negro population. Though not living with the negro, these Germans would give an example of European industry and skill, an entirely new concept of the white man for the negro, since the white man was either the owner of the plantation or held a superior position on it and never saw the labourer.

Myers was careful to bring out to Jamaica families composed nearly equally of males and females. The first group was from Wesel made up of eighteen able-bodied men, nineteen women, sixteen strong boys, and twelve girls.[12] Among their trades was that of loom-maker, two weavers of linen and one of damask, a miner, lapidary, coppersmith, and gunsmith; the rest were farmers. All the women were skilled spinners and knitters. Since military service was required of all able-bodied men in Germany, each man was armed with his rifle when he landed in Jamaica. They had also something to offer the negro in the moral order, for all the men and women were married, which was calculated to impress the apprentice negro with the sanctity of family life. Myers settled these Germans at Pleasant Mount in the civil parish of St. George, where he had constructed shelters and provided them with food until such time as they might clear three hundred acres of land in contiguous New Brunswick, named after their native duchy—Brunswick in the kingdom of Hanover.[13] But all was not altruism on the part of Myers, for he had made a verbal contract with the immigrants that they would reimburse him for expenses incurred or would work three years without pay.[14]

Seven months later, on 27 December 1834, another large contingent of 506 Germans arrived on the *Olberes* from the port of Bremen.[15] Healthy, cheerful, and anxious to proceed to their destination, these immigrants made a favourable impression on the reporter from the *Jamaica Despatch* sent to interview them. They were not allowed to disembark at Kingston but were placed on coastal vessels which carried them to their several destinations: Hamilton Brown transported 150 to St. Ann's Bay; Mr. Robert Watt 150 to Black River; James L. Hilton 45 to Dry Harbour Mountains in St. Ann; Samuel Anderson about 20 to Montego Bay; Dr. Spaulding and another proprietor 120, John Myers about 20 himself.[16] To meet Myers engagement with the captain of the ship for passage of the immigrants, the House of Assembly voted the sum of £3800 sterling.[17] This left Myers with a deficit of £338 currency which it was hoped that the Assembly would vote in his favour at the next meeting.

On Christmas morning, the immigrants, grateful for the kindness shown them by the captain, presented him with an address dated Kingston, 25 December 1834.

> To Captain Exter of the ship *Olberes* of Bremen
> Had not poverty exiled us from our native land, we would have tendered you a worthier gift than these lines: but circumstanced as we are we can only thus express the depth of our gratitude and trust you will accept the

> will for the deed. It is not flattery which prompts us to say that you have more than discharged your duty during our voyage from Bremen to Jamaica—you have been our father, our friend and adviser. Nor has your amiable lady (wife) been less ardent in discharging the duties of humanity by nursing and endeavouring to cheer them in their hour of sickness.
>
> Accept, we beseech you, the assurance of our gratitude which we can never repay, but which will daily call forth our prayers to the Almighty that He may reward you with blessing.
>
> We unite in wishing you a safe and speedy return to our native country and remain your ever grateful.[18]

All the passengers signed the address; three little girls dressed in native costume presented it to the captain.

Myers was not the only entrepreneur; a Dr. William Lemonius, also of German origin, became the second importer of immigrants.[19] A little more businesslike than Myers, he had an advance grant of £3750 from the Assembly to import 500 German labourers. Lemonius's contract read that he was to import these 500 German labourers within one calendar year beginning from 18 December 1834.

William Lemonius began his medical career as a doctor in the Duke of Brunswick-Oels Corps of the Austrian army in 1809. When the Brunswick Corps was incorporated into British service, Lemonius found himself in England and out of a job. Temporary employment was granted him in the Second Battalion Rifles of the King's German Legion. On 7 March 1811 Lemonius was appointed ensign in the York Light Infantry Volunteers stationed in the Windward Islands. When this regiment was disbanded in 1817, Major General O'Meara requested his services as Medical Officer on board one of the ships transporting O'Meara's regiment from Jamaica to England, and Lemonius accepted. So favourably was he impressed with Jamaica that he returned to the island in 1819, and in 1824 was appointed by his Grace the Duke of Manchester as justice of the peace and assistant judge for the civil Parish of Trelawny. This appointment brought him to the north coast of the island.

In 1831 a slave rebellion broke out in the western parishes of Jamaica, and Lemonius volunteered his services to the army. He was accepted and appointed to command a detail of the Twenty-second Regiment. Shortly afterwards he was transferred to Major General Hilton's brigade, which served the civil parishes of Trelawny and St. Ann. Since another uprising was expected in 1832, Lemonius was assigned to Montego Bay for the Christmas of that year.

In 1835 Lemonius was commissioned by the Jamaica House of Assembly to proceed to Europe and engage German immigrants for service in the island. Between 1835–37 Lemonius imported 800 German immigrants. This was a strategic move by the Assembly and had more reason behind it than the simple importation of Europeans to add to the skilled work force of Jamaica. It would appear that the government had an ulterior motive in selecting a military man for their agent and persuading Lord Seaford, owner of Montpelier estate, to settle them on Montpelier Mountain, twenty-four miles from Montego Bay. Situated in the hills south of Montego Bay, these armed Germans were required to drill once a week at Chester Castle as a powerful deterrent to any slave uprising like the one of 1831 which resulted in property damage to the value of £656,977.

We extract the following from the German Paper *Prymont,* 5 November 1836:

> A fortnight ago a caravan of 800 persons, men and women, youths and girls set out for Jamaica. Most of them were from Westphalia, only 28 being from the principality of Waldeck. The conditions they have agreed to are hard: they must labour as servants for five years for a few acres of land, at the expiration of which they enter into the possession of their little property. The future prospects are, therefore, not very brilliant.
>
> *Kingston Chronicle and City Advertiser*
> Friday Jan. 15, 1836

In 1793 Captain Sadler fashioned Montpelier estate out of five land grants in the civil Parish of St. James and Westmoreland. His widow, Janet, sold Montpelier to John Ellis on 26 December 1752 for £26,501. John Ellis, who died in 1782 or 1783, left his property in trust to educate his son Charles Rose Ellis, his widow receiving an annuity. Charles married Elizabeth Clifton, daughter and heiress of John Lord Hervey. In 1826 Charles Rose Ellis was created Baron Seaford. Here the Assembly settled Lemonius's German immigrants, not on the rich rolling land of the estate but in the mountainous backwoods where they could only eke out an existence.

These 800 immigrants came to Jamaica in two lots: the first, numbering 532, arrived from Bremen at Rio Bueno on 10 December 1835 on the ship *Olberes* under the command of Captain Exter; eighty-five of this number landed at Rio Bueno and were assigned to estates in the vicinity; 447 were taken to Montego Bay and of this number 198 were distributed to estate owners in the western end of Jamaica, while 249 were taken to Seaford Township. The second group numbering 250 were brought to Jamaica by Lemonious in 1836; some were assigned to Seaford Township, bringing the total to 300, the number reported by John Bierbusse in 1839 to William Cotham, S.J. at Spanish Town.

Lemonius had enticed these Germans to settle in Jamaica with a more rosy picture of the tropics than it deserved. Transported to a country whose language, customs, and climate were foreign to them, these early German settlers found the first few years most trying. Opinion spread throughout the community that Lemonius had duped them and threats of violence were uttered against his person should he ever set foot within the Seaford Township. Very few of those whom he had imported were accustomed to agricultural labour. The adult population was composed chiefly of disbanded soldiers and of craftsmen. Had it not been for John Bierbusse, schoolmaster and catechist, the whole project would have foundered. He kept up morale by conducting lay religious services on Sunday, and since he had a classical education was highly praised by the superintendent for schools for teaching thirty-two children in the village school on week days: special commendation came from his efforts to teach the children both English and German. Not only did he teach but he also gave good example to the settlers by cultivating the land allotted to him. He is recorded as having seventy-three hills of yams, one-half acre of cocoa and ginger, one hundred plantain trees, twenty roots of sugarcane, and 540 coffee trees. Although Bierbusse could confer the sacrament of baptism and offer religious instructions, he could not administer the sacraments of Penance and Holy Eucharist. The Catholics made a complaint to the government, and in September 1839 Bierbusse made the long journey of 120 miles to Kingston which resulted in Dupeyron's island-wide journeys to care spiritually for these Catholics scattered throughout the hills of Jamaica, covering a period of twenty-two years.

A little prosperity enabled some of the Germans to migrate to the more favourable climate of America, since from 1837–38 the Seaford Town community produced twenty-two thousand pounds of ginger, which brought some families as high as $300 for the year.[20] With this ready cash eighty-eight immigrants paid their passage to the United States from 1837–41.[21]

Although Lemonius had been voted £3750 by the Assembly,[22] he was given only £1800 to transact his business.[23] Instead of the projected five hundred settlers, only three hundred arrived. Of this number 260 were assigned to Seaford Town, two-thirds being Catholics.[24]

Had Lord Seaford settled the immigrants on arable land of his vast estate, the whole story of the Seaford Town settlement would have been one of success. Instead he assigned them five hundred acres of virgin bush land eleven miles south of his estate and in inaccessible mountain country, where they were indentured. They were allowed rations according to the army scale with an allowance of three shillings and four pence to the head of each family, two shillings and six pence to all children above the age of twelve, and one shilling and eight pence to all between the ages of eight and twelve years. For this grant they were required to work on the sixth day if so asked but with additional payment.

At Seaford Town a government commission was set up to make "regulations for the internal management of the township."[25] F. G. Hall was the first superintendent appointed, but within a year he had resigned. His place taken by Mr. Broadfast, and William Helsee, one of the immigrants, was placed in charge of government stores available to the settlers. An inventory revealed adzes, cutlasses, measures, locks, augurs, nails, hammers, scales, butcher knives, sieves for flour, different types of planes, steelyards, bellows, one anvil, one vice, an assortment of medicines, barrels of sugar, salt and rice. Helsee found work in the stores demanded so much of his attention that he was unable to cultivate his own land, and in lieu of this he was awarded double rations and double pay.[26] The name of Rev. W. Pfeiffer, a local Protestant minister, appears on the commissioner's list for having occasionally performed religious services for the non-Catholics from 1835–36, and for this he received £30.[27] There is no mention of the Catholic catechist receiving an emolument from the government, possibly because Bierbusse was not an ordained clergyman.

Not all went smoothly with the Meyers-Lemonius scheme. *The Jamaica Herald* for 6 May 1835 notes one such case:

> Mr. Hicks, a gentleman remarkable for his humane treatment of his servants, had engaged about 20 German immigrants, and located them on his coffee properties. There, we are assured, he had erected houses for their reception, given them lands, etc., and they were already beginning to gather in the fruits of their cultivation, when suddenly without any apparent cause of dissatisfaction, they left the property and came to Kingston. . . . It is plain enough that we require industrious field labourers, not weavers, spinners, brass and iron workers, musicians or those who may be out of employment and perhaps of dissolute habits to the bargain.[28]

Nor was there less dissatisfaction at Seaford Town, where bitterness at their slavelike treatment soured many. In a strange land, among a strange people, unable to understand, they learned the negro patois and forgot their native German after a generation or so. Their children grew up completely isolated from the town life of the island and lost all contact with Germany. It is not surprising that they welcomed the chance to migrate from here in the 1940s when Canada allowed the immigration of this sturdy German stock, leaving only a remnant in the island.

This was the township Dupeyron visited in 1839 with its problems of dissatisfaction, isolation, and lack of the religious services of a priest. On this first visit Dupeyron did not remain long at Seaford Town but continued on to another small settlement called Chesterfield, four miles to the east, where he performed one baptism on 26 November.[29] On the same and the following day he performed two more baptisms at Pisgah on his return trip to Kingston. Leaving Pisgah, he rode down the mountain trail to the lowlands where he performed eight baptisms at Denbigh estate, Clarendon on 5 December, the largest number of baptisms at any one place on this extensive missionary journey.[30] Now but forty miles from Kingston, he had made good time over level country and there at the presbytery gate in Kingston a warm welcome awaited the traveller from Fernandez, Duquesnay, and Cotham. Dupeyron's first extensive missionary journey had netted eighteen baptisms, one marriage, and an unrecorded number of confessions.[31] In actual number the results were small, but he had done something important for the Church in opening up for her the interior of the country: no longer would she be a stranger in the mountains and on the plantations, for from that moment it would mean progress for the faith, but it would be slow, imperceptible progress. Nevertheless it would be progress in the Jamaican countryside. For the next twenty-two years Dupeyron carried out this arduous apostolate single-handedly, covering every conceivable corner of the island. At one time or other he visited eighty-seven stations, a feat not surpassed in the days of modern transportation. When he retired in 1871, he left a legacy of hard, persevering labour seldom equalled in the annals of missionary work in Jamaica.

Government Grants for the Church

All of these missions were in need of financial support, and the most unlikely source would be from a professedly Protestant government, yet it was precisely from such a font that the mission in St. Thomas in the Vale received three hundred pounds sterling voted by the House of Assembly to construct a decent ecclesiastical edifice in place of the wattle hut used for worship up to that time.[32] The second grant was for the far western end of the island, where Catholic immigrants had settled on the great plantations. A committee representing the Catholic body in the County of Cornwall and the leeward, or western, portion of the County of Middlesex sent a petition dated 7 December 1842 to the House of Assembly stating that there were 750 Catholics scattered throughout that extensive territory.[33] They were principally Irish immigrants of humble circumstances who were suffering from the non-exercise of their religion; furthermore their children were debarred from the benefits of instruction and were in danger of growing up in evil ways. The expenses incurred by Fr. Dupeyron in attending to the spiritual needs of this scattered flock far exceeded his scanty means and that of his congregation. On the second reading in the House of Assembly, 13 December, it was passed.[34] One hundred fifty was voted to the Vicar Apostolic, Benito Fernandez, for the support of a priest to care for the spiritual welfare of the petitioners. This sum of £150 was voted annually until 23 March 1847, when it was reduced to £100.[35] The grant allowed Dupeyron to evangelize the countryside without adding to the financial burden of these poor immigrants and the vicar apostolic.

Educated English Catholics employed on the plantations, found this tenuous contact with the Church most disappointing. In 1842 a graduate of St. Edmund's College, England, was hired to work on a plantation in the County of Cornwall.[36] He assumed that a priest resided in the district, since the Assembly had voted £150 to maintain a priest in this western end of the island. Great was his disappointment to learn that Dupeyron visited the district only three or four times a year. Nor was this Catholic college graduate impressed by Dupeyron's faulty English or Fernandez's failure to express himself well in English after twenty years residence in Jamaica. He wrote to Fernandez pointing out the great spiritual desolation in the vicinity of Montego Bay, reminding the vicar apostolic that ample pecuniary means had been supplied by the government to remedy this deficiency.

Another graduate of St. Edmund's joined the first on the same estate in St. James but found the lack of spiritual aid amid gross immorality too much to endure, so he returned to England.[37] It was the custom of the day for the white male to live in concubinage with women of colour, a practice all but universal. The owner of the estate who employed these two St. Edmund's graduates had twenty-eight white persons working on his plantation in important positions.[38] The absentee owner had been informed that concubinage was dying out among the men in his service, but this Catholic young man discovered otherwise, for everyone kept a lady. For seven months he bore the taunts of these creatures because he would not conform to their loose way of life.[39] Complaints reached the owner in England with the result that fourteen married men were sent to replace those who had given themselves up to native women.[40]

Although he was interested in maintaining high moral standards on the plantation, this St. Edmund's graduate was chiefly concerned with the progress of the Church and claimed he foresaw the prospect of the advancement for the Church in Jamaica as "dull and cheerless as cold cocoa."[41]

Much of his disappointment stemmed from a reply from Jesuit superior William Cotham to a plan proposed by a zealous layman, Rudolphus W. Buchanan of Reading, to improve Church life in western Jamaica.[42] Buchanan wished to draw up a memorial addressed to the commander-in-chief of the British forces in Jamaica asking him to grant a salary to a Catholic chaplain who would serve the troops stationed in Maroon Town, Falmouth, and Lucea. The officers in charge of these barracks had recommended it and had promised to add their signatures to the memorial and expressed their hope that the British government would grant a yearly salary of £100 to such a chaplain.[43]

Cotham threw cold water on the whole idea, alleging that he thought it not worthwhile to petition the government for a Catholic salaried chaplain to serve the troops, since he had some experience in Kingston with Fr. Duquesnay who received £50 a year and for this grant was required to say Mass every Sunday for the troops, to visit the sick, and bury the dead, and at times make eight or ten trips to camp in a week. The government expected more service than the salary was worth. Again the government now granted £150 a year for the County of Cornwall; Cotham would be ashamed to ask more from the Assembly for the little Dupeyron did for the soldiers. Cotham ended with a bland cliché telling the enthusiastic youth that the vicariate was not interested: ". . . we thank you for making the suggestions as it proves the interest you take in the advancement of religion."[44] And promptly into the wastebasket went the youth's suggestions.

The St. Edmund's graduate kept on writing and on 19 November 1844 aired his grievances to a friend.

> I was at Montego Bay on Sunday to hear Mass, Monsieur Dupeyron having come down for three days in four months. He will be here again in March. . . . The want of some magnetic men here is a curse on the improvement in every way, and yet how noble is the field in which energy and ability might be employed. Mr. Buchanan is most anxious to have someone come here and would use all his endeavour to make him as comfortable as possible. In Montego Bay there is a large plot of ground with a house now used as a chapel when the padre comes down once in four months. With a couple of priests stationed here, the mission would soon require the building of a church. There is a great desire manifested by the coloured people to attend, and numbers were last Sunday disappointed for want of room. Would to heaven that something were done to relieve this great destitution.[45]

On 1 May 1844 action was taken to remedy the lack-of-priest situation by a London Catholic who offered to pay the expenses of educating a missionary for Jamaica.[46] This offer was made to Reverend John Hand, president of All Hallows College, Dublin. Sometime in July Hand wrote to Fernandez informing him of the kind offer from London, and at the same time he appointed a seminarian for the Jamaican mission. Within two years this very promising theologian would be ordained and ready for work in Jamaica. Christmas 1844 passed and Hand had not received a reply from the vicar apostolic. Hand acquainted Fernandez with a further offer to supply good priests for Jamaica if the vicar apostolic would contribute the small sum of £10 annually for support while they studied at All Hallows. Hand took it for granted that Fernandez would accept this very generous offer by the London benefactor. Fernandez seems not to have answered Hand. He may have lost all faith in Irish priests since Murphy, Gleeson, and Frost proved anything but exemplary representatives of the clerical state which they professed.

The St. Edmund's graduate never ceased his pitiful lament but, like many a hypercritic, he was blind to the heroic labours and difficulties of only four missionaries in the entire island. Utterly unfair was he to the accomplishments of this little band which so patiently bore burdens that would have discouraged the less valiant. On 27 September 1845 this same St. Edmund's graduate wrote to a friend complaining of the way the missionaries were partial to Catholic men living in sin.

> As to religion here, it is indeed at a very low ebb. The apathy is general and no instrument whether weak or strong must be brought into play to rouse the latent energies of the clergy. And the most influential men of the Catholic body are . . . all living in open infamy with black or brown women. Never do they frequent the sacraments. Seldom, as I myself witness, do they attend Church. . . .
>
> Oh what a low ebb must religion have sunk to when even her ministers are thus almost the defenders of the most abandoned sensuality and depravity. These men (in business and official life) have not the excuse urged by the planters that they cannot afford to marry since their income is not less than £1500 or £1600 a year. . . . No, the excuse of poverty would contrast badly with such facts I have laid down. It is the refinement of wallowing in sensuality that they can urge alone as the cause of their abominable life. Religion may go to the wall in the meantime before they contribute what they should and can afford. They have other channels into which their riches must flow, other duties on which to bestow their largess. Their God is their lust and they glory in their shame.[47]

The missionary is often faced with prominent Catholics living in concubinage. But should he thunder from the pulpit even without specific mention of names, everyone knows to whom the sermon is directed. And no amount of admonition ever seems to bring about their reformation of life; but faced with death, many do sincerely repent. Perhaps the complainant's youth urged him to fulminate against such men with these words:

> Can such a state continue? For my part as soon as I have a footing, I will stand to death against such abominations. It is this that prevents our holy faith from spreading far and wide. Undoubtedly the want of accommodations and room in our small churches has been a great impediment, but it cannot be said that everyone in search of truth would unsolicited enter a church whose ministers countenance and support infamy. Yes, countenance and support infamy in the language of the day. Unfortunately, I have heard it too often and from enlightened persons. Why is it said? Because these men are received with greatest affability by the priests and in second place because the priests, having taken good care not to offend the guilty by making use of the liberty which their position confers on them, are invited to dine at the houses of these persons and do dine with them, giving umbrage to all good Catholics.
>
> Were this intercourse to be the only means of reclaiming the lost sheep who have gone astray, it would then be meritorious. Oh but no, the delicate question is never stated, lest the gentlemen would be offended. Thus strengthened by the countenance they receive from the priests, these wretches are in a short time bold enough even to defend their conduct and that in the place of this countenance.[48]

State of the Church

In his report of 18 January 1842 to Cardinal Fransoni, prefect of Propaganda, Fernandez painted a rosier picture of the mission than did the graduate of St. Edmund. He claimed that the general state of religion on Jamaica, despite the lack of labourers, presented a rather flattering aspect. Although there were no conversions among the elite of society, the work among the middle and lower classes was not without fruit. In Kingston they could record 219 baptisms, 20 marriages, and 16 Protestants received into the Church. The sacraments were received daily by the people, and on Sundays the church was crowded. Four times a year Dupeyron made missionary trips into the interior to the great advantage of the faith, while his fellow Jesuit, Cotham, instructed the youth in the school which had recently been launched. Duquesnay, from time to time, visited the faithful at St. Thomas in the Vale, where a chapel and rather large school had been opened. He also conducted services at Spanish Town. Fernandez visited the mission at Rockfort. Gleeson served the chapel of St. Patrick and St. Martin while also acting as chaplain to the British troops. Fernandez had received a request from Catholics in the civil Parish of St. George that he send them a priest, and they promised to build a chapel at their own expense—a laudable project because there were three hundred Catholic negroes and some whites in the district, but the best he could do for the present was to despatch a priest several times a year.[49]

The Murphy Schism

Two years prior to this progress report, a sharp, discordant note sounded to disturb the harmony of the vicariate. Murphy returned to Jamaica on 22 November 1840. He presented his credentials to Fernandez and apologized privately for the scandal he had given. Had the vicar apostolic been of stern, unbending character, his troubles with Murphy would never have reopened. Although Fernandez secretly feared that Murphy might disturb the peace of the Church, he nevertheless accepted his apology as sincere and allowed him to take over his former chapel at Jasper Hall, High Holborn Street. Murphy owed his return chiefly to Dr. Thomas Griffiths, vicar apostolic of the London district, who persuaded Fernandez to allow the repentant priest to function once more in Jamaica.[50]

While Murphy's followers worshipped at Jasper Hall, they cast a covetous eye on the newly completed Chapel of St. Patrick and St. Martin on East Queen Street, whose cornerstone had been laid amid much pomp and circumstance by the governor of Jamaica before Murphy's hasty departure from the island with most of the funds for the chapel. These zealots held meetings at Jasper Hall and reasoned among themselves, with the help of Murphy, that since they originated this chapel, their pastor should be in charge of it.[51] A deputation was sent to Fernandez requesting that St. Patrick's be handed over to them, and Murphy appointed pastor. Although the vicar apostolic received them kindly, he replied firmly that Fr. Gleeson had been appointed pastor and would remain in that office.[52] Taking their grievances to the public they aired their imaginary wrongs in *The Morning Journal* of 18 January 1841.

> The Committee of St. Patrick's and St. Martin's chapel have received an answer from the Very Rev. Vicar Apostolic which instead of giving hopes of redressing the grievances, under which the Pastor and congregation have been so long suffering, tend to aggravate them the more and to inflame the discontent and disunion which have unhappily for too long a time distracted the Catholics of this city. . . . At a numerous and respectable Meeting of the Roman Catholics of St. Patrick's in Jasper Hall on the 24th inst., Thomas Shannon Esq., in the Chair, the Chairman immediately called upon Mr. J. Uter to state what had occurred during his absence from the island relative to the affairs of the new chapel. Mr. Uter then rose and stated that an outrage had been committed on that building by some parties who took forcible possession of it, and having further

> briefly and energetically alluded to insults and injuries they had committed on that building, he stated that they had continued to suffer from a few individuals who were interested in the subversion of the British Catholic Mission in this city. He stated that the object of this meeting was to protest against this continued persecution and seek legitimate redress.[53]

The resolutions passed at this meeting took the form of denouncing what they termed the illegal seizure of St. Patrick's from Shannon's attorney during Shannon's absence from Jamaica.[54] They would boycott St. Patrick's until it was restored to their pastor, Edmund Murphy. Firmly they called upon the spiritual head of the Catholic community to remove as speedily as possible those grievances which were likely to affect the unity of the Church.

Herein was the first hint of schism for, if Fernandez failed to accede to their wishes, they had instructed Shannon, who acted as trustee, creditor, and treasurer, to take such measures as would secure for them the peaceful return of St. Patrick's. Such brash resolutions were in defiance of all Church law for they had no right to tell the vicar apostolic how he should act in the official performance of his office. The Church in Jamaica was under his immediate jurisdiction, not that of a lay committee.

Result of These Resolutions

The real cause of all this trouble was Murphy, who cast covetous eyes at the new chapel. He would have it as his own, and the committee was a mere pawn to his personal end. The committee appointed to call upon Fernandez received a cool reception and was told by the vicar apostolic that he would acknowledge the incumbent, the Rev. James Gleeson. Fernandez recalled to their memory a point they may have forgotten, that he had appointed Gleeson as pastor of St. Patrick's at the request of this committee and at the desire of the three trustees: Bartholomew Seymour, Thomas Shannon, and E. Egan.[55] He concluded his remarks to the committee by expressing his disappointment at the harsh and threatening language in which they couched their resolutions.

Another meeting was held by the disaffected at Jasper Hall in which Fernandez was maligned, to quote the vicar apostolic:

> As these meetings were held in the house of Fr. Murphy, and as in one of the Resolutions there was a threat of schism, I imagined if Fr. Murphy were a good clergyman he would disapprove of them either publicly, as the proceedings appeared in the newspapers, or at least by writing to me. But he did neither, so that I felt myself imperatively called upon to withdraw his faculties. I wrote, therefore, to Fr. Murphy a letter for that

> purpose but he refused to receive it, and I was obliged to publish it in the newspapers.[56]

Withdrawal of faculties appeared under this form:

> To the Rev. Edmund Murphy Jan. 28, 1841
>
> Rev. Sir:
>
> The interests of the Roman Catholic Church, of which I am the Spiritual Head in this island and its dependencies, require me to withdraw from you, from this day forward, the permission I gave you to officiate as a Roman Catholic priest in my Diocese.
> I am, Rev. Sir, yours truly, [signed] Benito Fernandez.[57]

From the day Murphy ceased to have faculties to officiate, Fernandez sensed that tension was mounting. He was quite sure that the congregation at Jasper Hall was not quiet and that the troublemakers were a vociferous minority. He estimated the whole congregation, reckoning men, women and children, was not more than three hundred, a small part of the Catholic body of Kingston.[58]

In a memorandum Fernandez related subsequent events.

> Meetings were again held and, shameful to relate, on the night of the 5th–6th of March, 1841, forcible possession of the Chapel was taken. On the evening of the 6th March, the police tried to dislodge the rioters but were beaten off. The rioters then began to destroy the Chapel with bricks and stones and would have demolished it completely if a strong body of soldiers, accompanied by the Mayor, had not come forward. Twenty-five persons were taken prisoners, some of whom belong to the congregation of Jasper Hall. They will be tried at Quarter Sessions. On the evening of March 7th another meeting was held at Jasper Hall and resolution of it along with a letter from Fr. Murphy appeared in the newspaper, *The Jamaica Despatch*, of March 15th. A schism was to be completed on St. Patrick's Day at Jasper Hall.[59]

Fr. Clancy, a relative of the vicar apostolic of British Guiana, passing through on his way to Demerara, was appalled by the scandal created by his fellow countryman, Murphy.[60] Clancy entreated Murphy to seek the pardon of the vicar apostolic and end this obnoxious affair. It did have the effect of exacting from Murphy the promise to quit the island within the space of two months.[61] For this period the vicar apostolic granted Murphy his faculties to function as a priest in good standing. This was on 16 March.[62] On the following afternoon, 17 March, the vicar apostolic sent Gleeson to Murphy with the message that an apology was expected of him, which Fernandez would publish in the Kingston newspapers with an accompanying letter from himself.[63] The meeting was far from happy, for Murphy allowed his temper to express itself in a most shameful manner, abusing the much surprised Gleeson. He called the envoy the vilest of names. Murphy's change of heart may be explained in this manner: as soon as the zealots at Jasper Hall learned that Murphy had agreed to leave Jamaica, they persuaded him to reverse his plans. They argued that he was deserting them. Despite the unhappy turn of events, the vicar apostolic did not withdraw faculties granted for the two month period, hoping that Murphy would depart peacefully as promised.[64] The two months grace ended in May 1841, but Murphy remained in Jamaica and his faculties ceased.[65] A state of schism began and lasted during the next four years.[66] To the scandal of good Catholics, Murphy celebrated Mass, administered the sacraments, and preached at his chapel in Jasper Hall. Gradually, as hot heads cooled, many of his followers returned to the Church and popularity waned, Murphy became a disappointed man. On 9 May 1845 he sailed on the packet leaving at noon for England.[67] He went to Rome and laid his imagined grievances before Cardinal Fransoni, prefect of Propaganda. Fransoni consented to absolve him from censure when, in his own handwriting, he promised never again to set foot in Jamaica.[68] He returned to London and took up residence there. From London 15 March 1846 he wrote to his former adherents and begged them to return to the Church.

> I honestly pray that all the Catholics who were under my charge may return to their chief pastor, or at least submit to his jurisdiction. I deeply regret having been placed in a position where authority was set at defiance and I have left in the hands of Cardinal Fransoni, a retraction of the past.[69]

Without the presence of Murphy the schism quickly fell to pieces and its partisans divided according to their sincerity as Catholics, either returning to the jurisdiction of the vicar apostolic, or remaining so indifferent as to frequent no place of worship while some apostatized and made open profession of being Baptists or Methodists.[70]

Before Murphy had departed, another misfortune befell the Church. Fr. Gleeson, pastor of St. Patrick's and St. Martin's during the Murphy schism, defected. Duquesnay, writing to Rome on behalf of Fernandez, 22 February 1845, gave some details of this unfortunate event.

> Fr. J. Gleeson, an Irish priest, having obtained a statement from the Vicar Apostolic that he was a priest in good standing and not under any censure and that his morals were good, betook himself to the Protestant Bishop of this island and swore to the Thirty-nine Articles of the Anglican Church. When this terrible step was taken, he left the island carrying letters from the Protestant Bishop of Jamaica to the Bishop of Montreal (Toronto), Canada. There can be no doubt about this fact. Fr. Gleeson is a light-

headed, inconstant, careless, lazy person. He showed no fervour during the six years he had been attached to the mission. Nevertheless, his conduct had not been immoral, although not very edifying. On the other hand, the Vicar Apostolic believed he ought to give the statement spoken above. The apostasy took place in the early days of July 1844.[71]

The Great Fire

Murphy's schism and Gleeson's defection were only two of Fernandez's troubles during this turbulent period; a third was added, the Great Fire of 26 August 1840, which destroyed the entire structure of Holy Trinity Church on Duke and Sutton streets.[72] About twelve o'clock on Saturday afternoon, 26 August, an alarm was sounded for a fire at the foundry of James and Malcolm on Harbour near to East Street, and what started out as a minor blaze lasted all Saturday and into Sunday morning. It spread along the whole section between Harbour and port Royal streets, then up East Street, while the fire brigade was simultaneously fighting a fire at Mr. Jacob's house on Duke street, one at Mrs. Headly's on East street, and another at the Atheneum Club on Lawes Street, it extended to the whole block of houses around the square, from there to Sutton Street, crossing over Duke Street and consuming the two blocks of houses and Holy Trinity Church. When the fire finally spent itself, one eighth of the entire city had been burned.

Kingston fire August 26, 1840 started in an iron foundry belonging to William James and Co., situated at east end of Harbour St.—238 buildings destroyed.

Sunday Magazine-Sunday Gleaner,
22 August 1971

With Holy Trinity destroyed, there was no other place of worship for the Catholics except the controversial chapel of St. Patrick which for the next two years proved a blessing for the Kingston congregation until a grant of £500 from the House of Assembly and funds collected by the congregation raised a new Holy Trinity from the charred ruins of the old in 1845.

Dupeyron Becomes Coadjutor Vicar Apostolic

The Murphy affair and advancing years weighed so heavily upon Fernandez that he requested the Holy See for a coadjutor to help administer the ever-growing Catholic community with its steadily increasing responsibilities. Rome granted his request on 18 September 1841, when it named Arthur W. J. Duquesnay to that office, presenting the Church in Jamaica with an excellent opportunity to perpetuate itself through the medium of a native clergy by allowing Duquesnay to succeed Fernandez as vicar apostolic, thus setting a precedent under British colonial rule.

There was reason for this happy choice of a native Jamaican. Duquesnay had proved his administrative ability and had shown beyond doubt his intense interest in the progress of the Church by yeoman service under Fernandez. To him the Church owed all-important beginnings of Catholic education when, in September 1836 he opened a high school on Orange Street, Kingston. This educational institution under a native Jamaican had the potential of forming a corps of educated Catholics and through them of raising up a native clergy for the vicariate. In real life, this did not eventuate.

After labouring for eleven years in his native country, Duquesnay left Jamaica in the last week of July 1845 for Nassau, where he remained for four weeks before proceeding to New Orleans on 26 August. While at Nassau, which had not been visited since it became part of the Jamaican vicariate in 1837, Duquesnay found seventy-two Catholics who had raised £381 towards the construction of a church. He arrived in New Orleans on 5 October and wrote to Fernandez that he did not wish to return to Jamaica. Catholics in Kingston were much upset by his decision and no one more than Fernandez in losing such a dear companion, especially since the vicariate desperately needed priests. The hope of raising up a native clergy vanished with his departure.

In a letter written from New Orleans on 14 October 1845, Duquesnay explained his reasons of resignation to Cardinal Fransoni, prefect of Propaganda.

> It is after serious reflection before God, that I have decided to resign the office of Co-adjutor to the Vicar Apostolic of Jamaica. I humbly pray that you present my resignation also to the Holy Father, assuring his Holiness that I am well aware of the honour which he originally conferred on me. In resigning, I am not so much guided by the difficulties attached to the charge confided to me, as from the conviction that a new place will be better suited to me to raise my fallen spirits. Further my debility and illness grows worse each day, and obliges me to seek a change of climate. I would be very much dejected if Rome should think for a single instant that my decision was made by not being able to get along with the Vicar Apostolic. I say sincerely that I have never worked with a more sincere, more devoted priest worthy of my affection as he. I believe and declare here that the respect and reverence of the Catholics of Jamaica for his person, his piety and his zeal makes him the man proper to fill the office which is confided to him. I have placed in the hands of the Bishop of New Orleans the Apostolic Brief of Our Holy Father (by which His Holiness named me Co-adjutor of the Vicar of Jamaica) in order that he may make use of it as your Eminence shall instruct him.[73]

Duquesnay died 20 October 1858, pastor of St. Augustine's Church, New Orleans.

Duquesnay's estimate of Fernandez was well-founded and deserved for, from the moment of his elevation to the office of vicar apostolic, he had trod a stony path and through it all kept his equanimity which placed him head and shoulders above his critics offering to Jamaica the picture of a stalwart defender of the Church. No matter what his critics may have vehemently hurled against him, Fernandez stands out as one of the most apostolic men ever to tread Jamaican soil.

Fifteen

The Decade 1850–1860

Jesuit Education Comes to Jamaica

The scholastic reputation as one of Jamaica's best secondary schools enjoyed today by St. George's College could not have been predicted when it was founded in 1850. It laboured under two disadvantages: it was founded by foreigners, it was conducted by Jesuits. The first pupils were enrolled at St. George's while a bitter battle waged in the public press on the pros and cons of allowing Jesuits to operate a school in the island. A simple five-line advertisement inserted in *The Colonial Standard and Jamaica Despatch* roused a storm of bigotry when readers were informed.

> Kingston, Aug. 15, 1850
>
> St. George's Colonial College, 4 North Street. The above establishment will be opened for the reception of Pupils on Monday, the 2nd of September next.[1]

A group of Colombian Jesuits newly arrived from South America inserted this advertisement in the Kingston newspaper and thus launched a secondary school which would have happy results for the future of the Church. This cannot be called the first attempt at higher education—Duquesnay had opened his secondary school fourteen years previously; nor can it be called the first Jesuit attempt, since Cotham had assumed charge when Duquesnay devoted his full time to parish work.

By a decree of Colombian president José Lopez dated 18 May 1850, all Jesuits were ordered to abandon their colleges, churches, and residences, and leave Colombia within forty-eight hours. Later the time was lengthened to the generous space of ninety-six hours.[2]

On 25 June 1850 Fernandez welcomed to Jamaica two faculties, one from the College of Medellin and the other from Bogotá.[3] Fernandez was in full sympathy with these exiles, for twenty-nine years previously he himself had been a refugee. The leader of this Jesuit band, Emmanuel Gil, had paid a previous visit to Jamaica on 15 January 1847. The event was recorded by Cotham. "The famous Fr. Gil, Visitor of Ours in South America, arrived here on the 15th and sailed the following day for S. Martha, whence he was to sail up the Rio Magdalena on his way to Bogotá."[4]

Three years later Gil led this band of Jesuits out of Colombia to the more friendly shores of Jamaica. The welcome these exiles received was not universal as is evident from the skilled pen of a prominent citizen of Falmouth on the north coast.

Bigotry Raises Its Voice

The keen, practiced eye of John Castello, editor of the *Falmouth Post,* saw a threat to the commonweal of this peaceful island colony in the coming of the Jesuits. In a spirit of public righteousness, he warned his countrymen of the impending danger should the Jesuits establish their school. He voiced his alarm through his northside journal on 6 August 1850.

> The cause of Jamaican Tractarians is likely to be strengthened by the arrival in Kingston of eighteen or twenty Jesuits who have published in the daily papers an advertisement in which they announce the intention of establishing the 'St. George's Colonial College' for the education of youth. We deem it our duty to warn our fellow colonists of the danger of patronizing an institution which is superintended and conducted by men who are attached to one of the most infamous sects that have ever disgraced Christianity. . . . As many of our readers are ignorant of the nature and character of Jesuitism and therefore may be deceived with the specious prospectus which has been inserted in the journals of the southside, in order that parents may be induced to send their children to St. George's Colonial College for the purpose of being classically educated, we shall avail ourselves of an excellent work which is now before us to point out the principles of the individuals to whom public attention is now directed.[5]

Castello then proceeded to narrate all the defamation of three hundred years standing against the Society of Jesus. Others took up the calumnies and it developed into a battle of the press.

Fair-Minded Jamaican Answers Castello

Castello soon discovered that not all agreed with his point of view. One who signed himself Philalethes in a letter to *The Colonial Standard and Jamaica Despatch,* 14 August 1850, came to the defence of the Jesuits.

> Sir:
>
> It is with feelings of greatest pain that I have read in *The Morning Journal* today an article consisting of an extract from *The New York Commercial Advertizer* in which a most unwarrantable attempt has been made to create suspicion of the views and motives of the Roman Catholic Divines who are endeavouring to establish, or, as I ardently hope, have already established, a classical and scientific school (College) in Kingston on the enlightened system of European education.[6]

Philalethes considered Castello's charges unfounded in the absence of any direct proof that these Jesuits from South America were vile, unprincipled men.

> These Reverend gentlemen, who are entitled to the thanks and gratitude of Jamaica, have their motives impugned on grounds which appear perfectly preposterous, as not a single specific fact has been mentioned against them. In absence of every charge of this description, we must judge them by their overt acts and assuredly if their object is to propagate error and darkness they have adopted the most extraordinary means for this purpose that can well be imagined. . . . In sober truth, Mr. Editor, the establishment of this college in the chief town of Jamaica is the greatest and most important event that has taken place in the British West Indies since the abolition of slavery, the proof (if any be wanting) consists in this that should Protestants become alarmed at the possible diffusion of doctrines to which they are opposed, they have no conceivable way of preventing that diffusion but by adopting the very means employed by the Catholics themselves—by the establishment of the enlightened European system of an elevated classical and scientific education.

Editor of Daily Newspaper Comes to the Defense of the Jesuits

On Tuesday and Wednesday, 27 and 28 August, Castello read another defence of the Jesuits.[7] This time from the experienced pen of the editor of *The Colonial Standard and Jamaica Despatch*. The writer prefaced his editorial by acknowledging that the establishment of a classical college in Kingston under the superintendence of the Jesuits had created much excitement among the Evangelical Protestants. If the editor placed credence in all the communications received from the public, he would be inclined to believe that Antichrist had been formally installed in Kingston and that the whole morality of the island was about to be upset by these Jesuits. Since this was the era of Newman and the Tractarians, when the position of the Establishment was being seriously questioned, and defense of the Catholic Church was looked upon with suspicion and anyone who seemed to favour the Catholic position as a traitor. The editor had to assure his readers that he was not a Catholic nor a Catholic in disguise.

> We are not Roman Catholics. For the consolation of the very timid we may state that we are not even Tractarians. We have never read an Oxford Tract, and we have no feeling with Newman. Well, it may be asked if such be the case, why do we not lend our assistance to run down the Jesuit Priests who have found refuge in Jamaica from the persecution of a Revolutionary State in South America? We answer, because we have no sufficient reason assigned. On the contrary, the first offering they make us is one which we feel inclined to grasp at as a blessing rather than as evidence of offense. Jamaica has been a British Colony for nearly two hundred years, and to her reproach it must be said that no single establishment has ever existed at which the child of a gentleman could receive a gentleman's education, until an unfortunate body of Jesuits, hunted by a democratic Governor, goaded on by the very dregs of a South American Democracy, fled to Jamaica for protection and offered this boon to her inhabitants as some recompense for the shelter she has afforded them. Why should we hunt down such a body?[8]

From readers came old calumnies about the Jesuits resurrected from ancient documents which falsely accused them of a whole calendar of crimes. One reader sent a copy of 'Arrest du Parliament,' dated 5 March 1772.[9] This document proposed to examine Jesuit teaching and concluded they approved of theft, lies, perjury, impurity, homicide, patricide, and regicide, and that they upset religions in order to substitute their own superstitions, favouring magic, blasphemy, idolatry, and such an array of crimes which if proved, would be enough to exclude them from honourable society and even from civilization itself. The editor questioned that the rescript of the French Parliment applied to this little band of exiled Jesuits in Jamaica:

> But is the rescript of the French Parliament of 1772, authority in the present day? We really do not profess to know. We have read much of the Jesuits: perhaps as much as any one who is ready to stand forward as their reviler in Jamaica. And we have learned at any rate this of them that they challenge, perhaps, any other association, collegiate or clerical, to exhibit an equal amount of classical attainment or deeper intimacy with the intricacies of Metaphysics and Logic.[10]

Again the editor reminded his readers that he was neither a Jesuit nor did he have any affection for their doctrine. This theme runs through the editorial, lest he be thought to be some secret ally of the Jesuits or the Catholic Church.

> But let us not be misunderstood. We are not Jesuits, not lovers of the teaching of the Society of Jesus. We are Protestants who have lived for forty years under a constitution of unbounded toleration. We have been taught to believe that all men were free within the limits of the British Constitution to worship God according to their own conscience.[11]

He went on to claim that almost any fanatical sect would find itself protected by law in Jamaica and would be allowed to settle here disseminating their doctrine, however debased it might be, among the peasantry while the Jesuits whose training was of an excellent standard would be hunted out of the country. The editor asked that the Jesuits be granted the same fair trial as would be offered any religious body which desired to settle in Jamaica.

> An Anglican Churchman, of course, as a matter of faith could have no ecclesiastical communion with either [Jesuits or any sect]. Nor as regards the Jesuits, are they expected to do so. The persons who form the body in this island are literally unknown. It has not 'been our fortune' to meet one of them. But for the public notice that has been taken of them anonymously in the columns of a Contemporary, their presence in Jamaica would really have been unknown.
>
> St. George's College has been advertised, but who the professors were, that under the guardianship of the patron Saint of England had undertaken to teach the youth of the colony, when no one else would or could teach them, was unknown. We learn they are Jesuits, and 'good Churchmen' appeal to us incontinently to write them down. We cannot do so. We have no authority for doing so. They offer to teach the youth of the colony, to afford them classical advantages which they cannot at present obtain. Is it for this we are to aid in writing them down? No one of course who has his fears will send his child to St. George's College. He is not bound to do so, and, everything rests with himself. But the 'day scholars' may be sent to the classical classes and a child has access, therefore to the best means of education without residence. It is scarcely possible that with daily communication with his family, a child's mind could be so influenced as to lead to a change of faith.[12]

The editor thought that St. George's would give education in Jamaica the necessary prod to rouse it from the lethargy in which it had settled for many years.

> But if this Jesuit College be so pregnant with alarm to the ministry of our church may it not be the means of working something like real educational advancement in Jamaica? We have heard for years of a College—where is it? It is a disgrace to a country like Jamaica that a man must either send his child to England at an expense which ruins him, or let him grow up uneducated. St. George's College in the absence of any other sufficient establishment will be grasped at, in spite of prejudice by men who are neither Jesuits nor Tractarians but, who, watching carefully meanwhile over the spiritual intelligence of their children will avail themselves of the classical advantages offered by a foreign group who, whatever may be their theological opinions, are of all others best qualified for solid instruction. Let the Church of England, therefore, look to it.[13]

Such frank defense of St. George's drew down upon the editor of *The Colonial Standard and Jamaica Despatch* the rancor of an offended community. However, he was not one to retreat from a position which he judged to be just.[14] The editor knew he would arouse the ire of religious bigots but he had not reckoned with the schoolmasters of the community:

> We were prepared, we say, for all this but we confess that we had no expectation or intent of raising a pack of irate schoolmasters about our ears. These gentlemen, it appears, are offended at our statement that 'hitherto, to Jamaica's shame, there has been no Academic Institution in the island at which a gentleman's son could receive a gentleman's education.' We regret that offense should have been taken at such a statement, and the more so, as we cannot retract. In spite of Mr. Nathaniel Melhado's continental education and Mr. Solomon Meyer's sententious self-laudation, we maintain that up to the present hour it has been impossible for any gentleman to give his child a 'finished classical education' in Jamaica.
>
> If Mr. Meyers wishes to know what we mean by a 'finished education,' we may state that we mean a knowledge of the upper walks of Greek and Latin literature. We should like to see a child who has been turned out of either seminary [Melhado's and Myers's schools] who could take his stand in an Upper Form at Eton or Harrow, or could take his 'little go' at either University [Oxford or Cambridge].
>
> Show me one of these boys who could read a chorus in any one of the tragedies of Aeschylus or Sophocles, who could translate an ode of Pindar or wade through a chapter of Herodotus or a page of Aristophanes. We have no wish, far from it, to underrate the value of local schools. To the extent of their ordinary professions we believe them to be really valuable and as elementary academies they are of infinite use; but to expect to give a child a finished classical education at them, is not in reason. . . .
>
> Let Mr. Meyers and Mr. Melhado show us that they can offer the education which the public Schools of England impart in Latin and Greek alone, and they may be assured that they will not want in our support. We shall be too happy to assure our fellow-countrymen of a faculty which we believe at present not to exist, and then throw down the gauntlet to St. George's with impunity.[15]

The battle of words subsided, the air cleared. St. George's opened with an enrollment of thirty boarders and thirty-eight day students.[16] It was a propitious beginning for this new type of school, which offered a curriculum of Latin, Greek, French, Spanish, English, Rhetoric, History, Mathematics, Logic, Metaphysics, Ethics, Drawing, and Calligraphy.[17]

An academic year passed, and on 14 August 1851 the entire student body marched into an auditorium filled with proud parents and distinguished guests.[18] The occasion was a public examination in subjects studied during the year. One boy, Mario Valenzuela, who received a distinction in Ethics that afternoon, was to return to his native land, Colombia, and leave his mark indelibly in the annals of the Society of Jesus in that country. When he did return to his native country and tried to enter the Society of Jesus, he found that he had to face eight years of parental opposition before he became a Jesuit.

Born on 19 January 1836, of a union of two distinguished Colombian families, the Valenzuelas and the Pieschacons, he began his studies with the Jesuits at an early age.[19] When exile came he followed the Jesuits to Jamaica, but once back in Colombia, Mario entered the university, studying law and philosophy. Studies were interrupted on 4 April 1854, when General José Maria Melo proclaimed himself dictator. Mario joined the opposition and took part in the fighting which spelled defeat for Melo in August 1854. In 1857, Valenzuela chose the field of journalism, writing for *El Proviner,* and that same year was named a member of the Assembly which drew up the new constitution for the Province of Cundinamarca.

About this time he founded one of the great works of his career, a conference of the St. Vincent de Paul Society. Finding himself one day with friends in the cloisters of St. Dominic, he began to speak enthusiastically about the charitable work of the Vincentians. But how to begin it in Colombia? Mario took off his hat, passed it around, and with a few coins of little value the St. Vincent de Paul Society was born in that country.

Mario entered the Jesuit novitiate 2 May 1858, followed immediately by an odyssey through Central America. But in 1883 he returned to Bogotá, where parish work occupied his attention until the populace demanded a college. He opened the first in Pasto, then another in Medellin, and fianlly in Bogotá. From that point the Society of Jesus was back in Colombia with the blessing of the government, due principally to the persevering work of Mario Valenzuela, one of St. George's first pupils.

Faculty of St. George's Heroic Labour During the Cholera

St. George's had but opened its doors when the dread Asiatic cholera broke out in October 1850.[20] Kingston was particularly hard hit; by the end of the month one hundred deaths per day were reported. It worsened in November until the death toll reached one hundred fifty per day, and on two days of the same month six hundred victims died. The occasion gave the Jesuits an opportunity to prove what manner of men they were. The superior, Fr. Emmanuel Gil, set aside five priests and two coadjutor brothers to care for the stricken, and they were available at any hour of the day or night.[21] Often they found three or four cases where only one had been reported, and so many were the calls from door and window that they knew not which to attend first. Priests consoled the dying, exhorted them to repentance, heard their confessions, and administered Extreme Unction, then hurried on to the next house. When the scourge abated, Kingston counted 3,675 victims, more than one tenth of its total population.[22] The heroic charity displayed by these priests refuted the bigotry of editor Castello; the heart of all Kingston was won in their favour.

The bigotry aroused by the editor of the *Falmouth Post*, however, did not impede the progress of the Church. In Kingston there were two churches, Holy Trinity and St. Patrick's.[23] In the country, chapels began to mushroom: at Spanish Town, twelve miles from Kingston; at King's Weston, eighteen miles from Kingston; at Lovely Grove, Above Rocks, Cavaliers, Toll Gate, Rockfort, and Montego Bay. This was an impressive growth from the days when Araujo laid the foundations of Holy Trinity. Still, the best congregation centred around Holy Trinity, which was well attended by several hundred fervent Catholics, and at times was crowded to more than capacity, since everything was done to make the services attractive: good preaching, beautiful music, a variety of pious associations, together with expensive church ornaments which created a homey atmosphere of a mother Church.[24]

Cotham continued to serve St. Patrick's with not too much encouragement from the none too fervent congregation. Mass was celebrated there twice a week and on Sundays and holy days. In Spanish Town the lay committee had purchased an old house in 1838 and had reserved a large room for a chapel which had a congregation of 140; of that number thirty were regular communicants.[25] In October 1848 the vicar apostolic purchased a large house with eight acres of land at King's Weston for £27.7.0, and had spent fifty pounds sterling erecting a chapel which had a congregation of 165, and of that number 80 attended Mass regularly. Lovely Grove had a Catholic population of 160, and of this number 70 attended regularly. Cavaliers had 50 with 34 in regular attendance: Rockfort had 130 with 55 communicants. Toll Gate, 50 Catholics with 20 regulars. Above Rocks 200 members and 90 regular communicants; at Above Rocks on 13 July 1850, 55 received the sacrament of confirmation.

In Kingston the rectory of the vicar apostolic was 200 yards removed from Holy Trinity Church, so that he reserved the Blessed Sacrament in a small chapel in his King Street residence, where the Jesuits performed their religious duties.[26] They recited litanies after the morning examination of conscience at 11.45 a.m., followed by what was termed second breakfast. At 7.00 was first breakfast, consisting of coffee and bread; dinner was at 6.00 p.m. The difference between the second breakfast and dinner was that at second breakfast eggs were served and at dinner soup was added. But Dupeyron was rarely home to enjoy these community meals. He spent most of his time on horseback riding to his scattered missions, such as the journey he took in 1850 covering 578 miles which netted 181 confessions, 161 communions, 13 baptisms, and 6 marriages.[27] Three times a year he would make this arduous trip, staying on the road as long as nine weeks on each occasion. From such progress both in Kingston and in the country, Castello's tirade had little effect upon the Church.

But the time came when, of their own accord, the South American Jesuits terminated their stay in Jamaica. Acting upon an invitation from the archbishop of Guatemala, they left Jamaica in August 1852 to open a college in Central America.[28] They had been in the island a mere two years but in that time had laid the foundation of St. George's College which would prove a great boon for the Church. Five of the original faculty stayed on to acquaint Frs. Cotham and Simond with the administration of the college,[29] which was removed from 26 North Street to 74 King Street, Kingston.[30] The college for day students was opened on 2 August 1852 under Fr. Alexis Simond of the Province of Sardinia.[31] He became headmaster, assisted by Fr. Cotham, a lay teacher, and the five Spanish Jesuits who had not yet left for Guatemala. The student body was reduced to thirty pupils, most of whom were Catholics. Fr. Simond continued in the office of headmaster for the next fourteen years, so enhancing the reputation of the College that non-Catholic parents enrolled their boys there.[32]

The Jesuits were not the only religious body to enter the Jamaican educational field at this time. The Franciscan Sisters added their talent to the Church's increasing interest in education for the youth of the island. To Fr. Joseph Howell falls the honour of introducing these religious women to Jamaica.[33] Born in Yorkshire, England on 8 October 1790, Howell began his missionary career on 6 January 1856.[34] An article written in the first year of his ministry for the *Annals of the Propagation of the Faith,* Lyons, France, caught the eye of Mother Veronica Cordier, O.S.F.[35] French by birth, she and Mother Adelaide had left Tourcoing, Normandy on 2 June 1847 to take up educational work on Charlotte Street, Glasgow, Scotland at the invitation of Fr. Peter Forbes.[36] Two years later the Mother Superior was dead, a victim of the dread cholera. Ruin seemed imminent when Bishop John Murdock, vocar apostolic of Glasgow, came to their rescue.[37] Under his guidance the community prospered, so that within ten years they had forty professed in addition to a number of novices and postulants. They opened new convents, staffed schools, and inaugurated pioneer evening classes for poor mill girls who wished an education. At this stage in their development, Howell began a correspondence with Mother Veronica Cordier to convince her of the bright prospects awaiting her sisters in Jamaica. Mother Cordier brought the need for religious teachers in Jamaica to the attention of Bishop Murdock, who assigned four Franciscans to the mission: Mother Veronica Cordier, Sisters Paula Charlet, Philomena, and de Sales. On 5 November 1857 these new recruits disembarked at the port of Kingston.[38] It is claimed that they had only two shillings and sixpence in their purse.[39] If so, the lack of money was quickly remedied by a gift of ten pounds sterling from their first benefactor, the Honourable Richard O'Reilly.[40] Their first convent, a building located on East Queen Street, Kingston, where the Gaiety Theatre now stands, was put at their disposal by its owner, Henry Vendryes.[41] There the Immaculate Conception Academy, a school for the wealthier girls, opened January 1858.[42]

Although the Franciscans were content with their East Queen Street convent, Dupeyron envisioned a larger site where they might accommodate more pupils. For this purpose he purchased the home of the late Dr. Joseph Magrath on Duke Street north of St. Patrick's Church. By May 1859, the sisters were prospering with five new vocations, two from Scotland and three from Jamaica. Two of the Jamaican vocations were sisters, Josephine and Caroline D'Aquin, daughters of a Haitian refugee, who took the names of Sister Mary Joseph and Sister Mary Clare in religion. As a dowry, Henry D'Aquin gave them an estate in St. Andrew, contiguous to Kingston, but at that time considered to be in the country. Selling a wharf which he owned for £800, D'Aquin purchased "That Pen in St. Andrew Parish of Surrey, formerly called Islington, now by the name of Moringa Park, containing twenty-one acres."[43] This land proved of more utility than the wharf in the days to come. Renamed Alvernia, it served as a happy refuge when fire gutted their Duke Street convent, and it later became the site of St. Joseph's Training College for Teachers.

At the Academy, girls of the upper stratum of society were taught, but there was also a demand that the sisters teach the poor. An opportunity came in January 1860, when Dupeyron, who followed Fernandez as vicar apostolic, assigned the girls' department of his own school for poor children to the sisters. They renamed it St. Joseph's Girls' School with first classes held in the Assembly Room of the Holy Trinity Church.

After five years in Jamaica, Mother Cordier was advised to return to Europe to regain her health.[44] Perhaps the doctors were too solicitous, for in 1862 she reentered the convent she helped found in Glasgow and lived there until 15 November 1931, dying about the age of ninety-two[45] One of her companions, Sister Paula Charlet, succeeded as superior and held that office for the unbelievable period of fifty-two years.[46] Up to the end of her life she taught class, a total service of fifty-seven years to the youth of Jamaica. She died on 24 May 1914, at the age of eighty-one.[47]

Last Days of Benito Fernandez

For thirty-five years Fernandez had laboured continuously for the good of the Church and was never known to leave the vicariate, even for a holiday.[48] In all those years, loneliness, a schism, lack of priest personnel, and being a foreigner who had learned English as an adult may be counted among his many and varied troubles. Not to mention the day a negro struck his person,[49] subtle hostility towards the faith, and the perennial problem of concubinage among many of his flock. Yet through all this the one motive urging him to persevere so long was his intense love for the Church. Personal suffering mattered little as long as the Church made some advancement. And grow it did, from one priest in 1824 to eight Jesuits in 1855: William Cotham,[50] James Dupeyron, Alexis Simond, Joseph Bertolio, Joseph Howell, Stephen Ghersi, George Avvaro, and Joseph Dupont. Places of worship spread from Kingston to Spanish Town, Montego Bay, King's Weston, Lovely Grove, Toll Gate, Rockfort, Above Rocks, and Cavaliers.[51]

Fernandez had been ailing for some time and doctors had warned him that his condition was growing serious. He gave up all preaching[52] and limited himself to hearing confessions and singing a High Mass on Sundays. On Wednesday evening, 27 September 1855, he made his weekly confession and on the next day celebrated Mass. On the afternoon of Thursday, 28 September, while reciting the divine office, he died of a stroke.[53]

Word spread rapidly. Protestant, Jew, and Catholic expressed their grief—acts of charity and unbounded benevolence to all, irrespective of creed, and a spotless reputation made the good Benito, as he was affectionately called, a universal favourite.

The solemn tolling of the church bell officially announces the passing of a public figure. This was Kingston's custom. But Holy Trinity did not possess a bell, so a delegation of Catholic men together with Alderman Salom called on the rector of the Anglican church to ask if his church bell might be tolled.[54] He readily granted the favour. From Thursday afternoon until sunset, all day Friday, and on Saturday morning until interment, the Anglican church bell solemnly tolled for the Catholic prelate.[55] The Union Jack was flown at half-mast from the Commercial House, as were the flags of several consulates and ships in the harbour. At an early hour on Saturday, 30 September, the body of the vicar apostolic was placed under a canopy in one of the rectory apartments at 74 King Street.[56] At 8.30 a.m. the funeral procession moved from the rectory led by the sacristan bearing a large silver crucifix, followed by acolytes, then by 115 women dressed in white holding lighted candles.[57] The clergy immediately preceded the coffin which was borne by six men. At its side walked the pallbearers: Don Pedro Sasis, consul for Colombia; Don Juan Cantillo Jovellanos, consul for Spain; the Honorable Edward Chitty, chairman of Quarter Sessions; Lieutenant O'Flanagan of the First West India Regiment.[58] Walking three abreast was a vast concourse of people of all denominations following the coffin. The cortege passed down King Street, turned left at the centre of the Parade into East Queen Street, then up Duke Street to enter Sutton Street from the east. So vast was the throng before the Holy Trinity Church that the police under Inspector Leake experienced difficulty in clearing a passage for the funeral to enter. A solemn Requiem Mass was celebrated by the Reverend James E. Dupeyron with the Reverend Joseph Dupont as deacon and the Reverend Joseph Bertolio as subdeacon. Obsequies completed, Benito Fernandez was buried in the church he had so faithfully served, close to the main altar.[59] Other prelates would follow Fernandez, but none would equal his thirty-five years of unbroken service.

Much of the effort of Fernandez and Dupeyron during the years 1847–60 was dedicated to laying a solid foundation for the parish community. The principal focus of missionary endeavour was on parish duties such as might be incumbent upon priests in any large city of Europe or America. This was the method of evangelizing chosen by Fernandez and continued by his successor Dupeyron. With the strictly parish work came the consolations communicated by this type of apostolate in immediate, measurable results which could be expressed in numbers.

May 1847 opened with a ten-day mission preached by the priests attached to Holy Trinity Church.[60] It was the first of its kind ever given in Jamaica, and it had very happy results. Marriage was its central theme; so well did the missionaries press home their lesson that many couples living in concubinage asked to have their unions regularized. Three years later Dupeyron could write that the effects of the mission were still being felt and that during the period from May 1847 to July 1850 230 couples living in concubinage had been married.[61] Added to this were forty "honest marriages," as Dupeyron designated them.

In the following year, 1848, besides marriages Dupeyron recorded 337 baptisms, 160 converts, 60 confirmations, and 168 funerals. In his missionary excursions to the interior, Dupeyron heard 989 confessions, distributed 810 communions, baptized 119, and received 24 into the Church. In 1849 Kingston and environs netted 409 baptisms; of these 100 were converts. In his trips to the interior, Dupeyron heard 194 confessions, distributed 1,000 communions, baptized 65, married 15 couples, and received 15 converts into the Church, although at this time there were only nine chapels outside Kingston.

Jamaica in 1850 could boast of a population of 400,000, which was broken down into 305,000 negroes, 80,000 mulattoes, and 15,000 whites. The Anglicans had a great advantage, with 115 clergymen as compared to the handful of Catholic priests. The Catholic population at this time in history was 5,000.

Statistics for the next few years are meagre. The year 1852 produced 378 baptisms and 130 converts for Kingston and environs, while the record for the interior showed 406 baptisms and 6 converts. In Kingston and environs 260 funerals were conducted, 169 of them for victims of yellow fever.

The arrival of Fr. Joseph Howell, S. J. on Sunday, 6 January 1856 raised the number of missionaries to six.[62] The results of their labours from 11 December 1854 to 16 December 1855 showed 412 baptisms and 59 converts for Kingston, while Dupeyron's missionary excursions into the interior yielded 45 baptisms, 5 converts, and 11 marriages. Dupeyron complained that the Pascal communions were small for 1854, a mere 2,000. The following year, from 17 December 1855 to 21 December 1856, in Kingston and environs there were 489 baptisms, 68 converts, 162 funerals and the same number of Pascal communions, 2,000, in a total Catholic population of 5,000.[63] No further statistics are given until the year 1858 and these are scanty.

From 1 January to 5 December 1858, there were 494 baptisms and 153 funerals for Kingston, while for the interior the only statistic given is 75 baptisms. [64] In this year of 1858 is mentioned for the first time the conversion of the Chinese. No number is given except to say that the number of Africans and Chinese converts was 18. The Catholic population had now risen to 7,000 out of a total of 380,000.

From Passion Sunday to Palm Sunday, 1859, Dupeyron and Howell conducted a retreat for the congregation of Holy Trinity Church which yielded consoling spiritual results. From 6 December 1858 to 18 December 1859, 534 baptisms are recorded for Kingston; of this number 44 were converts while during this same period the missionaries conducted 144 funerals. From 19 December 1859 to 31 December 1860 in the whole of Jamaica there were 527 baptisms and 26 converts, while in Kingston there were 149 funerals.

The 1850–60 period posed a missionary problem which would

continue for a full century: what proportion of personnel and finances to assign to education and what to parish work? For the sisters, the question did not arise, because they were totally dedicated to education. But for the priests this was a serious decision. Unfortunately for education, parish work received the lion's share of men and money. But there was always a small group who fought hard to give education its rightful share in the scheme of things missionary. Despite their efforts, education was looked upon by the practical-minded missionary as a stepchild, since for them the numbers of baptisms, communions, confessions, confirmations, and marriages were more important than the long-range results which education would produce.

Sixteen

J. Sidney Woollett, S.J., and His Times

Dupeyron Vicar Apostolic

The death of Fernandez did not catch the Church unprepared as it had been when Quigly died in 1799 and again when Le Cun died in 1808. On 2 September 1851, during Fernandez' declining years, the Holy See appointed James E. Dupeyron coadjutor vicar apostolic with right of succession. With Fernandez's death Dupeyron became vicar apostolic of Jamaica, British Honduras, and the Bahamas.[1] It was a happy choice, for he knew every inch of the terrain, had met and was acquainted with people of every strata of society, from bush peasant to wealthy planter. Eventually his new office would end his missionary excursions; it would mean settling down to the routine of administration. For the time being, though, he had to continue his old way of life until someone came to relieve the burden. When he was absent from Kingston for long periods, Cotham acted as Jesuit superior, for Dupeyron now combined in his person the two offices of vicar apostolic and Jesuit superior.

In 1860 circumstances forced a change in the roving life of this itinerant missionary, limiting his activity to Kingston and environs. Cotham and Howell died within a month of each other, and to their deaths was added another, that of a missionary in British Honduras, reducing the Jamaican personnel to Dupeyron and Dupont. Cotham died on 19 November and Howell on 23 December. Dupeyron was visibly affected by Cotham's death, for since the day they sailed from Liverpool in October 1837 they had been intimate friends:

> My dear companion, I may say my dear Spiritual Father for the past twenty-eight years, whom I can never forget, Fr. William Cotham, died on Monday at twenty to ten p.m. after a few days illness. . . . Fr. Ressive at Belize and Fr. Cotham here. . . . Oh, God spare this poor mission.[2]

In December, Dupeyron again wrote in the same strain:

> Fr. Howell died on Sunday at 8.00 p.m. I was in the habit of saying Mass in his room and giving him Holy Communion in the form of viaticum. He was at a friend's residence (Mr. Artice) two miles from Kingston. . . . What a loss for the mission. We belong to the English province, but there is not a single English Father in the vicariate. Is there no one who would devote himself to this mission? I do not, and cannot expect one with the scientific, literary and oratorical talents of our dear departed that I am perfectly aware of. Oh send to us one who when he preaches in English, preaches in his mother tongue.[3]

Fr. J. Sidney Woollett, S.J.

This stirring appeal to the provincial of the English province had the happy effect of transferring Fr. Sidney Woollett from Demerara, British Guiana, to Jamaica. J. Sidney Woollett arrived in Jamaica on 3 June 1861 with the mature background of a former professional man.[4] His early environment was set in a mold different from the average missionary. Peering into his ancestry is historically rewarding. In a London garret, behind doors locked and barred, Sidney Marlow and his wife Mary Mangaar Marlow, maternal grandparents of Fr. Woollett, were received into the Church by Bishop Richard Challoner in 1772.[5] Royal blood ran in Woollett's veins, for Mary Mangaar Marlow was the daughter of Colonel Mangaar, son of a Danish king by a morganatic marriage. His father, John Mitchell Woollett, was a wealthy coal merchant who resided at Woolwich Common and carried on his export business in Ordinance Walk, Pedlars Acre, London.

Born on Easter Monday, 23 March 1818, Sidney was baptized three days later at St. George's Cathedral, Southwalk, by Fr. James Yorke Bramston. The elder Woollett enjoyed sufficient financial success to send his son to Jesuit Stonyhurst where he entered the class of elements at the age of ten, but remained only one year and then transferred to St. Edmund's College, Ware. Seven years later, at the age of eighteen, he received the tonsure from Bishop James Yorke Bramston. Then Sidney changed his mind and turned from the priesthood to medicine.[6] The reason might have been the death in 1839 of Dr. Marlow Sidney Woollett, his eldest brother, for it is conjectured that he thought he should represent his family in the medical profession. So in the year 1841, he matriculated at the University of London School of Medicine.[7] Sidney threw his whole energy into studies. He overcame repugnance which brought him face to face with the reality of the human body, not as something healthy and attractive but as diseased and even as a helpless corpse. He completed his studies with first-class honours,[8] won the coveted prize to serve as house surgeon and the further honour of working under Dr. Joseph Lister, father of Lord Lister, founder of antiseptic surgery. Woollett opened practice in Boulogne, France, possibly in a hospital conducted by nuns who had returned to France after several years exile in England.[9] Returning to England, he set up practice in Leamington, Warwickshire, at that time one of Britain's distinguished medical centres.[10] The celebrated Dr. Jephson took Woollett into his favour, and recommended surgical patients to the young surgeon, whom he considered of exceptional promise.[11] Not only was Woollett a clever surgeon but his charm of manner and well-grounded common sense made him popular with both men and women. He met Jane Matilda Patterson, the daughter of a leading Catholic lawyer, William F. Patterson, and married her on 24 April 1845, in the Catholic Chapel, Leamington.[12] But his newfound happiness lasted only two years, Jane dying of tuberculosis in 1847. Surgical ability, charm of manner, prospects of success, faded with Jane's death and thoughts of the priesthood again returned to his mind. In 1847 he came to a definite decision and at the age of twenty-nine entered the Jesuit novitiate at Hodder.[13] After studying philosophy at Stonyhurst and theology at St. Bueno's he was ordained a priest.

Chaplain in the Crimea

The holy oils were hardly dry on his consecrated hands when war broke out in the Crimea. On 4 March 1855 Woollett received word from his provincial, Fr. Joseph Johnson, that his offer to serve the troops had been accepted and he was to prepare to enter the army at once.[14] On 26 March he crossed the channel to Calais, travelled by rail to the port of embarkation, Marseilles, where the *Ottawa* conveyed him to the Crimea.[15] One far-reaching effect of Woollett's military career was the conversion of Fanny Taylor, foundress of the Poor Servants of the Mother of God. Her subsequent labours among the poor of England, Ireland, and Italy attest the value of this conversion. Miss Taylor became the first editor of the English publication *The Month,* and later founded her religious congregation,[16] while Woollett settled down to normal community life. But this was not for long. An order from his provincial sent him from his homeland to live in the tropics for thirty-three uninterrupted years.

Sending for Woollett on some routine business, Fr. Joseph Johnson, the provincial, had no intention of assigning him to the mission. But Woollett thought that this was the reason for the summons, since a vacancy had occurred in the mission Demerara, British Guiana, where one of the missionaries had died. Woollett, certain that his provincial was about to send him there, knelt in the chapel to ask divine assistance to cheerfully accept this faraway assignment. Before Johnson had time to speak, Woollett opened the conversation by saying "I know what you want me for. You wish me to go to Demerara. Well, I am ready." Only then did Woollett realize he had made a mistake when he read the puzzled look on the provincial's countenance. Into Johnson's mind leaped a new idea. Here was a man ready to leave England and spend the rest of his life in a difficult tropical mission. Why miss this golden opportunity? Quickly Johnson replied: "Really, I never thought of it. But you are just the man for the place."[17]

This simple sentence changed the whole life of J. Sidney Woollett, taking him from the comfortable fireside at home to a hard life in the saddle, first in Demerara, then in Jamaica. Yet not one line did he pen of complaint, neither when he crossed the Atlantic in 1858, nor on any other occasion during his long missionary career. Woollett was the type who could fit into any situation and never voiced the slightest dissatisfaction. He spent the year 1859 in Georgetown, British Guiana, where he acted as vicar general,[18] then one and a half years in neighbouring Berbice.[19]

Woollett's first assignment after landing in Jamaica was to teach English at St. George's College, and to act as chaplain at the military camp of British soldiers and at the convent of the Franciscan sisters.[20] He was very popular with men and officers, but his ministrations were not limited to the army, for when Her Majesty's sailors or American sailors hove into port, he was always ready to hear their confessions. The most noted American ship ever to dock at Port Royal was the *Alabama*. This ubiquitous Confederate warship, which single-handedly practically ruined the Union during the Civil War, was commanded by Admiral Raphael Semmes, a descendant of a pioneer Maryland family.[21]

Following a naval engagement with a Union ship, the *Hatteras*, the *Alabama* docked at Port Royal from 20–25 January 1863. Woollett, ever zealous for the military, tells in his own words of this famous ship.

> Friday, January 23, 1863
>
> The *Alabama* is at Port Royal after a splendid affair with a Federal man-o-war. Yesterday, I caught hold of an *Alabama* man, and walked him home and without any difficulty (for he seemed an honest character) got him to confessions. From him I learnt that several of the men were Catholics and some of the officers, including Captain Semmes himself. Again during the day I met some of the officers of the *Hatteras*, the sunken vessel, quite gentlemen and speaking of the officers of the *Alabama* as a gentlemanly set. The assistant surgeon of the *Hatteras* acknowledged himself a Catho-

> lic, but not a practicing one, but he told me Captain Semmes of the *Alabama*, is really a practical Catholic. I went down to Port Royal yesterday evening, and on board the *Alabama*, to try my chance among the Catholics. Captain Semmes was away on shore, but his First Lieutenant told me there were several Catholics on board including Semmes. He more than once repeated that he was sure Captain Semmes would be much disappointed in not seeing me. Most of the men were on shore. He entertained me in the Captain's cabin, and then introduced me to the men in the Ward Room. All seemed a quiet set; not a single boasting word, very polite. No wish to obtrude accounts of their doings, but not the slightest reserve in answering questions. The First Lieutenant (I think his name was Carey) gave an account of the recent action. The *Alabama* was not in Galveston but went there purposely to entice out a gunboat and have an action. She was sighted rather too soon by the *Hatteras* which came steaming out at full speed. A little confusion at first, and then she dodged the *Hatteras* till 25 miles out of Galveston, so that the guns might not be heard. It was dusk. In thirteen minutes, the *Hatteras* surrendered and in little more than an hour sank. Both vessels returned about six broadsides. Five shells went into the engine room of the *Hatteras*. She was on fire and beginning to sink when she surrendered. The *Alabama* was pretty well riddled; one man slightly wounded. She has heavy guns; one powerful rifled gun, no Armstrong. All the crew are English gunners and sailors from men-o-war.[22]

Semmes's exploits as a Confederate naval officer begot him fame; an admiral with sixty-seven enemy ships to his credit is a hero in any country.[23] But Semmes foreshadowed something more. Could he but lift the veil of the next century, he would gaze in surprise at a figure old and stooped, trudging the torrid streets of Kingston, up and down its narrow lanes, into hovels of the poor wherever the misery of want afflicted human beings. It was the figure of Fr. Oliver Semmes, S.J., grandson of the admiral. Fr. Semmes became just as much a hero to the outcasts of Kingston lanes as his grandfather had become a hero in the world of naval exploits. The name of Fr. Semmes was a byword of charity among the indigent of the city. When he died on 25 October 1949, these same poor lined the streets in such numbers to pay their last respects to their benefactor that it was judged one of the largest funerals ever witnessed in Kingston.[24]

Woollett Assigned to Missions

Woollett took Dupeyron's place as the circuit rider in 1861, for a man of Woollett's temperament was needed, one who could live for long intervals without the companionship of his sacerdotal brothers, one not afraid of the slow climb over Mt. Diablo, nor the trek up the valley to Pisgah, nor the burning tropical sun along the road to Montego Bay.[25] Woollett's singular contribution to the Jamaican mission is that he was the first to establish residence in the country, a forerunner of the seventeen resident missionaries who now serve these stations.

As it was Dupeyron's custom to stop at the plantations in lieu of hostel accommodation, Woollett followed the same convenient procedure and always found a warm welcome at the table of the Great House of both Protestant and Catholic, for his presence broke the monotony of isolation and furnished both companionship and news of the outer world.

Social Condition of Jamaican Peasantry

Woollett found the Church herself affected by conditions prevailing in the current social order. In prosperity and peace the faithful generously supported both priest and the varied programmes which called for financial aid; in depression and unrest, these same people had to curtail the support and limit aid to mere essentials. The 1860s were a time of depression and unrest in Jamaica.[26] Woollett had to pass through this period of social anarchy, for in 1838 the social system of slavery, upon which the economy of the colony so unequivocally depended, came to an end making the intervening years a period of readjustment for both planter and former slave. These twenty-two years should have been sufficient to readjust to the new order; instead they were an occasion of rapid deterioration. Slavery had ended by law, but no positive social reforms had been introduced, and society was left to drift by itself with no strong guiding hand until bourgeois and ex-slave faced each other in their representative champions: Eyre and Gordon.

Governor Eyre

Governor Edward J. Eyre was one of those hapless characters whose acumen did not befit the highest office in the colony at such a critical moment in Jamaican history. His character, temperament, and sympathies would have better served the island in the days of slavery. Friendly to the upper classes, he had a blind spot for the destitute peasant. As a young man, Eyre had migrated from England to Australia, where he won some fame as an explorer. In 1834 he joined the Australian government in the capacity of protector of aborigines and resident magistrate. In 1846 he was appointed lieutenant governor of New Zealand and later was sent to the West Indies where he served as protector of East Indian immigrant labourers in Trinidad. In 1860 we find him acting governor of the Leeward Islands; from this position he was appointed acting governor of Jamaica in 1862. In 1864 he assumed the full office of governor.

His appointment has been ascribed to an overwhelming desire for the position coupled with enough political astuteness to achieve his ambitious end. But he ventured upon a more troublesome career than he had anticipated, for Jamaica was experiencing daily worsening of economic conditions. The external cause was the American Civil War. Staple food supplies were cut off from the peasant. The internal cause was the reduction in the cultivation of sugarcane. Consequent upon this the number of employed labourers dropped to 30,000 out of a labouring population of 130,000.[27] Those fortunate enough to find work received the starvation wage of one shilling a day or even as low as nine pence.[28]

The House of Assembly was another obstacle to progress. This legislative body, whose duty it was to initiate reform, was totally unsympathetic to the dire necessities of the peasant class since it could hardly be claimed that its forty-seven members, chosen by a mere 1903 votes out of total population of half a million, was a governing body representative of the people.[29]

Gardner, the Jamaican historian, claimed

> For the past twenty years, the House [of Assembly] had been gradually deteriorating and its deliberations were often painfully interrupted by scenes of confusion and strife. The appointment of the Executive Committee had led to no permanent improvement, for after the first years a constant struggle for place and power was maintained and partisanship became more bitter than before. The community had grave reasons for complaint, for while the Assembly was wasting time in wrangling about its so-called privileges and rights, glaring abuses in almost all public institutions were unredressed, and very little done to promote the social elevation and true prosperity of the country.[30]

The one most responsible for bringing the deplorable conditions of the poor to the attention of the British Colonial Office was Dr. Edward Underhill, secretary of the Baptist Missionary Council of Great Britain. In January 1865, Underhill wrote to his brother-in-law, stating the facts as he himself had witnessed them and to this he added evidence from Baptist ministers in Jamaica.[31] This letter was referred back to Eyre. Anxious to make an authoritative reply, Eyre had copies printed and distributed to the custodes, clergymen, and prominent persons in the colony, asking for an appraisal of its contents. The letter became public and its contents warmly debated in the newspapers and at public meetings.

Early in 1865 the destitute peasants of St. Ann's civil parish drew up a petition to Queen Victoria depicting their dire poverty, worsened by recent drought and unemployment.[32] In it the peasants asked that they be granted the privilege of cultivating lands owned by the crown. Victoria's reply shocked and scandalized the island peasantry. She stated that the solution to their problem lay in their

> working for wages, not uncertainly or capriciously, but steadily and continuously at the time when their labour is wanted and for so long as it is wanted, and that it was from their own industry and prudence . . . not from any such schemes as have been suggested to them, that they must look for an improvement in their conditions.[33]

Eyre considered this reply a decisive victory for his own opinions. Fifty thousand copies were printed and distributed throughout the island.[34]

Protagonist—George William Gordon

George William Gordon, son of a negress slave and her white master, was Eyre's most formidable opponent.[35] Born in slavery, Gordon was emancipated about the age of eighteen years. He learned to read, write, and keep accounts, and his native ability enabled him to succeed rapidly in the produce business.[36] But politics and religion were his main avocations; the former led him to the House of Assembly, as an elected member of Kingston; the latter from the Anglican, to the Presbyterian, to the Congregationalist, and finally to the Baptist Church.

As a member of the Assembly, he fought strenuously for the indigent, underfed, out-of-work peasant. His language within the walls of the assembly was inflammatory: "If we are to be governed by such a governor much longer, the people will have to fly to arms and become self-governing."[37] His language outside the Assembly was milder, for he urged the populace to seek redress by legal means. Losing his seat in Kingston, he gained reelection to the assembly from the civil parish of St. Thomas, where he held the office of magistrate and representative member of the Anglican Church in the local vestry. The latter position was questioned by Rev. S. H. Cooke, the Anglican rector, who claimed that Gordon's election to the vestry was invalid since he was a Baptist, not an Anglican.

Rebellion

Cooke's opinion was sustained, but Gordon appealed the decision. Gordon continued to attend vestry meetings until Baron von Ketelhodt, custos of St. Thomas, an imtimate friend of Eyre, had

Gordon carried bodily out of the vestry meeting by the police.[38] This act against the popular Gordon by the unpopular von Ketelhodt was one of the contributing causes of the Morant Bay rebellion. To this humiliating act must be added hardships the peasants were enduring, lack of employment, high import tax on essential goods, unfair treatment of prisoners while awaiting trial, Victoria's disappointing reply, and the refusal of Eyre even to listen to a deputation of peasants who trudged the forty miles from Morant Bay to Spanish Town to present their grievances to the governor, only to retrace their steps to Morant Bay with nothing to show except a door slammed in their face. In this utter helplessness, with human nature strained to its limits, something had to break, and break it did on 11 October 1865.[39]

On Wednesday, 11 October, when the vestry was in session at Morant Bay Court House, an excited message was sent that an angry mob was approaching. Five hundred peasants had assembled that morning at Stony Gut, St. Thomas, under the leadership of Paul Bogle.[40] Dividing into two parties, they approached the town from the east and west, one stopping to sack the police stations for muskets and bayonets. The two parties met in the Parade, united, and proceeded to the court house. Custos von Ketelhodt faced the peasants and read the Riot Act when out of the mob came a stone cutting the head of one of the volunteers [militia] who had been hastily assembled to stop the advance of the rioters. The volunteers opened fire; rioters fell; the remainder rushed in on the volunteers, cutting down those who could not gain shelter within the court house. The school adjacent to the court house was set on fire, flames spread to the court house, and there was a mad scramble to escape. As they emerged, the mob cut them down. Von Ketelhodt was hacked to pieces and disorder spread throughout the countryside.[41] Gordon was brought from Kingston where martial law was not in force, to Morant Bay, where it was. Tried by a military tribunal, Gordon was convicted on flimsy evidence and with eighteen others, hanged before the court house. This was Monday, 23 October 1865.[42] On the following day Bogle was caught, sentenced, and hanged.

Fr. Woollett and the Barretts

This was the country, torn with unrest, that Woollett rode out to evangelize in the 1860s. It would be difficult for Woollett to ride the northwest sector of the island and not at one time or other lodge with the Barretts of Wimpole Street, for they were one of the great landowners on the north side and leading figures in West Indian plantocracy. One Charles Mouton-Barrett was to shape the picture of the

Church in the country parts. George Goodin Barrett in December 1793 had bought a 1,200 acre estate, The Retreat, St. Ann.[43] There Woollett would take up residence and set the precedent of a missionary living permanently in the country. Through the massive stone gateway of Retreat estate, Woollett rode into the life of proprietor Charles Moulton-Barrett, whose ancestral holdings dated back some two hundred years in Jamaican history.

Ancestry of the Barretts

Charles was the only Barrett of Wimpole Street ever to become a Catholic. By the year 1862 the Barretts, together with other West Indian planters, were experiencing an economic depression. These men failed to adjust their extravagant manner of life to rigid demands of paid labour and the obstructive Civil War in the United States and thus placed heavy burdens on the once opulent sugar industry.

At this unfortunate period in history, Charles Moulton-Barrett was the head of the house of Barrett. Born in Ledbury on 28 December 1814,[44] Charles spent most of his early life in England with the exception of the years he matriculated at the University of Glasgow. Although exceptionally bright, Charles refused to sit for his final public examination because of a speech impediment.

About 1856 Charles took up residence in Jamaica, first on the ancient family holdings at Cinnamon Hill and later at Retreat Estate in the perennial green hills of St. Ann. To Samuel, his younger brother, he assigned the cultivation of cane on the hot coastal lowland. This was a mistake, for Samuel refused to admit that the nineteenth-century planter could not live in the unlimited affluence of slavery days. He tired of the life and brought financial ruin to Charles. Affluence had waned with the passing of slavery. Distrust and low wages made the negro move into the hinterland where he could subsist independently of the great estate for the memory of cane cultivation was strong and stinging. In his mind it spelled slavery. Planters faced with shortage of labourers found their estates mere shells of the past, while disasters in the world of finance, upon which the planter depended, only worsened conditions. The days of the banquet-like table passed, and many a planter was glad to fare on the food which in former days only the slaves ate.

Charles Barrett was one of the great planters affected by the adverse economic conditions of the time when Woollett rode the circuit of the Jamaican missions. There is reason to believe that Woollett did not ride into the life of Barrett as a complete stranger. Possibly he was acquainted with Charles's sister-in-law, a native of Leamington, where Woollett once practiced surgery. Otherwise, it is difficult to account for Charles's almost immediate conversion, unless Dupeyron had already broken the ground and was instructing Barrett. On 14 October 1862 Woollett received into the Church Charles Moulton-Barrett and his two daughters Eva and Arabella at the family estate of Retreat, in the civil parish of St. Ann.[45]

Woollett Resides with Charles Moulton-Barrett

In 1866 Barrett invited Woollett to take up residence at Retreat estate and make this his headquarters for visiting mission stations in the interior. This event is recorded in an old Holy Trinity diary under date of 15 January 1866: ". . . on the following Tuesday Fr. Woollett will go to Retreat estate, St. Ann, to establish a mission station there." On this same day Woollett received the faculty of administering the sacrament of confirmation to all Catholics living in the interior.[46]

Retreat estate was one of those country seats removed even from the small settlement of Brown's Town. Fortunately we have a description of Retreat contemporary with the Woollett period:

> Retreat is the name of an estate about three miles [from Brownstown] belonging to a Catholic gentleman, and on this estate is Fr. Woollett's Church. The first sight of Retreat house and grounds is very pretty, but when you enter them you are delighted with the garden and picturesque negro huts scattered amongst the coconut trees, backed by a hill covered, as all hills are in Jamaica, with trees of every size and shape. The Church is about a stone's throw from the house and is a pretty little thing thirty by fourteen feet. It is gothic with a very steep roof, the eaves of which stretch over the sides, like those of a Swiss cottage. Over the entrance is a little belfry surrounded by a large and unmistakable cross. The staircase leading to the choir is formed of two remarkable slabs of cedar, not carved, but in their natural roughness. The pillars supporting the gallery are coconut trees barked and varnished, exhibiting a grain as good as the best imitation granite. The rafters are barked lance-wood in all their simplicity. A huge cross about twelve feet long, which strikes the eye, hangs on the wall over the altar. It delights everybody, and the nails at the hands and feet smeared with crimson help to reflection. This idea of Mr. Barrett's taken from an old legend which says that Our Lord's body was torn from the cross over the nails, which remained in the wood. A crown of thorns is attached to the centre. By way of making my holiday serviceable, Fr. Woollett had found a little occupation for me. The rustic architecture which had been begun, was to be carried out, and a Chinaman [Sing] went for this and a negro went for that, and the work commenced. In a short time we had raised a reredos, supported from the ground. No smoothing and planing, no mitring and closed measured joining for there were no tools, but the wood came from the bush, was stripped of its bark, and, with all its knots and twists, was fixed according to some design I would call rustic, but in its general lines, gothic.[47]

In order to show appreciation for what Charles Barrett had done for the Church, Leo XIII wished to confer upon him the distinction of knighthood. Although he regarded highly the Pope's desire to honour him, Charles declined the papal knighthood. Leo, still desirous to award the Jamaican who had opened his doors to the Church in the interior of the country, sent him a crystal crucifix whose four ends of the arm pieces were capped in filigree gold and encrusted with seventy-five rubies, while to the crystal was affixed a thin cross of gold, on which the corpus, also of gold, rested.

After serving the Church faithfully for many years Charles Barrett died at Clifton in the civil parish of St. Ann and was buried at his favourite estate, the Retreat, in the same civil parish. Over his grave his daughter Arabella erected a cross with this inscription at the base.

Beloved and Joyous memory
Charles John Moulton-Barrett
Born 28 Dec. 1815, Died 21 Jan. 1905
This cross is erected over his grave
By his daughter Arabella
He believed in Christ, Saviour and Lord
He lived to help others and the poor loved him
Make me worthy, O God, to dwell with him
In the glorious hereafter.

To Barrett and Woollett the Church in the interior of Jamaica owes much: Barrett for his generosity to itinerant missionaries, and Woollett because of his lifelong devotion to the people of the hinterland. Woollett, though physically resembling Barrett in height, was a giant of a man in physical endurance, tenacious perseverance, and universal affability. Endurance gave him strength to cover three quarters of Jamaica on horse, from the hot coastal plains to the almost inaccessible mountain interior while perseverance kept him a lone missionary for thirty-two years and affability gave him entrée to the heart of peasant and planter alike.

Bush Missionary

Methodical Woollett followed a definite schedule. On the first Sunday of every month he celebrated Mass and catechized at Retreat estate where he had fifty negroes under instruction; on the last Sunday of the month he officiated at the British military camp at Newcastle, eighty-five miles distant, overlooking the city of Kingston. Between the first and last Sunday he visited other stations, taking an alternative route so that each one might benefit periodically by instructions and the sacraments.[48] Choosing the route he sent advance word either by mail or messenger, noting the time of arrival and the length of time he would remain. This allowed scattered Catholics the opportunity to assemble from the surrounding country, attend Mass, receive the sacraments, have their children baptized, and their sick visited by the missionary. Within the yearly cycle Woollett covered some five thousand miles under piercing tropical sun, over dangerous mountain trails and backcountry bush paths. Woollett must be ranked among the great missionaries of the mid and late nineteenth century. In all his correspondence there is not one word carping or complaining about these physical hardships.

In 1866 Woollett wrote a description of these mission stations to his provincial in England.[49] In twenty-two of these places he managed to place vestments, begged from friends in Jamaica and England, which eliminated Dupeyron's awkward method of having to transport the mass kit by mule.

His first stations were in the civil parish of St. Ann where he listed five: one at Retreat where he was living; another on the coast in the chief town, St. Ann's Bay; a third at Dunbarton, on the road from Discovery Bay to Orange Valley; the fourth and fifth in the inaccessible Dry Harbour Mountains at Ballintoy and Armadale. These missions stretched from the low coastal plain to rugged mountain country. Notwithstanding miles of primitive travel from hot, palm-covered St. Ann's Bay to the high interior, only 108 Catholics could be found in this geographically extensive territory.

West of and contiguous to St. Ann is the civil parish of Trelawny, where Woollett had four stations. The first was at Oxford estate, a property owned by the Barretts where the majority were Portuguese immigrants to Jamaica who had arrived in the year 1833 to help supplement the dwindling negro labour market. On the estate of George's Valley, more Portuguese comprised his congregation. His third mission was in the hills at Greenside overlooking Falmouth. The fourth was in the capital town of Falmouth, which in the heyday of sugar had developed into the most important seaport town on the north side. Here Woollett hoped to build a church in 1866, a suggestion from an enthusiastic convert who dragooned his Protestant and Jewish townsmen to subscribe but apparently the sum was not enough to construct the type of church Woollett had in mind. In the hinterland he would have been satisfied with wattle and daub, but in the chief town he demanded a building of some architectural pretension. His dream had to wait one hundred years. There were 130 Catholics, mostly Portuguese, in the civil Parish of Trelawny.

Westward in the civil Parish of St. James, Woollett set up a mission station on the ancestral estate of the Barrett's at Cinnamon

Hill where Septimus, brother of Charles, welcomed the missionary with customary hospitality when he came to care for the spiritual needs of the Portuguese in his estate; while further inland at Content, on the Adelphi road, more Portuguese formed the nucleus of his congregation.

Three other stations in St. James demanded his attention. One was the old mission of St. Ignatius at Montego Bay, the other at the Buchanan estate, Reading, four miles west of Montego Bay. From Reading, Woollett moved on to the Maroon Town barracks in the cockpit country, where he cared for the British soldiers who had been stationed there to prevent the Maroons from overrunning and devastating the country. The total number of Catholics in the civil parish of St. James was small, a mere ninety-five.

The most westerly civil parish of Hanover had four stations; three of these were on sugar estates: New Milns, Chester Castle, and Tryall; the fourth in the chief town, Lucea. One hundred thirty-five Catholics, mostly Portuguese, formed these four congregations.

In the civil parish of Westmorland there were five stations: one at Glasgow, an estate on the border of Hanover and Westmorland and on the direct road which led south to another station, the old Spanish settlement of Savanna-la-Mar. West of Savanna-la-Mar, on the coast, was the station of Revival, known as one of the most Catholic districts in the country parts of the island. To the east, but in the same Parish of Westmorland, were two more stations: one at White House and the other at Belmont. In the German settlement of Seaford Town, Woollett gave the number of Catholics as 114.

The civil parish of St. Elizabeth had four stations: Holland; Emmaus; Black River, the principal town; and Pisgah, the mission of the ex-seminarian McDonald.

Far to the east in the civil parish of St. Mary was Preston Hill with its eighty-nine Catholics. In the last few lines of his report, Woollett did not identify the station's locality but merely mentioned that in the Parish of Manchester there were thirty-two Catholics, in the district of Vere, one, in the district of St. John and in the Parish of St. Catherine, twelve Catholics.

From January until August 1877 Woollett administered 145 baptisms, heard 515 confessions and distributed 337 communions.[50] The following year, 1878, he administered the sacrament of baptism 205 times, heard 1,010 confessions, distributed 811 communions, married 4 couples, received 4 converts into the Church, administered the sacrament of confirmation to 10 people, Extreme Unction to another 10 and conducted the funerals of 15 parishioners. He noted that there were 1,000 Catholics in all his missions, English, French, Irish, Portuguese, and Jamaicans. The distance he travelled on horse in 1867 was 5,000 miles.

Reading Estate

Woollett was not the only one who had the interest of the Church at heart on the north coast of Jamaica. A layman, Rodolphus Walter Buchanan, for thirty years had dreamed that a priest might one day reside in Montego Bay. On one occasion in 1844, he wrote to Kingston, but at that time no one could be spared. Buchanan felt that Kingston was monopolizing even the few missionaries there were in Jamaica. In one way he was thinking the same thoughts of the Jesuit Superior General, Fr. Peter Beckx, who felt that missionaries should reside at strategic points throughout the country and not be confined to residence in Kingston. In 1870 Buchanan was growing old.[51] His father, a lieutenant in the 13th Light Dragoons, had married Ann Scott of Jamaica on 19 May 1798. Two children were born of this union: a son, Rodolphus Walter, and a daughter, Ann Emily. Both eventually inherited Reading estate through their mother.

Woollett left a few descriptive lines of the estate:

> Reading is four miles from Montego Bay on the beautiful level shore road towards Lucea, has a wharf of its own, a house needing repairs, of easy access from the road than our house in Kingston is from the sea, and another [house] 600 feet above the sea, well furnished and [with] a fine library—this was Mr. Buchanan's residence—the drive road of which is very steep, but now more easy of ascent.[52]

Reading estate can be traced back to the Barnett family, early settlers in Jamaica, who like the Barretts received land grants from the crown.[53] The original grant of 227 acres entered in the Record Office on 16 January 1730 grew to 672 acres by 17 April 1740. He then sold out to John Markman of St. Elizabeth on 16 July 1741, for the sum of £500. Soon after making his will on 25 June 1747, Markman imprudently engaged in a duel with his neighbour Colonel Norwood Whitter of Bogue estate on a point of honour. The colonel alone survived. Inheritance eventually conveyed Reading to the Rev. Walter Scott Coward and his wife Emily Buchanan, who transferred it to Rodolphus Walter Buchanan on 12 November 1837.

Buchanan, a militant Catholic, had lived there a bachelor for thirty-three years when on 5 January 1870 he willed the property to the Church to be used for extending the faith in the County of Cornwall, and in particular in the civil Parish of St. James.[54] Reading was to be inherited by the Church after the death of his two nephews, Walter Vidal Coward and George Fletcher Coward; in the interim

Woollett was to use it as his residence. Woollett found living in a private family residence trying and welcomed the opportunity to change from Retreat estate to Reading.

It was one thing for Buchanan to make the Church the ultimate legatee and another to reckon with the human element in the two nephews. Walter Coward had gone to live in England; George had become a captain in the Jamaica constabulary, but both were of the opinion that Woollett had influenced their uncle in making his will. Added to this was mismanagement by Frederick Mortlock, trustee and attorney for the property. The income had dropped from £500 a year in Buchanan's day to £50 under Mortlock. This was an old Jamaican trick: the overseer would run the property into ruin, then purchase from the owner at a low price. Woollett, knowing Mortlock's designs urged the English Provincial Fr. Alfred Weld to buy out the life interests of Buchanan's nephews. On 4 July 1875 Woollett came to an agreement with George Coward, who also acted on behalf of his brother.[55] The purchase price was £1600, £400 more than Woollett had expected to pay. Therefore, negotiations dragged on until 18 November 1875, when Woollett wrote Weld, then the English assistant in Rome, that the procurator, Fr. Sidgreaves, was reluctant to loan money for the purchase because he had so much trouble with Jamaica in the past on the very point of loans. But Reading was purchased and Buchanan's dream of a resident priest in the western end of the island came true. This was the first residence the missionary could call his own in all the country parts of Jamaica and from this vantage point Jesuit missionaries worked the entire western area well into the 1920s.

Seventeen

Missionaries to the City

Missionary Workers in Kingston

Joseph Dupont, S.J., and Frederick Hathaway, S.J., his confrere, spent their lives in the service of the outcast: Dupont for forty years, Hathaway for twenty-four. Both helped much to identify the Church with the poor in Jamaica.

Fr. Joseph Dupont, S.J.

Born in Savoy, France, 9 August 1809, Joseph Dupont was a diocesan priest when he entered the Province of Lyons of the Society of Jesus on 16 June 1837.[1] Persecution drove him to seek asylum in England, where the English Jesuits kindly received him. Always longing for the missions, he was assigned to Jamaica, and on the Feast of the Purification, 2 February 1847, he disembarked at Kingston to begin an intensive forty years of missionary activity.[2] Dupont's charity embraced all men with special concern for the destitute. With the foundation of his life built on charity, the name Dupont became a household word for nearly half a century down the narrow lanes, in the yards, and in the hovels of Kingston and the nearby bush country. He had the gift of being at home with the poor in their native surroundings and of identifying himself with their daily problems. To all he was jovial, friendly, and deadly serious about their temporal and spiritual welfare.

Within the first week of arrival in Jamaica, Dupont faced a social problem of such magnitude that he kept working at it for the next forty years. It was not only the slum problem of chronic unemployment, nor the ghetto problem of inadequate housing, nor the family problem of illegitimacy—it lay deeper than these, for its roots were sunk within the human heart of every landholder, old and young, man and woman. It was a problem difficult to define, but it was there. It was the search for human understanding—human sympathy—the need for someone who would listen sympathetically to their day-by-day troubles and come up with a sympathetic answer. Dupont could hardly offer much relief to their stark poverty with his few pennies, for tomorrow their pennies would be gone and their poverty would still be with them, but he could project himself into their way of life, could think on their level and offer an impetus to the hopes and ambitions of these human, albeit poverty-riddled hearts. Here he excelled, and this was why he was so successful with these people. He could proffer them new hope for living, renew their ambitions to keep on fighting to overcome the disadvantages of their environment and revitalize a dead people weighed down under a mountain of cares. This is why he was so beloved up and down the city lanes for the name of "Dupont" spelt new hope in their hopeless lives.

A typical Dupont incident is related of him in the 1850s when cholera raced through Kingston and his inexhaustible energy was taxed to the very limit. On a stormy night Dr. Alexander Fiddes, one of Kingston's best-known physicians, was called to attend an urgent case of cholera at the waterfront near the Wherry Wharf. As the doctor rode along in his comfortable buggy, well-protected from the storm, he noticed the light of a lantern flickering in the distance. Someone was walking in this torrential rain, splashing through the ever-deepening waters, and soaked to the skin. Suddenly the light disappeared before one of the waterfront shacks. When the doctor arrived at his patient's hovel, he found Fr. Dupont there. He had trudged more than a mile on that stormy night to administer the last sacraments to a dying man. Fiddes said later that he weighed in his mind the contrast between Dupont and himself: the doctor in a sheltered carriage, the priest walking in the rain; the doctor expecting a fee for his services, the priest doing it for no earthly reward. It made such an impression on the physician that he remembered it to his dying day.[3]

The Jamaica "Yard"

The Jamaican yard where Dupont became such a familiar figure is a unique institution. In the thickly populated city districts, a family dwelling of one or two storeys, facing the street, will present an appearance of respectability. Hidden behind this facade will be a series of one-room shacks which line the fence on both sides of the yard. As many as ten, twelve, or even twenty one-room hovels, each ten feet by ten feet, which entire families call home, may be found in a single compound. It is with studied caution that one mounts the rickety stairs into these so-called apartments, where in a single room, with considerable crowding, is a bed, a chair, and a small table. These few essential pieces of furniture plus some wandering fowls occupy all available floor space. On the walls old newspapers cover rough, unpainted boards. On the necessarily crammed tabletop may be found the likeness of some priest especially beloved by the family, placed in an honoured position among the orderly stacked cups, saucers, and plates, the jar of homemade pickled peppers, the sugar bowl, the salt and pepper, the familiar bottle of ink with its accompanying pen, and the indispensable candle to dispel darkness should the kerosene lamp happen to fail. From hooks in the ceiling, or in the cross beam, hang the family wardrobe, bright coloured, neatly ironed dresses of the women being much in evidence. Out of doors, on a small portable stove, the family cooking is done. The local beef or mutton, the imported salt fish, the native ackees, plantains, sweet potatoes, and the Sunday afternoon special dish of rice and peas, were all prepared over a ten-inch diameter charcoal-fire stove. At one end of the yard was the only common faucet where tenants drew their water supply, a sort of village well in a restricted sense. Finally, through the rusty, squeakly, corrugated-iron gate, the yard's goats returned from their all-day exhaustive forage in the city's streets, always with doubtful success. Amid such poor and amid such surroundings Dupont spent his busy days.

Two Country Missions of Dupont

The city lanes were one area where Dupont became a familiar figure; another favourite mission was that of Above Rocks, in the district known as St. Thomas in-Ye-Vale in the early days of Duquesnay. Dupont was attracted to his poorer fellow countrymen from Haiti who had settled in this country district of St. Andrew, eighteen miles from Kingston. It was a relief from the depressing atmosphere of the city lanes and from the continual heat of the coast to spend a few days periodically in a friendly settlement where he could speak French to the people and bring them news of the mother country. Here Dupont built a church modelled on the one he had known so well in Savoy, a wooden structure, wedge shaped, ornamented with a generous share of gold paint and beautiful stained glass windows he had imported from France.

In the local government schoolteacher of Above Rocks, Mrs. Catherine Narcisse, Dupont had an efficient helper.[4] She was born in the district and knew both the people and the whole countryside. She not only taught catechism and conducted the choir, but she also acted as parish visitor. There was never a sick call but she answered in all sorts of bad weather and over terrible roads, always on foot, serving as nurse until the patient was well on the way to recovery. Her husband, Anable Narcisse, was official catechist for the mission and conducted services on the Sundays when the priest did not come. It was a well-organized mission with most of the people in the district professing the same faith and of the same ethnic origin, which made for harmony and gained for the mission the reputation of being one of the most Catholic in all Jamaica.

Dr. George I. Lescene, a graduate of St. George's College, noted his impressions of Fr. Dupont.

> It is difficult to describe this unique and original character. Personal charm of manner, he certainly had, a winning and engaging smile. But it was his wholehearted kindness, his utter selflessness and his all-embracing Christ-like charity which gave him the magnetic personality that drew all men to him, young and old, rich and poor, Catholic and non-Catholic alike. Little children followed after him holding on to his coat tails, receiving little presents. . . . The rich sought his advice in their doubts and accepted his answers as oracles. But it was the poor whom he loved, and as love begets love, they returned it in good measure.[5]

It must not be thought that he was a meek, spineless creature; on the contrary, he was not averse to administering corporal punishment when he thought it would do good. The story is told of a member of his congregation who continually absented himself from Mass and ill-treated his wife. Coming upon the culprit unexpectedly, Fr. Dupont questioned him on these two points. The poor fellow's answers were unsatisfactory. Fr. Dupont caught him by the collar and administered sound corporal punishment, punctuating his admonitions with: "You shall come to Mass. You shall not beat your wife. You are a bad man. You are wicked, wicked, wicked."[6] Only a person beloved by all could treat one of his parishioners as a child and administer the only correction the wicked man could understand.

Dupont's Golden Jubilee

On the occasion of his fiftieth anniversary as a priest, so large was the crowd that gathered at St. Joseph's School on Duke Street to pay him honour that most had to be content with glimpsing the ceremony from the school yard.[7] The principal speaker said that Father Dupont had both baptized and joined in wedlock most of the people gathered at St. Joseph's on that occasion. At that time he had spent thirty-seven years in Jamaica, and even at his age thought nothing of riding on horse to Above Rocks two or three times a week, of walking from one end of the city of Kingston to the other, day after day, or of getting out of bed at any time of the night when called to the sick. He was the first in the church when it opened in the morning and the last to leave the confessional at night. So great was his stamina that he was physically more powerful than most men half his age.

Monument to His Memory

On 11 September 1887, three years after this happy jubilee celebration, the whole city mourned the passing of Fr. Dupont.[8] Lest the memory of this beloved missionary fade and be forgotten by posterity, the people of Jamaica erected his likeness in the principal square of Kingston, the Parade. This was a singular honour, for no other clergyman, Catholic or non-Catholic, has ever had a monument erected to his memory in this public square. On Thursday, 2 June 1892, this event took place with appropriate demonstrations of public sympathy and genuine enthusiasm. Representatives from every walk of professional, commercial, and religious life were on the public platform erected before the monument.

> The streets hounding the north and east Parade were animate with a sea of sympathetic faces of every age and sex and condition—while this great human sea in its surging swell of warm, sympathetic emotion seemed to breathe a tribute of profound appreciation quite as significant as that which led to the preservation of the form of one of Kingston's greatest benefactors in the graceful lines and imperishable lineaments of the memorial marble.[9]

The orators of the occasion were fortunate in having for their theme the spotless character of this missionary priest and the nobility of his life among the poor. As one of those present expressed it, Dupont

> had raised for himself in thousands of individual breasts—and in the heart of the whole community—a monument more enduring than that which will be in the heart of the city for many generations. . . . Surely no orator could have wished for more sympathetic audience than that which crowded the parade last Thursday afternoon.[10]

When the covering fell from the monument, these people knew they had gathered to pay homage not to a philanthropist but to a sympathetic friend. The inscription on the monument condensed his work of a lifetime in a few words:

In Memory of
Father Joseph Dupont, S.J.
Born at Savoy, France
7th Aug. 1806

Died at Kingston, Jamaica, 11th Sept. 1887
A tribute of public gratitude and affection
to one who for over 40 years
laboured among us for
the good of all.[11]

A reporter for the local newspaper recalled Dupont's sympathetic understanding of the people and noted his self-denial which life among the poor demanded:

> Fr. Dupont was a living epistle—a practical evangel—of universal charity. Possessing a warm, sympathetic nature, he was regarded as a personal friend not only by the members of his own church, among whom he had for two generations ministered in holy things, mixing with them and sharing their vicissitudes of joy and sorrow at christenings, marriages, and in burials—but by all, and the all included almost the entire community who came within range and influence of his sunny temperament and gentle disposition. Father Dupont was Catholic in the best, broadest, and the highest sense of the term. His sympathy and Christian love went forth to the lowest dregs and the vilest scum of our city population. We do not believe that there was a pariah or outcast in Kingston that did not benefit in some way or other by the counsel or generous action of the good father. . . . The grandest feature of his character and life was to be found in what we may term supreme unselfishness—a sublime self-denial. . . . It is this quality that we attribute the wonderful triumph and apostolate won by a humble Savoyard priest in a community alien to him in religion and race.[12]

His memory still lives on in later generations whose ancestors recounted the sagas of the remarkable missionary to the poor of Kingston's lanes.

Fr. Frederick Hathaway, S.J.

Frederick Hathaway, Dupont's contemporary and fellow missionary to the poor of Kingston, had his early life cast in the unusual and the unique.[13] The transition from a fellow, dean, and bursar of Worcester College, Oxford, to a teacher of barefoot boys in the city of Kingston, makes Hathaway's life exciting. Had Frederick Hathaway remained at Oxford, his life would not have had the dramatic appeal that comes from turning one's back on a position of eminence to become a benefactor of the poor in Kingston's narrow lanes. Such a revolutionary change from the status of an Anglican minister to a Jesuit missionary on a tropical island, from Oxford to a one-room elementary school, could only be made by a man of Hathaway's love for the poor.

Frederick Hathaway was born in London on 3 October 1814, the eldest child of William Salas Hathaway, a physician, who lived and practiced in Wimbledon.

Anglican Years

At the age of twenty-two, Frederick went up to Oxford, entering Worcester College, where he held a scholarship from 1835–38. In Michaelmas term 1836, he took his A.B. degree, graduating with second-class honours. A throat ailment forced him to spend two winters in Madeira, delaying the earning of his M.A. degree until 1839. Then followed a series of academic appointments at his Alma Mater: first as a fellow, then in 1842 as dean, and in 1844 as bursar of Worcester Collge. His disposition for the ministry led him to accept Anglican orders and the consequent incumbency of Shadwell, a submissionary station in the vicariate of Thorner, near Leeds. This appointment brought him into close contact with the Oxford Movement, and the Tractarians profoundly affected Hathaway's religious views.

Imitating extreme Tractarian views carried out at Pusey's St. Saviour's Church, Hathaway catholicized his services and sermons only to find that his congregation did not look with favour on his advanced views, so that when he rang the bell for daily services, his faithful housekeeper was the sole member of the congregation to respond. He had to change the phrase "dearly beloved brethren" to "dearly beloved sister." On the wall of his oratory hung a painting of the Blessed Virgin Mary by John Pollen, a clergyman and fellow of Merton, and there Hathaway would recite the divine office together with his housekeeper who responded in English translations he had made.

Austerity and love for the poor dominated his daily life. He slept on the bare floor, wore a pointed chain next to his flesh, and took the discipline with constant regularity, while during Lent he fasted rigorously not taking anything until three in the afternoon, occasionally prolonging his fast until six in the evening.[14] Dr. Edward B. Pusey, professor of Hebrew at Oxford, his spiritual director, allowed gruel, milk, and potatoes during Lent, and meat only on Sundays. Although his income was £700 per year, Hathaway begrudged every penny spent on himself. He limited his personal expenses to one shilling per day. After paying his housekeeper, he gave the remainder to the poor. So shabby was his appearance that his mother and housekeeper and even the servants of his mother's household were dismayed at his shopworn clothes.

These practices drew him towards the Church. Austerity, love of the Catholic liturgy, devotion to the Blessed Virgin Mary, guided him to the final decision; it only remained for him to defend Papal authority. Opportunity presented itself when the Anglican Deanery of

Leeds met to hear Dr. Walter F. Hook, vicar of the parish Church, endeavour to pass a motion aligning the deanery against papal authority. The motion proposed by Hook brought a verbal protest from Hathaway. Surprise ran through assembly. Every eye turned on the objector. Hathaway was called to the platform where he clarified his position by an outspoken exposition in favour of papal authority. This was a bombshell, the one point of doctrine that would not be admitted. The excited audience yelled and hooted, calling Hathaway a Jesuit in disguise, while Hook added his own personal excoriation by calling him a traitor to the establishment. Hathaway remained calm, and when there was a lull he continued the same thread of his discourse.

His position would soon bring him into the Church. Although in April 1851, the clergy of St. Saviour's, with the exception of Pusey, came into the Church,[15] Hathaway did not follow them immediately. At this period in his life he accepted every Catholic belief but was still convinced of the validity of Anglican orders. In a Tract entitled *An Appeal to Rome,* he asked that the Catholic Church accept the Anglican liturgy and the married clergy. When the appeal failed, he felt he must come to a definite decision.

In August 1851, he gave up his ministry at Shadwell.[16] By November he had determined to become a Catholic and wrote Bishop Thomas Grant for an appointment. The two men had kindred interests. Grant led an austere life and had a reputation for scholarship. On 6 July 1851 Grant had been consecrated bishop.[17] On 13 November 1851, the feast of St. Stanislaus Kostka, Jesuit saint, Hathaway walked into St. George's Rectory to keep his appointment with Grant.[18]

> The first time I saw him [Bishop Grant], I was waiting for him at St. George's by appointment on a very cold afternoon and in a room without a fire. . . . He came in from a long journey carrying a heavy bag which he himself carried on foot from the railway station. He gave no reproof to the boy whose business it was to have his room ready for him, beyond saying with his usual sunny smile that he should like the fire to be lighted when convenient. . . . I was impressed with the degree in which, as soon as he knelt down with me to pray, he was absorbed in a sort of ecstasy of impassioned yet calm supplication, and that the words—very few indeed—which he addressed to me were just suited to my case. Those who tried their hands on me before, had either irritated me by imputing my motives for my delay which I was sure did not influence me, or lost their time in proving points about which I had already no doubt. The Bishop merely suggested to me, but in a very touching manner, that there must be such a thing as the sin of schism, distinct from that of heresy, and perhaps I had not prayed long enough to be enlightened as to what it was, and proposed that we should both kneel down and pray. When, after an interval of which I never knew whether it was minutes or hours, he arose

> and placed his crucifix on my head, I seemed to hear inside my soul, sounding very distinctly, the text 'Submit yourself to your prelates' with a sort of comment that I must choose at once between the Pope and the Archbishop of Westminster on the one side, and the Bishop of London and the Privy Council on the other. I answered that it was absurd to hesitate about such a choice. I chose the former. From that moment I never had a shadow of a doubt that I chose right.[19]

In a few minutes he was on his way with Bishop Grant to the oratory in King William Street. He had taken a particular dislike to the Oratorians on account of their style of singing and other matters of taste. Hathaway claimed that it was a simple test of his sincerity that he made his abjurations and received Communion in their chapel.

Hathaway Enters the Society of Jesus

Frederick Hathaway was thirty-seven years old when he entered the Society of Jesus at Hodder to begin his noviceship under Fr. Tracey Clarke, S.J.[20] It was a test of character for Hathaway to enter a religious order and sit as a learner among men just out of college. Freedom was restricted; every sound of the bell called promptly to some new duty. One saving feature about this particular novitiate was that most of the novices, like himself, were recent converts.

Impressions are made by the novices on other novices during the two years of close living, praying, and working together within a very confined area of society. No one could help observe Hathaway's devouring energy, his alacrity in performing even the most menial of duties, the caustic flavour of his wit, his austerity, and his rigorist views.[21] Essentially he was a man of good will and had come to the novitiate to have the rough edges of his character smoothed out by an intangible yet effective process. As he said, he "hoped . . . it would grind out of him all the grit of prepossessions, prejudices, peculiarities and his pet views which he knew he must be full of."[22]

From early childhood he had suffered from a constant racking cough. This defect did not impede the even flow of his rapid but most articulate language for a moment.[23] His pulpit exercises at the novitiate, in which every novice must take part, made a great impression upon his audience. Hathaway's knowledge of the Latin and Greek classics was a source of material for his sermons. One sermon delivered during dinner, as was the custom in the novitiate, contained a picturesque and eloquent description of the race taken from *Electra* of Sophocles.[24] So rapt was the attention of his audience that not a sound could be heard through the refectory; all had stopped to listen—a tribute to Hathaway's mastery of eloquence. One of those present made this comment:

> His spoken style was graphic, pictorial, vivid, very logical, and less cumbersome than his written style. I remember in after days an able priest who had been listening to him during a pastoral retreat at Oscott, say that every sentence might have been printed off as uttered and that for brilliancy of illustration, copiousness of diction, and cogency of argument, he never heard anyone to compare with him.[25]

He was ordained at St. Bueno's in 1857; then he went to Farm Street, London, and later to Westminster, where he was appointed, much to his delight, to care for the inmates of Middlesex prison.[26] On cold Sunday mornings in winter, the Catholic prisoners had the choice of remaining shivering in their cells or attending Protestant services in a comfortable chapel. Hathaway carried on an incessant war with the magistrates to secure justice for the Catholic prisoners.[27] So much of a hornet was he that they were happy to find an occasion to get rid of him. This opportunity presented itself when Hathaway gave a catechism to a non-Catholic prisoner. The prison authorities insisted upon dismissal. This coincided with his assignment to Jamaica, but it was thought that his constant, irritating throat ailment had more to do with leaving England than the prison incident. On 17 October 1868 he departed on the *Douro* for Kingston.[28]

Work in Kingston

Hathaway was assigned to parish work in Kingston and remained there until the close of his missionary career.[29] His natural propensity for the poor led him down the lanes to the crowded yards, into the hovels they called home. He soon realized these underprivileged were deprived of the rudiments of an education. In 1868 Hathaway opened St. Joseph's Elementary School for poor boys at 20 Heywood Street, Kingston.[30] He himself taught barefoot scholars the fundaments of reading, writing, and arithmetic. Commenting on his school ten years later in 1878, he remarked:

> My school here does not contain any of the scholars who came when I first opened it 10 years ago. Some are dead, some have left Jamaica, others are in business. Now and then a well-dressed young man stops to shake hands with me in the street, and I have no notion who he is, but on inquiry I find that nine or ten years ago he was one of the barefooted boys whom I was teaching to speak decent English, and to understand something about their religion. Several had got better situations as clerks and printers than their relatives before them and some are grateful for the education that helped them. I believe that no one has died without the sacraments, which is a great comfort. On the other hand, many have grown to be men, have fallen into the common practice here of neglecting their religion, and two are amongst the congregation of which I have charge in the General Penitentiary.[31]

On the Kingston waterfront at Fleet Street, high forbidding brick walls with ironclad entrance doors indicated that this was the General Penitentiary. To this prison Hathaway was attracted, sympathizing with the inmates deprived of their freedom. Most of the prisoners came from the underprivileged classes and had known stark poverty from the very day of birth, living as they did in the ghetto, a breeding place of crime. In *Recollections of Some Remarkable Conversions,* Hathaway narrates some of his Kingston prison experiences.

> In the November of this year [1867] I landed in Kingston, Jamaica, and I began at once, and have since continued, to visit the Catholic prisoners in the General Penitentiary; and the only conversions of all on my list that were witnessed by myself into the island took place in the prison.
>
> During each of the twenty years that I passed here, there have indeed been abundance of conversions, many of them very satisfactory, but they have been very much of the same class. A considerable number of natives seem to be of the opinion of the Swiss Reformer, that the Protestant religion is a good one to live in but a very bad one to die in; when they are sick, they accordingly apply to one of us, and they really in most cases receive the gift of faith. But of several thousands of such conversions I do not remember any distinguished by any special circumstances.
>
> The conversions in the Penitentiary, on the contrary, in the three years, 1869, 1870, and 1871 were mostly of men in good health and had this remarkable feature, they were the work under God, of a Protestant Minister, who never himself acted up to his own convictions. He used to stay and listen to the instructions given by me to the Catholics after his own congregation had retired, and was soon ready, like the 2nd Class in St. Ignatius' meditation, to make any sacrifice short of relinquishing his Chaplaincy. . . .
>
> The only conversion from Mahometanism that I have ever known, took place in the penitentiary. It was very remarkable from the absence of human agency. Seeing a coolie very ill in the Infirmary, I asked him if he were a Christian. He answered that he was a Mahometan, but wished to be baptized; but could not give any reason for the wish. Yet his delight and gratitude, as soon as he had received Baptism, as long as he survived, were unusually great.[32]

Hathaway and Alpha

Hathaway was to lay the foundation of an extraordinary work among the poor, the best known in Jamaica—Alpha. Few associate his name with this institution, yet it was Hathaway who instilled his own intense love for the poor into the hearts of four young Jamaican ladies: Jessie Ripoll, Josephine Ximines, Louise Dugiol, and Anne Llado. The first three became founders of the orphanage known as Alpha.

Long before the foundation of Alpha, young ladies of Kingston cooperated with Hathaway in organizing relief for the poor and the suffering.[33] Hathaway made them appreciate the value of self-sacrifice and taught them that everyone can be important in rendering assistance to the poor and unfortunate. A club for this purpose was organized with a president and officers, and committees were formed to take charge of the work in appointed districts.[34] Regular meetings at which progress reports were read helped keep enthusiasm at a high level. Anne Llado, as president, guided the organization, while Jessie Ripoll acted as secretary. At a room in the secretary's home, known as the 'Poor Relief Station,' supplies collected by begging were kept and from there they were distributed systematically by the committee in charge of the districts. High on the list were orphan children.[35] Evident need for some form of relief made the young women petition the vicar apostolic, Thomas Porter, that he allow them to open an orphanage for these unfortunate children. Porter granted permission,[36] and the orphanage known as Alpha came into existence with three of Hathaway's social workers, Jessie Ripoll, Josephine Ximenes, and Louise Dugiol forming the first staff. The Oxford don's love for the poor was crystalized in this institution which has been a haven for unfortunate children some ninety years.

Ill health and a hacking cough plagued Hathaway, and in 1879 he lost consciousness for a week and was anointed but recovered enough to spend some time at Montego Bay.[37] Returning to Kingston on one of the coastal ships, he fell on deck and injured his right thumb so severely that pain and consequent lack of sleep renewed his fever. The character of the man reveals itself in his self-abasement.

> My brains have hardly recovered from the addling effects of three weeks' fever and quinine. Often in my more frequent periods of helplessness or stupor, I can just manage to ask God to listen to the prayers of pious souls for me. His will be done. Young and active workers are taken away every day, and a worn out old hack, never of much use, and now of none, is again brought back from the grave and has to eat the food—and a good quantity of it—in idleness.[38]

In 1891 he was nearing his end, and the doctors pronounced recovery out of the question. He had fully recovered from his previous illness and was doing his usual round of work when the fatal attack took place. His chief trial was not pain of body, but his worry of being a nuisance in the rectory where everyone else was hard at work. He died at 10.00 a.m. on 6 November 1891.[39]

On the evening of his death, vespers of the dead were chanted, and the following morning a pontifical high Mass was celebrated. The eulogist, Fr. Patrick Hogan, illustrated Hathaway's devotion to duty by an appropriate story.

> A few days after his arrival in Jamaica, news came from Newcastle that a woman lay dying of Yellow Fever. There was no one in the house but the Vicar Apostolic, Fr. Dupeyron, then old and infirm, and Fr. Hathaway.

> Knowing the danger that an utter stranger would run in venturing in Newcastle at that hour, being already dark, Dupeyron hesitating between a sense of duty to the sick woman and the Father, merely said, 'I do not ask you to go, but I would like that you go, if you could.' That was enough, and in a few minutes, Fr. Hathaway was on horseback. The road to Newcastle was very different then from what it is now. Amongst other difficulties there were no bridges, and in fording one of these streams, the Father's horse stuck midway and refused to move. Not knowing the depth or width of the stream, Fr. Hathaway deemed it most prudent to wait until the horse got tired of its obstinacy. This proved a long time, but fortunately a man well-acquainted with the road happened to come up. Fr. Hathaway appealed for help and guidance, but the newcomer was no good Samaritan, and only saw a good opportunity of doing a little business, so he said he would guide the Father to Newcastle, to the place he was going at any rate, for twenty shillings. The Father was neither a simpleton nor a coward, so he said he preferred to take his chance rather than submit to extortion. At last, after parleying, a bargain was struck at a dollar, and Newcastle was reached in safety, and just in time, for the woman died that night.[40]

After the services at Holy Trinity Church, the funeral procession moved to the Catholic cemetery on Orange Street, where he was buried within the enclosure marked for the burial for priests.[41] Among the mourners were the orphan children from Alpha who by their tears showed how deeply they loved the one who had been a father to them. His grave was next to Dupont, who also had the same extraordinary love for the poor as Hathaway.

Gall's Weekly News Letter carried an article which held up Hathaway as a model to the clergy of Jamaica:

> What a lesson the death and funeral services of Father Hathaway, S.J. affords the Protestant clergy of this city! None can read the account thereof without emotion, that a brotherhood of ministers should be stirred by love, even in death, or that a whole community should be so moved by personal respects for one who had laboured earnestly among them. There must be some reason for this. Spontaneous outbursts of the kind spring from an inward impulse of respect; they afford evidence if nothing else does, how faithful and self-denying the ministry of such a man as Fr. Hathaway, S.J. must have been in his lifetime.
>
> The Roman Catholic clergy of this city today set a noble example to our Protestant clergy in respect to ministerial work. Every one of them, without exception, are earnest and devoted men in their work and life. They became priests from a sense of duty, not mere 'professional' to make money. Their mission is among the people and among these they toil from day to day. They never desert the poor for a higher atmosphere. We never find them with coffee plantations, preaching the gospel and selling coffee at the same time. We never find them in the coconut trade, the logwood business, or lending money on usury to their neighbours and small settlers. We never find them living up at Gallaway Hill all week when their mission field is Kingston. We never hear them refusing to

> preach the Gospel on Sunday because a shower of rain fell in the early morning, or refusing to visit the sick, or bury the dead because a buggy was not provided; nor their sending a student to perform services at the grave of a poor person because they had some bigger somebody to attend to. . . . The Catholics in this island at least . . . set us a noble example by missionary zeal, devotion to the poor, simplicity of life . . . they are doing more good in Kingston than all our Protestant clergymen put together. If any one of our Protestant clergymen were to die tomorrow, there is hardly one of them who would have the thousandth part of the tribute of public respect which was paid to the memory of poor Fr. Hathaway, S.J. on Friday last. . . . These incidents speak louder than words, and we Protestants with all these things before our eyes have reason to bury our heads in shame.[42]

One regret Frederick Hathaway had: none of his family ever followed him into the Church. A brother and sister did settle in Jamaica; the sister, like Frederick, was interested in social work and founded the British Sailors' Society Seaman's Club on Duke Street, Kingston.

Eighteen

Thomas Porter, S.J., 1877–1888

Porter and Alpha

The institution known as Alpha has become synonymous with concentrated effort in social and educational areas. Its orphanage and industrial schools, its basic and primary schools, its commercial and secondary schools—all on one compound—was a bold socio-educational experiment. Although Jessie Ripoll, under the inspiration of Frederick Hathaway, was its founder, we must give due credit to Thomas Porter for its success. Without his support it never would have left the planning board.

Porter's Early Life

Thomas Porter was born on Beaumont Street, Exeter, England, 1 November 1828, of parents who claimed Dumfries, Scotland, their ancestral home.[1] Possessing some affluence, they sent Thomas to Jesuit Stonyhurst and from there he entered the Society of Jesus on 7 September 1845, making his noviceship at Hodder where his elder brother George, the future archbishop of Bombay, had preceded him, and his younger brother, Joseph, followed him. Regency was spent both at Stonyhurst and at the Jesuit college in Malta. Two years of theology were made in France, the third at St. Bueno's, Wales, where Bishop Brown of Shrewsbury ordained him in the year 1860.[2] He returned to France and completed his final year of ascetical theology there. In 1862 he was back in England at St. Francis Xavier's, Liverpool, engaged in parish work, and in 1864, was assigned to St. Walburgis, Preston, where he completed the church by constructing the architecturally graceful spire. His first experience in pioneer work came in 1868, when he resided at Archer Street, Manchester, and ministered to Catholics over a wide area which eventually became the extensive Holy Name Mission. Here he laid the foundation of the

Church of the Gesú, an ornament to the city. His first administrative office was as rector of St. Francis Xavier's, Liverpool, an office he held from 27 September 1871 to 6 September 1877, the day when the Holy See chose him to be vicar apostolic of Jamaica. His departure from England occasioned widespread grief among his many friends who had come to love this affable priest of warm, genial disposition. On the voyage out he was accompanied by Fr. James Jones, former superior of the Jamaican mission and now provincial of the English province. They arrived in Jamaica in time to take part in a popular mission, a regular triennial renewal of Holy Trinity's spiritual life. After the mission, Porter devoted his attention to administrative problems: scarcity of priests, a competent headmaster for St. George's College, and the care of unfortunate offspring of illegitimate unions.

French Opposition to English Vicar Apostolic

Dupeyron's resignation had raised the question of his successor not only in ecclesiastical circles but also among some of the laity who were forming their judgment of the type of cleric they wished for the next vicar apostolic. When Porter was chosen, it was with dismay that the French of the congregation received the news, for they had suggested that one of their own be appointed, as may be seen from a letter written by H. J. Burger on 8 June 1872.

> Our Vicar Apostolic, the Reverend Father Dupeyron, has resigned his appointment and left the Colony—the acting Vicar is Rev'd Father Woollett, and it is said that either a Vicar will be sent out to us from England or that Father Woollett will be confirmed in the office. My object in addressing you is therefore to point out one of our most pressing wants here.
>
> We have had, from time to time, as missionary priests, Englishmen sent out to us: viz. Fathers Cotham, Howell, Woollett, Jones, Hathaway, and the late Father Barton—who was ordained in Demerara for this mission—but not one of these priests was able to discharge the duties which we esteem here as essentially those of the priesthood. They all could preach, more or less, eloquently, but not one of them could chant a High Mass, or a requiem, nor Vespers nor Funeral Service, nor at all discharge the functions those solemn and impressive—of Holy week. On such occasions they have to give place to our foreign Fathers, and content themselves, if the service permitted, with preaching. Eloquent as Father Howell was, and most remarkably so as was Father Jones, and impressively as is Father Hathaway, it is a well-known fact that few or none of us ever sought or seek them out in the confessional.
>
> Our congregation is of foreign origin—we are mostly descendants of Frenchmen or allied by marriage to persons of French descent; and our sympathies and tastes are entirely French, so that altho' we all speak English, and are educated as Englishmen, and appreciate most fully the advantage of having an English preacher, we nevertheless, resort to a

French or Italian priest when we desire the sacrament of penance. Under these circumstances you will readily understand that an English Vicar Apostolic is entirely unsuited to this mission, we desire to have a Vicar Apostolic who can discharge the duties of High Priest before the altar. If he is good as a preacher in English or French so much the better—but must be able to celebrate all the services of the Church with imposing dignity and voice, and not in the almost perfunctory manner of English priests who seem so out of place in all ceremonials. If our vicar cannot preach at all, he can delegate some one to do this for him, but not his other duties.

I may also state . . . that greater regard is paid to a Frenchman as a Catholic priest than to an Englishman as such. An English priest is, more or less, looked on as a renegade, notwithstanding that he, as well as his parents, might have been Catholics for generations past: the idea is always uppermost that an Englishman is out of place as a Catholic priest, and there is, more or less, unwillingness to make any concessions to him; but with a French priest all this is different—it is all quite proper. Much deference and respect were shown by the community to Father Dupeyron because he was a Frenchman—for the French are esteemed as a polite, clever, and agreeable people.

I therefore, pray you that in the appointment of a Vicar Apostolic for Jamaica—and such appointment should not be delayed one day longer than necessary—these facts should be borne in mind, for I express not merely my own opinion but those of the entire congregation.

At the end, Burger made some observations about the removal of the rectory from King Street to North Street:

Before concluding, permit me also to remark that the removal of the presbytery from King Street—a stone's throw from the Church—to North Street—the extreme end of the town—is a serious blunder. Our city is a very hot and dusty one—North Street is the street of the wealthy who are Protestant and it is a very tiresome journey for poor Catholics to go that distance to seek a priest, while it is equally tiresome for a priest to walk down to the dwellings of the poor in the lower part of the city. Where the Presbytery previously was, it suited all parties admirably.

That you will be pleased to consider these suggestions is the prayer of
Very Reverend Father
Your faithful servant in Christ,

H. J. Burger

To Peter Beckx, Superior General of the Society of Jesus.[3]

If Porter ever learned of this letter, he never revealed it publicly. Rather, he ignored such pettiness and turned to the immediate work of the vicariate.

Establishment of Alpha

One of Jamaica's social problems facing Porter had been anticipated by Jessie Ripoll, Josephine Ximines, and Louise Dugiol when the love of the poor instilled into their hearts by Hathaway grew into an enthusiastic desire to open an orphanage for the many underprivileged children they met in their daily contact with the outcasts of Kingston. After Porter had settled down to his office of vicar apostolic, these women made their plans known to him. He took immediate interest in their schemes and advised them to embark upon their enterprise as soon as they found it convenient. Further, he promised to ask sisters to come from Europe to complement their work and receive these Jamaican ladies into their religious congregation.

Early in 1880 a property on South Camp was offered for sale.[4] Like all property owners in those days, the owner had given it a name to distinguish it from neighboring estates. Evidently he had a classical turn of mind and since it was the first house on that road, gave it the Greek name of Alpha.[5] Porter asked Jessie Ripoll to inspect the property and give her opinion of its adaptability for an orphanage. Jessie reported it contained a small cottage with forty-three acres of brush land and would suit their purpose admirably.[6] Porter gave permission to purchase. From their own pockets, from offerings of friends added to what the vicar apostolic subscribed, the three young ladies purchased Alpha for £800.[7]

On 1 May 1880 Jessie Ripoll, holding by the hand one lone orphan whom she had named Mary, walked up the path to Alpha Cottage.[8] Thus simply and unostentatiously was begun the great social work which would bring wide acclaim from the Jamaican government, from the civic community, and from the poor, who knew their children would find a home should parents die and leave them orphans. Four months later, on 29 September, Josephine Ximines joined her friend, while Louise Dugiol was the last of the trio to take up residence at Alpha.[9] All hands were now needed to care for the ever increasing number of orphans being sent out to the institution.[10] Growing numbers brought problems of support. Hitherto the trio had relied solely upon donations from benefactors; now a more reliable source of income was necessary, so a laundry was opened, and to this venture was added the sale of produce from a vegetable garden.[11]

Another problem was education. In a few years the pioneer orphans had attained school age and their education was solved in the beginning by volunteer teachers who came daily to assist in the school.[12] The teaching staff was not satisfactorily solved until a decade later, when religious Sisters of Mercy came from England to give stability to the whole enterprise. During these ten intervening years the Jamaican trio lived heroically from day to day in the hope that Porter would persuade some religious congregation to help with their social and educational work which was having such a salutary effect on Kingston. The original group of three was inadequate and no new recruits were forthcoming from Jamaica.

El Cura Santa Cruz— Fr. Manuel Ignacio Santa Cruz y Loydi

Even before the problem of the Alpha Orphanage occupied Porter's attention, Fr. Manuel Loydi, one of the most colourful missionaries ever to labour in the colony, appeared on the Jamaican scene. He had arrived two years before Porter, when Woollett was acting vicar apostolic. Manuel Ignacio Santa Cruz y Loydi is known to Spanish history as El Cura Santa Cruz. On 1 January 1876 Woollett received a letter from Fr. James Jones, provincial of the English Province of the Society of Jesus, introducing Manuel Loydi, a Spanish diocesan priest who was to be received into the Jamaican mission. His thinning hair, a long heavy beard, broad shoulders, and stocky frame fitting snugly into a black clerical dress, offered no indication that this was El Santa Cruz, the most wanted man in Spain. For years the name of Santa Cruz had been a household word on the lips of every Spaniard, but it was soon to become one of the most lovable names in Jamaican missionary annals.

Early Career

Manuel Ignacio Santa Cruz y Loydi was born 23 March 1842, at Elduayen in the Basque province of Guipúzcoa, Spain.[13] A lover of nature and the outdoor life, Manuel grew up with an intimate knowledge of every nook and cranny of his Basque country. The early death of his parents threw the burden of his education on the shoulders of his uncle, a religious in the local monastery. At the age of nineteen years, Manuel entered the diocesan seminary at Vitoria to study for the priesthood. He was ordained 26 May 1866.[14] Loydi's first appointment was as a curate in the parish of Hernialde near Tolosa; upon the death of the pastor he succeeded to that office.

Political disturbances were mounting to a crisis during this period. Unrest smouldered as from tavern to saloon revolutionary politics was the subject. Tension ran high throughout the Basque country; rumours spread that priests were recruiting parishioners to serve in Don Carlos's army, so Don Carlos and the service of God became synonymous. This was cue for El Cura Santa Cruz to take up the cause. On the point of being arrested for imprudent utterances, fiery sermons, and diatribes against the Republican government, he managed to escape to France by a clever ruse. When he returned to

Spain, he considered himself no longer Santa Cruz, El Cura, but Santa Cruz, El Cabecilla—the leader of the guerillas. He collected enough men to form six military companies and, dividing his force into small units, instructed them to attack convoys, seize arms, and in every way possible harass government troops. Attack, retreat, scatter, rejoin, was the command of Santa Cruz, El Cabecilla to his troops.

Santa Cruz found himself in serious trouble by operating independently of his immediate chief, General Lazarraga, who denounced Santa Cruz and his followers as rebels, calling upon them to lay down their arms. Rather than risk dissension within the Carlist ranks, Santa Cruz made his submission and fled over the border to France.

Reconciliation with the Church

By engaging in active warfare, Loydi fell under ecclesiastical censure.[15] Once across the border, he was anxious to become a priest in good standing. It would appear that he went to Amiens, made a Long Retreat at the nearby Jesuit novitiate in Saint-Acheul, and was absolved from censures.[16] His confessor informed the bishop of Vitoria, Loydi's ordinary, that the guerilla chieftain desired to have his excommunication lifted. On 14 October 1874 the bishop expressed his happiness to learn of Loydi's change of heart and asked the confessor to apply to the Sacra Penitentiaria for absolution from censures and dispensation from irregularity.[17] Rome removed the censures and irregularity on the condition that Loydi have recourse to that body after two years.[18] But it was in the Jesuit chapel at St. Maur that Loydi celebrated his first Mass in three years on 9 June 1875, in the presence of some of his Carlist friends. From France, Loydi crossed the channel to England where he expressed his desire to do missionary work in Jamaica. Prudence motivated his request, for there was still a price on his head, and he dare not return to Spain or settle in a Spanish colony.

Missionary in Jamaica

In the many pages written about this popular guerilla hero, fourteen years of his life remain a blank. Literature fails to account for this lost period which was spent as a missionary in Jamaica. On 21 November 1876 Loydi arrived in Kingston at a time when his Spanish tongue proved most useful to the recently arrived Cuba refugees.[19] Fr. James Hayes had established a Cuban centre at old St. Patrick's on 15 August 1876, but a fall from a horse incapacitated him so that the care of these exiles devolved upon Loydi.[20] A school was opened for the forty Cuban boys and girls by Mary Lawrence at the southeast corner of Barry and Church Streets where Loydi gave weekly religious instructions.[21] On 30 June 1878 the mission terminated when the refugees returned to their native land at the end of the civil war in that country.[22]

Early Labours

A missionary was needed in British Honduras[23] and Loydi was assigned to it. On 14 January 1879 Loydi wrote to Porter saying that he had arrived in Belize on 9 January.[24] But during his one year at San Ignacio, Loydi failed to endear himself to the people since he was accustomed to work with Europeans of long-standing Catholic tradition and could not make allowance for Indians of the New World with primitive cultural ancestry.[25] He was assigned to Belize, but an old physical ailment returned to plague him. Since the doctors pronounced him incurable, he returned to Jamaica in 1880.[26]

Back in Jamaica

Loydi was perfectly content in the hills of Jamaica, for the terrain was much like his native Basque country and life in the saddle came naturally to him. Above Rocks, King Weston, Mt. Friendship, all within the same geographical area, experienced the missionary influence of Loydi. He so regulated his time that he spent four or five days a month at each mission station so thoroughly catechizing his parishioners that they came to know their religion better than in most mission stations. After their daily work, the people would gather for an explanation of the New Testament, church history and catechism, followed by the rosary and night prayers.[27] He was the first to introduce processions in which a statue of the Blessed Mother was carried publicly through the district, a devotion which became part of Catholic life of the island when on a Sunday in May the people marched in procession singing hymns to Mary.[28] Loydi maintained strict discipline in all his missions.[29] He would not countenance concubinage; either marry or separate was his undeviating rule, a stern directive in a country where seventy percent of the births were out of wedlock. For the poor he had a genuine love, and whenever they could not afford their staple food, rice, he would purchase a hundred pound bag and distribute to every needy family in the district.

In 1883, he moved further west into the Dry Harbour Mountains where at Alva he began the construction of a new church in 1883 by burning his own lime and cutting his own stone to construct the walls of the building.[30] The result was one of the most substantial churches in the country. Yet he never reformed his guerilla ways as Woollett experienced.

> I ought to mention that at All Saints [Refuge Mission] I missed the monstrance from the sacristy. Upon inquiry I was told that Fr. Loydi had come and taken it away. Perhaps he was authorized by your Lordship to do so, but it seems strange to me that Fr. Loydi did not communicate this permission to me. . . . It was a present from Mrs. Neal to the Retreat Mission, and doubtless presented out of regard and on account of Mr. Barrett's family, especially the Misses Barrett who were her pupils. The Barretts feel much, and I think naturally so, that Fr. Loydi has so unceremoniously taken possession of it 'annexed it'—as he would say, and especially as they just announced they would start a choir again. I think that if it is removed, a letter might be sent to Mrs. Neal at Florence to ascertain what she wished in the matter.[31]

Another facet of Loydi's character was that he was a capital beggar. Loydi also induced some Protestant women to sponsor a concert for him. On one occasion as he rode into the St. Ann cattle estate of George McGrath while the cows were being counted, he told the owner that he should donate one of his herd. McGrath consented. Loydi chose a fat animal and leaving it with McGrath asked him to sell it and send him the money.[32]

Memories of this guerilla chieftain turned missionary remained in the minds of his parishioners years after his death. Late in the year 1886 Loydi came to the mission of Avocat. Physically powerful, he carried his person with military dignity while his eyes reflected humility and friendliness. Religiously serious, Loydi occupied his time with instructing young and old. Since many were illiterate, only by constant repetition could they retain the fundaments of the Catholic faith.

Charles Ellis, who served as an acolyte, was always ready to relate his own experiences. He recalled his own position at Avocat as cook's helper, acolyte, and general factotum. He had to remain awake until 9:00 p.m. to recite night prayers with Loydi under the threat of a none too gentle prod should he nod or answer without thought. Although a strong man, Loydi was often attacked with severe pains in back and side. He would then send Ellis for white rum and small, red 'bird peppers' which he mixed and applied to the affected area, gaining some relief from the stubborn pain. Often he would take his choir boys from one mission to another, walking the whole distance, telling them they were on a pilgrimage and were making a sacrifice. At the end of the day he treated them to a grand fiesta with rice, peas, and fried chicken. These days Ellis never forgot though he served the mission for more than half a century as a catechist.[33]

A Man Without a Country

Behind Loydi's zeal and love for the poor was a gnawing realization that he was a man without a country. He dared not return to his native land, for that would mean imprisonment or death. Yet he was ever anxious to put himself in the good graces of the Spanish government. Constantly he was on the watch for a favourable opportunity, since he had no desire to remain for the rest of his life in exile, an outcast, a hunted man. He thought he saw this opportunity when the Spanish regent granted amnesty to all political offenders. Was Loydi included in this? He asked the vicar apostolic, Thomas Porter, to enquire through diplomatic channels. Porter wrote to the Hon. E. N. Walker, K.M.G., colonial secretary in Jamaica, on 21 January 1886.

> Sirs:
> The Reverend Manuel Santa Cruz, known here as Fr. Loydi, who had engaged in civil disturbances in Spain in the years 1872 and 1873, was obliged to leave Spain to escape the sentence of death to which he had been condemned by court martial. He was sent to this mission in the year 1876, and has done missionary work in British Honduras and Jamaica from then up to the present time. Having heard that an amnesty of all political offenders has been lately granted by the government of the Regent since the death of the King Alphonso, Fr. Loydi is anxious to know whether the amnesty is extended to him so that if he wished he might return to Spain without the danger of being arrested for the part he took in the war from 1872–1873. He, therefore, begs the Governor of Jamaica, or rather the Major-General administering the Government, to enquire of the Ambassador of Spain at the Court of St. James whether the Rev. Manuel Santa Cruz is included in the late amnesty above referred to. In case he is not included in the amnesty, Fr. Santa Cruz would beg the Government to ask on what conditions he could return to Spain seeing from the time of his arrival here he has taken no part in politics and is resolved to abstain from them in the future.[34]

The reply received 9 June 1886, from the Colonial Secretary brought bitter disappointment:

> The Rt. Rev. Fr. Porter S.J.
>
> Rt. Rev. Sir:
>
> With reference to my last letter No. 502/616 of the 27th January last, I am desired by the Governor to inform you that the Secretary of State for the Colonies has communicated to His Excellency the result of your Lordship's reference to the Spanish Ambassador in the case of Reverend Fr. Loydi, alias Don Manuel Santa Cruz. The Spanish Ambassador states that the pardon granted in virtue of the Royal decree on 9th December, 1885, although applicable to persons accused of rebellion, sedition, and other crimes therein mentioned does not include those who have committed common crimes.
>
> It is therefore necessary, the Ambassador states, in order to obtain the declaration desired by Fr. Loydi that he should petition Her Majesty, the Queen Regent, through the Spanish Consul at Kingston or at the place where he is at present living and state the number of criminal actions instituted against him and the courts which have cognizance of them, that

is to say if they come under the cognizance of the ordinary or military courts.

Hon. E. N. Walker,
Colonial Secretary.[35]

No pardon was forthcoming; the matter was placed in abeyance until a more favourable occasion might arise in the future.[36]

At this time Loydi sought entrance into the Society of Jesus and applied to Fr. Edward Purbrick, the English provincial, that he be allowed to make the thirty-day long retreat of the Spiritual Exercises of St. Ignatius as was customary for novices. The reply of 1 June 1887 said that he would be welcomed the following year and for this purpose, Loydi accompanied the vicar apostolic to London in 1888. But like the hope of pardon from the state, this desire of entering the Society of Jesus was shattered, for to accept a man still under a cloud would have been dangerous procedure at this period in history. Both political pardon and entrance into the Society of Jesus had to wait until the closing years of Loydi's life.

For fourteen years the familiar figure of Loydi on his horses, Surprise and Figgity, was seen throughout the mission country of Jamaica. From Alva in the civil parish of St. Ann to Avocat in Portland, he evangelized with the same energy characteristic of his earlier guerilla days. Then suddenly, one fine day, his rendezvous with Jamaica came to an abrupt end. He closed his career as a Jamaican missionary and departed. Why he left is not recorded. His catechist claimed that the vicar apostolic wished a Protestant teacher to live at Avocat and Loydi objected. It would rather appear that fourteen years in the mountains of Jamaica made him long for the companionship of men of his own nation.

To the mountain city of Pasto, Colombia, South America, he went, where the rector of the Jesuit College of San Francisco Javier received him as a missionary apostolic. From Monday to Friday he taught French, English, and religion in the college while Saturday and Sunday was spent at a nearby mission station ministering to the Indians. Each year he would apply for entrance into the Society of Jesus, and each year he would be refused, until he found a sympathetic superior, Fr. Camilo Gracia, a Basque like himself, who heard his pleas with favour and admitted Loydi into the Society of Jesus on 31 July 1920.[37] At the age of seventy-eight he began his novitiate, and two years later, at the age of eighty years, pronounced his vows of poverty, chastity, and obedience. In the whole history of the Society of Jesus there is no example of such prolonged, persevering persistence to enter her ranks as that of Manuel Ignacio Santa Cruz y Loydi.

But this was not the end. The end did not come until four years later when returning from his weekend trip to his favorite mission of San Ignacio, he fell critically ill. His companions knew he could never reach Pasto alive, so they retraced their steps hoping to reach the mission station before he died. He breathed his last on the mountain trail. The date was 10 August 1926, four days before the feast of the Assumption of her whom he had taught the mountain people of Jamaica and Colombia to love so tenderly.[38] He was eighty-four years of age.

Loydi was only one of the many missionaries who evangelized rural Jamaica at this time during the mid and late 1880s. Fr. James Splaine, S.J., was another who resided at Agualta Vale in the civil parish of St. Mary and covered the stations at May River, Preston Hill, and Avocat, all on the northeastern end of Jamaica.[39] All four missions in his district were noted for their bad health, bad roads, and bad rivers.[40] Speaking about a district known as St. George, Splaine claimed that anyone who could find a living elsewhere did not settle there. Not one Catholic of any social standing could be found in his beat, as he called it. The most respectable person was a brick mason named Elliot, a black man. As long as Splaine confined himself to Agualta Vale, he had both good shelter and sufficient food. But he had to visit other stations regularly if the people were to be kept in the fold, and so for effectiveness he would remain in these missions several days a month visiting the sick, baptizing, and becoming personally acquainted with the many problems which arise in such situations.

This meant he had to have a place to stay; it did not have to be pretentious, even a small bungalow containing a bed and table would amply satisfy his needs. But even this minimum did not exist at May River, St. Mary. The best he could do was to live in the room which also served as the confessional, a mere box seven feet square. Or he might find accommodation in the sacristy, which was even smaller and had the added disadvantage of being recently constructed of green lumber, and in a hurry, so that the sun had shriveled the planks, leaving openings which leaked during the rainy season.

But not every station had the luxury of a confessional in which to sleep. At Preston Hill he had to depend upon the parishioners for shelter.

> At Preston Hill I have to sleep in a negro's hut. The partitions within the hut are three feet high, and the bed is board covered with dried cow's hide. The ventilation is imperfect, considering six or seven negroes sleep in it with me. The windows consist of two little holes, neither of them six inches square, and the negroes shut the one on their side every night, for

they have a horror of the cool night air. They sing and smoke and talk, lying on their mats until about midnight, and then light up [their tobacco pipes] again about 4.00 a.m. After a night spent in this way, one is hardly in trim to begin the work of confessions, to give time to those who come long distances. It is the hardest work I have ever had to do. At the end of it, that is about 12.00 o'clock, I get something to eat. I would give anything for a private room where one could throw himself on the floor and have a sleep.[41]

Should the missionary wish to construct one of these country rectories, he would find it a complicated task, for the lumber would have to be sawn in the mountains and transported one plank at a time on the heads of men who would then leisurely construct the building, as Splaine discovered when he built at Preston Hill.

They seem all anxiety to carry out your desires. But turn your back for a quarter of an hour, and every jack man of them will put down his tool and begin to play and laugh and chatter like so many children. Pay them by the piece and they will split lumber with every nail they drive; pay them by the day and they will spend their time on the premises and not at their place of work. As for that honest pride in his work which you see in Europeans, it is quite unknown among these fellows. Their leading dominant idea is to out-fox Backra, to deceive the white man. And they think they have succeeded in doing so if you pay them for doing nothing. The only way to get anything done is to be your own overseer. So I mean to follow them into the bush and stop with them as much as possible while they are in my employ.[42]

Not only did humans give Splaine cause for concern, but nature added her share to his missionary trials. After heavy rain the Agualta River would cover the whole right bank of the commons, completely isolating Splaine from the rest of the district, and the mountain tracks behind the mission would become raging torrents an hour or so after the rains began to fall, so effecting the river as to raise its waters twelve feet above its banks. As these May or October rains continued, clothes became damp, shoes and books became covered with mildew, and a chill ran up Splaine's spine accompanied with nausea warning him that he had malaria. It was also a dangerous time for travelling as Splaine noted when during these heavy rains two people lost their lives in the Buff River on their way to St. George's Chapel, while two others were carried away in the same neighbourhood, one got to the shore and the other made for a small uninhabited island where the rains kept him prisoner for a day without food or shelter.[43]

Splaine related his own experience in attempting the journey to Kingston.

After a week of being confined here, I managed to ford the river and made off for Kingston. People on the road told me I could not go on, but I was

> resolved to try. In places the road was impassable for vehicles, and in one place it was entirely buried in a great avalanche of earth and rock. I dismounted and scrambled over, leaving my horse. But in Kingston I was little better off. The streets were often like rivers, quite impassable with dry feet . . . As soon as the rain broke, I rode across the mountainside to St. George's and there to May River. Between May River is Agualta Vale. There are only three fords by this route, which is bad enough, but the route is very bad if not impassable in the wet season. By the other route, which is bad enough, there are twelve or fourteen fords to St. George's.[44]

Jamaica was Porter's mission, and as vicar apostolic he had to make progress reports to Rome periodically. In 1882 he noted that there were 11,139 Catholics in the whole mission—approximately one thirtieth of the total population of 315,746.[45] Of the remainder, 300,156 were members of one or other Protestant denomination; a mere 4,455 were heathens. In this strongly entrenched Protestant island, the Church could only count 267 converts in 1883: 220 in Kingston and 47 in the country.

Porter was an active missionary almost up to the very day of his death. For more than a year and a half he had attended patients at the smallpox hospital where he witnessed as many as 190 patients in a ward.[46] At one of his mission stations twenty miles from Kingston he found seven with the dread disease, two of them Catholics. This was only part of his work, for every other Saturday he travelled to minister to the British troops at Newcastle, thirteen miles from Kingston and some four thousand feet high in the Blue Mountains.

Kingston of Porter's day had seven parochial schools, all under government supervision.[47] There were two poor houses, one general hospital, one military hospital, and a reformatory of girls. There was a boys' reformatory ten miles away, and a penitentiary where a priest conducted a daily service. Porter noted that there was plenty of work for young, healthy priests, but that his missionaries were aging. Two were seventy years of age, one sixty, and Porter himself fifty-nine. Poverty was part of both missionaries' and parishioners' lives. In this particular letter Porter said that, while at a country mission a piece of honeycomb was sent to him for breakfast with the request from the donor that the wax be returned to him. So poor were these country people that few owned a bed, and most slept on the bare floor. Porter ended this letter by a plea to pray for this poor mission and not forget the vicar apostolic.

In May 1888 Porter left Jamaica for Rome to render an account of his mission to the Holy See.[48] While there he fell ill. Thinking it a mere passing Roman fever, he began his return to Jamaica by stopping in London. After he arrived there, his illness was diagnosed as cancer, probably of long standing. A skillful operation by Dr. Roase gave hope of a cure, and he was sent to St. Bueno's, Wales, to recuperate. While in Wales he believed himself strong enough to join the community in their annual retreat but had to confine himself to his room after the first few exercises. He began to fail and Dr. Blankett was called from London. He pronounced his case hopeless, for cancerous tumours were present throughout his body. Confined to his room, then to bed, the end came on 28 September 1888 and brought to a close another chapter of the Church in Jamaica.[49]

Nineteen

British Honduras

The many miles of jungle coast from Yucatán to Honduras kept Spain's seventeenth-century security forces on the alert lest England, Holland, or France plant a settlement in some hidden nook or cranny. Despite vigilance, Spain could not possibly watch so many miles of uninhabited littoral where the Yucatán-Honduras coast provided a perfect refuge for buccaneers chased out of Tortuga and Old Providence islands. These smuggler pirates settled a town and named it Belize, in memory of their leader Bleuvelt, or so tradition claims. History pinpoints the year of Belize's founding as 1638.

When the buccaneers became a memory, this extensive logwood country then attracted the Scots who engaged in supplying this valuable source of purple dye to the English textile industry. But more than two hundred miles of coastline became disputed territory, for both England and Spain claimed the strip of land now known as Belize. Challenging England's claim, Spanish authorities in 1782 swooped down on the British loggers and imprisoned them in neighbouring Spanish Honduras. After their release they were allowed to settle in Jamaica under Governor Archibald Campbell. Four years later England reinforced her own claim by appointing a superintendent for the disputed territory. Hardly had England made the appointment when the hurricane of 2 September 1787 levelled the conglomeration of shacks known as Belize to the ground.

In 1812 a regular town plan, laying out Belize in rectangular form, injected some order into the mud and swamps.[1] Taking advantage of the new settlement, the Anglicans erected its first church in the territory. The Baptists, Methodists, and Presbyterians followed in the years 1822–50.[2] There was no Catholic Church. On 10 January 1837 the Holy See separated British Honduras from Trinidad and placed it under the vicariate of Jamaica. From that time it became Jamaica's responsibility to care spiritually for this Central American territory.[3]

Few Catholics lived in Belize, but just south of the town, at the Mullings River settlement, refugees from Honduras enjoyed the ministrations of Franciscan Friar Antonio Rosello from 1832–36.[4] He then returned to Spain Honduras, leaving the settlement without a priest. Since it was now Fernandez's obligation to supply priests to British Honduras, he sent Fr. James Gleeson, an Irish secular priest, to the mission in 1839.[5] Gleeson returned after a short sojourn, alleging that Catholics, especially the French and Spanish, showed no inclination to perform their religious duties. He added another reason; the state of his health could not endure the enervating heat of Belize.

In 1846 word reached Cotham, the Jesuit superior, that Spanish merchants at Belize greatly desired the services of a missionary, for seven years had passed since Gleeson had abandoned the mission and returned to Jamaica. To reinforce their demands, the Spaniards asked a young married couple who arrived in Kingston on 21 July 1846 to inform Cotham that many Catholics were attending Protestant services because there was no priest to minister to them.

In 1849 a sudden influx of Spaniards from Yucatán and other lands to the north changed the proportion of Catholics in British Honduras. Exasperated by the misgovernment of their Spanish masters, the Indian population had risen in revolution and ruthlessly massacred the Spanish inhabitants of Bacalar and the adjoining districts.[6] The remainder of the Spaniards fled down into British territory; most of them settled in the uninhabited northern frontier. Ranchos and pueblos now arose where previously only the woodcutter's axe had been heard.

These newly arrived Catholics also demanded attention, but nothing was done until August 1851, when Fernandez and Dupont made a missionary journey to British Honduras.[7] They remained there a month and returned to Kingston in September. A cursory survey of the mission territory by the two men revealed that a place of worship should take top priority, but getting the money for it would be a major problem. Optimistic Fernandez opened a fund-raising subscription, relying on the never-failing pennies of the poor and more substantial donations from wealthy Protestants to build the first Catholic church in this part of the world.

On 13 December 1851 Dupeyron, then the Jesuit superior, sailed from Kingston and arrived in Belize on 27 December. There he purchased a site for the church and remained until 21 January 1852. Dupeyron wrote to his superior in Rome on 10 February that the colony had a Catholic population of between eight and fifteen thousand; the greater part of them were Spanish mulattoes from Yucatán.[8] A church would suffice for adults, but the younger generation needed a school, since nothing could substitute for education in an effective mission.

On 15 March 1852 Dupeyron again sailed for Belize, this time accompanied by Fr. Joseph Bertolio, S.J., and a schoolmaster. Thus Catholic education began some time in March 1852. On this occasion Dupeyron contracted with a master carpenter to build Belize's first Catholic chapel.[9] A building sixty feet by thirty feet to be completed by 31 August. It was finished on schedule—a remarkable feat for the tropics. In the interim, the first storey of the rectory, a space thirty-six feet by thirty-five feet, had served as a temporary chapel.

Upon his departure from Belize, Dupeyron told Bertolio to expect a missionary companion shortly. Five months passed and no missionary came from Jamaica. In a letter to Dupeyron, Bertolio made it clear that he was not at all pleased with his assignment to the British Honduras mission as the sole priest. Dupeyron himself was in a quandary, for to leave Bertolio alone in an inaccessible mission country without a companion smacked of poor mission psychology. But what provision could he make? If he removed another priest from Jamaica, the island would be understaffed; yet he must send a man to Belize. Very real difficulties confronted mission superiors in the 1850s, especially in primitive British Honduras. Lack of money could be compensated for by some means or other but manpower was indispensable; this problem plagued the vicariate until the mid-twentieth century.

It was one thing to decide that another missionary was needed for Belize; it was another to activate the plan. Between the two stood serious obstacles. The only man Dupeyron could spare was Fr. George Avvaro, a missionary stationed at Spanish Town.[10] Dupeyron could not deny Avvaro's effectiveness at this mission when on 2 February he witnessed fifty people receive Holy Communion, a remarkable accomplishment in the 1850s, for at this same mission Cotham had complained that he had only two communions during his pastorate. If he removed Avvaro, this act would set the Spanish Town mission back twenty years. Dupeyron considered every missionary in Kingston as a possible replacement for Avvaro at Spanish Town. There was Cotham, pastor of St. Patrick's, but he carried on his work in very poor health. There was Dupont, but no one could assume Dupont's labours down Kingston's lanes among the outcasts of society. Simond taught French and Latin every day at the college, but only with great difficulty could he make himself understood in laboured English, so he could not replace Avvaro in the exclusively English-speaking congregation. Dupeyron himself had assumed the obligation of visiting Catholics throughout the island, supported by a yearly grant from the government, so he could not tie himself down to one mission station. Dupeyron compromised and sent Avvaro on a temporary assignment for two weeks, 8–23 August.[11]

When the Holy See assigned British Honduras to the vicariate of Jamaica, it did not settle the question as to what province of the Society of Jesus should be responsible for a supply of men and women. Propaganda Fide, a Roman curial office with jurisdiction over all missions throughout the world, assigns to some religious congregation a particular mission, leaving the congregation free to work out details as to which province shall be responsible for the mission territory. A doubt arose in Dupeyron's mind. Where did British Honduras fit into this pattern? To what provinces did the Society of Jesus assign the responsibility? A response from Father General Beckx dated 20 February 1852 placed full responsibility on the shoulders of the English province, which considered it a real burden since it was small in numbers and weak in finances.[12] For Dupeyron the scattered Catholic population of British Honduras merely offered a challenge to his missionary zeal since it was never satiated, no matter how arduous the task of ministering to his far-flung flock.[13]

Avvaro returned to Jamaica and again Bertolio was the only missionary resident in British Honduras. Patience is one of the most important assets for any missionary, and the moral degradation in a large percentage of Belize's population called for every ounce of patience in Bertolio's soul. These were the people for whom he was responsible, and their religious apathy caused Bertolio to question his own missionary effectiveness, for it appeared next to impossible to raise the moral tone of Belize's adult population. Dupeyron suggested as a remedy to Bertolio's discouragement that he make a missionary excursion into the interior where he would encounter a large percentage of non-Catholics, but he offered no reason for this plan.[14]

On 11 February 1853 Dupeyron paid another visit to British Honduras.[15] At Belize he found clear evidence of progress. The cry of the children had effected the change. The school, now seven months in operation, had made the difference. Under their competent Jamaican teacher of high moral character, the younger generation offered some hope of reform in contrast to waves of discouragement from adult Catholics. The people had been sadly destitute of religious instructions and the sacraments for years, so Dupeyron put the blame for adult immorality on these circumstances. But with the children conditions would be different, for they would enjoy the ministrations of a resident priest and the environment of a Catholic school, two powerful forces in forming a moral family life in the town of Belize. Nor could the adults be held entirely responsible for their faulty notions of morality, since on occasions they were visited by scandalous priests from the countries of Central America whose lives of concubinage belied their profession of celibacy.[16] Another good influence on public morality was Avvaro himself, for he returned to Belize on 13 March 1853, with full powers as superior of the mission.[17] No mission could ask for a more ideal missionary: quick to master a language, sympathetic and understanding with human failings, a perfect observer of religious discipline without being pharisaical, Avvaro became a Xavier to the populace of British Honduras. No better instrument could the Church ask to raise the moral standards of people to the level of decent Christian living than this Italian priest exiled from his native land.

With Avvaro at Belize, Bertolio devoted his energy and fluent Spanish to Yucatán refugees scattered in their pueblos throughout the northern districts of the colony. And to replace Avvaro in Jamaica, Fr. Stephen Ghersi, a Jesuit from St. Remo, a German diocese in Sardinia, arrived in Kingston 8 February 1853.[18] Fluent in both English and Spanish, his talents forecast a brilliant missionary career; but five weeks later, on 13 April only twenty-nine years old, he died of yellow fever. His death restricted missionary endeavours in British Honduras, forcing Dupeyron to await patiently another replacement for Avvaro.

On 10 April 1853 Dupeyron wrote to his provincial in England that conditions in British Honduras had improved over the first fruitless years; strong hope fortified with much patience had rewarded the labours of those employed on the mission.[19] This hope centered mainly on the sixty boys and girls attending Dupeyron's school conducted by Jamaicans. The young man taught the boys, his sister the girls, while their widowed mother acted as cook for the teachers and the priest.[20]

Lack of support for the mission perennially raised its unwelcome head; never did the question seem resolved. For a time it would lie dormant; then some demand from the English procurator, Sidgreaves, that payment was due, awakened the monster. Sidgreaves was a demanding treasurer. Even for the travel of missionaries from Europe to their destination in the West Indies, he sought payment by deducting their fare from the paltry amount allowed the vicar apostolic by the Lyon's Propagation of the Faith's fund. Dupeyron, on his part, made his own demands on the procurator that one hundred pounds sterling a year be allowed Avvaro and Bertolio to live in frugal comfort—what little the parishioners contributed could not possibly support the missionaries, no matter how carefully they exercised economy.[21] Within two years Dupeyron and Fernandez had spent twelve hundred pounds sterling to give the mission a start with a church, rectory, and school with money England managed to supply from its own slender resources.[22]

From financial worries Dupeyron had to turn to worries of health. Dupeyron thought he had removed all the mission's difficulties by frequent visitations to British Honduras. But he had not reckoned with Bertolio's health. So ill did the missionary become under the trying tropical climate that his life was in danger should he remain on the mission. Dupeyron had to recall him to Kingston. On 23 July 1855 he arrived in Jamaica where recovery came slowly.[23] As soon as he seemed to improve, he was sent to Spanish Town. Benedict Picardo, another Italian, replaced Bertolio.[24] He sailed to Belize on 7 May 1854, with orders to remain in British Honduras as long as Bertolio stayed in Jamaica. Bertolio never returned to Belize but died at Kingston, 19 April 1876.[25]

It remained a perennial effort by Avvaro to elevate the moral tone of both the logwood cutters and the outcasts of society by instilling a sense of Christian morality into a generation totally devoid of the concept of family life in the torrid tropics where vice was cheap and taken for granted by the general run of the populace. This became his life's work, a battle fought from pulpit and classroom. Just when it seemed as though victory was over the horizon, calamity struck Belize in July 1856. A fire destroyed the whole northern end of the town, leaving Avvaro without residence, school or church.[26] This condition lasted for two years. In vain he sought financial aid in Havana and Guatemala. Finally he turned to Europe for funds to replace his burnt buildings. By 25 September 1857, Dupeyron could express joy over progress of Avvaro's chapel, school and rectory as new buildings rose slowly from the foundations of the old.[27] Lack of lime at one stage and bricks at another prevented quick completion of the buildings. Yet Avvaro kept perseveringly on until all three essential structures were completed, two years after the disastrous fire.

Bricks and lime posed one problem; a friar another. Carmelite Antonio Roset suddenly appeared in British Honduras from Yucatán with a past veiled in mystery.[28] He alleged that he knew Fr. Pablo Blas, Jesuit superior of Guatemala—he had met him once in Panama. The friar made such a good case of identifying himself as a priest in good standing that Avvaro granted him faculties to preach and hear confessions. Suspicion was cast on Roset when he took improper liberties in the confessional. On another occasion, to the utter amazement of the congregation, he used a glass tumbler as a substitute for a chalice. Avvaro contacted the archbishop of Guatemala. The answer came back: born in a little town outside Barcelona, Roset entered the

Carmelites and was ordained deacon. While still a deacon, he betook himself to Central America where he deceived the authorities into believing that he was a priest. While he was acting as one, news came from Barcelona that he was only a deacon. Confronted with this revelation and challenged by civil authorities for impersonation, the rascally friar beat a hasty exit into Avvaro's territory of British Honduras. Even the civil superintendent of British Honduras expressed the hope that Roset would move onto greener fields, but he did not. Dupeyron briefed Governor Darling of Jamaica about the affair.[29] Under duress the friar changed his abode, but with no great celerity.

While Bertolio was still in British Honduras prior to the Roset incident, he himself had experienced like trouble when stationed at the Corozal mission. Swooping down from the north, excommunicated priests from Yucatán gave Bertolio so much opposition at his newly established mission that he had to abandon it and return to Belize. After a few months, when the settlers at Corozal saw more hireling than shepherd in the priests from Yucatán, they repented for having spurned Bertolio and asked for his return. But Bertolio was in no mood to accept their invitation. Instead, Fr. Charles Rossini, a newcomer, reopened the Corozal mission in 1858. One and half years later he was dead, worn out by the climate and exhausting missionary labours.

Three years later, in 1861, Fr. Ferdinand Parchi successfully established the mission on a sound basis. Trouble again came from the north. A Spanish priest apostatized, became a Wesleyan, and did much harm by distributing tracts vilifying the Church.[30] By preaching in their native Yucatán, he won over many to Wesleyanism. After two years this schism died out, and the greater number returned to the faith. Parchi tried his hand once more at Corozal but failed to make contact with these unstable Yucatáns, so he returned to Belize 25 March 1861.[31] They wanted a priest who spoke their Maya tongue, and no other would they accept. It was a constant, unanswerable question when these people would experience a change of heart. Dupeyron designated it the plaque spot of the vicariate. He thought that only time would solve the Corozal riddle.

Dupeyron sailed again from Kingston to Belize on 7 May 1861.[32] Already bothered by intermittent fever on account of the unusual fatigues of Lent, during which he had given a retreat to the Franciscan Sisters of Kingston, he found the heavy May rains which confined him to swampy Belize no cure for his recurring illness. The heavy rains let up long enough to allow Dupeyron and Parisi to make the slow trip south to Stann Creek, thirty-six miles from Belize. Dupeyron admitted that the work at the station was arduous but consoling. Still feeling the effects of the recent bout of fever, he returned to Belize, spending the whole night in an open boat exposed to rain and chilly weather. Of superb physical stamina, he rested for a while and then began the second leg of his missionary excursion to Corozal on 18 June. But the troublemaker Corozal offered neither consolation nor cure to the now very ill Dupeyron and on 27 June he was forced to return to Belize. Then began a furious bilious attack lasting forty-five days, while he was confined to bed or his room. When he returned to Jamaica on 12 August, he was still a very sick man. Reluctantly, the physically powerful Dupeyron admitted that even he could suffer one of the occupational hazards of missionary life in the tropics, malaria.

Italian Jesuits formed the bulk of missionaries in British Honduras. Political unrest in their own country had forced them to seek shelter elsewhere. This was providential, for the English Province would have been hard put to find an adequate supply of men among their own personnel at this period in history.

An addition to the growing list of Italians was Fr. Placide de Maestri, who arrived in Kingston from California on 20 September 1862.[33] He sailed for Belize on 8 October with instructions to join Parchi at Corozal and see if some spiritual sense could be instilled into these troublesome parishioners. Maestri knew Spanish well and could converse in French and English. All three languages were in constant use in British Honduras. To these exiled Italians the mission owed its success. Bertolio, Avvaro, Rossini, Parchi, Brindisi, Parisi, and Di Pietro rank among the all-time greats in British Honduras mission history.

A steady, permanent teaching staff often becomes a problem in the mission school. An example may be cited of the young man Avvaro hired to teach at Belize. Everything went well until May, when the fishing season opened. Without much ado he abandoned teaching for the more profitable avocation of turtle fishing off the Honduras coast, leaving Avvaro with the hope that he would resume teaching when the turtles ceased to run.[34] Such was the instability of the teaching staff until the arrival of Mark Quinn, a Jesuit coadjutor brother, to teach at Belize where his devotion to duty gave stability to this school from the year 1869.

Quinn was an excellent teacher, but his ears were sensitive to the sayings and doings of his Italian confreres. The aloof English world that had been Quinn's all his life was much in contrast to the effusive, colourful world of his Italian coworkers. He listened, he observed, he could bear it no longer. In a long letter to his superior, he gave vent to his thoughts and feelings. The Italians were constantly pointing out the faults of the English but, Quinn observed, the debit side of the ledger was not entirely filled with English faults; the Italians had theirs.[35] Victorian-minded Quinn sickened at the sight of an over-gaily decorated church in colours of blue, yellow, green, white, black, red, and pink which distinguished solemn feast days from ferials. Nor had he much taste for an Italianate Good Friday—a public holiday when people crowded the church as on no other day of the year. Lax Catholics who would not be seen in church until the next Good Friday, were in evident attendance, for it was both a social and religious day. People gathered at 2.00 o'clock in the afternoon and remained until 7.30 in the evening. Before the ceremonies began, the milling mob filled the spacious church grounds, talking, laughing, the children playing in and out among the gab-festing adults, and occasionally breaking into quarrels. Avvaro's long sermons were of particular aversion for Quinn. He would begin at 4.00 o'clock and continue without a break until 6.30. Then came the procession in which the whole congregation joined. Procession ended, Avvaro would preach again, this time in English, for another full hour. After several years in Belize and long letters of complaint to his superiors, Quinn was eventually assigned to Jamaica where he continued to teach elementary subjects in the Kingston Free School for boys.

When Dupeyron resigned in the 1870s, Woollett assumed Dupeyron's responsibilities and worries as pro-vicar apostolic. Whereas Dupeyron had allowed the individual missionary wide freedom, Woollett curtailed him. Dupeyron took a panoramic view of missionary activity, Woollett concentrated on the letter of the law. Italian thinking was more in accord with Dupeyron's manner, but now Woollett held the reins, so tightly that Di Pietro, superior of the mission, was reduced to a mere administrator.

Salvatore Di Pietro was born in Palermo, Sicily, 15 June 1830.[36] Educated by the Jesuits, he entered the Society of Jesus on 17 October 1854. In 1858 revolutions sweeping Europe drove Sicilian Jesuits to seek refuge within their own families. When the storm passed, Di Pietro resumed his studies and was ordained 2 June 1859. One year later, in 1860, Garibaldi dispersed the Sicilian province. Di Pietro spent a few months in Rome, then taught mathematics, chemistry, and philosophy for six years in Spain. In 1866 he returned to Sicily and opened the Episcopal Seminary at Gozo. At this time he volunteered for the missions and was on the point of leaving for Ecuador when a revolution in Spain prevented his departure. Appointed to British Honduras, he sailed from England in December 1868 in the company of Brother Mark Quinn. They arrived in Belize 22 March 1869, and Di Pietro was assigned to Corozal. Di Pietro contracted so severe a case of yellow fever that his doctor pronounced him unfit for the enervating climate of British Honduras.

In December 1869 Di Pietro left Belize to teach at the Colegio de la Merced, Guatemala, where he remained until a revolution forced him back to Punta Gorda, British Honduras, on 22 September 1871. In January 1872 Di Pietro again ventured into Spanish territory. This time he opened a mission station at Truxillo in neighbouring Spanish Honduras, but within six months a now rather routine revolution forced him to return to British Honduras. While at Truxillo, Di Pietro received word that he had been appointed superior of the British Honduras mission on 8 September 1872. Although superior of British Honduras, he was still under Woollett, who held the office of pro-vicar apostolic.

Di Pietro and Woollett never saw eye to eye on mission policy. Evidence of this occurred in the very September of Di Pietro's appointment. Woollett learned that Di Pietro and other British Honduras missionaries together with a missionary in Jamaica had actually engaged a community of nuns for Belize without Woollett's knowledge or consent. This so irritated Woollett that he immediately cancelled the engagement.[37] Di Pietro arrived in Kingston in a state of great agitation and expressed his determination to proceed to Cuba for the nuns without Woollett's sanction.[38] Woollett relented and allowed Di Pietro to proceed to Cuba. On this occasion Woollett's caution proved correct for the nuns were totally unsuited for mission work; subsequently Di Pietro had to refund the fare they had paid to Belize.

Woollett's narrow mission views brought about Di Pietro's resignation as mission superior only one and a half years after he had been appointed to the office. An Italian missionary was the occasion for his resignation. Brindisi was dying at Stann Creek and only the timely arrival of Di Pietro and the doctor saved his life. After Brindisi had convalesced at Belize, Di Pietro wished to send him back to England, but Woollett would not hear of it. Instead, he suggested that Brindisi be brought to Jamaica where he could recover at the Barrett estate of Retreat. He did come to Jamaica but in a dreadfully confused state of mind. After several months at the Barrett estate, he returned to Belize. Periods of good health interspersed with relapses made Di Pietro again suggest that Brindisi be sent home before a more serious relapse occurred. Woollett ignored Di Pietro's suggestion. Five months later the inevitable happened. On 12 September 1880 Brindisi died.[39]

Missions are persons, a composite of individuals. Not every successful missionary in Jamaica was an equal success in British

Honduras. Augustus Loontjens had done yeoman work in the western parishes of Jamaica, but in British Honduras he was a failure. Neither Di Pietro nor Parchi would have been acceptable in Jamaica.

Although the Spanish populace of British Honduras overlooked their halting Spanish, their poor command of English would never be acceptable to the people of Jamaica.[40] Woollett ascribed this to a proud Jamaican populace which considered itself on a par with the gentry of England, and for this reason he censured the Jamaicans. Only Corozal in British Honduras clamoured for a priest speaking their native Maya tongue; every other mission in that colony accepted faulty Spanish or the laboured English spoken by the Italians.

Language troubles were one problem at Corozal; Mr. Richard Fletcher, the Wesleyan minister, was another.[41] Antagonism developed between the Italians and the Englishman very early in the life of the mission, and the rivalry was carried on from the pulpit and the classroom where it waxed warmest, for both saw the man and woman of tomorrow in the school child of today. Prior to the coming of the Catholic school, Fletcher had settled down, satisfied that his own school would eventually spell complete success for the Wesleyan mission.

Uneasy was the calm when he witnessed brick and mortar transformed into a new Catholic school. Hurriedly Fletcher found a Belize benefactor who donated £2500 to make the Wesleyan school more presentable. There the rivals stood—Fletcher's renovated buildings and the newly constructed Catholic school. Buildings were important, but examinations showed the worth of an institution in colonial Britain. One hundred twenty-five Catholic children were presented to the government inspector in 1878; one hundred of them passed with the highest examination grade in the colony's school system. Rival Fletcher could only muster 103 for the examination; only five of them passed the examination. In three years Henry Gillet, S.J. had built up the Corozal school from nothing to such an enviable standard that the government inspector congratulated him and told Gillet to have confidence despite the character and language difficulties of the children he was teaching. He predicted that in a year or so Gillet would have the best school in the whole Corozal district.

Over in neighbouring Consejo, the local bastion of Wesleyanism, Fr. Dominic Chiarello, S.J., lacking a Catholic school, was experiencing his own difficulties with Wesleyan authorities.[42] In July 1878, Governor Frederick Palgrave Barlee visited Corozal and then rode out to look at Consejo. His sense of duty made him desire to know and see everything that was happening in the settlement. He was not pleased when he discovered that Catholic parents at Consejo were not sending their children to the Wesleyan school but allowing them to grow up illiterate. He expressed his opinion that parents could at least send their children to the Wesleyan school until the day when the padre might build his own school. The following day, the Wesleyan minister, accompanied by the mayor, visited Catholic families in the settlement, threatening with fine and imprisonment all who fail to send their children to the Wesleyan school. They offered as their authority the governor of the colony. Nothing could have upset the Catholics of Consejo more than falsification of the governor's words. One old lady and two children walked to Corozal to inform Gillet of the Wesleyan threat. Gillet's immediate reaction was to send word that the children were not to attend the Wesleyan school, and he himself would assume full responsibility to the governor for this line of action.

Arriving at Consejo next day, Gillet confronted the mayor, who denied the alleged threats. There the matter with Gillet immediately opening a school. Twenty-two children enrolled the first day; as the school grew, so attendance at Mass increased, raising the whole tone of the mission. Renegades, as Gillet termed the older people who had fallen away from the faith, were careful to call the priest when dying, in order to receive the last sacraments of the Church they had deserted. Before the school opened, these people would not even sell bread to the missionary; now with the school, they not only offered to sell bread but even offered choice cuts of beef to the missionary.

In Corozal bigotry died out, but not too gracefully. In September 1878 rumour reached Gillet's ears that Fletcher was about to accuse him before Lieutenant Governor Frederick Palgrave Barlee of some awful crime.[43] The "awful crime" turned out to be that Gillet had tried by unjust means to draw children from the Wesleyan to the Catholic school. This Gillet denied in a letter to the governor. Governor Barlee then ordered Fletcher to substantiate his charges, but no reply came from him. A second and a third letter from the governor brought no reply. Barlee then ordered Fletcher to prove his allegation or apologize to Gillet. This exoneration was just what the Catholic mission at Corozal needed to raise its esteem in the eyes of the populace, and it taught the old gentleman to make "awful accusations" with extreme caution.

A civil and an ecclesiastical blunder by Di Pietro lowered Woollett's esteem for the British Honduras superior.[44] Neither blunder was irreparable, but both loomed among the unforgivables in the provicar's imagination. In a civil matter, Di Pietro had wrongly instructed the Italian fathers in a matter concerning British Honduras's marriage laws. In the eyes of the government, these ecclesiastical marriages were invalid because the civil form was not followed. In ecclesiastical matters Di Pietro had delegated dispensations for which, according to Woollett, he had no faculty. But what Woollett dreaded most was Di Pietro's ever-increasing expenses. These showed up both in the accounts of individual missionaries and in Belize accounts sent by Di Pietro to the English province procurator, Sidgreaves. In order to curtail Di Pietro's spending propensities, Woollett, on 23 May 1874, appointed Fr. John Pittar, S.J., treasurer of the mission and ordered Di Pietro to hand over all accounts of money to the new procurator.

Di Pietro had enough of Woollett's stringent control of British Honduras. Forbidden to assign missionaries except with Woollett's approval and restricted in financial matters, Di Pietro resigned the office of mission superior on 10 May 1874. Di Pietro named Pittar as interim superior of the mission. Learning of the arrangement, Woollett sent a sharp note to Pittar dated 27 August 1874, reminding him that his appointment as superior did not begin until 1 September 1874, when he was to have it officially read in the refectory of Belize.[45]

Now it was Pittar's turn to experience Woollett's narrow-mindedness.[46] Woollett made it clear that the responsibility of assigning men rested solely with the vicar apostolic; hence Pittar could not appoint a missionary permanently to a station; should an emergency arise, and Pittar were forced to send one missionary to replace another, he must inform Woollett as soon as possible. As soon as the emergency ceased, the missionary must return to the post Woollett assigned him. He could not purchase property, nor erect a building, nor substantially alter an existing one without the pro-vicar's permission. Even if property were to be purchased, Pittar should submit the title to a lawyer, have his approbation, then convey the title rights to Woollett. Nor was Pittar to incur any debts nor borrow money even if the money be loaned without payment of interest. Included in these matters was the Carib Fund.[47] Every detail of the mission was under Woollett's strict surveillance. He allowed the British Honduras superior no initiative. All this was happening between men who, separated by 750 miles of water, could communicate only by slow-moving ship across the Caribbean Sea.

If money was a perennial headache for the support of the missions, more so was the problem of manpower. In 1875 there were only five priests to cover the three hundred miles of coastline of British Honduras territory. So few were the missionaries that the superior himself had to spend a month at a time in each mission assisting the priest and at the same time making his visitation to discover on occasion that not every missionary proved himself satisfactory to the environment, as for example Loydi, a Spanish secular priest who had made himself unacceptable to the people of the San Ignacio mission. Fresh from Europe, he could not adjust himself to the slow, plodding ways of people in the tropics. Impatience with their lack of response to his own superhuman efforts proved fatal to his missionary career in British Honduras, and after one year he returned to Jamaica where he did adjust himself to a most successful career of fourteen years among people living in her remote mountain terrain.

An important event in the routine life of the bush missionary is the visitation made by his superior. It proves to the missionary, removed from city or town civilization, that he is still remembered and has some contact with the civilized world of his day. Visitations, moreover, afford an opportunity to review the problems and difficulties of his own private life and those of his mission. Finally, it orients his work and gives it direction when so often it appears pointless to oppose the obstacles of ignorance and misunderstanding of a primitive-minded people.

In 1877 Thomas Porter, S.J., took Woollett's place as vicar apostolic. Whereas Woollett was a master of details, Porter cared little for minutiae. He carried this seeming lack of interest to include the British Honduras. Disappointment was voiced by all the British Honduras missionaries when Porter advised Di Pietro, who had been reappointed superior of the mission 2 October 1878, that he would postpone his first visitation.[48] This was a time when his presence would have acted as a stimulant, since all were either ill or much discouraged. Poverty was depressing and debts were mounting. Di Pietro spent many a restless night wondering how to meet these demands of his creditors. Would the whole mission end in bankruptcy? That it did not was due to the persevering and almost superhuman effort of Di Pietro.

Communities of sisters are a necessity for a successful mission. Two areas—education and nursing—have been their principal work. Practically all Catholic education has been in their hands, but their teaching has not been limited to the lower grades. Wherever a Catholic high school for girls is operating, it can be safely predicted that sisters are the teachers. Thus from his earliest missionary years, Di Pietro envisioned sisters conducting schools in British Honduras. Although his first attempts ended in failure, he did not give up. On 14 January 1880 he sent Gillet to New Orleans as his representative to attract sisters to the mission.[49]

In New Orleans Gillet met Fr. Francis Gautrelet, rector of Jesuit Immaculate Conception Church in that city, who recommended the Sisters of Mercy. Mother Austin, the superior, described by Gillet as clever and prudent, declined to give her consent until she had considered the British Honduras offer from all angles. After a week of serious thought, she made her decision. She was prepared to offer three choir sisters and one lay sister. However, the bishop of New Orleans objected. According to their rule, nine sisters were necessary to form a community. Would Gillet guarantee that within five years the sisters would have an increase of vocations in British Honduras to satisfy the rule? Gillet could give no such guarantee; the offer was withdrawn.

On 2 February 1882 Di Pietro handed over the reins of ecclesiastical government to Fr. John Martell, an English Jesuit.[50] Di Pietro wanted to further the interests of the mission in the matters of personnel and finances by a visit to his native Italy. He left for Europe on 8 June 1882 by way of New Orleans. While in that city he successfully negotiated for the Sisters of Mercy to go to British Honduras. On 20 January 1882 six sisters and their superior left for British Honduras; two more were to follow shortly, in keeping with the spirit of their rule.

Enthusiasm greeted the sisters from every quarter when they arrived in Belize. Even the government offered financial aid for their new school. Vicar Apostolic Porter sent his blessing and assured the sisters of his approval: thus the contention that marked the many years of Di Pietro's career was settled amicably.

Di Pietro had been the persevering hero of the British Honduras for thirty trying years. Avvaro, Bertolio, Parchi, Parisi, and Brindisi—the companions of his early days—were no more. Di Pietro alone remained of the pioneers. British Honduras was no longer the primitive land he had known when he first arrived in Belize; and he himself had become as native as the trees in her forests and the sand on her shores. The Holy See recognized that the Church in this colony had outgrown her pioneer days and had passed on to a more mature stage. Four years after British Honduras had become a crown colony, the Holy See separated the mission from the vicariate of Jamaica on 16 June 1888.[51] It became an autonomous prefecture and with Di Pietro as prefect apostolic.

In 1892, on the occasion of Leo XIII's episcopal jubilee, the colony despatched a congratulatory message to the Holy Father together with a petition that they be granted a bishop. Since Di Pietro was going to Rome, he was asked to present both congratulations and petition to His Holiness. Di Pietro left Belize on 15 July 1892 and was received by the Pope in audience on two occasions, on 12 September and on 23 November. On the occasion of the second audience, Leo XIII brought up the subject of a bishop for British Honduras. Di Pietro was told to convey the news to the Catholics of British Honduras that the Holy See would soon raise the prefecture to a vicariate.

Cardinal Ledóchowski expedited the business and even hinted to Di Pietro that he would be the best man for the office because of his long years of experience in the colony. Di Pietro protested and suggested that a younger man be made bishop. He even asked Fr. Luis Martin, Superior General of the Society of Jesus, to intercede on his behalf to have a younger priest nominated to the office.

Di Pietro sailed for Belize; while at sea, he was chosen by the consistory on 4 January 1893 as titular bishop of Eurea and vicar apostolic of British Honduras. On 30 January the bulls of the erection of British Honduras a vicariate and the election of Di Pietro as vicar apostolic were received in Belize. Di Pietro sent Gillet to ask neighbouring bishops to come to Belize for his consecration.

The ceremony took place on 16 April 1893, with Bishop Thomas A. Becker of Savannah, Georgia, as consecrator, assisted by the bishops of Natchez and Mobile, Most Reverend Thomas Heslin and Most Reverend Jeremiah O'Sullivan respectively. This was a day to remember in British Honduras, for no longer could Jamaica dictate or interfere in its ecclesiastical life.

Long had been Di Pietro's priestly mission career; short was his episcopate. This was to span a mere five years, with annual visits to the mission stations in order to encourage and evaluate the work of his missionaries, to preach, and to confirm. In 1898 his many years in this tropical country were beginning to tell on him physically. Twice he attempted to visit the mission stations during that year, and twice he had to give up. Each time he was forced to return to Belize on account of recurring heart attacks. On 6 August the local gentry called to congratulate him on his patronal feast day. On 7 August he took seriously ill and asked to receive the last sacraments. He was anointed on 14 August. During the afternoon of Tuesday, 20 August 1898 he passed quietly away.[52] He was buried in a vault under the cathedral floor in front of the Blessed Virgin's altar.

Twenty

The First Bishop 1889–1906

The Catholic Church in Jamaica was slowly reaching maturity, which the Holy See acknowledged by appointing a bishop as the next vicar apostolic. For some years Rome had been considering this step. It had come under serious consideration when Porter became vicar apostolic, for his provincial had told him that, should the Holy See wish to consecrate him bishop, he was to accept without protest. All during Porter's regime, the rumour persisted with the likely candidate shifting from Porter to Alfred Weld, the English assistant of the Society of Jesus, because of his interest in the Jamaican mission. The choice, however, fell on Charles Menzies Gordon, S.J.

Gordon's Early Life

Gordon was born in Glenlivet, Scotland, 5 March 1831, the son of Sir Charles Gordon, a barrister of Drinnan, Argyllshire, and a descendant of the Gordons of Minniore, a branch of the ancient ducal house of Gordon.[1] In early youth Charles was destined for a position in the renowned East India Company where his uncle was a director, but the death of his father altered his career from businessman in the tropical East to that of country squire in Scotland. Management of the family estates and the more or less uneventful task of promoter of the Highland Agricultural Society was his work-a-day life.

But Gordon never suffered dull monotony; in 1867, at the age of thirty-six, the call to arms roused him from the ancestral hearth to the defence of the Papal States against the usurper Garibaldi, for a man of Gordon's devotion to the Holy See could hardly sit at home and watch the Papal States go down to defeat. He raised a company of sixty men, paid their passage to Rome, and as their commander fought bravely for two years in the temporal service of the Pope, receiving serious wounds which he carried to the grave.

While in Rome he decided to join the Society of Jesus. On 4

November 1869, at the age of thirty-eight, Gordon began his course of studies as a Jesuit novice. Consideration was given to his age and the course abbreviated to nine years proceeding ordination. In 1878 he was ordained at St. Bueno's College, Wales. His first assignment, following tertianship, was parish priest at Galashiels, Edinburgh, in 1879; but the comfortable community life at Galashiels was abruptly interrupted by a call for missionaries to labour in South Africa. He volunteered and was accepted. He spent the year 1880 in Graaff-Reinet; the following year, 1881, in Zambesi. In 1882 he was recalled and assigned to Glasgow where at St. Aloysius' College, 21 Dalhouse Street, Garnet Hill, he acted as minister to the community and at the same time as parish priest. Although he never held the office of superior, he did prove in the work assigned him that he had administrative ability. Here was the person the Holy See was looking for to fill the office of vicar apostolic in Jamaica. Leo XIII signed the document appointing him vicar apostolic on 1 August 1889. Two weeks later on 15 August, Charles Gordon was consecrated titular bishop of Thyatira. The consecrating prelate was Archbishop Charles Eyre, and the ceremony took place in the Cathedral of St. Andrew, Glasgow. On 20 August his parishioners presented him with an address, a portable altar, a silver-gilt crosier, and a jewelled mitre, designed by the celebrated L. Cross of Bruges, while valuable personal gifts came from the archbishop of Glasgow, the bishop of Argyle, and the marquis of Bute.[2]

The first Catholic bishop of Jamaica did not delay long in Scotland, for the people were in daily expectation of the arrival of one whose noble ancestry placed him on a pedestal of high social elevation in this Victorian age of much pomp and circumstance. For two weeks the committee prepared for the arrival of "M' Lord." It was judged fitting that their bishop should be presented with an elegant gift: a fine carriage and a pair of horses. When the ship docked, a representative of the *Daily Gleaner* recorded the event under the date of 14 September 1889.

> The Rt. Rev. Bishop Gordon, the Vicar Apostolic of the Roman Catholic Church in this island, chosen by Pope Leo XIII, arrived yesterday in the Atlas' Company Steamer, *Adirondack,* from New York, accompanied by his chaplain Rev. H. Martyn Parker, S.J. of Stonyhurst College. His Lordship was met on board by the following gentlemen: Frs. Hogan, W. Spillman, P. Hasan, McCormick, and Brother Reddington; Mr. L. P. Branday, as chairman proceeded to read an address: "Many earnest prayers have been offered for a worthy successor to the able and energetic prelate Fr. Porter, S.J., whose loss we have for nearly a year been deploring, and with no less earnestness a prosperous journey has been implored in the intelligence of your Lordship's appointment being received by us. The joy that

the announcement of the new Vicar caused us was heightened by the intelligence that he was to be a Bishop."[3]

The new bishop replied to the welcome.

> I feel that God has indeed blessed my mission and that my future will be a future of happiness in His service, for whatever else may happen if the cause of the Church proceeds well I am quite happy, and I am sure it will proceed well. We do not seek to hinder others, we have only the greatest love and affection for all who may differ from us, and we will never have a word to say against them. At the same time we cannot forget our own affections, and I am certain therefore, that we shall promote this to the best of our power, but not in the slightest degree to offend the spirit of charity with regard to others. I dare say we shall find here, as I have found in other places, that however men differ from one another in points of faith, they all agree in promoting the works of charity, and as far as possible we shall do our best to aid our brethren in that and keep unity among ourselves and them, whether separated from us or not.[4]

This was the keynote of Gordon's life in Jamaica. His fixed determination was to intensify the interior life of the Church and to expand the Mystical Body of Christ. If he could not meet Protestants on religious grounds, he would promote with them the works of charity. From the pier the delegation proceeded to Holy Trinity Church where a vast throng had gathered to welcome their bishop. Red banners and green wreathes hung in the galleries of the church, at the west end of which the words "Ecce Sacerdos Magnus" were formed in foliage of various colours. The illuminated altar reflected the colours of the beautiful banners arranged along the walls of the sanctuary as the processional march proceeded down the main aisle of the church, led by an acolyte carrying a large crucifix, followed by the clergy and the first Catholic bishop of Jamaica. The Te Deum and benediction brought the afternoon ceremonies to a close.[5]

Gordon's Visitation of his Vicariate

The finely worded address of welcome, the generous gift of carriage and horse, the enthusiastic welcome at Holy Trinity, were all received by Gordon with the graciousness of a gentleman, but there was enough of the down-to-earth Scot in him to want to probe beneath the surface and see for himself the exact condition of the church he had been sent to govern. He began his visitation with Kingston. In the city he found conditions most satisfactory, all six priests were assiduously fulfilling their duties ministering to the congregation at Holy Trinity. The church had a seating capacity of eighteen hundred and a parish membership of seven thousand. Daily Mass was celebrated, confessions heard, baptisms and marriages performed, the dead buried. These works alone in a large parish would have been sufficient to keep six priests busy most of their waking hours; lest any time be called their own, there was the added care of serving the British soldiers at Newcastle, the sailors at the dockyard in Port Royal, the Convent of Franciscan Sisters, the orphanage of Alpha, The General Penitentiary, the Stony Hill Reformatory, the Alms House, and the nearby mission stations at St. Patrick's, Above Rocks, Harbour Head, Spanish Town, King Weston, White Hall, and Toll Gate.[6] All demanded their share of attention in the cycle of twenty-four hours.

St. George's College

St. George's College was the major disappointment. The one institution which should have highlighted the church's missionary effect had faded badly. Woollett's tenure as pro-vicar apostolic had been no help, for he was not interested in higher education. Uninterested or psychologically incapable headmasters followed the brilliant regime of Fr. James Jones, which was from 1865 to 1869. Had Jones not returned to England, St. George's would not have declined—such was the opinion of the Catholic populace. Finally Woollett closed the institution. It was reopened only in 1873, when Fr. Francis X. Jaeckel, a brilliant teacher and competent headmaster, took charge. Then came more trouble. Jaeckel disagreed with Woollett's policy, and went off on 21 May 1877 to open his own school as a secular priest. Porter then acted as headmaster of St. George's.

When Gordon appeared on the scene, he appointed Fr. H. Martyn Parker headmaster. Despite his degree from Oxford, Parker was an incompetent administrator and a poor teacher. Under his administration the number of pupils dwindled to sixteen, and even this insignificant number was claimed by the headmaster to be too many to manage. He refused to admit more pupils. Catholic boys were forced to find their education in non-Catholic schools. The bishop, who was also religious superior, could not allow this situation to continue; something had to be done. To solve the problem Gordon wrote to the English provincial, requesting that two teachers, well-trained at Stonyhurst, be sent to Jamaica to prepare boys for matriculation at the university. Should Jesuits be unable to supply a competent staff, the bishop proposed that the course be changed from a classical to a scientific-commercial one, and another religious congregation be given the charge.[7] The bishop's strongly worded letter brought the authorities in England to the realization that the lustre of St. George's had dimmed, and it was no longer a shining light in

Jamaican education. Action was taken immediately. Fr. William Hudson was sent out as headmaster, and under his guidance the college once again took its rightful place in the community as an institution capable of offering a complete classical education in preparation for the university.

Alpha Demands Attention

Gordon's visitation of Kingston revealed another institution that demanded his attention. Although in a flourishing condition in respect to numbers and physical plant, the Alpha orphanage was built on a shaky foundation. For ten years, 1880–90, three Jamaican ladies, Jessie Ripoll, Josephine Ximines, and Louise Dugiol, struggled to care for the orphans who had increased from one child in 1880 to forty in 1890.[8] In the same compound were two industrial schools; one was training fifty-eight girls, and the other school was training fifty-three boys. For ten years these devoted women had lived in expectations that one day they would become religious, but each year widened the gap between hope and fulfillment. In 1890 they were still in the same status as when they were founded. The rule Porter gave them was simple: obey the vicar apostolic and keep the Ten Commandments. If this was the total direction these women were ever to receive, the whole orphanage plan would fall apart.

Two solutions were proposed by Gordon: the first was to seek a community of English sisters to train young Jamaican ladies in the principles of religious life—once this foundation was laid, the Jamaicans would set up their own community. The second plan was to ask a religious community to come out from England and incorporate the four Jamaicans into their own community. The first and better scheme would have given Jamaica an exclusively native community in those early days, but it never got under way. The second plan was adopted after many delays and endless correspondence with many religious congregations.

The Way it Was Done

In the early days of his ministry at St. Aloysius' College, Gordon had made acquaintance with Fr. Peter Chandlery. Through Gordon, Chandlery developed a keen interest in the Jamaican mission, and to Chandlery it owes the introduction of the Sisters of Mercy. Knowing that he could rely on Chandlery's friendship, Gordon wrote asking for his help to solve the perplexing Alpha problem. If Chandlery thought he could secure sisters by merely asking the first congregation encountered, he was due for a rude awakening. He sought sisters from five congregations; all refused. On 27 April 1890 Chandlery wrote that he was trying to obtain Sisters of Mercy, Birmingham Nuns, for Jamaica; should these refuse, he planned to apply to the Sisters of St. Joseph of Cluny, though he thought Sisters of Mercy would best suit Gordon's orphanage.

His next letter, 24 May 1890, sounded a note of frustration. The Sisters of Mercy everywhere refused to spare any of their number for Jamaica. In near desperation he wrote on 20 July 1890, that he had tried everywhere to get nuns but did not succeed. The Cluny nuns, the Oblate nuns, the Franciscan nuns, the Daughters of the Holy Cross all sent the same answer: the Jamaican offer was most tempting and nothing would delight them more than to go to such a promising field of labour but—that wretched but—they had no sisters to spare. Chandlery advised Gordon that as a last resort he start his own community of sisters, then give them rules and a habit just as the bishop of Nottingham had done, and when these preliminaries had been taken care of, Gordon was to ask the Holy See's sanction.

A remarkable characteristic of Chandlery was his perseverance. On 20 July 1890 he wrote to Gordon saying that he was applying to the Sisters of Mercy of Bermondsey. A glimmer of hope shone in his letter of 4 August 1890. Good news at last. The Sisters of Bermondsey were going to write to Gordon for particulars of his proposed foundation. They would then consult their bishop, Dr. Butt, about the advisability of accepting the mission. Chandlery remarked that this community was noted for its apostolic spirit and in Bishop Grant's day had sent nuns to the Crimea.

Evidently Chandlery painted a very tempting picture of the Jamaican mission to the Sisters of Mercy, much to the amusement of Gordon. On 15 September 1890 hope became brighter. Gordon could not help being amused at Chandlery's remark that he had baited a hook with an appetizing bait to entice the sisters to Jamaica, but he added the protest that what he said was the truth and not exaggeration. A personal visit by Chandlery to Bermondsey turned the tables in favour of Jamaica, and the definitive decision was announced. "The Bermondsey Nuns have decided to go out to Jamaica, and I am sure you will be delighted with them. The new Jamaican superioress is quite a superior person, in fact one of the principal Nuns of the Community, and it is a great sacrifice to lose her. So there will be five in all, and six if Anne Grant, a postulant goes."[9]

Sisters of Mercy's Arrival in Jamaica

On the fifty-ninth anniversary of the founding of the Sisters of Mercy, the Bermondsey pioneers arrived in Kingston 12 December 1890, aboard the steamship *Don*. The new arrivals were Mother M. Winifred Aloysius (Furlong), Sister M. Clare Joseph (Mackey), Sister M. Aquinas (Kerns), Sister M. de Chantal (Higgins), and postulant Ellen Grey, who later took the name of Sister Mary Berchmans.[10] Coming from an English winter with its biting cold, its heavy damp fog and sunless skies, the five religious set foot in Jamaica during its most invigorating season: it was winter, but the West Indian winter of delightfully warm days, deep blue skies, and just enough cool breeze to temper the tropical sun. The contrast was reversed between the convent they had left in England and the convent that would be their home in Jamaica. Here England held the advantage. In England they had a long and well established convent with its regular daily order of work, prayer, and recreation, and a large community where personalities had less chance to clash and where they laboured among a people who were native to them in culture and thought. In Jamaica the sisters were just making a start; their convent was a tiny wooded cottage which crowded the six English sisters and four Jamaican ladies into its narrow rooms, where personalities would clash and one would be recalled to England.

Yet Jamaica did possess one advantage: for the newly arrived it was the land of the pioneer and a challenge to their dreams of heroic work. After incorporating the four Jamaican ladies into the congregation of the Sisters of Mercy, this small band of nine began their island-wide work for the poor. Each passing year brought an increase both in the number of new religious and the children assigned to their care. Alpha became a little world in itself: orphanage; industrial, primary, and basic Schools, a commercial school and an academy, all added up to the largest educational institution in Jamaica.

Gordon Continues his Visitation: in the Country

Gordon's visitation had produced advantageous results in the city; he now turned his attention to the country. A week's travel by carriage brought him to Reading, the centre of Woollett's missions. Slow travel by horse allowed him to stop periodically en route and evaluate the effectiveness of Woollett's missionary labours. Personal observation confirmed parishioners' complaints that all was not well: buildings everywhere badly needed repair, indicative of the general deterioration in all his missions. Congregations were displeased with the irregularity of his visits. They deplored the lack of interest Woollett showed by riding off immediately after Mass, offering them no opportunity of being instructed in Christian doctrines. Indifference and neglect brought calamitous results. Portuguese settlers were falling away from the Church and joining Protestant congregations. Gordon left a directive with Woollett: he was to visit his principal missions on fixed days; the remainder of his time was to be divided among his minor stations. The teaching of Christian doctrine was never to be omitted, no matter how pressing other business might be.[11] But this was not like the Woollett of old: something had happened. Blame for the generally run-down conditions of these missions cannot be placed entirely on Woollett's shoulders. For thirty years he had covered this wide mission territory alone. Only on two brief periods could he count on any help, once when Fr. John Tauer, S.J. took over some of the mission stations, and the other occasion when Fr. Augustus Loontjens, S.J., came to his aid. But both these missionaries found the work excessive, the loneliness unbearable, and the discouragements beyond their power of perseverance. After a fair trial Tauer and Loontjens asked to be sent to other fields of labour. Once they departed, the whole burden was again thrown on Woollett's shoulders. He was now seventy-two years old, an age when most men dream of an easier life by the comfortable fireside. But for him that day was yet two years distant; for the present he must still ride into those difficult, widely scattered mountain missions.

The stamina that allowed Woollett to ride 5,000 miles in a year was now on the wane. Gordon now faced the disagreeable task of replacing a missionary who had been on his own for thirty years and more, no easy chore to execute diplomatically. His opportunity came in 1891, when John Errington, who had just completed his tertianship, was assigned to Jamaica. Errington taught at St. George's College until early 1892, when he was sent to the Barrett estate to acclimatize him to missionary life and prepare him to live with Woollett at Reading.

The two missionaries met for the first time at Retreat estate, and it was an awkward encounter. When Errington broached the subject, saying that the bishop wished him to live with Woollett at Reading, the old missionary's manner "froze and he cut Errington short with the reply that he did not want to receive the Bishop's orders through a third party, refusing to glance at the written instructions Errington had in his possession."[12]

To avoid unpleasantness, Errington went to live at the nearby mission of Refuge, where he remained a month before taking up residence with Woollett at Reading on 30 May 1892. Although Errington found conditions at Reading unsatisfactory, he tried not to ruffle the old missionary by discussing controversial points. In the beginning Woollett disliked the change, but as time passed he saw the wisdom of Errington's taking most of the missionary burden. Despite Errington's help, Woollett's seventy years were exacting their toll from his once powerful physique. A change had to be made. Gordon thought he should have the advantage of community life in Kingston rather than the responsibility of the far-flung mission stations and tactfully suggested the change. Woollett took it like a soldier. On 2 May 1893 Woollett made known his decision to Errington. At first he considered driving over the road some 125 miles to Kingston, but such a trip would have been too exhausting for a man of his age. His final decision was to drive to Savanna-la-Mar and board the coastal steamer for Kingston.[13]

Early on the morning of 11 May 1893, just as dawn was breaking over the Caribbean, Woollett hitched horse to carriage, threw in his few effects, snapped the whip, and drove through the gates of Reading for the last time. Over Long Hill the serpentine road led to the village of Anchovy where Woollett had posted many a letter. Through Montpelier, Shettlewood, and Ramble, the road twisted and turned into the tiny village of Haddo, a sharp turn at Whithorn and another at Galloway, and he was down on the flat sugar lands of the south coast, where he passed through Petersfield, then to his destination, Savanna-la-Mar. It was a long trip of twenty-four slow miles. The afternoon sun was witness to this pioneer missionary riding down Great George Street for the last time. Woollett did not look back, there were too many fond memories in those hills. The coastal steamer grew faint on the horizon and with it ended the missionary life of Joseph Sidney Woollett.

The remainder of Woollett's life can be told very simply. Once he ceased to be in charge of the western missions, the question arose of his yearly grant of £100, voted by the House of Assembly for ministering to Catholics of Cornwall and Middlesex Counties. Protocol demanded that Woollett ask leave of absence from his duties. This he did through Gordon, who received a reply from King's House, 14 July 1892.

> I am directed by His Excellency the Governor to acknowledge the receipt of your letter of yesterday's date with reference to J. S. Woollett's leave of absence. The Governor has much pleasure in granting leave and the Colonial Secretary for the Colonies has been informed of the fact.[14]

Woollett remained but a few months in Kingston. He returned that year to the England he had not seen for thirty-eight years. After a short sojourn in London, he retired in 1893 to St. Mary's Hall, Stonyhurst College, where at the age of ten years he had launched his scholastic career. On 1 April 1894 the Jamaican government made

Woollett a final financial settlement of a yearly pension to the amount of fifty-eight pounds, six shillings and eightpence. He died at Stonyhurst College at the age of eighty-four on 7 February 1898.

Errington's Description of the Western Missions

Errington soon discovered that the mission stations willed him were no sinecure. Even travelling from his main station at Reading to headquarters in Kingston presented a problem. For this he had to ride a horse fifty miles, to the railway station at Balaclava, then board the cab of an engine because passenger trains were not operating as far as Balaclava in 1893. He rode in the cab until he reached a station where passengers were accommodated and he could continue the journey to Kingston under conditions more or less comfortable. He would then hire a horse and carriage in Kingston and return to Reading, stopping at his mission stations on the north coast to minister to his parishioners at such places as Somerton, Alva, and Refuge.

Somerton was a little village a few miles from Brown's Town settled by Irish immigrants. In Errington's day only one of them remained, a Mrs. Walshe, from near Ballina, County Mayo, Ireland. An Englishman, William Mears, had joined the Irish, and he too managed to survive. The rest had found the soil too barren and the labour under a tropical sun more than they could endure. Those survived migrated to more promising settlements in the island.

Thirteen miles higher into the dry Harbour Mountains, the mission of Alva was still flourishing in Errington's day because of the constant and careful catechizing by Loydi in the 1870s. The immigrants in all these stations had kept the faith despite the infrequency of visits by the missionary. An exception was All Saints, Refuge, where only a well-constructed church remained of a once-flourishing mission. It had been frequented by Portuguese, some of whom had removed to other parts of Jamaica and others had abandoned their faith. Errington assigned the scarcity of priests as the reason for these defections.

Despite discouragement of All Saints, Errington moved on to Seaford Town and arrived there two weeks later. In 1893 this German settlement was the most flourishing in rural Jamaica, for Fr. John Tauer, an Austrian Jesuit, had devoted much time to this mission and on 26 April 1882, had erected the first stone church, reopened the school, and set in motion the conversion of the Lutherans. Although Seaford Town had a high religious standard, in a civic sense it was in a lower bracket, for its population had not increased as it should have in the first years of colonization. Many of the pioneers had died from hardships brought on by the white man trying to perform the labour of the negro in gleaning a living from the stubborn mountain soil under a tropical sun. The second generation was more healthy than the first; in Errington's day, several generations later, these people had become enured to the tropical climate. Since these Germans were both intelligent and of high moral character, the extra time spent among them by the missionary paid substantial dividends in the frequent reception of the sacraments and a good family life. In contrast was the neighbouring village where lax morals were considered the standard practice.

A two-hour ride into the limestone hills where the people eked out a living from ground provisions—yams, sweet potatoes, corn, coco, and tomatoes—was the mission station of Pisgah, which could only be reached on horse over a narrow trail that clung serpent-like to the mountainside as it rose higher and higher. It reminded Errington of Cader Idris in Wales, where he had spent tertianship. Errington reached this remote village on Easter Sunday. There he found the people so poor that he thought that should they receive more frequent visits by the missionary, they would find it difficult to provide for him and his horse. The horse had to subsist on bamboo shoots during the visit. Errington observed that a Moravian school at Pisgah was doing well, but when he tried to open a Catholic school, it failed.

Riding onto a village twelve miles west of Savanna-la-Mar, Errington opened a Catholic school at Top Hill, Westmoreland, with an initial enrollment of thirty children. He saw the need for schools even in these remote missions and considered they performed a useful function if they could give these peasant children a good elementary education.

Errington's Description of the Western Missions

In a letter to his provincial in England, Errington described his first missionary venture into the interior, and ended on this note.

> Perhaps it will interest you to know how we travel from one mission to another. Hitherto I have had only one horse and saddle bags. The country is all fenced like England and Ireland, so that camping out in the American and Australian fashion is impossible. Outside the few large towns there is nothing in the way of an Inn. However, the planters and cattle farmers are very hospitable. At the mission itself there is generally a room attached to the Church, and someone in the neighbourhood provides the meals.[15]

While Errington was in charge of the western mission, the Jamaican Railway was constructing its last few miles of track connecting

Kingston and Montego Bay. Beginning at Kingston, the railway ran along the south coast on flat, level ground until it reached the town of May Pen. A few miles beyond May Pen it began to climb into the mountains—a gradual slope at first, then the real tortuous twists through high mountain country, reaching its peak at Greenvale; from this point began a descent to the terminus, Montego Bay. About five miles from Montego Bay, it passed through the Reading property. On 13 May 1892 Errington noted that labourers constructing the railway bed were doing much damage to the Reading property by stealing the citrus fruits. Errington warned Gordon that, unless they were checked, the Church would lose heavily. The mission depended on the sale of this fruit to sustain it. At this point, June 1892, the construction engineers offered to rent the Reading residence in order to live near their work. Errington readily accepted the lucrative offer and went to reside at Savanna-la-Mar. Finding Savanna-la-Mar too malarial, he rented a house in Lucea on 17 November 1892 at the normal payment of one pound and eight shillings per month, while the kindly Buchanan family provided his meals free.

For some time Errington had been suffering from a hernia which made riding a horse painful. On 22 February 1893 he wrote his provincial, saying that he could remain in Jamaica no longer. He stayed on until the end of the year, and then went to Barbados, where he resumed his missionary work.[16] Other missionaries followed Errington, some for a longer, others for a shorter time; no one ever surpassed the record set by Woollett.

Twenty-One

American Mission

Since 1837 the English province of the Society of Jesus had been supplying missionaries to Jamaica, vast British Guiana, and the Central American colony of British Honduras. A critical point in missionary personnel resources was reached when Zambezi in Africa was assigned to England. On 13 October 1893 John Clayton, provincial of the English province, wrote Gordon that for this reason Rome had entrusted Jamaica to the American province of Maryland-New York. But not until 10 December 1893 did Fr. Luis Martin, superior general of the Society of Jesus, officially inform Gordon himself of the change, a month after the Sacred Congregation of Propagation of the Faith had approved the transfer. Four months later, on Saturday morning, 7 April 1894, the first American Jesuits arrived: John Collins, Patrick F. X. Mulry, and Andrew Rapp.[1]

Their American Environment

To evaluate this early American period, it is well to place in proper perspective their environment, national views, training, and prejudices. The three new missionaries, from Kentucky, New York, and Maryland respectively, represented the culture of eastern United States, still a missionary country under Propaganda. The vast majority of American Catholics at this time were either immigrants or first generation Americans. From Europe they came, lured by more favourable economic and political conditions. Thousands of Germans, French, Irish, Italians, Lithuanians, and Poles flocked to urban United States in answer to the demand for cheap, unskilled labour in rapidly expanding industrial areas. Settling in cities from New York to San Francisco, they stretched thin the clerical resources of the Church. Its own gigantic territory, its internal growing pains, its effort to propagate the faith from Atlantic to Pacific, had forced the American hierarchy to think in terms of domestic problems and consider all extra-territorial missions foreign to its ecclesiastical obligations. Since most immigrants were only superficially acquainted with English, the hierarchy had to supply German-speaking, French-speaking, Italian-speaking, Lithuanian-speaking, Polish-speaking priests, and even national parishes for these ethnic groups. Such a gigantic task claimed all available clerical manpower within the continental United States. Should a young man aspire to a mission in a foreign country, the cry was raised immediately that there was enough work at home. Having been compelled by domestic missionary commitments to operate within the continental United States, no universal missionary tradition had been formed by 1893 in the American Church.

Foremost, these newly-arrived American missionaries in Jamaica had to bury their natural prejudices, for Jamaica was a British colony, ruled by Englishmen in all key colonial positions. These pioneer Americans and the majority who followed them were of Irish descent; they would have to rise above prejudice and assume a more benign, universal attitude towards other nationals. The years would eventually broaden their views, nationally and ecclesiastically.

Within a year the Americans were in conflict with Gordon, who deemed it serious enough to bypass provincial and general and appeal to the Sacred Congregation of Propaganda by writing to Cardinal Ledóchowski on 10 June 1895.

> The affairs of the Mission of Jamaica touch at present upon a point to which I find myself obliged to seek advice of your Excellency. Up to the present it has been enough for me to treat the affairs with the Provincial or the General of the Society of Jesus. The reason why I am acting otherwise is that since this Mission has been under the Province of Maryland-New York, the manner of acting has changed. For the first time one hears of them speaking of MINE and THINE and the diverse interests of the Mission and the Society. Under the regime of the Province of England, all was for the Mission. In view of this they treated it with generosity. Not only do they seek to seize their property but also separate the Bishop from his priests. For sixty years it has been the custom here that the Fathers of the Society of Jesus stay at the Bishop's residence. The author of an historical summary of this Mission writes how this custom was established by the first Jesuits who landed on this island. Frs. Cotham and Dupeyron, who after they vainly tried to make an establishment themselves, decided to accept the hospitality of the Vicar Apostolic who was not even of their Order. The writer also describes the results: it was a veritable family of friends or rather brothers established among themselves in lodging, table, and ecclesiastical functions. Everything was divided in perfect harmony under the Paternal authority. At present with a Jesuit bishop they complain that the Society is forced to stay with the Bishop as mere helpers or guests. It is regrettable that they take such an attitude instead of seeking the reason for such a custom, which ought to have a sufficiently strong reason, having had the approbation of so many Generals. No Provincial or local Superior complained of it. There is such a

> reason: it is simply that a poor Mission cannot support two establishments worthy of the capital city. At least the Bishop could not do it. . . . It seems to me that justice demands that the province of Maryland-New York enter upon the Mission under the condition which the Province of England left it, no more, no less. It is unworthy that a Province accept a Mission from the Holy Father in a mean or niggardly spirit.[2]

A second difficulty arose over property. The Maryland-New York provincial complained to Fr. Luis Martin, superior general, that he did not know which was vicariate property and which Jesuit property. Martin wrote Gordon 25 April 1895 about the complaint, saying that confusion arose because the bishop combined in his person the offices of vicar apostolic and religious superior. All property was held in his name and no distinction was made between the two owners, the vicariate and the Society of Jesus. The province of Maryland-New York was now asking for a clear distinction to be expressed in legal documents.

Although this was prescribed in the *Romanos Pontifices,* a little more diplomatic tact and less insistence on legal rights would have rendered the aging bishop more benevolent and docile. This rigid insistence on the letter of the law only alienated Gordon from the American missionaries. Within the following year, Gordon settled the matter. On 18 May and 26 July 1896, he sent to Rome all documents relating to the two estates, the vicariate and the Society of Jesus.[3]

Since the early days of Dupeyron, the offices of superior and vicar apostolic had been united in one person. Fr. Martin now wished to separate them. On 11 May 1897 he asked Gordon when such a separation could take effect. Up went Gordon's blood pressure. He asked how far would the jurisdiction of the religious superior extend? Would it overlap the jurisdiction of the vicar apostolic? Should this occur, there would be constant friction between superior and bishop. Martin allayed his fears; the religious superior would have no say in the government of the mission, which pertained to the office of vicar apostolic alone. Should the bishop wish to grant the superior some say in governing the mission, that would be his affair.

On 25 November 1898 a religious superior was appointed, Fr. James Noonan, S.J.[4] Noonan was a native of Ireland, born 13 March 1841. His first profession was as a teacher in the national schools of Ireland. Later he entered the St. Joseph's Society of the Sacred Heart (Josephites, Mill Hill Fathers), a congregation founded by Fr. Herbert Vaughan, later cardinal archbishop of Westminster, for service among the Negroes of Africa and North America. Vaughan sent Noonan as superior of the pioneer band of Josephites to St. Francis Xavier parish in Baltimore, Maryland. At the age of thirty-six, Noonan sought his release from the Josephites and entered the novitiate of the Society of Jesus at Frederick, Maryland.[5] As superior of the Jamaican Jesuits, Noonan tactfully smoothed over conflicts in the period of transition by his common sense and reasonableness in all borderline cases involving jurisdiction of superior and vicar apostolic. He so allayed Gordon's fears that no conflict of jurisdiction arose in his regime. Unhappily, difficulty arose during the following regime.

Agricultural College at Reading

Another concern of Gordon was his wish to train the youth in scientific farming, since Jamaica was an agricultural country. From Gordon's first visitation was born the conviction that Jamaica should have an agricultural college to train its youth. This he proposed to establish himself. His youthful Scottish environment was eminently suited for this project; yet, despite his keen interest and personal experience, the College of Agriculture would fail.

A question constantly on Gordon's mind was what to do for the orphan boys once they leave the care and protection of Alpha. As each year brought more boys into the orphanage, it also brought a proportionate number of those who had reached the age when they had to leave the only home they had ever known. Could they be incorporated into a wider social scheme which would raise their civic status and guarantee a more useful niche in the community? Gordon thought he held the key to the solution in an agricultural college, since ninety percent of the Jamaican economy rested on products of the soil: sugar, coffee, coconuts, pimento, citrus, and bananas. The greatest benefaction that could be offered Alpha graduates would be scientific training in farming; for this a school would be necessary. The Reading estate was the logical location.

In 1898, while John J. Broderick was in charge of Reading and the western missions, Gordon sent ten Alpha boys under a Jamaican, Mr. Thomas, to inaugurate the scheme. Thomas was unsatisfactory, the first attempt a failure. An agricultural school was not as simple as it looked on the drawing board. Teachers trained in scientific farming were needed for any success.

For help Gordon again turned to Chandlery who sought the Christian Brothers for the project, but they proved a disappointment. On 16 August 1891 he wrote Gordon

> I am sorry that the Christian Brothers have disappointed you. It is aggravating. I hope they have refunded the half of the expense of their journey out. I have been making enquiries, and someone recommended me to apply to the Salesian Fathers who are great at Industrial school work

and have a house at Battersea. I have arranged to go to see them on Thursday, and I hope to acquaint your Lordship with the results of my interview.[6]

On 18 August 1891 Chandlery reported on his visit to the Salesians at Battersea, where Fr. Charles Macey, the superior of the mission, received him and was deeply interested in all he learned about Jamaica. Chandlery observed that the brothers were skilled masons, carpenters, blacksmiths, and offered the further information that the brothers were never sent out alone. Two or three priests always went with them; while the brothers were employed in the workshops, the priests taught in the schools. The congregation turned out some two hundred artisans each year. Macey believed that Gordon had a fine chance of securing five or six priests and brothers if he made formal application to the superior general, Michael Rua. A good tempting letter with conditions clearly stated and special emphasis laid on the nobility of the work, was Macey's advice. To this letter Macey would add a personal word of encouragement when he visited the Turin headquarters three weeks hence. Property rights would pose a difficulty, for the Salesians wished to have ownership and management of the property. At this stage of the proceedings, Macey advised Gordon to apply for men to conduct his industrial school and merely hint at an agricultural college for the future. Had Gordon taken Macey's advice at this point, the Salesians would, perhaps, be in Jamaica today doing the admirable work for youth characteristic of their congregation. Chandlery warned Gordon that they were an exempt religious congregation, hence caution must be exercised in giving them a public church, should they ask for one; but, he believed, no complications would arise if they were confined to teaching and missionary work in the countryside.

Negotiations dragged on until 1892, when on 11 August Chanderly wrote to Gordon that, if Italian brothers would be acceptable, they might be more readily had than English Salesians; again these would be available for his industrial school. Gordon should jog the memory of the superior general about the attractiveness of Jamaica.

At the turn of the twentieth century, 12 December 1901, the Salesians arrived in Jamaica.[7] Persistent, persevering Chandlery had done it again. A new religious congregation was about to launch what should have proved one of the most important works for the Church in Jamaica to inaugurate. But before entering upon these labours, the Salesians signed a convention with Gordon. In this legal agreement, endorsed 2 July 1901, the nature of their work in Jamaica was described.

The purpose for which this agreement had been made in order to give, as far as possible, a satisfactory elementary education, and a good agricultural training to those male youths of Jamaica who may wish to participate in it. Its purpose is also to establish Catholic centres of young men who will become property owners, under the direction of the Salesians, by the work of their hands; and who will acquire enough land to live and raise a family in a becoming way. Besides the Salesians will maintain and spread the Catholic religion in the county of Cornwall.

In order to obtain its purpose better, and in order that the Salesians might be able to have a permanent dwelling in Jamaica, and the means to work with fruit in the task which they have undertaken to accomplish, the Bishop will put at their disposal the property at Reading, which contains from four to five hundred acres of land with cattle, horses, mules and other animals which are at present on this property, with all its harvests, and the houses with their furnishings, except the silver table service. The Bishop will also give them everything which is used in the service of the altars in the Missions of Cornwall, and their furnishings.

In the second place the Bishop will place at the disposal of the Salesians in Jamaica a thousand acres of the property of Donnington, as soon as they will be ready to begin its work, in order that it (the property) may be divided among the young (colonists) settlers into small pieces of property from five to ten acres. The acquisition of these thousand acres will be according to the cooperative system by which the profits of each year will be put aside to replace the sum given for the property. As soon as the enterprise begins to move ahead, the Bishop will purchase another property for the same purpose. Besides, the Bishop will attach to each settlement enough land to support the service of a Church and school.

In the third place, the Bishop will give a sum of twenty pounds sterling for the first year to each member of the Salesians in Jamaica. Lastly, the Bishop will pay the passage of all members who come to Jamaica, whether by railroad or by steamer.

The five promised this year will come to this island, Deo Volente, in the month of November, 1901.

signed:

Charles Gordon
Vicar Apostolic of Jamaica

Michael Rua
Superior General of the Salesians[8]

With much handshaking and well-turned phrases, bishop and Salesians greeted one another at Kingston's pier. The first arrivals were Fr. Antonio Riccardi, Superior; Fr. D. Guiseppe Valloggia; Mr. Thomas Deehan; Brother Eugenio Tedeschi, and Brother Giovanni Vulpinari. The congenial atmosphere blended perfectly with the beautiful tropical morning. The day after their arrival Gordon accompanied the new missionaries out to Reading by coastal steamer, and the party reached Montego Bay after a few days sailing on the Caribbean. Gordon remained with the Salesians at Reading until 26 December. He left with the feeling that the Salesians were perfectly satisfied with Reading and would embark with enthusiasm on their task training Jamaican youth in the methods of scientific farming.

The Human Factor

A more surprised Gordon could hardly be imagined as his eyes fell on the contents of the first letter from Reading, dated the very day he had left for Kingston, 26 December. In it the Salesian superior, Antonio Riccardi, expressed dissatisfaction and listed his complaints under four headings:

> That there had been a misunderstanding with reference to the primary and principal object of the agreement; namely, to obtain the aid of the Salesians for missionary work among adults.
>
> That a building capable of accommodating fifty to sixty youths and furnished with all the requisite convenience for a house of education does not exist at Reading.
>
> That the expense of enlarging the present boys' house and appointing it according to the Rules of the Salesians will necessitate a large outlay of money.
>
> The boys are not provided with suitable clothes and linen, and no provision has been made for cases of illness, or the expulsion of refractory boys.[9]

Riccardi's letter struck a blow at the very heart of Gordon's agricultural scheme. Stark reality had stripped the Gordon-Rua agreement of imagination and had left the pioneers face to face with a very primitive organization at Reading. After the bishop left, the Salesians had calmly evaluated their new home and quickly reached the conclusion that Reading was no Turin. One fair-sized cottage for their own living quarters, a barracks-like building for the boys, and some five hundred acres of land which, even in the days of slavery, required unremitting labour of strong negroes to yield even a modest income. That was their agricultural college.

From the bishop's point of view, the present task was merely to build for the future. He had no intention of furnishing all the modern conveniences they had known in Europe, for the foundation just begun in the hills overlooking Montego Bay. Riccardi's letter demanded a reply. Gordon answered it on 5 January 1902.

> Your letter of the 26th of December fills me with great astonishment, and if acted on will only create a great scandal and cause incalculable detriment to religion in Jamaica. . . . You must remember we are not here in a country where what is greviously wrong can pass unnoticed. You are in an important colony of the British Empire throughout which strict adherence to written compacts is expected, if we would be considered as

> honest men, and especially where large sums of money had been expended on the faith of those receiving them.
>
> Now what is the position between the Salesians and me . . .? The position is this: A Convention has been agreed between the Supreme head of the Salesian Order and the Bishop-Vicar Apostolic in Jamaica. In it the objects of the Convention are distinctly stated and the means of accomplishing it also. I have accomplished all that I promised strictly in as far as it could be done at present, and have expended large sums of money in doing so. Moreover I have staked my reputation as a man of prudence in trusting those upon whose faith I spent the money of my people. The Salesians present here have moreover confirmed this agreement by asking the delivery of the Reading property and the cattle as agreed on and have begun work on the place. Moreover they have expressed (the desire) to have the lower house where the boys live, furnished so they can occupy it. . . . On the 26th of December, having arranged all things amicably I took my departure. To my astonishment I received a letter dated 26th of December, a week after, in which the Superior announced that he intended going back on the Convention and all that had been arranged and only waited the answer of his superior in Turin to depart. This I feel sure will never be given. It would be too much an injustice to my people and too monstrous a blow to my reputation. What pleasure it would be to Protestants if such a fiasco were the results of my endeavour to benefit the cause of religion here. When the usual stories about monks and nuns were told here, as they are in all Protestant countries, my invariable reply was: do not believe what you hear but what you see . . .! What should I say now? What triumph for them! What scorn for me! Behold what trust in foreign monks has brought on you. No wonder they were expelled from France and barely tolerated in other Catholic countries! It is too awful to think of. All new enterprises are fraught with difficulties and the devil, moreover, opposes those undertakings for God. Don Bosco experienced troubles and fought them bravely and overcame. You, dear Father Superior, will do the same. Patience and trust in God will overcome your present difficulties.[10]

Later Gordon answered Riccardi's claim that there had been a misunderstanding of the primary object. Gordon countered with the reply that Riccardi himself was in error in thinking that priority should be given to adult missionary work. The agricultural education of boys and their subsequent settlement on the one-thousand-acre Donnington estate held equal rights. Riccardi had also drawn attention to the lack of school accommodations. He claimed there was no building capable of housing fifty to sixty youths and furnished with all the requisite conveniences for a boarding school; it just did not exist at Reading. Gordon explained there were accommodations suitable to make a start; one residence contained sitting room, bedrooms and library, serviced with kitchen, servant quarters, and stables. Contiguous to the house was a chapel, while two hundred yards away was a large building for the boys. This latter did not have to be pretentious but following the accepted custom for similar government institutions. The barracks was to serve a triple purpose: a dormitory at night, a school in the day, and a refectory for meals. The Salesians were reminded that they were not to expect all the conveniences, the comforts, and the appointments they had in Europe. The spirit of adaptability to environment should characterize these pioneers; gradually, Old World conditions would evolve from the rougher elements of Jamaica. On this philosophy the vicar apostolic had inaugurated his agricultural college plan, and never for a moment, he protested, did he lead the Salesians to believe they would find in Jamaica an institution such as they had in Turin, fully modernized and equipped with the latest mechanical teaching devices. The work here was to build up, not to carry on an already established institution. The bishop was fully aware of the difficulties confronting the new venture, but they would soon disappear if the pioneers would bend to the circumstances of life in Jamaica.

These difficuties were magnified by lack of facility in English, a want of proper understanding of the people and customs of a country quite different from Italy. A little time, a little patience, and all these obstacles would quickly disappear. Riccardi's final objection, that the boys were not provided with suitable clothing and linen, that no provision had been made for cases of illness or the expulsion of refractory boys, Gordon answered saying that for boys of this social class the minimum in quantity and quality of clothing was required; that there was a doctor at Montego Bay whose services might be retained; that the matter of discipline was a personal problem for the school authorities. As far as Gordon could see, he had done all in his power to make the scheme a success, even to the extent of giving the Salesians full control over the Reading property. He had handed it over to them unreservedly so that they might use it as security to obtain funds to erect buildings as they deemed necessary.[11]

Reputable men had been Gordon's advisors, and it was their opinion that a religious congregation skilled in agricultural methods would be beneficial to the community and enhance the status of the Church. Gordon begged Riccardi not to think of abandoning a cause fraught with such promising results for the Church.

However, neither argument nor personal appeal could change the stubborn mind of the superior, who was determined to abandon the Reading venture. When he suggested to his colleagues that they weigh anchor and sail for Mexico, they protested to him that they wished to live and die in Jamaica.

There was no stopping Riccardi. He left some time before 2 March 1902, for on that day Rua expressed his displeasure at both the departure and its manner; he begged the bishop's pardon, and promised to replace Riccardi with someone who spoke English.

Fr. Frederick Barni was the one Rua chose. On 14 May 1902 Barni wrote Gordon from Battersea, England, where he had been stationed after returning from Cape Town, South Africa. From a perusal of the bishop's letter to Rua and from oral informants, Barni had learned something of the needs of this recent foundation at Reading. He promised to carry out the bishop's wishes and correspond faithfully to the confidence Gordon had placed in the Salesians. Six months after Barni took charge of Reading, his enthusiasm for the scheme began to wane.

Frederick Barni, ordained 13 October 1891, had been one of the first Salesians Don Rua sent from Turin to Battersea, England. During his four years sojourn, 1892–96, he had learned to speak English, an asset his predecessor Riccardi did not possess. Both Gordon and Barni agreed that money would be needed to improve cultivation at Reading. Barni pointed out to Gordon that with all the good will in the world, if generous financial help was not forthcoming, the whole scheme would end in a fiasco.

Cultivation was only one problem; another was the trainees. Barni frankly told Gordon he thought the bishop had been fooled in the selection of these boys. Yaws and fever played havoc with them; they were never satisfied no matter what Barni did for them; they hated work and some, good for nothing, did not even wish to remain at Reading. Of the nine Barni had at Reading, two had been sent home because of yaws, two for fever, one for ill health, and one for being totally unfit. Two of the remaining boys were good for nothing, and only one showed any promise. He warned the bishop that since past experience with these boys was discouraging, more care should be exercised in selecting and admitting them, for to act otherwise would not be prudent. Whatever the present discouragements, Barni thought the plan deserved further trial, and no more boys would be admitted unless their character and physical health had been carefully scrutinized.[12] Barni also sent a critique of Reading to Don Rua, who had replied.

Barni's frank opinion so upset Gordon that he wrote a long reply on 3 December 1902.[13] Gordon regretted the letters had been written. He believed that Barni seemed to ignore the terms of the convention whereby the Salesians were in Jamaica, and the whole agreement now appeared about to be sabotaged. Rua had reaffirmed these terms some months after the Salesians had been in possession of Reading and had had the opportunity to estimate the difficulties from on-the-spot experience. Furthermore, this reaffirmation had been mentioned to Cardinal Ledochowski, prefect of Propaganda, who stated in a letter dated March 1902 that he was perfectly satisfied with the arrangements. Only a few months previously, Gordon had made a formal request for the Salesians to take possession of the Cornwall missions and for the Jesuits to retire from this district. This was verbally conceded by the Holy See on the occasion of Gordon's visit to Rome in July 1899, and embodied in the terms of the convention.

Gordon was convinced that he had carried out to the letter all that the convention had stipulated and that it was done at great personal expense. Clearly Gordon was upset that the trainees had been reduced to three boys, and he concluded that the work at Reading must be sadly neglected, the income diminished, and the whole estate lapsing into ruin. He reminded Barni that the establishment needed energy and constant careful management, and thought that only kind treatment of the boys would induce others to join the school. He believed that, for want of efficient management, the boys at the disposal of the Salesians would not be formed into fit instruments to carry out his plan in its final stages which would be to settle them as well-trained farmers on the large Donnington estate in St. Mary. Their work could not be accomplished without earnest, personal application and considerable self-sacrifice on the part of the Salesians, so thought Gordon. Gordon asked that Barni and his associates infuse more energy into their work and show results worthy of the well-established reputation for the care and kindness in management which Salesians enjoyed, and to further this end, Gordon withdrew the privilege of bination on Sundays and said he did not want them to do parish work unless they could spare the time from the main object of their being in Jamaica.

This verbal war had the effect of bringing both parties to an agreement on 15 December 1902.[14] The number of boys to be instructed in 1903 was to be restricted to four; new rules were to be drawn up for them; and his lordship was to advance sixty pounds sterling out of the two hundred pounds sterling he had promised to be applied in cultivating ten acres of bananas, corn, and tobacco. Building operations were to begin in January 1904, for which his lordship would give forty pounds sterling as the first installment of the final sum of one hundred pounds sterling. From the first week in June 1905 the number of boys was to be increased to a minimum of thirty trainees. Having fulfilled these promises, Gordon then cleared himself from further monetary obligations to carry out the terms of the covenant.

Dispute over Mission Stations

Beset by internal difficulties of administration, Gordon's scheme was now attacked by his Jesuit confreres. They had remained indifferent to his agricultural school at Reading, but when Gordon entrusted the mission stations of Seaford Town, Chester Castle, Top Hill, Lucea, Montego Bay, and eventually Falmouth and Refuge to the Salesians, the Jesuits objected.

At this period in history, when a territory was assigned to a religious order by the Holy See, it was looked upon as their own exclusive mission field. This seventeenth century ruling, dictated by friction among missionary societies in the Far East, had its handicaps. The entrenched missionary society might have too few personnel to evangelize the assigned territory, and in such a situation, the Church's growth might be stifled while pride or pettiness resisted outside aid. This was the difficulty in Jamaica. At most there were twelve Jesuit priests, who could by no means cover satisfactorily this mountainous island. But Fr. Patrick F. X. Mulry, S.J. looked askance at the western missions being withdrawn from Jesuit jurisdiction and placed under the care of the Salesians. On 22 April 1904 Mulry issued a formal protest.

> As Jesuit Superior of the Jamaican Mission, in the name of our Rev. Fr. Provincial and the Society of Jesus, I do hereby protest formally against the action of the Vicar Apostolic of Jamaica (Rt. Rev. Bishop Gordon) whereby he has introduced into the island of Jamaica religious priests, not of the Society of Jesus, and given them jurisdiction over certain Mission districts and the care of souls. I protest because this action has been taken without due authority and canonical mode of procedure and is therefore illegal and invalid. I protest too because such action is in violation of the rights and just claims of the Society of Jesus to whose care this Mission has been exclusively entrusted by the Holy See.
>
> *This canonical protest signed and sealed is hereby formally presented to the Rt. Rev. Vicar Apostolic of Jamaica in the presence of two witnesses to safeguard clearly and fully the rights and the just claims of the Society of Jesus in the Island of Jamaica.*
>
> Signed:
>
> *Fr. Patrick F. X. Mulry, S.J.*
> Jesuit Superior of the Jamaican Mission
>
> Witnesses:
>
> *Fr. J. Harpes, S.J.*
> *Fr. William F. Gregory, S.J.*[15]

Gordon was in a quandary. He alone stood firmly by his agricultural scheme; the Salesians doubted its practicability, the Jesuits offered no assistance. For the Jesuits, the crux was Gordon's failure to seek approval of the Sacred Congregation of Propaganda and the assent of his own religious order. Three documents refer to this matter. The first reference is a letter of 21 July 1893, from the English provincial, John Clayton, to Gordon. "You spoke of calling in another Order—Salesians, I think, and of giving them part of the island to look after. Do this as far as I am concerned."[16] There was no objection on the part of the English provincial, but this was before Maryland-New York took over the mission. The second reference is a letter dated 13 February 1899, from the Sacred Congregation of Propaganda to Gordon. "Concerning the proposal of you inviting the Salesian Fathers to Jamaica, this Congregation does not approve but it hopes it will turn out happily."[17] Gordon stated that later, in July 1899, on the occasion of his *ad limina* visit to Rome, he received oral approval from the Holy See.

The Sacred Congregation of Propaganda sent another letter to Gordon.

> The Congregation recalls through letters of September 13, 1899, in which you considered a good thing to call the Salesian Fathers to the Mission who would work together with you in the sacred ministry.
>
> If therefore as you report some of these praiseworthy Fathers should come to the Mission at the end of this year, I am quite sure that all things will turn out prosperously, and I trust that helped by their work you may be able to extend and propagate the Catholic Faith more and more in the Vicariate.[18]

Reason for Transfer of Western Missions

It was not without reason that Gordon assigned the western missions to the Salesians. Some disturbing facts were stated in a letter by Gordon to Martin, superior general of the Society of Jesus, dated 14 November 1901. He complained that the western missions under Fr. John J. Broderick, S.J. had been slowly passing out of existence. Seaford Town, Pisgah, and Top Hill, where there were formerly flourishing chapels, were on the point of being abandoned. Savanna-la-Mar had already been abandoned since the time of Andrew Rapp, Broderick's predecessor, and was only visited in passing by a priest on his way to the Top Hill mission. Pisgah was on the point of being given up, and Top Hill would not survive the loss of its school. In the whole district only two schools were functioning. As chief pastor Gordon could not sit idly by and watch these old established missions pass out of existence. He had to take effective measures to prevent their demise. Mulry would have been better advised if he had put aside *mine* and *thine* and cooperated with Gordon for the good of the whole mission. Obviously Mulry did not have sufficient personnel to man all the stations, since these missions were dying out before his very eyes. Should a more formal permission be required from the Sacred Congregation for the Propagation of the Faith than the one dated 21 July 1901, Mulry could have used his office to help the bishop secure the canonical division of the territory, giving part of it to the Salesians. It would also have helped Mulry to have reread the document he had signed on 1 June 1901, in which he consented to a religious congregation training boys at Reading estate.

> Reading Pen, in the Parish of St. James, was given by the late owner Mr. Buchanan for the purpose of advancing the Catholic religion in the County of Cornwall and especially St. James and for the purpose of effecting such object when practical and only as long as practical the property is to be used in the keeping and training of boys in habits of industry and morality with a view to locating them when competent upon the lands purchased wholly or partly out of the accumulations of their earnings. Provided that, if, in order to have the said property better worked and developed for the objects aforesaid, it shall seem expedient with the approval of the said Charles Gordon or any other Vicar Apostolic of Jamaica, for the time being they may transfer for a limited estate the said Reading Pen or any portion of it to any person or body of Religious persons willing to undertake the work of teaching and training youths in morals and industries and otherwise to work in the said religious and charitable mission of St. James.
>
> Signed:
> *Charles Gordon*
> *James Noonan*
> *Patrick Mulry*
> *Charles Ward*
> *W. Bourke.*[19]

Mulry could not claim he had not given his consent for Gordon to introduce a religious congregation such as the Salesians. The only grounds upon which to base his objections came when Gordon allowed the Salesians to take over the spiritual care of the mission stations in the County of Cornwall.

Gordon was not unaware of the problems confronting the Salesians in conducting an agricultural school and at the same time caring for such widely scattered missions as Seaford Town, Chester Castle, Top Hill, Lucea, Montego Bay, Falmouth, and Refuge. Teaching and widespread missionary work were too much for the limited Salesian personnel. If the boys were to be properly trained, the Salesians must devote their full time and energy to the school, for to travel over the whole western end of the island would not only drain their slender finances but so tax their physical energy that valuable effort would be taken from their principal object, the agricultural school. On one occasion Gordon had to caution them to do no missionary work unless they could spare time from their principal occupation of training boys at Reading and at this time withdrew all privileges until the school made progress. Clearly the mind of Gordon was that you cannot care for widely scattered missions and at the same time conduct a school with high standards.

Hope for the Scheme

Barni offered a glimmer of success for the agricultural scheme on 18 October 1905.

> The boys and missions we are managing are doing very well, and as the income from Reading property increases, much more will be done for the above objects. The method we are now using in dealing with boys . . . seems to be eminently successful, for it gives the boys an interest in his work, it makes him a trifle independent and rewards him according to his labours. The fishing which had begun a few months ago at the Reading Sea, proves a great help towards the boys' feeding. If bye and bye, a tannery, on a small scale, could be started it might prove another paying concern in which the boys can be successfully employed. I do not speak of our milk business which is gradually increasing in volume, by paying attention to keep the pasture in good order and by bestowing care on breeding our calves and cows. These, my Lord, are the divers items I have jotted down, and as time goes on other, profitable ones, might easily be added. We are here to do all in our power for you and most willing to spend our lives for the good of Jamaica. See, therefore, if the property can pass over to us, or at least give us security that nobody will destroy the work which cost us so much pain to build up. If you do this, you will have our lasting gratitude and the Salesians will be fixed in Jamaica.[20]

For four years longer the agricultural scheme continued in operation, then one fine day, 15 April 1909, the whole project came to an abrupt end.[21] Barni and his fellow Salesians pulled up stakes and returned to Italy. Conditions had reached such a low level that life in Jamaica became unbearable. Ill health and advanced age had forced Gordon to resign on 11 January 1906, and the interim between this and the selection of a new bishop was filled by an administrator, John J. Collins, S.J. Collins had his own ideas of effective means for propagating the faith, and Gordon's agricultural school was not one of them. With such an attitude on Collins's part, the whole scheme took a bad turn, when Barni, suffering from malaria which occasioned a melancholy state of mind, made him wonder why the Salesians had come to Jamaica in the first instance. Barni saw no alternative save to leave the island at once, even without informing Don Rua.

On 21 May 1909, Don Rua expressed his surprise and displeasure to Collins at the unexpected arrival of the Salesians.

> I was on the point of writing your Lordship even before the arrival of Signor Tedeschi, for I was not at all pleased that our confreres had come away from there without my having been acquainted with the matter beforehand, especially as I had already destined two other priests who were to go to their aid in the course of a few weeks. But Signor Tedeschi had handed me your kind letter which gave me satisfactory explanation of the steps taken and I am pleased with the convenient arrangement. I regret to know that Fr. Barni is enjoying indifferent health, but I hope that after a short rest and change of air he will be himself again. I beg to seize this opportunity of thanking your Lordship for your kindness to the spiritual children of the Venerable Don Bosco during their sojourn in the island of Jamaica. When your Lordship comes to Italy, we hope to have the pleasure and the honour of a visit at the Oratory in Turin where you will receive a hearty welcome.[22]

The letter which Collins wrote to Don Rua is preserved in the Salesian archives at Turin and dated 15 April 1909:

> I wish to express to your Reverence the great satisfaction I have in testifying to the splendid character of the men who laboured under me, namely, Fr. Barni, Mr. Tedeschi, and Mr. Vulpinari, for the past two years. As your Reverence is well aware, this is a poor mission. It was poor before the earthquake, and, naturally, it is much worse now; yet, out of a desire to express my gratitude to God, and to these excellent and capable men, I have made an offering to them of $400, $300 of which I have given to them in cash with the promise to pay the other hundred in six months time. I deeply regret their departure from the Island of Jamaica, where they have done excellent work, and where the fruits of their good work will, I am sure, remain long, because although the object of their advent here was, owing to conditions over which they had no control, a failure, yet, their lives on the Island have not been in any sense a failure, as their works and virtuous lives while here attest.[23]

Viewing Gordon's agricultural scheme historically, it is easy to be too critical of the venture, but there were evident flaws. It would have been wiser if Gordon had taken Chandlery's advice and placed the Salesians in charge of the Industrial school at Alpha and only broached the idea of an agricultural college to them later. Since Gordon was determined to begin with an agricultural centre, it would have been more businesslike to have invited a Salesian to make a preliminary survey of Reading and report on the feasibility of the scheme to Rua before signing the convention. Rua had only Gordon's word for the success of the scheme. It was the first superior, Fr. Riccardi, who sensed the insurmountable difficulties during his first week at Reading. Gordon uprooted Old World men and planted them in remote, isolated Reading, when they had no knowledge of the English language nor acquaintance with the customs of Jamaica. Again, the trainees from the orphanage of Alpha were likewise torn from their urban environment and made to dwell in the country for which they had no attraction. Isolated from the community life of social Kingston, they were made to live in a small rural community which was too much even for these orphan boys to bear. Then the selection had not been too careful: yaws and fever were prevalent; finally some of the boys were just good for nothing. Perhaps authorities at Alpha were only too glad to get such misfits off their hands and exile them to remote Reading. There is no evidence that Gordon ever paid Reading another visit once he had settled the first Salesians in December 1901. Instead he had formed all his judgments and made all his decisions from his office at 26 North Street, Kingston.

Twenty-two

John J. Collins, S.J., 1907–1918

The unhealthy calm of a tropical afternoon, an ominous quiet when a stiff breeze should have been stirring across the harbour, was the harbinger of the dread earthquake of 1907, bringing destruction to Kingston and to areas throughout the island. Its aftereffects were felt during the entire administration of John J. Collins, S.J.

First American Bishop

Gordon had retired on 11 January 1906, and the administration of the vicariate passed into the hands of John J. Collins, S.J., on 9 March 1906, who had the title of administrator apostolic. Collins was born in Maysville, Kentucky, 15 November 1856.[1] He gained his early education at St. Mary's of the West, Cincinnati, Ohio. Later he studied at Mount St. Mary's College, Emmetsburg, Maryland. On 5 December 1876 he entered the Jesuit novitiate at Frederick, Maryland. Philosophy and theology followed at Woodstock, Maryland, with the usual interim of regency made at St. John's College, Fordham, from 1883–89, where he taught algebra and commercial law, and later Latin in the special class. Cardinal Gibbons conferred Holy Orders upon him on 29 August 1891. The year 1893 found him one of the four pioneer American missionaries assigned to Jamaica, working in Kingston and the nearby district of Above Rocks. After eight years of service, he returned to the United States, spent two years on the Mission Band, and then was appointed rector of St. John's College, Fordham, 4 April 1904.

Collins was not the man to be satisfied with the status quo; progress was part of his nature. Under his administration St. John's moved up from the status of a college to that of a university. On 21 June 1904, with consent of the Regents of the University of the State of New York and the authorization of the board of trustees of St. John's, he announced the formation of the schools of law and medicine. Three years later, on 7 March 1907, Fordham was granted formal recognition as a university. Before his six-year term as president expired, he was chosen administrator apostolic for Jamaica by the Holy See. On 13 October 1907, he succeeded to the office of vicar apostolic. Fifteen days later, on 28 October 1907, he was consecrated bishop of Antiphellos at the Church of St. Francis Xavier, New York City. The Most Reverend John Farley, archbishop of New York, was consecrator; Bishop Thomas D. Beaven of Springfield, Massachusetts, and Bishop Charles E. McDonnell of Brooklyn, New York, coconsecrators.

Earthquake of 1907

Collins should have fallen heir to the stately brick-constructed Holy Trinity Church, boasting a seating capacity of eighteen hundred, to spacious Gordon Hall, opened on 11 August 1905 by his predecessor, to the Sisters of Mercy orphanage and schools at Alpha, to the Franciscan Immaculate Conception High School and their elementary schools for poorer children, to Jesuit-staffed St. George's College, to churches, chapels, and residences scattered throughout the island. These in the ordinary course of events would have been the monuments of the past upon which to build a more prosperous future. Instead he fell heir to their ruins and rubble, to cracked walls and insecure foundations, to gaunt pillars and roofless structures—the aftermath of the awful, destructive earthquake of 1907.

It was Sunday, 13 January 1907. William Stanton, Francis Goeding, Patrick McGuiney, and John F. Donovan, American Jesuits, had just closed a mission to the women at Holy Trinity Church, Kingston. The following night, 14 January, they were scheduled to open a mission for the men; they never did. At 3.29 p.m., Monday 14 January, life droned along as usual in the second largest city of the Indies; one minute later an earthquake, rivalling the intensity of the one of 1692, shook the whole island. By one frightful, nerve-racking shake, a thunderous sound of falling walls and choking dust enveloped the doomed city. In a matter of seconds, Kingston was in ruins. Tall buildings cracked, spewing their bricks into the streets. People cried with terror as they ran to safety, but eight hundred never reached beyond the debris that covered and silenced them in death. An eyewitness to this violent tremor recalled that

> The earthquake was heralded by an awful stillness, about a minute. Then with a low moan which almost instantly rose to a loud roar, the earth

> oscillated violently to the south. The next motion can be best described by the word 'circular.' The earth spun like a top for four or five seconds, then stopped with a frightful jerk. The succeeding oscillation was from the south, and this [was] followed by six or seven savage shocks—like a dog shaking a rat—the works of puny man could not stand the assault of nature, and Kingston was wrecked. After the shock came the fire which destroyed the ruins of commercial Kingston and all stocks in the stores. It was truly a dreadful spectacle—that volcano of seething roaring flame. But the stricken populace hardly noticed the great flame. Thousands upon thousands fled to the open Race Course, stood there and viewed the fiend-fire at its terrible work—viewed the greatest conflagration the vast majority had ever seen, many in silence while others discussed the cataclysm in awed whispers: the thing that had happened was too great for them. The sun set and the moon rose on a sea of blood and terrorized people. Those who had not fled the city sat down through that terrible Monday night watching the ruddy glow to the south, wishing that the day would dawn. It was truly a night of prayer, prayer to the Almighty that there will be no recurrence of the terrible shock—there were many shocks during the night, but none of sufficient strength to do further damage. The long looked-for dawn at last arrived, but the swaying of the earth and the tremors continued right up until yesterday [21 January], but as the hours drew along the shocks became less frequent. Two were recorded on Saturday. Sunday morning at 3.15 another very heavy shock was experienced, the heaviest since that which devastated the city. Once again people [who had returned to their shattered dwellings] fled in terror into the streets. Once again they were unnerved.[2]

Religious institutions suffered the same fate as commercial houses and family dwellings. The Franciscan Sisters were enjoying the long Christmas holidays at Alvernia, two miles distant from the centre of the city, when the disaster occurred. The old convent in Duke Street was reduced to a heap of ruins. Under its bricks and rafters, pupils and sisters of the Academy would have been pinned had school been in session. Even at their country convent, Alvernia, escape seemed miraculous, for every building was destroyed, but the children had time to run out on to the lawns before they fell. All the sisters escaped, some by taking refuge under tables, others by running into the open. Those outside on the grounds saw the earth heave up and down, then spin like a top as the large convent building rocked to and fro, then fell apart in huge sections. They fully expected to find more than one mangled corpse under the ruins. Struggling to stand on their feet, the sisters ran towards the convent: it was a moment of horror and dread; Mother Superior and Sister Isobel were the only ones buried under the building. The superior had been on the point of enclosing a scapular of Our Lady of Mount Carmel in a letter and held it tightly in her hand all through the quake. Several times both sisters tried to rush from the room, only to be prevented from doing so. Had they succeeded, they certainly would have been killed—bricks flew over them like so many flies but not one touched their heads. Although both were covered with debris, they had not a single bruise.

Sisters, children, and servants were all alive, but all was not so well in the British military camp a few hundred yards away, where flames and then shrieks of pain filled the air as companions tried to pull sick soldiers entrapped in the military hospital from the fire. A worse blaze to the south told that Kingston had become prey to merciless fire.

All during the night sisters and pupils sat on the ground at Alvernia looking towards the doomed city. They wondered what had become of their Duke Street convent, their relatives and friends. Shock succeeded shock and prayers were interrupted by refugees asking for the only shelter available—the grass and the starry heavens.

Morning brought the news that not a building was standing at the academy on Duke Street. The day continued with quakes and sad news.

The sisters had hardly retired to rest that night under the trees when a strange noise was heard passing before their compound; it sounded like a sea of human voices growing louder as it approached. Threatening rumours of escaped prisoners and inmates of the Insane Asylum had already reached their ears; and as the crowds, in thousands, were passing Alvernia's ruined gates, each sister wondered what new danger was at hand, afraid to communicate her thoughts to another. Then a man ran through the gates and breathlessly said that the governor had ordered the whole population of the city to move northwards towards the mountains, since a tidal wave was imminent.

The sisters were terrified, and the children more so. Among the boarders were a good number of young ladies from South America who understood English only imperfectly. When they heard the word 'governor' and were told to flee, they took it for granted that the government, like their own governments, had exiled the sisters. They begged to be allowed to follow their teachers into exile. It took some time to quiet them and explain what the real danger was. Since they were two miles from the waterfront and 250 feet above sea level, the superior decided all should remain at Alvernia. Quietly they again sat down under the trees and some had already fallen asleep when a messenger on horseback rode madly into the compound, saying that the sea had already covered the lower part of the city, and begged the sisters to run as fast as they could if they wished to save their lives. Each sister took as many children as she could and started on the march.

Hardly were they outside the gate when a constable came from the nearby police station with official news that no orders had been issued by the governor and that the sea was perfectly normal and calm even in the ocean beyond Port Royal. Who spread the false, terrifying news never became known. Back went the sisters and children to Alvernia, worn out by terror, and all fell asleep under the convent cottonwood trees.

In order to restore public confidence, schools reopened two weeks after the quake. Classes were held everywhere—under trees, in tents, among the ruins of buildings. As long as the weather continued fair, these makeshift classrooms served their purpose; but once the May rains began to fall, pupils had to be sheltered under repaired school roofs.[3]

The largest Catholic church in Jamaica, Holy Trinity, was a complete loss; only the east and south walls remained standing. Because the earthquake had occurred in the afternoon, only Miss Jeanette, the cleaner, had been in the church. With the sight and sound of falling bricks, she had run to the nearest shelter, one of the confessionals and had been buried under an avalanche of brick and timber. When extricated from her awkward position, Miss Jeanette was found unhurt. On the third day American sailors opened a passage, allowing one of the priests down to the tabernacle to rescue the Blessed Sacrament. Although the altar was broken and tabernacle door wrenched from its hinges, the sacred vessels were unharmed.

Within the ruined city, broken brick covered eight hundred dead, and thousands needed medical attention. The prime thought at this moment was medical relief which came on Thursday, 19 January, when two United States warships arrived. The following day, at the request of Bishop Collins, the naval medical men set up an emergency hospital at St. George's College. Joseph N. Dinand, one of the Jesuit missionaries, left us his account.

> Bishop Collins assigned me to meet Admiral C. H. Davis of the American Navy who came to the relief of the Islanders with two U.S. Gun-boats. He and his men were of great assistance until the British authorities could get help to the scene. The Admiral took possession of what remained of St. George's College and opened the first relief hospital here. U.S. Marines rebuilt the fallen walls and put the place in shape so that it could be used as a temporary hospital. Then the men went out with stretchers and brought in the injured, some of whom had been lying in the hills for three

> or four days. The surgeon at the time was Dr. Ames of the U.S. Navy, a native of Boston. The situation was tense. The convicts were threatening all sorts of trouble and outbreaks were in the making, but the U.S. Marines prevented any trouble of that kind.[4]

Administrator Apostolic Runs Counter to Government

Up at King's House the emergency hospital at St. George's was seen from a different point of view. On 20 January a letter from the governor asked Collins for an explanation. Sir Alexander Swettenham took an adverse view of American naval men setting up a hospital without his consent. The fact that they were on an errand of mercy was no reason why he should not have been informed. This left Admiral Davis no alternative save to withdraw his men. American newspapers featured the unpleasant incident, which came to the attention of the British Government. Swettenham resigned 3 May 1907. This was regrettable, for he is still considered to have been one of Jamaica's most capable governors.

After the departure of the American naval unit, Dr. Lecesne, a St. George's graduate, and Dr. Albert A. Ayton, assisted by Franciscan and Mercy sisters, continued to operate the emergency hospital at St. George's. But recurring shocks forced the removal of the hospital from the college building to large military tents supplied by the auditor general. Admitting more than fifty patients and treating three hundred at its outpatient department, this emergency medical station relieved congestion at the General Public Hospital. Yet official despatches made no mention of this work, possibly because of the unfavourable circumstances of its inception.

New Holy Trinity Cathedral

Twenty thousand Catholics of Kingston had no place to worship save one small chapel, St. Anne's in western Kingston. Holy Trinity was in ruins, but at nearby Gordon Hall, although the upper storey, a theatre, was destroyed, the lower part suffered little damage. Here a new roof was raised over the ground floor and altars installed to accommodate the worshippers.[5] A more challenging situation could not have presented itself to progressive Collins. But should the new 'cathedral'—so-called, although Kingston became a diocese only in 1956—be built on the old site, or on another? A notable shift in population had occurred since old Holy Trinity had been built. Kingston was experiencing growing pains, and Catholics were moving from the centre of the city to more rural areas like Franklin Pen, Campbell Pen, Allman Pen, and Passmore Pen. A cathedral near these districts would serve the congregation more conveniently, since transportation was a problem for those who did not own carriages. This meant they had to walk down dark streets for evening services from their new homes in northeastern Kingston to Holy Trinity on Duke and Sutton Street.

At the eastern extremity of North Street was a property called Colmar estate, owned by Mrs. Barrow and was now for sale; it offered a great advantage over the old site, since it was contiguous to Winchester Park, where the Jesuits had removed St. George's College in 1905. Since these teaching fathers served both institutions, college and church, it would mean a mere walk through the gate. The site was convenient for both people and priests. Collins bought the property. Suddenly arose the usual cry from the conservatives: Collins was building the cathedral in the country; he had no respect for the fond memories associated with the old site where all their forefathers were buried. One parishioner carried his complaint to the daily press, recording his dissatisfaction on 27 February 1908. But these voices were drowned out by those interested in progress.

Despite all complaints, Collins would build on the new site. Nor would he be satisfied with the mediocre. This would be the largest, the most costly, the most beautiful church in Jamaica; and it was.

On 13 December 1908 two thousand persons marched to the new site; two thousand more were awaiting their arrival. The assembled crowd listened to a dedicatory address by Patrick F. X. Mulry, after which the vicar apostolic blessed the cornerstone. The inscription composed by Francis A. Torndoff, S.J., an eminent epigramatist of Georgetown University, read:

> Citizens, strangers, all who come here to pray, earnestly beseech the Most Holy Trinity that this sacred edifice, erected in the place of the Temple that was shaken and leveled to the ground by an earthquake, and now restored by the offerings of the faithful, may upon its solid foundation, stand firm forever. 13th Dec. 1908.

Two years and one month later the church was completed. Romanesque, this massive reinforced concrete structure culminated in a copper-covered dome eighty-five feet high. Supporting the dome were four huge concrete pillars, each twelve feet in diameter. An architectural triumph of Raymond F. Almirall, New York, it presented a striking appearance on the Liquanea plain with the Blue Mountains as a backdrop, the most impressive ecclesiastical structure in all the British West Indies. Its interior was enriched by Brother Francis C.

Schroen, S.J., a native of Bavaria whose artistry is recognized in the hemispherical interior of the cupola from which rays of light emerge as though from some distant point in the open heavens. These rays grow broader and more defined as they descend, until they rest on life-sized forms of the four evangelists enthroned on the pendentives of the cupola on the base of which is inscribed: "This the Church of the living God, the Pillar and Ground of Truth."

Again Schroen's talent depicted allegorically on the vaulted arch above the high altar the transcending glory of the Most Holy Trinity, amid the nine choirs of angels singing the praise of the Triune God: "Sanctus, Sanctus, Sanctus, Dominus Deus Sabbaoth Hosanna in Excelsis. Gloria Patri, et Filio et Spiritui Sancto."

The high altar, Byzantine in style, was created by the Church Arts Works, New York, from Carrara marble. The donor, Theo Byndloss, spent well his £1160 sterling to erect this sacred table. Mass has been celebrated here daily for more than sixty years. The Honorable Lieutenant-Colonel Charles Ward, C.G.M., Custos of Kingston, gave £1,453 sterling for the great organ.

Several features might be grouped together: the bishop's throne, done in native mahogany with his coat of arms in relief; a gold-plated sanctuary lamp, the eighty pound sterling gift of Councilor Ivanhoe Gadpaille; a sanctuary rail wrought in brass, the gift of Charles Isaacs at the cost of 250 pounds sterling; the great bells, rich and solemn in cadence—now announcing joy, now sorrow—the gift of the Honorable George McGrath, who donated 500 pounds sterling for them.

Sunday 5 February 1911 was a triumphant day for Bishop Collins. Before him stood his monumental dream, the most magnificent, the largest, the costliest church in the British West Indies in which were 3000 people; 2400 seated, 600 standing for the 10.00 o'clock ceremonies. Outside there were as many more who could not even squeeze into the standing room. The governor of Jamaica was present and every class in the community represented, since all denominations had been invited.

It was a colourful procession, even for the colour-loving tropics that left Winchester Park for the Cathedral. Fifty acolytes in scarlet cassocks and white surplices led the way. The book, the mitre and crosier bearers added their own bright colours to the procession. Black-robed priests of the mission contrasted with purple-robed monsignors, while two bishops, Charles McDonnell of Brooklyn and John J. Nilan of Hartford, marched just before the officers of the Mass: William Gregory, subdeacon; Patrick F. X. Mulry, deacon; and John Harpes, assistant priest. His Lordship John J. Collins was celebrant. As the procession approached the main entrance it formed a semicircle. Bishop Collins walked to the door where he was met by Mr. W. O'Reilly Fogarty, who in the name of the Catholic workingmen of Kingston presented the bishop with a golden key with which he unlocked the door and made a solemn entry. Not until 12.30 p.m. were the ceremonies brought to a close. Never in all her ecclesiastical history had Kingston witnessed such a spectacle.[6]

Mission Stations 1908–1919

Bishop Collins did not rest after the construction of the cathedral. Inexhaustible energy, indomitable courage, joined with extraordinary love for the Church urged him to solve other vicariate problems. Among them was the question of mission stations. Hurricane, earthquake, and old age had reduced many a chapel to the state of utter ruin. From 1908–19 he erected nineteen chapels throughout the island, thirteen in districts where the Church had only barely penetrated, six replacements of dilapidated ones. This record would stand for the next forty years, but his most effective contribution was the establishment of St. Joseph's Hospital, then the only exclusively Catholic institution of its kind in all the British West Indies.

At May Pen, Clarendon, he had the cooperation of an intelligent and zealous layman, Judge Robert E. Noble, Resident Magistrate of the civil parish. Such a layman might be found in a large city parish, but in the country he was an exception. Out in the sleepy town of May Pen lived Judge Noble, son of the Anglican vicar of Brompton, Leicestershire, England. Called to the Bar of Inner Temple in 1896, he practised both in London and the Midlands before being appointed magistrate in British South Africa in 1906. Six years later he was promoted to the office of Attorney-General for St. Vincent, West Indies, where he acted as Chief Justice for a period of six months prior to his appointment as resident magistrate for Jamaica in 1914. From his conversion he had been active in Catholic affairs. In London he was prominent as an apologist and platform speaker for Catholic interests and frequently addressed large meetings under the auspices of the Catholic Federation, a committee appointed by Francis Cardinal Bourne. During the much disputed Education Bills he defended the Catholic cause with intelligent arguments, and while in St. Vincent chaired the committee which took a leading role in all matters connected with the welfare of the Church.

There was no priest and no chapel in the entire civil parish of Clarendon when Judge Noble arrived, but within six months he had changed the situation. The nearest priest, Fr. Frederick Grewen, lived in Spanish Town, twenty-three miles away. The judge persuaded him to celebrate Mass on one Sunday of the month in a private home and later to come one day each week for the same purpose. Not satisfied with this, his next move was to construct a chapel by persuading the leading merchant in town, Storks De Roux, to donate half an acre of land on Main Street and the Munn, Cassidy, Grinan, and O'Connor families to give cash. On Sunday, 21 August 1915, the chapel, dedicated to the saintly lawyer Thomas More, now St. Thomas More, was blessed by Bishop Collins. This same chapel served Catholics of this district for thirty-seven years until a more modern one was constructed in 1952.

What Collins accomplished in eleven years was not surpassed until very recent times; to him must be accredited an energetic impulse which reached into every corner of the island. Now every civil parish, with the exception of Manchester, could boast of church or chapel served regularly by a missionary. Upon this basic structure would rest all future expansion of the Church. Had Collins been the conservative type, he would have shied away from constructing massive Holy Trinity Cathedral; nor would he have constructed so many chapels, least of all a hospital. His was the pioneer spirit; his to accomplish the broad, general outlines and leave to his successor the details.

Financial Difficulties of Bishop Collins

Details in this case were the finances. Earthquake, hurricane, lesser storms, and World War I made it increasingly difficult to meet contracted debts. From £4,500 in March 1906, the vicariate debt in August 1917 rose to the precarious high of £60,000. This sent the panic-stricken among the conservative clergy to the only solution they could conceive. The Jesuit Superior, Patrick F. X. Mulry, sent a report to Rome wherein he enclosed a detailed history of the chief financial transactions of Collins together with other documents to show that in the administration of the vicariate he had made reckless, extravagant expenditures bringing the mission to the brink of bankruptcy. Should this happen, claimed Mulry, it would mean total destruction of a century of spiritual labour.

The main expenditure had been for the new Holy Trinity Cathedral at a cost of £30,000 which he detailed thus: £20,000 for the building and £10,000 for furnishings and decorations. To this must be added £2,000 for the site.

Another lament was that Collins purchased an abandoned sugar estate, Bushy Park, containing some 7,000 acres for the sum of £8,200.

Mulry had to admit this proved to be a gold mine, for Collins was able to sell it to the United Fruit Company for £16,000.

A dispute arose over £7,000 collected in the U.S.A. for earthquake-relief of 1907. The Jesuits claimed £2,240 of this sum for the restoration of St. George's College and the residence at Winchester Park. Since Collins was both administrator of the vicariate and also religious superior at that time, he used the money to restore schools and chapels belonging to the vicariate with no allocation for St. George's College. He even advanced loans to individuals who were in dire need—and to some, claimed Mulry, who were scoundrels preying upon the bishop's charitable nature. When a formal demand was made by the then Jesuit superior, Collins at first denied the claim of St. George's College and then acceded to it.

During the construction of the cathedral, two strangers came to Jamaica, set up a sawmill, and supplied much of the cathedral's woodwork. Although warned by reliable persons of the doubtful character of these individuals, Collins continued to trust them until upon leaving Jamaica they sold him the business for £2,700 from which he recovered only £1,600.

Collins had invested in two local newspapers which failed. Early in 1911 Collins joined with several others in purchasing an old newspaper. Under the new name *The Daily News,* it functioned but a few months. Again, in the autumn of 1911, he joined another gentleman in a further newspaper venture known as *The Daily Chronicle.* After no profits for several years, the bishop's partner withdrew. Collins refunded the money the other man had invested, only to find that his partner disputed the amount, brought suit against Collins, and recovered an additional £200 from the bishop.

Early in 1915 Collins got authorization from the government to issue bonds or script upon the security of the vicariate property to the extent of £19,000. This merely added to the rising debt.

When Collins learned the tenor of Mulry's report to Rome, he quietly reviewed the situation. He was sixty-two years old, had served Jamaica for a quarter of a century, his health was failing, and grave anxiety caused by the ever-mounting debt weighed heavily on his mind. On 13 March 1917 he wrote to the prefect of Propaganda, Cardinal Dominic Serfini, O.S.B., saying that he was convinced it would be to the advantage of the mission if he were to retire and a younger man take his place. A year passed before Benedict XV accepted Collins's resignation on 10 June 1918. The Holy Father asked Collins to continue as administrator until a new vicar apostolic was chosen.

News of Collins' resignation was received with regret by every class of the community, for Protestants, Jews, and Catholics were exceedingly fond of his warm friendly nature. A committee was formed under the chairmanship of the Honourable Robert W. Bryant, mayor of Kingston, who informed the bishop on 20 January 1920 that there was a universal desire among the general public to express their appreciation of the work he had done in and for the island, both at home and abroad. They wished this to take the form of something tangible.

The following day Collins replied that he had resigned because he felt that his health would not permit him to do justice to his duties as vicar apostolic, and he felt his poor health was due to the heavy debt he had to carry. This was caused chiefly by the disasters which plagued his regime right from the beginning. He thought the greatest satisfaction he could receive from the public of Jamaica would be a generous effort to reduce the burden of the debt for his successor.

A testimonial was given the bishop on Tuesday afternoon, 23 March 1920.[7] On the platform erected before the entrance to St. George's College were seated His Worship the Mayor, the Hon. Robert W. Bryant, the Hon. Ashley Eden, Secretary to the Governor, Dr. Lawson Gifford, Judge Robert E. Noble, Miss Anne Douglas, M.B.E., and Mrs. Catherine Bourne. The arrival of the governor was marked by the playing of the National Anthem by the Alpha Band. His Excellency, Governor Sir Leslie Prohyn, presented a beautiful testimonial scroll to Bishop Collins. As the ceremony was brought to a close, the governor presented Collins with a cheque to the amount of £4,095, with the promise that it would be rounded out to a full £5,000. The speakers on the occasion were loud in their praise of the bishop; he was a man of intense zeal, a man of warmhearted charity who had spent a quarter of a century for the good of Church and Country.

It is true that Collins incurred debt near to bankruptcy and that his simple trust in his fellow men led some unscrupulous characters to take advantage of his guilelessness. Despite these failings, Holy Trinity Cathedral has stood for more than sixty years as a great monument to his foresight, and many a cleric and layman has blessed him for establishing St. Joseph's Hospital, and the whole Catholic community can thank him for raising up chapels where they may worship. Despite the detailed criticism by those who should have had the courage to help solve his financial problems, his name remains blessed.

Collins was popular. Everyone loved him and it was a sad day when he left Jamaica. The institution known as Alpha could not let the occasion pass without a grand farewell which was reported by *The Daily Gleaner* under the date of 19 April 1920.

> This occasion was marked by the boys of Alpha . . . dressed as British Tars and carrying British flags. They marched down from Alpha . . . led by the Alpha band and were under charge of Rev. Fr. Pfister, S.J. They presented a very smart appearance and attracted considerable attention as they passed through the principal thoroughfares of the city and filed into No.2 Pier. Bishop Collins motorcaded down to the pier with His Lordship Bishop O'Hare and Very Rev. Fr.Delany, S.J. and was greeted by a number of prominent Catholic laymen who came to say goodbye to him.
>
> The Alpha boys were drawn up on the pier, and the band played some very enjoyable selections, receiving unstinted applause from the passengers aboard [the ship]. Especially appreciable were such old favourites "My Old Kentucky Home" and "Auld Lang Syne." As the ship swung round from the pier, the band played the National Anthem . . . Bishop Collins was too deeply moved to remain on deck and witness it.

It was a loss for the Church when, on Saturday afternoon 17 April 1920 Bishop Collins sailed on the United Fruit steamer *Tivives* for New York.[8] There he settled down to an uneventful life as spiritual director to the students of Fordham University where he had once held the office of president. There he died on 30 November 1934 at the age of seventy-eight years.

Twenty-three

William O'Hare, S.J., 1919–1926

Restless creditors, bankruptcy, and loss of mission property threatened the Church in Jamaica while pressing necessity compelled the Holy See to select a vicar apostolic whose proven ability would guarantee immediate reduction of the staggering debt. On 1 September 1919 Benedict XV appointed William F. O'Hare, S.J., the new vicar apostolic of Jamaica.

William F. O'Hare, S.J.

William Francis O'Hare, born in Boston, Massachusetts, 23 January 1870, was educated at Biglow Grammar School and English High School before matriculating at Boston College. He left college before completing the course to enter the Society of Jesus at Frederick, Maryland on 14 August 1888. After philosophical studies at Woodstock, he taught for a year (1897–98) at St. Francis Xavier's, New York, and then later at Fordham (1898–1900). He was ordained to the priesthood by Cardinal Gibbons in 1903. After completing his theological studies, he was named prefect of studies at St. Peter's College, Jersey City.

In 1906 O'Hare arrived in Jamaica and was appointed pastor of St. Ann's Church, Kingston, adding soon afterwards the duty of administrator of the Jesuit community at 26 North Street. Two years later he succeeded Joseph Dinand, S.J., as headmaster of St. George's College. With the exception of one year, 1909–10, when he returned to St. Peter's College to become prefect of studies, he held the position of headmaster of St. George's College until named superior of the mission on 17 August 1919.[1] On 25 February 1920 he was consecrated titular bishop of Maximinopolis at the Church of St. Ignatius, New York City. Archbishop Patrick J. Hayes of New York, the consecrating prelate, was assisted by co-consecrators Bishop Thomas O. Beavan of

Springfield, Massachusetts, and Bishop Edmund F. Gibbons of Albany, New York. A month elapsed before O'Hare arrived to take formal charge of his vicariate on 10 March 1920, during which time he had toured the eastern seaboard soliciting alms to reduce the debt. At 5.00 o'clock on the afternoon of his arrival, he marched in procession from the Jesuit residence at Winchester Park to the entrance of Holy Trinity Cathedral where an address of welcome was read by Aston Figeuroa, president of Men's Sodality.

Debt Reduced

The formalities over, O'Hare settled down to the serious business of reducing the vicariate's debt. This can best be told in his report to the Very Reverend Wlodimir Ledóchowski, superior general of the Society of Jesus, dated 8 December 1920.

> When I took up the administration of the vicariate, there was a debt of £60,000; the annual interest was £3,160 and this with securities for payment that had to be met, made it necessary that the Mission should raise £5,000 annually. Our total income was £2,000 leaving a deficit of £3,000 staring us in the face. First, when my predecessor resigned, all the people of the island, Protestants and Jews as well as Catholics, realized the cause of his resignation and feeling the greatest sympathy for him, determined to show their sympathy in a substantial way by helping reduce the debt he had accumulated. As he was very popular with non-Catholics, the sum of £5,000 was raised, most of it contributed by Protestants and Jews. In addition to this, at the time of my consecration in New York, I collected £3,000 in alms. Shortly afterwards an unusual opportunity presented itself of selling a farm [Donnington] owned by the vicariate for the past eighteen years, but which on account of hurricanes, drought, and bad management never yielded much revenue. When asked to sell I fixed a high price and got all our Religious and school children to pray that so that it was accepted without demur and paid viz: £20,000, although two years ago the property would not fetch £8,000. I Immediately applied all the monies I had to the reduction of the debt, so that our debt stands at £30,000, instead of £60,000.[2]

Thus within nine months after his consecration, O'Hare had reduced the debt to half its original.

Although it was of great import to satisfy creditors, it was of greater importance to broaden the frontiers of the Church that her influence might be felt in areas hitherto untouched. Port Maria on the north coast, chief town of the civil parish of St. Mary, was one such area. Historically the district conjured up the memory of buccaneer Henry Morgan, since it was at nearby Llanrumney estate that this terror of the Spanish Main, even after he had reformed, held rendezvous with his old cronies, now out-and-out pirates. It has been long suspected that Morgan, though outwardly an honest citizen, continued a close relationship with these predatory gentlemen. Whatever may be the truth of this suspicion, the Church was now setting permanent root close to the old Morgan estate. For two years the Catholics of Port Maria had been attending Mass once a month in the town hall, so that it was with eager interest they watched construction begin on 5 February 1923. The new church should have been ready for Easter Sunday services, but like many a tropical project, it was not completed until several months later, 17 June, on which day Bishop O'Hare blessed and dedicated the chapel to Mary, Star of the Sea.

Missionary Expansion

At Lucea, on the western tip of the island, conditions were really bad, the worst in Jamaica according to one observer. The poorest native hut was a mansion compared with the chapel. When he visited the place, he had such a war against rats, scorpions, land-crabs, and huge spiders that the best night's sleep he got was a few hours dozing in a chair. After the departure of the priest, the vermin again became masters of the chapel. Fr. Aloysius M. Thibbitts, S.J., the missionary, worked zealously and did succeed in making converts, but the chapel building was enough to try the faith of even loyal Catholics. These conditions spurred both missionary and bishop to erect a church of solid stone in the centre of the town at the cost of £1,000. The cornerstone was laid 3 June 1924 by O'Hare who dedicated it to his patron St. William.

O'Hare also opened a chapel in the civil parish of Manchester, the only district without one. Set amid English-like rolling countryside, the town of Mandeville, some two thousand feet above sea level, has a faultless climate, unparalleled anywhere in the world. Its predominantly English population made the number of Catholics a small minority of forty. Fr. Thomas A. Emmet, S.J., had begun to celebrate Mass at Mandeville in 1917 without the convenience of a public chapel, but antedating him was Fr. Charles F. Bridges, S.J., who visited the town and celebrated Mass in 1905. Occasionally thereafter Mass was celebrated in private homes or hotels. On Manchester Road O'Hare acquired a small stone building and dedicated it as a chapel for his limited Catholic congregation. This rounded out the network of chapels and churches covering every civil parish in the island. When Mass was offered in this new chapel for the first time on the fifth Sunday in June 1924, twenty-five persons were present; the pastor, Joseph Ford, S.J., was so enthusiastic that he predicted it would one day develop into a flourishing centre, but it would take forty years for his dream to come true.

Conversion of the Chinese

If the Jamaican countryside was experiencing an awakening to the faith, an equal and even more phenomenal growth was happening in Kingston. If one observed Holy Trinity any Sunday morning, one would note the ethnic variety of the congregation. Black, mulatto, white would elicit no surprise, for they seem natural to the country; but a large number of Chinese would attract attention. Two questions arise: how did they find their way halfway across the world to Jamaica, and how did they become Catholics?

Migration of the Chinese

The mid-nineteenth century witnessed Chinese migrations to the western hemisphere. One such was to the gold rush in California after 1848 where a few engaged in mining and others found domestic employment with Americans who valued their efficient, faithful service, and above all their acceptance of low wages. The other area was Panama. In May 1850 Henry Chauncey, an American financier, persuaded the Colombian government to grant him a franchise to construct a railroad running from Colón to Panama City, linking Atlantic with Pacific.[3] To lay tracks through jungle country, he recruited labourers from China. Unaccustomed to hard work nine degrees north of the equator, these Orientals found themselves fighting a losing battle against tropical disease and the burning sun, and with numbers decimated, they asked to be sent to a healthier climate. Jamaica was the country chosen. In 1854, 472 Chinese arrived here. Sickly when they came, they found Jamaica no panacea for their troubles. Severe working conditions and low basic pay dealt another blow to these unfortunates. Eventually most of them had to be admitted to the public hospitals of Kingston and Spanish Town where they died. Only thirty of this group survived; among them were Chin Pa-king (Robert Jackson), Chong Shin-pah, Lyn Sam, and Ho Shue. These laid the foundation of the first Chinese community in Jamaica. Chin Pa-king's boldness in opening a wholesale grocery on Pechon Street, Kingston, and his largess towards all newcomers helped to establish confidence and solidarity among the Chinese. Two others tested their business ability: Chang Shin-pah operated a grocery-dry goods store at the corner of Beckford and Orange Streets, Kingston, while Lyn Sam opened a grocery somewhere in Kingston whose exact location cannot be ascertained.

Second Migration

More Chinese arrived from other geographical areas between 1856–70. They had been indentured labourers recruited in China to work in the cane fields of Trinidad and British Guiana but were in a quandary when their contracts expired, for hurricanes and insects had wrought such havoc with the cane crop that planters were unable to reemploy them. Fortunately, American interests had started large-scale planting of coconuts, sugarcane, and bananas in Jamaica at this time, and about two hundred of these Chinese immigrated to this island. Upon expiration of their contracts, some continued to work on the plantations, while others opened small shops with the money they had saved. The entire stock of these shops would be worth £30 sterling, and the total weekly sales about £6, but it was a start for many who later rose to financial prominence in Jamaica, such as Lim Bang, who ruled the influential Chinese Benevolent Society; Wong Chong, also from British Guiana, who became a wholesale grocery merchant at the corner of Princess and Beckford Streets, Kingston; Arthur Hew, who became a tonic and wine merchant; and Dunbar Li-Kong, whose grocery at Barry Street and Mark Lane became the largest in the island.

Hard work and long hours were the keys to their success. At six o'clock in the morning, the shutters were taken down, and not until eleven o'clock at night did the shop close. They lived above the store to safeguard their goods below and to avoid the expense of another residence. Their small numbers kept them closely knit and promoted clannish cooperation among the community. Some of this group became Catholics in 1858.[4]

Third Migration

The third wave of immigrants formed the immediate ancestral basis of the Chinese Catholic community in Jamaica. These came to the island in 1884. At that time the Jamaican planters were experiencing a labour shortage due to the ex-slaves and their descendants' continued repugnance to plantation work. Planters requested the colonial secretary in Hong Kong to recruit labourers for the cane farms. Six hundred eighty came; 501 men, 105 women, 54 boys, seventeen girls and three infants. Twenty came from See-ip; the majority were Hakka people from Tung-kuan, Wei-yagn, and Poa-an in the province of Kwangtung.

On 8 May 1884 they left Hong Kong for Macao where they embarked on the SS. *Diamond*. Out in the Pacific the ship ran into a typhoon and limped into Vancouver with a broken mast and minus one labourer who was lost in the storm. Damage to S.S. *Diamond* was so serious that the passengers had to be transshipped to the German vessel S.S. *Prince Alexander* for the remainder of the voyage. After their hazardous trip, they landed in Kingston 12 July 1884.

Conditions Improve

No red carpet welcomed their disembarkation. They were sent under guard to the prison at Spanish Town. Roll was called; each one was assigned work on a particular plantation. They then discovered that years of their lives had been sold in exchange for passage to the island. One boy, nine years old, Wen Choy-pai, was told to work in the cane factory of Tuck and Field in the civil parish of St. Thomas. One hundred adults were assigned to the same plantation where they toiled from 6.00 o'clock in the morning until 6.00 o'clock in the evening.

Tropical heat forced the Chinese to protest, but management ignored their request for shorter hours. Then they staged a sit-down strike. In retaliation, the manager mustered sixty burly negroes and one hundred East Indians to compel the Chinese to work. A fight ensued; seven Chinese were wounded, one negro killed and several injured. One of the Chinese, Hu-lai, who knew English, acted as interpreter and arbitrated the dispute with the proprietors. Working hours were reduced to the more reasonable 7.00 a.m. to 4.00 p.m. day.[5]

More Chinese were needed and more came. Their relatives and friends sent them passage money, and thus made the indenture system obsolete. Each year the number of immigrants increased, since both Jamaica and Hong Kong were British colonies and no passport was required. Upon arrival they were free to choose their employment. Some found ready work on the plantations, others opened grocery shops. From retail grocery stores they blossomed into the wholesale business as their numbers increased to eight hundred in 1888.[6]

The Anglican Efforts

It was quite natural for a group of immigrants to acknowledge one of their number as leader and to turn to him for counsel and advice amid strange surroundings. Mr. Leahong was such a guide. Migrating from British Guiana in the 1880s, he had risen by dint of hard work from penury to wealth within his lifetime. His was the most influential family among the immigrants. The wife of this prominent Chinese became an Anglican, due to the fatherly interest in the Chinese manifested by the rector of the Kingston Parish Church. Influenced by her example, many of the Chinese community followed her decision. Conversions to the Anglican Church continued until 1920, when a change took place; the Anglican rector left Jamaica and his successors did not bestow the same paternal care upon the Chinese, so conversions diminished. Old age was telling on the good Mrs. Leahong and her active work ceased.

Microscopic Catholic Beginnings

During all this time the Catholic Church made no effort at converting the Chinese. They were turning from paganism to Anglicanism without the slightest exertion being made by the American missionaries. Now and then a lone Chinese did come into the Catholic Church, as is evinced from the tombstones in old Holy Trinity churchyard. The great mass conversion of the Chinese, however, was thrust upon them in a providential manner.

In the rear room of a Glengoff village grocery store, a daughter was born to Mr. and Mrs. Daniel Acquee on 25 August 1904, by name, Blanche. Blanche's birth went unnoticed in the newsy *Daily Gleaner* of Kingston, so unimportant was this passing incident in the great events of the day. Even the village folk expressed no interest: she was just another Chinese girl.

Blanche's grandfather, Kong Fook, had emigrated from China in the 1880s and had opened a grocery shop in the village of Lawrence Tavern. Her grandmother, Chin See Moy, had come to Jamaica as an indentured servant about the same time and was assigned to work on a sugar estate on the Stony Hill Road at the Old Water works. But life became intolerable on that plantation, so she ran away. Her first stop was the village of Lawrence Tavern not too many miles distant, where Kong Fook took her in, paid off her bond, and married her. From this union Blanche's mother was born. Blanche's father, Daniel Acquee, came from Ho Yeng, a village in Kwangtung. A match was made by Blanche's grandparents and the couple married. Mr. and Mrs. Daniel Acquee opened a grocery shop at Glengoff, not too many miles from Lawrence Tavern. Three girls and one boy were born of this union.

In the village of Glengoff, one of Acquee's most cherished friends was a Mr. Ximines, an exemplary Catholic. Mrs. Acquee asked him to arrange to have Blanche baptized in the Catholic Church. Fr. Peter

Kayser, S.J., was the missionary consulted, but he hesitated since both parents were pagans and had not the remotest Catholic connections. Two factors persuaded him that he might safely baptize Blanche. First, Mrs. Acquee had given her word of honour she would be brought up a Catholic. Secondly, the catechist at Cassava River, Mr. Eustace McNeil, would be the godfather. So on the feast of St. Stanislaus Kostka, 13 November 1904, Blanche Acquee was baptized in the Church of the Holy Family, Cassava River. This one baptism set in motion the conversion of the Chinese on Jamaica.

A few years later the Acquee family moved to Kingston and opened a grocery shop at 49 North Street.[7] This was within a stone's throw of St. Anne's School, conducted by the Franciscan Sisters. Mrs. Acquee had told Blanche that she had been baptized a Catholic and she in turn informed Sister Agatha, O.S.F., the school's principal, who placed her under the care of Miss Marie da Costa to prepare Blanche for her First Holy Communion. Later Blanche received the sacrament of confirmation from the hands of Bishop Collins. From this point in her life, she became an enthusiastic apostle.

Another little Chinese girl, Doris Lee Young, came to live with the Acquee family, and the Catholic Church became the all-absorbing subject among the children of the Acquee household. Blanche brought Doris and her own older sister Eva, who had just finished her elementary education at St. Anne's, to Fr. Leo Butler, S.J., the pastor of the church, for instructions. In 1918, another child, Blossom, was born in the Acquee family. Blanche carried her to the church for baptism. Eva now joined Blanche in her work of conversions and induced several young Chinese to attend instructions under Fr. Butler. Within a short time he had baptized a dozen children. For him it was the beginning of an era, introducing him to an apostolate among the Chinese which would continue for forty years.

More came for instructions, boys and girls. Fr. Butler, now headmaster of St. George's College, turned to Sister Sylvia, O.S.F., and before the end of the year, twenty-five had come into the Church. In 1924 the Chinese youth had formed themselves into the Oslyn Troupe to provide entertainment for the community. Sr. Sylvia was asked to train them. The first concert was held at St. George's College with such remarkable success that the following day they played at the Ward Theatre, the Carnegie Hall of Jamaica. All the more remarkable was the conversion of these young Chinese entertainers. In the original cast there were but four Catholics out of twenty-four, but one year later the whole troupe had come into the Church. Again it was Blanche, a member of the troupe, who played a major role in the conversion of her fellow troupers.[8]

More impetus was given these mounting conversions by Fr. Simon Tang, S.J., of Canton, China. In 1925 Fr. Tang, while making tertianship at St. Andrew-on-Hudson, New York, was asked to conduct a mission among his countrymen in Jamaica. For six weeks, beginning in March 1927, he toured the island, telling the Chinese about the Church. Forty adult converts were the result of his efforts. After Fr. Tang left, one influential Chinese, William Pinchin, who owned a business at the corner of Barry Street and Matthew's Lane, Kingston, acted as instructor to convey the fundaments of Christian doctrine to adult Chinese who knew little English.

The Tang mission's result of forty converts lifted the movement from the teenage group and placed it among the mature segment of the community. But what was needed was a follow-up in which the faith could be explained in detail. Gordon Hall was placed at the disposal of the Chinese, where every Sunday afternoon Fr. Butler and Sr. Sylvia conducted regular instruction classes. From Gordon Hall the centre was removed to St. Anthony's School, 80–84 Orange Street. This location was more convenient to the Chinese community focused on nearby Barry Street. At this centre Blanche, who had sparked the movement, continued her interest. Every opportunity to advance the faith was zealously used by this young apostle. Through the medium of *Catholic Opinion,* she asked that all Chinese attending instructions bring along with them at least one other non-Catholic, and on another occasion using the same *Catholic Opinion,* she wrote "It is the hope of our little Mission, thus started, may be the beginning of a great work among our Chinese brethren."[9] Truly it was for the number of Chinese Catholics increased to three thousand by the year 1925.

Education of the Chinese

Another powerful instrument of conversion was the Catholic school. Chinese parents, strongly attached to their children, learned to entrust them to the sisters and fathers, for not only was the intellect disciplined, but they were given a solid moral training as well, which was greatly appreciated by the Chinese since virtues which had been handed down to them by their ancestors were being instilled into their children by the Catholic Church. In the beginning, contact with the Catholic school was on the elementary level, since most Chinese children of the first two generations were forced by circumstances to terminate their education at an early age in order to help their parents in the family grocery shop. Yet these few years in the Catholic elementary school had the effect of implanting the faith solidly in these children. This generation, with its greater financial security, was able to keep the following generation in school for a longer period. Even parents who needed the help of their children in the shop before and after school hours managed to extend the education of their children beyond the stage enjoyed by mother and father. There was, however, one handicap. Chinese parents desired that their children should learn the Chinese language and customs. Since the language was not taught in Jamaica, the child was sent back to China at an early age. For some this meant a return to a pagan atmosphere which had an adverse effect on their faith. It might also mean attending a Protestant school in China, where all the efforts in Jamaica were undone. Within recent years this plan ran into a snag: World War II and Communistic occupation prevented sending children to the mainland. Gradually the Chinese language became almost unknown to the rising generation. A Chinese Public School opened in Kingston failed to satisfy the need, since only a limited number of children attended the school, and the institution was found incapable of imparting a knowledge of the Chinese language and at the same time of preparing the child to pass the public examinations so necessary both in business and the intellectual world of Jamaica.

Parents then turned to Jamaican schools where the child was prepared for the public examinations but where no Chinese was taught. For the boys, the favourite was St. George's College where Fr. Butler was headmaster; for the girls the Immaculate Conception High School and Alpha Academy were the choice. Ambitious, studious, and industrious, these pupils used their native ability to the utmost, and what their fathers accomplished in the business world, their sons and daughters achieved in the intellectual. From high school to university was the logical step, some matriculating in English, others in Canadian and American universities. These higher studies broadened their horizons and opened the professions to them. The result has been doctors, lawyers, architects, engineers, and seminarians and priests. Within the past decade ninety-two Chinese graduates of St. George's College have either attained their university degree or are in the process of doing so. Three have won their Ph.D.'s and three more are in course. One attained the distinction of a Rhodes' Scholarship. Called to the bar at Gray's Inn, Maurice Tenn is a practicing barrister in Kingston.[10]

Organization

From St. Anthony's School on busy Orange Street, the Chinese Centre moved to Holy Trinity Cathedral in 1945, where spacious facilities for both instruction and recreation were available. Here Fr. Raymond

Fox, S.J., administrator of the cathedral, joined Fr. Butler in the work among the Chinese in the same year. Working chiefly with the youth, Fr. Fox organized them into a very effective Chinese Catholic Action and directed them to visit hospitals, alms houses, and private homes of the sick where they made their faith felt throughout the Chinese community. Every Sunday the same association conducted catechism class at St. George's College Hall for Chinese children who did not enjoy the advantage of a Catholic education.

Fr. Fox's death on 19 August 1945 left the Chinese without a director. When no one was appointed to continue the work, a Protestant evangelical group formed an organization and invited the young Chinese to join. Blanche once more stepped into the breach and informed ecclesiastical authorities of the harmful situation and stressed the need for a director to continue the work of Fr. Fox. The vicar apostolic, Bishop John J. McEleney, S.J., acted promptly by appointing Fr. Thomas Glavin, S.J., pastor of St. Theresa's Church, as director. The centre, now moved to his parish, became the focal point for Chinese activity.

Ronald Chen, Blanche's son, became president of the revived Chinese Catholic Action Association. Like his mother, he had much influence among the Chinese youth, which he helped organize into a powerful adjunct of the Church in Jamaica. The association issued a monthly mimeographed *Bulletin* which cemented the organization by encouraging the youth to express their views on current problems affecting the Chinese community in its relation to the Church. Once organized, this society drew the attention of Chinese Catholic groups outside Jamaica.

In 1952 the Chinese Catholics of the West Coast of the United States met to work out a solution to problems affecting Chinese communities and the Church. San Francisco was the first rendezvous, drawing delegates from Vancouver, Hawaii, and various parts of California. At this meeting the Pacific Regional Conference, including the West Coast of the United States and Hawaii, was organized. So overwhelming was the response that the conference voted to return to San Francisco the following year, and again it was well received. Vancouver offered to act as host to the third meeting. At this conference it was voted that San Francisco should be the site every other year.

In the spring of 1957, Rachel Chun, chairman of the conference, made a trip across the United States and Canada to acquaint the Chinese centres with the work of the conference. Chicago, Philadelphia, Washington, Boston, New York, Montreal, and Quebec were the cities visited. New York sent four representatives to the sixth conference in San Francisco. Chicago caught the fever and invited the conference to that city for the seventh annual meeting. Since the East Coast of the United States was now included in the conference, the name was changed to the Chinese Catholic Conference, and it was noted that San Francisco should be host henceforth once every third year. It was at the eighth conference in New York that Jamaica became involved in the organization. In the following year, the ninth conference was held in Kingston, Jamaica, from 28 July to 1 August 1960. The theme of the conference was the lay apostolate. Its purpose was to exchange ideas, discuss common problems, and promote a better understanding of the Catholic faith among the Chinese laity. Again, in 1966, Jamaica was host to the conference, which by this time had gained great momentum in the Chinese communities across the United States, for it brought the Church into sharp focus with China, the most populous nation in the world, and offered a challenge to the modern Church that she make the work among the Chinese her major apostolate of the century.[11]

From the Chinese Catholic Action Association flowered the first vocation. Kenneth Kong, the youngest son of Mr. and Mrs. Kong Back Lee was ordained to the priesthood by Bishop Carter on Thursday evening, 16 June 1966. Educated at St. Anthony's School, where so many Chinese began their elementary education, he later entered St. George's College, received his Cambridge School Certificate, and was graduated in 1954. That same year he joined the staff of John Crook Ltd., a business firm in Kingston. Two years later he entered St. Michael's Seminary, where he completed his humanistic and philosophical courses before studying theology at St. John's Seminary, Brighton, Massachusetts. His first solemn Mass was offered at Holy Trinity Cathedral, Kingston, with Jesuit Fathers Alwyn Harry and Joseph Brennan, diocesan priests Alphonso Bygrave and Kenneth Ramsay concelebrating with him. Four Chinese took part in the offertory procession: Dudley Chai Onn, William Lock Hong, Carmen and Marene Kong.[12] For Blanche Acquee Chen this day was the fulfillment of her life's hopes and desires, for from the tiny seed she planted among her early schoolmates, the number of Chinese Catholics had increased to twenty thousand, and to climax her work one was now a priest.

Just as there had been a notable Catholic increase among the Chinese, so there was also a growth among the general population in conversions to the Church. Over the ten years 1915–25, the Church increased from 31,760 to 40,000.[13] It was the country parts which contributed most to this increase where forty-five percent of the Catholics now lived. Growth in the country was due to the new chapels which brought the missionaries into closer contact with the people. Strategically placed, these substations were the focal points of the Church in the surrounding countryside, providing more instructions for the faithful and giving them greater opportunity to frequent the sacraments. To this natural growth of Catholics were added many non-Catholics favourably disposed towards the Church who sought and received instructions from the missionaries.

Yet during this same ten-year period personnel showed an increase of only one missionary. In 1915 there were twenty-one priests and one bishop; in 1925 there were twenty priests, three scholastics and one bishop.[14] The opening of new schools and colleges and the addition of an extensive mission in the Philippines, where within four years forty Jesuits were assigned, restricted the manpower of the New York-Maryland Province. In Jamaica this meant much labour in a tropical country for twenty-one men to serve seventy-nine churches and chapels in addition to St. George's College, which was now almost entirely staffed by Jesuits.

For Jamaica to lose even one missionary during this 1915–25 period was to curtail seriously the work of the mission. Such a loss occurred when Patrick F. X. Mulry died at St. Elizabeth's Hospital, New York, on Thursday, 2 November 1922. Mulry, whose missionary career extended over a period of twenty-seven years, had returned to the United States to recuperate his health for what was thought to be a stomach ulcer but later was diagnosed as cancer. When his doctors revealed its serious extent to him, he took the news with the courage of a soldier.

On Saturday, 4 November, in the Church of St. Francis Xavier, New York, Bishop Collins presided at the funeral of his onetime companion on the Jamaican mission. The requiem Mass was celebrated by Mulry's nephew, Fr. Joseph A. Mulry, at which one hundred priests were present, while apart from the immediate family were delegations of sisters, laymen and women representing the charitable organizations with which the Mulry family had long been identified in New York. His remains were borne to the Jesuit cemetery of St. Andrew-on-Hudson at Poughkeepsie, New York.

Born on West Street, New York, 3 December 1860, he received his early education under the Christian Brothers. On 6 August 1877 he entered the Society of Jesus at West Park, New York. Ordained to the priesthood in June 1893 by Cardinal Gibbons, he was assigned to Jamaica the following year. While engaged in parochial work at Holy Trinity, he also took charge of the Spanish Town mission, covering the twenty-four-mile round-trip on bicycle. He later devoted much time to the missions in the civil parishes of St. Ann and Portland. Appointed superior in October 1903, demands of administration confined his work to Kingston. There he became identified with the League of the Sacred Heart, the St. Vincent de Paul Society, and the Knights of St. John. To these duties he added the office of editor of *Catholic Opinion,* a monthly published by Jamaican Jesuits. Close by were the missions of Matilda's Corner and Gordon Town, which were his favourite haunts within the city limits.[15] Keen mental powers and a burning love for the Church were combined with an attractive personality, which were brought to bear on the works he undertook, whether guiding a fellow Jesuit or encouraging some country catechist.

O'Hare's Death

Four years later the mission lost its chief pastor, Bishop O'Hare. An editorial in *Catholic Opinion,* at the beginning of his regime, expressed the view that he would bring vigour and ardour to the office by reason of his good health. The expectation was groundless, for at one of his first public appearances in the cathedral he fell into unconsciousness. From that day the fear of a fatal collapse shadowed all his efforts. Beside chronic stomach trouble and a weak heart, he also had a slight lesion of the brain which brought on sudden fainting spells and occasionally long periods of unconsciousness with complete physical collapse.

One of these attacks proved fatal on 11 October 1926. O'Hare had attended the Eucharistic Congress in Chicago, June 1925. After the congress he had spent several weeks in the archdiocese of Philadelphia making appeals for funds. Twice he had to give up his attempt to raise money for the mission due to recurring illness. It appeared for a time that a stomach operation would be necessary, but medical treatment at St. Vincent's Hospital, New York, postponed surgery. Doctors promised him a moderate degree of health if he followed their diet. He was also advised not to return to the tropics, but he rejected this advice and sailed for Jamaica, where he arrived unexpectedly on 4 October 1925.

He returned to Jamaica not to work but to die. His healthy looks deceived many who commented on how well he seemed after his trip to the United States. On Monday morning, 11 October, he told his chauffeur to drive him to a beach some six miles distant where he followed his doctor's orders to sea bathe frequently.

Just across the street from St. George's College, he had purchased a new residence where he intended to live apart from the fathers attached to the college. New furniture had been bought in New York, and he had stopped to give instructions to the caretaker about the arrangement of the room, leaving what he thought to be his future home. He rode until he reached the Church of St. Benedict the Moor at Harbour Head, where just beyond this point the car turned into a private beach. It was a good half mile farther to the spot where he could swim, so he told his chauffeur to wait in the car for him. He stopped a few minutes to talk to the caretaker of the beach and then walked to a rough thatched shelter to change into his bathing suit.

The stretch of beach was deserted except for a group of women doing their Monday wash where the Cane River empties into the sea. One woman sent her young daughter back to the house on an errand; on the child's return to her horror she saw the still form of a man at the water's edge rollling to and fro with the waves washing the shore. The frightened child ran back to her home and told her father what she had seen. The father, a fisherman, reluctant to believe his child, walked down to the beach only after much persuasion. The child's report was true, for on the beach was a dead man. The news spread rapidly and a crowd gathered. Up to that time, no one had recognized the bishop, but when the car was discovered at the roadside, someone informed the chauffeur. He hurried down to identify him. Removing the body from the water, the bystanders placed it in a sheltered spot and covered it with palm branches. The chauffeur hurried back to Kingston and returned with Fr. Francis Kelly who, hoping the bishop was yet alive, administered the last sacraments.

It was some time before police and medical authorities reached the spot, and after an examination the doctor allowed the body to be removed to St. Joseph's Hospital where a postmortem was performed by the district medical officer, Dr. Atkinson. He reported that the bishop's death was due to chronic inflammation, hardening of the arteries, and heart trouble arising from the above causes. He did not drown—no water was found in stomach or lungs.

Possibly the bishop did not go far into the water but was sitting on the shore allowing the waves to wash over him when the attack occurred, for his eyeglasses and shoes were found beside him and his episcopal ring was in one of his shoes when his body was discovered. No more than three-quarters of an hour had elapsed between the time he had left the chauffeur and the time the child found him.[16]

News of the tragedy spread quickly throughout the city, and messages of condolence began to pour in from all parts of Jamaica. The governor's read:

> Very Rev. Sir:
>
> I have received with great regret the news of the death of your greatly respected bishop. Permit me to express my respectful sympathy with your

Church in the loss which it has suffered, a loss which will be felt by the whole community of Jamaica.

Yours very truly,
[sgd.] *R. E. Stubbs*[17]

From the Anglican coadjutor bishop came the following:

St. Peter's College
Cross Roads. P.O.

11.10.26

Dear Fr. Kelly,
Will you please accept and convey to your clergy and people an expression of my heartfelt sorrow and profound sympathy with you in the sudden passing of your beloved Bishop. I have been in Jamaica nearly ten years and during that time have been privileged to know Bishop O'Hare as a real friend. His knowledge and readiness to help in any cause for the welfare of the people of the island generally, will cause his memory long to be revered. May he rest in peace, and may God's special blessing be upon you at this time. I am sure that the [Anglican] Bishop of Jamaica who is at present in England, would wish me to express on his behalf his sincere and deepest sympathy. I hope to be present at the funeral.

Believe me to be
Yours very sincerely
[sgd.] *David W. Bently, Bishop*[18]

In Jamaica, burial takes place as soon as possible. On Thursday morning, 12 October, a solemn High Mass of Requiem was celebrated at 6.30 A.M. with Very Reverend Francis J. Kelly as celebrant, Fr. Joseph Ford, deacon, and Fr. Leo Butler as subdeacon. The solemn absolution was deferred until the afternoon to allow missionaries in the country time to arrive for the burial. From 1.00 P.M. until 4.00 P.M. the body lay in state at the cathedral where thousands viewed their bishop for the last time. Youths whom he had taught at St. George's College, now respected business and professional men, passed by the bier, remembering his kindness to them in and out of the classroom. Over in England, four Jesuit novices, the fruit of his administration, bemoaned the death and blessed the memory of him who so faithfully fostered their vocations. Then there was the great mass of common folk who had known him in the confessional, at the altar, and in the pulpit. Lastly, the very, very poor who knew him as a kind father, zealous priest, a devoted shepherd, and a self-sacrificing apostle. All filed silently by his body as it lay in state.

Promptly at four o'clock the great bell in the cathedral belfry began its doleful, measured tolling. It was echoed by the bells on all the Protestant churches. Thousands were packed into the benches and aisles of the cathedral; thousands more, unable to gain admission, stood outside on the cathedral grounds and on North Street. The funeral procession left the cathedral about 4:30 P.M. It was one of the largest funerals ever witnessed in Jamaica. The whole three miles from the cathedral to the Catholic cemetery was lined with people. There were more than three hundred autos and carriages in the cortege. It is estimated that fully fifteen thousand people attended the final obsequies in the cemetery. The fact that there was scarcely a dry eye in the vast assembly as the coffin was lowered into the grave was eloquent testimony that the good Bishop had won their hearts and affections. Scores of wreaths from all classes of Jamaicans, Protestant as well as Catholics, were heaped upon his grave. If sorrow can be made tangible and visible, it was certainly visible and tangible in that vast throng of mourners as they withdrew from the cemetery.[19]

To lose a missionary is always a blow to the limited personnel of the mission, but to lose its chief missionary is a serious and added blow, for O'Hare had administrative ability above the average. His financial capabilities could never be questioned and, given a few more years, he could have wiped out completely the debt of his predecessor. His quiet, unassuming personality won friends in every level of society, a necessary characteristic for a man in his position. Another whose talents rivalled O'Hare's would have to be chosen, one whose ability to raise funds would be combined with a pleasing personality which would cement the varied ethnic elements into harmonious unity.

Twenty-four

Bishop Dinand and the Native Sisters

More than a decade had elapsed since World War I. While the European nations were recovering from their wounds, the United States was experiencing an economic boom unparalleled in its history. During this same period the Church in the United States was blessed with an affluence of vocations.

In 1925 there were ninety-eight Jesuit scholastic novices in the Maryland-New York Province, in addition to fifty-three more in the Vice Province of New England.[1] The following year, 1926, it was decreed to separate Maryland-New York from New England, the latter becoming an independent province. The Philippine Islands were assigned to Maryland-New York and Jamaica to New England as missions. The Maryland-New York jurisdiction over Jamaica ended with O'Hare; the Province of New England was called upon to supply the next vicar apostolic.

Dinand Chosen Bishop

On Sunday, 21 August 1927, it was announced at all Masses in Jamaica that His Holiness, Pius XI, had chosen Joseph N. Dinand Vicar Apostolic of Jamaica. Dinand was then the president of Holy Cross College, Worcester, Massachusetts.[2] Twenty years previously Dinand, as a tenderfoot missionary in Jamaica, had witnessed the devastating earthquake of 1907. The long interval had not erased from the minds of Jamaicans the memory of his sympathetic ministrations during the disaster, nor had they forgotten his eloquent sermons in Holy Trinity Cathedral.

Dinand's Early Years

Dinand was born in Boston, Massachusetts on the feast of St. Francis Xavier, 3 December 1869.[3] When he completed his grammar school education, he won a scholarship to Boston College High School. Four years later he entered Boston College to study for a bachelor of arts degree, but after his third year he entered the novitiate of the Society of Jesus at Frederick, Maryland, on 13 August 1887. At Woodstock, only a few miles to the west of Frederick, where he spent the next three years, Dinand was subject to an intensive course in scholastic philosophy and a not too demanding course in the physical sciences. During regency, which followed philosophical studies, he was assigned to teach such diverse subjects as classics and mathematics at the College of St. Francis Xavier on West 16th Street, New York City. Five years of regency made the assignment to study theology at Woodstock seem like a well-earned vacation, until pressure of classes, repetitions, circles, and disputations proved it was no sinecure.

But this demanding attention to studies proved worthwhile when on 25 June 1903, he received Holy Orders at the hands of Cardinal Gibbons. A fourth year of dogmatic theology, followed by a year of ascetical theology at St. Andrew-on-Hudson, New York, prepared him for missionary work in Jamaica.

St. George's College, to which he was assigned, discovered it could boast of both an efficient teacher and a skilled athletic director who won the admiration of the young students; this was from 1905–08.

In 1908 Jamaica lost one of her most promising missionaries, for Dinand returned to the United States where he was assigned as administrator for young men who had just entered the Society of Jesus at St. Andrew-on-Hudson and later was appointed socius to the provincial of the Maryland-New York Province.

On 9 October 1911 came the opportunity to prove his administrative ability: he was appointed president of Holy Cross College. Eloquent and of magnetic personality, Dinand's public appearances drew alumni audiences to a public awareness of Holy Cross as he campaigned across the United States for funds to construct a new chapel, science halls, library, faculty residence, dormitories and classrooms, some of which were erected in his own regime, while others had to await the regime of Fr. James J. Carlin, his immediate successor.

Dinand returned to the office of president of Holy Cross on 31 July 1924. During his second term the library—since renamed Dinand Library—was built at a cost of $750,000. His other contribution was to broaden the curriculum and enlarge the faculty in order to meet the increasing needs of the growing student body and to establish on the campus a friendly spirit between professor and student, both of whom always found in their college president a wise and prudent counselor.

Consecration

On 30 October 1927, in the Memorial Chapel of Holy Cross College, Joseph N. Dinand was consecrated titular bishop of Selinas by the Rt. Rev. Thomas M. O'Leary, bishop of Springfield, Massachusetts, assisted by Rt. Rev. Joseph A. Murphy, S.J., vicar apostolic of British Honduras and Rt. Rev. John G. Murphy, bishop of Portland, Maine. Since Dinand was beloved by the student body and alumni, they took the occasion of a farewell banquet to express by encomia all he had accomplished for the college. When the final word of the last speaker died on the Worcester air that evening, Bishop Dinand rose to address the gathering with such vehement eloquence that the memory of that night lingered long in the minds of his audience.

With praises still ringing in his ears, Bishop Dinand sailed out of New York for Kingston on 7 December 1927.[4] A few days on the Atlantic and the temperature changed from freezing to the 80s when his ship the *S.S. Sixaola* berthed at the United Fruit Pier, Kingston, on the evening of 12 December.[5]

Jamaica

The sight of this tropical city awakened memories of twenty years past; but the years had changed both place and people. Scars of the 1907 earthquake had healed, and the Church had made notable advances in new structures and new converts. Among the many who came to welcome him, the bishop noted that the vast majority were strangers. As the tropical sun was sinking behind palm and mountain, state and ecclesiastical dignitaries gathered at Winchester Park to honour the new vicar apostolic in a civic welcome. His Excellency, Sir Edward Stubbs, Bishop de Carteret of the Anglican Church, and Bishop Joseph Murphy, S.J, of British Honduras, were among the prominent guests on the platform when an address was read by Fred Kennedy representing the Catholic laymen. The final expression of welcome was reserved for His excellency, the Governor, in the name of the government and the colony of Jamaica. That afternoon augured well for the future of the Church under Dinand. He had collected $17,000 from friends in the United States, part of which was used to purchase the Argyle property at Half Way Tree, St. Andrew.

Bishop Dinand plunged at once into the work of the vicariate with seemingly inexhaustible energy: affairs of administration, official ceremonies, confirmations, and long hours in the cathedral confessional made such a demand upon his physical strength that no human constitution could withstand the strain. A mere five months later, his health broke under the pressure of work in this tropical country.

Dinand Leaves Jamaica

On 11 May 1928 Bishop Dinand left Jamaica to fulfill engagements on behalf of the mission.[6] So badly was he in need of rest that he had to cancel all commitments and submit to doctor's orders that he resign himself to an indefinite period of inactivity and quiet. He made plans to return to Jamaica in the early autumn of 1928, but ill health lengthened the rest into twelve long months. He then resigned the office of vicar apostolic on 4 October 1929.[7] He had given much promise of a brilliant future about to dawn for the Church; now these hopes lay shattered with his health, simply because he had failed to learn to adjust himself to life in the tropics.

Native Religious Congregation

Although it had been a much-discussed idea among previous vicars apostolic, it was reserved to Bishop Dinand to launch the project of a native religious congregation. He took it from the planning board and gave it the reality of substance, reasoning that should the Church depend wholly on foreign sources of personnel, the natives of the country would always regard her with at least a hint of suspicion. This sagacious act of Bishop Dinand not only dispelled xenophobia but also tapped a potential for vocations hitherto unmined by the Church. It was Dinand's great work to inaugurate a native congregation of religious before he resigned.

Tiny Seed

It is of interest to review the early days of this organization and piece together the varied elements which contributed to its birth. The sowing of the first seeds are best told by Mother Mary Alocoque, superior of the Franciscans in Jamaica.

> When Bishop Dinand came to see me in 1928, about giving him a Franciscan Sister to make possible the foundation of a native Sisterhood, I told him that I thoroughly agreed with the project and would write to Rev. Mother Dominica, the Superior General, stating his request for a Sister to begin the work. I remarked, however, that I had no Sister to offer him at

> present. Bishop Dinand left very happy and confident of the ultimate success of his great desire. Shortly afterwards, when the reply from Mother Dominica arrived, I went at once to see the Bishop and told him that Mother General had granted permission, instructing me to do everything possible to assist him. On this occasion I took as my companion Sister Humiliana. Bishop Dinand was delighted with my promise of letting him have a Sister as soon as I could. Just before leaving, the thought occurred to me of offering the services of my companion, Sister Humiliana to the Bishop. This I did, remarking that due to a slight eye infection she was at the moment free from any special duty. I added that being a Jamaican herself, she would be a great asset for the project. I know what I said must have taken Sister Humiliana by surprise. But before she could express herself, Bishop Dinand had accepted my offer. Upon our departure, we left a very happy Bishop ready to begin at once the realization of his heart's desire, the founding of a native Franciscan Community.[8]

Once the formality of approval was complete, Sister Humiliana settled down to the practical work of organizing the congregation. Two sources of vocations were personally available to her: one was the Holy Trinity Sunday School which was under her charge; the other was St. Joseph's Girls' School, where she taught. Both were potential sources of native vocations. In order to acquaint Jamaican girls with the aims and advantages of religious life, evening instructions were begun at the Franciscan Duke Street School. The inaugural meeting of the new congregation took place on 19 February 1929, at which twelve young ladies were present, together with Frs. Francis J. Kelly, S.J. in whose hands Bishop Dinand had placed the destiny of the congregation before leaving Jamaica for the United States, Joseph Dougherty, S.J., George McDonald, S.J., Charles Bridges, S.J., and Joseph Kelly, S.J.[9]

On 6 August 1929 Francis J. Kelly wrote Cardinal Van Rossum, C.SS.R., Prefect of Propaganda, concerning the new congregation.

> The undersigned Apostolic Administrator of Jamaica following the wish of the Vicar (Apostolic) himself, reverently informs your Eminence that there are three Religious Communities of Sisters in the Vicariate, namely: A Third Order of Franciscan Sisters, Sisters of Mercy, and Dominican Sisters who with much zeal strive for spiritual good among the faithful in school and hospitals. Nevertheless, it must be said with sorrow, that considering the place and the customs of the people, it is almost impossible for native Jamaican women to be admitted into these Religious Institutes, although vocations to the religious state are not lacking among the natives. In order that the religious state may be open also to the natives, and that the faithful in the interior of the Vicariate may be provided with (spiritual) necessities (there is no doubt but that native Sisters will produce great fruit for the spiritual good of Jamaica), the Administrator, following the (will) of the Vicar (Apostolic) himself considers it would be useful and even necessary that a Congregation be established which

would admit principally native women of Jamaica. There are now at hand constitutions which were written according to the norms of Canon Law and approved temporarily by the Administrator, if it should please the Holy See to grant the faculty of instituting this new Congregation under the title of Franciscan Missionaries of Our Lady of Perpetual Help. The habit worn by the professed will be white in colour, and a veil of the same colour with a black cincture and beads. The habit of the novices will be nearly the same; the veil will be blue.

Besides striving for perfection, it will be the duty of the Sisters to instruct the youth in the schools, to visit the sick in hospitals, to direct homes for women, especially working girls. All care will be used that in exercising these works every caution will be observed for protecting the Sisters themselves so that nothing be done that is not edifying. Especially will it never be permitted that the Sisters exercise these works by themselves without a companion, nor will they be allowed to exercise these works at night.

Although the Congregation cited above (Franciscans, Mercy, and Dominicans) are doing good work, nevertheless, the number of these Sisters is entirely unequal to the demands of the Vicariate. Nor is there any hope that they will increase in number to satisfy the demands without native Sisters, who once admitted, will undoubtedly increase in vocations daily.

Again means of support will not be lacking, which may be had from daily donations of the faithful or remunerations of the Sisters' labours, or from extraordinary gifts from pious benefactors.

In order that the beginning of this new Congregation may be more efficacious, the Administrator has obtained from the Superior General of the Franciscan Sisters (whose Mother House is in Allegany, New York) that the new Congregation be governed for five years by a professed Sister of the same Order, when a superior general and a mistress of novices is to be chosen from among the natives, unless in the judgment of the Vicar General the government of the new institute should continue to be ruled for another five years by a Franciscan Sister.

The Administrator requests of the Sacred Congregation the faculty to erect canonically this new Institute. In the meantime, awaiting approbation, he will carry on the experiment with seven suitable ladies under a professed Franciscan Sister.

Signed,

Francis J. Kelly, S.J.
Administrator Apostolic[10]

Definite approbation for Sister Humiliana to direct the new institute came from Mother M. Dominica, O.S.F. of St. Elizabeth's Convent, New York, on 22 August 1929.[11] In writing to the administrator apostolic, she reminded him of the desire and intention of Bishop Dinand to establish a community of native Sisters and of his anxiety to obtain Sister Humiliana to direct the training of its members in religious life. In this letter the Mother General granted formal permission for Sister Humiliana to take charge of the new foundation with the understanding that her work with the Community was to be directly and wholly under the guidance of the bishop or his representative relating to both the spiritual and temporal interests of the institute. Later she said Sister M. Michael, O.S.F., would be assigned to assist with school work. Sister Michael never came. Mother M. Dominica made the wise suggestion that no more than six or eight members be admitted in the beginning with the view that when these were formed and had grown accustomed to religious observance, they would serve as examples to subsequent candidates.

Early Days

Every religious institute looks back to the cradle of its birth with nostalgic memories of its early struggles, pioneer experiences, and the unbounded hopes it had for success. Down at 16 Lissant Road, Kingston, was a small cottage owned by a Mary Lawrence, who had agreed to rent it to Mother Humiliana for £8.0.0. per month.[12] Eight pounds sterling loomed as an astronomical sum in the mind of the new superior. She begged here and there to obtain the first month's rent so the cottage was hired and the convent came into being. Cramped convent quarters called for ingenious use of all available space. The room facing Lissant Road served the dual purpose of recreation for the sisters and a parlour for visitors; the room leading off this, a mere 10 feet by 12 feet, had a multiple purpose: at night it was a dormitory for two sisters but they had to rise early and allow it to be used as a sacristy for the priest. After Mass it was turned into a refectory, and as soon as breakfast was finished, it became a classroom. Crowded into another small room were cots for the other three sisters, while the smallest of all, just large enough to hold a bed, was reserved for Mother Humiliana. The chapel could hardly be called a room, for it was only six feet square containing an altar and one kneeling bench for the community.

Five young ladies formed the nucleus of the Lissant Road Community. From here they walked daily to the Franciscan Convent on Duke Street while making a retreat under the direction of Fr. Joseph Dougherty in preparation for their formal founding as a religious congregation.[13] Fortunately, the retreat master buoyed up the discouraged spirits of these pioneers, attacked as they were by wagging tongues predicting an early death to the whole project. Fr. Dougherty urged them to pay no heed to such unfavourable comment, and as Christ had founded his Church amid much adverse criticism, so He would use the example of this new congregation to impress upon Jamaicans the need for indigenous sisters and priests if the Church in this island were to be independent of foreign aid. The retreat was climaxed by the formal reception of candidates: Julia Leon of Spanish Town, Ivy Bogle of Kingston, Rita De Souza of Kingston, Gertrude Narcisse of Above Rocks, and Adina Hamilton of Kingston by Jesuit superior and administrator apostolic Francis J. Kelly into the Franciscan Missionary Sisters of Our Lady of Perpetual Help at 4.00 P.M. on 8 September 1929 at Holy Trinity Cathedral.[14]

Even such serious business as founding a religious congregation has its humourous side. One such episode happened the morning after the inaugural ceremony when after Mass the sisters sat down to breakfast with thoughts of hot coffee and homemade rolls. A surprise awaited them: there was no coffee, no rolls, nor could they detect the slightest sign of activity in the kitchen. Five hungry glances were cast at Sister Perpetua who only at that moment awoke to the remembrance that she has been appointed housekeeper for that week.

A more serious incident occurred sometime later when the sisters discovered that not everybody in Kingston welcomed the new congregation: some were violently opposed to their way of life. Before opening their school in January 1930, the sisters began visiting the sick and poor as part of their religious programme.[15] One afternoon while they were returning from an errand of mercy, a window was raised in Wildman street and a stone hurled at the passing nuns, nearly striking Mother Humiliana.[16]

A newly-established congregation has to discover some means of support. From September to December 1929 the community had depended on alms. When the question of a steady income was proposed to Mother Humiliana, she thought that the solution lay in opening a kindergarten, since no private school of this type was conducted by the Church, and the field was completely free in this area.

Entry into Education

On 21 January 1930 the native sisters ventured into the field of education by opening Holy Childhood Kindergarten School in a tiny room of their overcrowded convent. Five pupils formed the first class; the following week they added two more children—a Chinese boy and a grand-niece of Mother Humiliana. After two years of conducting the school under the crowded conditions of Lissant Road, the sisters were convinced that they had to find more ample accommodations. The memoirs of Mother Humiliana record that a novena was begun to St. Joseph; and on the ninth day an advertisement appeared in *The Daily Gleaner* offering for rent a house at 37 Old Hope Road,

Kingston.[17] Inspection of the premises brought from the owner the surprising statement that the house was for sale rather than for rent, but purchase by the sisters was out of the question. The owner then proposed the alternative that he would rent the house, provided the sisters paid a year's rent in advance. The money was raised, and 37 Old Hope Road became the new site for convent and school. Soon the owner's motive for wanting ready cash became apparent. Shortly after the sisters had occupied the premises, the bailiff appeared to levy all the furnishings because the property had been heavily mortgaged, and the owner was grossly in debt. Mother Humiliana showed the rental receipt to the bailiff, and being of the gentlemanly type he apologized for the error and went to bag his quarry in some other part of the city. This storm passed, and the school settled down to the usual drill of reading, writing, and arithmetic until one fine, hot morning the children reported there was no water. They were correct, for the water commission had shut off the water for nonpayment of rates; as was their custom, they had acted without informing the occupants. A hurried call sent to the Jesuit superior, Charles Arnold, soon had the water running again when he assured the commission of immediate payment of the rates.[18]

The Sisters Move Again

The year at 37 Old Hope Road was drawing to a close; move they must or be evicted by the holder of the heavy mortgage on the property. House hunting once again became part of the daily routine for the sisters, and every possibility was investigated but nothing was found suitable for a school and convent. Fr. Arnold solved the problem by suggesting to the vicar apostolic that he build a convent on the four acres of bush land at the Holy Cross mission, Half Way Tree, St. Andrew.[19] William Spooner completed construction of the convent on 29 March 1932.[20]

Two days later the sisters occupied it and ended their gypsy-like existence. The school was a small dilapidated wooden garage, the property of the Holy Cross Mission which had been converted into two classrooms to meet the opening of the summer term classes. The garage-converted classrooms did not endanger the school's popularity, for enrollment increased to twenty-five pupils.[21]

Not for long did the school remain in the garage. Fr. Joseph Keller, S.J., a former missionary in Jamaica, organized a Little Flower Missionary Club of Boston and sent $400 as his first donation towards a new school building. With this and other donations, the sisters were able to complete a modest classroom building in January 1933.[22] The native congregation was only four years old, yet it had a thriving school and a membership of twelve sisters.[23]

Expansion

Once established, a religious congregation finds itself overburdened with demands on its personnel. Requests are so numerous that it becomes a matter of careful selection to screen the genuinely urgent from the less important. With scarcely enough sisters to properly staff the growing Holy Childhood School, Mother Humiliana received an urgent call from Fr. George McDonald, manager of the government denominational school at White Hall, St. Andrew. He wanted her to send teachers to replace the lay staff, with whom he was having some difficulty. The number of pupils had fallen to twelve, and the government had threatened to withdraw its financial grant unless effective measures were taken to improve the situation. The offer was accepted, and on 15 June 1931 the Blue Sisters made their debut into the government school system. But not until January 1932 were they officially recognized by the government as competent to take full responsibility of the school. With this recognition they received the same salaries as other qualified teachers. This move not only gave them prestige in the teaching profession but also provided the convent with a steady income. Their teaching ability was proved to the government when they raised the number of pupils at White Hall School from twelve to one hundred by April 1932, nine months after Fr. McDonald had called upon their assistance.[24]

Further expansion came in the same year of 1932, when they assumed charge of the parochial school at St. Peter and Paul in St. Andrew. The school had fifty-five pupils, but the sisters were not successful in this venture, for so few students could not financially support a private school. They closed it in 1937.

One of their most successful educational ventures began on 9 September 1941 when Fr. William Coleman, S.J., invited the sisters to take charge of Holy Rosary, a parochial school on Windward Road, Kingston. Here they conducted a school independent of government aid, relying solely on tuition from the pupils. Freedom from government supervision allowed the sisters to conduct the school according to traditional Catholic conventions without being told by the state what curriculum they must follow or what teachers they must hire or what time limits must be placed on religious instruction. Holy Rosary became one of the most influential Catholic schools in Kingston through both academic freedom and its limited enrollment of 458 pupils, thereby allowing the teacher a more personal contact with the pupil, an educational advantage lacking in many government schools whose enrollment reached as high as two thousand.

The next progressive step was taken by Fr. Cornelius Shea, S.J., of the Above Rocks mission, who on 31 October 1944 entrusted St. Mary's Elementary school to Sister Ann Marie, Sister Mary Charles, and Sister Gertrude Maria.[25] The early days at Above Rocks were trying for the sisters, because they lived in very cramped quarters with no modern conveniences. The next pastor made an effort to improve conditions by constructing a two-storey convent of doubtful architectural design which never seemed to be completed. The mission, although only eighteen miles from Kingston, was nevertheless in the bush and its people were extremely poor, eking out a living from ground provisions grown in a sandy soil. Something more than an elementary education was needed for children who found themselves with nothing profitable to do once they completed St. Mary's at the age of fifteen years, so the sisters started a craft centre where they taught the girls the art of weaving native jippi-jappa into straw hats, baskets, and other articles to sell the tourists at the Government Straw Market in Kingston.

Another mission of the Above Rocks type was at Alva, St. Ann, where the sisters began their educational work in the Dry Harbour Mountains at the invitation of Fr. Robert I. Burke, S.J.[26] He assigned the infant school at St. Boniface's mission to them on 31 March 1948. It was not until 1956 that the sisters assumed charge of the government grant-in-aid elementary school in the same compound and received government salaries for their teaching. Two years later, in March 1950, the native congregation ventured into May Pen, the most populous town in the Parish of Clarendon.[27] There, at St. Thomas More Academy, they experienced strong prejudice from the predominantly non-Catholic community which looked upon the sisters as intruders. But constantly meeting these cheerful religious on the streets, in the marketplace, and in the shops, changed the town's hostile attitude to devoted loyalty; indeed, a universal protest greeted a rumour that the sisters might abandon May Pen. Their first convent in May Pen was in a rented house on Storkes Street. In 1960 the pastor, Fr. Philip Branon, S.J., built a convent of modern design near the newly constructed church and rectory on the Fernleigh estate.

Only nine months after taking charge of St. Thomas More Academy, the new congregation moved farther up country to Balaclava, where they opened the first Catholic school in the district on 8 December 1950. Here Sister Margaret Mary, a capable teacher, set a high scholastic standard. So appreciative were the town's people that they sent their children in large numbers to the new institution in preference to other more established schools.

The Church in Jamaica owes much to Bishop Dinand's foresight in establishing a native religious congregation, for remarkable has been their growth from the one tiny classroom on Lissant Road to today's seven modern schools: Holy Childhood in St. Andrew, with classes ranging from kindergarten to high school; St. Thomas Aquinas at White Hall; Holy Rosary, Kingston; St. Mary's, Above Rocks; St. Boniface, Alva; St. Thomas More, May Pen; St. Gabriel's, Balaclava. All these educational institutions justified Dinand's judgment that Jamaica possessed latent vocations which up to his time remained untapped.

Social Work

From its inception, Dinand had planned that the native sisters should engage not only in educational but also in social work. These two objectives were incorporated into their constitutions in 1957, which said that

> The special object is active cooperation in the propagation of the Catholic faith, and the provision for the spiritual and temporal welfare of the sisters:
>
> a) by education of children in schools.
> b) by taking care of the sick in hospitals.
> c) by conducting nurseries for babies, homes for aged women and working girls.[28]

Although from their inception the sisters had engaged in social work by visiting and instructing the poor in their homes, they did not open a home for aged women until Villa Maria was established in a rented house at 75 Half Way Tree Road, St. Andrew, in 4 August 1947.[29] Its aim was to put some measure of happiness into the sunset lives of these good people by providing them with care and pleasant surroundings. A few years later the home was so inadequate that a more spacious residence was opened on 33 Seymour Avenue, St. Andrew.[30] This property was purchased to accommodate the increasing number of aged who could afford to pay something towards their support either from their own savings or by the help of relatives who wanted to take advantage of the Social Centre.

There was another class of aged who were so poor that the sunset of their lives had to be spent in the gloomy surroundings of a government alms house. These unfortunates had engaged the attention of the St. Vincent de Paul Society for several years. Intimate contact with these old people had convinced them of how many people dreaded the prospect of spending their old age as state wards. The Particular Council decided to open a home for them at 72 Half Way Tree Road, St. Andrew, in a residence owned by the Narcisse family. The home, called Ozanam Home for the Aged, was opened 19 July 1953.[31] This new social venture was entrusted to the native sisters, whose growing reputation for such work made them the logical choice. Just as the first home for the aged outgrew its limited accommodations, so the Ozanam Home experienced the same growing pains, and a new building had to be constructed at 38 Mannings Hill Road, St. Andrew.[32]

Another rule of the native congregation read that they were to conduct nurseries for babies. Ever so many mothers in the poorer districts of Kingston found it increasingly necessary to augment their husband's wages by full-time work of their own. What to do with their infants during the day was a constant question. For the most part these tiny children were left in the care of a friendly neighbour whose attention to the child depended largely upon the demands made on her own time; for some children it meant a mere passing glance to see that they were in no serious trouble. To the rescue of these mothers came the Dupont Creche (day nursery), which was opened in that impoverished district of Kingston known as Cockburn Pen on 1 March 1955.[33] Sixty children were placed in the daily care of the native sisters, who provided these infants with substantial meals and more than watchful care. Little by little the purpose for which the congregation was founded was implemented by undertaking the works prescribed by its constitutions.

Mother Humiliana Retires

Mother Humiliana's work with the native congregation was nearing the quarter century mark and the community had grown under her guidance from the original five to fifty. Yet the demands for the services of the sisters in both educational and social work were far beyond their resources. All this was taxing to the strength of Mother Humiliana, who had observed her golden jubilee as a Franciscan on 9 April 1947.[34] It was evident that a younger Franciscan should assume the burden of guiding the native sisters until such time as they might be able to select one of their own as superior. The choice fell on Mother M. Xavier, O.F.S., who assumed the office vacated by Mother Humiliana on 8 September 1951.[35]

Mother Humiliana had accomplished a pioneer work in Jamaica. It was fortunate that she had been selected to guide the first footsteps of the new congregation, since she, as a native Jamaican, understood both the mentality and capabilities of her people. Mother Humiliana was of French-Jamaican ancestry, the third child of Mr. and Mrs. Victor Boileau Sorapure.[36] Agnes Jessie Sorapure was born on 23 April 1875, on Hanover Street where the Kingston Technical School now stands—the site of Le Cun's chapel and the place where he died in 1808. Agnes Jessie Sorapure entered the Franciscan Convent, Duke Street, Kingston, on the feast of St.Raphael, 24 October 1896, and it is recorded that it was at six o'clock in the evening. Six months later, 25 April 1897, Agnes Sorapure received the habit and the name in religion of Sister Mary Humiliana. Her first teaching assignment was one year at St. Aloysius Boys' School, and after profession she moved around the circuit: St. Joseph's Girls' School; St. Catherine's, Spanish Town; a return to St. Joseph's; then St. Anne's, Holy Family, and finally the Immaculate Conception High School, where she was stationed when appointed to form the native congregation.[37]

No one will deny that Mother Humiliana devoted all her energy during the best years of her life to the task of forming young Jamaican ladies into good religious. But, like all pioneers, she came in for her share of criticism. These fault-finders were content with mere words and would never lift a finger to help shape the congregation to their lofty ideals. Their chief criticism was that she admitted girls of the servant class into the community. Under colonialism a distinct brand was placed on such a girl and marked her for life as a domestic, a servant of the plantocracy. Mother Humiliana acknowledged she did admit this type of girl; but what her critics failed to realize was that she never intended that this class of girl should teach. Her plan was that the congregation should have two types: teaching sisters from the upper classes of society, and what she termed 'House sisters' from the lower classes who were to devote their lives to the domestic work of the convent by cooking, washing, and general household work, leaving the teachers free to concentrate all their efforts on education. In her memoirs, Mother Humiliana mentions seven such sisters who performed yeoman service for the congregation. The Jamaican Franciscan Missionary Sisters of Our Lady of Perpetual Help have made remarkable progress as may be seen from the statistics of 1970.[38]

Government Grant-in-Aid Secondary School:	
Holy Childhood High School, St. Andrew	472 pupils
Government Grant-in-Aid Elementary Schools:	
St. Richard's, St. Andrew	794 pupils
St. Mary's, Above Rocks	845 pupils
St. Benedict the Moor, Harbour Head	500 pupils
St. Boniface, Alva	938 pupils

Private Preparatory Schools:	
Holy Childhood, St. Andrew	685 pupils
Holy Rosary, Kingston	448 pupils
St. Thomas More, May Pen	250 pupils
St. Gabriel's, Balaclava	50 pupils
Private Kindergarten School:	
Stella Maris, St. Andrew	60 pupils
Infant Centre:	
St. Boniface, Alva	159 pupils
Social Centres:	
Dupont Creche, Kingston	60 infants
Villa Maria Home for the Aged, St. Andrew	18 ladies
Ozanam Home for Aged Poor, St. Andrew	36 ladies

From the very foundation of the congregation, it was envisaged that one day Jamaicans would assume complete control of the organization. Bishop John J. McEleney, S.J., took this progressive step on 16 September 1961, when the sisters elected Sister Peter Claver their first Mother General.[39] This completed the final step in the great work envisioned by Bishop Dinand in 1928. Bishop Dinand's dream has come true in the Congregation of native sisters he founded, and because of that dream thousands of young Jamaicans will have a better love both for God and country.

Twenty-five

Thomas Addis Emmet, S.J.

The nineteen years from 1930–49 may be characterized as an era of excessive caution in financial matters. In his first missionary post, Thomas A. Emmet had been in charge of the material needs of St. George's College during the Collins regime; to his dying day he carried the memory of that anxious period when impending ruin hung over the whole mission. The very thought of that hectic period was so seared into his memory that it carried the constant warning: never go into debt. "Pay as you go" became the vicariate policy. The individual could initiate projects, could build, only if he assured Emmet that he could finance everything undertaken.

Thomas Addis Emmet was born in Boston, Massachusetts, 23 August 1873, the eighth of nine children of Edward and Julia Emmet. Early in life Thomas was introduced to the world of books, first at Lincoln Grammar School, and later at Boston College High School. After high school he entered the Society of Jesus at Frederick, Maryland, on 15 August 1893. Of his class of twenty-four novices, fifteen were from Boston.

Five years at old Frederick left him with such fond memories that in his declining years he would speak of them with nostalgic emotion. He could recall the Thursday holiday walks which brought him to his favourite spot on the south side of the Monacacy River near Araby, where the juniors would mount a rock-hewn rostrum to imitate the orators of ancient Greece and Rome. Constant practice in public speaking, combined with a natural talent, made Thomas Emmet a polished orator whose cleverness, depth, and maturity of thought held his audience captive.

Frederick was followed by three years at Woodstock where Thomas studied philosophy and the physical sciences. Then came a teaching period, first at St. Francis Xavier's, New York City, then at Georgetown, Washington, D.C., where for three years he acted as prefect in the preparatory department. Regency completed, he returned to Woodstock for his course in theology, which culminated in ordination to the priesthood by Cardinal Gibbons on 30 July 1909. The following three years were again spent at Georgetown where he filled the position of dean of men.

His tertianship was made at Tullamore, Ireland, the country of his Protestant ancestor patriots, Robert and Thomas Addis Emmet. After tertianship he resumed his duties at Georgetown as dean of men; in this difficult office, he won the confidence and respect of hundreds of young men by the tactful manner in which he managed the student body. As long as he lived he felt a deep affection for Georgetown University and the many friends he had won in Washington.

When Emmet read the status for the year 1916, he found himself assigned to St. George's College, Kingston, as administrator. For the next four years he lived at Winchester Park where he not only administered the material needs of the Jesuit community but also took his turn acting as missionary at Morant Bay, May Pen, and Mandeville. His extraordinary preaching ability drew large crowds of both Catholics and non-Catholics to Holy Trinity Cathedral, where a good sermon was held in high esteem.

The Jamaican appreciation of good oratory belies the distorted picture the public receives from popular mission propaganda. The civilization that is Jamaica is deeply rooted in more than three hundred years of English culture; those years have formed the Jamaican into a courteous, respectful, well-mannered person. Such an audience appreciated the eloquence of Thomas Emmet.

After four years in Jamaica, Emmet was recalled in 1921 to the Maryland-New York Province, where his talent for preaching was utilized in conducting popular missions in New York and the Middle Atlantic States. In this capacity he continued to labour until 1923, when he became headmaster of Georgetown Preparatory School. Once again he was in his beloved Washington, where he spent the next six years grappling with the problems of a growing institution—problems of construction, problems of curriculum, and even the problems of the individual students. All were thrown upon his shoulders for a final decision. So efficiently did he solve these questions that Georgetown Preparatory School became one of the leading schools of its type in the country.

Completing his duty as headmaster, Emmet returned to popular missionary work in November 1929. While conducting a retreat for the Sisters of Charity, he received word on 28 June 1930 that the Holy See had chosen him to succeed Bishop Dinand as vicar apostolic of Jamaica.

Since the office of vicar apostolic carried with it episcopal dignity, Thomas A. Emmet was consecrated titular bishop of Tuscamia 21 September 1930, at St. Mary's Church, Boston, by His Eminence, William Cardinal O'Connell, assisted by the Very Reverend John W. McNamara, auxiliary bishop of Baltimore and Rt. Rev. John B. Peterson, Auxiliary Bishop of Boston. The sermon was preached by the future cardinal, Richard Cushing.[1] Before the advent of air service, the popular medium of travel to Jamaica was a United Fruit steamer. On Monday morning, 20 October 1930, the new vicar apostolic arrived in Kingston aboard the *S.S. Sixaola*. In the afternoon, at a service in Holy Trinity Cathedral, the brief appointing him to his office was read; thus Emmet took formal possession of his vicariate.

Emmett Takes up Duties in Jamaica

In his address to the people, the bishop expressed deep gratitude to God for the honour conferred by the Holy See. He thanked his friends and his flock for their sincere congratulations and prayers, and expressed his deep appreciation to Francis J. Kelly, S.J., for loyal service rendered the vicariate during the illness of Bishop Dinand.

Festivities to welcome Bishop Emmet were concluded the following afternoon with a civic celebration when Sir William Morrison, a non-Catholic, presided over the vast concourse of Jamaicans assembled at Winchester Park to listen to prominent citizens voice the praises of the new bishop. As the afternoon sun sank behind the tropical palms, the cheers ended; Bishop Emmet was now ready to settle down to the everyday routine of vicariate business.

The decade beginning in 1929 opened with financial disaster and closed with social unrest. Jamaican merchants who had invested in the New York stock market awoke one day to find their golden nuggets were worthless dross; even the merchant who had no New York investments found himself engulfed in the oncoming tidal wave of the Great Depression, with tight credit and no market for his produce. Bananas, coconuts, coffee, and sugar went begging for a buyer. Caught in this maelstrom was the Church with twenty-three missionary priests and one hundred sisters to support, and with churches and chapels to maintain. Funds from the United States all but came to a stand-still, and contributions from the faithful in Jamaica reached a new low. Squarely upon the shoulders of Bishop Emmet fell the unenviable task of supporting the vicariate. Carefully nurturing his slender resources, Emmet successfully weathered the threatened storm. He had learned the lesson of those dark financial days of his early career of 1917. The Church was fortunate to have at its helm in this period a missionary of caution and prudence in financial matters.

At the end of the decade, another obstacle lay in his path: social unrest was spreading throughout Jamaica. The world of colonialism was changing, with a new era of nationalism appearing on the horizon. Colonials were no longer satisfied with being subjects; they would be rulers, governing themselves and their native lands. Colonialism had ruled Jamaica for some 275 years, but a new nation was being born from the pains of a disturbed social order.

Initial rumblings were heard from the labouring classes. Prices of food and clothing were on the rise, and wages were at a standstill. The labourer demanded that his starvation wage of two shillings per day be increased to three shillings; the old, standard reply came from the great sugar estates that a one shilling increase would ruin their business. Strikes, riots, violence spread throughout the land. A weak colonial governor, Sir Edward Denham, unable to solve the general unrest, succumbed under the strain and was buried at sea 3 June 1938.

Unique Social Service to Jamaica

The British Colonial Office eyed with concern the growing unrest in Jamaica. Into the melee it threw the best it had, the most experienced and capable governor in its service, Sir Arthur Richards. Worldwide experience in all corners of the globe marked him as a man who could, with diplomatic finesse, manage a difficult situation. Fourteen times he invoked the Paramount Importance Clause to stabilize the government of Jamaica. Quick to perceive a state of affairs, courageous to act with adamant determination, he would allow no difficulty to stand in his way if he thought the situation could be remedied to the benefit of the community.

One crux was the government leper colony at Spanish Town. The office of governor brought Richards into close contact with all government institutions in the colony. Periodic visitations provided him with more firsthand information than all the official reports which crossed his desk. A visit to Spanish Town Leper Colony shocked Richards. He saw squalor, bad management, lack of proper medical attention, and utter indifference for the afflicted inmates. As governor, he could not allow such a situation to continue. He must find a remedy. His first act was to hold prolonged investigations into conditions at the Leper Home. It was suggested that the institution be removed from Spanish Town to another part of the island, but second thought showed that Spanish Town possessed so many natural advantages that Richards decided to allow it to remain on that site. But he did propose sweeping changes in the institution's organization. This could best be effected, he thought, if the colony were entrusted to a religious society experienced in the work of caring for lepers. Two possibilities were explored: the Salvation Army and a Catholic religious congregation. Enquiries were sent to the head of the Salvation Army and to Bishop Emmet, asking the conditions under which they might be prepared to assume charge of the lepers.

On 22 July 1939, Emmet replied to Richards, saying that he had an interest in the matter and was making enquiries among religious specializing in the work.[2] Richards favoured a congregation of sisters to take charge of the lepers. He had good reason for his preference since, as governor of the Fiji Islands, he had witnessed the heroic work of the Marist Sisters among the lepers. Richards asked Emmet to bring this congregation to Jamaica.

Fortuitous circumstances favoured the request. The Marists had established themselves in the archdiocese of Boston, and in charge of the Propagation of the Faith for that archdiocese was Fr. Richard Cushing, friend and fellow townsman of Emmet. The urgency of Richard's request was pointed to Cushing, who set the wheels in motion for the introduction of the sisters into Jamaica.

Proposal to Government

Steps for securing the Marists progressed rapidly. On 5 March 1940, His Excellency Governor Richards sent a message to the legislative council informing that body that the government proposed to improve conditions at the leper home and, that as a result of this decision, representatives of the Marists had visited Jamaica in mid-July 1939 to examine conditions at firsthand and to exchange views with government.

The sisters agreed to undertake the work on a nonreligious basis as a work of mercy; they would serve as government employees at a salary of £150 per year for each sister and would replace the present superintendant and the matron, managing the institution themselves under the general control of a government medical officer. The home would be considered as a government nonsectarian institution under the usual financial control; should the government approve, the sisters would be prepared to take charge any time after 1 May 1940.[3]

In addressing the Legislative Council, Richards said he was satisfied with the proposed arrangements which, if followed, would result in considerable improvement to the Leper Home in the care and comfort of the inmates. If Sir Arthur Richards thought that the mere proposal of his plan to place the Marist sisters in charge of the Leper Home would win unanimous approval from the Legislative Council, he was due for an astounding surprise. He had not reckoned with that formidable foe, bigotry, the same bigotry that had raised its head against the opening of St. George's College ninety years before and now manifested itself against the sisters.

On 8 March 1940, five days after Richards had revealed his plan to the Legislative Council, he wrote privately to Bishop Emmet.

> I thought I had lost all power of feeling surprised, but Jamaica is unique. . . . It must be the original home of envy, hatred, malice and all uncharitableness. I am very angry and a little sad about the opposition which has been engendered and at the contemptible efforts to stimulate both racial and religious prejudice. However, it does not embarrass me in the least. I am determined to do this for the lepers and will not allow any golden opportunity to be destroyed. My fear is that the Sisters may not be willing to come if the atmosphere is so heated.[4]

Richards was not a man to allow bigotry to defeat his social plan to improve the lazaretto. Heated opposition turned the discussion into an all-day debate on Wednesday, 27 March 1940, when members from Kingston, St. Andrew, Trelawny, St. Ann, Manchester, and Clarendon opposed the government's wish to admit the Marists. Publicly they protested they were not swayed by religious bigotry, yet the evidence was so clear that even the press called it a religious debate. There was some opposition to the opposition. This came from McNeil, the member from St. Catherine, in whose constituency the Leper Home was located. He had long campaigned for improvements at the institution; if his colleagues were violently opposed, he was just as enthusiastically in favour of the sisters. Carrying his enthusiasm to the floor, he berated his fellow members and proclaimed his faith in the Marists in clear, unmistakable language. There was no doubt where McNeil stood; if Kingston, St. Andrew, Trelawny, St. Ann, Manchester, Hanover, and Clarendon were opposed, St. Catherine was just as strongly in favour.

At this point Governor Richards asked that he be heard by the council on the subject.

> I think at this stage it is perhaps desirable for me to intervene because I am, in a peculiar sense, personally responsible for these arrangements. I found the Lepers' Home in a state that admittedly is a public disgrace. The doctor told me that it would be powerless to remedy that without an expert staff and not a staff which is liable to come today and go tomorrow, but a staff he could rely on for continuous and expert and devoted work. So, obviously, the first thing to do was to engage that staff.
>
> It is here that my own personal experience came in. My first experience was in the Malay States and the Straits Settlements, in the Far East. There we had originally two leper islands where lepers were sent by the government and housed in huts of native construction. They had proved

difficult to administer. The lepers were miserable and suitable supervision was hard to obtain. The Federated Malay States Government then decided to build a model leper settlement within ten miles of Kuala Lumpur, the capital town of the Federated Malay States. Large sums of money were spent on it, and in time it represented everything that money could buy. But it was not a complete success. It had too much atmosphere of a prison, and the difficulties of a proper subordinate supervision were immense. It required something more than good housing and normal performance of duty which a government salary can buy to make a leper home other than a dismal lazaretto.

My next experience was in Borneo where we kept our lepers again on an island in native huts. There too we could not obtain proper supervision. Money alone cannot buy continuous devotion in such distressing surroundings. This settlement, despite visits from kindly persons in addition to the doctor, was a place of unhappy exile. I ask you to follow me across the world to West Africa. In my travels up country in Gambia I found lepers in every village sharing the same huts and using the same pots and spreading contagion. We organized one or two leper village camps and succeeded in a certain amount of voluntary segregation under regular visits from the doctor, but of course there was no proper supervision and attendants could not be induced to take the jobs. These camps did something to prevent the indiscriminate spreading of contagion and helped to arrest the disease in the sufferers, but I cannot claim that they represented much hope of cure or were really more than a beginning. We aimed at educating the people to regard leprosy as an avoidable thing, to be controlled by segregation, and ultimately to be cured by the institution of a properly equipped Home.

At this stage I must take you across to the Pacific. I found there that one of the Fiji Islands had been set aside as a Leper's Home, a small island of great beauty, a few hours sail from Suva, the capital town of Fiji. This leper settlement received lepers from all the Pacific Islands under the administration of Fiji, New Zealand, and Australia. It is managed by the Government of Fiji with a resident Medical Officer and an administrative staff of Marist Sisters. I wish you could see those wards, gentlemen, and compare them with the squalid misery of our own Leper Home, or even, if the comparison is not fair, with the soulless material efficiency of the Malayan Home. Clean, airy, beautifully kept wards, where advanced cases are not mixed with the early stages . . .

In recognition of their work, His Majesty the King, has bestowed the Order of the British Empire on the Mother Superior whose visit here in July was the cause of so much criticism in this country. . . .

One point more, before I finish—the most important of them all. The government aims at stamping out leprosy in this island. I have medical opinion solidly behind me in saying that there is no reason why in a period of two or three generations we should not free Jamaica from this scourge. It is perfectly possible in so small an area. But an essential condition is a Model Leper Home where patients would go willingly in the confident expectation of loving care and reasonable comfort and, for those in the early stages, the hope of cure. Will you allow irrelevant sectarian jealousy to deflect you from your duty to the present and to posterity? I am sure you will not do this thing, Gentlemen.

At this point, one of the elected members interrupted the governor with the remark that he was preaching to them. But Richards ignored him and concluded his talk by saying

> We do not realize—we cannot realize, what life in a Leper Settlement is like. It is not so much the fear of possible infection. That seems a small thing compared with the pain, the pity, and the disgust of the surroundings, and the atmosphere of affliction, disease and physical disgrace. Butt ends of human beings, some of them almost unrecognizable, but still breathing, still thinking, still remembering.
>
> Gentlemen, we are not all expected to be Marist Sisters. A man may conceive his duty more narrowly—he may love his comforts better, but none will cast a stone at him for that. But in the name of public decency, Gentlemen, in the name of all that is left of chivalry, do not let us minimize such work or say that £150 a year is princely to pay for it.
>
> I appeal to you, Gentlemen, in Mercy's name, in the name of suffering humanity, for the sake of the men and women—yes, and children too, of your own race, afflicted through no fault of their own with the most loathsome disease known to man—and I am sure that I shall not make this appeal in vain.[5]

Richards did not make his appeal in vain, for immediately the whole legislature broke into thunderous applause of approval. It was impossible for the council to answer Sir Richard's wide experience by arguments from the imaginary fear of Catholic Sisters. When on 27 March 1940 the question was put to a vote, it was clearly in favour of the Marists by twenty to seven. Given a little time, the sisters changed the Spanish Town lazaretto into a model leper home rivalling in cleanliness, efficiency, and heroic work their institution in the Fiji Islands.

Hardly had the Leper Home controversy cooled than another incident provoked contention. In order to understand this event, we must trace our steps to the year 1937 when on Saturday, 23 October at 3.30 o'clock in the afternoon, a fierce fire destroyed the Franciscan convent and schools on Duke Street, Kingston. All seven buildings in the block were reduced to ashes. The Franciscan community was evacuated to Alvernia on the Old Hope Road, where, three days after the fire, the schools were reopened.

One year later, in 1938, Mother M. Joan, O.S.F., began reconstruction of St. Joseph's Girls' School, St. Joseph's Infant School, and St. Aloysius' Boys' School on the fire-scarred Duke Street. Facilities for the high school were so cramped at Duke Street that more spacious accommodations had to be found.

At this time Constant Spring Hotel in St. Andrew, owned and operated by the colonial government, was for sale. Tourist trade had dropped to a depressingly low level, and, with few guests, the hotel had lost money over a period of years. The government was willing to sell for £45,000. Mother Joan approached Governor Richards with an offer to purchase the Constant Spring Hotel, believing it provided ideal school premises. On 31 August 1940, the Franciscan Sisters Council of Allegany, New York, concurred with Mother Joan's decision and made a definite bid to purchase the hotel. Their plan was then made known to Richards, assuring His Excellency they would continue their educational work on the premises for the good of the Jamaican youth.

The earlier letter of 30 July and the later one of 31 August 1940, were passed on by Richards to the colonial secretary with the request to have the details of purchase drawn up in a formal agreement. The general outline was to follow the contents of the correspondence between Governor Richards and Mother Joan which had begun on 23 March 1940. The price was to be £40,000 plus the site of St. Aloysius's School premises on East Street, Kingston. This would equate the price of £45,000 asked by the government.

Once the sisters' intention to purchase became public, the dormant interest of other parties in Jamaica was suddenly awakened. Richards replied to these interested parties telling them that since the sisters had begun to make definite negotiations, he would not now be in a position to consider a counter offer from the Chamber of Commerce and the Imperial Association. If these interested bodies wished to remedy their past indifference, they must negotiate directly with the sisters; only if the sisters expressed a readiness to withdraw from the purchase would Richards enter into the matter. Neither Richards nor Emmet could see sufficient reason why the sisters should withdraw from the purchase. This counter offer seemed insincere to Richards. Joseph G. Keiffer, a representative of the Chamber of Commerce and the Imperial Association, approached Richards, saying that he had a good offer from one Mr. Christie, a Canadian with large sums to invest. It appeared from conversation that Christie would open and operate the hotel during the war, but he hoped that a local group would take it over and finance it. If this failed, Christie might, though reluctantly, finance it himself. Added to this was a further request from Keiffer that the government cancel taxes on the hotel during the war.

Amid all this verbiage Richards repeated his statement that he would act with reason, and would only consider a new situation if the sisters offered to withdraw; the negotiations could then be reopened for a new offer to purchase. In any case, Keiffer was told to negotiate with the sisters because Richards could not forecast decisions on a mere hypothesis. In a letter to Emmet, Richards remarked that he was not allowing this controversy to alter his blood pressure.[6] Richards was not the only one bothered by these champions of the commonweal. Now it was Emmet's turn. Pressure was brought to bear on the bishop that he might dissuade the sisters from purchasing. Herbert G. De Lisser, editor of *The Daily Gleaner,* acting as a representative of the Chamber of Commerce and the Imperial Association, was sent to Emmet. Emmet wisely replied that the Franciscan Order was recognized as an independent corporation in both canon and civil law, and that the incorporation of that body was separate from the Roman Catholic bishop. Hence Emmet pointed out to De Lisser that he had no alternative but to abstain from interfering unwarrantedly in this matter and advised De Lisser to deal directly with the mother superior of the Franciscan sisters.[7]

Not content with contact on the local level, the opponents sent delegates to Rev. Mother Jean Marie, O.S.F., in Allegany, New York. On 31 August 1940, Mother Jean Marie revealed the details of this visit in a letter to Bishop Emmet. The unwelcome visitors had come and gone. Trying to be gracious to them without yielding to their entreaties had strained the diplomatic suavity of the sisters.

A prominent Jamaican Catholic arrived first, saying that it was the wish of his party that he be the first to present himself for the conference. Evidently, thought Mother Jean Marie, his religion was to be used as a softener to make the sisters benevolent. The following day the British consul of New York accompanied him. They were an insistent pair. It appeared that they wished the sisters to live in the hotel for a few years or give it up altogether. They argued that the sisters were greatly harming the general public by purchasing the hotel and turning it into a school.

This point the sisters failed to see. Weren't they merely trying to find a suitable place for a high school where they might educate Jamaican girls? This could hardly be considered as harmful to the island. The sisters had spent close to a century educating Jamaicans; there should be no protest if they wanted to continue this education in a more spacious location.

Such were the replies of Mother Jean Marie to the representatives of the Chamber of Commerce and the Imperial Association. One more point the sisters made clear to the delegates was that they themselves first approached Governor Richards with the offer to purchase; he did not make the initial move. This was to prevent rumours to the contrary. Only one concession would Mother Jean Marie make: she allowed the delegates to draft their proposition, which she promised to present to the Franciscan Council. She did this but the council rejected their proposal.[8]

One last attempt to stop the sale was made. A caveat was placed on the sale, delaying action, while a cable was sent to Mr. Becket of the British Colonial Office. It stated that there was serious widespread concern over the conversion of the Constant Spring Hotel to a Catholic school, claiming without foundation that a unanimous opinion favoured cancellation of the sale, and that the Chamber of Commerce had succeeded in obtaining a counteroffer of £45,000 from a Canadian company prepared to guarantee Constant Spring as a hotel in perpetuity, and further bemoaning the fact that the Chamber of Commerce and the Imperial Association had unsuccessfully sent representatives to New York to persuade the sisters to cancel the negotiations. It also noted that both governor and bishop had refused to use their influence to have the sisters withdraw from the sale and it also hinted that secret negotiations had been conducted between the government and the sisters without reference to the Legislative Council, the Privy Council, or the Tourist Board. It claimed that the government had no right to make an important decision without consulting the taxpayers' representatives; if the sale were not cancelled, the question should be taken up in the House of Commons as a test case involving the democratic rights of British Colonial subjects.[9]

Not content with protesting openly, the disgruntled representatives undertook a whispering campaign. The familiar propaganda was so overdone that some members of the Legislative Council became tired of being threatened and cajoled. The member from Manchester related an amusing story to Richards. He was present when a number of men were discussing the Constant Spring affair. One witless fellow asserted that he knew for a fact that the governor had received £2,000, and each elected member of the council who supported him was given £100 from the Catholic mission. Richard's answer was that he thought the division of the spoils decidedly unequal, and he had no idea that Bishop Emmet was so financially reckless.

Any chance that the sale would be stopped was slim, for the matter was already in the hands of lawyers and the colonial secretary. Richards took action to have the caveat removed. Final success for the sisters could hardly be doubted, for the Privy Council had unanimously endorsed the governor's action.

Mother Joan, the Franciscan superior in Jamaica, proceeded with legal documents which the colonial secretary signed, closing the negotiations in favour of the Franciscans.[10]

The protectors of the commonweal had to be satisfied with the comment in *The Daily Gleaner* dated 16 November 1940. "So the fate of our lovely hotel is sealed. Constant Spring has been legally transferred to the Franciscan Sisters and the public opinion in this island flouted by the Government and the Catholics."[11]

A Christian Design for Living

Back in the 1940s Fr. Raymond Sullivan, S.J., made up his mind to remedy the deplorable housing conditions found among the very poor of his Brown's Town missions. Thatched one-room wattlehuts where the poor were born, spent their lives, and died were hardly conducive to high Christian morality. One bed—the family bed—one chair at most and a tiny table were all that could be squeezed into these miserable, ten foot square, huts.

Fr. Sullivan had merely to consult government census statistics for the officially recognized fact that seventy percent of the children of Jamaica were born out of wedlock. If these one-room shacks were not the cause, at least they were a strong contributing factor to this frightening moral condition. Sullivan was one missionary who was not content to sit down and let a problem work itself out. If there was an issue he must solve it, and here was a very vexing problem within his own mission.

Eleven miles from Brown's Town, on the road to Kingston, was a large property known as Chippenham Park. Here, Sullivan thought, would be an ideal spot to establish a model Christian community, so he acquired 115 acres in 1940 to construct one hundred model homes in a Christian homestead. Begging $6,000 from friends to pay for the land, he had the property surveyed and cut into lots of one acre for each home. On this one acre of rich soil, sufficient vegetables could be grown for each family's table use. But costs were mounting and the survey had added another $1,000 to the debt. Some organization had to be formed to collect funds. Fortunately, Sullivan's two brothers, Russell and Harold, both Jesuits, came to his rescue. An office, opened at 755 Boylston Street, Boston, Massachusetts, became the focal point for raising funds. Possessed of the same inexhaustible energy as Raymond, his brothers collected $82,971 by 1 June 1952, just four years after ground had been broken for Holy Name Homestead.

Before building could begin, a cement-block factory and a storehouse had to be set up, together with a catchment and reservoir capable of holding 250,000 gallons of water. This cost $4,216, while another $3,200 was used to purchase woodworking machinery for shaping beams, cutting and planing lumber for floors, doors and windows. Once the preliminary necessities had been obtained, actual construction of the model houses began. For a description Fr. Sullivan had this to say:

> In a mountainous area where one or two-room houses are the rule, these modern, moral homes have four bedrooms, a large combination living and dining room, an inside kitchen and bathroom, front and back porches and electricity. In these buildings any timber used is seasoned, native hardwood. In an area where people buy water, four gallons at a time, each family has a 1200 gallon overhead concrete tank. In drought periods each home can obtain water from a quarter million gallon reservoir, centrally located in the Holy Name township. Each home has running water, kitchen, toilet, basin and shower conveniences hitherto unknown in this area. Each home is surrounded by its own acre of arable land where food for its own consumption is grown.[12]

No down payment was made by these very poor people on the homes. One dollar a week was all that was asked from each family with taxes and insurance included in this dollar. After twenty-five years the family would own house and land. All payments made by home owners were set aside in a revolving fund to build other homes and thus keep the scheme going indefinitely.

By 1 January 1952, twenty-two model homes had been constructed. This was the result of hard, daily labour of one missionary over a four-year period. Unfortunately, internal difficulties brought this laudable project to a standstill. There it remains, with seventy-eight houses still on the planning board awaiting the day when the original scheme for abetting the poor will receive a more favourable review for its intrinsic merits. (Government has purchased the unused land for its own housing scheme, 1978.)

Life at the Homestead

For humans who seldom ventured beyond their shacks and native hills, Holy Name Homestead was a new experience. But from this experience arose sociological problems, since it demanded an adaptation of the family to a higher social status. This meant change, and change is always irksome to adults grown accustomed to a particular culture set in a particular environment. Into the homestead they carried the social customs of the bush. Back in the hills they had cultivated small patches of never-varied vegetables for their own personal use. If they sought work it was within the district where they lived in order to supply themselves with a few shillings of ready cash. Life after dark was spent at the crossroads rum shop where, under flickering kerosene lamps, all problems, local and international, were facilely solved. Life was easy. There was no serious competition, no overvaulting ambition. With just enough clothes to cover their backs and just enough food to satisfy the pangs of hunger, these simple people lived simple lives.

They found the four-bedroom house at the homestead such a luxury that many wished to live in one room and rent the remainder to other families. Why not? They had been living in one-room houses for generations. In order to forestall any such scheme, the homestead tenants had to sign a formal agreement. They were to use the dwelling for residential purposes under the following conditions:

> Not to cook elsewhere than in the room provided for use as a kitchen. To keep all buildings and lands in a thoroughly sanitary state and in substantial repair. . . . Not to make any alterations whatever, temporary or otherwise, to existing buildings or lands, not enclose any verandah or gallery, and not to erect any other house or building on the land, nor carry out any repairs without the written consent of the landlord (pastor).[13]

Learning to care for the homestead property was just one area where the obvious had to be stressed. This, fortunately, could be controlled by a set of rules, but what could not be conventionalized was the inner man. Many carried into their new environment the lack of personal ambition and a lack of pride of attaining a reasonable goal in life. They were still content with their vegetable patches, their occasional day's work. Their social life still centred around the village rum shop, while the children of these ambitionless fathers were inclined to grow up with the same lackadaisical outlook on life. In contrast to these unfortunate creatures were the families who took just pride in caring for their homes, who worked at steady jobs, and who were intent upon sending their children to high school, even if it entailed much sacrifice. The future of the homestead will, undoubtedly, be built upon these latter.

While Fr. Sullivan was in the process of planning his Holy Name Homestead, World War II was in progress and had an effect upon Jamaica, for it provided a place of refuge for civilians dwelling on the Rock—that impregnable British bastion, Gibraltar—who found themselves unwanted in the land of their birth lest they prove an obstacle to military action. In July 1940 Gibraltar could no longer guarantee the safety of civilians, and another place had to be found. Some were transported to England, and Jamaica was asked to take her share. When Governor Richards received the official request from the British secretary of state, he enlisted the aid of Fr. Thomas Feeney, S.J., Jesuit superior and acting vicar apostolic. Most of the evacuees were Catholics.

The government acquired 250 acres of choice St. Andrew land in the district of Mona for a camp for the Gibraltarians, where they were to settle for the duration of the war in an environment much like their mountainous home, for the backdrop of the Blue Mountains would be a constant reminder of Gibraltar.

A group of two thousand were due in September 1940, another two thousand shortly afterwards. But, as with many wartime arrangements, the first evacuees numbering 1,100 did not arrive until late October. This gave the Public Works Department breathing space to draw plans, engage contractors, and perform the amazing feat of constructing fully-furnished accommodations for four thousand people within seven weeks.

The first evacuees to disembark at Kingston gave the impression of cheerfulness and gratitude to the British Government for its solicitous care. The second set of arrivals, four hundred in number, came on 26 October where an orderly procedure, due in no small measure to the cheerful conduct of the evacuees, brought them in record time from the ship to Camp Gibraltar where relatives and friends gave them a tumultuous welcome. Children jumped on the sides of the buses, their ebullient Latin spirits so impatient that they could not wait for the bus doors to open. So happy was the show of welcome that the arrivals had to push their way through the enthusiastic crowd.

For living accommodations long huts of twenty-eight rooms, fourteen on either side, had been constructed with open verandahs running on both sides of the living quarters. Three large recreation rooms complete with stage and dressing rooms were part of the camp facilities with one of these recreation rooms used as a Catholic chapel, for nearly 95 percent of the Gibraltarians were Catholics, while the remainder was divided between the Anglican and Jewish faiths. This large Catholic majority prompted Richards to ask the Catholic authorities to provide personnel for religious, educational and recreational services.

The camp administration covered a variety of offices: commissariat, municipal services, medical and dental, accounting department, stores, sanitation, canteen, police, post, telegraph and savings bank. Most important of these services was that of the commissariat which was responsible for three dining rooms and three kitchens where fourteen hundred evacuees were served daily in cafeteria style.

Other facilities offered to the evacuees consisted of an eight-room infirmary and two other huts converted into wards with a capacity of 120 beds under the supervision of two Dominican sisters aided by young ladies of the camp who went into training for the nursing profession. The canteen consisted of a dry-goods department where clothes and shoes were sold, a general store which combined grocery, stationery, candy, and tobacco shops with an added drug store. This facility offered employment to nine evacuees and two natives, while a number of evacuees were recruited to keep the grounds in condition by cutting the grass, planting shrubs, trees and flowers—all with the idea that there should be no idle hands among those physically able to work.

The spiritual life of the camp was well taken care of by one daily Mass and three Masses on Sunday; sodalities for men and women, Sacred Heart devotions, missions, novenas, and retreats which gave a Catholic atmosphere to their exile.

For the school, six sisters were employed: two Franciscans, two Sisters of Mercy, and two from the native congregation. Classes were opened in January 1941, with 331 pupils. Since most of the adult evacuees spoke only Spanish, evening classes were conducted for those who wished to study English. Although British subjects, they required the services of priests who spoke Spanish. Fortunately, there were five such missionaries in Jamaica: William Feeney, Leo Butler, John Buckley, Thomas Hennessey, and John Williams, all Jesuits.

The evacuees left for home in October 1944, writing into their record ninety-three baptisms, fifty-two confirmations, nine marriages, and ninety-three burials.

Five years after the departure of these evacuees, on 3 April 1949, Bishop Emmet resigned. The times through which he had guided the Church had been fraught with major difficulties. In 1930, when he assumed office, there were only twenty priests in Jamaica. Eight were assigned to eight country mission stations and these eight ministered to thirty-eight substations outside Kingston. From 1931–38 there was a slight growth in manpower; but in 1939 ten men were added to the Jamaican mission. The following year eight more men brought up the total to fifty-four, the largest number ever assigned to the mission until then. During this period the main mission stations increased to eleven, and the substations to sixty-one.[14]

Lack of manpower had been one difficulty, but the Church had a more subtle adversary: the civic and social milieu in which she found herself in this island. The milieu was colonialism, waging its last-ditch fight to maintain its status, but strong enough during the whole of Emmet's regime to have a decided effect on the social order.

Under British colonialism the Church occupied, at best, an inferior place in civic and social life. The Anglican Church, though disestablished, was by consent of government always accorded the place of honour at all civic and social functions. It reinforced a caste mentality in the colonials. In their mind the Catholic Church did not fit into the highest echelon, for few of its members were among the social, financial, or professional elect. Anglicanism was a fortress whose strong walls the Catholic Church could not breach, for it was protected by colonial governors and others in high positions in the colony.

This had a psychological effect. The Catholic Church had little attraction for those in the upper classes of society; as a result, there were few converts among them. So the Church turned to the lower social classes for the majority of her conversions. It was slow work, with instructions ranging from a hundred or so in the convert classes to a mere handful in remote country stations. Most converts had a minimum of education—graduates of the elementary school system at the age of fifteen years. This postulated knowledge of the faith gleaned from a penny catechism; this slight knowledge was the most they could grasp. The whole Church, for the most part, rested on the lower classes; she had to adapt her instructions to this level. This meant there was no serious teaching in the field of philosophy or the heights of theology.

Such restriction also deterred vocations. Catholic boys had only one high school—St. George's College—where enrollment in this period was never high and where no serious effort was made to foster the badly needed vocations to the diocesan clergy. A few graduates entered the Society of Jesus.

The crunch was the small number of graduates and its inadequate faculty, for its teaching staff in 1930 consisted of thirteen Jesuits provided by the New England Province, and two native laymen. This was an unsatisfactory situation for the school depended upon a foreign country for its core faculty. Again, the short periods of service of those assigned caused a rapid turnover of personnel, much to the detriment of the efficiency of the institution. If effective missionary work was to be done, this bottleneck had to be broken. This would come in the following regime.

Emmett Resigns

The Church, like any organization in which humans play a part, bears careful scrutiny periodically. Such business-like procedure helps maintain efficiency within the human element. Is progress being made? If not, why not? Are her leaders functioning efficiently or not? These were the questions Bishop Edward Meyers, auxiliary bishop of Westminster, had to ask himself as official representative of the Holy See to make a visitation of the Church in the Caribbean.

It had been known for some time that Emmet's health was poor. Since that day of 10 January 1937, when he collapsed celebrating Mass in thanksgiving for the hundredth anniversary of the vicariate, he had found it increasingly difficult to carry the burden of office. Several months after Meyers' visitation Emmet was informed of the unfavourable tenor of his report; Emmet mailed his resignation to Rome on 17 October 1948. It was accepted, but he was asked to remain at his post until a successor might be appointed.

Emmet left Jamaica at the end of March 1950. On Thursday evening, 5 October 1950, he collapsed at the New England provincial's residence in Boston. He died of a coronary thrombosis within minutes.[15]

Twenty-six

Social Order 1938–1966

When a definitive history of Jamaica is written, historians will probably designate 1938 as the decisive year, the pivotal year in which the old order of oligarchic rule by plantocracy and powerful business interests yielded to the more democratic rule by the man in the street, the labourer in the cane and banana field, and the stevedore on the docks. It will be remembered as a year of the most momentous social revolution since the days of emancipation, a corollary to the 1838 event, manifesting its logical effect a century later to the very year. It gave to emancipation the maturity of democratic government wherein neither wealth, nor planters' interests, nor ancient family name would be the prerequisite to sit in legislative councils. Through universal suffrage the common man would make the laws of the land.

However, 1938 marked the birth not the completion of this social revolution; fulfillment would only come after many years of slow advances. This new constitutional era was ushered in by what began as a mere local labour dispute at the British-owned sugar estate of Tate and Lyle at Frome, Westmoreland. On this estate a new central sugar factory was being constructed, and labourers demanded four shillings in place of their disreputable wages of two shillings per day. Even in 1938 two shillings per day could hardly keep a working man from starvation, not to speak of his trying to support a family and live according to any decent social standard. When their demands were not met, one thousand men refused to work, bringing the operation of the entire estate to a standstill. The *Daily Gleaner* reported that "On Tuesday morning, May 3rd, at 8.00 o'clock in the morning, all hell broke loose at Frome; a full-blooded riot is now in progress."[1]

Men and women armed with everything from machetes to revolvers, exploded into mob violence, leaving the police no alternative save to fire on the rioters, killing four, wounding nine, and sending eighty-nine to jail. Throughout the Frome countryside people were in an angry mood: cars were stopped, occupants molested, and the unruly element joined forces with the strikers to create a Roman holiday of violent sport.

Several causes were assigned for this unrest. First, there was the domineering and overbearing attitude manifested by employers of the Frome estate towards their employees. Secondly, though Jamaican labourers were accustomed to work for low wages, they worked only four or at most five days per week, while the remainder of the time allowed workers to cultivate their small farms and raise enough food to augment their pittance wage; but this extra time was now not allowed by Tate and Lyle. Instead, the labourers were required to work the full week at these same low wages with no time free to cultivate their own farms. Thirdly, living conditions on the estate were bad; workers were provided with so few huts that many were forced to sleep in the open in hammocks, in striking contrast to the comfortable quarters provided for their bosses. Fourthly, the workers resented the labour-saving machines being introduced, for this led to fewer available jobs. Fifthly, the workers were not satisfied with the low contract wages offered by Tate and Lyle. Sixthly, they lacked a genuine labour organization and capable leaders; not having them, they were led into violence and anarchy by mischievous agitators.[2]

Turmoil died down in Westmoreland; but a few days later, on 9 May, there was trouble in Kingston. Here the star of a new and powerful labour leader, William Alexander Bustamante, was rising rapidly to prominence. Addressing a crowd of two thousand at the Kingston Race Course, he placed the blame for the woes on Governor Edward Denham, whom Bustamante demanded be recalled to England.[3] It was a fiery speech, such as would characterize him for years to come.

Unrest beset the whole of Kingston, the unrest that comes from frustration of unemployment and low wages. Labourers wanted work, but there was none to be had even at three shillings per day. In Trench Town, a district of Kingston, new roads were being cut through the bush preparatory to the building of a low-income housing project. Three hundred fifty had expected to find employment on this government venture; only sixty were hired.[4] When the sixty reported for work, they found a huge crowd in a menacing mood, angry that they themselves had not been hired—angry also because of the very low wage contract of three shillings a day that was being offered. This was 13 May; two days later on 15 May, labour unrest again flared up with thousands of unemployed walking from place to place in the city seeking work, and work was not to be had.

Out on the Kingston Parade, Bustamante again addressed a

large crowd of unemployed on their dire condition, while down on the waterfront a strike was rearing its menacing head.

On 23 May the storm broke. At dawn mobs of striking waterfront and sanitary workers, their ranks swelled by thousands of men and women from the slums and the underworld, filled the city streets and virtually took possession of Kingston, forcing banks, business houses, and stores to close their doors.[5]

The *Daily Gleaner* recorded the event.

> Households in the city awoke this morning to unaccustomed shouts and sounds of turmoil which seemed to be coming from all directions at once. The cause was quickly learned. Large bands of striking sanitary workers, street cleaners, and cart men employed by the Kingston-St. Andrew Corporation who went on strike yesterday demanding an increase of pay from 18/– and 21/– to 30/– and permanent weekly employment, had been joined by thousands drawn from the city's slum areas. In bands of thirty to forty they were covering Kingston from end to end, kicking over and destroying garbage receptacles and throwing the contents on the already refuse-littered streets which quickly assumed a terrible looking state indeed, which is already bordering on the dangerous. . . . The city streets reek with filth. . . . Armed police are out at the Coronation Market holding back the huge mob who are evidently bent on raiding the place. . . . A detachment of Sherwood Foresters arrived at the Central Police Station at 10.45. They are now parading the streets in service kit with rifles.[6]

As late as 25 May the situation remained grave as "crowds composed to a large extent of rowdies and youths, still paraded the streets and in many places attacked the police with stones and bricks."[7]

By 28 May the waterfront strike had been settled, and the city returned to normal. Once violence had spent its energy, the peoples' leader organized the labourers into the Bustamante Industrial Trade Union. Now the workers were knit into a consolidated body which gave them unified strength to demand higher wages and better living conditions by arbitration and proper social legislation.

Bustamante next formed his Jamaica Labour Party, which he associated with the Bustamante Industrial Trade Union. The two organizations for all practical purposes were interchangeable. His cousin, Norman Washington Manley, a leading Jamaican barrister, likewise inaugurated his Peoples' National Party, to which he conjoined the Trades Union Council, and, in later years, the National Workers' Union.

Jamaica now had two powerful trade unions and, linked with them, two equally dynamic political parties. From the island-wide influence of these organizations would come a new Jamaica, fashioned politically, socially, and economically by the united strength of an organized populace.

The Cooperative Credit Union Movement

While the man in the street profited considerably from the new order, there were areas in his life which still needed expert guidance and direction. One of these was the economic field. Many a worker felt a serious need of a personal financial reserve which he might call on in time of need, rather than rely on loan sharks who were willing to accommodate at such an exorbitant rate of interest that the victim remained in debt for years. Help and guidance came in the person of Fr. John Peter Sullivan, S.J., who pioneered Cooperative Credit Unions, making it possible for the worker to have financial security and a source from which he might borrow money at a low rate of interest.[8]

Many of the world's most effective benefits have had humble, almost microscopic beginnings. This was especially true of the Cooperative Credit Union movement in Jamaica. It was initiated not by a degreed economist, but by a tyro missionary with no technical training, who had to learn credit union technique from its ABCs.

The movement began with a handful and spread to thousands of workers, and it became one of the most effective social benefits not only to Jamaicans but to labourers throughout the Caribbean. Full credit must be given to Sullivan and his well-trained lay leaders. Their contribution to the improvement of Jamaica's social order makes a captivating story.

Sullivan arrived in Kingston on 6 August 1939 aboard the *S.S. Jamaica*.[9] Rising behind the city were Jamaica's famous Blue Mountains; so close did they appear to the newcomer that it seemed he might reach out and touch them. Perhaps he could not make physical contact with the mountains, but he would reach them with his Credit Unions and effect the people living in them. They would never be too far away from the influence of his basic social reforms; he would reach into the lives of these people and offer new confidence, a new hope amid their stark poverty. By means of his island-wide effort of more than a quarter of a century, he clearly demonstrated that the Church was keenly interested in their social prosperity.

John Peter Sullivan's first assignment was to St. George's College, where he taught English and at the same time acted as spiritual director to the Young Men's Sodality of Holy Trinity Parish. This sodality, numbering fifteen Jamaicans whose average was twenty-four years, had been founded by Joseph Krim, S. J., in 1935.[10] So thoroughly had director Krim trained these young men in sodality technique that, when Sullivan assumed charge, they were restless for action. Sullivan felt that a deeper appreciation of motivation, as distinct from action, should form the next step in their development. For nearly one year the fifteen Sodalists, studied the *Encyclical on the Mystical Body of Christ* under Sullivan's direction, until they were thoroughly imbued with its contents.[11] Intensive study of internal motivation manifested itself externally when permission was sought and obtained from the vicar apostolic to introduce a full-fledged dialogue Mass into the cathedral parish.

So rapidly did this spread to other Jamaican parishes that Gerard Ellard, S. J., publicized the success of these sodalists in his book, *Dialogue Mass*. They had learned from the doctrine of the Mystical Body of Christ to think not in terms of their own microscopic selves, but of the wide, limitless horizon of all mankind. They felt that they must translate the challenge of the *Ite, missa est* from the altar to the office, to the shops, to the docks, to the plantations. They would make their communal Mass bear down hard and effectively on the economic problems of their depressed brothers in Christ.

The next step was the blunt translation of cooperative worship into cooperative work. Late in 1940 the same young men who had put themselves through a course in the Mystical Body of Christ now began to study co-ops.[12]

What did they begin with? Practically nothing; no literature except for a few rudimentary pamphlets, no local precedent, no cooperative law, no money, and only the guidance of an amateur economist. The avid group of fifteen met every Tuesday night for thirteen months and, as more literature became available, their acquaintance with the historical background and techniques of Cooperative Credit Unions grew apace.[13]

In March 1941 the sodality group decided to save as they continued to study.[14] It was a memorable night. Each member contributed his first six pence, and the share capital that night stood at seven shillings and six pence. It marked a turning point. The transition from mere theory to the actual establishment of the first Credit Union in Jamaica was made, the dawn of a socioeconomic movement which would accelerate into more extensive membership and greater funds with the passing of the years.

Three years later this tiny Sodality Credit Union had grown from the original fifteen to a membership of 130, and from the initial share capital of $1.87 to $6,000.[15] From July 1942 to Christmas 1943, they had loaned close to $10,000; and this in a Jamaica where the average weekly salary of the sodality group was $10.

Within a few brief years these enthusiastic sodalists had leaped from the confines of their narrow circle and were instrumental in establishing credit unions in shops, land settlements, and plantations. One striking example of expanding influence was the Credit Union at Port Royal. Port Royal, once the wealthiest city of the Indies, was now a poor little village of some eight hundred people. Three hundred of these were children, and of the five hundred adults, approximately one hundred had only intermittent employment, while the average wage for those fortunate to have occasional employment was $6.00 per week.[16] Appeals for government subsidy and even private charities brought no response.

One Sunday after Mass Charles Judah, S. J., in charge of this mission, gathered the men and women to spin them the story of the successful Nova Scotia cooperatives.[17]

By way of a follow-up, Aston Bailey, topflight sodality co-op organizer, pushed off Sunday after Sunday in a boat to Port Royal across the harbour from Kingston.[18] For a year Bailey put the Port Royal co-op pioneers through a stiff study club course on the subject of credit unions. In April 1943 there were ten members and $150 in share capital;[19] one year later, the membership stood at 208, and the total savings slightly under $6,000.[20] By June 1947 this membership increased to 266 with a total savings of $12,455; a truly amazing figure for any town in Jamaica, and more so for depressed Port Royal.[21] In addition, this same credit union had loaned $27,750 without a serious loss from bad debts.[22]

Much of credit union success in Jamaica stems from the indefatigable, persevering, personal labour of John P. Sullivan, S. J. If his trained sodalists worked sedulously, their leader laboured with equal industry invading every known area where the working class might be found in order to establish credit unions for them. Standing on a box as an improvised rostrum, he would explain to one hundred women workers in a tobacco factory, earning no more than $4.00 per week, the economic advantages a credit union would bring into their lives. Or he might be seen in such an unlikely place as a rum manufactory, demonstrating to the owner the boon a credit union would be for the hundred or so employees in his Kingston bars. Again he would be at police headquarters to obtain permission from the superintendent to organize the local constabulary; or Sullivan would drive forty miles into the country in order to present the value of a credit union to hundreds of workers on a sprawling 35,000 acre sugar estate.

This was the practical side. The academic side of the movement was incorporated under the aegis of St. George's College Extension School in September 1944 where four experts offered courses in cooperative credit, consumer cooperatives, cooperative marketing, and cooperative housing.[23]

How the Credit Union Functions

A cooperative credit union is a society which furnishes its members with a convenient, safe means of saving money and of obtaining credit at reasonable rates of interest.[24] It is organized within a group already united by common bond and fairly well-known to each other, such as workers in a factory, residents of the same community, or members of a parish or club. The credit union offers its members three primary services: first, a system for accumulating savings by encouraging its members to make regular deposits of small amounts depending upon their circumstances; secondly, a source of credit by providing members with loans when they need money for provident and productive purposes: thirdly, it gives members an education in the management and control of money.

Between the commercial bank and the credit unions there is marked difference. Banks are owned and operated by people who save and invest money for profit; credit unions are owned and operated by people who save to help themselves. Shareholders of banks vote according to the number of shares held; each member of a credit union has only one vote, regardless of the number of shares he holds. Banks in 1940 were not particularly concerned with catering to the small account and in granting small loans, whereas the credit union is precisely concerned in the small loan. Banks issue yearly consolidated statements but do not reveal the amount of business done in a given area through a branch office; a credit union must publish a monthly statement of its affairs; hence the general membership is kept constantly informed of the state of its finances.

Honesty, industry, and good character are the requisites for membership along with the further requirement that the applicant must come within the group serviced by the particular credit union. If it is a factory credit union, the members must be employed in the factory; if a community credit union, he must be a resident of the particular territory served.

The capital consists of shares and deposits made by members. The value of a share in Jamaica is £1.0.0, paid weekly, fortnightly, or monthly. A member may purchase a share outright by paying the amount in full while the installment plan enables members of slender means to buy shares gradually and thus promote thrift, which is one of the prime requisites of the successful credit union.

From interest on loans by borrowing, interest on bank balance and dividends, the credit union derives its own income. Each year before the declaration of dividends, twenty percent of the net earnings are set aside as a reserve fund which is designed to protect members against a bad loan. Only members in good standing may borrow, and these loans must be made for productive or provident purposes. A provident loan is one which, in the best judgment of the credit committee, promises to be of real benefit to the borrower. His purpose must be stated in the loan application. The size of the loans is limited by the ability of the credit union to advance them; where there are more loan demands than available funds, the smaller loan is always given preference. The great attraction for the working man is the low rate of interest, one per cent per month on the unpaid balance.

For the general management of a credit union, a board of directors is responsible which acts on application for membership, determines interest rates on loans, fixes amounts of surety bond for officers handling money, declares dividends, has charge of investments, and designates the bank in which funds shall be deposited. It is, however, the credit union committee which has general supervision of all loans and which must examine and determine what security shall be required for each, and it is also the duty of this committee to enquire into the financial position of the borrower and ascertain his ability to repay fully and promptly the obligations assumed. The supervisory committee has for its primary work the checking of books so that any error made by the treasurer be detected and corrected as soon as possible. It also sees that the treasurer accounts for all money collected and lodges it within twenty-four hours, and finally that the credit union is operating in accordance with its rules.

The structural composite of the credit union conforms to the architecture of Jamaica's New Social Order, since it is essentially a democratic organization giving to the people full responsibility of management; it becomes their own. Success or failure rests upon the interest manifested by the members. With the growth of so many credit unions throughout the island, a percentage of failures was inevitable, but lapses were surprisingly few, due principally to educational precautions taken before any credit union was allowed to function.

The principal opponent of the credit union in Jamaica was the loan shark. The loan shark held a real advantage, since he asked no questions and had no concern how the victim might spend the loan.

His chief concern was the payment of 120 percent interest by his client. In contrast, the credit union was bound by its rules to pry into the client's business and judge whether the proposed loan conformed to credit union regulations.

Some found this distasteful, even after they had been rescued from the loan shark; they fell back into the easier, albeit more expensive, way of getting money in time of need. Such a member was the exception; the average member was solid and dependable. His pennies, shillings, and pounds built up the organization to its present social effectiveness.

Credit Unions Organize into a League

Up to this point in development, credit unions in Jamaica functioned as separate units. Director Sullivan discovered that, just as an individual found financial strength and security in joining a credit union, so credit unions united in a league would carry more weight and be more effective.

This idea stemmed from the second convention of Jamaican credit unions held at St. George's College in July 1942. Then, by unanimous agreement, five organizational members, the Clerks, the Holy Trinity Sodality, Holy Rosary Parish, the Kingston Teachers, and the Jamaican Welfare Services, set up an educational council.[25] It was evident that the credit union idea was spreading rapidly, and the convention delegates agreed unanimously that the common bond of a league would unite the credit unions and render their socio-economic work more effective.

Although formed in 1942, the league did not become a registered society under the Industrial and Provident Societies of Jamaica Law until 1947, when it adopted the official name of the Jamaica Credit Union League, Ltd.[26]

The League set forth definite aims: to promote organization and development, to encourage cooperation among credit unions, to disseminate information and foster their common good, to approve bookkeeping forms and records with a view to maintaining a uniform system of accountancy, to protect the funds from loss by bonding and insuring officers in positions of trust, to collaborate with other cooperative groups working on Rochdale principles for the promotion of common interests in a manner that may be mutually agreed upon from time to time, and lastly to make loans to credit unions or to individual members through the deposit and loan section of the League.

Spread of Credit Unions Throughout the Caribbean

The socially conscious lay leaders of the Jamaican credit union movement could not stand idle when the same economic conditions that existed in their own country were also found in other Caribbean lands. They would share with others the solutions to such problems which they found so effective in Jamaica. Founder-director Sullivan was sent to make personal contact in over twenty territories of the Caribbean area. Urged on by the thought of the unreached millions, he visited every conceivable spot washed by the blue Caribbean, to sell these millions the credit union scheme as a solution for their economic morass.

As in Jamaica, so throughout the rest of the Caribbean, Sullivan placed special emphasis on total participation by members themselves. They would control the organization, do the work; the credit union was theirs. It did not belong to the clergy. If the clergy were involved in the movement, they were to act as guides, as an inspiration to the laity, giving proper motivation to all engaged in this apostolate. Wherever he stopped, Sullivan called the attention of his trained leaders to the obligation that was theirs from baptism and confirmation to work for the most fundamental, profound type of activity, namely, the growing together in Christ.

Statistically, the first complete scientific census ever taken in Jamaica revealed that, in 1943, one out of every three persons, able and willing to work, was fortunate enough to have a job, and that, of these wage earners, 77.8 percent earned from a few cents to $4.00 weekly.[27]

With the exception of some parts of Trinidad, and the whole area of the Netherlands' West Indies, the statistics showed that the economic and social depression in Jamaica was duplicated all over the Caribbean and, in some territories, was much worse. In many Caribbean areas specific social action movements were doing magnificent work in light of their respective problems and resources, but all were suffering from severe limitations. Most ecclesiastical social movements were confined to urban areas, whereas the Caribbean as a whole was overwhelmingly rural. Further, these social movements, for the most part, affected only the middle class, and the middle class throughout the Caribbean was only a very small percentage of the population: it was the lower-class wage earner, counted in the millions, that was untouched.

In spreading the influence of credit unions throughout the Caribbean, Sullivan stressed that current Catholic Action movements must be reinforced widely, deeply, and immediately, with socio-economic programmes like cooperatives, rural life movements, and allied techniques, aimed simultaneously at spreading security, with special emphasis on adult education and all its comprehensive implications. Otherwise the papal concept of a mission Church growing to full maturity might never be realized in the twentieth century.

The tiny seed planted on that night of March 1941, when fifteen sodalists inaugurated the first credit union in Jamaica, grew and spread its branches of influence throughout the Caribbean. Help was sought from Jamaica by twenty territories extending as far as South America.[28] Representing the Credit Union League, Sullivan visited six islands in 1946: the Dominican Republic, at the invitation of their pioneer credit unions; St. Lucia, at the invitation of the government; Grenada, at the request of the peasant clubs; the Dutch island of Curaçao, at the invitation of a private agency; Trinidad and Barbados. In 1948 other territories sought advice: the Bahama Islands, at the invitation of the bishop; Dutch Guiana—now Surinam—where the Belgian Redemptorists wished to establish a social action programme; adjacent British Guiana—now Guyana—at the request of both bishop and government; then north to Puerto Rico, to most government co-op leaders; Haiti, where the Oblate Fathers were working the credit union organization; finally, repeated stops at Trinidad and Barbados.

The highlight of 1951 came when Sullivan was sent as special representative of the Holy See to the Food and Agricultural Organization of the United Nations Caribbean Commission Cooperative Conference convened at Trinidad.[29] In 1953 the Latin American Rural Life Congress at Maizales, Colombia, drew delegates from all Latin America. Although Jamaica is not classed as a Latin American country, Sullivan received a special invitation.

The only island visited in 1954 was Dominica, on direct invitation from both the local government and that of the United Kingdom. Here advice was given on various aspects of co-op and credit union movements. The notable event of 1955 was the Cooperative Workshop in Panama, embracing Caribbean and Central American countries. In 1956, Trinidad, Puerto Rico, and the Dominican Republic called for help and advice, but the chief event of that year was the fact that Sullivan again officiated as special representative of the Holy See for territories served by the Caribbean Commission. This was held in British Guiana and jointly sponsored by the FAO and the Caribbean Commission. In the same year, 1956, Jamaica played host to delegates and observers convening for the plenary session of a committee created in Panama in April 1955 and commissioned to activate a Caribbean-wide Cooperative Confederation. Another important socioeconomic step was Jamaican collaboration with CUNA in organizing the first British West Indies Credit Union seminar, held at

St. George's College Extension School, which brought together credit union leaders from British Guiana, Trinidad, Grenada, St. Vincent, St. Lucia, Barbados, Dominica, and British Honduras.

Antigua was added to the growing sphere of influence in 1957 when this tiny island in the northeast Caribbean received assistance in the development of a young credit union. In that same year Sullivan was sent as delegate to two important conventions: one in Puerto Rico where he represented the Jamaica Credit Union at the first constitutional convention of the Caribbean Cooperative Confederation: the other in Trinidad where Jamaica as co-sponsor with CUNA formally ratified the constitutions for the West Indian Credit Union Confederation, a British West Indies-wide organization of actual and potential credit union leagues. Those participating and ratifying the constitutions were British Guiana, Barbados, Trinidad, Grenada, St. Lucia, St. Vincent, Dominica, and Jamaica.

Twenty-five years of growth from fifteen to sixty-five thousand members, spread throughout the entire Caribbean, from an initial share capital of $1.87 to the astonishing figure of $6,000,000 is a story of hard work by hundreds of socially-minded lay leaders.[30] Their labours in the credit union movement coincided with a worldwide reawakening of interest in the reconstruction of the social order that greater social justice might find its way into the life of the working man.

The architect of this Caribbean social structure, in keeping with his ideal of giving complete control to lay leaders when prepared to accept the responsibility, retired as active head of the Jamaica Credit Union League at the nineteenth annual convention held at St. George's College, when he became managing director emeritus. The goal, set in 1940, was reached in 1959 when the entire organization was placed in the hands of responsible lay officers. He even witnessed one of his original fifteen, Aston Bailey, become a full-time professional field man for the West Indian Confederation of Credit Unions. Bailey had come a long way from the days when he first rowed across Kingston Harbour to establish the credit union at Port Royal.

Sullivan's work was of such a nature that it could not but attract the attention of government. On the occasion of his retirement, the Chief Minister, Norman W. Manley, publicly expressed his appreciation.

> My association with Fr. John P. Sullivan goes back to the days when I was more familiar with the co-operative movement and other aspects of social welfare than with the sort of business which has come to take up the greater part of my life.
>
> These are exciting days, but those days were exciting too, and of consuming interest.

I can never forget the dedicated enthusiasm of Fr. John Sullivan for the work he was doing for the co-operative movement. He represented faith and confidence in their most contagious aspect. At the same time, no one more fully understood or more carefully practiced the requirements of attention to detail and maintenance of method, both at the organizational level and at the business level as he did. No one better understands that, although the cooperative movement is born of an idea, success depends upon the mastery of efficient business techniques.

It is for these reasons that the movement in Jamaica owes so much to Fr. John Sullivan and it is a great tribute to his work that the Credit Union movement has proved to be one of the most successful, if not the most successful, branches of co-operative movement in Jamaica. . . .

We will miss him greatly but I am sure that the movement, built on sound foundations and now possessing first-class leadership, has a great future before it, and will endure in our country.

(signed)
N. W. Manley
Chief Minister
16th June, 1959[31]

Training Centre for Leaders in Social Work

Sullivan's resignation did not mean that he would retire to the comfort of the fireside; rather he would devote his entire time and energetic personality to the training of indigenous leaders to carry on his socio-economic programme in order to build men of tolerance, breadth of view, civic awareness, and community-mindedness—leaders of imagination and courage. Without such, the international credit union movement would become just another finance company. Having saved every penny that friends donated during the previous twelve years, he purchased a spacious residence in the suburbs of Kingston as a centre with live-in training facilities for qualified students drawn from the four language groups of the Caribbean with heavy priority placed on the development of West Indian credit union leadership.

Sullivan now envisaged a fresh approach to old, persistent problems. He had advanced from the amateur to the professional. Twenty-five years of social work had elevated him to the unique position of the best-informed person in the Caribbean on socioeconomic matters. "Give us leaders, and we give you the future," became the rallying slogan of his new vision. Indigenous leaders trained through the organization of relatively small groups whose prime target was the satisfaction of some specific need strongly felt by the people in the group, spelled the whole programme he now envisaged.

Yet is was not entirely new for the general overall plan had been suggested at a credit union discussion as early as 1945, but immediate plans for the centre were not projected until 1950. It was not until 1958 that the scheme actually got off the ground.

A suitable location was considered of prime importance, so an estate removed from the city yet within its precincts was acquired at 2 Olivier Road, Kingston. With this basic necessity settled, the scheme moved forward as Sullivan had envisaged it. Concurrently, the centre would serve to foster family credit, develop the spirit of thrift, and attempt a bona fide housing project. The same overall phases of self-help which started the movement on the way to success were now merely being expanded. Vatican II became the touchstone of these new ventures, yet Sullivan had anticipated the council by a quarter of a century.

Collaboration between Catholics and non-Catholics had been a fundamental principle of the early movement since its inception in 1942, when Sullivan had helped establish many a credit union under distinct Protestant auspices.

The question which always arises is whether this centre turns out degreed graduates of university level? And the answer is always no. A degreed course is not the object of the Social Action Centre, since Sullivan himself wanted to develop community leadership on a non-academic basis which would affect those levels of society wherein two great dynamics might be utilized: in the area of economic need and in the area of leadership potential among the middle and lower-middle classes. This was in fact an extension of the original credit union work, both having the basic idea of establishing leadership among the common people.

The whole scheme, like any pioneer project, was fraught with difficulties. Foremost was the atmosphere of old colonialism which still pervaded the air of this independent nation, for people tend to lean too heavily on government for help in any scheme projected by themselves; to overcome this inertia was one of the fundamental objects of the Social Action Centre. In itself this was a difficult, hidden work, and had to precede the more important phase of developing indigenous leaders. Lack of promotional resources was another serious roadblock, as well as the opposition of vested interests and inadequate legislation.

The newly constructed Social Action Centre headquarters comprised an administration block containing a lecture hall capable of seating one hundred persons, modern kitchen and dining facilities, library, committee rooms, and staff offices. The dormitory possessed accommodation for twenty-eight students. The whole complex is situated in suburban Kingston and is conducive to leisurely discussion and undistracted decision.[32]

For six years, 1960–66, a group of young men drawn from business and the professions met twice a month for research and follow-up discussion on such issues as population problems, distribution of

Jamaican wealth, comparative wage rates, and unemployment.[33] This had been designated by the centre as a Civic Affairs Cell. Added to this were the term courses in cooperative law, cooperative management, credit union business management, and accountancy. One of the more recent services offered by the SAC was the promotion of cooperative housing, with over one thousand persons involved in this scheme.

The SAC also served as managing director and the source of professional advice for the training of cooperative housing societies with the professional aid of architects, engineers, contractors, and other personnel needed to promote the housing institute.

Leadership courses are fundamental to the SAC for they mark the high point in the effort to assist in the socioeconomic development of the island. The curriculum consists of economics of change, a basic theory applied to economic growth in the Caribbean; Jamaican economic history, a backdrop by which current and future growth may be better understood; cooperative systems and programmes, an explanation of cooperative institutions; organization and management, with emphasis on how credit unions and cooperatives lead to a better life for Jamaica; Jamaican economic development, an introduction to the efforts of private and government agencies involved in assisting the island's economic growth; law and the layman, which offers a course in the general principles of civil and criminal law, sources of law and constitutional structures; trade unionism, which relates the history and practices of labour unions in Jamaica; industrial relations methods, which offers an investigation into the ways of improving labour-management relations in the Caribbean; social ethics with concrete application of moral responsibility in the areas of economic, social and political morality; and finally, field trips which introduce students to various Jamaican institutions involved in the growth of the nation.

John Peter Sullivan had come a long way since that day in August 1939 when he first set foot on Jamaican soil and inaugurated that socioeconomic programme which placed him among the giants of Catholic missionary endeavour. So effective has Sullivan's work been that in 1970 the Cooperative Credit Union in Jamaica alone had a share capital of $8,639,703 subscribed to by 43,000 members. This prompted the Minister of Agriculture and Fisheries, the Hon. John P. Gyles, to pay tribute to the movement for its substantial contribution to the economic and social development of the island.

From one credit union with a membership of fifteen, in 1941 the credit unions now number 261 in Jamaica, a membership of 306,000 and a share capital and deposit of $502,000,000 in 1987.[34]

Twenty-Seven

Education 1519–1894

The Spanish Era

Education in sixteenth-century Europe was for the few. It was the common opinion that the farmer in the field, the labourer at his task, the artisan at his trade, could manage with little formal education. The Spanish conquistadors carried this idea to the New World. The discovery of Jamaica in 1494 brought the Spaniards into contact with Arawak Indian tribes; some 150 settlements ringed the island, governed by local chieftains called caciques. Keen of intellect, the Arawaks quickly mastered whatever the Spaniards taught them, whether it was how to make bricks, to cut stone, or to assist in the construction of buildings. As one official letter noted, they were "of very clear understanding." The rank and file Arawak were taught manual skills, but children of the caciques received a higher education, and to them the Spaniard revealed the wonderful world of books.

As early as 29 August 1516, Charles I wrote Governor Garay, "I approve and thank you . . . for having made the children of the caciques to read and write."[1] Before education came to the mainland, before schools, colleges, or universities had even taken seed in North or South America, here on the shores of a Caribbean island, sons of semi-savage Indians were engaged in a programme that antedated all other educational endeavours in the western hemisphere, preceded chronologically by similar efforts in Hispaniola.

However, the hidalgo could hardly be entrusted with the task of educating youth, since writing his name laboriously was a sufficient embellishment for his not too lofty social status. It would appear that the Franciscan missionaries who conducted schools for Indian children in neighbouring Hispaniola were also the teachers of the sons of caciques in Jamaica and that the locale of the school was certainly at Seville, the chief town at this period in Jamaican history.[2]

As year succeeded year in Spanish Jamaica, we can only infer from tenuous evidence that the Franciscans, and later the Dominicans, conducted schools at their respective monasteries in the capital town of Santiago de la Vega after the year 1534. This slender evidence rests on the fact that education is necessary to qualify for the priesthood, and in 1611 we find young men in their studies at Santiago de la Vega where "many young men had entered the monasteries, inspired with the desire to serve God."[3] But, realizing that the goal could not be readily attained, not from the lack of educational facilities, but simply because they had no bishop to ordain them, they returned after a time to secular life. Dr. Alonzo de Espanosa Centeno, a native of Jamaica, noted that he studied for his degree at the Royal University of Mexico;[4] probably he made his preparatory studies in his home land.

Haitian Refugee Schools

For more detailed information on Jamaican Catholic education, we have to turn to the English period. Since the Church was looked upon with disfavour from the English conquest until the arrival of Fr. Quigly in 1792, we can presume that Catholic schools were nonexistent during this time. As for the brief period when Fr. Churchill was in Jamaica in the year 1688, he was so busy with parochial work that he had little time to devote to education. Nor is there any indication that Quigly opened a school during his few years in Kingston from 1792 to 1799. But we do know that French refugees who came to Jamaica opened their own private schools, for a list is available beginning in 1792.[5]

Mrs. Gallbraith	Duke Street	27 pupils
Mrs. Dejeant	Princess Street	26 pupils
Mrs. Bugueil	Temple Lane	11 pupils
Miss Villieir	Princess Street	14 pupils
Miss Cochard	Princess Street	11 pupils
Mrs. Shreyer	Parade	20 pupils
Mrs. Laroque	White Street	14 pupils
Miss Laulanix	High Holborn Street	14 pupils

Since these schools were private and of elementary standard, their scholastic worth depended upon the quality of the individual conducting the school. These schools were not unlike similar institutions conducted today throughout Jamaica by private persons. We find them in the rooms and on the porches of private homes, or even under a convenient shade tree, for parents who can afford the few shillings tuition prefer to entrust their children to private schools under a well-considered teacher than send them in their early years to a government school where education is on the mass-production plan.

Although these Haitian refugee schools ranged from High Holborn to Princess Streets, they were well within Kingston's residential area of the day. At one of these Haitian schools young Duquesnay, the future coadjutor vicar apostolic, learned his ABCs; later the elder Duquesnay sent his son Arthur William to the Jesuit College of St. Aloysius, Montmorillon, Poitou, France. Upon completion of his secondary education, Arthur entered the Society of Jesus, but withdrew as a novice to pursue his vocation to the priesthood at the seminary of Rouen, where he was ordained a secular priest in 1833. He returned to Jamaica in 1834.[6]

Duquesnay's School

Early nineteenth-century Kingston needed a secondary school such as Duquesnay had attended in France. Not every Kingstonian was financially as fortunate as the elder Duquesnay; most had to be content with an elementary education unless they wished to send them to a school under Protestant or Jewish tuition. Most of the Haitians preferred not to do this.

Duquesnay, graduate of St. Aloysius, and former Jesuit novice, seminary trained, and ordained priest, was just the one to open such a school for Catholics, since he possessed the qualifying background, if any Catholic did in Jamaica. He saw the need; he opened the school.

Classes began in September 1836, with forty pupils enrolled at 63 Orange Street, Kingston.[7] The following year the school was removed to more spacious quarters at 5 Upper King Street, the site also of the presbytery where Duquesnay and Fernandez lived. Kingston Catholics, writing to Pius VIII on the condition of the Church in Jamaica, expressed their satisfaction with the new school. "The young priest [Duquesnay] for the past eight months had opened a school where Catholics [boys], while being fortified solidly in the principles of religion, learn English, French, Spanish and Latin."[8]

Duquesnay may well be considered the father of modern Catholic education in Jamaica, but the idea of a secondary school originated in the mind of the vicar apostolic, who not only gave the project his blessing but also took an active part by teaching Spanish.

Despite the favourable acclamations of his fellow Haitians, Duquesnay had his periods of discouragement when he questioned whether the school would ever produce any good.[9] Duquesnay's lament, the lament of every teacher, was addressed to a Jesuit friend in Rome. Would his daily labour of instructing Catholic youth have any lasting effect upon their individual lives and through them a permanent effect upon society? In Duquesnay's case it had, for in 1836 was laid the foundation stone of the structure of Catholic education which spread to every part of the island and proved an invaluable contribution to the intellectual, social, and religious life of the community.

Duquesnay launched his school when Catholics were in a distinct minority. Fewer than one in twenty-five of those who were members of a religious body—Baptists, Methodists, Presbyterians, and Anglicans—were Catholics; of the total island population, only one in forty was a Catholic. However, most of the Catholic population was concentrated in Kingston, a distinct advantage for a day school.

Soon after Cotham's arrival in December 1837, he also began to teach at Duquesnay's school, but lack of suitable textbooks was a handicap which Cotham remedied by writing to England asking for the following, used at Stonyhurst.

1 dozen Ruddiman's *Latin Grammar*
1 dozen Eutropius
½ dozen Cornelius Nepos
2 dozen Chambaud's *French Grammar*
2 dozen *Introduction to the Lecteur Français*
2 dozen Hutton's *Arithmetic*
1 or 2 copies Hutton's *Mathematics*
3 dozen School Geographies[10]

For a few months in 1838, Cotham was assigned to the mission of Spanish Town, but since it proved a failure, he was back again in the school. In January 1842 he was placed in charge of Duquesnay's institution.[11] Cotham reported that this school died a natural death on 13 December 1844, since it had few scholars willing to pay the tuition.

The Colombian Jesuits' School

The year 1850 was the second important date in Jamaican Catholic education when twenty-one Jesuits, twelve from the College of San Bartholomé, Bogotá, Colombia, and nine from the College of Santa Fe, Medellin, Colombia, offered the experience of their teaching to the youth of Kingston.[12]

Priests:

Emmanuel Gil, superior
Franciscus Sauri
Ignatius Assensi
Aloysius Amoross

Benedictus Moral
Emmanuel Fernandez
Josephus Cotanilla
Joachim Freire
Leo Tornero
Nicasius Eguiluz
Paulus Pujadas
Petrus Garcia
Stephanus Parrondo

Scholastic:

Michael Ruiz

Coadjutors:

Angelus Chacon
Gabriel Trobat
Joannes Cenarruzabeitia
Josephus Saracco
Josephus Tirado
Michael Pares
Raphael Fortun

Classes began at St. George's Colonial College on 2 September 1850 and progressed normally until the middle of October, when they were interrupted by the scourge of cholera which swept the city of Kingston for a full month. Once this had abated, the students settled down to the routine of daily classes but kept in mind that on the following August 15, they must present themselves for a public examination in their subjects. On that day several professors attached to the College, the clergy of the mission, and prominent laymen would be their examiners. On that day, Peter Galway, Esq., of Manchester, chaired the examination in the morning, while the Honourable Edward Chitty chaired it in the afternoon. Following the examination, prizes were awarded such scholars as showed proficiency in their respective subjects.

Fortunately, *The Colonial Standard and Jamaica Despatch* has preserved this data.[13]

Mathematics—Algebraic Course
Prize—Antonio Jaspe
Distinguished—Victor Sorapure and José M. Peña
Interrogators—Fr. Stephen Parrondo, Fr. James Dupeyron, and Mr. W. Carter

Latin
Prize—First Class—William Roux
Prize—Second Class—Edmund Burke
Distinguished—P. Galway
Interrogators—Fr. William Cotham, Fr. James Dupeyron, and Fr. Moral

French
Prize—Charles Rubion
Distinguished—Peter Rubion, Augustus Roux, Alexander Carvalho

Interrogators—Fr. Dupeyron, Fr. Sauri, Fr. Simond
Questions and answers given in French

English Reading and Recitation
Prize—Charles Rubion
Distinguished—José M. Peña, Masters Gunter and Cardoza

English Grammar
English Students—Second Class
Prize—José M. Peña
Distinguished—Charles Rubion, Peter Rubion, Alexander Carvalho, Augustus Roux, Albert Alexander, John Ryan, and Eulisse Duquesnay
Interrogators—Fr. Sauri and Fr. Parrondo

Spanish Students—First Class
Prize—José M. Peña
Spanish Students—Second Class
Prize—Tomas Locava
Interrogator—Fr. Sauri

Drawing
Prizes—Manuel A. Arruble, Rafael Garcia

Logic and Metaphysics
Prize—José M. Peña
Interrogator—Fr. Garcia

Moral Philosophy
Distinguished—Mario Valenzuela, Rafael Garcia, and Joaquin Salas
Interrogator—Fr. Garcia

Calligraphy
with a demonstration of the principles of the art of the proper construction of letters by geometrical analysis of lines and angles exhibited in specimens of penmanship produced.
Prize—Francis Alvarez
Distinguished—Augustus Roux, John Ryan, Alexander Carvalho, and Francis May
Interrogator—Mr. William Carter

Unfortunate for Catholic Jamaica, these experienced teachers remained for only two years.[14] A generous, tempting offer from the archbishop of Guatemala swayed them in favour of that Central American country.[15] Because they were far more proficient in the Spanish language, the decision of Fr. Emmanuel Gil, the Superior, cannot be criticized too harshly. Departure was not sudden, for five professors remained in Jamaica during the next school year to acquaint the new headmaster, Fr. Alexis Simond, and his two assistants, William Cotham and Joseph Howell, with the system they had set up at St. George's College.[16]

St. George's was now removed from 26 North Street to 5 Upper King Street where it became known as the Presbytery or Middle

School. Parents who had sent their boys to St. George's College on North Street continued to support the Presbytery Secondary School under the English Jesuits where twenty-five pupils, nearly all Catholics, followed the same curriculum under the English as they did under the Spanish Jesuits. The names of Sorapure, Duquesnay, Roux, and Carvalho found in the 1850 catalogue appear also in that of 1858, along with new names such as Lewis, Burger, Branday, Laroque, and Pouyat—family names which have been prominent for generations in the Catholic history of Jamaica.

Simond's fourteen years as headmaster terminated abruptly in January 1866, and the school was closed.[17] What happened? Did he have a difference of opinion with regard to the value of education as a missionary instrument with the noneducationally minded Dupeyron? Or was the school a financial burden for the vicariate? Whatever the cause, Simond sailed for the French atmosphere of New Orleans that very month. We know these were trying years, socially and economically, for Jamaica; Civil War in the United States hampered the flow of such staples as salt fish and cheap cotton cloth; then the Morant Bay rebellion, indicative of deep-rooted social unrest, was not solved by the explosion of violence Governor Eyre directed against it.

Fortunately, the newly appointed Jesuit superior, Fr. James Jones, a graduate of Stonyhurst College, valued education as an effective missionary instrument. He reopened St. George's College on 2 March 1868, the curriculum and faculty being listed in the *Handbook of Jamaica*.[18]

Professor of Physics and Mathematics	Very Rev. J. Jones
Professor of Latin and Italian	Rev. J. Mosia
Professor of French	Rev. J. Dupont
Professor of Spanish	Rev. J. Bertolio
Professor of English	Rev. J. Barton
Professor of Book-keeping	Mr. Mosur
Professor of Music	Mr. Vilain

Fr. James Jones had succeeded Duquesnay as superior of the mission on 24 June 1865, and he also assumed the duties as headmaster of St. George's College.[19] His keen interest in education predicted a brilliant revival for the only Catholic secondary school for boys in Jamaica. From Haiti, from Central America, from the country parts of Jamaica, came students to sit beside boys from the city of Kingston. All formed one happy community, inspired by Jones's contagious enthusiasm. Once more he placed St. George's in its honoured niche of the leading secondary school in Jamaica.

Three years later, in 1871, this promising future was scuttled. Jones had been recalled to England in September 1869, and Dupeyron, who again became superior on 25 September 1869, had little enthusiasm for St. George's College. When boarders and day scholars left for the Christmas holidays in 1871, they departed with heavy hearts, for their college closed its doors once more.[20] Why the demise of such an important institution in the life of Catholic Jamaica? The answer is in a letter of the English provincial, Edward Whitty, to Woollett, dated 1 March 1872. "Some of our Fathers in England have understood from impartial persons the College has proved a failure through the undisguised opposition of Fr. Dupeyron—that had Fr. Jones remained in Kingston the College would have lived on—that Fr. Barton through weak health and youth was unable to meet the opposition of Fr. Dupeyron and perhaps others."[21] But Catholics of Kingston would not accept the defeat of St. George's, and so they sent a petition to Fr. Edward Whitty, the English provincial.

Kingston, Jamaica
April, 1873

To The Reverend Fr. Whitty
No. 111 Mount Street
London, West

Very Reverend Father,

We your undersigned faithful servants of the Catholic faith, residing in the Island of Jamaica, on behalf of the Catholic community of our island, beg most respectfully earnestly to solicit your kind attention to this prayer for your intervention and aid to our spiritual and material benefit. A favour we feel bold in asking as being in the furtherance and development of your peculiar province, that of propagating the faith and of watching and maintaining it wherever established.

The Catholic community of this island had long suffered from the want of a properly established Catholic School or College, whereat to train their youth until the Spring of 1868 under the distinguished guidance of our much respected Father Jones, a College was started to supply this our great need. The College so established rose rapidly into repute and bade fair to eclipse all others here through the influence of manner and ability of Father Jones which made him popular, alike among Catholics, Protestants and Jews, and by the superior class of education so peculiar to Jesuit teaching, when to our astonishment, we were suddenly deprived of this benefit and were suffered, nay bid again to subject the faith of our youth to the corrupting influence of Protestant Schools.

Because of the comparatively small number of our community and its poverty, we have hitherto feared to intrude ourselves upon your attention, believing that the careful watchfulness for us of you, and those deputed by you to minister to our spiritual wants would not omit to press this our great necessity upon your consideration. That this has been done, we do not doubt, for within the past few months, with pleasure (but with anxious forebodings) we have observed that the College is again reopened under the direction of Father Jaeckel, a worthy successor of Father Jones, who, like his predecessor is truly esteemed and respected by all who have had the pleasure of knowing him and who, with his perfect knowledge of several languages, is peculiarly suited for teaching in or directing a College here, where from our geographical position and constant communication with different peoples such a qualification is almost indispensable.

What we wish to press upon you, Very Reverend Father, is the need in which we stand of a College or School, firmly established among us, where we can honestly complete our obligation to the Church and our young ones of having them well-educated without exposing their faith to the corroding influence of heresy. And in consequence of the paucity of our numbers, and we may add, comparative poverty, we would recommend that the College be supplied with a sufficient number of professors to enable the community at large, and our friends, and coreligionists of the neighbouring Islands on the Spanish Main, to avail themselves of the superior advantages a Jesuit College affords, and which they had the opportunity of appreciating during the brief existence of Father Jones' College.

We would also (if we may be allowed the liberty) suggest the name of Father Jones as one whose presence here would materially assist and further the cause on account of the profound esteem in which he is held by all classes of the community here.

Again most respectfully praying of you to aid Father Jaekel and further his views in this present most laudable attempt to revive the College among us, we take pleasure in subscribing ourselves.

Very Reverend Father
Your devoted servants in Christ,
[Here follow ninety-two signatures][22]

Whitty wrote immediately to Woollett, then both pro-vicar apostolic and Jesuit superior, the following letter.

About ninety names of men in Kingston are appended to an address praying for a Jesuit College. Could you not assemble them and ascertain their views on it and their wants. Both Fr. Weld and I think that your Reverence's objection to a College, namely, that the men should be regarded by the English Province as given to the Mission is founded on very narrow grounds. It would be ruined certainly if the superiors of the Mission did not look on the Mission and College as one concern. If the College is worth having at all, it should become an important element in the Mission. Wherever the money or men come from, there should be no distinction in the interest taken in them.[23]

Whitty's suggestion to Woollett that he call a meeting of the ninety-two petitioners, met with no response from the pro-vicar apostolic. Impatient with delay, another letter was written, this time to the superior general of the Jesuits.[24]

Kingston, Jamaica
9th June, 1874

Al Signore
Pietro Beckx

Very Reverend Father,

It is now a year ago that together with the other Catholic gentlemen of this community we addressed a petition to the Reverend Father Whitty, then the English provincial of this mission, drawing his attention to the necessity of establishing here a Catholic College for our Catholic boys. We were answered that the matter would be considered, giving us at the same time, every hope for the establishment of the said College.

Knowing as we do that your representatives here, Father Woollett and Father Hathaway, are opposed to the establishment of the College, we fear that so important a subject as that we have been obliged to take up will be allowed to pass without the serious attention which the proper education of Catholic youth in a Protestant country deserves from you as the head of this mission.

The College attempted to be started by Father Jaeckel, of which we made mention in our petition, is struggling for existence and with the opposition it is meeting from your representatives here without a sufficient complement of teachers will in all probability be soon abandoned to the spiritual death of our rising generation.

I have therefore to ask you Very Reverend Father considering the importance of the subject that moves me to excuse me while again on behalf of myself and the other petitioners pray your Reverence's particular consideration in the matter.

I have the honour to be
Very Reverend Father
Your obedient and respectful
Servant in Christ
B. C. Carvalho[25]

The Fr. Francis X. Jaeckel mentioned in the petition was a German Jesuit of the Belgium province who had made his tertianship at St. Bueno's, Wales in 1861, was assigned to British Honduras, but being dissatisfied with that mission, had requested to be transferred to Jamaica. The English provincial said of this character

> Fr. Jaeckel is a mine of energy and talent. He is capable of anything, whether as a teacher or missionary and has all the drudgery of a German. . . .
>
> My own idea is that teaching would be more in his line than a mission. If you try him at all, it would be well to give him some independent work in which he would not be liable to be fettered by other Fathers.[26]

His judgment was correct; Jaeckel had almost unlimited talent, but he was also gifted with a very strong will. Once he had charted his course, he adhered to it despite difficulties and opposition. This trait was to lead him into trouble with his local superior.

The closing of St. George's College so upset Jaeckel that he wrote a strong note of protest to the superior general, Peter Beckx, saying that the whole population of Kingston—Catholics, Jews, and Protestants to the number of 40,000—resented the demise of so influential an institution where many of them had been educated. Jaeckel proposed to Woollett that he be allowed to reopen St. George's. Woollett admitted that both the English provincial and the superior general were in favour of making a new start and said he would approve, provided Jaeckel could obtain the backing of ten Catholic families. But this was to be done privately with no publicity in the newspapers. Jaeckel contacted the Catholic families, who responded enthusiastically.

St. George's did reopen, and Jaeckel became headmaster in March 1873. Although no advertisements appeared in the daily newspapers, the *Handbook of Jamaica* identified it as a high school for boys located at 26 North Street.[27] Its curriculum embraced all the studies requisite for entering a university such as Oxford or Cambridge—an ambitious programme for a colonial college. Jaeckel set a high standard as headmaster, and as a teacher he gained the respect, love, and loyalty of his students. In all Jamaica there was not his equal.

Within a month of the reopening of St. George's, a difference of opinion arose between Jaeckel and Woollett. When news of the disagreement reached England, Whitty wrote a sharp note to Woollett on 1 July 1873:

> There is no use in my discussing the existence or nonexistence of the College. I must have expressed myself with singular felicity if I gave you the impression that I had decided in favour of the College. But what puzzles me more than all is that you allowed Jaeckel to reopen a College so soon without more deliberation. Had I been asked I should certainly have advised you to pause, seeing that we had so recently closed it. As things are I gather that your Reverence's mind is in favour of a merely limited and purely Catholic College. And the question now seems to lie, seeing what has been done, between the existence of this College such as it is or its existence in the sense Fr. Jaeckel proposes.[28]

Not only had Woollett committed himself to the reopening of St. George's College but he had done so without much consultation. He failed to take into account Jaeckel's views on the policy to be pursued.

A further obstacle was Woollett's remoteness from Kingston. Instead of residing in Kingston, as pro-vicar apostolic, he chose to live at Reading, more than 120 miles removed from the city. Nor could he always be found at Reading, for he was constantly on the road, covering the whole western end of the island in his missionary excursions. At best communications were very slow and Woollett a difficult man to contact. Woollett had deputed Hathaway to act as superior in Kingston, but Jaeckel was not fond of Hathaway's judgments in practical matters.[29] Situations could arise in Kingston and Woollett would not have heard of them until *post factum*—a long time *post factum*.

The Woollett-Jaeckel situation was bad, and it deteriorated as fundamental problems arose to worsen the situation from 1874–77.[30] The question was constantly asked as to what precise form should St. George's take: was it to be a small secondary school with one or two masters or was it to be a full-fledged college with a complete staff in all departments? Then who was eligible for admission? Was the institution to be limited to Catholics or were Protestants and Jews to be admitted? What were to be the financial arrangements?

Jaeckel was for a full-fledged college with complete staff; Woollett was not. Jaeckel was for admitting Protestants and Jews; Woollett would limit the school to Catholic boys. Jaeckel thought St. George's should have its own bank account, and he alone should be responsible for disbursement of funds; Woollett would not agree. Woollett looked upon the college as outside his jurisdiction, yet in practice he followed the opposite policy.

Letters to the provincial, to the assistant in Rome, and even to the superior general himself failed to settle the controversial issues; neither Jaeckel nor Woollett would yield.[31] Jaeckel could only see his own small world and not the many commitments the English province had in its already established and flourishing schools which were constantly crying for teachers. Woollett characterized Jaeckel as a strange character with an exalted idea of his worth, works, and capabilities. Yet Woollett cannot be exonerated, for he had set his mind fixedly on serving the parish mission and would give the struggling school only what he was obliged to, and that begrudgingly. When the superior general insisted that Woollett assign more teachers to help Jaeckel, Woollett considered the directive a mere suggestion which he was at liberty to follow or not. Jaeckel's assistant, Thomas Little, was practically useless; he taught only two hours a day. Ill health plagued him, but not so seriously that he could not spend hours at the Spanish Town mission because it was much to his liking. Little bluntly admitted teaching was repugnant to him. So the burden of conducting classes for five hours every day fell to Jaeckel.

On 21 May 1877, the unhappy situation came to a head. Jaeckel simply walked out with the notice that he would have no further part with the Society of Jesus.[32] On 27 September 1877, Fr. Peter Beckx wrote Jaeckel, telling him to return to Belgium.[33] But Jaeckel decided to remain in Jamaica and open his own school on 37 Duke Street with the aid of two lay teachers, N. E. Ellis and H. Harris. Later the school was removed to Upper Church Street, a place called Maryvilla.[34] Many of his pupils at St. George's followed him and continued their education under his direction. Always a success, his school flourished until his death in 1888.[35]

St. George's College would certainly have nailed the 'closed' to its doors for a fourth time had it not been for the timely arrival of Fr. Thomas Porter, S. J., the newly appointed vicar apostolic. He landed in Jamaica shortly before 23 September 1877, for on that date he and his companion, Fr. James Jones, former headmaster of St. George's, opened a mission at Holy Trinity Church. It appears that Jones urged on Porter the necessity of continuing St. George's College despite the Jaeckel debacle.

Immediately assuming the office of headmaster, in addition to that of vicar apostolic, Porter assured the continuity of the college.[36] Before the end of 1877, Fr. George Higgins, S. J., had taken over the office of headmaster, leaving Porter free to administer the vicariate. Then followed Fr. John Ryan in 1878, William Burns in 1885, Henry Parker in 1889, William Hudson in 1891, and lastly W. F. Fitzgerald, a layman with an M. A. from Oxford.

Despite the rapid change of headmasters, the college did make scholastic progress and offered a solid curriculum, as is evidenced from the *Handbook of Jamaica*.

> St. George's College 1889–1890
> The course comprehends 24 hours weekly
>
> 1) Latin, Greek, English, French
> 2) Arithmetic, Geometry, Algebra, Trigonometry, Bookkeeping
> 3) History, Geography, Natural Philosophy
> 4) Calligraphy, Drawing
> 5) Declamation, Ex Tempore Speaking
> 6) Vocal Music
> 7) Religion
>
> The terms are £2.10. per quarter, paid in advance. For brothers £2.00. Books and stationery extra. Vacations are about 3 weeks at Christmas, 4 in June and one week at Easter.[37]

This was the course of studies offered at St. George's College when the Maryland-New York province took charge of the institution. It would prove an important feature of the Jamaican mission, the basis upon which would rest an educated laity and a native clergy.

At this period in Jamaican history, secondary schools were for the boy or girl of ample financial means. This type of school did not number among its pupils the barefoot boy of Kingston, nor the farmer's son in the country; a less sophisticated school suited their minimal educational needs. Not until Benito Fernandez inaugurated his Free School for boys and girls did the Church venture into this type of education. This got its start at 20 Heywood Street, Kingston, when in 1844 Fernandez opened his first Elementary School for ragged little ones of questionable social background, who spoke a most difficult to understand dialect and gave no promise of becoming social or civic "greats" in later life.[38] In 1867, Fernandez's school, now named St. Joseph's Free School, changed its location from Heywood Street to 5 Upper King Street and was placed under the direction of coadjutor Brother Daniel Reynolds, S.J.[39] Financing the Free School was a vexing problem until the Church found the solution in the Jamaica Catholic Association, established in 1867 by Fr. Jones, which agreed to support the 130 boys attending St. Joseph's School by allocating £100 per year for their education.

In 1868, Fr. Hathaway appeared on the educational scene. Whether he opened his own school or took over the existing St. Joseph's Free School is not clear, but in 1875 the *Handbook of Jamaica* locates Hathaway's school at the corner of Hanover and East Queen Streets.[40] It was called the Catholic Elementary School, where Hathaway was assisted by Brother Reynolds and a Miss Anne Llado.

In the year 1880 Hathaway had given up teaching; the school, now named St. Joseph's Elementary, was under the direction of Thomas Porter, assisted by Brother Reynolds and Miss Anne Llado, but with its location now returned to 20 Heywood Street, Kingston.[41]

The advent of religious sisters placed elementary education on a firm foundation. First came the Franciscans from Scotland and later the Sisters of Mercy from England. The Franciscans perceived the necessity of a school for the poor soon after their arrival.[42] They held their first classes in the assembly room of Holy Trinity Church in 1859, and in January 1860 incorporated Fernandez's school for poor girls into their original assembly room institution. Sheer devotion to duty so enhanced the reputation of their schools that they ranked scholastically with the best in Jamaica.

In 1862 the Franciscans could count more than four hundred poor children under their tutelage.[43] The assembly room school had become St. Joseph's Girls' School and the boys' division of Hathaway's school had become St. Aloysius'. They also opened St. Anne's in western Kingston, the poorest section of the city. Moving out to Spanish Town in 1890, they closed the educational gap left by Fr. R. Walters, an Irish secular priest who had taken charge of the Spanish Town mission on 27 June 1843.[44] Shortly after his arrival he opened the first elementary school in Spanish Town with an enrollment of forty pupils. On 6 April 1844, Fr. Cotham commented that Walters was still doing excellent work in Spanish Town. The school continued for two years, then Walters got himself into trouble so serious that Benito Fernandez, vicar apostolic, had to revoke his faculties. Walters left for Trinidad on 8 August 1845, and his promising school closed its doors. It reopened in 1890.[45] Then it was so firmly established that it has functioned continuously for eighty years, first under the Franciscan Sisters and then under the Sisters of Mercy.

Although the Sisters of Mercy did not arrive until 1890, elementary education became a functional part of their programme from the day they assumed charge of the Orphanage and Industrial School at Alpha. Within two years, in 1892, fifty-three boys and fifty girls were being educated at that institution.[46] Government inspection of these schools officially commended these hard-working Sisters of Mercy and offered official government encouragement amid discouraging problems that arose trying to teach these children who came from the destitute poor or from broken homes, and resented the confining atmosphere of classroom walls; for the street and the open lots was their school. But these children came a long way under the devoted guidance of the sisters, for within one year they had won a good medal for artwork in the Jamaica Exposition of 1891.[47] Within three years they had won both a gold medal and a diploma at the World's Fair, Chicago, 1893, for their same kind of artwork.[48]

Education of city children was only part of the Church's endeavour to form a literate populace. Out in the hills, where most Jamaicans lived, were thousands of children growing up without the advantage of even an elementary education. These the Church had to include in her educational programme, no matter how poor or how modest might be the beginnings. From the year 1836, schools began to assume an important role in the country community.[49] On the elementary level, they imparted knowledge within the ambit of the three Rs; since they were taught by teachers whose own education seldom attained the secondary level, and hence there was no hope of imparting anything beyond the bare essentials.

Out in Seaford Town, at the western end of Jamaica in deep bush country, John Bierbusse had opened a school for the children of German immigrants: a mere fifteen attended his first classes conducted in the German language.[50] Four years later Bierbusse still taught at Seaford Town with an increase of pupils, but he suddenly vanished from the scene, diasppointed with the reality which did not live up to the publicity given the project by the recruiting agents in Hanover, Germany. At the eastern end of the island, the District of St.

George was not too fortunate in its initial educational attempts. In 1842 a Haitian settlement of coffee planters in this quiet and unperturbed mountain country had for its first teacher one Mr. Fitzgibbons, whose severe interpretation of the text about sparing the rod and spoiling the child appears to have been the explanation of his speedy and prudent departure from the district.[51] Teacher Balfour followed stern Fitzgibbons; since he was of kindlier disposition, he gained the confidence of parent and pupil.[52]

Though they taught mere fundamentals, these country government schools were important, for they offered the boy or girl an opportunity to learn to read and write. When residence in the city became possible, the pupil could continue education at a secondary school. Some of these country pupils left their names in the field of learning—a country boy from the district of Goshen, Adam C. Welsh, became one of the great Hebrew scholars of his day.[53]

The country school at Avocat in the district of St. George's offered excellent service to the community. When the whole mission was removed several miles lower down to Trinity Valley, to a spot purchased from Pierre Malabre by Dupeyron, Robert Murray took over the task of teaching.[54] For the next thirty-six years, he devoted his life to the education of these country children. Continuity such as this greatly benefitted the district and gave to the school a stability necessary for the efficient imparting of knowledge.

Woollett, who had shown unmistakable opposition to Jaeckel's St. George's College, was zealous in promoting country education. On the Retreat estate owned by Charles Barrett, Woollett set up his first school. He hired a former St. George's teacher and with funds furnished by the kindly Barrett educated thirty-six children, giving them an advantage not possible in the days of their slave ancestors. Soon the numbers rose to fifty, who took advantage of the combined efforts of Woollett and Barrett to produce literate boys and girls in these mountains above St. Ann's Bay.[55]

By the year 1868 Woollett had extended his educational programme to include his mission at Seaford Town, where he improved conditions at the existing school by adding new desks, furniture, and a good supply of texts. The school could now accommodate one hundred pupils, an improvement over the one begun by the German immigrant Bierbusse. Woollett planned schools for his missions in the town of Falmouth and the remote district of Alva in the Dry Harbour Mountains. At. Pisgah, the nearest mission to Seaford Town but the farthest removed from urban community life, there was a schoolmaster and thirty-two pupils due to his efforts.[56]

But parents were so poor that the entire support for the school had to be assumed by the missionary. What Woollett paid as salary to the teacher must have been meagre, for he had to augment his wages by cultivating tobacco and yams which he sold in the local market. The overall number of children profiting by Church sponsored schools was not large, but it did indicate that the poor boy and girl living far from the advantages of the city were not entirely neglected, though it meant personal sacrifice on the part of the missionary.

One may wonder if these early educational efforts, so soon after emancipation, produced satisfactory results or were they wasted on the country air? One authority, Charles J. Latrobe, wrote on 19 October 1837 that the children of slaves showed remarkable facility in the attainment of the elementary branches of instruction taught them, and this was especially true of writing and arithmetic.[57] Yet to maintain these schools was a perennial problem for the missionary who, convinced of their value to the community, relied principally on the weekly fees collected from the pupils.

Top Hill, Westmoreland, was such a school. Opened in January 1892, it had to compete with St. Paul's, a Protestant school only three miles distant. Beginning with a wooden structure thirty feet by eighteen feet, the school had twenty-five pupils, two thirds of whom were Catholics.[58] Miss Myrie, the teacher, lived as poorly as any of her pupils on the salary of £2.0.0 per month. Finding it impossible to live on this wage, she left in March 1894, and the school was without a teacher. Thereupon Bishop Gordon persuaded a Thomas Buchanan, the teacher at White Hall, Kingston, to take Miss Myrie's place. Buchanan regretted the change as soon as he arrived at the country school on 12 March 1894, for Top Hill had no blackboards, no alphabet charts, no reading charts, nor even an attendance register.[59]

A constant lament of teachers in nineteenth-century parochial schools in Jamaica was that they were underpaid, even by the standard of the common labourer. It could not be denied that the Church was building her country educational system on low basic pay for the teacher. Teachers suffered; pupils suffered, for the type of teacher employed was either a person who totally disregarded such mundane considerations as money and worked out of pure devotion to the training of youth, or one who could find no better employment. Too often, he was of the latter class. Youth was being entrusted, in its formative years, to men and women who were intellectually inferior to trained teachers. The wonder is that the Church has been able to raise her mission schools to their present high standard. This never could have been done had not most of these schools been incorporated into the government educational system, whereby the salaries of the teachers, both religious and lay, were paid by the Ministry of

Education, which also made substantial grants for construction and maintenance.

During the fifty-eight years from 1836 to 1894, the Church opened twenty-one schools both in Kingston and in the country. Some were successes, others failures. The main cause of failure was lack of financial support. A list of these schools is as follows:

IN KINGSTON

Duquesnay's School
Fernandez's School for poor boys and girls
St. George's College
Immaculate Conception Academy
Hathaway's School
St. Joseph's Girls' School
St. Aloysius' Boys' School
Alpha Boys' School
Alpha Girls' School
Alpha Academy
St. Anne's School
White Hall School

OUTSIDE KINGSTON

Walter's School, Spanish Town
St. Catherine's School, Spanish Town
Retreat Estate School, Brown's Town
St. Boniface's School, Alva
Top Hill School
Seaford Town School
Pisgah School
Black River School

The next phase of education began with the Americans who were fortunate to arrive in Jamaica at a time when the government offered generous grants to Catholic schools.

Twenty-eight

Education 1894–1970

For more than one hundred years, the educational system in Jamaica had been modelled on that of England. The problems Jamaica encountered were the same as England's, and she accepted England's answers to these difficulties.

English education was divided into primary, secondary, and university.[1] Primary education, however, was divided into elementary schools for the lower classes and preparatory schools for the upper classes. Elementary schools for the poor provided them with a terminal education, while the preparatory schools were an introduction to the higher education of the secondary schools for the upper classes of the gentry. Beginning at an early age, English education indoctrinated its students with a sense of class distinction, and this was the determining factor separating the early education of youth into different schools for the upper and lower classes of society. To pass from one to the other was next to impossible. A child born into the lower classes of society was not expected to pursue his education at the secondary school level, much less at the university level.[2] The entire orbit of his formal education centered around those years of his young life from the age of four years to sixteen years, while the content of his education embraced just enough reading, writing, and arithmetic for his place in society within the labouring class.

This classification was faithfully reflected in the elementary school system in Jamaica, which aimed to prepare the child for a place among the labouring classes of the island. Entering the infant department at the age of four years, the child passed into first standard of elementary school at the age of six years and remained in this school until he completed sixth standard at the age of fifteen years and thus terminated his formal education. He was considered fit for his position in life.

The pattern followed by the boy of the upper social classes was quite different. Instead of being sent to a government school for his early education, he was tutored privately at home or sent to a preparatory school conducted by a competent teacher. At the age of ten years he was ready for first form in a secondary school. Completing fifth form, he sat for a public examination. At this point his formal education might terminate, at what in the American system would be the equivalent of completing high school. If he elected to continue his formal education, though, two more years were available to him in secondary school which was called "higher schools."[3] At its completion he sat for another public examination. Successfully passing this examination, he might matriculate at a university where an academic degree awaited him upon completion of the course.[4] This same system was followed in Jamaica, the one exception was that the student had to travel abroad to seek university education until the establishment of the University of the West Indies (University College) in 1948.

For a clear knowledge of Jamaican education, a look at the problem which confronted England will help. In the 1880s, elementary education in England was torn between two interested parties, those who wanted a purely secular system, and the determined opposition of the churches, which fought to maintain control of the schools.[5] Those in favour of purely government-controlled schools based their argument on the alarming shortage of schools in England, believing that the Churches could not provide adequately for the education of the nation.[6] This would later be reflected in Jamaica, when government would assume more and more control over the educational system. Government hostility in England injected new life into ecclesiastically controlled schools; Anglicans in particular began an extensive school expansion programme.[7]

But not only were the number of buildings in England inadequate; the educational standards had also deteriorated. A religious dispute prevented the denominations from receiving substantial government help which would have raised their standards by offering an attractive salary to the more qualified teacher. The crux of the dispute centered around the teaching of religious knowledge.[8] The question arose: if Protestant bodies were to pool their resources in a common school system and thus receive substantial help from the British government, what religious tenets should be taught in these schools? The Anglicans proposed their tenets; the Nonconformists, theirs. Failure to agree on such a fundamental issue precluded government aid and brought educational progress to an impasse which weakened the whole English school system.[9] Since neither Anglicans nor Nonconformists would agree on the fundamentals of religion to be taught in these schools, the plan for an interdenominational school system came to naught. In 1852 the English Government took a firm step towards resolving the impasse between Anglicans and Nonconformists. A ruling was handed down that no financial grant would be paid to any school unless a "Conscience Clause" was inserted into the institution's constitution. This ruling guaranteed to any child attending these schools the liberty of absenting himself from religion classes should tenets contrary to his faith be taught.

Jamaica modelled its reform after the British precedent of 1852, and made this a requirement in 1870 for all schools receiving government aid.[10] The "Conscience Clause"[11] is displayed prominently in every classroom and reads:

> It shall not be required as a condition of admission or continuance of any child in a Public elementary school:
>
> 1) That he shall attend or abstain from attending any Sunday School or Place of Religious Worship.
> 2) That he shall if his parent or guardian objects attend any Religious observance or any instruction in Religious subjects in the school or elsewhere.
> 3) That he shall attend school on any day specially set apart for Religious Worship by the Religious body to which he belongs.[12]

The second level of English education was the secondary school. This posed two problems. The first, how to integrate the elementary with the secondary school so as to make secondary education available to the lower classes; and secondly, how to break down the social buffer between elementary and secondary schools. The establishment of universal free education on the elementary level produced an unexpected problem in England. When this system of free education was introduced, it was assumed that it would provide for the first stage in the education of poor boys of ability who were to receive a secondary education after being selected from the elementary schools. The primary difficulty came from independent secondary "Public Schools," which were a complete class preserve in themselves. There was no provision at all for education among them. It was the secondary grammar government-aided schools which drew a large percentage of their pupils from the elementary schools, but admission was gained only after a competitive examination had selected the fortunate ones. Some objected to this procedure which made the whole educational future of the child depend upon the performance in a single examination taken at the age of eleven years.

Since Jamaican education was based on the English prototype, the same two problems which confronted the English also faced the Jamaican namely, social distinction, and how to integrate the elementary with the secondary system. Like England, Jamaica too was losing a vast reserve of talent by depriving a majority of pupils of a secondary education simply because they did not happen to be born into the upper classes of society. By solving the social distinction question, Jamaica moved on to solve the integration of the elementary and secondary systems. In order to assure fairness to all, the Government decreed that all places in Grant-in-Aid secondary schools should be filled by competitive examinations open to all children of Jamaica who had reached the age of ten years. Government set, supervised, and corrected, the examination carried a number assigned to each student which guaranteed fairness by government-sponsored correctors. On the basis of this examination, students from any elementary school, whether government or private, would be admitted to a secondary school. The student might signify the school of his choice and if practicable, government would assign him to that school. This fair system tended to break down class distinction and offered to everyone who qualified the opportunity of a secondary school education.

Then came the cry from parents and students that there were not enough secondary schools in Jamaica to place all boys willing and capable of pursuing higher education. Government faced the situation by providing additional schools and more teachers competent in instructing in secondary school subjects.

American Jesuits were introduced to this English-Jamaican system of education in 1894 when they assumed control of St. George's College. Completely ignorant of the system which placed increasing emphasis on the Cambridge external examination, they followed the curriculum and method familiar to them from their experience in the American system of education where emphasis at this time was placed on the individual school setting the standard of excellence by its own examinations.

St. George's College up to 1894 could not be considered an unqualified success. On three occasions it had to acknowledge failure since it reneged on its public promises and had to close its doors. Failure could be laid to one principle cause, a lack of interest by superiors in the institution. Without their full, constant support, St. George's College could never become a successful educational institution, and this lack of interest stemmed from the fallacy of concentrating on the immediate needs of the time to the exclusion of a clear vision of the future. Superiors failed to see the solid effect an institution like St. George's College would have on the combined civic and religious life of Jamaica.

Jones was the first to evaluate the potentialities of St. George's and to clearly gauge the worth of secondary school education as an important missionary ancillary.[13] Gordon too was of the same opinion as Jones. Combining in his person both the office of Jesuit superior and vicar apostolic, Gordon took the occasion of the arrival of American Jesuits to raise St. George's College to its rightful niche in Jamaican education. But even he failed to realize how long and slow a process it would be. He might give it a start, but it would take the sweat and persevering efforts of many American Jesuits to make St. George's College one of the leading secondary schools in Jamaica.

With the opening of the scholastic year of 1894–95, St. George's College was given a new look; teaching staff and curriculum were reorganized, a new headmaster, Fr. Patrick H. Kelly, S.J., assisted by a competent staff, was appointed to teach Latin, Greek, English, French, history, mathematics, the natural sciences, and religion. The school advertised that it would prepare students for the public examinations of the Cambridge Locals as well as the civil service and the Jamaica scholarship examinations. At that time St. George's was located at the northwest corner of North and East streets, Kingston. Kelly lasted only one year as headmaster, though he continued on the staff as a teacher. He was replaced by the very competent William Gregory, S.J., who successfully guided thirteen students through the Cambridge Local examinations. Fr. Edward Purbrick, provincial of the Maryland-New York province, expressed his delight that Gregory had so successfully prepared his students for this difficult English-based examination.[14] Since he was an Englishman educated under the English system, Purbrick realized how assiduously an American had to work to accomplish this intellectual feat.

Augustus J. Duarte, S.J., and Joseph N. Dinand, S.J., followed Gregory in succession. Each by his own personality added a little more strength, a little more stability to the evolving institution now accepted as an integral part of the mission. This brought an increase in both faculty and student body. It was evident that the faculty residence at 25 North Street and the school premises at North and East streets were inadequate for an expanding institution. Like a stroke of good fortune, Winchester Park, containing nineteen acres, was for sale and was purchased from Alfred Pawsey on 11 February 1905 while Duarte was headmaster.[15] First classes were held in the Pawsey residence (the old building at 25 North Street was now inadequate) on Monday, 27 March 1905, while the faculty continued to reside at 25 North Street.[16] For the next two years they had to be transported daily to Winchester Park situated at the far eastern end of North Street, for there was a legal snag in disposing of the 26 North Street property.

The question was who owned it—the vicariate or the Society of Jesus? The 26 North Street property had been purchased for £800, half of which was given as a loan by Fr. Weld, the provincial of the English province. The other half had been borrowed, and the loan was repaid from school fees. When Jones became provincial, he deeded 25 North Street to Gordon, on 22 December 1891. But Gordon never paid the £500, the agreed sale figure.[17] In writing to Propaganda Fide, Rome, on 10 June 1895, Gordon claimed that Jones remitted the £500 debt, the justice of which the Jesuit superior general, Luis Martin, questioned in a letter to Gordon 23 April 1895.[18] Martin admitted that the vicariate legally possessed the residence, but the nonpayment of the debt by the vicariate being doubtful, the presumption was in favour of the Jesuits.[19] The question of this debt was a matter of controversy in the following regime of John L. Collins.

O'Hare, Patrick Collins,[20] and again O'Hare guided St. George's College from 1908–15. In O'Hare's first term as headmaster the new St. George's rose in architectural splendor on the campus, for the College had outgrown its cramped quarters in the old Pawsey house and was crying for a new building, constructed exclusively for classroom use. On 19 March 1913 a contract was signed between Fr. John Harpes and two alumni of the college, Eustace and Clement Fielding, for construction of the new building.[21] The architect was Brahman Judah, whose two sons, Sydney and Charles, had entered the Society of Jesus in 1923 and 1924. Beyond the actual edifice itself, it reflected a new departure in mission thought in Jamaica, for priority was now afforded secondary education, admitting that it could play a major role in mission planning. The first sod was broken 3 March 1913. So historic did *Catholic Opinion* consider the event that it carefully noted that the ceremony took place at 3.20 in the afternoon.[22]

In the opinion of American professors, a well-rounded liberal arts course in the classics, modern languages, and mathematics was of more importance than preparing students for external examinations sent out from England by the Cambridge University Syndicate. Such was the attitude in 1915, and so it is not surprising that only five St. George's boys sat for the public examinations that year. But the importance of the Cambridge examination would grow with the years and so influence both content and method of teaching that one day these examinations would become the scholastic criteria of the worth of a secondary school.

In vain secondary schools protested that external examinations must not dictate curriculum; but in practice they actually did. No matter how much resistance was offered, public examinations did subtly influence content and method. For a period of years, St. George's College had set its own examinations, its own curriculum, and offered its own diploma in proof that its graduates had successfully completed the prescribed course of studies. In the 1940s public examinations like the Cambridge Locals assumed such importance for the scholastic community that to resist the trend would have so isolated St. George's from the intellectual segment of Jamaica that her student body would have dwindled and have been forced a fourth time to close her doors. Growing emphasis placed on these examinations as a requirement for entrance to the university, for positions in government and banking services, and even for employment in commercial houses, forced educators to prepare their students to pass successfully such examinations. St. George's had to adopt an attitude of interest and base its curriculum on the subjects recommended by the Cambridge Syndicate. The value of Oxford-Cambridge examination increased when their potential was recognized by the education world of England.[23]

At the close of the eighteenth century, English universities were in a state of doldrums, and from this inertia were rescued by introducing a series of examinations much like those conducted in universities today. In the 1850s further interest was awakened by applying the university system of examinations to secondary schools in order to raise their standards in like manner. Oxford and Cambridge answered the plea of local school committees by setting examinations for students not members of the universities.[24] The purpose was not to qualify the student for the university; rather these examinations were to act as an incentive for the secondary schools to raise their standards so that their students could pass these examinations set by the Oxford-Cambridge Syndicate. In 1858 an examination was set by Oxford and Cambridge universities which qualified successful candidates for the civil service.[25] From this experiment, the value of external examinations was learned and applied to secondary schools. The name "Cambridge Locals" stems from the custom of conducting these examinations at local centres; thus Jamaica would be a local centre of the examinations for the Caribbean area.

One influential effect of the Cambridge Locals was to stress the ever-growing importance of science in the curriculum. The years beginning in 1938 may be characterized as the age of physical sciences at St. George's College. Science was asserting itself in Jamaican education just as it was in the English and American systems. In the initial stages the total content of the liberal arts subjects was not reduced, but as time passed biology, chemistry, and physics clamoured for more than a minor role in the curriculum. This placed pressure on the headmaster to provide competent science professors, men trained as specialists in their subjects.

Fr. John Blatchford, S.J., started the era of able science masters at St. George's College in 1935 by teaching chemistry.[26] At first the school could not offer him much in the way of a laboratory, a mere makeshift in the old Pawsey residence; but four years later St. George's did have a laboratory which any school in Jamaica would be proud to possess. Ground was broken in 1936. In March 1939 the building was dedicated amid much fanfare. Governor Sir Arthur Richards and other notables extolled its many merits—a model of excellence in construction, good taste, and equipment, the only building to be erected on the campus in a quarter of a century. It forecast a departure from an exclusively liberal arts curriculum to a new venture into the world of science. Fr. Leo Butler, S.J., sounded the keynote by declaring there was sound reason for introducing science into the course of studies in a major role.[27] For some years the universities had taught not only advanced courses in science but had to add both elementary and intermediate courses in science because students coming from secondary schools were not properly prepared in these subjects. It was now judged by the universities that the time had arrived for secondary schools to bear the burden of introducing students to the sciences on the elementary and intermediate levels, so that the university might concentrate on advanced courses. Students planning a career in medicine or engineering discovered that the university required a science studied in a secondary school as a prerequisite for matriculation. In opening the new science building this requisite was uppermost in the mind of Butler, for a student's competence was determined by his success in passing the Cambridge Local Examination which was placing increased emphasis on science.

Planners of the new chemistry laboratory had to keep in mind that they were not only to prepare students on the elementary level, but also on the intermediate level. This necessitated apparatus for qualitative and volumetric analysis, physical and organic chemistry. Through the years the original building underwent improvements based on the long-range policy to bring it to a level of the highest standard of course offered in chemistry in the secondary school system.[28]

Biology was introduced into the curriculum in 1941 when Fr. Blatchford began classes in January, using his own chemistry laboratory as a temporary arrangement until the newly appointed professor of biology, Fr. Gerald Hennessey, S.J., arrived from Fordham University, where he received his master's degree.[29] In September 1941 Hennessey assumed charge of St. George's biology department, having arrived on the 20 August with $5,000 worth of equipment contributed by personal friends, the College of the Holy Cross and Boston College.

Hardly had classes begun to function when a request came from a number of secondary teachers for a course to prepare them to enter the field of biology. Hennessey agreed and the course also began in September 1941.[30] In October came another request, this time from Dr. Kenneth Evans, director of the Government Bacteriological Laboratory, asking Hennessey to instruct fifteen of his technicians. Still another request came from a group of religious sisters; they too wanted a course in biology.[31] These demands forecast a bright future for the subject of biology under the tutorship of Hennessey, who continued to offer his teaching services to the public for the next thirty years.

The science of physics antedated biology by a full year, Blatchford, an all-around scientist, began as early as 1940 in his chemistry laboratory, using it for both classes and experiments. In September of that same year, Fr. Francis Dutram, S.J., arrived from Boston to take up his duty as physics master.[32] Classes were transferred from the chemistry laboratory to crowded quarters at the south end of the administration building. Here Dutram taught until 1947, when he was succeeded by Fr. Raymond McCluskey, S.J., who immediately planned a new science building. Leonard Chang, a graduate of St. George's College and the California Institute of Technology, both designed and constructed the new laboratory in 1950. It became the centre of much student interest, particularly for Chinese students, whose natural talent for mathematical science found a ready outlet in physics.

In 1940 sixty-seven students had been enrolled in the physics course, but in 1966 the number had risen to 230.[33] The faculty of 6 Jesuits at St. George's College which preceded the advent of the science laboratories was increased to 11 members in 1940, to 17 in 1951. By the year 1960 there were 40 Jesuits and 12 lay professors with a student body numbering 868. In 1970 there were 35 Jesuits, 26 lay professors and a student body of 950. In 1960, 91 students passed the Cambridge Examination at the ordinary level and 13 at the advanced level, with more and more emphasis being placed on this latter level for prestige to both students and school.

A large number of Chinese students enrolled at St. George's during the 1940–60 era. Now that their parents had reached the comfortable financial status whereby they might dispense with the sons' help in the family grocery shop, more opportunity was offered the children for higher education. Of the ninety-one students who passed the Cambridge Locals in 1960, forty-seven were Chinese, while five of the thirteen who passed the same examination at the advanced level were of the same ethnic group. These people were pragmatic, and since St. George's College had well-equipped laboratories and excellent science courses, it offered a bright promise of passing the Cambridge examinations—all important factors for the engineering and medical professions. They represented forty-three percent of the student body in 1950.

Extension School

Increasing demands on the biology department of St. George's for courses outside the regular day classes gave birth to the idea of an extension school for adults in the mind of Thomas A. Feeney, S.J., president of the college. On the evening of 5 October 1942, he formally opened the Extension Department, taught by Jesuit and lay faculty from 4.30 p.m. to 9.00 p.m. every day from Monday to Friday during the regular school term.[34] For some reason or another, hundreds of young men and women had never finished secondary education. Faced with a life of unfulfilled ambitions, they recognized the extension school as a step towards the realization of their desires. In the first year 126 took advantage of the twelve courses offered.

Philosophy	Physics	Law
Chemistry	Journalism	History
Public Speaking	Sociology	Biology
Economics	Mathematics	Cooperatives

Early in its history the Extension School plotted a curriculum adapted to the special needs of its students. The adult did not seek an integrated course such as was offered in the day division of St. George's; rather he selected individual subjects in the arts and sciences which enabled him to pass, in the shortest time possible, the exams of his choice in the General Certificate of Education, Higher Schools Certificate, University College or Vocational school entrance. These serious-minded adults progressed so commendably in the pursuit of an education that they have taken their places in Jamaican life as doctors, lawyers, dentists, engineers, biologists, chemists, teachers, agronomists, and business men and women.

Some predicted an end to the usefulness of St. George's College Extension School once the University of the West Indies opened its extramural department. They were wrong, for not only did it survive but it grew so in numbers that students had to be turned away for lack of space. Fees were kept to a minimum, so low that even the poorest could afford the tuition. In the beginning most of the faculty were Jesuits who were also engaged in teaching in the day division of St. George's. This placed a heavy burden on these teachers; so great did the demand for courses in the Extension School become that more lay faculty were added to the staff.

Throughout the years, while the majority of courses have been offered without interruption, new ones have been introduced and old ones discarded according to the demands of the student body and the availability of teachers. The following table shows this trend.[35]

SUBJECT	NUMBER OF STUDENTS ENROLLED IN EACH SUBJECT						
	1949	1952	1958	1967	1968	1969	1970
Biology	90	94	169	71	73	77	104
Chemistry	50	78	119	126	120	118	113
Physics	35	63	70	134	128	120	119
Mathematics	52	118	248	439	456	576	531
Spanish	51	64	101	100	87	49	31
Latin	20	45	45	—	—	—	—
Philosophy	5	15	45	—	—	—	—
Economics	10	22	55	105	131	161	145
Public Speaking	15	28	—	—	—	—	—
Law	67	—	—	—	—	—	—
Journalism	15	—	—	—	—	—	—
Music Appreciation	9	—	—	—	—	—	—
French	5	—	—	—	—	—	—
German	—	—	11	—	—	—	—
Geography	—	—	25	43	45	52	51
Aviation	—	—	36	—	—	—	—
Accounting	—	—	7	69	109	132	167
English	25	45	139	513	484	558	453
English Literature	—	—	—	—	—	—	—
Zoology	—	—	—	60	51	53	31
Botany	—	—	—	20	36	26	16
Health Science	—	—	—	121	116	129	120
History	—	—	—	54	93	111	95
Commerce	—	—	—	43	32	27	33
Computer Systems	—	—	—	26	21	—	—
Leadership	—	—	—	—	—	—	12

The Extension school has proved a boon to the community. In its many years of existence, more than 20,000 students have passed through its portals, reaching an all-time high in 1970, when 1,135 were enrolled for that year. Of the sixteen Jamaicans admitted to the University College of the West Indies when it first opened its doors in October 1948, eight of these had taken courses at St. George's Extension School. Howard, McGill, Edinburgh, and Columbia universities are examples of the many institutions which have admitted students from St. George's Extension School. In the field of scholarships, they have been awarded the Jamaica Scholarship, the Issa Scholarship, the

Public Works Scholarship, the Cooperative Scholarship, and the Medical Scholarship.

Campion

In 1957 St. George's College faced a governmental control problem which it had to solve. The root of this problem lay in 1936, when St. George's accepted grant-in-aid, and became a part of the Government education system. The Jamaican government paid the salary of the lay faculty, and also assumed seventy-five percent of the cost of new construction. For these services it would want some say in the administration of the college. From 1936–56, although it was a grant-in-aid school, St. George's set and corrected its own entrance examinations, and on that basis admitted students it judged qualified. Then, in 1957, the Ministry of Education set its own examination.[36] From the results it judged those students qualified to be admitted to Grant-in-Aid Secondary Schools. No longer did St. George's have the option of admitting students; it had to take whomever the government sent to the college. The student might signify the college of his choice and, as far as possible, the Ministry of Education honoured that choice. But in the final judgment, it was the responsibility of government to assign the student to the institution. This was good for the boy who qualified by the standard set by the Ministry of Education, but for those who failed, there was no Catholic secondary school to attend.

A clamour of protests went up from parents whose sons had failed the government examination. They could hardly be ignored, and in response to their petition, Campion College came into being. It followed the same academic course as St. George's and prepared students for the same Cambridge General Certificate of Education, but it had no financial dependence on the Ministry of Education. This meant that the school was free to accept or reject applicants solely on the standards which this private school had set as requirements for admission. Parents had to face the fact that the student calibre would be lower than that of a Grant-in-Aid Secondary School whose student body had passed the entrance requirements set by the Ministry of Education. As the years passed, a better type, intellectually speaking, did seek admission to Campion College. This raised the standard with the result that the school experienced remarkable success in the Cambridge examinations. It opened at the Jesuit superior's residence, 105 Hope Road, January 1960, with a handful of students and four Jesuits for faculty.[37] It has grown to a faculty of fifteen Jesuits assisted by twenty-four lay teachers, with a student body of 535 in 1970. This remarkable growth of a privately-conducted secondary school independent of government aid is indicative of its importance in the field of Jamaican education. (Note: In 1987 Campion College is a Grant-in-Aid Government denominational school with an enrollment of 1300.)

In this modern era, when St. George's and Campion colleges were playing a distinctive role in education, the Sisters of Mercy were making their educational expertise recognized throughout all classes of society. This is evident at such a centre as Alpha, 26 South Camp Road, Kingston, where some 3,000 boys and girls from every stratum of society attend classes which range from preparatory, to primary, to the secondary level, all under the direction of the Sisters of Mercy.

Students enter Alpha to begin their preparatory or primary education in the three Rs and continue until the age of ten years when they take a government Common Entrance examination which qualifies them for a government-sponsored high school. Should a girl select Alpha Academy, she would continue her education on the same compound, 26 Camp Road, Kingston, where she would study English, mathematics, history, geography, science, and modern and ancient languages until she completed fifth form and would then take her first public examination, designated as "Ordinary Level" and which some colleges and universities accept as entrance requirements. Should the student choose to continue her studies at Alpha, she would enroll in a programme known as Higher Schools, which would prepare her for matriculation at most English universities.

Near the Alpha compound, but located on Emerald Road, Kingston, is an example of a recent type of school, the junior secondary school. Holy Trinity Junior Secondary School is conducted by the Sisters of Mercy, assisted by thirty-one lay teachers with an enrollment of 1,591 boys and girls. Here a course of studies is offered which equates the first three years of a senior secondary school and which is proving very popular in the government educational system of the island.

On Laws street, Kingston, the heart of the inner city, the Sisters of Mercy are active at Holy Family Mission, where pupils may begin their education at kindergarten and complete it at primary school level. Here one thousand boys and girls are taking advantage of this type of education.

In such diverse places as Spanish Town, Mandeville, Hatfield, Black River, and Savanna-la-Mar, the Sisters of Mercy conduct kindergarten to primary level schools serving some 2,500 boys and girls in these areas outside Kingston.

Corresponding to the Alpha compound is the attractive Constant Spring campus of the Immaculate Conception High School conducted by the Franciscan Sisters where a student may gain a full education from kindergarten to junior college at an establishment which has been in existence since 1857 and where 1,346 girls are taking advantage of these sisters' long experience in educating Jamaicans.

Like the Sisters of Mercy, the Franciscans have a junior secondary school at St. Anne's Parish, another inner city, with an enrollment of 429 pupils and where there is also a kindergarten-primary school numbering 1,537 boys and girls. At St. Aloysius (boys)—St. Joseph (girls) School compound at the old convent grounds Duke Street, Kingston, the Franciscans can boast of the largest Catholic school in Jamaica with an enrollment of 4,192 pupils.[38]

Out at Highgate, in the civil parish of St. Mary, the Franciscans conduct Marymount Academy, which with its preparatory school has an enrollment of 204. At Montego Bay the Mt. Alvernia High School and its preparatory department has grown to 621 students.

Twenty-nine

New Vistas

A new era opened for the Catholic Church in Jamaica on 5 February 1971, when Samuel E. Carter, S.J., the first native archbishop of Kingston was installed in Holy Trinity Cathedral by Archbishop Barbarito, the Papal Delegate to the Antilles. This event marked a definite break with the past and an end to the non-Jamaican hierarchy. Now Jamaica could proudly point to a native son chosen by the Holy See to administer the Church in the archdiocese.

Jamaica is a mission where the Church for many years depended on a foreign clergy, a definite weak point in her organization. Over the years the Church should have fostered a native clergy and not have relied so greatly on foreign priests.

Jamaica, the third largest island of the Greater Antilles, is surpassed geographically by Hispaniola and Cuba. It has a total population of 2,100,000 with only 187,222 (1980) Catholics, which represent a cross section of racial mixture, for ninety-five percent of the people are of African origin; with a small number of Chinese, East Indians (from India), Levantine, and white European and North Americans of less than five percent.

The archdiocese of Kingston covers a geographical area of six civil parishes—Kingston-St. Andrew, St. Catherine, Clarendon, St. Thomas, Portland, and St. Mary. Falling within the jurisdiction of the archdiocese are the Cayman Islands: Grand Cayman, Little Cayman, and Cayman Brac, an area of 100 square miles. Under the archdiocese are the suffragan sees of Belize, Hamilton in Bermuda, Montego Bay, and Nassau.

A British colony since 1655, Jamaica has been a self-governing, independent nation since 6 August 1962, within the Commonwealth of Nations. The Queen of England is titular head of the country and the local Governor-General her representative. Jamaica has a democratic form of government similar to the British parliamentary system with a Prime Minister and a House of Representatives elected by the people. The long English domination of Jamaica has left its impress on the language and culture of the people.

Constitutionally, Jamaica is now ruled by her own sons and daughters. Likewise for the Church to be governed by her own native clergy is of the utmost importance, for they know the language with all its nuances; they know the customs and can incorporate the Church into the milieu better than any foreign clergy. If the dioceses of the United States had to depend on a foreign clergy, the Church would be neither as numerous nor as strong as she is today in that country. This can be applied to every nation in the world. Given a native clergy, you have the opportunity of proving to the people that the Church is not foreign to the land, for the people see a concrete example in their sons ordained priests and bringing the Good News to them in their native tongue.

Let us look at the position of the Church when Archbishop Carter assumed office from Archbishop McEleney in 1970. Catholics numbered some eight percent of the total population. This appears a low figure, since the Church has functioned uninterruptedly since 1792, a period of 178 years. Several factors account for this low percentage of Catholics. When the Church received a new birth in 1792, the only priest on the island was Fr. Anthony Quigly, a Recollect, sent out by Bishop Douglass of the London District to minister to a handful of Catholics: French refugees from Haiti and Spanish merchants from South America with a few Irish and English. He confined his apostolic labours to the Catholics of Kingston, with no thought of evangelizing the rest of the island.

Even if Quigly tried to evangelize the Jamaicans, he would have found a formidable foe in the monolithic Anglican Church, ensconced in every civil parish, where worship centred around the parish church. Members of the Anglican Church were of the upper stratum of society, including the governor-general, and a Church which jealously guarded its religious prerogatives as a status symbol harbouring only the elite.

Vast numbers of slaves could have no part in Anglican worship; they were excluded from baptism by the very high stole fee a slave owner had to pay should he want his slaves baptized Anglicans. Not until the advent of the Moravians and the Baptists who admitted slaves into their communions did the Anglican Church also baptize slaves, lest the non-Conformists gather all of them into their folds.

A lack of priests was another obstacle preventing the advance of the Church in Jamaica. Quigly died in 1799 and was followed by several refugee priests, some of whom remained for a short time before moving on to greener pastures. This offered little stability to the Church in Jamaica.

Benito Fernandez, a Franciscan, was another refugee priest who was exiled from New Granada (Colombia) in 1821. Unlike his predecessors, he settled in Kingston and remained until his death in 1855.

Early in his pastorate he saw the need for religious priests who would supply men for the mission and offer it stability. He applied to the Holy See for such priests; Rome assigned Jamaica to the Society of Jesus as a mission. Rome also asked the Society of Jesus to send English, French, and Spanish priests to minister to their respective ethnic groups. Religious priests, all foreigners, did not satisfy the basic need for the development of a native clergy.

This state of the Church remained until 1952 when Archbishop McEleney opened St. Michael's Seminary at Bellevue in the Red Hills, overlooking Kingston. Latin, English, history, and religion were the initial subjects; later philosophy was added to the curriculum. For theology, the seminarians were sent abroad.

To move a young seminarian from his native environment and expose him to a strange culture can be a mistake. Once he experiences a higher culture in the environment of another land, either he does not want to return to his native country, or, if he does return, it is with a heavy heart. Archbishop McEleney saw this difficulty and transferred St. Michael's to a new location adjacent to the University of the West Indies, Kingston, and added theology to the curriculum. He also arranged that the seminarians should be awarded degrees from the university.

This was a decided advance in the development of a native clergy and the stage at which Archbishop Carter found the seminary when he assumed office. He now had a firm base on which to build a native clergy, for the entire seminary course was made in the young man's native environment.

The first years of St. Michael's Major Seminary were not without difficulties. To find a suitable faculty was one; to attract young Jamaicans to the institution was another. For a period of years no one was ordained. Promising young men came but they departed, their reasons known only to themselves. Two excellent professors were found: David Sanders, O.P., who taught theology, and Joseph Brennan, S.J., who taught philosophy. They gave stability to the nascent seminary under its Jamaican rector, Alwyn Harry, S.J.

Although the intellectual life of the seminary is of utmost importance, unless it rests on a firm spiritual foundation, it will be like sounding brass and tingling cymbals. For the life of the future priest is more than intellect; the will must be trained to conform to the divine Will. The Second Vatican Council had this to say on the subject:

> Spiritual formation should be closely linked with doctrinal and pastoral training. Especially with the help of the spiritual director, such formation should help the seminarians to learn to live in familiar and constant companionship with the Father through Jesus Christ, His Son, in the Holy Spirit. By sacred ordination they will be molded in the likeness of Christ, the Priest. . . . They should live His paschal mystery in such a way that they know how to initiate into it the people entrusted to them. . . . With the trust of a son, they should love and honor the most Blessed Virgin Mary who was given as a mother to his disciples as He hung on the cross.[1]

Archbishop Carter made this spiritual dimension the very life of St. Michael's Seminary as one of the means for carrying out the will of the Council. As a means of improving the spiritual life at St. Michael's, Archbishop Carter required all candidates for the major seminary to spend two years in basic spiritual training at St. James' Minor Seminary, Montego Bay diocese.

The words of Pope Pius XI have been put into effect in Jamaica. Addressing his words to the bishops of the world, the Pope said:

> First of all, let us recall to your attention how important it is that you build a native clergy. If you do not work with all your might to accomplish this, we maintain that your apostolate will not only be crippled, but will prove to be an obstacle and an impediment for the establishment and organization of the Church in those countries. We are more than willing to admit and recognize that in some places steps have been taken to overcome this obstacle by the erection of seminaries in which native youths of good promise are duly instructed and prepared to ascend to the dignity of the priesthood.[2]

In recent years St. Michael's has broadened its curriculum to include not only a programme for permanent deacons but also the training of lay ministers—parish assistants such as readers, catechists, special ministers of the Eucharist, prayer-group leaders, and acolytes. The seminary also offers extension courses in scripture and theology for the laity.

Religious sisters are included in the seminary programme by courses in systematic and moral theology, Church history, and pastoral training, thereby obtaining a bachelor's degree from the University of the West Indies.

In the continuing education of the clergy, St. Michael's helps plan and assist in workshops and conferences held throughout the year. While as a preparation for Lent it has introduced special Lenten courses in some aspects of Holy Scripture.

On 29 September 1985 Archbishop Carter ordained three seminarians to the priesthood at Holy Trinity Cathedral: Paul Owen Collier, Alfred George Lee, and Kenneth David Richards. What was surprising was not the ordination of these young men but the huge crowd of Jamaican laity that so filled the sacred edifice that it overflowed out onto the outside grounds. Here was a public manifestation of the laity's interest in their Church by coming to witness their native sons raised to the priesthood that they might care spiritually for the people of Jamaica and by their zeal to extend the kingdom of God throughout their native land. Pope Pius XI thought a native clergy so important that he said he would rather ordain one priest than convert fifty thousand people.

Although the clergy is a very important component of the Church, it is not the whole Church, for in the people of God is included the laity which constitutes the more numerous element in the Mystical Body of Christ. Like the clergy, the laity also has a vocation in the Church. *Lumen Gentium* indicates that the place of the laity is not on the periphery but in the very heart of the Church.

> The term laity is here understood to mean all the faithful except those in holy orders and those in a religious state sanctioned by the Church. These faithful are by baptism made one body with Christ. . . . They carry out their own part in the mission of the whole Christian people with respect to the Church and the world.[3]

The distinguishing mark of the laity is the secular nature of their vocation.

> The laity, by their very vocation, seek the kingdom of God by engaging in temporal affairs and by ordering them according to the plan of God. They live in the world, that is, in each and all of the secular professions and occupations. They live in the ordinary circumstances of family and social life, from which the very web of their existence is woven.[4]

Archbishop Carter employed the local synod as a means of inducing the laity to participate in the life of the Church. The aim of the synod was to provide an annual assembly of the people of God for examining and discussing important issues affecting the Church in the Archdiocese of Kingston. All city parishes were allotted two delegates each, while rural parishes having less than three mission stations were allowed two delegates, and those with more than three mission stations were entitled to three delegates.

An important component of every synod was its theme. For example, the theme of the 1981 synod was "Building up the Church Community." This was to be done through means of the family, youth and catechesis:

> Family togetherness is vital—praying, worshipping, eating, working, playing, sharing together in such a way that develops a loving Christian attitude by regular family prayer, the teaching of the faith by word and example, eating together at least one daily meal which begins with grace, involvement with the Church and community projects, learning to communicate by word and example with consistent concern for each other.[5]

Youth must always be given more consideration in parochial development, for youth is the Church of tomorrow. Yet youth tends to take second place because youth and immaturity are equated. Fortunately, youth has played an important role in every Jamaican synod.

The vision these synods have offered is a well-planned programme of activities which involved youth spiritually, culturally, and educationally in the life of the Church. It was proposed that one Sunday a month be designated Youth Sunday wherein all activities as far as allowed, be carried out by young people.

Regular retreats and days of recollection were suggested and that youth be allowed more involvement in parish work such as visiting the sick and elderly and being encouraged to hold meetings with their parents persuading them to offer more attention to the activities of youth. Nor were delinquent youth to be neglected. For them a programme suited to their needs was to be established.

Where you find a strong catechetical programme, you discover a healthy Church; where it is neglected, you may look for weak faith and even the falling away from the Church as happened on the occasion of the Reformation.

The Synod of 1981 suggested that in the Archdiocese of Kingston there be ongoing religious education both in the day and Sunday schools as well as in the home. It was envisioned that parents be so informed about their Catholic faith that "the responsibility for early and continuing catechesis be in the home."

For personnel, the synod asked that a "body of persons, Religious and Lay, be trained to offer catechetical instruction both in Catholic and in Government Grant-in-Aid Schools under Protestant denominations, since it is allowed by law to teach Catholic students their religion in these schools." This would mean more trained personnel to become part of the Archdiocesan Catechetical Team. For this structure the Synod proposed "an Archdiocesan syllabus with teacher-learning guidelines, simple illustrated literature, inter-island and inter-regional Catechetical Camps for youth."

In the proposals made at the local synods, education was considered a very important factor in the Jamaican Pastoral Plan, since the

Church conducts eighty-eight schools from infant to secondary level, island wide, educating 52,588 boys and girls.

Vatican II also reminds us of the importance of schools in education when it says:

> Among all the agencies of education the school has a special importance. By virtue of its very purpose, while it cultivates the intellect with unremitting attention, the school ripens the capacity for right judgment, provides an introduction into the cultural heritage won by past generations, promotes a sense of values, and readies for professional life. By creating friendly contacts between students of diverse temperament and background, the school fosters among them a willingness to understand one another. Moreover, the school sets up a kind of center whose operation and progress deserve to engage the joint participation of families, teachers, various kinds of cultural, civic, and religious groups, civil society, and the entire human community.[6]

To place all Catholic education in Jamaica under one agency, Most Rev. John J. McEleney, S.J., in 1956 commissioned a group of Catholic educators, both religious and lay, to form an association representing the viewpoint of the Church in education. He saw the need for a professional body because the Church was beginning to realize that leadership in Catholic institutions should come from Jamaicans engaged in this profession. Again, the Church through its religious congregations owned and operated many schools which needed an agency to bring them under one portfolio, thus unifying Catholic education in the island.

Each year the association chose a theme for its Annual General Meeting, such as: 1. Understanding the Child 2. Education for Nationhood 3. Education for International Understanding 4. Education, Hope of the Nation 5. Education to Meet Our Expanding Needs.

When Archbishop Carter returned to Jamaica after his theological studies in the United States, he was elected President of the Jamaican Catholic Educational Association. It was with much satisfaction that he was able to set his approval on the Association's Ten Year Plan dating from 1982–92.

The plan identified the goal to be attained and the means to accomplish it—"The overall purpose of the Plan is a spiritual renewal that by 1992 will develop the People of God of the Archdiocese into a Church truly and fully alive." The primary means are six: catechesis, prayer life, family life, stewardship, youth development, and social justice.

Further the Ten Year Plan states that: 1. The value of the Catholic

School is affirmed 2. Every Catholic School should be a true Catholic School 3. Every Catholic has a right to a Catholic education 4. The School shall be seen as a major apostolic work of the parish, and therefore there is need to integrate the parish and the school.[7] How far this Plan will succeed will be seen in retrospect from its final year 1992.

Jamaica is a Christian country, albeit a strongly Protestant Christian nation, so that the Church's missionary approach must be by way of ecumenism through the school, the parish, and individual efforts. It cannot be otherwise, for the number of pagans in this country is a mere handful.

Protestant Christianity was first introduced among the slaves by Moravian missionaries, followed closely by Baptists, and later by Anglicans. To these denominations we must now add the United Church (Presbyterians/Congregationalists), Methodists, and a variety of Pentecostals.

There is a strong ecumenical bond among these Christian Churches as well as an ecumenical bond with the Catholic Church. Together they comprise a very energetic ecumenical council—the Jamaica Council of Churches—with the Catholic Church an active member.

Special note must be made of the excellent relationship between the Anglican and the Catholic communities. This rapport began with a friendship between the former head of the Anglican Church, Bishop Percival Gibson, an alumnus of St. George's College, and Archbishop McEleney.

To Archbishop McEleney, who encouraged Catholics to become involved in the ecumenical movement, the Church owes her initial interest. Particularly, he exhorted the clergy to join the Ministers' Fraternal Associations in their respective civil parishes, bringing the priest into close alliance with his Protestant brothers.

Robert I. Burke, S.J., pastor of the Highgate missions in the parish of St. Mary welcomed Archbishop McEleney's invitation to join with his Protestant brothers in the Ministers' Fraternal Association of that parish and became a very active member of it. The pastor of the Annotto Bay mission in the same parish of St. Mary followed Burke's example and joined the MFA.

At Annotto Bay there were four churches: Baptist, Methodist, Anglican, and Catholic. The respective pastors proposed that the Unity Octave from 18–25 January be observed by all Christians of the town. Each evening a service was conducted in one of the four churches with one of the pastors as guest preacher.

This proved so successful that the four pastors decided to repeat the ecumenical services during the Wednesdays of Lent. The Lenten services followed the same pattern as the Unity Octave with the Sacred Passion as the theme and a guest preacher every week.

The first Lenten service was held not in a church but in the open public market to allow those of no church affiliation to attend without embarrassment. The final service was a candlelight procession through the town to the spacious Anglican church where the Catholic priest preached the sermon.

In 1976 the Friars of the Atonement, initiators of the Church Unity Octave, at the invitation of Archbishop Carter opened a foundation in the civil parish of St. Catherine, Jamaica. Prior to their arrival, Mass had been celebrated in private homes and even in a room made available for the Sacred Liturgy at the Caymanas Park Race Track through the courtesy of Mr. Joseph Armond, a Catholic.

While Archbishop Carter and Fr. Donald Reece, rector of St. Michael's, were attending a special seminary seminar in Rome, Fr. Reece, a former member of the Atonement Congregation, introduced the archbishop to the friars at San Onofries, their Roman residence. As a result of the meeting, the archbishop wrote the following to the Friars of the Atonement:

> I believe we have here in Kingston the ideal ministry for the Friars of your Congregation. In the Archdiocese of Kingston we are embarking on a new exciting ecumenical venture. Across the Kingston harbour, to the west, there is a new extension of the City—the Portmore Development Project. When completed it will form a complex of four to five communities with several hundreds of homes. The Roman Catholic Church and the Anglican Church have joined together to form an Ecumenical Holding Company. We have selected a site where we will build a Church to be used jointly by both Anglicans and Roman Catholics.[8]

The Church of Reconciliation is novel in Catholic-Anglican relations, since from the beginning it was planned as a sacred edifice to be used jointly by both communities. The area served covers the districts of Bridgeport, Edgewater, Port Henderson, Garveymeade, Naggo's Head, Newlands, Passage Fort, and Southboro.

The Church of Reconciliation is unique. It has both Anglican and Roman Catholic congregations. Both communities share the same worship space and engage in joint spiritual, pastoral, social and fundraising activities. The first meeting of the joint Anglican-Roman Catholic community was held on 12 January 1977. Both communities joined hands and hearts in a ministry of Reconciliation which hopefully would become a beacon of faith to the Christian world.[9]

On Saturday, 18 June 1977, Mass was celebrated for the first time in the new Church of Reconciliation; on 2 July 1977, the first Catholic marriage ceremony was performed in the church. On Sunday, 4 September 1977, the official dedication was presided over by the Most Rev. Samuel E. Carter, S.J., and the Rt. Rev. Herbert D. Edmondson, Anglican Bishop of Jamaica.

The friars extended their labours by constructing the Church of the Atonement at Independence City, principally through the efforts of Mr. and Mrs. Riley Hibbert, who came to live there in 1969 and immediately canvassed the neighbourhood for other Catholics. A good number were found and the Sacred Liturgy was celebrated for the first time in the Hibbert home on 27 June 1970 by Rev. John Caskin, S.J.

The congregation outgrew the available space at the Hibbert home, and it was at this point that Mr. Joseph Armond offered the use of a large room at the Caymanas Race Track for Sunday Mass. When Fr. Richard Albert, S.A., became pastor, a suitable church site was selected at the Waterford Housing Scheme where construction was begun and completed in 1986. Fr. James Olley, S.A., celebrated the first Mass there on 13 July 1986.

Archbishop Carter is a degreed social worker from the Boston College Graduate School of Social Work. So it was only natural for him to interest himself in the social welfare projects of his archdiocese.

One of the oldest established services is St. Joseph's Hospital, founded by the Sisters of St. Dominic, who came to Jamaica on 19 October 1911 from the mother house at Hoboken, New Jersey, which had been established twenty years previously by Dominican sisters from France. Although they came to Jamaica as cloistered nuns, they found they had to open a private school to support themselves. This school was established at their convent at Devon Villa, Orange Street, above Torrington Bridge, Kingston. In the course of the year, St. Joseph's was opened and the sisters given charge.

For some seventy-five years St. Joseph's has offered its services to both Catholics and non-Catholics who otherwise would have been forced to seek medical care either at a Protestant or government hospital, neither of which provided the same medical and religious care they received at St. Joseph's.

For many years the sisters had to rise early in the morning, milk their herd of cows and sell the milk in Kingston to keep the hospital financially sound and the cost of medical services at a minimum for the patient.

In 1970 the Dominican Sisters handed over the administration and operation of the hospital to the archdiocese, since they could no longer maintain it, principally due to lack of vocations. In the same year funds were raised by public subscription for its expansion. In

1976 the construction of the new wing of fifty beds was undertaken but the cost of materials soared. Added to the cost of new construction was the debt of $350,000 for operating the hospital. Twelve percent interest on the total liability placed the institution in dire financial straits.

Fortunately, the Jamaican Government, in November 1977, offered to subsidize the hospital by $438,000 per annum for the use of thirty beds by poor patients who could not afford to pay.

The present (1986) St. Joseph's Hospital with the new James Becker Wing for patients and administration has the most modern operating room in Jamaica. On its spacious grounds a number of doctors have established a medical center where the sick may consult specialists. The Hospital treats on the average some four thousand inpatients and some seven thousand out-patients a year.

Another valuable social service is the Roper Centre, named for a diocesan priest, Clarence Roper, who died of cancer in 1963. Opened in 1964, it has proved a benefit for the poor, offering counselling and general welfare service for discharged prisoners, men and women, often regarded as social outcasts by their more fortunate brethren. At the centre a training programme in handicrafts and sewing for unemployed women has been developed, supported mainly by funds supplied by the Catholic Women's League.

Three social institutions are conducted by the Jamaican Franciscan Missionary Sisters: the Ozanam Home for Aged Women, located at 30 Mannings Hill Road, Kingston; another, the St. Clair Home for Aged Men, both funded by the St. Vincent de Paul Society; and a third, the Villa Maria for Aged Women, located at 33 Seymour Avenue, Kingston, financed by the sisters from fees charged the inmates.

The Alpha Boys' School at 26 South Camp Road, Kingston, is conducted by the Sisters of Mercy for orphans and boys from broken homes. Here 250 boys are taught a variety of productive trades to prepare them to be useful Jamaican citizens. The Home-School has been in existence for nearly one hundred years, and for these boys the only home they have ever known. Hence, they are devotedly loyal to the Sisters of Mercy, their foster mothers.

Another institution in Kingston for boys is the Vidal Home, named for a diocesan priest who spent his priestly life ministering to the poor of Kingston. Fifteen boys are in residence. This institution is conducted by the archdiocese. Both the Vidal Home and the Alpha Boys' School are subsidized by the Jamaican government.

The Social Action Centre was founded by Rev. John P. Sullivan, S.J., with generous help from the German bishops' organization Misereor, to form leaders not only for the credit union cooperative movement but also for other social services. Since Sullivan's death in 1975, it has been managed by a lay group with generous help of staff and money from the Society of Jesus, which help has diminished in the last six years.

Marriage is not only a sacramental institution but a social one as well, affecting all people. Despite attempts at the archdiocesan level insisting upon a careful preparation for marriage, it varied widely from parish to parish and from mission station to mission station. Some pastors required a very careful period of instruction; others did little more than fill out the formal questionnaire to assure canonical freedom to marry. Updating courses for pastors on marriage tribunal work by Fr. Maurice Walsh, S.J., changed the haphazard procedure by the promulgation of new guidelines in preparation for marriage which required that those planning marriage be given a minimum of six instructions after they had served a three month notice of their intention of marrying. Exception from these instructions could only be had from the chancery. The promulgation of these guidelines helped make the faithful more aware of the seriousness of the sacrament of marriage.

Because Catholics are a minority group in Jamaica, more than 50 percent of all marriages are contracted with non-Catholics. In 1977 there were 348 marriages; of these 235 were mixed marriages. With rare exceptions, the children of such marriages are baptized and brought up Catholics. There is less difficulty in Jamaica with mixed marriages than in some other countries because of our cordial ecumenical relations with other Christian communities. Occasionally this gives rise to indifferentism, but the positive advantages of the ecumenical spirit far outweighs any disadvantages that might occur.

In the 1978–82 period there were 1,001 marriages in the archdiocese; of that number 749 were mixed marriages. Despite this high percentage of mixed marriages, no significant number of Catholics gave up the practice of their faith.

Both priests and sisters have over their long years in Jamaica been very zealous and devoted to the poor in their schools, their parishes, and their social works. Wherever the poor were found, their priests and sisters made their presence felt; it can never be alleged that the Church in Jamaica neglected the poor. Yet no religious congregation was devoted exclusively to the poor until Fr. Richard HoLung in 1984 founded the Brothers of the Poor, a pious union committed to living religious life in community and working for the poor as their main apostolate. They work in five major areas: 1. a faith centre for homeless people, and education of youth; 2. prisons; 3. Eventide Home, a government project for the aged; 4. Mona Commons; 5. White Wing

Apostolate, near St. Pius X Church. They have established their community centre at 25 Munroe Road, Kingston.

A most welcome religious congregation, devoted exclusively to the poor, the Sisters of Mother Teresa of Calcutta, India, opened a house among the poorest of the poor in Kingston in the year 1986.

Several years ago, His Grace, Archbishop Carter wrote to Mother Teresa of Calcutta, requesting some of the sisters for ministry among the poor of Kingston. Mother Teresa wrote Archbishop early in 1985, and on May 4th Sr. Dolores, Regional Supervisor, along with Sr. Georgia arrived to select a spot for the sisters to minister. After examining several areas of the city, Sr. Dolores selected that of Law and Tower Streets. The four sisters (Sr. Ernestine, Sr. Ronald, Sr. Wilfred, and Sr. Noncita) returned in late July and took up residence in an old factory which had been cleaned up and secured. The sisters now spend a great deal of time caring for the sick, visiting the elderly, instructing the children, and offering the gentle touch of the Lord to a poverty-stricken area.[10]

On Monday, 30 June 1986, Mother Teresa, Nobel prize winner for peace, visited Jamaica and spent two nights and three days in Kingston. Many people say Jamaica will never be the same, and others have been heard to say it was a moment of grace, and people like Erica Allen of J.B.C. television said, "I felt God's presence in a new and beautiful way." The Governor-General said that he considered her as one of the greatest visitors to King's House since he has been Governor-General. All these comments were about a small, bent-over Yugoslavian woman popularly known as Mother Teresa of Calcutta.[11]

This remarkable woman came as a missionary sister to teach in a Calcutta school for the well-to-do, but her attention was attracted to the poverty and misery beyond the convent school. Twenty-seven years ago she applied for a dispensation to leave her convent and work among Calcutta's poor. With only five rupees in her purse, but with complete trust in divine Providence, she began her work which in two years developed into a religious congregation—the Missionary Sisters of Charity. Today there are 2,500 sisters of thirty-five nationalities serving the poor in twenty-seven countries.

The 1970–86 period has been a time of much progress for the Church in Jamaica. This is primarily due to Vatican II, which placed the missions from the peripheral position they had previously occupied into the very centre of the Church's life, saying "The Pilgrim Church is missionary by her very nature."

The present generation has entered into a new phase in profane history and again Vatican II agrees: "The present historical situation is leading humanity into a new stage and the Church is summoned with special energy to save and renew every creature." This new phase of profane history is the desire of all people for self-government, to be ruled by their own sons and daughters, independent of foreign influence in their internal affairs. This led Jamaica to seek independence from Great Britain in 1962.

The Holy See has acknowledged this new stage by fostering an indigenous clergy. No longer does she favour foreigners holding ecclesiastical offices when competent natives can be found to fill these offices.

The Holy See ended foreign domination of the Church in Jamaica when she appointed Samuel E. Carter, S.J., archbishop of Kingston and Edgerton R. Clarke, a diocesan priest, bishop of Montego Bay.

This was a major step for the Church, since her hierarchy is now in the hands of native bishops who, having knowledge of and sympathy for their own people, will guide the Church through the latter years of this century into the bright years of the twenty-first century.

Appendix A

Successsion of Prelates

1.	Don Sancho de Matienzo (Abbot)	1516–1522
2.	Don Andres Lopez Frias (Abbot)	1522–1523
3.	Don Luis de Figueroa (Abbot)	1523–1524
4.	Don Pedro Martir de Angleria (Abbot)	1524–1526
5.	Fray Miguel Ramirez, O.P. (Abbot)	1527–1535
6.	Don Amador de Samano (Abbot)	1535–1539
7.	Johanes Davila (Abbot)	1554–?
8.	Don Francisco Osorio Mercado (Abbot)	1561–1573
9.	Don Mateo Santiago (Abbot)	1573–1578
10.	Lic. Luis Munoz (Abbot)	1578–?
11.	Don Francisco Marquez de Villalobos (Abbot)	1581–1606
12.	Don Bernardo de Balbuena (Abbot)	1608–1619
13.	Don Mateo de Medina Moreno (Abbot)	1622–1650
14.	Thomas Churchill (Pastor-Vicar General)	1688–?
15.	Anthony Quigly, Franciscan Reccollet (Pastor)	1792–1799
16.	William Le Cun, O.P. (Pastor)	1799–1807
17.	Juan Jacinto Rodriguez de Araujo, O.S.A. (Pastor)	1808–1824
18.	Benito Fernandez	
	(Pastor)	1824–1837
	(Vicar Apostolic)	1837–1855
19.	James E. Dupeyron, S.J. (Vicar Apostolic)	1855–?
20.	Joseph Sidney Woollett, S.J. (Pro Vicar Apostolic)	1871–1877
21.	Thomas Porter, S.J. (Vicar Apostolic)	1877–1888
22.	Charles Gordon, S.J. (Bishop)	1889–1906
23.	John J. Collins, S.J. (Bishop)	1907–1918
24.	William F. O'Hare, S.J. (Bishop)	1919–1926
25.	Joseph N. Dinand, S.J. (Bishop)	1927–1929
26.	Thomas A. Emmet, S.J. (Bishop)	1930–1949
27.	John J. McEleney, S.J.	
	(Bishop)	1950–1967
	(Archbishop)	1967–1970
28.	Edgerton R. Clarke (Bishop, Montego Bay Diocese)	1967–
29.	Samuel E. Carter, S.J. (Archbishop, Kingston)	1971–

Appendix B

Documentary Sources

Archivo General de Indias, Seville, (AGI)

Public Record Office, London

Calendar of State Papers (Col.)

Archives of the Archdiocese of Kingston, Jamaica

Sacra Congregatio de Propaganda Fide (S.P.C. America, Antille)

Archives of the Society of Jesus, Rome (Jamaica)

Archives of the English Province, Society of Jesus

Journals of the Assembly—Institute of Jamaica

Votes of the Assembly—Institute of Jamaica

Vital Records of Carlisle, Massachusetts, U.S.A.

Massachusetts Historical Society Proceedings, U.S.A.

Ponticia Universidad Catolica Javeriana, Bogota, Colombia, S.A.
Cartes Edificantes de la Provincia de Colombia.

Archivo Generale, Salesiani Don Bosco (AGSDB), Turin, Italy.

Archives of the Society of Jesus (Jamaica)

Appendix C

Provincial Synod—1622—Santo Domingo

Historical background

The first Provincial Synod of the Caribbean region was convened at Santo Domingo in 1622. A letter dated October 10, 1600, from the Dean and Chapter of Santo Domingo, Hispaniola, to King Philip III of Spain narrated the many problems besetting the island, such as: the recent attack by Francis Drake on the city when he robbed the inhabitants and destroyed churches and private dwellings. Not satisfied with this wantonness, the Sea Rover set fire to the heart of the city, which suffered a loss estimated at 120,000 ducats. To these troubles was added a severe plague which decimated the negro population. Further disasters were experienced from three hurricanes which devastated farms and dwellings. Tithes dropped to a mere 100 ducats in the year 1600. Beef and clothing imported from Castile were very expensive, and some clergy were experiencing the pangs of hunger. If it were not for the prospect of a benefice, many of the clergy would have departed Hispaniola.

During these calamitous times Friar Agustin Davilla y Padella, O.P., born in Mexico, was Archbishop of Santo Domingo. Davilla died on July 26, 1604 and a succession of prelates followed him in the See of Santo Domingo: Friar Domingo de Valderrama, O.P. arrived in Hispaniola early in November 1607, but was transferred to the Archdiocese of La Pas. Valderrama was followed by Friar Cristobal Rodriques y Suarez, O.P. who arrived June 30, 1610, held a Diocesan Synod, but was transferred in October to the See of Arequipa. He died en route to Peru November 4, 1613. His successor, Friar Diego de Conteres, a Mexican Augustinian, was consecrated in Mexico, stopped at Havana, and died there September 1, 1616; he probably lost his life in a hurricane. The vacant See was not filled until December 15, 1619, when Friar Pedro Solier arrived from Rome; but he died before his confirmation arrived. Solier had held the See on a previous occasion. He was followed by the Benedictine Friar Pedro de Oviedo, whose date of appointment and arrival is not known but must have been before 1621. It appears he carried with him a Brief from Gregory XV, a royal cedula (decree) calling for a Provincial Synod which he convened at Santo Domingo in 1622.

The Synod

The proceedings of the Provincial Synod held at Santo Domingo, Hispaniola, in 1622 opened with these words: In the Name of the Most Holy Trinity, of the Father, and of the Son and of the Holy Spirit; in the city of Santo Domingo in the island of the West Indies situated in the Ocean Sea, commonly called Hispaniola, on the Feast of the glorious Apostle and Evangelist Matthew, the 21st day of the month of September 1622, this Synod was convened.

The Most Reverend Master Dr. Peter de Oviedo, Archbishop of the aforesaid island, Primate of the Indies, and member of the Royal Council, summoned into this city all the suffragan Bishops to celebrate a Provincial Synod according to the will of Trent. The Council was long desired by our Catholic King, Philip IV, who by royal decree to the aforesaid Archbishop and the Reverend Suffragan Bishops, encouraged and requested this, and assigned the date of the aforesaid Provincial Synod, sending out the customary notices required by law and convoking the persons due to assist, both those having consultative and those having deliberative vote, assembling them together with the Most Reverend Master Don Gundisalva de Angulo, Bishop of Venezuela; Don Doctor Bernardo de Balbuena, Bishop of Puerto Rico; the Most Reverend Licentiate Francisco de Medina Moreno, Great Abbot of Jamaica; and the Most Reverend Don Alphonso Enrique de Toledo, Bishop of Cuba. The Bishop of Cuba asked to be excused by reason of advanced age and ill health. Don Augustino Pimentel, Canon of the Cuban Cathedral and Provisor-General of Havana, substituted for him.

Having completed the customary procession with the Most Reverend Bishop in mitre and staff, the Pontificial High Mass was celebrated by the Most Reverend Bishop of Puerto Rico, and the sermon was preached by Friar Didaco de Soria, Provincial of the Order of Mercedarians of the Blessed Virgin Mary before a large gathering of joyous people.

The members of the Synod then assembled in the hall of the Cathedral for the proceedings of the Synod, occupying their places according to protocol, that is, the Most Reverend Archbishop, President of the Synod; Didaco Gomez de Sandoval, the constituted civic head of Hispaniola; Doctor Bernardo de Balbuena, Bishop of Puerto Rico, then all others in their respective order according to their qualifications. Lastly many clerics and those assisting the bishops were present.

Following the procedure of Trent, the statute concerning the conducting of Provincial Synods was read. The Secretary and other officials were chosen. Then the presiding secular official of Hispaniola, Dr. Didaco de Sandoval, presented his Majesty's document to the Synod which was read by the Secretary and received with joyful demonstrations by those present. This document expressed the singular honour from the King and particularly the honour afforded them by the presence of Don Didaco de Sandoval, sent in the name of the King.

The Most Illustrious Peter de Oviedo, Master of Theology, gave thanks to the Apostolic See and with firm conviction professed all and each article of the Creed. He made avowal of the seven sacraments—all the Council of Trent declared concerning original sin and justification. He professed that in the Mass there is offered to the true God a propitiary sacrifice for the living and the dead, and that in the sacrament of the Holy Eucharist is truly, really and substantially the Body and Blood together with the soul and divinity of Our Lord Jesus Christ.

After Don Peter de Oviedo had sworn to uphold and profess all which the Catholic Church held and professed, each Bishop in turn made the same avowal of faith.

Second Session, November 6, 1622—The Sacraments

Baptism

Although there were comparatively few parish churches within this vast territory under the jurisdiction of the Synodal Fathers, it was decreed that solemn baptism was not to be conferred in private homes but only in the parish church at a font which had been erected for the purpose. At baptism there was to be no ostentatious display of wealth such as the infant wearing shoes of gold texture, nor to have undergarments of the same material; nor was the church to be decorated with gaudy ornaments such as silk banners, neither was the organ to be played as relatives sang birthday songs while the infant was being carried to the sacred font. Children born in the country, two leucas from the parish church might be baptized privately when in danger of death and as soon as possible brought to the church for completion of the ceremonies.

Since midwives were often called upon to baptize children in danger of death, it was necessary that they should know the ritual. Hence to test this knowledge they were to appear before the Vicar of the District and pass an examination. Should they fail they were to be deprived of their office.

In all baptisms a strict record was to be kept by the pastor in a baptismal register in which he was to inscribe the name of the child, parents, and godparents. Should he fail in this duty, he was to be subject to a fine of three ounces of silver.

Experience had taught that negroes were transported from Africa without the benefit of baptism. But if slave merchants claimed that negroes had been baptised before landing in the Indies, whether prior to leaving Africa or on the high seas, or any place the ship may have stopped, inquiry was to be made into the instructions given by the person who conferred the sacrament and the intention of the negroes receiving the sacrament, whether it was received voluntarily or forced upon them. Should any defect be discovered they were to be baptised conditionally.

Adult negoes were not to be baptized unless instructed in the Apostles' Creed, the Lord's prayer, the ten commandments, and the seven sacraments, with special emphasis on baptism. If through some defect the negroes could not grasp all these doctrines after they had had two or three months instruction, then the priest might baptize as long as they knew the chief mysteries necessary for salvation, were sorry for their sins, and knew after a fashion the efficacy of baptism.

When negroes were brought into a West Indian port, they were to be catechized immediately by a priest. It often happened that negroes transported to the Indies were left unsold, and during this time lived without baptism, jeopardizing their eternal salvation. The Synod decreed that the bishop of the port or his vicar should assign a priest to instruct negroes in the fundamental doctrines of the Church, so that later they might be baptized when they arrived at the terminus of their voyage. The bishop was to assign a stipend to the port chaplain, and the merchants were to pay it. Should they neglect to do so, they were to be visited with censures or other canonical penalties.

Evidently the sacrament of confirmation was neglected by the colonists for a certain contempt was noted: ". . . great negligence is seen in the reception of this sacrament either through failure to intellectually grasp its importance or because of the spirit of the age." The Synod asked priests to exhort the faithful of whatsoever social condition to receive confirmation, and should there be any relaxation of its reception which amounted to contempt, the bishop was to correct this attitude by an admonition or if necessary by a precept. Negroes were also to be prepared for confirmation and brought to the centre where the sacrament was to be conferred.

When the Synod came to consider Holy Orders, it made a blunt statement concerning negroes of the first and second generation born in the New World. Such "black persons are not to be admitted to sacred Orders." There was reason for this. Negroes had been brought to the New World as slaves and hence not able to act freely as is required of one in sacred Orders. Their religion was animism, and to eradicate the superstitition in which their ancestors had been steeped would require several generations. Further the Synod attached these conditions to ordination: the negro must, like his white counterpart, not have been condemned by the Holy Inquisition on his father's side in the first and second degree, and on his mother's side in the first degree; he must be free from servitude and possess sacredotal virtues.

The ordination of Indians was also taken under consideration. Neither newly converted Indians nor their sons were to be admitted to ordination. The reason: nothing attracts people to a love and reverence of the sacraments more than virtue and modesty in the priest. These virtues were lacking in Indians and their children, who by their very nature were prone to drunkenness, impurity, and idolatry as had been observed by bishops on their visitation to Indian missions where they saw how easily these aborigines lapsed into idolatry. The Synod Fathers had a very poor opinion of these Indians claiming ". . . they are the most vicious of people, so that negroes in respect to them are superior. Hence this Synod reverencing the dignity of the priesthood forbids sons of Indians and their grandsons to be raised to this celestial state . . ." However, mestizos (of Spanish and Indian blood) were allowed to become priests.

The financial support of diocesan priests labouring in the Indies was a serious problem for bishops. Anyone desiring to enter the diocesan priesthood had to have some means of livelihood. How was he to support himself among a people who had little of this world's goods to sustain even themselves? The only solution bishops saw was a patrimony (a family inheritance/pension) or a benefice. Otherwise their support would fall on local bishops who found it difficult to finance their diocesan commitments. So it was enacted by the Synod that every candidate for the diocesan priesthood had to offer proof that he possessed a patrimony or benefice. But there were individuals who were not above practicing deception, claiming a benefice when they had none. They would reach an agreement with the holder of a legitimate benefice to claim this benefice as their own and once ordained would return the benefice to the real owner. Should such a person through fraud be advanced to the priesthood, he was to be suspended for a period of three years and all persons involved in the fraud were to be punished according to the judgement of the bishop.

A serious lack of priests to cultivate the Antillean vineyard caused bishops to accept ecclesiastical candidates for the priesthood who swore they had a domicile in another diocese but could not show dimissory letters. In some cases bishops later found these persons were wanderers with no fixed abode and had entered the ecclesiastical state not so much for the Church as for their own personal gain. They had left their diocese and wandered from place to place with no fixed domicile. Bishops were warned not to accept such persons merely on their own sworn testimony. Rather they were to demand approval in writing from the candidate's bishop. Should such a person be ordained fraudently, he was to be suspended from the exercise of his priesthood, and if he had obtained a benefice, was to lose it. His suspension was to last for three years.

Matrimony

The subject of matrimony was the cause of much discussion. The Synod held marriage in high esteem because it signified the union of Christ and His Church, declaring that the matrimonial bond was so firm that it could not be broken by man. ". . . those whom God has joined together, let no man put assunder." In cases where couples wished to separate, the cause was to be made known to the bishop, and if the parties lived in a remote area, more than ten miles from the bishop, his vicar was to be informed of the reasons of the litigation and this information was to be relayed to the bishop. In the interim, the woman was to be sent to a safe place away from molestation if she were in fear of the man.

No vagrant was allowed to contract marriage unless his status of freedom had been proved by two witnesses whom the bishop himself or his vicar was to examine. Only in rare cases should the bishop dispense with the examination of these witnesses.

On occasion it happened that a man wished to marry a girl hastily, and from this scandal might arise, particularly if the girl were of the nobility. The Fathers of the Synod were warned that they were not to proceed impulsively in such cases, but to follow the rules laid down by the Council of Trent in regard to the publication of banns of marriage, and only in grave cases should they dispense from the publication of these banns.

Since it sometimes happened that negroes had contracted marriage before a priest without having been baptised, or a probable doubt arose about their baptism, the Synod declared that if such a marriage was celebrated after the alleged baptism of one of the contracting parties, a new consent must be given and the ceremony repeated according to the Catholic rite.

Penance

The Synod cautioned priests to study with care how penance was to be administered after the example of the Heavenly Physician, keeping in mind that they had been granted powers not given to the angels. Since many negroes were ignorant and lacked learning, priests were allowed to grant them absolution as long as they held firmly to the articles contained in the Apostles Creed and knew the meaning of the sacrament of penance.

Since it had become a custom for priests to hear the confessions of women at night, the Synod thought this practice should stop since the ". . . most unbecoming situations might arise from confessions of women heard at night or in darkness. We order such confessions to be heard from morning until evening." Nor were such confessions to be heard in a private dwelling with the penitent standing before the confessor.

There were occasions when confessors, desiring Mass stipends, did not observe the proper manner of imposing sacramental penance especially when the penitent had some obligation to fulfill, but accepted stipends in lieu of the obligation. Confessors were warned not to accept Mass stipends under such circumstances either by themselves or through a third party. This would eliminate cupidity on the part of the confessor, and the priest would give no suspicion of avarice.

Since the care of souls is the art of arts, both diocesan and religious priests were to be examined in Canon Law and in all the rules which the Council of Trent had decreed concerning the knowledge that confessors should possess.

Although confessors were forbidden to absolve in cases reserved to the bishop, an exception was made for negroes, in which case the confessor was granted the faculty to absolve in such reserved cases. So that any priest who possesed faculties of the diocese might not only absolve negroes at present reserved to the bishop but also in any future cases which might be reserved to the bishop.

There were other decrees which may be summarized as follows: Physicians and those caring for the sick were held to exhort the sick to go to confession; that the tabernacle for the Eucharist be fittingly furnished; that the Holy Eucharist be renewed every eight days; that two clerics in surplices accompany the priest when he carried Viaticum to the sick; that on the feast of Corpus Christi and Holy Thursday ecclesiastical ministers be appointed who were to keep watch before the Blessed Sacrament; that Extreme Unction was to be conferred on all Christian negroes, and the priest was to enlighten them with a clear knowledge of the sacrament both as to its fruit and its effect; Extreme Unction was to be administered to the wounded and others affected lethally.

The second Session ended with all the Synod Fathers approving all its decrees.

Third Session—November 3, 1622

This session opened with a consideration of five mandates of the Church: the hearing of Mass, feast days of precept, annual confession, precept of the Eucharist, fasting, and tithes. Added to these were some related subjects.

Hearing Mass

"Notwithstanding that God is a spirit, not only must He be worshiped and adored by internal acts of faith, hope, and love, but He must also be worshiped by external acts so that both mind and heart may proclaim His praises and offer thanks for benefits conferred by Him. Prayers and sacrifices are to be offered by ministers of the Church, among which the Holy Sacrifice of the Mass holds place of honour." With these words the Synod opened the third session.

Attendance at Mass

For some people attendence at Mass had been so neglected that they hardly fulfilled their obligation once a year. All, both men and women of whatsoever social strata, even unwed girls who were not hindered by some genuine impediment, were obliged to fulfill the precept of attending Mass on Sundays and holydays of obligation.

A custom had grown up which allowed a widow to absent herself from Mass for a period of several months after the death of her husband. The Synod corrected this by saying that confessors were to warn the faithful that a widow was allowed to remain at home for one month only, following the death of her husband.

Another custom which had been introduced was the playing of games in the vicinity of the church while Mass was being celebrated. The Synod declared that no one was to indulge in games on a day of precept from morning until afternoon, and should anyone violate this decree, he was to be fined ten ounces of silver, one third of which was to go to the informer. Not only were games forbidden during Mass, but the same prohibition held while Divine Office was being recited in the church. There was to be no strident noise or excited shouting or any kind of game in the plaza before the church. Bishops might impose a fine of ten ounces of silver or any other penalty, depending upon the quality of the guilty person.

Whoever lived one leuca away from the Church was bound to hear Mass, but the bishop could modify this rule. Negroes who worked at a far distance from the Church were obliged to hear Mass at least six times during the year, on days of precept. During these times they were to be taught Christian doctrine by the pastor on account of the danger to salvation to which these negroes were exposed in out-of-the-way places. If the slave owner was unwilling to allow them to attend Mass and instructions, the bishop might impose penalties to remedy the situation. No negro was to do servile work on Sundays or holydays of obligation. The slave master was to be fined ten ounces of silver for the first offense and excommunication for the second offense.

The function of a tavern in a mission station was to sell not only merchandise but also to operate a workshop wherein goods were manufactured for the community. Taverns were showing boldness by remaining open on days of precept. Hence the Synod decreed that workshops were to be closed on such days and no goods sold except what was necessary for the livelihood of the community. A fine of four ounces of silver was to be placed on those who would violate this order.

Feast Days to Be Observed Throughout the Year

". . . because of our debt of cult and honour to God and His saints, feast days were to be observed by refraining from all servile work, and the faithful were held to hear the entire Mass under pain of mortal sin. The Indians were excepted. The Synod would speak of their obligations later."

"In the first place, Sundays on which the glory of the Resurrection has always been observed in the primitive Church up to our own day, are considered the most important of all feasts."

Feasts to be observed from precept:

January	Circumcision Epiphany
February	Purification
March	St. Joseph
April	St. Mark, Evangelist

May	Sts. Philip and James, apostles Finding of the Holy Cross
June	St. Barnabas, Apostle St. John the Baptist Sts. Peter and Paul
July	St. Mary Magdalene St. James, Apostle St. Anne
August	Transfiguration St. Lawrence, martyr Assumption St. Bartholomew
September	Nativity of Blessed Virgin Mary St. Matthew, Apostle
October	St. Luke, Evangelist Sts. Simon and Jude, Apostles
November	All Saints St. Andrew, Apostle
December	Immaculate Conception St. Thomas, Apostle Christmas Day, with two following days St. Stephen, Proto-martyr St. John, Apostle
Moveable Feasts	Resurrection, with two following days Ascension Pentecost, with two following days Corpus Christi.

Feasts of the patron of the cathedral and parish churches must be observed everywhere in Spanish states. Also those feasts which because of a vow are accustomed to be observed with the consent of the bishop.

Mindful that those in authority wielded a powerful influence by their example, the Synod made specific mention of governors and magistrates ". . . who preside over the State . . . as they surpass others in civic dignity, they ought to outshine them by the example of their lives." Bishops were exhorted to take care that governors and magistrates be present at Mass on specific feast days: Christmas, Circumcision, Epiphany, Holy Week, Easter, Ascension, Pentecost, and Corpus Christi. Not only were they to be present at Mass but also were to attend the Divine Office of Vespers on those days.

Annual Confession

The Synod decreed an extraordinary means to insure that the faithful confess once a year: ". . . because many omit annual confession, the Synod prescribes that all bring a letter containing a testimony of confession from their confessor, without which the Holy Eucharist will not be administered to them." Further the pastor was to write out a list of names of those who had fulfilled this precept, and he was to show it to the Bishop after Easter so that transgressors might be punished.

Sailors were not exempt from fulfilling this obligation of annual confession. Since many were neglectful in this matter, the bishop was to gather them together so that those about to go to sea might fulfill their obligation of annual confession and Easter communion. He was to do likewise for sailors just returned from a long voyage. This same method also applied to people living in remote districts outside cities and towns.

Holy Eucharist

Holy Communion was to be received at least once a year during Paschal time or when a person was in danger of death. In order that it might be known with certainty that every parishioner had made his Easter duty, a schedule with names of those who had made their Easter duty was to be published and which the parish priest was to renew on the third Sunday after Easter so that the bishop might know anyone who had not fulfilled his duty.

Mass was not allowed to be celebrated in a private home for the purpose of administering Viaticum to the sick. "All the faithful who have reached the age of reason are obliged to receive the Holy Eucharist at least once in their lifetime, and since this is not always fulfilled by children, if they are *in periculo mortis,* let the Holy Eucharist be administered to them, after having been to confession, although they may not have made their first Holy Communion.

Fasting

The Synod was very strict on fasting. Neither diocesan nor religious priests were allowed to eat eggs or milk products during Lent. Even for the afternoon collation, cheese was not allowed. This was ". . . because corporal fasting purges the mind, elevates the senses, and subjects the flesh to the spirit, makes the heart contrite and humble."

Tithes

Tithes and first fruits were to be paid according to a custom of forty years or more. When this time element was sufficiently established, tithes and first fruits were to be paid for the decent subsistence of the clergy such as: wheat, cocoa, maize, and arroz. Negroes were also to pay tithes of first fruits when through an explicit or tacit consent of their masters, they cultivated fields or raised sheep.

Churches

". . . the principle and end of all things—the Lord—ought to be venerated in the Church in which God wills to dwell and pours forth in a special manner spiritual graces." In order that the church might be held sacred, all confabs, profane gadding about, and the conducting of secular business was forbidden under pain of excommunication lest the House of Prayer become a house of business. Parishioners were reminded that all loud noise be far removed from the sacristy which "is dedicated to priests preparing for sacred functions, so that they may be recollected and silently engage in prayer without distraction".

Several other points may be listed under one heading, such as: no one shall remain in church all night; nor shall Mass be celebrated at night not even those called "aguinaldo"; parish Churches were to follow the Cathedral in the divine office, ceremonies, and the ringing of the Angelus; Churches shall be so ornamented that they will help raise the mind to God; vestments shall not be used for profane purposes under pain of a fine of eight ounces of silver. "Right of sanctuary" was in common practice so that a wrongdoer might seek refuge in a Church and no one, not even civil authority, might remove him as long as he behaved himself such as: no playing of cards, no prolonged discussions, no conversations with women, no contempt shown to civil authorities. Should he be guilty of conduct unbecoming the sacred precincts, he was to be warned three times, and if he persisted in his conduct he was to be evicted from the church.

Images

Since "Holy Mother Church teaches that the saints reigning with Christ offer prayers to God for mankind, it is good and useful to invoke them and humbly venerate their images and relics. Let the bishop diligently take care that relics are kept in a decent and clean place in the Church, and all superstition be avoided, and no one be allowed to place in the Church any strange images, but only those approved by the bishop."

After the Bishop of Venezuela had publicly read the proceedings of this session, the Fathers were asked if they consented to what was declared, defined, and ruled. All answered that they did approve.

Fourth Session—November 21, 1622

The fourth session considered such subjects as bishops, canonical visitors, clerics, religious, preaching the Word of God, and finances.

Bishops

Bishops were reminded that they were the leaders of the Church and that the Holy Spirit had placed them over the flock to rule the Church and they should do all in their power for the flock and not desert the sheep as do mercenaries, but rather take up residence among them as recommended by the Council of Trent whose decrees the Synod reiterated. They were not to receive money for conferring Holy Orders, in order to close the door to simony, even though such money be a freewill offering, since all should be ordained who had qualified for the ministry without having the stigma of avarice attached to it.

Visitation

Bishops were reminded that they should inspect their sheep personally. But should they be hindered by some unforeseen cause, they were not to choose a nondescript person to represent them but one eminent in virtue and learning. The bishop was allowed to appoint a vicar-general either for a period of time or for a particular place, whichever seemed of more advantage. A vicar-general was to be prudent, virtuous, and learned in the law. Should the Visitor learn of any grave business demanding the judgment of the bishop, he should inform the bishop at once. These Visitors were to give no suspicion of being businessmen, nor were they to associate with gamblers, nor allow them into their houses. All these admonitions were to be observed under pain of excommunication.

Prudence

Since the expense customarily incurred by a visitation was very great, the bishop was to be excused from personally making the visitation. Visitors were to consult least of all their own aggrandizement and were in no way to be deterred from performing their duty by artful excuses. When the vicar-general, as visitor, shall have despatched his letters of admonition, he shall order that attention be given to that part necessary for the particular region and shall not promulgate it unless in accordance with the law, taking into consideration what is of honour to his subjects and what scandal might arise and what could be avoided so that the intended effect might be carried out with suavity and prudence.

At this point in the proceedings a note was inserted, deploring what the Synod called a "vicious custom which has wandered from the right path in these regions and daily tends to grow strong and must be wiped out—that by which some women seek alms freely at night, by which they can be offensive to a Christian people." Ecclesiastical judges were warned to forbid women from seeking alms from door to door after the Angelus under pain of censure. The Synod did take into consideration the more wretched and really indigent, asking bishops or ecclesiastical judges to note officially such persons that they might succor them in their necessity.

Marital Status of New Arrivals

Colonists arriving from Spain, if accompanied by a woman, presented a problem. The Synod advised parish priests to enquire diligently and prudently into their relationship, and if not in one another's company legitimately they were to be told to separate. This was especially true of clerics. If they refused, they were to be considered contumacious and were to be punished with the penalty for concubinage.

Should it happen that married men came to the Indies without their wives, their names were to be entered in a special register, and when the time permitted for them to stay was up, they were to be forced to return to their wives.

Diocesan Examiners

In order that diocesan examiners of the clergy might conduct themselves faithfully and truthfully in their duties, they were to take an oath to fulfill their ministry honestly setting aside all ill will and inordinate affection. They were to beware of accepting money or any other form of bribery by reason of the examination or the decision which they would pronounce in approving or disapproving the examinee, and this under pain of excommunication.

Examiners were warned that neither directly nor indirectly were they to reveal in advance the questions of the examination to the examinee; and the one about to be examined was not to be examined by a relative either of consanguinity or affinity or even friendship to the examiner. Should the bishop learn of such a case, he was to find a substitute for the examiner.

No cleric was to be admitted to the examination unless he had a letter from his bishop testifying to his previous Orders, and this letter was to be countersigned by a notary. Should the examiner fail to carry out these orders, he was to be deprived of his office; other punishments might also be added by the bishop.

Miscellany

Several considerations of the Synod in this session may be grouped together such as:

Stipends, "if in the past one shall have taken stipends in excess of the official amount, or if the person is still taking such stipends at present, the cleric must be warned and corrected at once by the bishop." **The Parish Priest** "should take up residence in his parish since he is shepherd of his flock, nor is he to dwell in a nearby city though it should be only a mile distant from his parish, nor can the bishop give permission that the parish priest have a substitute act for him for any length of time." **Christian Doctrine,** at least on Sundays and feast days, the parish priest was to explain the gospel. In Advent and Lent after the Angelus he was to gather together the negroes and other unlearned people in the church where he was to explain to them Christian doctrine. **Registers,** the parish priest was to have four registers—Baptismal, Confirmation, Marriage, and Burial—in which he was to enter details particular to each book. **Holy Oils,** parish priests living near the Cathedral were either themselves or by a cleric to come for the Holy Oils on Holy Thursday, bringing silver containers. Some of the Holy Oils were to be handed on to the parish priest living next to the first one, and so this process was to be repeated until all in the diocese had received the Oils. This process was to be completed within a period of three months. **Stipends,** nothing beyond the customary alms was to be accepted for the administration of the sacraments in order that all stain of avarice be banished from ecclesiastics. The Synod forbade both diocesan and religious clergy from accepting such either by themselves or through a third party under any subterfuge. Violating this decree in the first instance, they were to be fined two ounces of silver; a second offense would bring suspension for three years; a third carried the penalty of exile from the ecclesiastical province for a period of four years—beyond that they were to be considered in a state of simony.

Preaching

The Word of God was given lengthy consideration by the Synod since it is one of the principal duties of a priest.

Method Preachers of the Word of God were reminded of the sublimity of their office and were cautioned to interpret Holy Scripture according to the mind of the Church and especially the early Fathers.

Among the aborigines there was great ignorance of the mysteries of the faith, so on occasions such as the Circumcision, Transfiguration, Incarnation etc., after reading the gospel, the preacher was to make clear the hidden meaning of the feast, thus correcting ignorance so that religion might enjoy greater increase among the Indians.

License No license was to be granted to a diocesan priest to preach the Word of God without a previous examination at which the bishop or his vicar was to be present. Because of the gravity of recommending an ecclesiastic as competent to preach the Word of God, the Synod placed this burden on the judgement of the bishop or his vicar. The form to be in accordance with the Bull of Leo X and set forth in the Lateran Council with special reference to the Council of Trent.

Hearing sermons Many inhabitants of the Indies neglected hearing the Word of God, so that people even of mature age may have heard only one or two sermons during their whole lifetime, and by this neglect they endangered their salvation. The Synod made special appeal to all the faithful to hear the Word of God in Advent, Lent, and on feasts of the Church. Should they persist in deliberately remaining in their ignorance, the Synod decreed that under pain of anathema they hear at least three or four sermons during their lifetime unless legitimately impeded. Sermons called "de tabla" were preached by religious priests on regular occasions in the Cathedral and parish churches wherein they catechized and explained the gospel. This service was in appreciation to the Spanish King, who from state funds had erected and maintained monasteries where the friars lived. But this service had fallen into neglect resulting in great spiritual loss to the faithful. The Synod exhorted religious priests to renew this custom, and should they not heed this paternal admonition, bishops were to compel such recalcitrant friars by suspending their faculty to preach even in their own churches.

Probity of Clerics

Concerning the probity of clerics, the Synod had this to say: "We wish to admonish all clerics, especially those in Major Orders, of the necessity of following the example of holy men, not the example of licentious persons. For this reason we exhort them to cultivate the actions of the saints. Let their light shine before men, and let them show proof of their profession by the style of their dress so that the propriety of externals may indicate the virtue of their internal character. They shall not adorn themselves with silk collars, commonly called "harnesses"; their collars shall not exceed the width of one finger, and their handkerchiefs, commonly called "puntas" shall not be adorned with pointed lace; they shall not wear their hair loosened like a woman, nor cultivate a beard, but wear the tonsure on the crown of the head. Let them have a smoothly shaven face without a beard according to the Lateran Council. Nor shall they wear red or green undershirts. Finally let them abstain from those things which are contrary to the same Council under pain of a fine of ten ounces of silver, and other penalties the diocese may impose."

Wandering Clerics

As late as the 1600s the Indies were a haven for adventurers; clerics were no exception. Some wandered into this territory without license from their bishop, others brought authentic letters. All were to be examined carefully by the Ordinary before faculties to celebrate Mass or perform other clerical duties was granted them. Faculties were to be granted only after mature consideration and a strict examination accompanied by a testimony from their own bishop. Should they attempt to hear confessions or preach without episcopal authorization, even if so allowed by the parish priest, they would incur the penalty of excommunication.

Academic Degrees

Since an academic degree opened the world to greater preferment, some clerics were not adverse to claim a degree when they had none. "Many inflamed with a deceitful desire, fictitiously claim they have been honoured with the degree of Baccalaureate, Licentiate, Magister, and Doctor, which falsehoods bring great harm. And so we forbid anyone the use of subscribing to his name any degree until he has shown the title of the grade to his bishop or vicar, and this under penalty of a fine of fifty ounces of silver."

Again several minor decrees of the Synod may be placed under general headings. Rules: Testimony of ordination or granting of faculties was to be given free of cost by a notary appointed by the bishop. Should vagrant priests appear, the parish priest or vicar was with all diligence to persuade them to enter the nearest monastery of their

Order and so inform the bishop. Should they refuse, the bishop was to compel them to betake themselves to the monastery and thus be handed over to the religious superior. Priests expelled from a Religious Order were not to be granted benefices. And the final decree: Religious were to show reverence and obedience to the bishop.

After a reading of this session's proceedings, the Fathers were asked by the Bishop of Puerto Rico if they approved the decrees. All answered that they approved.

Fifth Session—December 19, 1622
Concerning the reformation of certain matters which come under the care and guidance of the Bishops

The fifth session devoted itself to chaplaincies, wills, legacies, and parish priests.

Chaplaincies

Chaplaincies which had been established could have the chaplain nominated by the Founder, if still alive. It was thought by the Synod that a diocesan priest should be installed as chaplain and not a religious priest who was not subject to the bishop. Should the chaplaincy become vacant and should the patron not nominate a priest within a prescribed time, the bishop was to use his privilege and assign a suitable diocesan priest to the post.

Chaplains were warned not to allow goods or money accruing to the chaplaincy either to himself or his relatives in the first or second degree of kindred; for this, the Synod noted, would greatly hinder the perpetuity of the chaplaincy. Should this happen, he was to return the goods or money to the general coffers. The patron in charge of the chaplaincy was to make an annual assessment of all monies and goods belonging to the chaplaincy. This inventory might also be made by the bishop.

The bishop or visitor might demand an oath from chaplains whether they had duly executed their office in celebrating Masses and observing anniversaries. Where this was not the case, the bishop was to choose someone to carry out the duties with greater care and diligence so that Masses and anniversaries might be conscientiously celebrated.

Chapels were to be repaired annually from the income of stipends. The bishop was to insure the stability and perpetuity of the said chapels.

Wills

In order to remove abuses and corruption which had been creeping into these regions, namely, in the case of Wills in which a clause was inserted to prevent the bishop from seeing such Wills on his visitation and in which the jurisdiction of the bishop was undermined, clearly contravening the Council of Trent, the Synod decreed that testators could not validly leave pious legacies on the condition that the bishop or his visitor was not to see the contents, or view them before their execution.

The Will of the testator was always to be made known to the bishop so that he might execute it piously and faithfully, since such a Will was to be effected according to the sacred canons of Trent. Abuses had crept into this matter which greatly vexed the Synod since some chaplains, prompted by cupidity, hindered the Will of the testator by declaring the Will invalid so that Mass stipends and their disposable property were assigned to themselves, for example, they would celebrate only one Mass, commonly called "de cuerpo presente," when money had been bequeathed for two or even four Masses.

Such chaplains tried by devious means to discharge the least of their debt owed to the Church ritually and canonically by disposing of such money and goods according to their own will, and they even prevented the bishop and his duly appointed legate from making a visitation. Further it was clear that stipend Masses were not being celebrated or priests, dioceses or Religious, were asked to celebrate Masses for less than the customary stipend, and this amount was determined by the chaplain himself. Nor was the Church given the one sixth part of the alms, nor was restitution made, nor did they allot pious bequests to any other than the chaplain himself.

The Synod Fathers were anxious to cure such a malady, hence admonished all who had the faculty of drawing up Wills that there was to be no secret covenant contrary to justice from which something illegal might arise. The Synod Fathers commanded under excommunication after three canonical warnings that the faithful of any state, condition, or dignity should in no way coerce the testator or persuade him to make such a secret covenant. Should it happen that despite warning some should persuade testators to insert a secret clause and should this come to the knowledge of seculars or religious, they were held to make it known within three days to the bishop or parish priest of the place so that the pious legacy might be executed according to the will of Trent, lest there be any fraud perpetuated by this act. The Synod declared that this decree be put in writing so that all concerned might be held to call this to the attention of the testator.

Sixth Session—December 26, 1622

The entire sixth session was devoted to the Indians, providing an insight into what Church leaders thought about the aborigines, their problems, and the solutions to ecclesiastical difficulties met by the Church in dealing with these same Indians. Hence the Synod opened the session with this statement: "It is the desire of the Fathers in order to be more nearly conformed to the Divine will, not only to consider carefully the flock of Christ but also to lead others into her fold so that there may be one fold and one shepherd to praise the Omnipotent God. The Fathers of the Synod express these opinions by declaring and establishing the following for the profit of both neophyte and faithful":—

Baptism

Parish priests were not to administer baptism to Indians without a surplice and stole, nor outside a Church unless necessity so urge, or the infant was born a distance of two or more miles from the Church. For those baptized in a private home, care was to be taken that the child be brought to the Church within the space of a month so that the ceremonies might be completed.

For adult Indians, the priest was not to confer baptism until they had learned the Lord's prayer, the Hail Mary, the Apostles' Creed, and the Ten Commandments. For Indians who could not learn such, they should be made to understand what is necessary for salvation and believe that by receiving baptism they become heirs of heaven. They should have sorrow for their sins.

In order to avoid impediments arising from spiritual relationship, the parish priest was to appoint in parochial cities men and women of mature age who would act as godparents. They were to admit only one man or one woman as sponsors, or at most one man *and* one woman.

In each parish Church there was to be a stone baptismal font which was to have a locked cover; further the parish priest was to keep a register in which the name of the baptised, parents and godparents were to be written, noting the day, month and year of baptism.

Confirmation

The Indians were to be transported to the place where confirmation was to be administered. Since Indian towns were located at a great distance from one another, and many lived in forsaken places, the sacrament of confirmation could only be administered during the visitation of the bishop. So the sponsors were advised to bring the Indian candidates to the parish or place where the bishop was to confer the sacrament. Sponsors refusing to do so were to be subject to punishment determined by the bishop.

Penance

The more ignorant the Indian neophytes were, the more care should the parish priest use in instructing them, especially in the sacrament of penance. He was to prepare them to have the correct dispositions to make a good confession. Parish priests were held to administer the sacrament of penance not only during Lent but also throughout the year whenever the Indians sought it; and this was to be done in clerical vestments and in the church unless administered to the sick. The priest was not to impose such penance as attendance at Mass or the performance of good works.

Each year on Septuagesima Sunday the parish priest was to write out a list of those Indians who were to satisfy the precept of the Church, and fifteen days prior to Low Sunday they were to inquire of the Indians if they had fulfilled the precept. If some had not done so, the parish priest was to teach them the virtue and efficacy of the sacrament and the obligation of annual confession.

Reserved Cases

The Synod granted faculty to parish priests to absolve Indians from cases reserved to the bishop.

The Eucharist

The Synod contended that the behaviour of the Indians and the negligence of parish priests caused them to lack knowledge and proper dispositions for receiving the Most Holy Sacrament of the Eucharist. Parish priests, as teachers, were called upon to instruct them in the faith that Christ, the Lord, really lives in this sacrament. Further, they were to teach the Indian that purity was necessary for its reception. Concerning Viaticum the Synod had this to say: "Since up to the present it has not been the custom to confer this sacrament as Viaticum, the Synod now considering the question in a more favourable light and lest we deprive sick Indians of the Heavenly Food when they have the capacity of confessing their sins and believe in this sacrament, orders that the Holy Eucharist be administered in parishes where the Ordinary has not yet permitted the Sacred Species to be reserved. It shall be brought to the sick in the morning after the celebration of the parish Mass, the Roman ritual being observed."

Extreme Unction

Faithful Indians who had reached the use of reason and were in danger of death from illness or old age were to be administered the sacrament of Extreme Unction by the priest dressed in surplice and stole. Nor was the priest to wait until the Indian was unconscious, so that being in full use of his senses he might explain the efficacy of the sacrament to the dying person.

Matrimony

Parish priests were admonished that under no circumstances were they to omit the banns of marriage wherein also were to be declared the impediments to marriage; and this because of the ignorance of the Indians.

The ceremony of matrimony was to be performed according to the decrees of the Council of Trent, and a register kept where the names of the contracting parties were to be inscribed.

Since many Indians had been married before becoming Christians, the parish priest was to enquire into the legitimate custom of the pagan rite; how consent was given: by nods of the head, by exchange of gifts, or by words? If these were the legitimate customs whereby the contracting parties gave consent, then the marriage was valid.

But there were also customs among the Indians which would invalidate the marriage contract, and hence some Indians would be free to marry after being received into the Church. Should the parish priest doubt the validity of the pagan marriage and be unable to solve the doubt, he was to consult the bishop or his vicar.

In the case of two infidels joined in matrimony before one becomes a Christian, if the pagan does not attempt to make the Christian apostatize, or if the pagan shows signs of wishing to become a Christian, they may be allowed to live together. If on the contrary there should be danger of the Christian losing the faith, they were to separate and the Christian might legitimately enter into another marriage. The bishop was to be consulted in each case.

Indians Who Contract Marriages Outside Cities

In order to avoid legal controversy and like troubles, it was decreed that when an Indian contracted marriage with an Indian of another city, the husband should cohabitate with his wife in the domicile of the woman. This was not to be understood of Indians called cacqiues (chiefs). In this case the wife was held to live with her husband in the domicile of the cacique.

Language

Parish priests both diocesan and religious who as parish priests were held by the official decrees of the Synod, were to learn the language of the Indians and were to be examined in knowledge of the language before receiving a benefice. Those ignorant of the language were not to be appointed parish priests, for a speaking knowledge was very necessary that they might evangelize the Indians and that progress might be made through evangelization.

Drunkenness

Since there had crept in among the Indians the habit of getting drunk when they gathered for feasts from which both temporal and spiritual harm resulted, under no circumstances was such drunkenness to be countenanced by the parish priest. On the contrary they were to teach the Indians to celebrate marriage and other feasts according to Christian morality.

Education

The Synod asked parish priests to establish schools for boys where they might learn to read and write Spanish. In these schools they were also to be taught Christian doctrine. Children were not to be forced to attend these schools through fear of punishment.

School masters were warned that schools were not to be an occasion of slavery for Indian boys. Indeed, they might help provide for the Church and even gather fodder for the horses, but under no circumstances were the boys to work for the comendarii before completing the age of twelve years, and this according to royal edict.

Girls were not to attend catechism class before the age of nine years unless accompanied by their mothers, and then only on feast days.

Visitation of the Sick

Parish priests were urged to visit the sick Indians frequently and encourage and console the dying.

The parish priest was to demand nothing for himself from the goods of a deceased Indian beyond what was willed by the person. Should an Indian die intestate, his heirs were free to bequeath whatsoever they wished. But they were to be reminded they should donate a fifth part of the inheritance for suffrages for the deceased, and this according to law. Should they refuse to do so, they were not to be pressed.

The parish priest was to celebrate one Mass for each deceased Indian, man or woman, who had reached the age of nine years, and the commendarius was to pay the stipend.

Offerings and Stipends

Since at the time of this Synod, 1622, the stipend assigned to the parish priest was what the commendarius was to pay. No parish priest was to exact a stipend from the Indians by reason of administration of the sacraments such as baptism, nor for conducting funerals. Further, should the Indian donate a white cloth and candle on the occasion of a baptism, the parish priest was forbidden to accept such unless it was given spontaneously. Whoever should violate this decree was to be fined double the amount he had accepted in the first instance, and greater in the second instance according to the judgement of the Orindary.

Catechesis

The Synod claimed that ignorance of the principal mysteries of the faith, which Indians should know and love, was the reason why they were so undisciplined and wicked, for they would revert to their idols and again plunge into infidelity. The Synod urged parish priests to apply a remedy to such evil.

Method They were to assemble boys up to the age of twelve years and girls up to the age of nine years every morning and afternoon for two hours and older ones at least on feast days and teach them according to the Roman Catechism, namely: the Our Father, Hail Mary, Apostles Creed, the Ten Commandments and the precepts of the Church. Should these Indian children not be able to retain all of this, they were to be taught to know and believe the chief mysteries of the faith; namely, there is one God, the author of all things who rewards with eternal life those who keep His mandates, and on those who do not He inflicts eternal punishment; that the Father is God, the Son is God, the Holy Spirit is God; three Persons, one and the same God; that the Second Person, Jesus Christ, is the Lord, who for the salvation of men became Incarnate by the Virgin Mary, who remained a virgin before birth, during birth, and after birth. Christ suffered died and was buried, rose from the dead, and ascended into heaven. All are saved by this Faith when sin is detected, and baptism, a sacrament of the Church is received. If he is a former pagan who is baptized, and sins after baptism, and receives the sacrament of penance, he will attain eternal life. These doctrines were to be so uniformally taught that the neophytes were to hear nothing discordant in word, books, sermons or tracts. And they were not to be translated into native languages unless seen and approved by the bishop.

Negroes and Visitors not to be Allowed to Live Among the Indians

Ethiopians and people of dark colour, called mulattoes, were seldom permitted in Indian towns; nor were wandering clerics or gamblers allowed. The parish priest was not to entertain people of questionable character so that peace and tranquility might be preserved among the Indians. In order that sin be avoided and that Indian women, because of fraility, be not easily led into sin, no secular visitor was to stay more than three days in the priest's rectory; nor were his relatives, except his mother and sister, allowed lest the newly converted Indians be given scandal since they might be ignorant of the kinship with the priest.

Parish Priest not to Engage in Trade or Business

The sacred canons placed an interdict on ecclesiastics who engaged in business or became merchants among the Indians. This was more of a danger among diocesan priests, so the Synod ordered under pain of excommunication that no parish priest by himself or through a third party cultivate fields, become merchants buying or selling mules or horses, or exercise any species of trade when the Indians came to do work for the mission. It made one exception: he might justly sell food for the sustenance of Indian families or raise sheep for this purpose.

Residence of Parish Priest

The Fathers strictly forbad any parish priest from leaving his Indian parish without permission of the bishop or his vicar unless for reason of confession, illness, or forced by some necessity. If in the latter case he could not inform the bishop or vicar before leaving, he was to present himself to the bishop or vicar when he returned. If anyone, incardinated into a diocese, contrary to this decree, shall have departed from his parish, in addition to a fine of ten ounces of silver, he was not to enjoy the fruit of his benefice during the time he was absent. Should he, without written permission from his bishop, desert his parish, he was subject to excommunication.

Inaxcessible places, rugged terrain, and the greater good of the Indians compelled bishops to spread their personnel over great areas which limited the number of priests assigned to individual churches. It was decreed that the parish priest reside at times in those remote settlements lest the Indians die without the sacraments, since they could not be brought into the town where they would have the sacraments administered to them. Unless infirmity impeded the priest, he was to visit such Indians each month and this under holy obedience and a fine of four ounces of silver. He was to visit the sick more often in order to fortify them with the sacraments and offer spiritual and temporal aid.

Imprisonment and Punishment of Indians

"The condition and nature of the Indians is such that they readily shrink from the parish priest when they know they are to be corrected by punishment. When and if it should happen that through some human fraility they should err, let the parish priest entreat, reprove, and chide in all patience since this often helps much more in correcting than sternness. If a grave fault is committed by the Indians and the rod be thought by some to be necessary, neither this nor imprisonment is to be used, nor shall the parish priest permit the comendarii to use punishments, and this under pain of excommunication. We forbid the incarceration and physical punishment of Indians of whatsoever status and condition they may be so that the loss of souls may be avoided, and they may not be precipitated headlong by such punishments or encouraged to return to idolatry. Concerning public sinners such as those living in concubinage and practicing magic and the like, the parish priest shall inform the bishop together with names of witnesses so that a remedy may be provided."

Explanation of Gospel at High Mass

"As God has planted the Church of the Indies as a new celestial seed, He gives the increase. Adhering to the Council of Trent, this Synod prescribes that during High Mass on feast days when Indians are gathered together, the parish priest shall explain the gospel and give warning of salvation covering it with wax, as it were, that these truths may remain in their hearts. After the explanation, the priest shall ask useful questions and endeavour to make the Indians better acquainted with the Divine Law."

Qualifications of Religious Chosen to be Parish Priests among the Indians

Since religious priests were commissioned by the Holy See and a rescript of the Catholic King to act as parish priests among the Indians, the Fathers superior and the Provincials were exhorted that in choosing such subjects in their Chapters, they be men of mature age, of solid virtue, that they know the language of the Indians, and are distinguished in knowledge and doctrine. Such religious were to be presented by superiors to the bishop.

Holy Days of Obligation to be Observed by the Indians

Paul III, taking into consideration the poor state of the Indians, did not oblige them to observe all the Holy days observed by the Spaniards. For this reason he deputed the bishops to accommodate the feasts to the Indians. So they were under precept to observe only the following:

All Sundays

Christmas, without the following two days
Circumcision
Epiphany
Easter, without the following two days
Ascension

Pentecost, without the following two days
Corpus Christi

Nativity of the Blessed Virgin Mary
Assumption
Sts. Peter and Paul

Feast of titular Church in their territory

The observance of other feasts which obliged the Spaniards was left to the voluntary devotion of the Indians.

Lest the Spaniards take the occasion when the Indians did not have to attend Mass on the rest of the feasts required of the Spaniards and make the Indians work on these days, it was decreed that the Indians would work a minimal period of time and not on the Spanish estates unless this was allowed by the bishop, or from other faculties.

"Whatever promotes the worship of God and the observance of feast days is to be cultivated. For it is necessary in these regions to arouse greater devotion, looking to preserve and augment such devotion among neophytes in so far as devotion is deficient. The Synod, therefore, prohibits under pain of a fine of four ounces of silver that no one of whatsoever state, condition, or quality force the Indians to labour on feast days or send them out of town the previous day if they cannot come to a place where they can hear Mass the following day."

Canonical Visitation

Since the special purpose of a canonical visitation was to safeguard good morals and correct evils, this could be done best by one not in charge of the mission. The bishops were cautioned to choose men of learning and mature age for this duty, men who would reject political preferment, friendship, and bothersome expenses in their visitation.

They were neither to barter, sell, buy, or look for any emolument even spontaneously offered beyond their food. Whosoever should violate this decree would be held to pay double the amount in restitution within a month of the offense, and he was to be removed from his office and suspended from his benefice according to the Constitution of Gregory X at the Council of Lyons.

Establishment of Indian Towns

Experience taught and it was the common consensus of theologians and confessors that the Indian neophytes were swayed now one way, now another in the matter of salvation where they lived alone in forsaken areas and apart from the society of Christians and where they could not be taught things necessary for salvation or helped by the reception of the sacraments. Seeming to be by nature something like wild animals, they hardly attained to mediocrity in doctrine after having been catechized assiduously. How, therefore, could they learn at all dispersed throughout wild places without the aid of preaching?

Hence King Philip, on whose shoulders fell the duty of governing these gentiles, wishing to ease his conscience of this burden, commanded that these Indians be gathered into towns throughout these territories. Such a method was the only one used by the Provincial Synods in the New World. "It is because of the neglect of this precept that we are groaning. The King's serious mandate has not been put into execution in their provinces by those whose duty it is to provide solicitously for the Indians lest they lose these lambs of Christ and allow them to be torn asunder by demons who act like cruel and raging wolves. Hence this Synod orders and exhorts magistrates, governor, and judges who by their office or commission are held to establish towns for the Indians, that they set aside human respect and quickly gather the Indians into towns in which their wild manners may be subdued and they grow accustomed to Christian life and civilized institutions; and through daily instructions come to a full knowledge of the faith and observe the Commandments of God." The Synod further reminded bishops that their ministry would not excuse them from fulfilling this mandate nor would they have a clear conscience unless they strove to apply this remedy to the present evil and to the greater evil which would arise in the future from its neglect.

Construction of Churches

"Among the hindrances which harm the salvation of the Indians and by which they are oppressed by the devil, this holds first place: the great negligence in building churches and the lack of donating necessary ornaments for the administration of the sacraments. Because of these defects the Indians are not taught Christian doctrine, nor are the sacraments administered, nor the dead given Christian burial in many places. Therefore the Fathers of the Synod, whose concern this is, exhort those whose duty it is to build churches that they begin without delay and provide them properly with what is necessary for teaching the Indians and for the administration of the sacraments as our Catholic King has commanded."

Transport of Indians

"Some comendarii are so filled with cupidity that they place their own interests before the advantages of the Indians. They are accustomed to transport Indians from their places of residence to other places, and from this act arises great inconveniences due to the lack of necessities of life by which the Indians are affected while they await new harvests in the new locations. More often the places to which they are sent are less healthy and many die. Further, there would be no priest who would know their dialect and who might administer the sacraments to them. From this also arises much confusion of ecclesiastical jurisdiction concerning parish priests, and for this reason parishes are left deserted. Lest Indians be transferred from their own native villages or designated domicile without approval of the bishops, let the judges warn and exhort colonists that this decree, made after mature consideration, is inviolable and cannot under any circumstances be broken. Let judges seriously weigh petitions of comendarii for transferring of Indians from one place to another."

Stipends for Parish Priests (of Indians)

Colonists were held to offer the parish priest the customary stipend in the form of money. In the case of Indians, money being deficient among them, they were held to offer useful produce. Where it happened that stipends could not sufficiently support the priest, that bishop was to allow a portion of his funds for the priest as was recommended by the sacred canons. This was to be augmented according to the necessity of the place, but it was to be assigned temporarily.

War against the Indians

"Although a just war is permitted, nevertheless, it is a sin to engage in war for spoils alone. Many, led by this cupidity in these regions, extort from governors permission to wage war on Indians under the pretext of punishing criminals, contrary to the will of the King expressed in his interdicts. War against the Indians is sometimes undertaken when they neither despise the Christian religion nor impede the passage of travellers, nor lay ambush for them. These Indians are unjustly forced from their own territory into diverse localities, despoiled of fortune and home by unjust wars so that they hate the very name of Christian. Thus they flee into caves and forsaken places in the mountains where, without food and under freezing conditions and hard labour, they perish. Such irreparable injury this Synod deplores. Considering the seriousness of the act, no remedy in the past has been satisfactory, and there will be none unless ecclesiastical jurisdiction immediately forbids the use of the sword, and therefore it does so forbid by this present decree that no officer, soldier, or anyone else of whatsoever status or condition be allowed to wage war on Indians who are not waging war on us, or who have done no criminal act which would make them be considered criminals, nor shall anyone abduct them from their homes. All transgressors of this decree fall under excommunication, L.S. Let them be denounced through vicars to the Inquisition before whom they shall appear and by whom they shall not be absolved until they return the children and adults to their own domiciles. Thus under the pain of excommunication, which shall fall on the principal transgressors and those who carry out their orders, they shall not be absolved from these censures until the Indians are returned to their homelands. Finally, Spaniards shall not sell Indians captured in a just war, nor buy nor exchange them with a tacit understanding of receipt of money."

A Review of Certain Privileges from Various Pontificial Decrees Granted in Favour of Indians

a) From the decree of Paul III, the Indians are not held to fasting anytime during the year except on days of Lent, Holy Saturday, and the vigil of Christmas.

b) From the decree of Paul III, Indians may eat meat in Lent and other days of abstinence, which is granted by the Bulla Cruciata.

c) From the decree of Paul III, Indians may contract marriage within the third and fourth degree of consanguinity and affinity.

d) From the decree of Pius IV, Bishops in the lands of the Indians may use for chrism that which is called "balsam" in these regions but really is not balsam.

e) From the decree of Clement VIII, it is allowed secular and religious priests stationed twenty miles from where Chrism and the Oil of Catechumens is consecrated to use the old Chrism and the Oil of Catechumens even after a period of four years from the time it was blessed.

f) From the decree of Gregory XIII, it is granted to archbishops and bishops of the Indians, and others to whom is accorded this faculty, to absolve from the crime of heresy and idolatry and from whatsoever reserved cases both in the internal and external forum, all Indians both men and women and children born of them, having imposed a salutary penance for the soothing of conscience.

Seventh Session—January 1, 1623

Execution of the Decrees

"Since nothing effectively will come of the laws and statutes established by this Synod unless the laws and decrees shall bind under strict obligation of fulfilment as a burden incumbent upon the bishops, we exhort them that they make every effort that they be observed and that they enforce them with all their power. Let them carry out those things which pertain to the said decree, if they are not contrary to already established laws. Let them enforce all these canonical remedies for keeping the law, especially the most onerous if subjects are contumacious and recidivous."

"If in the future there should arise doubts about these decrees and constitutions, we confide the interpretations and explanations to the archbishops and bishops and their successors."

"Lest ignorance be used as an excuse by anyone concerning the decrees of this Synod, as soon as the Holy See gives approval and they shall be confirmed, the bishops shall declare so in writing or through their vicars and make it known in the Cathedral and in parish churches in Spanish cities. Here the decrees shall be promulgated, and after having done so, shall come into effect two months later."

"The Synod protests, nor does it intend anything in these decrees other than obedience to the Roman Pontiff and observance of the Council of Trent."

"Since this first Provincial Dominican Synod has been constituted legitimately under obedience to the Apostolic See, it affirms and protests that it never intended nor does it intend to contradict any decrees of the General Councils, nor oppose in the slightest manner any holy and salutary decree. The Synod declares wholeheartedly that it does not wish either in part or in whole to detract from the right of patronage granted by the Apostolic See to Philip of Spain, our Catholic King, to whom has been committed the western world, that he may govern it in peace and tranquility and with singular magnificence and piety may he subdue these barbarous nations and enemies of the Church. May God grant him a long life for the happiness of the State."

"Each and every thing which has been acted upon and decreed in this Provincial Council, through which we owe obedience, reverence, authority, and judgement to the Holy Roman Church, Mother of all the Churches, we submit all the decrees to her as a Teacher for emmendation and correction."

Friar Peter de Oviedo, Archbishop of Santo Domingo
Friar Gundisalvus de Angulo, Bishop of Venezuela
Dr. Bernardo de Balbuena, Bishop of Puerto Rico
Dr. Augustine Serrano Pimentel, signed for Bishop of Cuba
Franciscus Serrano y Baraes, signed for Abbot of Jamaica

Ref. Boletin Eclesiastico de la Arquidiocesis de Santo Domingo-Primada de America

Notes

NOTES TO CHAPTER 1

1. Samuel Eliot Morison, *Admiral of the Ocean Sea* (Boston: Little, Brown and Co., 1949), 451.
2. Ibid.
3. Ibid.
4. Ibid.
5. Ibid.
6. Morison, *Admiral of the Ocean Sea,* 103.
7. Morison, *Admiral of the Ocean Sea,* 34.
8. Ibid.
9. Morison, *Admiral of the Ocean Sea,* 452.
10. Ibid.
11. Narrative of Fernando Colón, *History of the Life of Christopher Columbus* (London, 1732).
12. Morison, *Admiral of the Ocean Sea,* 453.
13. Ibid.
14. King to Diego Velázquez, 24 Feb. 1515. AGI 139-1-5, t. 5, fol. 169v, Indiferente General-Registros-Libros generalisimos de Reales ordenes, nombramientos gracias etc. 1512–18.
15. Peter Martyr, *De Novo Orbe,* Fifth Decade. Translated by R. Eden (London 1912).
16. Ibid.
17. Steven M. Donovan, "Bernardo Buil," *CE* 3:40–41.
18. Morison, *Admiral of the Ocean Sea,* 453.
19. Peter Martyr, *De Novo Orbe,* Fifth Decade.
20. Morison, *Admiral of the Ocean Sea,* map opposite 452.
21. A.G.I. 139-1-5. Tomo 4, folio 51 v. Años 1512–18. The king to Gil González Dávila, 10 Dec. 1512.
22. Morison, *Admiral of the Ocean Sea,* map opposite 452.
23. Morison, *Admiral of the Ocean Sea,* 639.
24. Morison, *Admiral of the Ocean Sea,* 640.
25. Morison, *Admiral of the Ocean Sea,* 631–34.
26. Colón, *Christopher Columbus.*
27. Colón, *Christopher Columbus.*

28. Morison, *Admiral of the Ocean Sea*, 648–49.
29. Morison, *Admiral of the Ocean Sea*, 650.
30. Morison, *Admiral of the Ocean Sea*, 650–53.
31. Morison, *Admiral of the Ocean Sea*, 658.
32. Robert Howard, *Arawak Village site,* White Marl, Jamaica. Jamaica Historical Society, *Bulletin*. Vol iii, No 4, December, 1961, pages 59–62 and Vol. iii, No 45 March, 1962, pages 79–82. Also—Archaeological Society of Jamaica. *News Letter*—1958–1986. James W. Lee, Editor.
33. Irving Rouse, *Prehistory of the West Indies*. Reprinted from *Science,* May 1, 1964 Vol. 144, No. 3618, page 502.
34. Rouse, *"Entry of Man into the West Indies."* Yale University Publications in Anthropology No 61. pages 3 to 24.
35. Ibid.
36. Ronald Vanderwal, "Problem of Jamaican Prehistory," *Jamaica Journal*, 1968, pages 10 to 13.
37. Francisco Morales Padrón-Jamaica Española-Sevilla, 1952. Only four caciques are known p. 29.
38. Dr. Elizabeth Wing, University of Florida, Gainesville, Florida. Personal communication. *Letter—Dec. 7, 1964.*
39. Rouse, *Prehistory of the West Indies—Science,* May 1, 1964, No. 3618, page 509.
40. Ibid.
41. Ronald Vanderwal, *Problem of Jamaican Prehistory, Jamaica Journal* Sept. 1968, p. 11.
42. C. Bernard Lewis. The Jamaica Historical Society—*Bulletin*. Vol II, No. 1 March 1957, p. 28.
43. Ibid. Also: Samuel Eliot Morison—*Admiral of the Ocean Sea*. Boston: Little, Brown and Co., 1949. pages 451 and 452.

44 and 45. Stone grinder-artifacts at Institute of Jamaica, Kingston, Jamaica.

46. C. Bernard Lewis. The Jamaica Historical Society—*Bulletin* Vol. II, No. 1 March 1957, p. 28.
47. J. S. Tyndal Biscoe, *The Jamaican Arawak. The Jamaican Historical Review* Vol iii, No 3. March 1962, p. 4.
48. Ibid.
49. Peter Martyr, *De Novo Orbe,* Fifth Decade. Translated by R. Eden (London 1912) No pagination.
50. Ibid.
51. Ibid.
52. Ibid.
53. Ibid.
54. Ibid.
55. No explanation is offered as to the method of observation.
56. Peter Martyr, *De Novo Orbe,* Fifth Decade.
57. Ibid.
58. Ibid.

59. Ibid.
60. Colón, *Christopher Columbus.*
61. Samuel Eliot Morison, "Address at St. Ann's Bay," Jamaica, 12 Oct. 1960 from Morison's written manuscript unpublished.
62. Discovered and photographed by author—1955. Photograph at Arawak Museum, White Marl. Jamaica.
63. Samuel Eliot Morison, "Address at St. Ann's Bay," Jamaica, 12 Oct. 1960.

NOTES TO CHAPTER 2

1. Frank Cundall, *Chronological Outlines of Jamaica History, 1492–1926* (Institute of Jamaica, 1927), 2.
2. W. Eugene Shiels, S.J., *King and Church: The Rise and Fall of the Patronato Real* (Chicago: Loyola University Press, 1961), 66.
3. Shiels, *King and Church,* 64–65.
4. Shiels, *King and Church,* 66–67.
5. Shiels, *King and Church,* 113–15.
6. Shiels, *King and Church,* 74.
7. Shiels, *King and Church,* 78–91.
8. Shiels, *King and Church,* 100–12.
9. Horace de la Costa, S.J. *The Jesuits in the Philippines, 1581–1868* (Cambridge, Mass.: Harvard University Press, 1961), under the word *Patronato.*
10. Frank Cundall and Joseph L. Pietersz, *Jamaica Under the Spaniards* (Kingston: Institute of Jamaica, 1919), 1.
11. Cundall, *Chronological Outlines of Jamaica History,* 2.
12. Ibid.
13. Cundall and Pietersz, *Jamaica Under the Spaniards,* 12.
14. Francisco Morales Padrón, *Jamaica Española.* (Seville: Escuela de Estudios Hispano-Americanas de Seville, 1952), 90.
15. Morales Padrón, *Jamaica Española,* 88, 90.
16. Cundall, *Chronological Outlines of Jamaica History,* 2; Cundall and Pietersz, *Jamaica Under the Spaniards,* 1; William J. Gardner, *A History of Jamaica* (T. Fisher Unwin: London, 1909), 8.
17. Morales Padrón, *Jamaica Española,* 89.
18. Morales Padrón, *Jamaica Española,* 88, 90.
19. Geraint Casserly discovered the ruins of the plaza in 1937.
20. Eric Williams, ed., *Documents of West Indian History* (Port of Spain: PNM Publishing Co., 1963), 101.
21. De la Costa, *The Jesuits in the Philippines,* 13.
22. Ferdinand to Diego Colón, 25 July 1511. AGI leg. 418, bk. 3, fol. 128.
23. Ibid.
24. Morales Padrón, *Jamaica Española,* 288; AGI 139-1-5, Años 1512–18. Document not dated but preceding document is dated 3 May 1513, and the following document is dated 15 May 1513.

25. Morales Padrón, *Jamaica Española,* 91.
26. Morales Padrón, *Jamaica Española,* 156.
27. Morales Padrón, *Jamaica Española,* 156, n. 3.
28. Ibid.
29. King to Gil Gonzales Dávila, 10 Dec. 1512. AGI leg. 418, t. 4, fol. 45v. 1512.
30. King to Gil Gonzales Dávila, 10 Dec. 1512. AGI leg. 418, t. 4, fol. 45v.
31. Morales Padrón, *Jamaica Española,* 92.
32. 36 Morales Padrón, *Jamaica Española,* 91. 37 AGI 139-1-5, tomo 4, f. 45v. King to Diego Colón, 12 Dec. 1512.
33. King to Diego Colón, 12 Dec. 1512. AGI 139-1-5, t.4, fol. 45v.
34. AGI, King to Diego Colon. A.G.I. 139-1-5 t. 4. fol. 45v Document not dated but preceeding one is dated May 3, 1513 and following one May 15, 1513.
35. AGI 139-1-6, t. 8, fol. 303v. Años 1518–26. 20 July 1512.
36. Morales Padrón, *Jamaica Española,* 94.
37. Don Francisco Garay, 11 June 1515. AGI 1-1-27, Simancas Secular-Gobierno. Años 1515–94.
38. Garay, 11 June 1515, AGI 1-1-27, Simancas Secular-Gobierno. Años 1515–94.
39. Garay, 11 June 1515. AGI 1-1-27, t. 8, fol. 303v. Años 1518–94.
40. Ibid.
41. Ibid.
42. Ibid.
43. Ibid.
44. Ibid.
45. AGI 139-1-6, t. 8, fol. 125. Años 1518–26. 6 Sept. 1519, 49 AGI 1-1-27, tomo 8, f 303v. Años 1518–94. Don Francisco Garay June 11, 1515.
46. AGI 139-1-6, t. 8, fol. 125. Años 1518–26, 6 Sept. 1519.
47. AGI 139-1-6, Tomo 8, Folio 125. Años 1518–26. 6 Sept. 1519.
48. King to Francisco Garay, 6 Sept. 1521. AGI 139-1-6, t. 8, fol. 316. Años 1518–26. See also AGI 109-1-6, t. 8, fol. 55. Años 1527–35. Garay had already left for Mexico.
49. King to governor and officials in Jamaica. 9 Sept. 1526. AGI 139-1-7. t. 11, fol. 157v. Años 1526–28.
50. Morales Padrón, *Jamaica Española, 282, n. 63.*
51. King to Diego Colón, 20 July 1518. AGI 139-1-5. t. 5, fol. 208v. Años 1512–18.
52. King to his officials, from his castle at Valladolid. 5 June 1513. AGI 139-1-5. t. 4, fol. 167v. Años 1512–18.
53. Seville Papers—Vol. 5, 2nd Series, 27, 20 Feb. 1524. Also, King to Francisco Garay. AGI 139-1-5. t. 8, fol. 193. Años 1512–18.
54. King to Francisco Garay. AGI 139-1-6. t. 8, fol. 123v. Años 1518–26.
55. Seville Papers—vol. 3, first series, part II, 45. 29 Aug. 1519.
56. Hans Sloane, *Catalogus plantarum quae in Insula Jamaica sponte proveniunt, vel vulgo coluntur, cum earundum synonymis et locis natalibus* (London, 1696). Section devoted to Sloane's personal observations of Seville.
57. Cundall and Pietersz, *Jamaica under the Spaniards,* 4.

58. Francisco Lopez de Gomara, *Cortez: Life of the Conqueror* (Berkeley & Los Angeles: University of California Press, 1964), 21–22.
59. Morales claims expedition under Garay left Jamaica 26 June 1523—*Jamaica Española,* 74.
60. Lopez de Gomara, *Cortés,* 21–22.
61. 67
62. King to Diego Colón, AGI 139-1-6. t. 9, fol. 29. Años 1518–26.
63. Queen, 16 Feb. 1533. AGI 79-4-1. t. Y 1, fol. 133. Años 1529–50.
64. Ibid.
65. Ibid.
66. Ibid.
67. Ibid.
68. Ibid.
69. Ibid.
70. Ibid.
71. Ibid.

NOTES TO CHAPTER 3

1. King to Don Geronymo, Vichy, 29 Jan. 1515. AGI 139-1-5, t. 5, fol. 145v. Años 1512–18.
2. Morales Padrón, *Jamaica Española,* 155; King to Vichy, 29 Jan. 1515. AGI 139-1-5, t. 5, fol. 145v. Años 1512–18.
3. Morales Padrón, *Jamaica Española,* 155; AGI 139-1-5, t. 5, fol. 145v. 29 Jan. 1515.
4. AGI 139-1-5, t. 5, fol. 145v. 29 Jan. 1515; Morales Padrón, *Jamaica Española,* 159.
5. King to Vichy, 22 Aug. 1515. AGI 139-1-5. t. 5, fol. 214. Años 1512–18.
6. King to Vichy, 12 Aug. 1515. AGI 139-1-5. t. 6, fol. 7. Años 1512–18.
7. King and queen to Diego Colón, 17 July 1516. AGI 139-1-5. t. 6, fol. 7. Años 1512–18.
8. King and queen to Diego Colón, 17 July 1516. AGI 139-1-5. t. 6, fol. 7. Años 1512–18.
9. King and queen to Diego Colón, 17 July 1516. AGI 139-1-5. t. 6, fol. 7. Años 1512–18.
10. A.G.I. 139-1-6. Tomo 9, Folio 239. Dec 24, 1523 King to officials in Jamaica Años 1518–1526.
11. A.G.I. 139-1-6. Tomo 9. Folio 239 Años 1518–1526. King to officials in Jamaica Dec. 24, 1523.
12. A.G.I. 139-1-6. Tomo 9. Folio 112. Años 1518–1526. King to Duke his cousin March 27, 1523.
13. Eric Williams. *Documents of West Indian History* 1492–1655. PNM Publishing Co. Ltd 90 Frederick St. Port-of-Spain (1963) p. 137.
14. AGI 139-1-5. Tomo 6. Folio 22. Años 1518–1526. King to Governor Juan de Mendegurren. March 27, 1523.
15. AGI 139-1-5. t. 6, fol. 22, Años 1512–18, King and Queen to Governor Francisco de Garay, 13 28., 27 March 1523. AGI 139-1-5. t. 6, fol. 22. Años 1512–18. Sept. 1516.

16. AGI 139-1-6. t. 9, fol. 239. Años 1518–26. King to governor and officials in Jamaica, 24 Dec. 1523.
17. AGI 139-1-6, t. 9, fol. 239. Años 1518–26. King to governor and officials in Jamaica. 24 Dec. 1523.
18. King to governor and officials in Jamaica, 24 Dec. 1523. AGI 139-1-6. t. 9, fol. 239. Años 1518–26.
19. Seville Papers, no. 52, 5 Nov. 1524.
20. Morales Padrón, *Jamaica Española,* 198.
21. Morales Padrón, *Jamaica Española,* 165, 198.
22. Morales Padrón, *Jamaica Española,* 165.
23. Seville Papers, 1st series, vol. 3, 46. 21 March 1524.
24. King to governor and officials, 24 Dec. 1523. AGI 139-1-6. t. 9, fol. 239. Años 1518–26. King to governor and officials, 9 Sept. 1526. AGI 139-1-7, t. 11, fol. 144. Años 1526–28.
25. Seville Papers, vol. 3, 1st Series, 46. 21 March 1524. King to governor and officials, 24 Dec. 1523. AGI 139-1-6. t. 9, fol. 239. Años 1518–26.
26. King to governor and officials, 24 Dec. 1523. AGI 139-1-6. t. 9, fol. 239. Años 1518–26.
27. King to governor and officials, 24 Dec. 1523. AGI 139-1-6. t. 9, fol. 239. Años 1518–26.
28. King to governor and officials, 9 Sept. 1526. AGI 139-1-7, t. 11, fol. 144. Años 1526–28.
29. King to governor and officials 9 Sept. 1526. A.G.I. 139-1-7. t. 11, fol. 144.Años 1526–28.
30. King to governor and officials, 9 Sept. 1526. AGI 139-1-7, t. 11, fol. 144. Años 1526–28.
31. Peter Martyr to Charles I. King to governor and officials, 9 Sept. 1526. AGI 139-1-7, t. 11, fol. 164. Años 1526–28.
32. Charles I to officials in Jamaica 15. Oct. 1526. AGI 139-1-7. t. 12, fol. 112. Años 1526–28.
33. King to governor and officials, 9 Sept. 1526. AGI 139-1-7. t. 11 fol. 145. Años 1526–28.
34. Queen to Gil Gonzales, 16 Feb. 1533. AGI 79-4-1. t. Y-1, fol. 128.
35. Sloane, *Catalogus plantarum,* lxvi.
36. *News Letter,* Archaeological Society of Jamaica 1965–1986, James W. Lee, editor, Kingston.
37. King to Fray Miguel Ramirez, 20 March 1528. AGI 139-1-7. t. 13, fol. 68, Años 1526–28; Morales Padrón *Jamaica Española,* 166.
38. King to governor and officials, 20 March 1528. AGI 139-1-7. t. 13, fol. 68v. Años. 1526–28.
39. AGI 79-4-1, 22 Dec. 1530.
40. Queen to Ramirez, 22 Dec. 1530. Seville papers. vol. 2, 1st Series, part I, lot V.
41. Queen to Ramirez, 22 Dec. 1530. Seville papers. vol. 2, 1st Series, part I, lot V. Queen to Gil Gonzales, 4 Feb. 1533. AGI 79-4-1. t. Y-1, fol. 118. Años 1529–50.

42. AGI 79-4-1, t. Y-2, fol. 22; see also fol. 23v, 19 July 1534.
43. King to governor and officials, 9 Sept. 1526. AGI 139-1-7, t. 11, fol. 144. Años 1526–28.
44. *News Letter.* Archaeological Society of Jamaica 1965–1986, James W. Lee. editor. "There is only one town in it [Jamaica] named Santiago of la Vega." Dr. Alonso de Espinosa Centeno, Seville Papers, lot xv, 1644.
45. Morales Padrón, *Jamaica Española,* map p. 280. May Pen also claimed to be Guatibacoa.
46. King to Governor Juan de Mendegurren and officials, 9 Sept. 1526. AGI 139-1-7. t. 11, fol. 157v.
47. Queen to Gil González, 4 Feb. 1533. AGI 79-4-1, t. Y-1, fol. 118, Años 1529–50.
48. AGI 54-3-28. Audiencia de Santo Domingo. Simancas-Secular. 1536–1634.
49. AGI 54-3-28. Audiencia de Santo Domingo. Simancas-Secular. 1536–1634.

NOTES TO CHAPTER 4

1. Audiencia de Santo Domingo-Cuba-Registros of oficio y partes—Reales ordines dirigidas a las autoridades ye corporaciones of la ysla. t. Y-2, fol. 31v. AGI 79-4-1. Años 1529–50.
2. Audiencia de Santo Domingo-Cuba-Registros de oficio y partes—Reales ordines dirigidas a las autoridades y corporaciónes de la ysla. t. Y-2, f. 31v. AGI 79-4-1. Años 1529–50.
3. AGI 54-3-28. Años 1536–1634.
4. AGI 79-4-1 t. Y-2, f. 136v. Años 1529–50. Also f. 146.
5. Don Carlos to governor and officials, 23 March 1535. AGI 79-4-1. t. Y-2, fol. 34v. Años 1529–50.
6. Ibid.
7. Morales Padrón, *Jamaica Española,* 199.
8. Queen to the cardinal archbishop of Seville, Spain, 12 April 1535. AGI 79-4-1, t. Y-2, f. 35. AGI 79-4-1. t. Y-2, fol. 35v. Años 1529–50. La Reyna-nuestros oficiales qui resides en ciudad de Seville in casa de la contratación de las Indias, 22 April 1535.
9. Queen to officials in Seville of the board of trade with the Indies. 22 April 1535. AGI 79-4-1. t. Y-2, fol. 35v. Años 1529–50. 12. Queen to Amador de Samano, abbot of Jamaica. 22 April 1535. AGI 79-4-1. t. Y-2, fol. 36v. Años 1529–50.
10. Queen to de Samano, 22 April 1535. AGI 79-4-1. t. Y-2, fol 36v. Años 1529–50.
11. Queen to Governor Manuel de Rojas A.G.I. 79-44-1 Audiencia de Santo Domingo-Cuba, Tomo Y-2. Folio 79 Anos 1529–1540 8 Sept. 1536.
12. AGI 54-3-28. Años 1536–1634. 8 Sept. 1536.
13. AGI 54-3-28. Años 1536–1634. 8 Sept. 1536.
14. Morales Padrón, *Jamaica Española,* 128, 185.
15. King to Pedro Cano, 5 Sept. 1539. AGI 79-4-1. t. Y-2, fol. 148, Años 1529–50.
16. Ibid.
17. Ibid.
18. King to Pedro Cano, 5 Sept. 1539. AGI 79-4-1. t. Y-2, fol. 148. Años 1529–50. Also,

King to abbot of Jamaica, 5 Sept. 1539. AGI 79-4-1. t. Y-2, fol. 147v. Also, Edward Long, *History of Jamaica* (London, 1774, 3 Vols.), vol. 2, bk. 3, c. 7, 3–4.

19. Documents pertaining to Admiral of the Indies Don Luis Colón. AGI Sevilla-Simancas. Años 1528–57.
20. AGI 54-2-8. Años 1607–9.
21. Villalobos to king, 8 Nov. 1582. AGI 54-3-28, Santo Domingo leg 177. Años 1536–1634.
22. Morales Padrón, *Jamaica Española,* 169–70.
23. 1577. Documents pertaining to the conservation of the privileges of Admiral of the Indies Don Luis Colón. [AGI Sevilla-Simancas.] Años 1528–57.
24. Morales Padrón, *Jamaica Española,* 173.
25. Ibid.
26. **Morales Padrón, *Jamaica Española,* 173, Also, Santo Domingo. AGI 54-3-28. Años 1536–1635. See also AGI 54-2-8. 20 July 1608. AGI 54-3-28. Audiencia de Santo Domingo. Años 1536-1635. See also AGI 54-2-8. 20 July 1608.**
27. AGI 54-3-28. Audiencia de Santo Domingo. Años 1536–1635. See also AGI 54-2-8.20 July 1608.
28. Villalobos to Philip II AGI 54-3-28. Anos 1536–1634. Audiencia de Santo Simancas-Secular. 8 Nov. 1582.
29. Seville Papers Vol. III, 1st Series, part ii, lot x West Indian Reference Library, Kingston.
30. AGI 139-1-5. t. 4, fol. 157v. Años 1512–18. 5 June 1513.
31. King to F. Bermejo 13 Dec. 1527. AGI 139-1-7, t. 12, fol. 250v. Años 1526–28. AGI 139-1-7, t. 12, f. 250v. Años 1526–28. King to F. Bermejo 13 Dec. 1527.
32. Seville Papers, 39.
33. King to abbot of Jamaica. AGI 54-3-28. 1 April 22. Años 1536–1634.
34. Abbot Mateo Santiago to king. AGI Santo Domingo Leg. 177.

NOTES TO CHAPTER 5

1. Villalobos to king, 8 Nov. 1582. AGI 54-3-28. Audiencia de Santo Domingo Simancas-Secular-Cartes y expedientes del distrito de la Isla de Jamaica. Años 1536–1634.
2. Ibid.
3. Ibid. Also, Thomas Gage, *Travels in the New World,* edited by J. Eric Thompson (Norman: University of Oklahoma Press, 1958), 16.
4. Morales Padrón, *Jamaica Española,* 309.
5. Ibid. Also, Morales Padrón, *Jamaica Española,* 305.
6. Villalobos to King, 8 Nov. 1582. AGI 54-3-28. Audiencia de Santo Domingo Simancas-Secular-Cartes y expedientes del distrito of la Isla of Jamaica. Años 1536–1634.
7. Ibid.
8. Ibid.
9. Ibid.
10. Ibid.
11. Ibid.
12. Ibid.

13. Ibid.
14. Ibid.
15. Ibid.
16. Ibid.
17. Ibid.
18. Ibid.
19. Ibid.
20. Ibid.
21. Ibid.
22. Ibid.
23. Ibid.
24. Sir Alan Burns, *History of the British West Indies* (London: Allen and Unwin, 1954), 213 ff.
25. Morales Padrón, *Jamaica Española*, 280.
26. Cundall and Pietersz, *Jamaica Under the Spaniards*, 35. Also, Villalobos to king, 8 Nov. 1582.
27. Villalobos to king, 8 Nov. 1582. AGI 54-3-28. Audiencia de Santo Domingo Simancas-Secular-Cartes y expedientes del distrito de la Isla de Jamaica. Años 1536–1634.
28. Ibid.
29. Ibid.
30. Ibid.
31. Ibid.
32. Ibid.
33. Ibid.
34. Ibid.
35. Ibid.
36. Ibid.
37. Ibid.
38. Ibid. Also AGI Santo Domingo 177; Also see Morales Pardón, *Jamaica Española*, 179; Sir Anthony Shirley's attack on Jamaica.
39. AGI Santo Domingo 177; Also: Morales Padrŏn, op. cit, 179; Sir Anthony Shirley's attack on Jamaica.
40. Ibid.
41. Ibid.
42. Morales Padrón, *Jamaica Española*—Seville 1952, p. 179.
43. Audiencia de Santo Domingo. Documents and files issued by the governors of Havana and Cuba approved in counsil. AGI 54-1-16. Años 1522–1608. 13 June 1603.
44. Ibid.
45. Ibid.
46. Ibid.
47. Ibid.

48. Ibid.
49. Ibid.
50. Ibid.
51. Ibid.
52. Ibid.
53. Ibid.
54. Ibid.
55. Villalobos to the king, 8 Nov. 1582. AGI 54-3-28. Años 1536–1634.
56. Ibid.
57. Ibid.
58. King to officials in Panama, 28 June 1599. AGI 79-4-6. Años 1581–1673.
59. 88. Audiencia de Santo Domingo, 8 Nov. 1582. AGI 54-3-28. Años 1536–1634. Also king to officials in Panama, 28 June 1599. AGI 79-4-6. Años 1581–1673.
60. Edward Long, *History of Jamaica,* vol. 2, bk. 3, c. 7, 3–4.
61. Fernando Melgarejo de Córdoba, 26 Dec. 1597. AGI 54-3-28. Años 1536–1634.
62. Morales Padrón, *Jamaica Española,* page 181.
63. Audiencia de Santo Domingo, 8 July 1607. AGI 54-3-28. Años 1536–1634.
64. Bishop of Cuba, Juan de las Coliezas Altamirando, to the king. From Havana, 23 Aug. 1608. AGI 54-2-8. Audiencia de Santo Domingo. Años 1607–9 Cartes expedientes of personas secular of la Isla of Cuba vistos en el cosejo. Simancas-Secular.
65. A.G.I. 54-2-8. Audiencia de Santo Domingo. Anos 1607–1609. Bishop of Cuba Juan de las Coliezas Altamirando to King. From Havana 20 July 1608.
66. Ibid.
67. Ibid.
68. Ibid.
69. Ibid.
70. Ibid.
71. AGI 54-2-28. Audiencia de Santo Domingo—Isla de Jamaica—Ramo secular y eclesiastico—cartes y expedientes del distrito de laico Isla 1536–1634. Don Fernando Melargejo Córdoba to king, 12 July 1598.
72. Ibid.
73. Ibid.
74. Ibid.
75. Ibid.
76. Ibid.

NOTES TO CHAPTER 6

1. John van Horne, "Bernardo de Balbuena in Jamaica," *Daily Gleaner,* 5 June 1934.
2. Ibid.
3. España-Simancas-Audiencia de Santo Domingo. Petitiones memoriales y otros documentos indiferentes. De Roma 24 Aug. 1608. AGI 53-2-10. Años 1608–16.
4. Van Horne, "Bernardo de Balbuena in Jamaica," *Daily Gleaner,* 5 June 1934.

5. Ibid.
6. Ibid.
7. Ibid.
8. Ibid.
9. Audiencia de Santo Domingo. 16 May 1609. AGI 79-4-6. Años 1581–1673.
10. Ibid.
11. Ibid.
12. Van Horne, "Bernardo de Balbuena in Jamaica," *Daily Gleaner,* 5 June 1934.
13. Ibid.
14. Ibid.
15. Ibid.
16. Ibid.
17. Ibid.
18. Ibid.
19. King to his Council, 26 May 1609. Audiencia de Santo Domingo. AGI 79-4-6. Años 1581–1673.
20. Van Horne, "Bernardo de Balbuena in Jamaica," *Daily Gleaner,* 5 June 1934.
21. Ibid.
22. Ibid.
23. Ibid.
24. Ibid.
25. Ibid.
26. Ibid.
27. Ibid.
28. Ibid.
29. Morales Padrón, *Jamaica Española,* 181.
30. De Roma 24 Aug. 1608. AGI 52-2-10, Años 1608–16.
31. Don Alonso de Espinosa Centeno, 1644. AGI 54-3-29.
32. Ibid.
33. Ibid.
34. Balbuena to king, 14 July 1611. AGI 54-3-28; Audiencia de Santo Domingo Simancas-Secular, Años 1536–1634.
35. Ibid.
36. Ibid.
37. One hundred fifty Arawak settlements existed at time of discovery.
38. Morales Padrón, *Jamaica Española,* 464.
39. Balbuena to king, 14 July 1611. AGI 54-3-28; Audiencia de Santo Domingo Simancas-Secular. Años 1536–1634.
40. Ibid.
41. Ibid.
42. Ibid.

43. AGI 54-3-28; Audiencia de Santo Domingo. Años 1536–1634. 17 July 1611
44. Ibid.
45. Balbuena to king, 14 July 1611. AGI 54-3-28; Audiencia de Santo Domingo Simancas-Secular. Años 1536–1634. 44.
46. Morales Padrón, *Jamaica Española*, 198.
47. Morales Padrón, *Jamaica Española*, 199–200.
48. Ibid., p. 187.
49. Van Horne, "Bernardo de Balbuena in Jamaica," *Daily Gleaner* 5 June 1934.

NOTES TO CHAPTER 7

1. Morales Padrón, *Jamaica Española*. p. 187.
2. Ibid.
3. Audiencia de Santo Domingo, April 1622. AGI 79-4-6. Años 1581–1673.
4. Provincial Synod—Santo Domingo—1622 Audiencia de Santo Domingo—AGI 78-2-3—1622–1623.
5. AGI 79-4-6. Audiencia de Santo Domingo. Anos 1581–1673. 1 August 1626.
6. King to governor of Jamaica.
7. Morales Padrón, *Jamaica Española*, p. 188.
8. AGI 79-2-3. Audiencia de Santo Domingo Anos 1581–1673.
9. Morales Padrón, *Jamaica Española*, p. 152.
10. Ibid.
11. Don Alonso de Espinosa Centeno, 1644. AGI 54-3-29.
12. Ibid.
13. Ibid.
14. Don Alonso de Espinosa Centeno, 1644. AGI 54-3-29. Also see Morales Padrón, *Jamaica Española*, 382.
15. Cundall and Pietersz, *Jamaica Under the Spaniards*, 40.
16. Ibid.
17. Ibid. Also see AGI 54-3-29.
18. Don Alonzo de Espinosa Centeno. AGI 54-3-29. 1644.
19. Cundall and Pietersz, *Jamaica Under the Spaniards*, 40. Also see AGI 54-3-29.
20. Morales Padrón, *Jamaica Española* 144.
21. King to his officials. Audiencia de Santo Domingo. AGI 79-4-6. Años 1581–1673.
22. Ibid.
23. Ibid.
24. Ibid.
25. Ibid.
26. Ibid.
27. Ibid.
28. Ibid.

29. Audiencia de Santo Domingo-Simancas-Secular. Documents from 8 Jan. 1649 to 21 July 1651. AGI 79-4-6. Años 1634–78.
30. Ibid.
31. Ibid.
32. Ibid.
33. AGI 79-4-6. Audiencia de Santo Domingo-Simancas-Secular. Años 1634–1678. July 21, 1651.

NOTES TO CHAPTER 8

1. Thomas Gage, *Travels in the New World,* edited by J. Eric Thompson (Norman, Oklahoma: University of Oklahoma Press, 1958), xlii.
2. Ibid., xiii.
3. Ibid., xlii–xliii.
4. Ibid., xxvi.
5. Ibid., xxiv.
6. Ibid., xxix. Also, 7–8.
7. Ibid., 15.
8. Ibid., 32.
9. Ibid., 102–37.
10. Ibid.
11. Ibid., 125–31, 136 n. 16. See also, 136.
12. Ibid., xv.
13. Ibid., xxxiii.
14. Ibid., 297.
15. Ibid., xxxiv.
16. Ibid., 341, 344.
17. Ibid., xxxv–xxxvi.
18. Ibid., xxxvi.
19. Ibid., xxxviii.
20. Ibid., xl.
21. Ibid., xxxviii.
22. Ibid., xliii.
23. Edward Long, *History of Jamaica* (London, 1774), vol. 1, bk. 1, c. 11, 225.
24. Ibid.
25. Gage, *Travels in the New World,* xliv.
26. S. A. G. Taylor, *The Western Design* (Institute of Jamaica and the Jamaica Historical Society: Kingston, 1965), 19.
27. Ibid.
28. Ibid.
29. Ibid., 52.
30. Long, *History of Jamaica,* 1:1:11, 225.

31. Ibid.
32. AGI 54-3-29. Audiencia de Santo Domingo—Simancas-Secular-Documentos correspondientes a la perdida of la isla Jamaica. Años 1634–78. Letter written by a British captain from Jamaica to a friend in England. 1 June 1656.
33. Ibid.
34. Ibid.
35. Ibid.
36. Narrative of General Venables, *Robert Venables*. Edited by C. A. Firth for the Royal Historical Society. London 1900.
37. Ibid.
38. Ibid.
39. Narrative of Captain Julian of Castilla concerning events from 20 May 1655 to 3 July 1656. AGI 54-3-29. Audiencia de Santo Domingo—Simancas—Secular. Años 1634–78.
40. Morales Padrón, *Jamaica Española*, 463–65.
41. *"Narrative of General Venables."*
42. Morales Padrón, *Jamaica Española*, 326.
43. "Narrative of Captain Castilla." AGI 54-3-29.
44. Ibid.
45. Ibid.
46. Ibid.
47. Ibid.
48. Ibid.
49. Ibid.
50. Ibid.
51. Ibid.
52. Ibid.
53. Ibid.
54. Ibid.
55. Ibid.
56. Ibid.
57. Ibid.
58. Ibid.
59. Ibid.
60. Ibid.
61. Ibid.
62. Ibid.
63. *Calendar of State Papers*, (Colonial), 110, no. 260.
64. Ibid.
65. *Calendar of State Papers*, (Colonial), 261. Names of officers and soldiers engaged in the American expedition who during the year 1656 applied for arrears of pay on

whose account such applications were made by their widows or representatives. Mary, widow of Thos. Gage, chaplain, 18 July 1656. Also see 26 March 1656. Interregnum Entry Bk. Vol. 110.

NOTES TO CHAPTER 9

1. AGI 54-3-29. Audiencia de Santo Domingo. Simancas-Secular-Documentos correspondientes a la Isla Jamaica. Años 1634–78. Signed by Don Cristóbal Ysasi y Proenza, 9 July 1659.
2. Ibid.
3. Ibid.
4. Ibid.
5. Cundall and Pietersz, *Jamaica Under the Spaniards*, 86.
6. AGI 54-3-29. Audiencia de Santo Domingo. Ysasi y Proenza, 9 July 1659.
7. Ibid.
8. Ibid.
9. Ibid.
10. AGI 54-3-29. Audiencia de Santo Domingo. Ysasi y Proenza, 9 July 1659. Written from Vera Cruz by Domingo Rodriguez of Vera, 24 July 1657. See also Letter by Captain Juan de los Reyes and Don Domingo de Silva to Ysasi. 8 Aug. 1657.
11. Ibid.
12. Ibid.
13. Ibid.
14. Ibid.
15. Taylor, *Western Design*, 163.
16. AGI 54-3-29.
17. Ibid.
18. Ibid.
19. Ibid.
20. Ibid.
21. Ibid.
22. Ibid.
23. Ibid.
24. Ibid.
25. Ibid.
26. Ibid.
27. AGI 54-3-29. The Spaniards claimed that there were ten ships.
28. AGI 54-3-29.
29. 32 32 Taylor, *Western Design*, 175.
30. *JHR*, 3: no. 1, 12.
31. AGI 54-3-29.
32. Ibid.

33. Ibid.
34. Cundall, *Chronological Outlines of Jamaica History,* 12.
35. *Journals of Jamaica Assembly,* 1:1.
36. *JHR,* 3: no. 1, 31.
37. *JHR,* 3: no. 1, 23.
38. *Journals of the Assembly,* 1:1.
39. *JHR,* 3: no. 1, 31.
40. *JHR,* 3: no. 1, 21.
41. *JHR,* 3: no. 1, 26.
42. *JHR,* 3: no. 1, 27–28.
43. *Journals of the Assembly,* 1: Appendix Statistics, 20.
44. Ibid.
45. Ibid.
46. 50 Frank Cundall, *The Governors of Jamaica in the Seventeenth Century* (West India Committee, London, 1936, p. 14. Also. Cundall. *Chronological Outlines of Jamaica History.* p. 10.
47. James Burney, *History of the Buccaneers of America* (London, 1902), 20.
48. Ibid. 57.
49. Ibid. 77–81.
50. Ibid.
51. Ibid.
52. Ibid.
53. *Journals of the Assembly,* Vol. 1: 1677–78 and 1680–82.
54. *Journals of the Assembly,* Vol. 1: 1677–78 and 1680–82. Appendix: Statistical Papers, 20.
55. *Journals of the Assembly,* Vol. 1: 1677–78 and 1680–82. Appendix: Statistical Papers, 42.
56. Ibid.

NOTES TO CHAPTER 10

1. Cundall, *Governors of Jamaica in the Seventeenth Century,* 15.
2. *Catholicon* 4:198–291. The Old Brotherhood of the English Secular Clergy. (1683) (131)
3. Ibid.
4. Ibid.
5. Ibid.
6. Ibid.
7. Calendar of State Papers (Col.) No. 571, 23 Oct. 1663.
8. Churchill was granted faculties by Bishop Leyburn, Vicar Apostolic of the London District. See Faculties of 1687, Vol. XXXV. No. 65. Archdiocese of Westminster Archives.
9. Public Record Office, London. S/N 233, C.O. 138/5.

10. Cundall, *Governors of Jamaica in the Seventeenth Century,* p. 110. Cundall, also: Chronological Outline of Jamaica History p. 14.
11. Document B/N, Institute of Jamaica.
12. Liber 20, of Deeds, Folio 2, 21 March 1687/8. CAST.
13. *Catholicon,* 4:198–201.
14. Calendar of State Papers (Col.) No. 299, July 1689.
15. James Castillo to Marqués de los Velez, 25 Oct. 1688, Seville Papers.
16. K. G. Davies, *The Royal African Company.* London: Longmans, Green & Co. 1957 p. 59.
17. Ibid. p. 13–14.
18. Ibid. p. 97.
19. Ibid.
20. Calendar of State Papers (Col.) No. 548, 1683.
21. Calendar of State Papers (Col.) No. 548, 1683.
22. *Journals of the Assembly,* 1:130–31.
23. Ibid.
24. Public Record Office, England, S/N 234 and S/M 1652, C.O. 1/64.
25. Ibid.
26. Public Record Office, London,—S/N 234, C.O. 1/64, Sheet No. 9.
27. Castillo to de los Velez, 25 Oct. 1688, Seville Papers.
28. Public Record Office, Manifesto—S/N 234, C.O. 1/64, Sheets Nos. 5 and 6.
29. Ibid., Sheet No. 6. 32.
30. Ibid., Sheet No. 3.
31. Publc Record Office, London—S/N 235, C.O. 140/4, Sheet No 4.
32. Public Record Office, Manifesto—S/N 235, C.O. 1/64, Sheet No. 3.
33. Ibid., Sheet No. 2.
34. Calendar of State Papers (Col.) 1699 (1753), 546.
35. Public Record Office, Manifesto—S/N 234, C.O. 1/64, Sheet No. 7.
36. Ibid.
37. Ibid., Sheet No. 7, 39
38. Castillo to de los Velez, 25 Oct. 1688, Seville Papers.
39. Calendar of State Papers. 1699 (1753).
40. Public Record Office, Manifesto—S/N 234, C.O. 1/64, Sheet No. 10.
41. Ibid.
42. Ibid.
43. *Journals of the Assembly,* 1:22.
44. *Journals of the Assembly,* Vol. i p. 126.
45. Castillo to de los Velez, 25 Oct. 1688, Seville Papers.
46. Calendar of State Papers, No. 299, July 1689.
47. *Journals of the Assembly,* 1:130–32.

48. 51
49. Estella Frances Ward, *Christopher Monck, Duke of Albermarle,* book 8, 327–28. London 1915.
50. *Journals of the Assembly,* 1:135, 3 June 1689.
51. *Catholicon* 4:198–201.
52. Charles Leslie, *New History of Jamaica* (London, 1740), Letter No. 8, 252.
53. Taylor manuscript—Institute of Jamaica
54. The Reverend Mr. Heath's Account of Earthquake, Port Royal 1692. Institute of Jamaica.
55. Heath's Account of Earthquake.
56. Land patented by Charles Whitfield who sold it to Fotherly, who sold it to Kelly, who sold it to Castillo, Cundall, *Government of 17th Cent.* p. 153.
57. *Journals of the Assembly,* 2:47. See also Cundall, *Governors of Jamaica in Seventeenth Century,* 153.
58. *Journals of the Assembly,* 2:47.
59. *Journals of the Assembly,* 2:47.
60. *Journals of the Assembly,* 2:47, 28 July 1711.
61. *Journals of the Assembly,* 2:38 2 June 1711.
62. *Journals of the Assembly,* 1:380 5 Oct. 1705.
63. Ibid.
64. Peter Guilday, *Life and Times of John Carroll, 1735–1815* (Westminster, Md.: Newman Press, 1954), 250–57.
65. Ibid.
66. Ibid.

NOTES TO CHAPTER 11

1. *Journals of the Assembly,* 2:32, 36.
2. W. Adolphe Roberts, ed., *Capitals of Jamaica* (Kingston: Pioneer Press, 1955); Frank Casserly *Kingston in the Nineteenth Century,* 64.
3. Cundall, *The Governors of Jamaica in the Seventeenth Century,* 206.
4. *Journals of the Assembly,* 9:83.
5. *Journals of the Assembly,* 9:235.
6. Bryan Edwards, *History Civil and Commercial of the British Colonies in the West Indies* (London: John Stockdale, 1801).
7. A person in charge of estate for owner
8. Edwards, *History of British Colonies in the West Indies.*
9. Ibid.
10. Ibid.
11. Ibid.
12. Ibid.
13. Cundall, *Governors of Jamaica in the Seventeenth Century,* 26.
14. *Journals of the Assembly.*

15. Ibid.
16. Ibid.
17. Tax Rolls for Years 1791–1805, CAST.
18. *The Caribbean Catholic Directory* (Kingston: Metro Press Ltd., 1967), 40.
19. SPC 3:380–81.
20. Ibid.
21. Ibid.
22. Burial and baptismal records of Holy Trinity Cathedral, Kingston, 1792–99. AKA.
23. Baptismal Register, 1799. AKA.
24. Baptismal Register 1800– frontispiece.
25. Burial Register, vol. 1 (1795). AKA.
26. Ibid.
27. Burial Register, Archdiocese, vol. 1 (1798). Also, SPC Am. Ant. 3:f. 291.
28. SPC Am. Ant. 3:f. 271. Someone claims Le Cun arrived on Jamaica 25 Aug. 1798.
29. Ibid.
30. SPC Am. Ant. 3:f. 361.
31. Ibid.
32. AKA.
33. AKA.
34. SPC Am. Ant. 3:f. 271.
35. Ibid.
36. SPC Am. Ant. 3:f. 254. Also, SPC Am. Ant. 3:f. 298.
37. SPC Am. Ant. 3:f. 291.
38. SPC Am. Ant. 3:f. 254.
39. SPC Am. Ant. 3:f. 254–56.
40. Ibid.
41. SPC Am. Ant. 3:f. 271–72. Also, SPC Am. Ant. 3:f. 256.
42. SPC Am. Ant. 3:f. 257.
43. SPC Am. Ant. 3:f. 295.
44. SPC Am. Ant. 3:f. 295.
45. SPC Am. Ant. 3:362.
46. SPC Am. Ant. 3:f. 290.
47. SPC Am. Ant. 3:f. 295.
48. SPC Am. Ant. 3:f. 362. Also, SPC Am. Ant. 3:f. 287.
49. SPC Am. Ant. 3:f. 295.
50. Baptismal Records, 1800. AKA.
51. L. Concannen to W. Le Cun, 28 Feb. 1800.
52. AKA.
53. AKA.
54. SPC Am. Ant. 3:f. 369.

55. Ibid.
56. Cundall, *Governors of Jamaica in the Seventeenth Century,* 26.
57. AKA.
58. Baptismal Records, 1804. AKA.
59. Baltimore Cathedral Archives, Case 5-e 7; printed in *Records,* 20:62–63.
60. Burial Records, AKA, 2 Aug. 1795–19 Jan. 1873, p. 57.
61. AKA.
62. Le Cun to Governor Sir Eyrie Coote, 19 June 1807. AKA.
63. Walshe to Le Cun, 27 June 1807. AKA.
64. AKA.
65. AKA.

NOTES TO CHAPTER 12

1. SPC Am. Ant. 5:f. 840.
2. Ibid.
3. Roberts, ed., *Capitals of Jamaica,* 61.
4. AKA.
5. Roberts, ed., *Capitals of Jamaica,* 63.
6. Ibid., 64.
7. Ibid.
8. Ibid., 58.
9. Deed of Holy Trinity property. AKA.
10. 11 SPC 6:f. 365. D. O'Reilly. (11)
11. *Morning Journal,* 26 Aug. 1843.
12. (Note: Morning Journal claims Church completely destroyed.) *Morning Journal.* 26 Aug. 1843.
13. Baptismal Records 1808–24. AKA.
14. Marriage Records 1816, p. 17. AKA.
15. *Massachusetts Historical Society Proceedings.* (1881–82), Vol. XIX.
16. *Vital Records of Carlisle, Massachusetts, U.S.A.* to 1849.
17. Ibid.
18. Ibid.
19. Ibid.
20. Ibid.
21. Baptismal Records 1816. AKA.
22. Marriage Records 1818. AKA.
23. Baptismal Records 1818. AKA. See also, *Vital Records of Carlisle, Massachusetts, U.S.A.* to 1849. Also, *Massachusetts Historical Society Proceedings.* (1881–82), Vol. XIX.
24. Burial records 1814. AKA.
25. R. B. Le Page and David De Camp, *Jamaican Creole* "Creole Language Studies No. 1" (London: Macmillan, 1960), 74.
26. Ibid.

27. Ibid., 82.
28. Clinton V. Black, *History of Jamaica,* 103. See also, Le Page and De Camp, *Jamaican Creole,* 82.
29. Joseph Shore, *In Old St. James,* (Kingston: John Stewart, 1911), 98.
30. Ibid.
31. Joseph J. Williams, S.J. *Hebrewisms of West Africa* (New York: Dial Press, 1931), 71–72.
32. Ibid., 7.
33. Joseph J. Williams, S.J. *Voodoos and Obeah* (New York: Dial Press, 1932), 112.
34. Ibid., 110–12.
35. Ibid.
36. Journals of the Assembly (Jamaica) vol. 1. Appendix: Statistical Papers, 21.
37. Gardner, *History of Jamaica,* 331.
38. Cundall, *Chronological Outlines,* 20.
39. Gardner, *History of Jamaica,* 201.
40. Ibid., 343.
41. Ibid.
42. Ibid.
43. Ibid., 344.
44. Ibid.
45. Ibid.
46. Ibid., 358.
47. Cundall, *Chronological Outlines,* 28.
48. Gardner, *History of Jamaica,* 359–60.
49. Ibid., 360.
50. Gardner, *History of Jamaica,* 345.
51. Ibid.
52. Ibid., 344–47.
53. Williams, *Voodoos and Obeah,* 110–12.
54. Burns, *History of the British West Indies,* 621.
55. Ibid.
56. Baptismal Records of Slaves. AKA.
57. Baptismal Records of Slaves. AKA.
58. Cundall, *Chronological Outlines,* 30. Also, Baptismal Records, 1821. AKA. 62.
59. Baptismal Records, 1820. AKA.
60. Louis Bodoano, Ms History of Church in Jamaica, AKA.
61. Baptismal Records, 1824. AKA.
62. SPC Am. Ant. 9:f. 163.

NOTES TO CHAPTER 13

1. Cardinal Odescalchi to Benito Fernandez, 28 Aug. 1828. AKA.
2. Fernandez to MacDonnell Sept. 7, 1829, AKA

3. MacDonnell to Fernandez, 4 May 1830. AKA.
4. Memorial of MacDonnell's visitation, June, 1831. AKA.
5. AKA.
6. MacDonnell to Fernandez, 15 June 1832. AKA.
7. SPC Am. Ant. 6:120–21.
8. Cundall, *Historic Jamaica*, (London, 1915), p. 179
9. MacDonnell to Fernandez, 5 May 1833. AKA.
10. Murphy to Fernandez, 24 May 1833. AKA.
11. Louis Bodoano, History of Church in Jamaica (MS.) AKA.
12. AKA.
13. *JD*, 21 March 1833.
14. JD, 21 March 1833. Also, SPC Am. Ant. 5:918. 13
15. SPC Am. Ant. 5:919.
16. Ibid., 997.
17. Ibid., 940–41.
18. Ibid., 995.
19. SPC Am. Ant. 6:50–51.
20. Holy See to Fernandez, 21 May 1837. AKA. The accepted date when Benito Fernandez was appointed vicar apostolic is 10 Jan. 1837; however, he is not named in this document, but he is named in the document dated 21 May 1837.
21. Records of the English Province of the Society of Jesus, General Statistics and Collectanea, Part the First, 173 ASJR. 21 Cotham to Jenkins, 8 Sept. 1837. ASJE.
22. Cotham to Roothaan, 6 Dec. 1837. ASJR. Jam. 1,I,18.
23. Cotham to Jenkins, 26 Dec. 1837. ASJE.
24. Dupeyron to Roothaan, 6 Dec. 1837. ASJR. Jam. 1,I,15. See also, *Jamaica Almanack, 1837–1838*.
25. SPC Am. Ant. 6:f. 190.
26. SPC Am. Ant. 6:f. 204 and 190.
27. *The Caribbean Catholic Directory* (Kingston: Wayne HoSang Press, 1980), 81 and 90.
28. Cundall, *Chronological Outline*, 29.
29. Stipendiary Magistrates Jamaica—HMSO London, 1840.
30. (Note: used in Jamaica Of.-*Jamaica Despatch and Shannon's Daily Messenger* Fri. June 6, 1831.
31. Black, *History of Jamaica, 165–66;* Burns, *History of the British West Indies*, 631 n.
32. William J. Gardner, *History of Jamaica* (1873) p. 312
33. Cundall, *Chronological Outline*," 32. See also, William J. Gardner, *History of Jamaica*, 386–396.
34. Black, *History of Jamaica*, 171–72.
35. Burns, *History of the British West Indies*, 659.
36. Votes of the Assembly—Jamaica. 1833, p. 40.
37. Cotham to Jenkins, 13 May 1838. ASJE.

38. Cotham to Roothaan, 29 July 1838. ASJR. Jam. 1,II,4.
39. Cotham to Jenkins, 13 May 1838. ASJE.
40. Cotham to Roothaan, 18 March 1839. ASJR. Jam. 1,II,8.
41. Cotham to Jenkins, 3 Feb. 1839. ASJE.
42. Dupeyron to Roothaan, 25 May 1839. ASJR. Jam. 1,II,9.
43. Cotham to Jenkins, 29 July 1838. ASJE.
44. Cotham to Roothaan, 6 Dec. 1839. ASJR. Jam. 1,I,18.
45. Cotham to Roothaan, 6 Dec. 1839. ASJR. Jan. 1,I,18. See also, Cotham to Jenkins, 1 Jan. 1839. ASJE.
46. Cotham to Roothaan, 13 Aug. 1840. ASJR. Jan. 1,II,21.

NOTES TO CHAPTER 14

1. Cotham to Roothaan, 30 Jan. 1840, ASJR, Jam. 1-11,17.
2. Cotham to Jenkins, 1 Oct. 1839, ASJE.
3. Missio Jamaicensis, Jamaica 1-11,17, Cotham to Roothaan, 6 Dec. 1839. ASJR.
4. Baptismal and Marriage Records, 1839. AKA.
5. Cotham to Jenkins, 8 Nov. 1839, ASJE.
6. Baptismal and Marriage Records, 1839. AKA.
7. Ibid.
8. Ibid.
9. Listed as John Myers in Jamaica Almanacs 1833–40 but called Solomon Myers by Governor Sligo—22 Feb. 1838—C.O. 137/197
10. *JASDM,* 27 May 1834.
11. Ibid.
12. *JASDM,* 9 June 1834.
13. Ibid.
14.
15. Ibid. see also, *JDNC,* 29 Dec. 1834.
16. *JDNC,* 2 Jan. 1835.
17. Votes of the Assembly (Jamaica), 1836; see also *JDNC,* 2 Jan. 1835.
18. *St. Jago de la Vega Gazette,* 10 Jan. 1835. The Bremen ship *Olberes* from Bremen arrived at Rio Bueno on 10 inst with 500 immigrants—then sailed for Kingston.
19. Dr. William Lemonius's Memorandum of Army Services, CAST, Jamaica.
20. *Report for the Seaford Township,* Jan. 1836–30 Sept. 1841.
21. Ibid.; see also C.O. 137/209—Sligo to Glenelg, 12 Feb. 1836.
22. *JDNC,* 2 Jan. 1835, and 29 Dec. 1834.
23. *St. Jago de la Vega Gazette,* 12–15 Dec. 1835.
24. Cotham to Roothaan, 6 Dec. 1839. ASJE, Jam. 1-11,14. In 1793 Capt. Sadler fashioned Montpelier estate out of five land grants, Seaford Town being part of the estate.)
25. *Report for the Seaford Township,* 1 Jan. 1836.

26. 2
27. *Report for the Seaford Township,* 1 Jan. 1836.
28. *Jamaica Herald,* 6 May 1835.
29. Baptismal and Marriage Records, 1839. AKA.
30. Ibid.
31. Ibid.
32. ASJE, *passim.* See also, Fernandez to McDonnell, 19 April 1841. AKA. 31
33. *Acts of the Jamaica Assembly,* 7 Dec. 1842.
34. *Acts of the Jamaica Assembly,* 16 Dec. 1842.
35. *Acts of the Jamaica Assembly,* Votes of the Assembly—Jamaica. March 1847, 204.
36. 4 Aug. 1844. ASJE.
37. Ibid.
38. Ibid.
39. Ibid.
40. Ibid.
41. 7 Aug. 1844. ASJE.
42. Ibid.
43. Ibid.
44. Cotham to Buchanan, 10 July 1844. ASJE.
45. 18 Nov. 1844. ASJE.
46. 19 Nov. 1844. ASJE.
47. 27 Sept. 1844. ASJE.
48. Ibid.
49. SPC Am. Ant. 7:f. 21.
50. Cotham to Jenkins, 28 Dec. 1840. ASJE.
51. Dupeyron to Roothaan, 11 Feb. 1841. ASJR, Jam. 1-111,1.
52. *MJ,* 28 Jan. 1841.
53. Ibid.
54. Ibid.
55. Ibid.
56. Ibid.
57. Ibid.
58. Dupeyron to Roothaan, 11 Feb. 1841. ASJR, Jam. 1-111,1.
59. AKA.
60. ASJR, Jam. 1-111,2.
61. Ibid.
62. Ibid.
63. Ibid.
64. *MJ* (Kingston), 30 Jan. 1841.
65. Ibid.

66. Cotham to Jenkins, 8 May 1845, ASJE.
67. Ibid. Murphy left Jamaica 9 May 1845.
68. SPC Am. Ant. 7:f. 883.
69. SPC Am. Ant. 7:f. 882. See also *MJ*, 15 March 1841.
70. Cotham to Roothaan, 6 Oct. 1845. ASJR, Jam. 1-111,28.
71. APC Am. Ant. 7:f. 701.
72. *MJ* 27 Aug. 1843.
73. *Acts of the Jamaica Assembly,* Votes of the Assembly—Jamaica, 1843; see also Cotham to Jenkins, 7 April 1844. ASJE. 75 SPC Am. Ant. 7:f. 885. 75

NOTES TO CHAPTER 15

1. *CSJD*, 15 Aug. 1850. There were 7 advertisements before this date. Hence the date discrepencies in *Falmouth Post* and the *Colonial Standard and Jamaica Despatch*
2 Harold Brownlow, *A Brief History of St. George's College*—1925, Kingston—p. 3.
3. William H. Feeney, S. J., private notes *AKA*. St. George's College
4. Falmouth Post and Jamaica General Advertizer, 6 Aug. 1850.
5. *CSJD*, 14 Aug. 1850.
6. *CSJD*, 28 Aug. 1850.
7. Ibid.
8. Ibid.
9. Ibid.
10. Ibid.
11. Ibid.
12. Ibid.
13. Ibid.
14. *CSJD*, 4 Sept. 1850.
15. Ibid.
16. Ibid.
17. Dupreyron to Johnson, 18 May 1854. ASJE.
18. William H. Feeney, S. J. "First Staff and Early Years of St. George's College," private notes. AKA
19. Daniel Restrepo, S.J. *Vida del Padre Valenzuela,* (Bogotá: La Editorial Pax, 1946) p. 12.
20. Feeney, "First Staff and Early Years of St. George's College," 2–3.
21. William H. Feeney, S.J., "St. George's College," private notes. AKA.
22. Frank L. Casserly, *The Capitals of Jamaica: Kingston in the Eighteenth Century,* 7.
23. Cotham to Roothaan, 29 Jan. 1850. ASJE.
24. Ibid.
25. Ibid.
26. Ibid.
27. Ibid.
28. Dupeyron to John Eldridge, 13 May 1852. ASJE.

29. Ibid.
30. *History of St. George's College,* Centennial Number, 1850–1950 (Kingston, 1950), 1.
31. Ibid.
32. Dupeyron to Jenkins, 26 Sept. 1852. ASJE.
33. *Franciscan Centenary: 1857–1957* (Kingston: Gleaner Company, 1957), 7.
34. Dupeyron to Beckx, 9 Jan. 1856. ASJR, Jam. 1-V,1.
35. *Annals of the Propagation of the Faith,* (1856), pages.
36. *Franciscan Centenary: 1857–1957* (Kingston: Gleaner Company, 1957), 7, 12.
37. Ibid.
38. Ibid.
39. Ibid.
40. Ibid.
41. Ibid., 18.
42. Ibid., 7.
43. Spanish Town Liber, Old Series 944, folio 38. CAST.
44. *Franciscan Centenary,* 13.
45. Ibid.
46. Ibid.
47. *Franciscan Centenary,* 13; AKA.
48. Ibid.
49. SPC Am. Ant. 9:164.
50. *Catalogue of the English Province of the Society of Jesus.*
51. Ibid.
52. Dupeyron to Johnson, 10 Oct. 1855. ASJE.
53. Ibid.
54. *MJ,* 1 Oct. 1855.
55. Ibid.
56. Ibid.
57. Ibid.
58. Ibid.
59. Ibid.
60. Dupeyron to Roothaan, 31 May 1847. ASJR, Jam. 1-IV,4.
61. Dupont to Roothaan, 17 July 1850. ASJR, Jam. 1-IV,9.
62. Cotham to Roothaan, 16 Aug. 1849. ASJR, Jam. 1-IV,6. See also, Dupeyron to Roothaan, 6 Feb. 1853. ASJR, Jam. 1-IV,20. Also, Dupeyron to Beckx, 9 Jan. 1856. ASJR, Jam. 1-IV,1.
63. Dupeyron to Beckx, 9 Jan. 1856. ASJR, Jam. 1-IV,1. Also, Dupeyron to Beckx, 26 Jan. 1857. ASJR, Jam. 1-V,4.
64. Dupeyron to Beckx, 10 Dec. 1858. ASJR, Jam. 1-V,9.

NOTES TO CHAPTER 16

1. Alessandro Cardinal Barnabo, ASJR. Jam. 1-IV,13.

2. Dupeyron to Weld, 23 Nov. 1860, and 23 Dec. 1860. ASJE.
3. Dupeyron to Weld, 23 Nov. 1860. ASJE.
4. Dupeyron to Weld, 7 Sept. 1861. ASJE.
5. Joseph S. Woollett, AKA.
6. *Letters and Notices of the English Province*, (April 1898) 34: 416–24.
7. Ibid.
8. Ibid.
9. Ibid.
10. Ibid.
11. Ibid.
12. Ibid.; also Copy of Marriage—TB 595553, County of Warwick No. 108, Register Book of Marriages No. 1, Catholic Chapel, Leamington.
13. *Letters and Notices of the English Province*, (April 1898) 34:416–24.
14. Ibid.
15. Ibid.
16. *Liturgical Arts* (Feb. 1951) 19, No. 2.
17. *Letters and Notices of the English Province*, (April 1898) 34:416–24.
18. Ibid.
19. Ibid.
20. *Catalogue of the English Province of the Society of Jesus*, 1851.
21. Thomas F. Meehan, "Raphael Semmes," *CE* 13:712.
22. AKA.
23. Meehan, "Raphael Semmes," *CE* 13:712.
24. *CO* (Kingston) Oct. 1949.
25. House Diary, Winchester Park, Jamaica, 1861.
26. William J. Gardner, *A History of Jamaica* (London: T. Fisher Unwin, 1909), 471–72.
27. The Morant Bay Rebellion, Institute of Jamaica.
28. Clinton V. Black, *History of Jamaica*, (London and Glasgow: Collins, 1958), 193.
29. Black, *History of Jamaica*, 193.
30. Gardner, *History of Jamaica*, 471.
31. Ibid., 472.
32. Sydney Olivier, *Myth of Governor Eyre* (London: Hogarth Press, 1933), 21.
33. Ibid.
34. Black, *History of Jamaica*, 194.
35. Ibid., 187.
36. Ibid.
37. Ibid., 191.
38. Morant Bay Rebellion (Institute of Jamaica Reference Library).
39. *Report of the Jamaica Royal Commission Respecting Disturbances in the Island* (London: HMSO, 1866).
40. AKA.

41. *Report of the Jamaica Royal Commission,*
42. Ibid.
43. Island Record Office, CAST, lib. 414, folio 1414.
44. Jeannette Marks, *The Family of the Barretts* (New York: Macmillian, 1938), 537.
45. Baptism Records, 1862. AKA.
46. House Diary, Winchester Park, Jamaica, 1866.
47. "Gillet to Whitty," *Letters and Notices of the English Province,* 9:239–49.
48. Woollett to Weld, 16 Aug. 1866. AKA.
49. Ibid.
50. 54
51. Woollett to Weld, 16 Aug. 1866. AKA. See also, Biography of Rodolphus Walter Buchanan (Institute of Jamaica Reference Library).
52. Woollett to Weld, 16 Aug. 1866. AKA.
53. Ibid.
54. Ibid. AKA.
55. Woollett to Gallwey, 2 April 1875. ASJE.

NOTES TO CHAPTER 17

1. Cotham to Roothaan, 20 Jan. 1850. ASJE.
2. Ibid.
3. Joseph Pieterez, Private Notes.
4. George I. Lescene, Reminiscences of Old Above Rocks.
5. Ibid.
6. Ibid.
7. *CSJD,* 31 May 1883.
8. *CSJD,* 11 Sept. 1883.
9. *CSJD,* 2 June 1883.
10. Ibid.
11. Ibid. The date of birth is incorrect. Correct date is 7 Aug. 1809.
12. Ibid.
13. *Letters and Notices,* (1892) 28:254–81.
14. Ibid.
15. Ibid.
16. Ibid.
17. Ibid.
18. Ibid.
19. Ibid.
20. Ibid.
21. Ibid.
22. Ibid.
23. Ibid.

24. Ibid.
25. Ibid.
26. Joseph Pieterez, private notes.
27. Ibid.
28. Ibid.
29. Ibid.
30. Ibid.
31. Ibid.
32. Frederick Hathaway, S.J., *Recollections of Some Remarkable Conversions* (Kingston: Mortimer C. De Souza,).
33. *CO,* May 1930, 10–11.
34. Ibid.
35. Ibid.
36. Ibid.
37. *Letters and Notices of the English Province,* (1892) 28:254–81.
38. Ibid.
39. Ibid.
40. *Gall's Weekly News Letter,* (Kingston, Jamaica), 14 Nov. 1891.
41. Ibid.
42. Ibid.

NOTES TO CHAPTER 18

1. *Notices and Letters,* 7:153–54.
2. Ibid.
3. Burger to Beckx, 8 June 1872. ASJR, Jam. I-VI,50.
4. *Notices and Letters,* 7:153–54.
5. Historical Account of the Beginning of Alpha. ASMKJ.
6. Ibid.
7. Ibid.
8. Porter would not allow Jessie Ripoll to remain over night at Alpha without an adult companion; Mrs. Greenwood, her aunt, came to live with her. Historical Account of the Beginning of Alpha. ASMKJ.
9. Ibid.
10. 1 March 1887, Porter wrote to friends in England telling of new building at Alpha.
11. Historical Account of the Beginning of Alpha. ASMKJ.
12. Ibid.
13. Pontificia Universidad Catolica Javeriana, *Cartras Edificantes de la Provincia de Colombia* (Bogatá: PUCJ, 1927), 11:224.
14. Ibid.
15. Canon Law
16. 14 Oct. 1874. AKA.

17. Ibid.
18. Ibid.
19. Ibid.
20. Ibid.
21. Ibid.
22. William H. Feeney, S.J. *El Cura Santa Cruz in Jamaica* (Kingston: AAMM).
23. AKA: a. Loydi to Porter, 14 Jan. 1879. b. Di Pietro to Porter, 11 Feb. 1879, c. Di Pietro to Porter, 15 March 1879. d. Di Pietro to Loydi, 14 April 1879. e. Di Pietro to Loydi, 14 Jan. 1880.
24. Ibid.
25. Ibid.
26. Ibid.
27. Charles Ellis, private notes.
28. Ibid.
29. Ibid.
30. *Notices and Letters*, 7:153–54.
31. Woollett to Gordon, 12 June 1870. AKA.
32. *Notices and Letters*, 28 (1892): 403–4.
33. Charles Ellis, private notes.
34. Porter to Walker, 21 Jan. 1886. AKA.
35. Ibid.
36. PUCJ, *Cartas Edificantes*, 11:224.
37. Ibid.
38. Ibid.
39. *Notices and Letters*, 7:153–54.
40. Ibid.
41. Ibid.
42. Ibid.
43. Ibid.
44. Ibid.
45. *Notices and letters*, (1883) 16.
46. *Notices and Letters*, (1887–88) 19:66–67.
47. Ibid.
48. *Notices and Letters*, (1887–88) 19:624.
49. Ibid.

NOTES TO CHAPTER 19

1. *Readings in Belizean History*, Vol. I. Published by BISRA, Belize City, July 1978, pp. 7–21. Edited by John Maher, S.J.
2. *CHR* (October 1918) 4,3:304.
3. AKA.

4. *CHR* (October 1918) 4,3:304.
5. SPC Am. Ant. 6:409.
6. *CHR* (October 1918) 4,3:304–05.
7. Dupeyron to John Etheridge, 10 Feb. 1852. ASJE.
8. Ibid., 20 Feb. 1852.
9. Ibid., 1 May 1852.
10. Ibid., 1 May 1852.
11. Ibid., 26 Aug. 1852.
12. Ibid., 1 May 1852.
13. Ibid., 20 Feb. 1852.
14. Ibid., 28 Aug. 1852.
15. Ibid., 10 April 1853.
16. Ibid.
17. Ibid.
18. Ibid.
19. Ibid.
20. Dupeyron to Etheridge, 25 April 1853. ASJE.
21. Ibid.
22. Ibid.
23. Ibid.
24. Ibid., 18 May 1853.
25. AKA.
26. *CHR* (October 1918), 4,3:307.
27. Dupeyron to Johnson, 25 Sept. 1857. ASJE.
28. Ibid.
29. Ibid.
30. *CHR* 4,3 (October 1918):307.
31. Duperon to Seed, 11 March 1861. APASJ.
32. Ibid., 7 Sept. 1861.
33. Ibid., 9 Oct. 1862.
34. Quinn to Whitty, 39 May 1870. APASJ.
35. Ibid.
36. *The Angelus,* Sept. 1898 (Belize, British Honduras).
37. Woollett to Gallwey, 19 March 1874. APASJ.
38. Ibid.
39. Di Pietro to Porter, 12 Sept. 1880. AAK.
40. Woollett to Galwey, 19 March 1874. APASJ.
41. Gillet to Porter, 8 Nov. 1878. AKA.
42. Ibid.
43. Ibid.

44. Woollett to Gallway, 23 May 1874. APASJ.
45. Woollett to Pittar, 27 Aug. 1874. AAPSJ.
46. Ibid.
47. Duperyron to Cardinal, Prefect of Propaganda.
48. Di Pietro to Porter, 15 March 1879. AKA.
49. Di Pietro to Porter, 14 Jan. 1880. AKA.
50. Di Pietro to Porter, 2 Feb. 1882. AKA.
51. *CHR*, 4,3:305.
52. *CHR*, 4,3:306.

NOTES TO CHAPTER 20

1. *Letters and Notices*, 42:19–21.
2. Ibid.
3. *DG*, 14 Sept. 1889.
4. Ibid.
5. Ibid.
6. *Letters and Notices*, 42:19–21.
7. ASJKJ.
8. Marie Oliver joined them later.
9. ASJKJ; also, ASMKJ.
10. ASMKJ.
11. Gordon to Woollett, 1890. AKA.
12. Barni to Gordon, 14 May 1902. AKA.
13. Ibid.
14. Ibid.
15. *Letters and Notices*, (April 1898) 34:416–24. See also, *Letters and Notices*, (1892) 28:413–7.
16. *Letters and Notices*, (1892), 28:413–17.

NOTES TO CHAPTER 21

1. *DG*, 8 April 1894.
2. Gordon to Ledóchowski 5 June 1895. AKA.
3. Ibid., 18 May 1896, 26 July 1896. AKA.
4. *Woodstock Letters*, Vol 28, (1899) p. 339.
5. S.J. Catalog, Maryland-New York, 1877.
6. Chandlery to Gordon, 16 Aug. 1891. AKA.
7. AGSDB Turin, Italy 389: Montego Bay, Jamaica.
8. 2 July 1901. AKA.
9. Riccardi to Gordon, 26 Dec. 1901. AKA.
10. Gordon to Riccardi, 5 Jan. 1902. AKA.
11. Ibid., 26 Dec. 1901 AKA

12. Barni to Gordon, 14 May 1902. AKA.
13. Gordon to Barni, 3 Dec. 1902. AKA.
14. Agreement between Gordon to Barni, 15 Dec. 1902. AKA.
15. F. X. Mulry, S.J., 22 April 1904. ASJKJ.
16. Clayton to Gordon, 21 July 1893. AKA.
17. Ledóchowski to Gordon, 13 Feb. 1899. AKA.
18. Ledóchowski to Gordon, 27 July 1901. AKA.
19. Gordon et al. 1 June 1901. AKA.
20. Barni to Gordon, 18 Oct. 1905. AKA.
21. Ibid.
22. Rua to Gordon, 21 May 1905. AKA.
23. Collins to Rua, 15 April 1909. edito da Don Ceria, o.oc, p. 202. AGSDB.

NOTES TO CHAPTER 22

1. *WL* 64 (June 1935): 258.
2. *Jamaica Daily Telagraph-Anglo American Herald*, 22 Jan. 1907.
3. Sister M. Conception, O.S.F. Account of Earthquake, 17 June 1907, AKA.
4. *Banner of Mary* (Kingston, Jamaica), May 1907.
5. Ibid.
6. *DG*, 8 April 1894.
7. *CO*, Sept. 1915. See also, AKA. Also, Collins to Serfini, 13 March 1917. AKA. Also, *DG*, 24 March 1920.
8. *DG*, 19 April 1920.

NOTES TO CHAPTER 23

1. *WL* 56:52–53.
2. O'Hare to Ledóchowski, 8 Dec. 1920. AKA.
3. *CO*, April 1924, 15. Also, *The Chinese in Jamaica* (Kingston: Lee Tom Yin Co., 1957), 10.
4. ASJR. Jamaica 1-V,9.
5. *Chinese in Jamaica*, 11–12.
6. Ibid.
7. Personal communication, Mrs. Daniel Acquee.
8. Personal communication, Blanche Acque Chen.
9. *CO*.
10. *Record of Old Boys St. George's College: With Degrees—Graduate-Undergraduate and in Course* (Kingston: Jamaica: St. George's College, 1960).
11. *Ninth Annual Chinese Catholic Conference: July 28–Aug. 1, 1960* (Kingston: Printex W.I. Ltd., 1960).
12. *CO*, 24 June 1966.
13. *The Handbook of Jamaica* (Kingston: Government Printing Office, 1915–25).
14. *Catalogue of Maryland–New York Province, Society of Jesus*, 1926.

15. Delany, *History of the Catholic Church in Jamaica*, 220–22.
16. *WL* 56: 47–52.
17. Stubbs to Kelly, 11 Oct. 1926. AKA.
18. Bentley to Kelly, 11 Oct. 1926. AKA.
19. *WL* 56:47–52; also *DG*, 13 Oct. 1926.

NOTES TO CHAPTER 24

1. *Catalogue of Maryland–New York Province, Society of Jesus*, 1926.
2. Walter J. Meagher, S.J., and William J. Grattan, *The Spires of Fenwick: A History of the College of the Holy Cross*, (New York: Vantage, 1966), page 255.
3. Ibid., page 198.
4. *DG*, 13 Dec. 1927.
5. *DG*, 14 Dec. 1927.
6. *CO*, June 1928.
7. AKA, 1930.
8. Personal communication.
9. *CO*, March 1929.
10. Kelly to Van Rossum, 6 Aug. 1929. AKA.
11. Mother M. Dominica to Kelly, 22 Aug. 1929. AKA.
12. Memoirs of Mother M. Humiliana, O.S.F. (unpublished).
13. Ibid.
14. Ibid.
15. Ibid.
16. Ibid.
17. *Souvenir of Silver Jubilee of Franciscan Missionary Sisters of Our Lady of Perpetual Help: September 8, 1929–1954* (Kingston: The Gleaner Co., 1954) 7. Also, Memoirs of Mother M. Humiliana, O.S.F.
18. Memoirs of Mother M. Humiliana, O.S.F.
19. Ibid.
20. Ibid.
21. Ibid.
22. Ibid.
23. Ibid.
24. Ibid. Also, *Souvenir of Silver Juvilee of Franciscan Missionary Sisters*, 7.
25. Ibid.
26. Ibid.
27. Ibid.
28. *Constitutions of Franciscan Missionary Sisters of Our Lady of Perpetual Help.*
29. *Souvenir of Silver Jubilee of Franciscan Missionary Sisters*, 7.
30. *Souvenir Magazine of the Ozanam Home for the Aged, 1953–1961* (Kingston: United Printers, 1961), 10.

31. Having been operational since Feb. 22 1953.
32. *Souvenir Magazine of the Ozanam Home for the Aged*, 4.
33. AKA.
34. *CO*, 13 April 1947.
35. *Souvenir of Silver Jubilee of Franciscan Missionary Sisters*, 8.
36. *Franciscan Centenary, 1857–1957* (Kingston: The Gleaner Co., Ltd., 1957), 38.
37. Memoirs of Mother M. Humiliana, O.S.F.
38. AKA.
39. AKA; also *CO*, 22 Sept. 1961.

NOTES TO CHAPTER 25

1. *WL* 80 (1951): 236–37.
2. Emmet to Richards, 22 July, 1939. AKA.
3. Ibid.
4. Richards to Emmet, 8 March 1940. AKA.
5. *DG*,, 28 March 1940.
6. Correspondence between Richards and Mother Joan, O.S.F., 1940. AKA.
7. Emmet to DeLissser, AKA.
8. Mother Jean Marie, O.S.F., to Emmet, 31 Aug. 1940. AKA.
9. Kirkwood to Becket. Nov. 1940, AKA.
10. Registrar of Titles, Kingston, Nov. 5, 1940. Vol. 314, Folio 84.
11. *DG*,, 16 Nov. 1940.
12. Raymond R. Sullivan, S.J., *Special Report on Holy Name Homestead* (Kingston: Sec. 34.66, P.L & R. Jan 1, 1952. eight pages unnumbered
13. AKA.
14. William H. Feeney, S.J., Notes on Gibraltar Camp, Jamaica.
15. *Catalog of the New England Province of the Society of Jesus*, (Boston, MA.: Privately printed, 1930–40). Also, *WL* (1951) Vol 80, p.243–44, July 1951. John H. Collins, S.J., author.

NOTES TO CHAPTER 26

1. *DG*, 3 May 1938.
2. *DG*, 9 May 1938.
3. Ibid.
4. *DG*, 13 May 1938.
5. *DG*, 23 May 1938.
6. Ibid.
7. *DG*, 25 May 1938.
8. Hugo W. Durst, S.J., *Credit Union for Self-Help, West Indian Style*. Credit Union Series #7. St. George's College Extension School.
9. DG, 4 Aug. 1939.

10. John Peter Sullivan, S.J., *Song of the Islands.* Social Action Series 5. (Kingston: Social Action Department of St. George's College Extension School, 1955).
11. Ibid.
12. Ibid.
13. Ibid.
14. Ibid.
15. Ibid.
16. Ibid.
17. Ibid.
18. Ibid.
19. Ibid.
20. Ibid.
21. Ibid.
22. Ibid.
23. Faculty of St. George's College Extension School, Co-operative Department.
24. Hugo W. Durst, S.J., *Credit Union for Self-Help, West Indian Style.* Credit Union Series 7 (Kingston: St. George's College Extension School, Co-operative Department, 1951).
25. Sullivan, S.J., *Song of the Islands;* see also his *What is the Jamaica Credit Union League?* Social Action Series 27.
26. Cf. Jamaica Credit Union League, Ltd, registered 1947 under the Industrial and Provident Societies of Jamaica. Kingston, Jamaica 1947.
27. John Peter Sullivan, S.J., *What of the Millions Unreached?* Social Action Series 9. (Kingston: Social Action Department of St. George's College Extension School, 1956).
28. John Peter Sullivan, S.J., *Wings Over the Caribbean,* (Kingston: Social Action Department of St. George's College Extension School, 1957).
29. Ibid.
30. *Sodality Co-op Silver Jubilee, January 27, 1967,* 9 (£2,500,000).
31. An appreciation by N. W. Manley, Chief Minister of Jamaica. *AKA.*
32. Personal communication.
33. Personal communication.
34. Credit Union League-Kingston 1987.

NOTES TO CHAPTER 27

1. Seville Papers, First Series, Part 1, Lot 12.
2. Ibid.
3. Seville Papers, First Series, Part 2, Lot 17.
4. AGI 54-3-29. Don Alonso de Espinsa Ceneno, 1644.
5. *Handbook of Jamaica,* 1792.
6. AKA.
7. SPC Am Ant. 6:189–90.

8. SPC Am Ant. 6:189–90.
9. SPC Am Ant. 6:205.
10. Cotham to Jenkins, 26 Dec. 1837. ASJE.
11. Cotham to Jenkins, 18 Dec. 1841. ASJE.
12. 1850, unnumbered document. ASJR.
13. *CSJD,* 15 Aug. 1841.
14. *St. George's College Anniversary: 1850–1950,* (Kingston: Gleaner Printery, 1950), 1.
15. William H. Feeney, S.J., Account of St. George's College, 19 March 1950.
16. *St. George's College Anniversary,* 1.
17. *L&N,* Barton to Weld, 26 Feb. 1868.
18. *Handbook of Jamaica,* 1870.
19. *Catalogue of the English Province of the Society of Jesus,* 1870.
20. Chitty to Woollett, 16 Oct. 1871. AKA.
21. Whitty to Woollett, 1 March 1872. AKA.
22. Jesuits in Jamaica to Whitty, April, 1873. AKA.
23. Whitty to Woollett, 16 May 1873. AKA.
24. AKA.
25. Carvalho to Beckx, 9 June 1874. AKA.
26. Whitty to Woollett, 16 Oct. 1871. AKA.
27. *Handbook of Jamaica,* 1870.
28. Whitty to Woollett, 16 Oct. 1871. AKA.
29. ASJE.
30. Whitty to Woollett, 16 Oct. 1871. AKA. Also, Woollett to Gallwey, 5 June 1874. ASJE.
31. 10 March 1874. ASJE.
32. 21 May 1877. AKA.
33. May 1877, Beckx to Jaeckel. AKA.
34. *Handbook of Jamaica,* 1878, 1880.
35. *St. George's College Anniversary,* 2.
36. *Catalogue of the English Province of the Society of Jesus,* 1878, 1880, 1886, 1892.
37. *Handbook of Jamaica,* 1889, 1890.
38. Louis Bodoano, History of Catholic Church in Jamaica, ms pp. 54–56, AKA.
39. Ibid.
40. *Handbook of Jamaica,* 1875.
41. *Handbook of Jamaica,* 1880.
42. *Franciscan Centenary,* 18.
43. Dupeyron's report to Congregatio de Propaganda Fidei, 1862. AKA.
44. Cotham to Rome, 2 Aug. 1843. ASJR, Jam. 1-111. See also Cotham to Jenkins, 23 July 1845 and 7 Oct. 1845 ASJE; Fernandez to Congregatio de Propaganda Fidei, 8 Dec. 1845. AKA.

45. *Franciscan Centenary,* 18.
46. *Handbook of Jamaica,* 1896.
47. *Ibid.*
48. *Ibid.*
49. *Charles J. Latrobe, Negro Education, Jamaica* (Kingston: House of Commons. 7 Feb. 1838), 66.
50. *Cotham,* April 1913, p. 28.
51. Ibid.
52. Ibid.
53. *Dictionary of National Biography,* s.v. "Welsh, Adam C."
54. *Cotham,* April 1913, p. 26.
55. Latrobe, *Negro Education, Jamaica* 85.
56. Woollett to Weld, 19 Feb. 1868. AKA.
57. Latrobe, *Negro Education, Jamaica* 85.
58. Buchanan to Gordon, 14 March 1899. AKA.
59. Elizabeth Dennis to Gordon, 1894. AKA.

NOTES TO CHAPTER 28

1. Alexander D. C. Peterson, *One Hundred Years of Education* (London: Duckworth, 1952). Primary, 10–18; secondary, 122–50; university, 167–98.
2. Ibid., 137–50.
3. Ibid., student must pass Advance Level exams.
4. Ibid.
5. Ibid., 36.
6. Ibid., 35.
7. Ibid.
8. Ibid.
9. Ibid., 36.
10. Ministry of Education, Jamaica.
11. Ibid.
12. Ibid.
13. AKA.
14. AKA.
15. 11 Feb. 1905. ASJK.
16. 27 March 1905. AKA.
17. Martin to Gordon, 23 April 1895. AKA.
18. Ibid.
19. Hansleman to Collins, ASJK.
20. Sidney L. Bury, "Historical Sketch," *St. George's College Anniversary,* 1.
21. *CO,* April 1913, p. 23.
22. Ibid.

23. Peterson, *One Hundred Years of Education*, p. 250.
24. Ibid.
25. Ibid.
26. *Catalogue of the New England Province of the Society of Jesus*, 1936.
27. William H. Feeney, S.J., Private notes, 17 Jan. 1950.
28. Ibid. and CO, 1941.
29. William H. Feeney, S.J., Private notes, 17 Jan. 1950.
30. Ibid.
31. Ibid.
32. Ibid.
33. Ibid.
34. St. George's College Extension School, Headmaster's Office Record.
35. Ibid.
36. Ministry of Education, Jamaica.
37. *Catalogue of the New England Province of the Society of Jesus*, 1961.
38. For educational work of Franciscan Missionary Sisters, see chapter twenty-four.

NOTES TO CHAPTER 29

1. Vatican II, *Decree on Priestly Formation (Optatam Totius)*, c. 4 The Deepening of Spiritual Formation, sec. 8.
2. Pius XI, *Rerum Ecclesiae*, No. 20.
3. Ibid.
4. Ibid.
5. *Handbook, Ninth Annual Synod 1982*. Kingston. p. 13.
6. Vatican II, *Declaration on Christian Education (Gravissimum Educationis), sec. 5.*
7. *Jamaica Catholic Education Association*, 1982, 22–24.
8. *Tenth Anniversary Souvenir Booklet*, St. Francis Communities, Bridgeport. 4 October 1986, p. 2.
9. Ibid.
10. *Catholic Opinion*, October 1985.
11. *Catholic Opinion*, July–August 1986.

Bibliography

Anstruther, O.P., Godfrey. *A Hundred Homeless Years*. London: Blackfriars Publications, 1958.

Black, Clinton V. *History of Jamaica*. London and Glasgow: Collins, 1958.

Burney, James. *History of the Buccaneers of America*, London, 1902.

Burns, Sir Alan. *History of the West Indies*. London: Allen, Unwin, 1954.

Cundall, Frank. *Historic Jamaica*. Kingston: Institute of Jamaica, 1915.

Cundall, Frank and Pietersz, Joseph. *Jamaica under the Spaniards*. Kingston: Institute of Jamaica, 1919.

Cundall, Frank. *The Governors of Jamaica in the Seventeenth Century.* London: West India Committee, 1936.

Cundall, Frank. *The Governors of Jamaica in the First Half of the Eighteenth Century.* London: West India Committee, 1937.

Edwards, Bryan. *History of the West Indies*. 3 Vols. London: John Stockdale, 1801.

Gage, Thomas. *Thomas Gage's Travels in the New World*. J. Eric. S. Thompson, ed. Norman: University of Oklahoma Press, 1958.

Gardner, William J. *A History of Jamaica*. London: Fisher Unwin, 1909.

Gomara, Francisco Lopez de. *Cortes—Life of the Conqueror.* Berkeley: University of California Press, 1964.

Leslie, Charles. *New History of Jamaica*. London: 1740.

Long, Edward. *History of Jamaica*. London: 1774.

Marks, Jeannette. *The Family of the Barretts*. New York: Macmillan, 1938.

Morales Padron, Francisco. *Jamaica Espaniola*. Seville: Escuela de Estudios Hispano-Americanos De Sevilla, 1952.

Morison, Samuel Eliot. *Admiral of the Ocean Sea*. Boston: Little, Brown and Co., 1949.

Nugent, Lady Maria. *Lady Nugent's Journal*. Philip Wright, ed. Kingston: Institute of Jamaica, 1966.

Oliver, Sydney. *Myth of Governor Eyre*. London: Hogarth Press, 1933.

Le Page, R. B. and De. Camp, David. *Jamaican Creole*. London: Macmillan and Co., 1960.

Peterson, Alexander D. C. *One Hundred Years of Education*. London: Duckworth, 1952.

Roberts, W. Adolph, ed. *The Capitals of Jamaica*. Kingston: Pioneer Press, 1955.

Sheils, S.J., W. Eugene. *King and Church*. Chicago: Loyola University Press, 1961.

Sherlock, Philip. *The Aborigines of Jamaica*. Kingston: Institute of Jamaica, 1939.

Shore, Joseph. *In Old St. James (Jamaica).* John Stewart, ed. Kingston: Sangster's, 1911.

Smith, M. C., Augier, Roy, and Nettleford, Rex. *The Ras Tafari Movement in Jamaica.* Institute of Social and Economic Research, University College of West Indies, 1960.

Taylor, S. A. G. *The Western Design.* The Hague: Mouton and Company, 1965.

Ward, Estella. *Christopher Monck, Duke of Albemarle.* London: 1915.

Williams, S.J., Joseph J. *Hebrewism of West Africa.* New York: The Dial Press, 1931.

Williams, S. J., Joseph J. *Voodoos and Obeah.* New York: MacVeagh, Dial Press, 1932.

Index

C

D

E

I

J

K

N